Peter Norton's™

Complete Guide to
PC Upgrades
Second Edition

Peter Norton
Michael Desmond

SAMS

201 West 103rd Street, Indianapolis, Indiana 46290 USA

Peter Norton's® Complete Guide to PC Upgrades, Second Edition

Copyright© 1999 by Peter Norton

International Standard Book Number: 0-672-31483-5

Library of Congress Catalog Card Number: 98-87673

Printed in the United States of America

First Printing: January 1999

00 99 98   4 3 2 1

Trademarks

Executive Editor
Jim Minatel

Acquisitions Editor
Jill Byus

Development Editor
Steve Schafer

Managing Editor
Thomas F. Hayes

Project Editor
Sossity Smith

Copy Editors
Victoria Elzey
Krista Hansing
Kay Hoskin

Indexer
Cheryl A. Jackson

Technical Editor
Lloyd Case

Layout Technician
Brad Lenser

Proofreader
Tricia Sterling

Contents at a Glance

Contents

Dedication

To my wife Anne, for helping me believe, and my brother Jim, for making sure I remember to laugh.

—Michael Desmond

About the Authors

Computer software entrepreneur and writer **Peter Norton** established his technical expertise and accessible style from the earliest days of the PC. His *Norton Utilities* was the first product of its kind, giving early computer owners control over their hardware and protection against myriad problems. His flagship titles, *Peter Norton's DOS Guide* and *Peter Norton's Inside the PC* (Sams Publishing) have provided the same insight and education to computer users worldwide for nearly two decades. Peter's books, like his many software products, are among the best-selling and most-respected in the history of personal computing.

Peter Norton's former column in *PC Week* was among the highest-regarded in that magazine's history. His expanding series of computer books continues to bring superior education to users, always in Peter's trademark style, which is never condescending nor pedantic. From their earliest days, changing the "black box" into a "glass box," Peter's books, like his software, remain among the most powerful tools available to beginners and experienced users, alike.

In 1990, Peter sold his software development business to Symantec Corporation, allowing him to devote more time to his family, civic affairs, philanthropy, and art collecting. He lives with his wife, Eileen, and two children in Santa Monica, California.

Michael Desmond is an award-winning writer and contributing editor for *PC World* magazine, the world's largest circulation monthly computing publication with over 1.2 million readers. His work has appeared in *The New York Times*, the *Chicago Tribune*, *US News & World Report*, and *Spin* magazine. He has also contributed to numerous books, and was co-author of *Platinum Edition Using Windows 95* from Que Publishing. In 1998, Desmond was honored by the American Society of Business Press Editors for Best Technical Article and earned second-place for his contributions in the Best News Series category. In the same year, the first edition of this book was honored as runner-up in the Computer Press Awards for Best Advanced How-To Book. Desmond has twice been recognized as a runner-up in the prestigious Jesse H. Neal Awards from the American Business Press—for best news article in 1998 and for best investigative article in 1996.

Previously senior editor of news at *PC World* and executive editor at *Multimedia World* magazine, Desmond has an M.S. in Journalism from Northwestern University's Medill School of Journalism, and a B.A. in Soviet Studies from Middlebury College in Vermont. In 1998, Desmond stepped down as president of the Computer Press Association after a four-year term on the board of directors. Desmond lives in Burlington, Vermont, with his wife Anne, sons Kevin and Patrick, and a yellow labrador retriever named Finnigan. You can visit his Web site of his company, MichaelDesmond Communications, at www.MichaelDesmond.com.

Acknowledgments

Believe me, books don't write themselves, and neither do revisions. This second edition of *Peter Norton's Complete Guide to PC Upgrades* was made possible by the dedicated efforts of a team of writers, editors, vendors, and industry experts. I'd like to thank Development Editor Steven Schafer, whose timely edits, sharp eye, and keen knowledge of gaming hardware helped improve the coverage of PC hardware in this edition. Credit also goes to Acquisitions Editor Jill Byus, who remained patient yet insistent as the deadlines wore on. Sharp technical edits from Lloyd Case helped keep the contact accurate and on track. Dell's Brian Zucker also earns mention, for his heads-up comments during this book's first run. Of course, I must once again thank my agent at Waterside Productions, David Fugate, for landing me this project. It has made all the difference.

Many hard-working public relations, marketing, and technical professionals helped make this book possible by responding to my always-urgent calls for photos and information. I owe deep thanks to all the people who dropped everything to get me the materials I needed before deadline. Here are the companies who contributed to this book: 1394 Trade Association; 3Com Corp.; ACTiSYS Corp.; Adaptec, Inc.; Altec-Lansing; AMD; American Power Conversion; ATI Technologies; CH Products; Cirque Corporation; Cirrus Logic; CMD Technology, Inc.; Creative Labs, Cyrix; Data Translation; Dell Computer; Diamond Multimedia; Epson America, Inc.; Hewlett-Packard; Hitachi America; IBM PC Corp.; Intel Corp.; Iomega; Kingston Technology; Lexmark International, Inc.; Logitech, Inc.; Micron Electronics, Inc.; Micronics; Microsoft Corp.; NMB Technologies; Olympus America; PC Power and Cooling; Pinnacle Micro Corp.; Plextor Corp.; Quantum Corporation; Ricoh America; Seagate Corp.; UMAX Corp.; Viewsonic Corporation; Winnov, Inc.; and Wireless Computing.

Finally, I want to thank my wife, Anne without whom I never could have finished this book. She put up with a lot of late nights and lost weekends, remaining incredibly supportive even as the months wore on and the deadlines grew desperate. Thank You.

—Michael Desmond

Tell Us What You Think!

As the reader of this book, you are our most important critic and commentator. We value your opinion and want to know what we're doing right, what we could do better, what areas you'd like to see us publish in, and any other words of wisdom you're willing to pass our way.

As the Executive Editor for the General Desktop Applications team at Macmillan Computer Publishing, I welcome your comments. You can fax, email, or write me directly to let me know what you did or didn't like about this book—as well as what we can do to make our books stronger.

Please note that I cannot help you with technical problems related to the topic of this book, and that due to the high volume of mail I receive, I might not be able to reply to every message.

When you write, please be sure to include this book's title and author as well as your name and phone or fax number. I will carefully review your comments and share them with the author and editors who worked on the book.

Fax:	317-817-7448
Email:	hardware@mcp.com
Mail:	Executive Editor
	General Desktop Applications
	201 West 103rd Street
	Indianapolis, IN 46290 USA

Introduction

The PC is an appliance—at least that's what computer manufacturers want you to think. You buy the box, plug it in, and suddenly life is good.

In reality, buying and installing PC hardware is more daunting than ever before. A plethora of new devices—scanners, photo printers, even personal digital assistants—make mainstream PC configurations more complex than ever. At the same time, new peripherals like AGP graphics cards, DVD-ROM drives, and any number of USB devices make buying decisions more difficult. What's more, these new product classes add to the long list of things that can go wrong with your PC.

All this comes on top of the usual barrage of confusing acronyms and dubious benchmarks. That's a distressing thought when you consider that PCs have become as ubiquitous as TVs and toaster ovens. Also, with the ascendance of the Internet, we now rely on our computers for so many things. Connected PCs bring us the news, let us submit projects under deadline, and even help keep us in touch with far-flung family and friends. As we rely on PCs more and more, it becomes critical for users to understand how to solve the everyday challenges without placing a call to the local service center.

This book will help you understand the workings of PC hardware, ranging from CPUs to printers, so that you can choose the products that will best help extend and enhance the life of your PC. You'll also find step-by-step instructions for installing and maintaining these devices. Along the way, you'll find tips to help you get the most out of your PC.

Who Should Read This Book?

This book's intended audience is intermediate-to-advanced Windows 95 and 98 users who want to get the most out of their investment in PC hardware. Step-by-step instructions help negotiate tricky installations, and useful explanations of products and technology help make informed buying decisions. Whether you have a PC at home or in the office (or both), this book provides the information you need to handle your PC jobs yourself.

This is not a book for rocket scientists or system engineers. It is intended for people who rely on PCs to do their jobs and get things done at home—even if it's just roaming the halls of Quake.

The focus is on PCs running Windows 95 and Windows 98 because these are the most pervasive operating system versions for individual desktop PCs. However, you will find that the insights provided here also apply to other operating systems.

What You'll Learn

Here are some of the topics covered in this book:

- Step-by-step instructions for installing a wide variety of PC devices
- Comprehensible explanations of PC hardware and technology
- Useful advice for buying new products
- Strategies and tips for resolving hardware conflicts and breakdowns
- Advice for making the most effective upgrades for a wide variety of systems and applications
- An introduction to emerging PC technologies, including DVD, Universal Serial Bus (USB), FireWire, Accelerated Graphics Port (AGP), and high-speed Internet access via DSL and modems
- Repair and maintenance advice for PCs and peripherals

A typical chapter covers a single topic, such as modems or monitors, in depth. Each chapter begins with an overview of the hardware technology and products, enabling you to understand how things work before you move on. Each chapter also includes a buying section focussing on cost-effective upgrades, as well as on making sure you get a fair deal when you buy new hardware.

Each chapter also includes a section covering upgrades, providing step-by-step installation and setup instructions for devices. Finally, a troubleshooting and repair section helps you deal with adversity when it arrives, providing hands-on instructions and tips.

How This Book Is Organized

This book is broken into sections by broad product categories. For example, chapters covering data storage are grouped together, making it easy to explore related PC hardware and technology. In addition, you'll find an introductory section providing an overview of PC hardware, an introduction to the Windows 95 operating system, and strategies for troubleshooting and repairing PCs.

Part I: Introduction

Part I provides an overview of what is to come. Here you will gain useful insights into PC technology, as well as key strategies for managing PC hardware. Chapters covering general upgrade and repair strategies (later covered in depth in chapters concerning specific hardware devices) will help you understand the issues raised later in the book. This part also includes a discussion of the Windows 95/98 and Windows NT operating systems because the OS plays a critical role in the management and operation of any hardware device.

Part II: Core Components

The tour of PC hardware starts at ground zero, the CPU. The most critical and expensive component of your system gets in-depth treatment. You'll learn why a 300MHz Pentium II is faster at running 3D games than an AMD K6 CPU of the same clock speed, and you'll learn how to tell if a faster CPU might be the fix you need for your aging system.

From the processor, we'll move on to other critical performance building blocks. We'll cover system RAM and cache memory, both critical players in application performance and compatibility, helping determine what you need to run your software. Memory in particular is critical, because a boost in the amount of RAM can be the most profound performance upgrade you can perform.

Also included in Part II is a chapter on PC power supplies and peripherals. Bringing it all together is the chapter on motherboards, the component that serves as the platform upon which all other components are connected. You'll find out why chipsets, rarely popularized in advertising, are perhaps the most important ingredient of your PC.

Part III: Basic Data Storage

This part introduces the workhorse storage devices inside your PC—hard disks, floppy drives, and CD-ROM drives. You will learn the role of these ubiquitous drives and how they work. Step-by-step installation instructions guide you through sometimes-tricky hard disk installations and help you deal with the complexities of master-slave relationships for IDE drives.

Virtually all these media run under one of two buses—IDE or SCSI—so Part III begins with a chapter discussing IDE and SCSI controllers. You need to understand the key performance and compatibility issues of these bus types before you commit to buying a certain type of hardware. With an eye toward the future, this part includes a chapter on DVD drives. Here you'll find critical updates on compatibility problems with DVD, as well as useful tips to help you avoid disaster during the installation of these newest drives.

Part IV: Advanced Data Storage

Storage coverage continues in Part IV, with specialized removable storage solutions. From slow-but-affordable tape backup drives to rewritable optical formats like CD-RW and DVD-RAM, this part provides information on storage options critical to protecting and archiving your valuable data. Of considerable concern: This section covers tape and optical formats so that you can work with media that will remain compatible for years to come.

Part V: Multimedia

Part V covers a variety of popular upgrade candidates, including sound cards, graphics and video boards, and monitors. You'll learn why a 3D graphics card is so important to acceptable multimedia performance and gameplay. You'll learn about Intel's Accelerated Graphics Port (AGP) bus for high-speed and detailed 3D graphics, and you'll learn what improvements are planned for this technology. Also covered are video capture boards and videoconferencing products, including monitor-top cameras that can be used to take digital snapshots.

The big news among displays is flat-panel technology, which after years of promise is finally becoming affordable. I'll tell you when it might be worth—or not worth—your while to shell out an extra $500 for a crisp LCD monitor for your desktop and also warn you about the failings of flat panels running off the analog VGA port used by today's CRT monitors. You'll also learn how the balance between the monitor and the graphics board is crucial, receive useful advice on ergonomics, and even get helpful buying advice on power-saving products.

Sound cards have transitioned from the persnickety ISA bus to the Plug and Play PCI bus, and they've added some new tricks in the process. You'll learn about positional 3D audio, which takes your games to the next level of immersion, as well as about AC-3 surround sound for the latest DVD-based titles and movies. We'll also take a peek at USB digital speakers, which do away with the sound card entirely and promise to deliver unparalleled PC audio quality.

Part VI: Connectivity

More than ever before, PCs are the center of communication. Part VI helps you outfit your PC for the coming millennium, when virtually every PC will be connected to multiple devices and networks. The chapter on modems explains what you need to gain reasonable access to the Internet, while the chapter on digital connectivity gives you a heads up on cable modems, digital subscriber line (DSL) service, and satellite-based access. You'll see how to protect yourself when buying a 56K modem, and you'll get a glimpse of the intriguing digital technologies that lie underneath.

The chapter about I/O add-ons introduces some emerging bus standards promising to revolutionize PC connections. You'll also see how you can add this new technology to your existing PCs using simple PCI card upgrades. The office networking chapter gives you a run-down of Ethernet-based networking, and includes all the steps you need to wire your own. New in this revision is coverage of intriguing and affordable home networking products, which link PCs over your home's existing power or phone lines, as well as via radio signals. You'll learn how you can share data, applications, and hardware devices such as printers.

Part VII: Input and Output

This section covers devices enabling you to move data in and out of your PC. Input devices such as mice, keyboards, and game controllers get a close look, with an in-depth discussion of ergonomic issues and tips for avoiding painful hand, wrist, and shoulder injuries. You'll also learn about exciting innovations in the game controller market—such as force feedback joysticks and other game controllers that shake—as well as 3D mice and keyboards with built-in pointing devices.

If you want to turn your PC into a digital photo studio, look no further than the chapters on scanners and digital cameras. You'll get a realistic assessment of the quality of these devices, as well as an eye-opening discussion of the confusing specifications that vendors often publish. You'll also find out why anyone looking for top quality will want to buy a good scanner.

The chapter on printers will help you make sense of the confusing variety of printers available for PCs. You'll learn why color ink jets are such a terrific value for home PC owners, and why office users might want to stick with a fast and reliable laser printer. You'll learn how to get the best quality out of your existing printer, and you'll see why you need to look closely at the cost of paper and media when choosing a printer.

Appendix and Glossary

This book finishes with an appendix on what to do with a PC that you don't want anymore. One intriguing option is to donate your system to a charity for a nifty tax deduction. You'll also find a useful glossary that can help you understand the fog of acronyms and technical jargon that go with any discussion of PC hardware.

Conventions Used in This Book

This book uses the following conventions:

Menus and the selections on them are separated by a comma. For example, "Select File, Open" means "Pull down the File menu and choose Open."

Words that you must type or words that you see onscreen appear in a `monospace` font.

New terms appear in *italic*.

MBps stands for "megabytes per second." Mbps stands for "megabits per second." KBps stands for "kilobytes per second." Kbps stands for "kilobits per second." GBps stands for "gigabytes per second." Gbps stands for "gigabits per second."

Icons

This book contains many icons that help you identify certain types of information. The following paragraphs describe the purpose of each icon.

Note: Notes bring interesting facts to your attention. I use Note boxes to explore useful tangents and provide information that I've picked up while using PC hardware.

Peter's Principle: Critical Information for PC Owners

These sidebars convey vital insights about important hardware issues. Boxes that have this icon might discuss key buying issues or help unravel confusing technical standards, but the focus is always on critical information with immediate value to PC owners.

Tip: Tips show you new ways of doing things that you might not have thought about before. Tip boxes also provide an alternative way of doing something that you might like better than the first approach I provided.

TROUBLESHOOTING

Everyone encounters problems occasionally, and this book is here to help. You'll find the Troubleshooting icon wherever there are useful tips and instructions for fixing hardware that has gone awry. In addition, every device-specific chapter includes a troubleshooting and repair section where you will find valuable advice for handling common hardware problems.

Caution: Cautions almost always tell you about some kind of hardware or data damage that will occur if you perform a certain action (or fail to perform others). Make sure that you understand a Caution thoroughly before you follow any instructions following it.

PART I

Introduction

The PC: An Overview

Not since the invention of the automobile has the introduction of a new device changed our society as much as the personal computer. More incredibly, the PC has become virtually ubiquitous in just 15 years, since its invention in 1982. From Fortune 100 businesses to home offices to college dorm rooms, PCs are a fixture in our day-to-day life.

There is just one problem: Most people are intimidated by PCs. It's no wonder. Some pretty amazing engineering goes into those putty-beige boxes. The rocket scientists over at Intel, for example, make their living from submicron magic, crafting intricate data-handling engines out of semiconducting silicon. For a populace stymied by VCR clocks, it's a small wonder that the enormously powerful and complex PC can be very intimidating.

It doesn't have to be that way. This chapter will help break the ice by providing an overview of how PCs work. You will learn:

- How the PC got its start from a modest beginning as an in-house project at IBM
- About the workings of modern PCs, including all the requirements to meet the new PC99 specification
- About notebook PCs and how they work
- What to expect from PC technology in the future

What Is a PC, Anyway?

Today, personal computers are more powerful and diverse than ever before. From handheld personal digital assistants to multiprocessing Web servers and workstations, you will find a wide variety of devices that can legitimately be called personal computers. The vast majority of these devices, however, fit the description of personal computer that people are accustomed to—affordable desktop-based computers that are designed for general-purpose tasks ranging from spreadsheets and word processing to games and communications.

First, a Bit of History

The PC got its real start in 1981, when IBM released a modest little box by the name of The IBM PC. At the time, no one knew that the IBM PC was destined to create a multi-billion–dollar market that would help power one of the greatest economic upturns in American history. Rather, it was regarded as the latest in a series of hobby computers—devices catering to an audience of ardent programmers, tinkerers, and electronics nuts.

Then what helped propel the IBM PC beyond that fate of the dead-end computers that preceded it, including the Tandy TRS-80 and MIPS Altair? Two things:

- An open hardware architecture
- A third-party operating system and application market

Hawking Hardware

The IBM PC group took a very un-IBM–like approach to their little creation. The company's then-successful mainframe business made its fortune by requiring buyers to get everything from IBM. Everything from the new computer to replacement parts to operating system software all came directly from IBM. There was no competitive market of products or developers. When you bought IBM, you were committed to its products for the life of the machine.

Working on a shoestring budget, the IBM PC people cut deals with hardware companies to provide components for their PC. That decision would have an enormous impact on the nascent PC market and on the larger American business landscape. Here's one example: IBM single-handedly launched the rise of semiconductor powerhouse Intel Corporation when it tapped the company's 8080 chip to serve as the central processing unit (CPU) of the IBM PC.

More importantly, IBM invited other companies to build and sell products for its computer. Add-in card slots let companies such as Hercules create high-resolution graphics cards for early PCs. The result was that a cottage industry of peripherals arose making the IBM PC an attractive option for business users.

Microsoft Gets Its Start

Along the way to launching the PC, IBM managed to give a start to another small company, Microsoft Corporation. IBM needed software to control its new machine, thus the computing giant turned to a small Seattle company owned by Paul Allen and Bill Gates.

At the time, Microsoft had been creating programming tools—specifically, the Basic programming language—for the old CP/M platform. But when IBM came calling, Gates and company quickly changed directions and started working on the first operating system for the IBM PC, which they called Disk Operating System, or DOS.

DOS became the software brains of the IBM PC. Behind every keystroke, file transfer, and screen display was Microsoft's DOS software. Most importantly, Microsoft kept the rights to its new creation, allowing it to later sell DOS and succeeding products to makers of IBM-compatible PCs.

The upshot was that both the hardware and the operating system software that were needed to make IBM-compatible PCs were both in the open. IBM held precious little control of the PC market it had just launched.

In Between

Today, literally thousands of companies are hard at work creating systems, peripherals, software, and tools for IBM-compatible PCs. Whether you're buying a brand-new system or making the best of one that is several years old, you enjoy a wide choice of products and vendors.

Hardware: The One-Cent Tour

No doubt about it—PCs can be intimidating. And it only gets worse when you find that you must upgrade or troubleshoot your system. Inside the chassis, you'll find a lot of delicate—and expensive—electronics. It can seem awfully complex and dangerous, but it doesn't have to be.

It helps to think of your PC in terms of its component subsystems. This quick outline of the PC's components can help put things in perspective:

- Outside the PC: You'll see the display, keyboard, mouse, and the PC's case, as shown in Figure 1.1. The case holds all the PC's vital components, and it also provides access to CD-ROM and floppy drives on the front and various ports along the back. The case also shields you from electromagnetic radiation produced by internal components and allows for channeled airflow to reduce overheating problems.

FIGURE 1.1.

Minitower PCs such as this Micron system provide easy access to components while minimizing footprint. (Photo courtesy of Micron Electronics, Inc.)

- CPU: The *central processing unit,* or *processor,* handles all the arithmetic that drives your PC. The speed of the CPU, combined with its internal design, determines how quickly and efficiently the CPU can process data and program code.

- System memory: Called *random access memory,* or *RAM,* system memory stores the code and data being used by your PC. The more memory you have, the better your performance.

- Hard disk: The PC's permanent storage device. Programs and data held on the hard disk are transferred to system RAM for use. Today's hard disks feature capacities of 5GB and higher.

- CD-ROM drives: The ubiquitous large-capacity removable-media drive. CD-ROM drives let PC users access multimedia content, install large applications, and work with enormous databases and other resources. This technology is being replaced by DVD-ROM drives, which offer even larger data capacities.

- Graphics adapter: Everything you see on the display goes through the graphics adapter. This hardware component speeds the display of 2D graphics, 3D graphics, and video playback. A good graphics adapter is critical to fast performance.

- Audio adapter: Anything beyond the basic beeps from your PC speaker go through the audio subsystem. Sound cards let you play digital audio through your PC speakers, as well as record analog sounds to digital format.

- Modem: Allows your PC to talk to the Internet, fax machines, and other PCs using a standard phone line. It can be either an internal add-in card or an external box.

- Network interface card: Also called NICs, these add-in cards are used to connect a PC to a local area network, which is common in offices. More and more home PCs are featuring network cards as cable and xDSL modems connect to your PC via a fast network card.

- Display: The TV-like cathode ray tube (CRT) display found on almost all desktop PCs. Today, 15- and 17-inch displays are most common, though 19-inch models are popular on high-end consumer systems. Larger monitors provide much better viewing.

- Keyboard and mouse: The primary input devices for your PC. Almost all PCs require—and come with—a keyboard and a mouse.

The Software Side

This being a hardware book, it's easy to lose sight of the importance of software in the operation of the PC. But, in fact, you can't separate hardware from software when talking about PCs. Software literally gives life to inanimate hardware.

In fact, your interaction with much of the hardware inside the PC comes through software. Graphics and sound-card features, for example, are accessed through on-screen control panels.

There are three types of software:

- Applications
- Operating systems
- Drivers

Applications

These are the programs you use every day, whether Quicken accounting software or Quake II. Application code and files are stored permanently on your hard disk or CD-ROM drive until you launch them. At that point, the bits are moved into system memory, where the CPU can quickly access the data and code it needs to perform actions.

Applications, particularly multimedia titles and games, interact with virtually every part of your PC. The keyboard and mouse provide input for the application, and files and data are accessed from the hard disk, CD-ROM drive, floppy disks, or even from the Internet through a modem. Graphics are sent to the display to let you view and manipulate program controls and features, collectively known as the *interface*. This is where the cycle closes: The graphical display enables you to view your input and access on-screen controls.

The Operating System

You might think your applications access your PC's hardware. After all, when you click the disk icon, the program saves the current file to disk. In fact, the operating system sits between your applications and hardware, providing a common set of rules for applications. This layer of software below your applications defines how applications access memory and the CPU, which can have a huge impact on functionality and performance.

It can be difficult to overstate the importance of the operating system, also called the OS. The OS breathes life into your hardware, providing a common set of services and software-access systems that make it possible for your programs to perform their magic. What's more, the OS determines exactly what your applications and hardware can and can't do.

Here's a case in point: If you are running Windows 98, you can buy scanners and other devices that plug into the two Universal Serial Bus ports on the back of most PCs. But Windows NT 4.0, Microsoft's corporate-minded operating system, doesn't recognize USB. However, if you want to make use of multiple processors—say, for high-end 3D graphics, you'll need Windows NT or another optimized OS—Windows 98 can only "see" one processor.

Drivers

Finally, there is the software you don't see. Device drivers are the diplomats of hardware, opening lines of communication between your peripherals and the operating system. They are also the most under-appreciated component of hardware performance. If you want to get the most out of your hardware, you need to be aware of the driver software that makes it run.

Why do you need drivers? Although operating systems such as Windows 98 and NT provide a standard set of rules for applications, each hardware device has its own particular talents and ways of doing things. It would simply be too complicated to provide support for every single peripheral in the OS itself, so drivers bridge the gap. Driver software is usually written by the hardware company because the company knows its products intimately.

> **Tip:** Device drivers get updated frequently—to add features, improve performance, and fix bugs. For this reason, it's a good idea to occasionally check your peripheral vendors' Web sites for updates. In almost all cases, driver updates are available for free download—essentially a free upgrade.

The PC Today

You've seen a quick outline of what goes into a personal computer, but this is hardly the complete picture. The PC is constantly evolving, adding capabilities and getting faster every year. In fact, this evolution is part of what makes buying and upgrading computers very difficult.

Are you looking for some help? There is a bit forthcoming from Intel, Microsoft, and other companies who sponsor the PC99 specification. PC99 is the latest in a series of system guidelines designed to help system and peripheral manufacturers improve the functionality of PCs. At the same time, PC99 is an excellent indication of what to expect in the year or so to come.

Actually, there are five flavors of PC99:

- Consumer PC99: Describes home or small office/home office (SOHO) PCs. Generally assumed to be standalone systems, the spec assumes a modem-based Internet connection.

- Office PC99: Describes networked systems designed to run productivity applications. Remote configuration and management features help reduce operating costs.

- Entertainment PC99: Includes requirements for TV in and out, high-speed digital connections, remote pointing devices, and other features.

- Mobile PC99: Focused on notebook computers, Mobile PC99 mandates intelligent power management features and accessible expansion through various slots and ports.

- Workstation PC99: This category is specific to systems running Windows NT Workstation, and calls for additional tweaks such as error correcting code (ECC) system RAM, SCSI-based disk storage, and multiple hard disk drives.

A basic PC99 specification serves as the common ground for all the subcategories. The baseline includes a 300MHz processor with 128K Level 2 (L2) cache. Although Consumer PC99 systems can have 32MB of RAM, Office PC99 demands 64MB. The Workstation PC99 spec boosts that to a 400MHz CPU with 256KB of L2 cache and 128MB of system RAM. Advanced power management and BIOS are required across the board, allowing intelligent system operation and power down. Two USB ports are called for on all desktops (notebooks require one USB port).

PC99 Explained

Regardless of the kind of desktop system you want to buy, PC99 provides a set of common guidelines that apply. The technologies PC99 demands for new PCs include the following:

- 300MHz Pentium II CPU: The baseline performance for desktop PCs is 300MHz, while notebooks start at 233MHz.

- Universal Serial Bus (USB): An external Plug and Play bus that will replace serial and parallel ports, as well as provide connections for keyboards and mice.

- Digital Versatile Disk (DVD) ready: This high-capacity optical drive format is the successor to CD-ROM drives and is recommended for all platforms. (See Figure 1.2.)

- 3D graphics support: Driver support for 3D graphics, allowing use of 3D games and titles. It also mandates using PCI or AGP bus to host the graphics hardware.

- MPEG-2 video capability: Hardware that allows the display of high-resolution video used on DVD-based titles and applications.

- 56Kbps v.90-compliant modem: PC99 requires that modems comply to the international v.90 standard for 56Kbps modem operation.

- Device Bay: A standard for the easy installation and removal of peripheral devices, using Plug and Play USB and FireWire buses. This is recommended for all system types.

FIGURE 1.2.
DVD-ROM drives are among the exciting consumer technologies endorsed by the PC99 specification. (Photo courtesy of Creative Labs)

In addition, the PC99 specification abolishes the venerable ISA (industry standard architecture) bus. ISA dates back to the very beginnings of the PC. If you look inside your PC, you can see three or four ISA slots, which accept compatible cards.

> You can learn more about the ISA, PCI, and other PC buses in Chapter 9, "Understanding Motherboards and Chipsets."

Although there are many ISA-compatible add-in cards, the bus is limited to a paltry 5MBps of data throughput. That might be fine for modems and low-end audio, but it won't do for graphics, networking, or multichannel audio. What's more, the aging ISA spec lacks built-in support for Plug and Play, bus mastering, and other important capabilities found in newer bus architectures such as PCI and AGP.

Note: Notebooks also get a nod in the PC99 scheme, with the inclusion of the CardBus. The successor to the successful PC Card specification, CardBus provides a fast 32-bit expansion bus for notebook PCs. Best of all, the peripherals comply with a svelte, credit-card sized format, which makes them perfect for mobile computers.

Consumer PC99

The Consumer PC99 adds a few tweaks to this baseline. This version of the specification deals with PCs intended for the home and therefore stresses multimedia features common in educational and gaming titles.

One thing the Consumer PC99 spec adds to the basic menu is the requirement of a fast 32X CD-ROM drive. However, it is worth noting that a 32X CD-ROM drive is hardly cutting edge—in fact, today's drives often run at top speeds of 40 times that of the original 1X CD-ROM spec. However, the faster drive speed ensures that the PC can play virtually all CD-ROM-based titles.

In addition, the Consumer PC99 spec recommends the following:

- IEEE 1394 FireWire: A high-speed external bus that offers Plug and Play and that is suitable for video capture, external storage devices, and simple networking.
- Accelerated Graphics Port (AGP): A high-speed dedicated graphics bus that allows for faster, more realistic 3D graphics.
- TV capability: An analog TV tuner and TV-out capability to allow viewing directly from the PC's monitor.
- DVD-ROM drive: A next-generation optical disk drive that improves upon the 650MB CD-ROM drive by offering 3.7GB to 17GB of storage, depending on the type of media being employed.

- Accelerated 3D hardware: The graphics subsystem includes hardware to speed up and enhance the performance of 3D graphics.

Office PC99

It's no surprise that the Office PC99 spec deals with business-oriented PCs. Here, networking, reliable operation, and cost of ownership are paramount. Although multimedia capabilities are nice to have, they aren't critical to the mission of most business PCs.

Office PC99 demands two specific features:

- Manageability enhancements to the PC's BIOS and the motherboard that allow IS managers to control and configure PCs over the network, as well as install software.
- A network interface card with NDIS 5 driver support that ensures full compatibility with Windows 95 and NT.

In addition, the Office PC99 spec recommends many of the same features included in the Consumer PC99 version. Among them:

- IEEE 1394 FireWire
- Device Bay
- Accelerated Graphics Port (AGP)
- TV capability
- DVD-ROM drive
- Accelerated 3D hardware

Entertainment PC99

Microsoft and Intel aren't content with the traditional PC market. They want a slice of the home electronics business too—stereo equipment, TVs and VCRs, and game consoles. PC99 is an important step toward melding the PC to these traditional devices (see Figure 1.3).

Entertainment PC99 demands the following capabilities not found on other PC99 PCs:

- Two USB and FireWire ports, including one of each mounted on the front of the PC for easy access.
- Bundled joystick and game pad, which conform to the standard human interface device specification governing USB-based input devices.
- Remote control hardware: Wireless mouse and keyboard are needed.
- MPEG-2 video playback capability and TV tuner.
- DVD-ROM drive.
- Compliance with the OnNow specification, which provides for low-power sleep mode so that PCs can be left on permanently.

FIGURE 1.3.
Gateway 2000's Destination line of PCs, which broke new ground in consumer convergence, looks more like a consumer video setup than a traditional PC. (Photo courtesy of Gateway 2000)

In addition, Entertainment PC99 recommends several features, including the following:

- Device Bay
- Accelerated Graphics Port (AGP)
- TV capability
- DVD-ROM drive
- Accelerated 3D hardware

Mobile PC99

When it comes to mobile computing, the PC99 specifications once again provide a minimal configuration. No surprise, the compact notebook form factor demands some compromises. CPU speeds are slower, hard disks smaller, and expansion requirements are tailored to the tight spaces of laptop PCs.

For example, Mobile PC99 is the only specification still allowing for Pentium MMX class CPUs, with a 233-MHz Pentium MMX as the minimal notebook target. Perhaps most critical, the specification demands that notebooks use 32-bit PC Cards for adding modems and other peripherals, and include IR and USB ports for connecting to devices such as printers, scanners, and desktop PCs.

Workstation PC99

This subset of the Office PC99 spec calls for a beefier configuration that is in line with the demands of the Windows NT operating system. Minimum processors run at 400MHz (versus 300MHz), while system RAM starts at 128MB. The assumption for Workstation class systems is that they are involved in heavy-duty multitasking, high-end graphics, and other processor intensive tasks.

Workstation PCs also call for more advanced disk subsystems, with SCSI used to host multiple hard disks, for example. IEEE 1394 is also recommended for disk drives, though this technology is probably a couple years away from widespread adoption.

The PC Tomorrow

You now know what's on the menu for 1999, but what about a couple years from now? If you're like most buyers, you want your system purchases and upgrades to keep you a step ahead of the obsolescence freight train. The following sections describe a few key applications and technologies to look out for.

Voice Recognition

There are two categories of voice recognition:

- Voice command and control
- Voice dictation

Just as the mouse helped redefine the PC interface, expect voice command and control to add a new dimension to PC interfaces. Voice control of PCs has existed for years, but less-than-perfect recognition and hefty performance overhead made it a clumsy solution. As PCs get faster and audio capabilities become better integrated, voice command becomes a viable option.

Perhaps the biggest stumbling block has been the inability of PCs to understand anything other than the exact words or phrases required to recognize a command. Say "File New," and your word processor will open a new document, but say "Create a file," and you'll get an error message. This creates more problems than it solves.

Voice dictation, on the other hand, is the vocal equivalent of typing in a word processor or spreadsheet. Here, the task gets much tougher, because the PC must understand tens of thousands of words on-the-fly. What's more, it must deal with grammatical nuances and pesky homonyms—words that sound alike but mean different things.

If you want voice recognition today, you'll want the fastest Pentium II processor you can afford and a lot of system memory. Also look for a good sound board with a headset microphone for optimal gain.

High Bandwidth Net Access

The modem of the future will be all-digital—no more screeching telephone signals. Cable modems are being rolled out in select markets nationwide, while the telephone companies are testing digital subscriber line (DSL) service. Although DSL data rates vary, even the most affordable plans offer digital service that is many times faster than current 56Kbps access. However, deployment remains scattered.

The good news is that today's PCs will be able to access these technologies with simple card-based upgrades. That said, you'll want a fast CPU and a big hard disk to manage the larger data pipes.

Bigger Monitors

Expect bigger displays for both CRT and flat-panel LCD- (liquid crystal display) type screens. 19-inch CRTs have become a viable midrange buy for people who want to spend a little extra to get the most display area.

More significantly, flat-panel display prices are finally falling, with the screens becoming a real option for desktop PCs . Today, 15-inch desktop LCD displays are selling for about $1,000, and prices should continue to fall. Analysts expect LCD markets to become a mainstream player around 2002. These flat panel screens are lighter, more energy efficient, and easier on the eyes than traditional CRTs. Image quality is also superior. Still, CRTs will remain less expensive for the foreseeable future.

Better Buses

USB is here today, but look for FireWire to emerge on multimedia desktop PCs. During the next few years, FireWire will improve from its current minimum of 200MBps to more than 1 gigabit per second (gbps), making it a match for the most demanding operations.

Inside the PC, the new AGP is getting better. Intel 4x AGP (or AGP Pro) has emerged on workstation-class systems based on the Xeon processor. Although targeted at 3D graphics design and other high-end operations, AGP 4x should play in the mainstream market by 2000. We've also seen fast-and-wide PCI buses on server-class systems, allowing faster access to high-speed network interface cards (NICs) and hard disk drives. This standard allows 133MHz operation (versus 66MHz) over a wide 64-bit bus.

Device Bay

It may be part of the PC99 spec, but expect the Device Bay to be something that comes into serious play during the next two years. This standard approach to peripheral installations hopes to make swapping in drives and peripheral modules as easy as inserting a VHS tape. Plug and Play and on-the-fly system configuration (called *hot swapping*) both figure prominently in this technology.

A Note on Notebooks

No discussion of PC technology is complete without covering portable PCs. Notebooks occupy a growing segment of the market and are becoming more affordable as manufacturers get better.

In general, the same technologies and somewhat-altered components are used in notebooks as in desktop PCs. The main issues impacting notebooks are

- Compact size and light weight
- Low power consumption
- Low heat dissipation

The Package Defined

Because notebooks need to be small, you won't find any ISA or PCI bus slots for adding peripheral cards—unless you purchase a separate docking station unit that serves as a desktop home base for your notebook PC. Nor will you see any 5¼-inch disk drives and bays. Notebooks are complete dead ends when it comes to performance and upgrades (see Figure 1.4).

FIGURE 1.4.

The compact design of notebook PCs makes them more expensive to build and more difficult to upgrade than their desktop counterparts.

A typical notebook weighs between 6 and 12 pounds, including all the accouterments such as battery packs, power bricks, and other components. The chassis is about 10 inches by 12 inches, or a little larger than a typical sheet of paper, and the height can range between 1 and 2 inches. As a rule, the faster and more feature-rich your PC, the more weight and size you'll have to contend with. For this reason, if you travel a lot, you might want to compromise features to improve portability.

Otherwise, a notebook is similar to a desktop. There is a CPU, hard disk, display, keyboard, and even a pointing device (although it's not a mouse). You'll also find serial and parallel ports, as well as USB ports on some newer models, and virtually all notebooks now include integrated sound and speakers. Many notebooks today also include a modem and CD-ROM drive, making them the functional equivalent of desktop PCs.

Components

Notebooks might feature the same component set as desktops, but there are differences. Table 1.1 lists them.

Table 1.1. What's the difference?

Component	Desktop	Notebook
CPU	3.3 or 2.9 volt operation	2.2 volt operation, compact design
Display	15- to 19-inch CRT	12- to 15-inch LCD
Hard disk	3½-inch width	2½-inch width
PCI bus	Three to four add-in slots	Integrated bus, expansion slots available with external docking stations
PC Card bus	Not present	Two or more slots of PC Card peripherals
Pointing device	Mouse	Integrated pointer, port for using optional mouse
Power supply	200+ watt power supply	Lithium ion battery

Notebook PCs might have many of the same components as desktop systems, but that doesn't mean the two are on equal footing. The low-power and space requirements of notebook PCs means the newest technologies take some time to get to notebooks. In general, expect notebooks to be slower than their desktop counterparts and to be more expensive to upgrade with additional RAM or larger hard disks.

If you use your notebook mostly in the office, you can get around the expansion limitations of the notebook form factor. Docking stations plug into an expansion port on the back of many notebook PCs, allowing users to plug in add-in cards, various input devices, and other peripherals. The drawback? Docking stations add $400 or more to the cost of a notebook.

Summary

PCs are complex beasts, but they are not this way without reason. If you want to make sense of what makes a PC tick, you need to understand the parts that comprise it. When you do, it's much easier to know what you need for your particular applications and needs.

Of course, PC technology is hardly standing still. The PC99 specification advances the capabilities and ease of use of the PC platform. As these technologies mature and propagate, PCs will begin to look more like consumer electronic devices and less like complex electronics gear aimed at hobbyists and programmers. In the meantime, it pays to stay on top of the acronyms and cryptic standards at the heart of PC products.

Inside Windows 95 and 98

I admit it—I'm a hardware freak. I love megahertz, gigabytes, and the subtle science of submicron physics. There's something really neat about the fact that processor power essentially doubles every 18 months. But there is one simple fact even hard-core hardware junkies must come to terms with: Software makes the world go 'round.

More specifically, operating systems and applications make hardware worth buying. The real value of a PC isn't in the hot new Pentium II processor with MMX technology or in the huge 16GB hard disk. What matters is what the software enables you to do. If you can create better documents more quickly or play better games and titles, the hardware means something.

Ultimately, the operating system determines what your programs can do, so it really pays to be aware of what you're running. In addition, the OS provides key facilities and talents for configuring and troubleshooting your hardware. The good news is that Under Windows 95, users have more resources available to them than ever before.

In this chapter, you will learn about:

- The operating system's role in the operation of your PC and its applications
- The evolution of the Windows operating system and its key features
- Windows 98
- Features within Windows 95 that can help you manage and configure your hardware

Windows 95: The Operating System that Reinvented the PC

When Windows 95 arrived in August of 1995, it was a very big deal. The successor to the hugely successful Windows 3.x operating environment, Windows 95 brought a number of key features to the mainstream desktop PC. And these features continue to define later OSs, like Windows 98 and Windows NT 4.0. Among the key features:

- 32-bit addressing: The 32-bit address scheme vastly simplified program code and eliminated key weaknesses in 16-bit Windows that invited frequent system crashes.

- Plug and Play: Perhaps the most important innovation in the history of personal computing, Plug and Play eased the treacherous game of trial and error that usually accompanied a hardware upgrade.

- Multitasking and multithreading: These features let capable programs do more than one thing at once, speeding performance when running multiple applications as well as when doing several things within a single application (for example, printing and scrolling at the same time).

- Hardware Abstraction Layer (HAL): This software layer sits between applications and hardware, preventing conflicts and problems that can arise when many applications try to work directly with many hardware products. Hardware makers provide an interface between their hardware and the OS, while applications use standard pathways to reach hardware.

- Hardware management: Windows 95 tracks and provides an interface for managing hardware settings—features that previously were available only in third-party utilities.

- Integrated operating system: For the first time, Windows worked without separate DOS underpinnings. Although the DOS core still existed, Windows 95 presented a cleaner and more reliable structure to both users and programmers.

- Dynamic device drivers: Windows 95 VxDs allow hardware drivers to load and unload without restarting the system, making it possible to hot-swap components or share resources. This talent is particularly useful in notebooks.

32-bit Revolution

Intel processors have provided 32-bit addressing since the 386 was introduced in 1988. Yet almost all PC software written before August 1995 was based on 16-bit addressing schemes. The reason is that without a popular 32-bit operating system, applications couldn't reach the full feature set of Intel's 32-bit CPUs.

Applications Get Better

What's so important about the number of address bits available to programs? For one thing, 16-bit addresses are too small to easily access all the data and code applications typically in use. In order to find data in memory, programmers had to resort to segmented addressing, a time-consuming scheme that takes several steps to hone in on bits stored in memory. Segmented addressing not only took longer to write, but it also hurt application performance.

32-bit addressing freed programmers to worry about other things. Large data sets could be addressed in a single chunk, not parsed and recombined after the fact. The result was faster, more stable, and less complex code. For users, it simply meant better software and better performance.

The Secure Operating System

In addition, the 32-bit Windows 95 operating system provides a much more stable environment than previous DOS-based systems. With the large address space provided by the 32-bit address scheme, Windows 95 can build secure walls around its applications.

Properly-written Windows 95 programs can crash and conflict all they want, but they can do so only within their own piece of memory real estate. The program itself might crash, but the bits owned by Windows 95 or other running applications won't get touched. No more wholesale system lockups and nasty Windows 3.1-style general protection faults (GPFs). In theory, at least, Windows 95's memory space is secure from application blow-ups.

Windows 95 also provides far greater resources for applications than the 16-bit version did. Applications under Windows 3.1 had to register themselves within memory stacks, which the OS used to track program activity. Unfortunately, not enough capacity was left to run more than a few large applications, leading to confusing out-of-memory errors, even on systems with 16 or 32MB of RAM. Windows 95 greatly increased the capacity of these stacks, enhancing stability when multitasking (see Figure 2.1).

FIGURE 2.1.
You can't see the reworked application resource infrastructure in Windows 95, but its effect is evident when you're multitasking. Now, Windows 95 stays stable even when you're running several large applications.

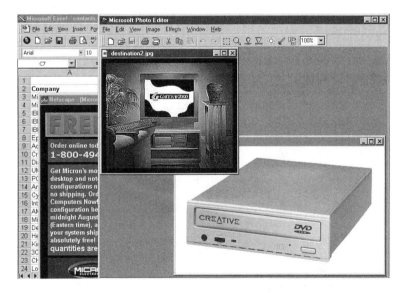

The truth is not quite so pretty. For one thing, Microsoft had to provide almost complete compatibility with the thousands of 16-bit DOS and Windows 3.1 applications. To do this, Microsoft exposed some of the Windows 95 memory space to these older programs.

The technical details aren't important. What is important is that Microsoft essentially built a soft underbelly to its Windows 95 OS—one that continues to exist in Windows 98. If a program crashes and mucks with this shared memory space, the entire OS and other running applications can be compromised.

> **Note:** Windows 95 kicked off the 32-bit software revolution, but it was hardly the first to market. In fact, IBM beat Microsoft to the punch by about four years. The OS/2 operating system provided true 32-bit support and outstanding DOS compatibility long before Windows 95 arrived. Although OS/2 remains a factor in mission-critical applications such as banking, corporate database management, and government applications, it failed to catch fire in the mainstream. Hefty hardware requirements and some very shrewd maneuvering by Microsoft helped keep OS/2 in the corner of the market despite its early lead.
>
> Microsoft's other operating system, Windows NT, actually does the 32-bit thing better than Windows 95. Like OS/2, NT is aimed at corporate heavyweights and workstations. Despite its name, it bears little structural resemblance to Windows 95. NT forgoes 16-bit compatibility to provide a nearly bulletproof environment. So although your games and many older programs won't run under NT, no program gets to jump into shared memory space and topple the operating system. This kind of security is critical for businesses, who need their networks running every minute of every day. The constant watchdogging also affects performance and demands more system memory and other resources.

Multitasking

In addition to stabler, more feature-rich programs, the 32-bit OS helps boost performance. Windows 95 provides multitasking and multithreading, allowing several applications and operations to run simultaneously. There are two kinds of multitasking:

- Cooperative
- Preemptive

Cooperative multitasking, provided in Windows 3.1, basically gives the processor's attention to each running application. If an application happens to grab the system for a long time, other applications or operations might fail as they become starved for attention. The result is a scheme that can result in crashes or system lock-ups.

Preemptive multitasking allows software to butt in and grab the CPU, thus preempting the running operation. This scheme ensures that Internet downloads, for example, won't fail because a big spreadsheet recalculation is taking up 100 percent of the CPU. Instead, Windows 95 will make sure that the OS will stop working on the recalculation task for a bit to ensure that the big download gets the attention it needs.

Finally, *multithreading* provides smooth handling of multiple tasks within an application. For programs designed to have multiple threads, the OS can let Excel conduct a monster recalculation even as it spools a print job and saves a separate file. As with preemptive multitasking, the threads are tracked to ensure that none is forsaken.

Hardware Handling

Here is where the rubber meets the road. Windows 95 changed the hardware rule book, and almost entirely for the better. Better device management, better compatibility, and Plug and Play all make Windows 95 a vastly superior platform for hardware.

Plug and Play

The single most important innovation was the introduction of Plug and Play, or PnP. Windows 95 is actually just one leg of the PnP standard, which was formulated by Microsoft, Intel, Compaq, and others to provide automated recognition and configuration of hardware in the PC. Here are the three components:

> **Note:** Windows NT 4.0 doesn't include Plug and Play technology, but its successor—NT 5.0—does. The addition of automated hardware detection and configuration in NT 5.0 should go a long way toward making NT a more popular mainstream operating system. Of course, Windows 98 uses the same PnP technology found in Windows 95.

- Hardware: PnP boards and devices include ROM that stores unique identifiers enabling the OS and BIOS to know the type of device, its manufacturer, and other key elements. Additional hardware allows for software-based configuration and the storing of data.

- BIOS: Because hardware must be polled and preconfigured before Windows 95 even starts, the BIOS must be set up to handle PnP hardware. The BIOS enumerates PnP devices, eventually handing its work over to Windows 95.

- Windows 95: The operating system interacts with the BIOS to ensure proper device configuration and includes facilities for automatically detecting new PnP devices.

In general, PC owners running Windows 95 fall into three categories when it comes to Plug and Play:

- Out of luck: Those with older 486 and Pentium systems probably lack PnP BIOS support. Without the PnP BIOS, neither the PnP logic on peripherals nor the PnP capabilities of Windows 95 can come into play. If your BIOS is Plug and Play, you should see the words "Plug and Play" appear along with the BIOS version number during startup. You can also check the BIOS version number against your system documentation to see if it supports Plug and Play.

- Mixed bag: Most users with new systems running Windows 95 will have a PnP BIOS in place. But there will be a mixture of PnP and non-PnP devices, often called *legacy hardware*. Windows 95 deals with legacy devices by moving PnP settings around the immovable resources of the older peripherals.

- Pure PnP: The best possible scenario. All the hardware and software can interact to determine the best settings for each device. Problems are reduced because hardwired resource settings don't force other devices into odd configurations.

> If you have a system with a mixture of PnP and legacy hardware, make a point of upgrading to devices that include PnP capability. By adding intelligent hardware over time, you will end up with a system that is more stable and easier to configure.

Device Management

As mentioned earlier, operating systems like Windows 95, 98, and NT put a standard layer between applications and all the hardware. The main benefit is that your applications don't need to support every hardware device on the market. Instead, they just need to talk to the operating system.

The key to this scheme is the driver software that comes with peripherals. Hardware vendors write specific driver software for their products, allowing programs to access hardware features. In the past, vendors have had to write separate drivers for the Windows 95/98 and NT operating systems, but Microsoft has since rolled out a common driver model enabling one driver to handle both OS families. In order to offer top performance and capabilities, hardware vendors frequently update their drivers.

Windows 95 and 98 offer extensive compatibility. Three types of drivers work under the operating systems:

- 16-bit Windows 3.1 drivers
- 32-bit virtual device drivers (VxDs) for Windows 95
- 32-bit Win32 Driver Model (WDM) device drivers for Windows 95 and NT

16-bit Drivers

Also called *real-mode* or *DOS-compatible drivers,* 16-bit drivers are written to work with Windows 3.1. Microsoft designed Windows 95 to be compatible with existing hardware, allowing it to work with device drivers written for Windows 3.1. The benefit is obvious: If a peripheral lacks a native Windows 95 driver, it will still work on Windows 95 systems using the original software.

Although you can usually get by with the old drivers, you won't want to. 16-bit drivers provide slower performance than native 32-bit drivers, meaning that disk drives, graphics cards, and other peripherals will fail to operate at optimal levels. More important, 16-bit drivers often lack features available in their contemporary counterparts. Graphics boards, for instance, feature drivers for switching resolutions or managing the desktop area—but those probably won't be available on 16-bit drivers.

32-bit Windows 95/98 Drivers

Today, most peripherals use drivers crafted specifically for Windows 95/98. Called *virtual device drivers,* or VxDs, this software provides direct support for hardware within Windows 95/98. It's no surprise that these drivers deliver optimized performance and include the full feature set.

One key talent of 32-bit drivers is their ability to load and unload without requiring the system to restart. This dynamic driver scheme allows Windows 95 PCs to effectively share resources and add capabilities when called upon. Notebook PCs, for instance, can recognize and initialize a PC Card modem the instant it is popped into the slot. Likewise, desktops can access a portable scanner when it is plugged in—memory-consuming drivers need not be loaded all the time in the expectation that the scanner might be activated.

Win32 Driver Model: The New 32-bit Driver

Perhaps most important of all, Microsoft has created a new driver scheme called Win32 Driver Model (WDM) that allows a single device driver to work under Windows 95/98 and NT. This emerging class of 32-bit drivers is a big boost for Windows NT, since vendors in the past have often passed on writing NT-specific drivers to focus on the larger Windows 9x market.

Why haven't some hardware vendors bothered to write NT drivers? For one thing, writing drivers isn't easy—in fact, it can border on black magic. Rapid-fire advancements in PC technology mean that driver software is simply trying to keep pace with the latest versions of hardware and software. If you add a second OS, the workload for a hardware company doubles.

Predictably, the OS with less market share gets less attention. This means Windows NT often gets saddled with aging, less-than-polished drivers for the hardware running under it. Now WDM helps bring NT into parity with Windows 9x, since a driver written for one OS will work equally well for another. That said, some devices will not be able to use the common driver model. Expect graphics and audio drivers to require distinct Windows 9x and NT versions for some time to come.

Peter's Principle: The Applications Make the OS

Often, deciding on an operating system can be a calculated risk. If you purchase a computer that has an OS on the wane—say, OS/2 or, to a lesser extent, a Macintosh—you might be unable to use the best hardware and software. In fact, the market for software and driver development behaves a lot like the stock market: When confidence among developers of a certain OS wanes, the relative value of the operating system often declines.

Take the Mac OS, for example. Today, many software vendors won't invest their resources in a marketplace that is a fraction of that of Windows 95. Even firms that made their fortune as Apple developers, such as Adobe and Macromedia, now release Windows 95 or NT versions of their products either before or at the same time as their Mac counterparts. The reasoning is simple: Companies can realize greater returns by honing their products for Windows 95 rather than shifting to the Mac OS.

Before you buy a Mac or a PC, you should consider the health of the operating system you want to use. If you want to play fast-action games, the Mac is a dead end. Likewise, NT is not a good option. If you want home-education software, Windows 95 is your best bet, with the Mac close behind. Once again, NT's corporate focus means that many CD-ROM games and home peripherals (such as programmable joysticks or keyboards for children) might not work on the OS.

Often the story is told on store shelves. Just as VHS beat out Betamax as the home-video recording standard, Windows 95 and other OSs constantly jockey for market position. As a general rule, the OS with the most software wins. And in this case, that OS is Windows 95—while compatibility makes Windows NT the next choice. Despite its woes, the Mac OS continues to offer excellent software for creative endeavors such as desktop publishing and image editing. Before you commit to an operating system, make sure you know what software vendors are supporting.

Windows 98: An Incremental Step

The latest update to Windows 95—called Windows 98—really amounts to a series of incremental improvements to the earlier OS. The most important new features in Windows 98 are:

- A Web-savvy interface, including a Web-like browser view and desktop "channels" that turn your display into a cross between a PC monitor and Web-savvy TV (see Figure 2.2).

- FAT32 hard disk support, which eliminates the need for multiple drive letters on disk drives greater than 2GB. It also reduces the amount of wasted space, called *slack*, that is accrued with small files (generally less than 16KB).

FIGURE 2.2.

If you right-click the Windows 98 desktop, select Properties, and select the Web tab, you can set your system to automatically access Web-based channels for the latest content.

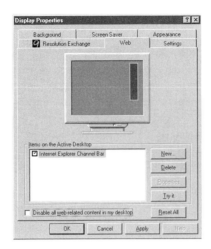

- Advanced bus support, including USB, AGP, IEEE 1394 (also known as FireWire), and fast IR.

- Enhanced multimedia capabilities, including MMX accelerated code built into key Windows 98 components, such as the video- and audio-handling subsystems. The new ActiveMovie interface delivers better control than the old Media Player, while DirectX drivers provide hooks for compelling game play and multimedia playback.

- Native DVD drive support. DVD-ROM drives under Windows 98 are no longer seen as CD-ROM devices, as is the case with Windows 95.

- WebTV software for viewing television broadcasts on your PC—provided you have a TV tuner card installed. This feature lets you view programs, select and search from a downloadable TV schedule, and set up a custom viewing schedule.

- Advanced power management, including sleep mode for desktop PCs. PC Card peripherals also gain better low-power operation.

Is Windows 98 a slam-dunk upgrade? Maybe not. For one thing, many features of the operating system have been available from Microsoft's Web site or on new PCs for months or even years. It's very likely that many of these features are already on your system. If you've already downloaded Internet Explorer 4.0 (IE4), the DirectX 6.0 driver set, and the PowerToys utilities, you're well on your way to having Windows 98 on your desktop.

That said, there is something to be said for a wholesale upgrade. Core components of the OS get retrofitted, and the all-in-one update can ensure that you have the best of everything. This is also the only realistic option for people who ply the Web with a 28.8KBps modem. IE4 is over 22MB in size—a nearly impossible download for analog surfers.

So what makes Windows 98 worth buying? Two things, FAT32 and USB. The following is a rundown for these critical technologies, so you can decide if they are important enough for you to consider a Windows 98 upgrade.

Exploring FAT32

Perhaps the most critical improvement is the introduction of a new file system, called FAT32. Previously, the only file system available to Windows 95 users was FAT16, which suffered from key limitations. FAT 16 can only recognize 2GB per logical partition. Which means that in order to use a hard disk larger than 2GB in size, you had to break it into a series of drive letters. Today's 16GB drives, therefore, would require 8 drive letters under FAT16.

For more on working with file systems, see Chapter 11, "Taking Hard Disks for a Spin."

In addition to allowing large disk partitions, FAT32 cuts down the amount of wasted space on a drive. Under FAT16, even the smallest file on a 2GB drive will consume 32KB of space. This minimum file increment—called a cluster—means that tens of megabytes of usable space can be wasted in a single partition. FAT32, by contrast, limits the cluster size to 8KB on disk partitions up to 8GB. Table 2.1 compares the cluster sizes of FAT16 and FAT32.

Table 2.1. Slacker: FAT16 wastes bits as partitions grow in size.

Partition Size	FAT16 Cluster Size	FAT32 Cluster Size
16MB-128MB	2KB	4KB
128MB-256MB	4KB	4KB
256MB-512MB	8KB	8KB
512MB-1GB	16KB	8KB
1GB-2GB	32KB	8KB
2GB-8GB	n/a	8KB
8GB-60GB	n/a	16KB
60GB-2,000GB	n/a	32KB

Windows 98 also adds some intelligence to its handling of files on a FAT32 partition. The OS monitors activity to determine which applications and files are most often accessed. These files are moved to the outer edge of the physical disk platters, where the higher rotation rates enable faster loading and access. Automated disk defragmentation helps maintain top performance.

During the Windows 98 upgrade, you are given the choice whether or not to move your FAT16 disk partitions to FAT32. However, you should be aware that some of your existing software may not work properly under FAT32. System utilities—and particularly disk utilities—may conflict with FAT32 since the new file system changes underlying data structures. Older DOS software may also not work with FAT32, since these programs expect to have direct access to a hard disk that is assumed to be built on FAT16.

Finally, it's worth noting that once you upgrade to FAT32, you can not easily move back. If you find that valuable programs will not work, you'll either need to upgrade your software or reformat the hard disk, reinstate FAT16, and then rebuild your applications and data.

USB to the Rescue

If you own a Pentium MMX or faster system, Windows 98 should also give you access to an exciting new class of peripherals that run off the Universal Serial Bus (USB). This external Plug and Play bus is designed to replace your serial, parallel, keyboard, and mouse ports. You can tell if your system has USB by checking the back of the PC. You should see a pair of small, rectangular ports.

What makes USB important? For one thing, Windows 98 can instantly detect and load any device that's plugged into the port, without having to reboot. In addition, USB can support up to 127 separate devices, which can be attached to each other daisy-chain fashion. This feature fixes the problem with current peripherals, which must often be physically swapped out, as multiple devices make use of a single parallel or serial port. The bus performance is also better than that of existing parallel ports, with a 12Mbps data rate that is more than 50 percent faster than the fastest parallel port technology.

But wait, there's more. Many USB devices can draw power directly from the USB wire, doing away with bulky power cords and plugs. Scanners, modems, and force feedback joysticks are all more streamlined in their USB incarnation.

While USB is supported under Windows 95, the support is not complete. Device makers must provide additional software to work with the older OS, posing enough concerns and cost that many vendors are not supporting it. By contrast, Windows 98 has proven a very stable platform for USB, automatically detecting, installing, and configuring USB peripherals.

Windows NT: Microsoft's Buttoned-Down Operating System

Where Windows 95 was targeted at mainstream users, Windows NT caters to a more discerning crowd. Microsoft's bulletproof OS is designed to run in heavy-duty systems that demand complete reliability. Among them are

- Network servers
- Web servers
- Graphics workstations
- Heavy-duty corporate desktops

Windows NT will certainly run on standalone home and office machines, but most such users won't be tempted to move from Windows 95. Why? For one thing, NT demands more resources than Windows 95—32MB of RAM is a good starting point, for example—meaning that many users would face a stiff hardware upgrade in order to run NT effectively.

There are actually two flavors of NT:

- Windows NT Workstation
- Windows NT Server

The two employ the same core code, but you'll find a greater range of networking features in the NT Server package. NT 4.0 Server can do duty as a full Web server platform, but Workstation is limited in the number of connected systems it can support. You'll also find greater symmetric multiprocessing (SMP) support in NT Server. Unlike Windows 95, which can recognize only a single processor, NT can recognize four CPUs at once.

Advantages of Windows NT

Like Windows 95, Windows NT is a multithreaded, multitasking operating system, meaning it can smoothly juggle many tasks at once. And with version 4.0, Windows NT even looks like Windows 95—a significant improvement over the Windows 3.1 look of its predecessor. NT 4.0 uses familiar tools such as Control Panel, Device Manager, and the Start button.

Most important, NT is a true mission-critical operating system, unlike Windows 95, which incorporates 16-bit code and a fragile memory structure in order to ensure compatibility. Windows NT was designed from the ground up to be bulletproof. Applications running under NT have no access to memory used by other applications or the operating system. If Excel crashes, it won't take NT down with it.

In fact, the core function of the operating system (called the *kernel*) is protected by an abstraction layer preventing programs from fiddling with the OS. Instead, commands are handed off by applications and then handled internally by the operating system. The result is a sort of relay race in which the baton is handed to the OS to handle a function and then handed back to the application as soon as the task is complete. The drawback is that NT takes a lot of time to switch between internal and external operation, resulting in slower performance than under Windows 95 or 98.

How important is the reliability of NT? Businesses such as banks require that their systems run without fail, often 24 hours a day, seven days a week. Occasional reboots and the odd system crash aren't annoyances—they are service disruptions resulting in lost sales and clients. NT is the first operating system from Microsoft that is delivering that kind of rock-solid performance. Business users and developers also find that NT Workstation allows them to run their desktops all day without rebooting. Windows 95 and 98, by contrast, must occasionally be restarted when running several applications in order to recapture lost resources.

Perhaps most important, NT uses a familiar code base. Developers can write their applications for both Windows 95 and NT using the same code, creating an immediate and enormous market of NT-compatible software. Called Win32, this application programming interface (API) attracts more developer effort than any other in the market.

Drawbacks of Windows NT

NT isn't perfect. Mainstream users are still put off by NT's stiff hardware requirements and slower performance than Windows 95. What's more, although NT features the Windows 95 interface, it lacks Plug and Play capability. Hardware installations and resource settings must be handled manually, resulting in much more trial and error.

NT also lacks compatibility with some hardware and software—a big reason why the OS hasn't moved into the mainstream desktop market. Hardware devices must use NT-specific device drivers in order to work with the OS, requiring additional effort some companies are unwilling to undertake. Although the roster of NT-compatible devices is growing quickly, buyers with NT systems must still be careful to make sure that the hardware they purchase will work with the operating system.

Software compatibility is a problem for games. Windows NT's strict security slows performance and rules out the kind of direct access most games require. Microsoft is addressing part of this problem by bringing its DirectX technologies over NT, but the transition is not immediate. Windows 95 typically enjoys a long feature lead over NT in handling games and multimedia; in some cases, games might not run at all under NT. If you have a PC that needs to run both business apps and entertainment titles, you'll need to stick with Windows 95.

Coming Up

Like Windows 95 and 98, NT is evolving. Microsoft has added multimedia savvy to the operating system with the DirectX technology set. The addition of DirectX should also further software compatibility. In addition, the Win32 Driver Model (WDM) eases the driver development burden. WDM allows a single driver to work on both Windows 9x and NT, so a vendor needs to write a driver just once in order to reach both operating systems.

For many users, NT becomes a real option with the arrival of Windows NT 5.0. This version finally adds Plug and Play to the NT family, as well as support for USB, advanced power management, and DirectX multimedia technology. In effect, with 5.0, NT finally catches up to Windows 95/98 in supporting cutting edge technologies.

Is NT for you? If you run server applications or do heavy-duty graphical work such as 3D computer-aided design (CAD) or video editing, it might be. And if you want to run Windows applications on a multiprocessor PC, NT is the only real choice. These advantages, plus the fact that NT uses the familiar Windows 95 interface, make NT an attractive option for businesses and professionals.

Living with Windows 95 and 98

Unless you're an affirmed UNIX junkie, you probably welcomed the move to Windows 95. The 32-bit OS mostly did away with the inscrutable command-line interface and the teetering Windows-on-DOS structure that was so prone to crashing. In many ways, Windows 95 actually surpasses the vaunted Mac OS, with features such as Plug and Play.

That said, Windows 95 has its share of problems. The interface might be vastly improved from Windows 3.1, but accessing hardware settings can be a trial. The Control Panel facility—the central repository for hardware configuration—is a veritable dumping ground of icons. Likewise, Plug and Play can fail spectacularly, creating greater problems than it solves. The following sections will help guide you toward the features in Windows 95 that can help you.

Microsoft improved things a bit by rolling out an upgrade to Windows 95 called Windows 98. However, the new OS version is hardly a large step forward. Rather, Windows 98 presents a variety of tweaks, fixes, and enhancements that help improve upon the original—revolutionary—design.

Control Panel

If you're dealing with hardware, no resource is more important than the Windows 95 Control Panel. Control Panel provides one-stop shopping for finding and adjusting hardware settings, adding and removing peripherals, and changing drivers. Whether you plan on upgrading your hardware or keeping abreast of the latest driver software, you should be familiar with the Windows 95 Control Panel.

> **Note:** The Windows 95 and 98 Control Panels and other facilities are largely similar. While some changes have occurred in the individual Properties windows, readers will be able to follow these Windows 95-specific instruction for either OS.

To access Control Panel, simply select Start, Settings, Control Panel. You will see a window with over a dozen icons, representing hardware devices and Windows 95 facilities (see Figure 2.3). When you double-click an icon, you are taken to the appropriate properties sheet. Here you will find crucial information for the device, such as driver versions, system resource settings (IRQ, DMA, and so on), and device settings.

Over time, you might notice additional icons appear under Control Panel. Graphics card drivers, for example, might install a new icon in Control Panel. These new icons often provide enhanced features for installed hardware or address a peripheral type not supplied in the default Control Panel setup.

FIGURE 2.3.
From Control Panel, you can gain access to virtually every peripheral attached to your PC.

Control Panel also contains key upgrade facilities under the Add New Hardware and the Add/Remove Programs icons. We will step through some of these resources.

Accessing Device Properties Using Control Panel

Let's walk through this quickly. To access the properties of a device—say, a modem—do the following:

1. Select Start, Settings, Control Panel.

2. Double-click the Modems icon.

3. In the Modems properties sheet, click the modem you want to inspect. (You can have multiple modems set up.)

4. Click the Properties button to view the specific settings for this device.

5. In this case, the screen that appears provides information on COM port settings, device speeds, and speaker volume. You can also follow the Connections tab to inspect dialing settings for the device.

Once you get to the properties sheet, you'll see different interfaces for each device. After all, a graphics card doesn't use the same resources as a modem or a printer. A little digging should make you familiar with where the information is stored.

Adding New Hardware

This being an upgrade book and all, it seems logical to step through the procedure for adding devices to your PC. Windows 95 and 98's Add New Hardware icon is your upgrade gateway. This icon launches the Add New Hardware Wizard, a step-by-step interactive installation guide that prompts you to tell Windows what you're installing and how you want it done. This useful resource also fires up Windows 95's Plug and Play, so you can let the operating system do the installation automatically.

Actually, there are three ways to install new hardware, and it can get confusing. Here are the options you might face:

- New hardware detected at boot-up: The Add New Hardware Wizard launches when you start Windows 95 or 98.

- Use the Add New Hardware icon: You tell Windows 95 or 98 to fire up the Add New Hardware Wizard by using the generic hardware install facility.

- Use the specific device icon: You tell Windows 95 or 98 to install a specific device by clicking the Add button found on the properties sheet of the device type you want to install.

The most common upgrade is for Windows to sense new hardware when it is started. After all, any internal device upgrade will require you to reboot the system. In this example, we will install a new sound card. Note that internal components such as ISA modems usually don't require you to click the Add New Hardware button. That's because Windows 95's Plug and Play will detect the new device and launch the Add New Hardware Wizard at startup.

1. First, install the new card into your PC. Of course, you must shut down the system, remove the power cord, and open the case to do this.

2. Once the sound card is in, start up Windows. The operating system will detect the new hardware at boot-up and launch the Add New Hardware Wizard.

3. Click the Next button to kick things off.

4. Windows 95 asks to detect the hardware. Click the Yes radio button and then click Next to let Windows 95's Plug and Play go to work.

UPGRADE ADVICE

> You can speed up the upgrade process by telling Windows not to detect new hardware. If you do this, make sure you know exactly which device you're working with, the manufacturer name, and the model name. Also, make sure you have the driver disk handy so that you can load the device drivers and other utilities when prompted. Skipping the detection step can save up to several minutes of waiting around. Be careful, though. If you've just removed an older card and replaced it with a newer model, you should let PnP do its work so that Windows knows about the change to the old hardware. It's worth noting that Windows 98 relies heavily on auto-detection of hardware—you may simply want to let Windows 98 handle setup on its own.

5. Get a cup of coffee, or something. The detection process can take a while, particularly on slower machines.

6. Windows will prompt you with the name of the manufacturer and model of the device it detected. If this information is correct, click Next.

7. When prompted to install device drivers, use the Browse button to select the drivers from the supplied floppy disk or CD-ROM. This usually means pointing the installation to the appropriate drive and (sometimes) directory.

8. Wait while the drivers load. You might need to restart your system in order for the new device to work. Keep a close watch during this process.

9. Once everything is loaded, restart your system (even if you are not prompted to do so) in order to ensure that all changes take effect. Also, test newly installed hardware immediately after setup. For the sound card, try playing some system sounds or MIDI files. You can also access the properties sheet from Control Panel to check the resources that Windows 95 has assigned.

If you are replacing an existing device, there are a few issues to consider. For one thing, you should make sure Windows 9x registers the removal of the old hardware before plugging in the new product. That will help reduce the chance for error in the detection process. The first thing you should do is uninstall any dedicated software for the device, using a provided uninstall facility (if available) or Windows' own Add/Remove facility (if not). For example, a Matrox graphics card might install PowerDesk graphics tools, which you will want to remove prior to removing the hardware.

Next, out with the hardware. For internal cards, that means shutting down the PC, pulling out the board, and then restarting. The auto-detection feature will sense the change and remove the hardware settings from the Windows 9x Registry. You should then check the Device Manager (under Start, Settings, Control Panel) to make sure that no reference to the old device is present.

Once these steps are done, you can once again shut down the PC and install the new internal hardware. At this point, simply follow the steps as described previously. Windows' hardware auto-detection should be able to handle the new configuration smoothly.

Things are a bit simpler for external devices such as printers, scanners, and modems. You'll want to unplug the device from the PC (while running) and then manually remove the device from the Windows Device Manager properties box. To do this, click Start, Settings, Control Panel, open the System icon and click the Device Manager tab. Find the device type you are replacing in the scrolling list box, double-click it, and then select the specific item entry. Click the Remove button. While you can usually hook up the new hardware and install the drivers, you may want to restart Windows to ensure that the Registry has fully reflected the device removal.

> **Tip:** If you are installing a new graphics card, you need to be extra careful. Your new card may not work with the graphics settings Windows has been using with the old one. If you install the new hardware without moving to a compatible graphics setting, you will likely see a severely distorted screen and could invite damage to your hardware. Before you remove the old graphics card, make sure you set the screen resolution to simple VGA (640 by 480 pixels). This will ensure that your new card will be able to immediately display the screen, allowing you to then readjust the resolution to optimal settings.

The Add/Remove Programs Facility

Control Panel also contains the Add/Remove Programs icon. This useful resource guides you through software installation and, more importantly, provides a way to remove programs from your PC. These are your upgrade gateways, providing a structured approach to updating your system.

Double-click the Add/Remove Programs icon. You will see a dialog box that has three tabs, as shown in Figure 2.4.

Figure 2.4.

The Add/Remove Programs Properties dialog box is a powerful resource for updating Windows with new software.

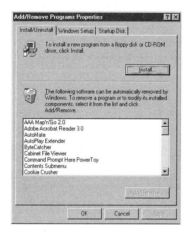

- Install/Uninstall: Adds and removes applications
- Windows Setup: Adds and removes Windows 95 utilities and features
- Startup Disk: Creates an emergency boot disk for troubleshooting problems

As with the Add New Hardware process, a wizard interface guides you through the installation step-by-step. This useful approach can help keep novices out of trouble. But as with adding hardware, you don't have to use this facility to install new software. It's just one option.

Here are the common methods that an application installation routine may start:

- CD-ROM setup file detected: Windows 95's AutoPlay feature detects a new CD-ROM disc and automatically fires up the installation wizard after you insert the disc.
- Use the Add/Remove Programs icon: You tell Windows 95 to fire up the installation wizard by double-clicking the Add/Remove Programs icon and clicking the Install button on the Install/Uninstall tab.
- Double-click the SETUP.EXE file directly: You bypass the wizard and launch the appropriate SETUP.EXE file by double-clicking it.

All these approaches yield the same result. And provided that the application conforms to Windows 95's guidelines for installation, you'll be able to uninstall the program using the Add/Remove Programs resource.

The System Tray

Another place to access hardware settings is from the system tray, which is found on the Windows 95 Taskbar (see Figure 2.5). Small icons on the far right of the Taskbar denote hardware with a system tray interface. Graphics card settings, sound card volume and settings, and the PC's system clock can generally be accessed from here. In addition, custom graphics and joystick drivers might place an icon in the system tray. Active print and fax jobs are displayed in the tray as well.

FIGURE 2.5.
The small icons at the far-right of the Taskbar provide instant access to volume controls, desktop icons, display settings, and modem status, among other things.

Tip: You can enhance the Taskbar using Microsoft's PowerToys software. This free utility adds a Taskbar-based monitor icon for switching colors and resolutions on-the-fly, as well as an icon for accessing desktop elements without having to close application windows. You can download the PowerToys utilities at the Microsoft Web site at:

```
http://www.microsoft.com/windows/downloads/contents/PowerToys/
W95PwrToysSet/
```

Device Manager

Perhaps the single most important element when it comes to managing hardware under Windows is Device Manager. Considering its importance in keeping track of resource settings and installed devices, Device Manager is surprisingly difficult to access. You will find it buried within the System Properties dialog box. There are two ways to get to Device Manager—from Control Panel and from the Windows 95 desktop.

To access Device Manager from Control Panel, do the following:

1. Open Control Panel and double-click the Systems icon.
2. In the System Properties dialog box, choose the Device Manager tab.

To access Device Manager from the Windows 95 desktop, do the following:

1. Right-click the My Computer icon on the desktop and choose Properties from the context menu that appears.

2. The System Properties dialog box appears. Choose the Device Manager tab.

> **Tip:** If you're too impatient to wait for context menus, you can fire up the System Properties dialog box by selecting the My Computer icon on the desktop and pressing Alt-Enter. The System Properties dialog box will come up right away.

Device Manager Explained

Device Manager provides a list of all the various hardware devices stored on your PC. Everything from CD-ROM drives to network adapters has an icon in this list. By clicking the + symbol next to the desired device type, you can see what hardware is installed on your system in the selected device category. Double-click the revealed devices, and you'll be transported to a useful configuration sheet that includes resource settings and driver information for the device. You can even change settings directly from this facility, making it easy to hunt down and resolve conflicts.

Most importantly, Device Manager enables you to ferret out conflicts and problems. If a device is in conflict with another device, a yellow circle with a question mark appears next to the affected devices, as shown in Figure 2.6. This is an effective visual cue that immediately guides the user to hardware problems. For example, the driver software may not be properly installed. A red "x" indicates an item that has been disabled.

FIGURE 2.6.

Helpful icons draw your attention to devices that need troubleshooting— a big help when you're trying to get to the bottom of a mystery.

You'll also find an icon called System at the bottom of the list. Here you will find nitty-gritty details on resources for things such as the PCI bus, the ISA Plug and Play enumerator, and the system clock. In general, you won't need to—and won't want to—mess with these low-level settings. Still, you can browse these devices.

Print Settings

One of the most useful features is the ability to print your current system configuration directly from Device Manager. To do so, follow these steps:

1. Double-click the Systems icon in Control Panel. In the System Properties dialog box, choose the Device Manager tab, shown in Figure 2.7.

FIGURE 2.7.
Make a point to periodically record your system configuration using Device Manager's excellent system summary tool.

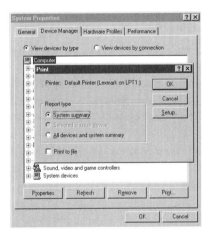

2. Click the Print button.
3. If you want a complete report, click the All devices and system summary radio button. Otherwise, click the System summary radio button.

Windows 95/98 Utilities

In addition to the hardware-specific talents found in Control Panel and Device Manager, Windows 95 provides utilities to monitor and optimize your PC. These helpful applets are the result of years of agglomeration as Microsoft has incorporated more and more tools inside its DOS and then Windows operating systems. Today, Windows 95 and 98 come with enough tools that you can do without third-party utilities—although these products still provide added value over those built into the OS.

Most of the useful programs can be found on the Start menu. Select Start, Programs, Accessories, System Tools. The fly-out menu will display up to a dozen or so icons, which represent built-in utilities.

Adding and Removing Utilities

Windows doesn't install all the monitoring and management software by default. You need to tell it to add many of these programs. If you have the available hard disk space for them, you can add these applets in one of two ways:

- During the Windows installation routine, select the Full Install option. All the utilities will be installed and available to you.
- After Windows is installed, use the Add/Remove Programs Properties dialog box to selectively add some or all of the utilities.

To add utilities using the Add/Remove Programs Properties dialog box, do the following:

1. Select Start, Settings, Control Panel. In the Control Panel window, double-click the Add/Remove Programs icon.

2. In the Add/Remove Programs Properties dialog box, choose the Windows Setup tab.

3. You'll find utilities under the Accessories and Disk Tools items. To view the options, choose one of these items and click Details. A list of available applets will be displayed. Any item without a check in the box is not installed and is unavailable.

4. To install applets, go to the item you want to add, either within the individual component's Details view or from the main Components view. Check the boxes of items you want to add.

5. Click OK, and then click OK or Apply. Windows will install the item you want. Depending on the item installed, you might need to restart your system in order for changes to take effect.

6. To remove an item (say, to save disk space), simply go to the specific utility or component and click the appropriate box so that no check appears. Again, click OK and then click OK or Apply. Windows will remove the utility.

Windows's Inner Talents

Before you spend $50 on a third-party utility suite, it pays to know what Windows 95 and 98 can do themselves. Many of its features are more than adequate for the majority of users. Of course, advanced users and inveterate tinkerers will want the extended features and optimizations offered by products such as Symantec's Norton Utilities.

Windows 95's Accessories

Windows 95 and 98 provide a common suite of utilities for managing your system. In the Add/Remove Programs Properties dialog box, in the Windows Setup tab, you will find an Accessories facility that has nearly 20 individual items. We'll cover additional Windows 98-only utilities in the next section. The following will help you manage your Windows 95 and 98 systems:

- Backup: Enables you to archive hard disk data to floppy disks or tape drives. Includes facilities for scheduling and customizing backup routines.

- Disk Defragmenter: Moves hard disk data together into contiguous sections, which reduces disk head travel and improves performance. You should defragment periodically to keep your hard disk running smoothly.

Tip: You should run both Defragmenter and ScanDisk periodically. Defragmenter will optimize performance by grouping related data on the disk. ScanDisk can catch flaws in media before they become critical and result in data

- DriveSpace: On-the-fly hard disk compression helps make room for more data on smaller hard disks. Compression ratios can reach about 2 to 1, although ratios of 1.5 to 1 or 1.7 to 1 are more common. Be aware that the OSR2 version of Windows 95 is incompatible with DriveSpace, so compressed drives won't work on this later version of the OS.

Peter's Principle: Disk Compression Hurts Performance But Offers Real Benefits

Avoid using on-the-fly disk compression if you can. Any hard disk compression scheme will hurt performance, because the CPU must encode and decode all the data that comes to and from the hard disk. The added workload really hurts older 486 and Pentium PCs, but even the newest systems will suffer when running demanding games and multimedia software titles. Hard disk compression also adds complexity to your data management, because the disk must be partitioned to allow compression to occur. These changes can confuse older utilities and might cause problems with DOS-based software.

If you find yourself unable or unwilling to move to a larger hard disk, compression can help. DriveSpace enables you to define the level and type of compression, allowing you to balance smaller file sizes against better performance. You can even identify levels of compression for particular file types.

- Inbox Repair Tool: Tries to repair corrupted inbox files (.PST) used by Microsoft's Exchange mail facility.

- Netwatcher: Enables you to monitor the identity of connected systems on a network.

- Resource Meter: Enables you to track available resources, which can run out as you run multiple applications. Can be helpful in avoiding system crashes.

- System Monitor: Enables you to selectively observe the activity level of system components. Tracks CPU usage, memory transactions, and data flow to and from the hard disk, modem, and network interfaces, among other things. Useful for sniffing out bottlenecks.

All these tools are well worth installing; most take up very little space on your hard disk. The System Monitor and Resource Meter applets, for example, take up about 300KB combined. Although ScanDisk and Defragmenter are larger, they are well worth installing because they play a key role in preserving your critical data.

Windows 98's Additional Tools

Added tools are not a core reason for making the Windows 98 upgrade. After all, a third-party utility can add functionality at less expense and risk than an OS upgrade. But there are some welcome enhancements in the newer OS, listed next:

- System Maintenance Wizard: Automatically performs hard disk house cleaning. File defragmentation, disk surface error checking, and temp file clean up can all be scheduled to ensure optimal performance and reliability.

- FAT32 Conversion Utility: Allows you to switch your FAT16 hard disk drive to FAT32 format. While Windows OSR2 includes FAT32 support, Windows 98 is the only one to allow conversion of existing FAT16 partitions. Be warned: The utility only converts one way, from FAT16 to FAT32—there's no going back after the fact.

- Registry Checker: Not only does this automatically back up your Registry, it can also search out and resolve problems.

- Windows Update: This Start button item lets you find the latest device drivers, Windows patches, and feature upgrades online from Microsoft's Web site. Useful for those committed to keeping their systems up-to-date.

- System Info: Previously included with Microsoft Office, Windows 98 now features a much improved version of this system diagnostic software. You can get detailed and well-organized information on CPU, hard disk, BIOS, and other critical subsystems. In fact, System Information obsolete the Device Manager as the best source of overall configuration data for Windows 98 systems.

Summary

Windows 95 was a quantum improvement over the sorry state of affairs under DOS and Windows 3.1. Intelligent device management, Plug and Play, and the performance and reliability of the 32-bit code base all combined to make Windows 95 a critical improvement. Windows 98 provides an incremental extension of those gains, adding useful utilities, greater hardware support, and a boatload of fixes.

One thing is for sure, Windows 95 effectively transitioned the PC industry to 32-bit computing. The savvy combination of 16-bit compatibility and 32-bit native operation have helped thousands of hardware and software companies make the transition to 32-bit computing. While Windows 98 continues this line of backward compatibility and 32-bit operation.

Consider this: When IBM touted its OS/2 operating system as an advanced 32-bit environment, developers stayed away in droves. The problem was that their OS/2-optimized applications wouldn't work under Windows 3.1, and Windows 3.1 applications wouldn't work optimally under OS/2. This combination stunted OS/2 application development and killed the market for OS/2-equipped PCs. Microsoft got its 32-bit operating systems onto PCs by ensuring that they could run 16-bit code, and system vendors and users were not faced with making the large universe of 16-bit code obsolete. Once Windows 95 was on enough PCs, software makers—led by Microsoft, not surprisingly—began cranking out 32-bit applications of their own.

If you're using Windows 95, you are probably well on your way to making the 32-bit transition. If you're considering a hardware upgrade, replace your older non-PnP devices first. Also make sure all your device drivers are up-to-date, because older 16-bit drivers can slow performance, hamper features, and invite conflicts. By the same token, you'll see vastly improved performance—particularly in multitasking—if you use only 32-bit applications.

Should you consider Windows 98 or NT? For home users, Windows 98 is a good idea if you want access to USB peripherals, which can ease peripheral installation and setup, or have a large hard disk drive. Windows 98 also supports DVD-ROM drives and adds tweaks for catching system breakdowns. But an upgrade can pose compatibility problems, particularly with older systems. If your system is over three years old, I'd recommend sticking with what works.

Meanwhile, NT continues to sidle toward the mainstream. But even NT 5.0 will remain corporate focused, and users must contend with NT's stiff hardware requirements. If you need reliable operation—which means, no reboots for weeks or months on end—and advanced security features, NT is a great choice for your desktop. It also provides advantages for professional workstation applications like 3D graphics and image editing.

Upgrade Strategies

If you own a PC, an upgrade is probably in your future. After all, you're likely to spend more time and money upgrading your PC than you will repairing or maintaining it. The reason is simple. When something goes wrong with a PC component, it's simply less expensive to replace it than to try to repair it.

But upgrading isn't easy. It often involves fishing around in the guts of your PC, removing cards and adding new ones. You also need to install drivers and update the operating system. These aren't trivial tasks; they all include some level of risk. For this reason, it's a good idea to think before you upgrade. This chapter will help you master the upgrade landscape. You will learn:

- When an upgrade is called for and when it's better to buy a new system
- About the different types of upgrades
- How to best approach a hardware upgrade, including general strategies and tips

When Are Upgrades Worth It?

For most PC owners, upgrades are a fact of life. Old parts might need to be replaced, or new software might require additional resources. Whatever the case, any PC owner who expects to keep his or her machine for three or more years will probably end up investing in updated hardware.

In general, there are three reasons to upgrade a PC:

- To improve performance
- To add new functionality
- To replace a failing part

Performance Upgrades

Probably the most-talked-about upgrades are those that target performance. After all, when you boost the speed of your PC, the results are evident immediately. Windows 95 boots faster, programs snap to life, and complex graphics update without delay. No doubt about it, a certain satisfaction comes from improving your system's performance.

Sure a move to Windows 98 can help boost your system's performance. Windows 98's FAT32 file system and intelligent disk management, for example, can optimize hard disk operation by placing the most used files and programs along the fast-spinning outer edge of the disk. Likewise, support for AGP graphics opens the door to advanced 3D games and software when using AGP graphics cards.

Certainly, there is always a need to consider performance upgrades. Every year, the software your PC runs gets bigger and more complex. Today's word processors—with their built-in grammar checkers, on-the-fly corrections, and whizbang graphics and layout tools—are a long way from modest DOS programs such as WordStar. And I have no doubt that word processors will continue to get more complex.

Peter's Principle: Don't Expect Too Much from Upgrades

It's important not to expect too much from your performance upgrades. Remember, replacing a CPU doesn't eliminate other performance bottlenecks, such as slower RAM, lack of secondary cache, or slow hard disk response. Don't expect an upgrade to make your PC as fast as new systems. Instead, a hardware upgrade can help extend the useful life of your PC for another year or two—long enough to enable you to gain access to some hot new technologies that might have yet to reach the market.

Keep in mind that you can spend a lot of money on upgrades that deliver only marginal or temporary performance gains. When planning an upgrade, you should always try to get the most for your money. For example, with RAM prices at a historic low, adding memory to your PC might be the best option. Also be careful not to buy into technology that is soon to be replaced. For example, a graphics card upgrade that lacks 3D features will leave your system without the ability to play some of the most popular games.

When I talk about performance upgrades, I am talking about speed, pure and simple. These are upgrades that shorten boot times, accelerate graphics displays, and smooth out jerky video playback. The following components are prime performance candidates:

- CPU and L2 cache
- System RAM
- Graphics card
- Hard disk
- CD-ROM drive
- Modem

Table 3.1 guides you to the proper upgrade for your needs.

Table 3.1. Performance upgrades at a glance.

Component	What It's Best For	Drawbacks
CPU	Overall performance, games, graphics, and spreadsheets	Expensive, risky upgrade
L2 cache	Overall performance	Cache sockets are sometimes unavailable
RAM	Overall performance, multitasking	Older PCs can't accept fast RAM
Graphics card	Graphics, video, and 3D display	Limited impact on many applications
Hard disk	Database and multimedia operations	Older systems will require a separate add-in card for best results
CD-ROM drive	Multimedia applications	Many titles won't benefit beyond 8X spin rates
Modem	Internet access	Significant impact on Web browsing and file downloads; no benefit to application performance

CPU and L2 Cache

CPU and secondary cache upgrades have the main advantage of affecting performance across the board. From word processing to game play, a faster CPU and larger L2 cache will benefit your computing experience. But a new CPU can be quite pricey. Intel's Pentium MMX OverDrive upgrade, for example, can cost about one-quarter the price for an entirely new Celeron-333 system.

A CPU upgrade can boost performance in several ways. Older Pentium systems can gain access to the latest MMX software by adding a new CPU, and the faster internal clock helps speed virtually all PC transactions. The newest CPUs also feature larger internal L1 caches, which help cut down bottlenecks in memory.

Any CPU upgrade is serious business. Depending on the type of CPU, you might encounter BIOS conflicts and other "gotchas." You should check the CPU vendor's documentation carefully to make sure your PC will work with the new processor.

System RAM

This is perhaps the best upgrade for machines that are on the downside of their careers. RAM is affordable—about $10 per megabyte—and it's particularly crucial for large multitasking operating systems such as Windows 95/8 and NT. With many people running Internet browsers alongside their other applications, the additional RAM can help relieve chronic disk swapping.

RAM is easy to install and well-standardized, but not all systems can access the latest, greatest stuff. Older systems use 30-pin sockets that won't work with the EDO DRAM technology (see Figure 3.1) used in many Pentium Classic and some Pentium MMX PCs. Likewise, older PCs won't be able to take advantage of today's sync DRAM (SDRAM) memory. Still, adding RAM can be the most effective performance boost you can buy. Although both Windows 95 and 98 can run in 8MB of RAM, 16MB is a good minimum, while 32MB of RAM provides the best combination of performance and affordability. If you want to use advanced Windows 98 features like Active Desktop, you'll certainly want 32MB on hand. Windows NT, meanwhile, requires 32MB of RAM but runs better in 64MB. Of course, more RAM is always better.

> **Note:** With RAM so inexpensive, you may be tempted to upgrade to 128MB of RAM. However, you should first check your system's chipset, since some are only able to cache up to 64MB. If your Pentium or Pentium MMX system uses the 430TX or 430VX chipset, you'll suffer a major performance hit if you upgrade RAM beyond that 64MB limit.

FIGURE 3.1.
Often the most effective upgrade, adding RAM to a PC, can really speed up multitasking operations. But this 168-pin DIMM won't fit into older Pentium PCs designed for 70-pin SIMMs. (Photo courtesy of Kingston Technology)

INSTANT REFERENCE | For more information on system memory and chipsets, see Chapter 7, "Exploring System Memory and Cache" and Chapter 9, "Understanding Motherboards and Chipsets."

Graphics Card

All cards sold during the last two years provide adequate 2D graphics handling. But the emergence of 3D games and titles is making graphics card upgrades a hot item again. 3D cards can add impressive rendering capabilities to your PC, allowing realistic and smooth game play for software using a compatible 3D display scheme.

Adding a card is easy, but 3D technology is moving fast. You'll want to make sure the card you purchase will work well with the games and software you own or intend to buy. You'll also want to decide whether or not you want to get a card offering 3D graphics alongside 2D graphics and video, or if you want a dedicated 3D graphics card that may offer superior game performance but requires you to have a second 2D board installed. If you're trying to get a card for an ISA or VL-bus machine, you will have a hard time finding a decent 3D graphics card. My advice: Upgrade to a PCI, or preferably, AGP equipped motherboard, or get a whole new machine.

INSTANT REFERENCE | For more information on graphics cards, see Chapter 17, "New Dimensions: Graphics Accelerators."

Hard Disk

A new hard disk will probably affect your ability to access files and programs more than it will affect performance. That said, today's disks spin faster, respond quicker, and move data more smoothly than ever before. The key spec is access time, measured in milliseconds (ms). Today's drives run at 9ms to 12ms, up to twice the speed provided by older drives. But if performance is your main concern, you should consider adding RAM before installing a new hard disk.

A good enhanced IDE drive (see Figure 3.2) will suffice for virtually all mainstream applications, but if you want to capture video or do other professional-level work, consider a SCSI drive. These drives enjoy higher top data rates than their IDE cousins, and they can also move data without tying up the CPU. Of course, bigger is always better for hard disks, and you should look in the range of 4GB and above when buying a new drive.

INSTANT REFERENCE | For more information on hard disks, see Chapter 11, "Taking Hard Disks for a Spin."

CD-ROM Drives

Speeds keep going up—from 8X just a couple years ago to 32X and faster now. Don't be fooled. The higher spin rates aren't really accessed by most software, and in any case, access times are really the key to responsive performance. What's more, some of these fast drives suffer from vibration problems when spinning CD-ROMs. Finally, faster drives may spin down after periods of inactivity, creating additional delays that can be particularly annoying for game players.

Figure 3.2.

The newest IDE hard disks, such as the Quantum Bigfoot shown here, use the new ATA-33 specifica- tion to more than double maximum data transfer rates. (Photo courtesy of Quantum Corp.)

While the spin rate can help boost application installs and file transfers, look for low access times (below 200ms) for optimal performance. The best SCSI-based drives can provide 150ms access times for quicker accesses. In addition, SCSI drives will improve multitasking performance (effectively juggling hard disk and CD-ROM access) but won't make much of a difference otherwise.

Of course, the optical storage buying decision is clouded by other device types. DVD-ROM offers enormous capacities, nifty multimedia talents, and full compatibility with existing CD-ROMs. Prices are even low enough to make it the smart mainstream pur- chase, though you'll want to make sure you get a second or third generation drive to ensure adequate performance. Finally, those who want to back up or share data—or make copies of discs—will want to consider a CD-Recordable (CD-R) or CD-Rewritable (CD-RW) drive. While these devices will read and write CD-ROM discs, both cost more and run more slowly than their read-only counterparts.

Instant Reference

For more information on optical storage, see Chapter 12, "CD-ROM Drives," Chapter 14, "DVD: The Future Arrives," and Chapter 15, "Recordable Optical Storage."

Modems

If you spend a lot of time browsing the Web, a 56Kbps modem upgrade is probably a ter- rific idea. The higher downstream data rate can save valuable minutes and hours off your day-to-day downloads, even if upstream speeds stay at 33.6Kbps. The best news is the fact that an international standard, in the form of the v.90 specification, is in place to ensure interoperability between previously discordant technologies.

If you are running a 28.8Kbps or slower modem, you shouldn't hesitate to upgrade to a 56Kbps model. Those with 33.6Kbps modems should see if they can upgrade their existing hardware—often you can download a free firmware upgrade to gain the performance boost. If you already have a 56Kbps modem that uses one of the two proprietary communication format (x2 and K56Flex), you should check with your vendor to see if you can't get a free upgrade to the internationally-recognized v.90 standard. That will help ensure that you get top performance with all your connections.

Feature Upgrades

Feature upgrades can add new dimensions to your PC, letting you do things you couldn't do before. In fact, many performance upgrades provide a feature benefit. For example, an OverDrive MMX upgrade enables your older Pentium system to play MMX-enhanced games and titles—a feature it didn't support before. Likewise, 3D graphics cards might add support for previously inaccessible software.

In general, expect to get more value out of feature upgrades than performance upgrades—to an extent. An aging 33MHz 486 will gain only moderate benefit from that capacious 7GB hard disk or 24X CD-ROM drive. The main thing is to make sure your upgrades fit your needs and that they will work within your system.

The following are typical feature upgrade alternatives:

- Displays
- Video peripherals
- Input devices
- Data storage

Table 3.2 guides you to the proper upgrade for your needs.

Table 3.2. Feature upgrades at a glance.

Component	What It's Best For	Drawbacks
Display	Increased display area, higher resolutions	Expensive; large size
Sound card	Enhanced audio output, compatibility with newest games and titles	None
Video peripherals	Videoconferencing, editing videotapes	Video files are large; complex installations
Printer	Paper-based output	Color printers are slower and cost more to operate than monochrome laser printers

continues

Table 3.2. Continued.

Component	What It's Best For	Drawbacks
Digital cameras	Capture images for use in desktop and Web publishing	Expensive, regular film-based cameras provide better image quality
Input devices	Ergonomic design, better control	None
Data storage	Greater capacity, multimedia features	Expensive; soon to be replaced with more advanced products

Displays

One of the most compelling overall feature upgrades you can make is to the display. A larger monitor can make a world of difference, whether you're working on spreadsheets or playing fast-action games. It's not like getting a larger television screen. You can pack much more information onto a larger monitor—more tasks and more columns of data. Anyone who runs multiple programs or works with complex applications will want the space afforded by a 17-inch or even 19-inch monitor. Just be sure that the graphics board can handle the load. You'll need at least 2MB of graphics memory and fast refresh rates in order to enjoy the full benefit of the larger screen.

Video Peripherals

Fast entering the mainstream are video cameras enabling you to make video calls to other similarly equipped PCs. Connectix's QuickCam and Intel's Create and Share kits provide a monitor-top video camera and conferencing software. These packages can also be used to capture video or stills to your hard disk, but you're limited by the length of the camera cord.

If you're creative, you might want to add a video capture card, which enables you to record broadcast or taped analog video to your hard disk. The digital video may be sent to tape or digitally edited and enhanced with special effects and transitions. The good news: Prices on these cards have dropped sharply over the past two years—today, a $300 or $400 video capture card can produce good quality video. For those wanting to capture video stills or short clips from VHS tape, consider products like Iomega's Buz or Play Inc.'s Snappy devices, which let you grab video over the parallel port.

INSTANT REFERENCE   For more information on video capture, see Chapter 20, "Digital Video Capture."

Inputs

If you use your PC for game play, a joystick or other game upgrade can really improve your level of play. You'll find everything from Nintendo-like gamepads to force feedback joysticks that actually buffet and resist to emulate the feeling of high-G turns and other effects. Likewise, 3D input devices such as Diamond's GyroMouse are terrific for games such as Descent, in which you need to be able to quickly move up and down, side to side, and forward and backward without cramping your fingers on obscure keyboard codes.

For more mundane tasks, ergonomic keyboards can help prevent painful repetitive strain injuries (RSI). Split models such as the Microsoft Natural Keyboard are the most common. Also look for enhanced mice, trackballs, and touchpads that simplify scrolling (by way of integrated scroll wheels, for example) and provide automated operation through programmable keys. Remote keyboards use IR or radio waves to let you input from across the room, while more and more peripherals make use of the Universal Serial Bus to ensure compatibility with future systems.

INSTANT REFERENCE   For more information on input devices, see Chapter 26, "Keyboards," and Chapter 27, "Point and Shoot: Of Mice, Joysticks, and Other Controllers."

Data Storage

The big news here is DVD, shown in Figure 3.3, which stands for *digital versatile disk*. This high-density optical media provides data capacities of 4.7GB and beyond. If you're looking for convenient archiving and distribution, emerging CD-Rewritable (CD-RW) and DVD-RAM drives both enable you to write to standard optical media.

FIGURE 3.3.
PC software makers and Hollywood studios are both excited about DVD, which can hold over two hours of terrific-quality video and store from 4.7 to 17GB of data. (Photo courtesy of Diamond Multimedia)

INSTANT REFERENCE   For more information on data storage, see Chapter 12 and Chapter 14.

Repair Upgrades

The last type of upgrade is really a repair. Do you try to fix a 3-year-old graphics board when it goes down? Of course not. It would cost more to have a tech noodle with the thing than the hardware itself is worth. By replacing the dead or dying component, you not only address the functional problem, but you also end up enhancing the PC itself.

In fact, when it comes to PCs, *repair* often means *replace*. Solid-state circuitry can't easily be fixed once it's fried, and disk drives and other sealed components are expensive to service. Given that PC components quickly fall behind the feature and performance curve, it makes sense to replace these failed components.

But before you decide to replace an ailing component, you should make sure that a less-drastic solution isn't available. What looks like a dead hard disk or CD-ROM drive, for instance, might simply be a loose cable or an improperly set IDE jumper. Here are a few things to consider before you run to the computer store:

- Check that all cables are snug and properly connected. Loose cables are a common cause of mysterious failures.
- Ensure that fans are operating and that proper ventilation is available to the PC. Overheating can cause intermittent and chronic failures in a variety of components.
- For drive problems, check the on-board jumper settings and the system BIOS to make sure the drive is properly configured.
- Also try shutting down the PC and reseating boards and wires. Repeated heating and cooling of components over time can cause small movements which interrupt connections.
- Try installing updated drivers for appropriate peripherals. Driver conflicts can render devices inoperable.

General Upgrade Tips

Upgrading a PC can be a harrowing task, particularly when it involves internal components and messy driver installations. You can ease the pain by keeping a few general rules in mind both before and during the process. The following sections contain a few tips.

Preparation

Preparation is the key to any upgrade. From compiling the right tools to making sure that you have an up-to-date backup, a little preparation can save both time and data.

Weekend Warriors: Give Yourself Time

Complicated upgrades don't happen quickly. You need to give yourself enough time to remove the old components, install the new ones, and conduct all the troubleshooting and testing to make sure you've got things right. For anything more than an external printer or modem upgrade, try to give yourself the weekend or several nights to get the job done.

Also, it's worth checking to see if the manufacturer of the component you're installing provides weekend and/or evening support hours. Depending on the company, telephone tech support can range from 24-hour toll-free support seven days a week to weekday-only support available just eight or nine hours a day via a toll call. If you think you'll need help with a weekend or evening upgrade, it's best to go with a company that provides phone support when you need it.

Save the Data

Don't be fooled by slick documentation and colorful packaging. Upgrades can go seriously wrong. You can prepare yourself for the worst by saving your important files and applications. There are two things you need to do to protect yourself:

- Make a startup disk
- Make a full data backup

Make a Startup Disk

Windows 95 and 98 both provide a facility for making a startup disk, containing files needed to start Windows 95 from a floppy disk. In addition to startup and configuration files, this disk contains utilities for managing the hard disk and resolving problems that might be preventing normal operation.

To create a startup disk, do the following:

1. Go to Control Panel by selecting Start, Settings, Control Panel.
2. Double-click the Add/Remove Software icon, and then choose the Startup Disk tab.
3. Click the Create Disk button.
4. Insert a floppy disk into your system's A: drive.
5. Once the files are done copying, mark the disk as a startup disk and note the date on the disk. Store it in a safe location.

Tip: Remarkably, older versions of Windows 95 fail to include drivers for the installed CD-ROM drives on the startup disk. The result is that if you need to use the startup disk to recover your system, you won't be able to access the Windows 95 CD-ROM disk—making a reinstallation impossible! After you're done creating a startup disk, make a point to copy the file MSCDEX.EXE from your hard disk to a separate floppy. Windows 98 and newer Windows 95 versions fix this glaring oversight. If your version of Windows 95 is designated as a "b" or "c" in the System Properties dialog box, then you have a newer version.

Back Up Your Data

You don't need to have a dedicated backup software system in order to protect your data. Windows 95 and 98 include a utility—cleverly named Backup—enabling you to archive your data to tape or floppy disks. Since most people don't own tape backup drives, the floppy disk feature can be very attractive.

There's one hitch. Your Windows setup might not have installed the Backup utility. If you want to use this utility to back up your data, you can install it as follows:

1. Insert the Windows 95 CD-ROM disc into the CD-ROM drive (or, for floppy installations, have your disks handy).

2. Go to Control Panel (select Start, Settings, Control Panel) and double-click the Add/Remove Software icon.

3. Choose the Windows Setup tab.

4. In the Components scroll-down list, select the disk tools item and click the Details button.

5. In the sheet that appears, click the Backup entry. A check should appear in the box to the left of the description.

6. Click OK, and then click Apply. Windows 95 will search the CD-ROM for the drivers. You might have to prompt the program to find the right drive and directory.

Once Backup is installed, you can archive your data. Here's an example of how to do so:

1. Select Start, Programs, Accessories, System Tools. Select Backup to launch the program.

2. If you intend to use floppy disks for your backup, the program will notify you that it doesn't detect a tape backup drive. Simply click OK and disregard the message.

3. In the Explorer-like interface, click the empty check boxes next to the folders and drives you want to back up, as shown in Figure 3.4. If you want to back up an entire drive, simply click the check box next to the drive icon.

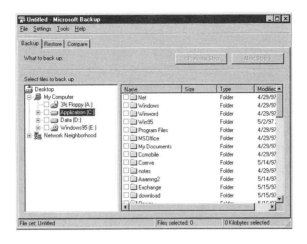

FIGURE 3.4.
Microsoft Backup's familiar Explorer-like interface makes it easy to set up intelligent backup routines that can save time and preserve data.

4. Windows 95 Backup will go through the files and begin the backup process.

5. When you're done, store the disks or tape media in a safe, cool place. Make sure that you mark the media with the date and a description of the backup.

INSTANT REFERENCE   For more information on backing up your data, see Chapter 16, "Tape Backup."

If you have your original system disks and a startup disk, you don't have to copy over the entire hard disk. You can simply copy relevant data files and keep them in a safe place. You can reinstall your applications from their respective CD-ROM disks if disaster strikes. This can help cut down the time involved in backing up your data, particularly if you're relying on floppy disks for this task.

Get Your Tools

Before you start working, think about what you'll need. Most internal upgrades require at least a Phillips-head screwdriver for removing the case and expansion backplates. You'll also want to use a static mat with a wristband if you expect to go fishing around inside your PC. The static mat serves as a grounding device, eliminating the chance of a damaging static discharge.

A good way become properly equipped is to pick up a simple PC toolkit. Ranging from less than $20 to $100 or more, a toolkit will often include the following useful items in a small carrying case:

- Bit driver
- $1/8$-inch and $3/16$-inch Phillips bits
- $1/8$-inch and $3/16$-inch flathead bits
- Torx T10 and T15 bits
- Chip extractor

- Chip inserter
- Tweezers
- Spare parts tube
- Parts extractor

More expensive kits will include items such as a flashlight, wire cutters and crimper, exacto knife, and an extended set of bits. Soldering tools, including a soldering iron, solder sucker, and solder material, might also be included. You can purchase a repair kit from any computer catalog vendor, such as CDW or PC Warehouse.

It's also a good idea to have all your documentation handy. Before you start opening the PC and making a mess of things, go through the new upgrade product first. Make sure that all the required parts are there, and review the documentation for the upgrade procedure. You might find some very useful tips able to save you time and trouble. Also be sure to keep your system documentation handy in case you need to set motherboard jumpers or make changes to resource settings of installed components. Without these documents, you will be flying blind.

Another handy tip: Print out your current system configuration from the Windows 95 Device Manager or from the Windows 98 System Info utility. You should also make note of your current jumper settings, SCSI ID numbers, and other device-specific settings before you start tinkering.

Split Decisions: What to Upgrade

Upgrading a PC poses some difficult choices. Do you bump to a faster CPU or buy more RAM? Does a faster CD-ROM drive make sense, or will a bigger and faster hard disk do the trick? Unfortunately, there are no easy answers.

Essentially, any upgrade can help your PC perform faster and provide more features and capabilities. But some upgrades are better than others. Some of them—depending on your specific situation—can be a waste of time and money, so you need to think before you purchase.

First, you need to ask yourself some questions:

- Can your PC really be upgraded enough to do the job effectively? Remember, older 486 systems might lack performance for some tasks, but be perfectly fine for others.
- Do you need to upgrade for performance or to add functionality?
- Will a single component upgrade provide the enhancement you need, or will it take two or more component upgrades?
- How much do you plan to spend on the upgrade? If it's more than $500, think hard about what you're doing. After all, you can get reasonable performance from a new PC for less than $1,000.

You Know You Need an Upgrade When...

How do you know what kind of upgrade you need? That's easy. Just observe. Table 3.3 describes common PC behaviors and the upgrades that can help resolve them.

Table 3.3. Symptoms and solutions.

Symptom	Possible Upgrade Solution
Incessant hard disk activity when you switch applications or open menus	Add more RAM (32MB is best for moderate Windows 95 use; 64MB is best for multimedia applications; 128MB for very heavy multitasking and graphics)
Freezing of onscreen windows when you scroll through or switch windows	Consider a faster graphics card or CPU; add RAM
Digital video is jerky and grainy	Get a video-capable graphics card
Painfully slow Internet downloads	Install a 56Kbps-capable modem
Eye discomfort and headaches	Use a 17- or 19-inch monitor with high refresh rates for stable display (no flicker)
Slow loading of multimedia titles	Buy a fast 32XC CD-ROM drive or DVD-ROM drive
You can't hear sound on DOS-only applications	Switch to a Sound Blaster-compatible sound card
Out of disk space	Install a second hard disk
You can't play 3D or MMX-enhanced games	Upgrade to a 3D-capable graphics card and/or install an OverDrive MMX or other MMX-enhanced CPU

Just following the advice in Table 3.3 won't cut it, however. The effectiveness of any upgrade depends on the PC being upgraded. For example, on systems with a 430VX or 430TX chipset, pushing RAM to 128MB will actually slow you down. And adding 32MB of RAM to a 25MHz 486 system won't resolve issues with the underpowered processor or the tiny 250MB hard disk. By the same token, upgrading a 166MHz Pentium to 233MHz Pentium MMX will be a wasted effort if all you have installed is 8MB or even 16MB of RAM.

For this reason, you should try to prioritize your performance upgrades carefully. Assuming you are running Windows 95, here is a list of suggested upgrades, in order of diminishing returns:

- Upgrade 8MB of RAM to 16MB
- Replace a 486 CPU with a Pentium-class CPU
- Upgrade 16MB of RAM to 32MB
- Replace a Pentium-class CPU with Pentium MMX-class CPU
- Replace an old graphics card with one that has 4MB and 3D capability
- Boost an L2 cache to 256KB or 512KB, if possible
- Replace an old CD-ROM drive with one running at 24X or higher
- Add a new multigigabyte hard disk that has access times below 10ms

It's About RAM, Stupid

Many people get excited about CPU upgrades, but the slogan of every upgrader should be "It's about RAM, stupid." Anything less than 16MB of RAM will condemn you to long waits while the hard disk swaps out memory needed by applications. Demanding applications and heavy multitasking will require at least 32MB of RAM.

The culprit is Windows virtual memory scheme. Windows enables you to make use of more bits than you have RAM to handle by using your hard disk as a kind of RAM pool. Code that Windows doesn't think is needed gets sent to the hard disk to make room for active stuff. The drawback is that when that code is needed again—say, when you switch over to a background application—it can take long seconds of furious disk activity to restore those bits to fast main memory.

This slowdown isn't hard to understand. Even the fastest hard disk is much slower than solid-state system RAM. Transfers that took nanoseconds now take milliseconds as the disk head hunts and pecks for the necessary bits on the disk. By eliminating virtual-memory transactions, you can see an immediate benefit greater than any CPU upgrade. In fact, CPU upgrades will do little to improve things on a system that has too little RAM.

So how much RAM do you need? Windows 95 and 98 consume about 12MB of memory, leaving a meager 4MB for applications. So 8MB machines are already in the hole and must store hunks of active Windows 95 code on the hard disk just to allow the machine to operate at all. 16MB is OK for single-tasking, but anyone running multiple applications will want to go with 32MB.

When Not to Upgrade

Perhaps the hardest decision is the upgrade you don't make. At some point, the cumulative wear and tear and mounting bottlenecks on an aging PC make upgrades unworkable. A fast new CPU will only strangle on the narrow and slow motherboard bus, while the dwindling selection of VL bus peripherals makes it difficult to find decent graphics cards.

Right now, millions of 486 owners face tough decisions. Although products exist to help 486s stay afloat, the aging infrastructure results in diminishing returns. At this point, anyone running new Windows 95 applications on a 486 needs to think in terms of months, not years. For example, an upgrade can help stretch your system until the next financial quarter or can let you wait until the arrival of neat technologies you want built into your next PC. But don't expect any upgrade to turn your aging warhorse into a modern workstation. Short of a new motherboard, no upgrade can overcome the ravages of time.

Why aren't 486 systems prime upgrade candidates now? Table 3.4 shows the bottlenecks on 486s that can't be resolved short of a motherboard upgrade.

Table 3.4. Bottlenecks that require a motherboard upgrade to eliminate.

Aging System	Today's PCs
80 to 100ns fast-page-mode RAM	50ns SDRAM
L2 cache is lacking or slow	512KB pipeline burst cache
ISA and VL-bus slots	PCI and AGP bus slots
33MHz motherboard speed	66MHz and 100MHz motherboard speed
32-bit system bus	64-bit system bus

The cumulative effect of these bottlenecks will limit the impact of any upgrade. Even the fastest MMX-enhanced CPU will be forced to wait for slow system memory to move data across the slow and thin system bus. The lack of fast L2 cache (or any L2 cache in some cases) means that faster CPUs will simply sit idle, waiting for the rest of the system to catch up.

If your needs are very modest, a 486 can serve well, provided it has enough RAM and hard disk space to do the job. But if you want to multitask large applications and work with big files, you will need to reconsider your platform. Multimedia titles and most games will be out of the question, and even the latest versions of Web browsers will outmatch a 486.

Disassembling Your PC

Upgrading or Repairing a PC often means pulling it apart. After all, you typically have to remove that aging CPU or add-in card before you can replace it with something better. This section will provide a step-by-step approach to breaking down your PC.

External Disassembly

We'll start from the outside and work our way in. Here we're worried about external devices like the display, keyboard, mouse, and various peripherals. If you are moving to a new system, these devices are often easily transferred to the new PC. That means you can save money by not purchasing the same hardware for the new system. To break down the external components, do the following:

1. Shut down your PC and unplug the power cord from the wall.

2. Unplug the modem's phone cord from the wall outlet. If the modem is an external model, also unplug the modem power cord and the serial cable connection to the PC. Set the modem aside.

3. Unplug the printer's parallel cable, mouse and keyboard connectors, and speaker wires from the back of the PC. Also remove the microphone cord, if present.

4. Disconnect gaming devices. A joystick or game device should be removed from the MIDI/game port of your sound board.

5. If your system has any USB or SCSI devices, you'll want to unplug the cables at the source as well. USB connectors are compact, rectangular plugs located next to the PS/2 keyboard connector. SCSI connectors are typically larger and are found on one of the add-in card backplanes.

6. Unplug the monitor's power cord from the wall and then unplug the 15-pin VGA connector from the graphics card backplane. You may need to loosen the two in-place screws to get the cable free.

7. Now move the PC chassis itself into a clear space. If you have a sturdy and clear desk (that you're not afraid to scratch up) it is convenient to place the PC there. Otherwise, set the system down on a stable and level surface.

8. Remove the case. Older systems will require a Philips screwdriver to remove four to six small screws along the back edge of the chassis. Newer models can be removed by loosening a single, central thumbscrew or by pressing a pair of tabs and pulling the case back. If you are unsure how to remove the case, check your documentation.

9. Work the case off the PC chassis, being careful not to tip or drop the PC. Set the case aside.

Removing Add-In Cards

Now that your PC's case is removed, the dismantling tour continues with the internal components. You can't just pull out whatever at this point, though. IDE and power cables block access to disk drives, for example. Remove the add-in cards first, since they are easiest to access and will help free up room for the tight spaces around the drive bays. Before we get started, however, you must ensure that you are properly grounded in order to avoid discharging a static shock that could damage components. The best way to do this is to use a grounding strap that attaches to your wrist and provides a path for electricity to run from you to a grounded object. These can be found in any electronics or computer store or catalog.

1. Make sure the PC is resting with the motherboard facing up.

2. Use a Philips screwdriver to remove the screw holding in one of the add-in cards. It is best to start with a card that has a free space next to it, since this will provide additional room for gripping the board when pulling it out.

3. Be careful to keep the screw on top of the card backplane as you finish removing it from its hole. These little buggers have a way of dropping into the motherboard and becoming a nuisance to recover.

4. Lift the screw off the backplane and set it aside.

5. Disconnect any internal wires, such as the audio patch cable that runs from the sound board to the CD-ROM drive, or the internal cable that runs from a SCSI adapter to the SCSI hard disk drive. Set the wire or cable aside with the screw.

6. Remove the card by gripping it along the top at the backplane edge and the inner-most edge. Pull upward first from the inner edge so that the card rises slightly to one side.

7. Now pull both edges, adding a bit more force to the backplane edge. The card should come free.

8. If the card is in tight, try pulling first one edge and then the other until you feel the connection come free. Be careful not to force it.

9. Once removed, set the card aside with its screw and any cables. When possible, place cards into their original anti-static bags.

10. Repeat this process for each card.

Removing Drives

By now, things are starting to look pretty empty in the PC. However, the hard disk, CD-ROM drive and floppy drives are still to go. We'll address these next. Once again, you'll need a Philips screwdriver to remove these devices. We'll start with the externally-accessible drives and then address internal drives. At this point, we'll use masking tape and a pen to mark disconnected cables so we can mate them with their respective components later. This is a real time saver when putting things back together down the road.

1. In some cases, you may have to remove the front bezel of the PC to get at the external drive bays. If this is the case, find plastic tabs where the plastic bezel meets the metal chassis. Pinch these and pull the bezel away from the chassis. The bezel will come free. Set the bezel aside.

2. Unplug the white power connector from each of the drives by pulling at the flared edges of the connector. Do not pull the connector by the wires, as this may damage the plug. You may need to exert a little left-and-right pressure to get the plug free. Identify each connector by marking a piece of tape and affixing it to the wire.

3. Unplug the bus interface cables. In most systems, this is a 40-pin, gray colored ribbon cable with a red marking along one edge. Find the black connector that plugs into the back of the drive.

4. Use two hands if necessary to apply force to each edge of the connector. As with the power plugs, you may need to apply a little left-and-right force to work the contact free. Again, tag the cables.

5. Remove any other wires or cables. Your CD-ROM drive, for instance, may still have the audio patch cable connected to it. Again, do not pull by the wire. Apply force on the white plug. You'll want to tag all disconnected wires.

6. Use a Philips screwdriver to loosen the two screws that fix each of the externally-accessible drives (CD-ROM, floppy, and so on) to their respective bays. Set the screws aside.

7. The drive should be ready to come out. First, push evenly on the back of the drive to begin sliding it out the front of the chassis. Go easy—you don't want to damage anything or fire the drive out the front.

8. Once the drive is partway out, shift to the front of the system. Use both hands to grasp the front portion of the drive body (not just the edge of the plastic bezel) and pull it straight out of the bay.

9. Set the drive aside with the screws and any patch cables.

10. Repeat as necessary for each externally accessible device.

Internal drives should be treated much the same, except that they won't slide straight out the front of the PC chassis. Rather, you may have to disassemble a drive assembly inside the chassis to effectively remove the hardware. As before, you'll disconnect the interface, power, and any patch wires. If the drive is accessible in the chassis, you can simply unscrew the retaining screws and pull the drive free.

> **Caution:** If the drive is suspended in a drive bay, be very careful to support it while removing the screws. Otherwise, the drive may drop suddenly, possibly causing damage and imperiling your data.

Remove the Power Supply

The power supply is probably the easiest component to find on the PC. The large, rectangular gray-metal box includes air vents and a fan that pushes hot air out the back. While several of the power leads have already been disconnected, you'll need to address the wires attached to the motherboard.

1. Locate the power cables going to the motherboard and remove the connectors from the board. Be sure to tag each wire, noting its exact position, so that you do not accidentally reverse the wiring when reinstalling. Doing so can permanently damage the motherboard.

2. Be careful not to pull the power connectors by the wire. Rather, grasp the white plastic connector with two fingers and pull straight up. Apply a slight back-and-forth pressure if needed.

3. Remove any auxiliary power wires. This includes wires connecting the mother-board to the fan, as well as the wire leading from the power supply to the front panel switch and indicator lights.

4. Locate the screws attaching the power supply to the chassis. The heads should be visible from the outside of the back of the PC.

5. Unscrew the Philips screws, being careful to support the power supply to prevent an accidental drop. Impact could damage both the supply and the motherboard.

6. Set the power supply aside.

Remove the RAM

When the silicon starts coming out, you know you're getting serious. By now, the inside of your PC is looking like a pretty lonely place (though the rest of the room is no doubt a mess). Once the CPU and RAM are removed, all that's left is the motherboard and its surrounding chassis.

1. Locate the RAM modules.

2. Starting with the most accessible module, find the small tabs at either end of the modules that hold the RAM in place. Systems with RAM SIMMs will have silver-colored tin tabs, while newer DIMMs will use vertically-oriented plastic tabs.

3. For SIMMs, place your thumb behind the back of the first module and use the index finger of each hand to press the tab back.

4. Once the tab is clear of the module, use your thumb to press the module forward. The module will rest at a 45 degree angle.

5. For DIMMs, simply press the tabs straight down until they click into the released position.

6. Grasp the module card by the edges and pull it straight up out of the socket. Set the RAM aside.

7. Repeat this process for each module.

Pull the Processor

Finally, time to pull the CPU. These instructions apply to socket based systems, including 486, Pentium, Pentium Pro, Pentium MMX, and all AMD and Cyrix CPUs. If you're lucky, your system uses a CPU with a zero insertion force (ZIF) socket. If so, this is easy work. Here's what you do.

1. Locate the system CPU. If the processor has a fan or heat sink with a wire attached to the motherboard, you need to detach the wire first.

2. Find the ZIF lever (the metal lever with a plastic tip that lies next to the socket) and gently pull it up. The CPU leads should now be free in the socket.

3. Making sure that you're well-grounded, grasp the CPU with your thumb and fore-finger and pull straight upward. Avoid raising one edge or the other, because this can result in bent or broken pins.

4. Set the CPU aside.

If you have an older system, you may not have a ZIF socket in place. In this case, you'll need a special chip pulling tool enabling you to get under the CPU body to apply an even upward force. Do the following.

1. Locate the system CPU. If the processor has a fan or heat sink with a wire attached, you need to detach it first.

2. Grasp the chip puller with your thumb and forefinger, and lower the tool so that the tongs are level with the bottom of the processor. Squeeze the tongs between the CPU and socket, working them so that the tong teeth fit between the CPU pins.

3. Once you're confident that the tongs have a good grip, pull evenly and gently, straight up toward your body. To help unseat the pins, you can pull one side up slightly and then even up the opposite side. Be very careful, because tipping the CPU too far to one side will bend or break the pins!

4. You may have to work all four edges of the processor to get an even pull. To do this, spread the tongs, get clear of the CPU, and then reorient around the two other sides. Repeat steps 2 and 3.

5. Keep at it until the CPU comes free. Take your time and work slowly. Forcing the CPU will invite broken pins, which will destroy the CPU.

Putting It Back Together

To reassemble your PC, you simply reverse the order of steps provided here. The key is to avoid boxing yourself out by installing, say, disk drives before you've added RAM and the CPU to the motherboard. Add back devices in this order:

1. CPU and RAM
2. Power supply and connectors
3. Internal drives
4. Externally-accessible drives
5. Add-in cards
6. External devices (printers, monitor, speakers, and so on)

As before, you need to make sure you are properly grounded when handling internal components. You should also take particular care when reconnecting the power supply leads, since it is sometimes easy to mislay the connectors on older motherboards. Such a mistake can fry your hardware.

Summary

Upgrading a PC requires thought and planning. Play devil's advocate and ask yourself the hard questions. Often, people trying to avoid a $2,000 purchase end up wasting $500 on an upgrade that doesn't work. The result is that they end up spending $2,500.

Remember to consider the cost of the upgrade when planning. Does a $500 expenditure make sense for a component that will add 6 or 12 months to the life of your PC? And be sure to consider the fact that the extended life might not be perfect. You might have to forgo the newest applications and titles on that aging system, despite the upgrade, although your bread-and-butter programs might work fine.

If you keep that perspective, you should be able to make proper decisions. Try to think strategically. Do you expect to buy a new PC a year or three down the road? If you plan your upgrades, you should make the most of your money. Be careful out there.

Troubleshooting and Repair Strategies

Many users will never have to face the prospect of repairing their PCs. Properly maintained, the solid-state components inside the case can run for 5 or 10 years, or more—certainly longer than the useful life of the system itself. At the same time, moving parts such as hard disks and CD-ROM drives have grown more reliable and durable. The net result is fewer repairs and less downtime.

That said, PCs still fall victim to a wide variety of maladies. Poor maintenance can result in overheating, which over time can destroy sensitive electronics. The working environment can be a major factor: Dirty work areas can gum up power supplies, floppy drives, and other moving parts, and restrict the airflow and thermal conduction needed for silicon chips.

This chapter helps you deal with hardware maladies and shows you how to address them without replacing the components. Just be aware that very often, the age of affected hardware means it would be less expensive to simply replace the item than to try to get it serviced or repaired. Not only will the new component be as good as new, but it will also offer performance and features superior to the original part, upgrading overall system behavior.

This chapter covers the following topics:

- Common causes of hardware breakdowns and how to avoid them
- Do-it-yourself repair opportunities for PC components
- A symptom guide for repair jobs

Looking for Trouble: What Causes Breakdowns

As the old saying goes, an ounce of prevention is worth a pound of cure. When it comes to protecting your data, you'll want all the prevention you can lift. After all, when you're trying to repair a component, you're probably in a position where your data has been put at risk—not a pleasant feeling.

You can save yourself much anxiety by making frequent backups and taking proper care of your PC. If you know what can cause problems, you can take steps to ensure that problems don't crop up. Yes, occasional failures happen—hard disks will crash, power supplies will get tired, and RAM modules will punk out—but you can help avoid nasty surprises.

The Law of Averages

The key is to spare your PC any unnecessary stress. Although daily wear and tear will take their toll—and aging components sometimes fail without apparent cause—a properly maintained PC will tip the law of averages to work substantially in your favor. After all, a typical CD-ROM or hard drive sold today boasts a projected working life—called *mean time between failure,* or MTBF—of hundreds of thousands of hours.

Do the math. A device with an MTBF of 100,000 hours is rated to run 4,167 days. This is nearly 11½ years of constant, nonstop operation—no downtime, no vacation, and no weekends off. Consider the fact that most corporations depreciate PC hardware over five or even three years, and you find that much of the hardware inside a PC is rated for twice the useful life of the system itself.

> **Note:** Don't be misled: MTBF is not a realistic projection of the life of your hardware. After all, a manufacturer can't know that a product that has existed for only six months will last for 10 years or more. What mean time between failure defines is the amount of time at which exactly half of the units might be expected to fail. In other words, for a hard disk line rated at 100,000 hours, half of the drives are statistically expected to die before 100,000 hours of operation, and half are expected to die after 100,000 hours of operation. A drive could fail after 300,000 hours or after just three hours (but, statistically, that possibility is very remote).

Another predictor of usable product life is the warranty. After all, when a company warrants a product against failure, it's putting its money where its marketing is. Until about three years ago, three-year warranties on PCs were all but unheard of. The hardware was just too unreliable for vendors to cover repairs beyond the first year. Today, most larger PC vendors offer three-year parts-and-labor warranties, and some extend that coverage to five or six years on solid-state components such as RAM and CPUs. They know that, once a device is installed and working properly, it will probably continue to work fine for the remaining life of the system or beyond.

When you purchase a new hardware device, look for products that have longer parts-and-labor warranties. Three years is a good minimum for most components.

Clean Up the Environment

Generally, things happen for a reason. Perhaps the most common cause of component breakdown with PCs is exposure to a hostile environment. A number of factors—alone or in combination—can place undue stress on your hardware. Key factors among these are

- Heat
- Airborne hazards (dust, dirt, smoke, and pet hair)
- Electrical stress

By reducing your hardware's level of exposure to these factors, you can significantly reduce the likelihood of having to repair or replace components.

Heat

Heat is the most consistent enemy of your solid-state hardware. Without moving parts, components such as the CPU, RAM, L2 cache, and graphics and sound boards are free of the debilitating effects of friction and kinetic stress. But semiconductors such as silicon chips operate best when they are cool. As these chips heat up, their conductive properties can break down, eventually leading to complete failure. The threat of thermal damage is the reason why you see massive heat sinks and extra fans mounted on Pentium and faster CPUs, and why so many new PCs feature one or more fans to provide internal airflow.

The components most affected by heat are

- CPU
- L2 cache and RAM
- Motherboard chipsets and traces
- Hard disk drives
- Adapter cards

It's not just heat that is an issue. As PCs are turned on and off, the components inside must endure a repeated cycle of warming and cooling. It's no surprise that materials expand and contract with each cycle. Over thousands of on/off cycles, motherboard traces can crack, silicon chips can be damaged, and connector pins can creep out of alignment.

> **Peter's Principle:** Leave It On or Turn It Off?
>
> As long as there have been PCs, there's been a debate about whether it's better to keep a PC turned on all the time or to shut it down when it's not in use. The arguments cut both ways. PCs that are turned on and off are subject to some stress as power surges through circuitry and components are heated and cooled. Over time, this on-and-off cycle can stress sensitive PC hardware such as silicon chips.
>
> Leaving a PC on reduces cumulative stress but invites other problems. For one, you'll face steeper electric bills as a result of constant operation—although newer PCs with energy-saving monitors and low-power sleep modes can ease the pain. A PC left on all the time is also exposed to variations in the power coming into your office or home, so a good surge protector or (preferably) a backup power supply would be a good idea. Finally, constantly running PCs is more likely to create problems in dirty environments, where the additional hours of operation draw more dust and particulates into the case.
>
> > **Caution:** If you are using a backup power supply, make sure you plug it directly into a wall, and not into an intervening surge suppressor. If a UPS is plugged into a surge suppressor, the protective circuitry may get bypassed, resulting in increased risk to your hardware.
>
> There is no right or wrong answer. If your applications demand that the PC be ready at all hours to handle incoming faxes or voice mail, your best bet is to leave the system on.

To avoid thermal damage, the inside of the PC must be kept cool, preferably under 110 degrees Fahrenheit. The best bet is to work in a cool environment. A PC in an air-conditioned office, for example, is less likely to suffer failure from overheating than one serving in a hot warehouse during the summer.

This is not to say that, for example, you must cool your warehouse if you have PCs in service there. After all, PCs are in regular use on shop floors, in steel mills, on ships and boats, and even on the battlefield. Don't let the possibility of system failure stop you from turning on the machine. Just realize that as environmental stresses increase, the threat of failure rises too. Remember that the precious part of your computer is your hard-won data. Keep good backups.

Follow these tips to avoid overheating:

- Work in an air-conditioned area where the room temperature doesn't go over 80 degrees Fahrenheit.

- Ensure proper ventilation. Make sure that all fans are working and that the case is properly sealed to optimize airflow. If you've taken a peripheral out of a drive bay, replace it with a face plate so that air will circulate as it is meant to. If you pull out an internal modem or other adapter card, replace the backplane shield before putting the cover back on.

- Ensure that dust and debris don't block air vents and that the PC isn't placed such that air intake and outflow are restricted. Also, don't stack books or other objects in front of fan or ventilation outlets, and be aware that PCs sitting on the floor gather more dust than those mounted on desktops.

Tip: Pets can be a major source of particulate build-up in a PC. If you own cats or dogs or other shedding animals, you should try to keep them out of the room where the PC is set up. Failing that, mount the PC on a desk so that it is not on the floor, where it will attract the most hair and fur.

- In hot environments, use a temperature sensor and alarm to notify you when the internal temperature gets too high (see Figure 4.1). Some models will automatically shut down the PC.

FIGURE 4.1.
Internal temperature alarms like this one can help avoid hundreds or thousands of dollars in damage. (Photo courtesy of PC Power and Cooling)

Symptoms of overheating include

- Intermittent system crashes and failures, including memory parity errors, system lock-ups, and random reboots
- System failures that consistently occur after several hours or minutes of operation
- Failure of a system to reboot after several hours or minutes of operation

Tip: One way heat becomes a problem is when the power supply's fan fails. If your system box seems hot, makes an unfamiliar noise (or doesn't make the noises you associate with normal operation), or is otherwise behaving oddly, and if you haven't made any changes to it lately, put your hand over the air vent on the back of the machine. If you can see the back of the system unit without moving the machine, you should see a fan there. You should feel a gentle air flow through that vent. If you don't, even if your office temperature is normal, system failure is imminent. If the fan mechanism has failed, you need to replace the power supply immediately in order to avoid thermal damage to the PC during operation. In addition, if the power supply itself overheats, your system might be exposed to severe electrical stress.

Peter's Principle: Identifying Hot and Cold Breakdowns

Whenever I encounter mysterious behavior with my PC, I stick to the "hot and cold rule" of troubleshooting. You see, heat causes problems with silicon (CPU, RAM, cache), and cold causes problems with hardware (hard disk, CD-ROM drive). As a rule, heat-related problems occur after hours of use, while cold problems usually happen at first boot-up.

Keeping hot and cold in mind can help you figure out what seems to be unfathomable behaviors from your PC. For example, if a PC consistently fails to find the hard disk on the first boot attempt but boots normally thereafter, it's a safe bet that the drive isn't powering up quickly enough to be on call when the system BIOS reaches for it. The extra seconds afforded by the second boot give the sluggish component enough time to recover and respond. Behavior like this might be your system's way of telling you that the disk drive is wearing out or that the power supply is overtaxed. Likewise, system lock-ups or memory parity errors that occur consistently late in the day might be the result of cumulative thermal stress to the RAM chips or L2 cache.

By noticing when things happen, and not just what happens, you stand a good chance of narrowing down the potential culprit. And often you might find that the problem isn't with the pricey hard disk or RAM modules but with an inexpensive power supply or a $20 fan.

Problems occurring after several hours of use can often be tracked to silicon, and those occurring immediately after start-up can usually be tracked to hardware devices such as disk drives.

Dust and Dirt Devils

Another common cause of failure is dirty operating environments. PCs are designed to move air through the chassis in order to keep components cool. But if that air is dusty or dirty, particulates in the air stream will blanket internal components, impeding electrical connections and helping trap heat. Over time, dirt can gum up components such as the power supply fan or CPU fan, inviting potentially catastrophic failure. Static electricity built up within the case can also cause dust to adhere to components.

The components most susceptible to dirt-related problems are

- Power supply
- CPU and other fans
- Floppy disk drive
- CD-ROM drive
- Add-in card connections
- Cable and ribbon connectors
- Mouse and keyboard

Unfortunately, there might not be a lot you can do to clean up your environment. Dust or pollen might be a part of your everyday life. But there are some helpful tips that can really cut down on the PC's exposure to airborne dirt and grime:

- Make sure that all add-in card backplane slots are sealed tight. Open backplane slots allow unwanted material to gather in empty and occupied card slots, as shown in Figure 4.2.

- Place the PC on a desk or other raised platform. Dirt settles on the floor, so a PC set low will pull in unwanted material through its air vents.

- Always operate the PC with the case on. An open PC chassis will allow dirt to settle on top of all components. The open case also negates airflow, inviting thermal damage.

- Periodically clear dust from components. Use a soft, dry paint brush to loosen dirt lodged on the surfaces of cards and circuit boards, in card slots, and in CD-ROM and disk drive mechanisms, and then either blow it away with a compressed air canister or use a service vacuum or other hosed vacuum to draw the dust out. Also blow dust out of the power supply, but don't intentionally spin the fan blade, because doing so works dust into the spindle of the fan motor, increasing friction and the possibility of failure.

- Periodically clean out the socket where the mouse ball sits. Cumulative grime will shorten the life of the mouse. Also avoid eating or drinking on the desktop. Food spills are among the most common causes of input device failure.

FIGURE 4.2.
Missing back-plates like the one shown here can allow dust to gather on the motherboard, clogging sockets and trapping heat.

How do you know when dirt is attacking your PC? Often you can tell by the looks of it. If the keyboard, mouse, and monitor all bear a nasty brownish film, your PC probably needs a good cleaning. After all, what has settled on the outside of the system has probably worked its way inside as well.

TROUBLESHOOTING

> Dirt problems often present themselves as heat-related problems, because dirt insulates components and causes them to trap heat. If you discover that your PC is overheating, make sure you take time to clean all internal components. Use compressed air to blow debris and dust out of the motherboard.

Here are some symptoms of a dirty PC:

- Failure to boot because the electrical contact to the graphics card or other key peripheral has been blocked. Dust bunnies were created for exactly this purpose.
- Failure of sound card or some other nonbooting device due to blocked contacts.
- Heat-related symptoms.
- Excess fan noise or lack of fan noise.
- A sticking mouse or sticking keyboard keys.

A Shock to the System

Although almost everyone knows that a severe electrical spike can fry system components, fewer people are aware of the cumulative effects that long-term exposure to uneven power can have. Over time, the stress of slight under- and over-voltages can strain power supplies, chipsets, and disk drives. The result is a shortened operating life that occurs with virtually no visible symptoms.

Cumulative Power Problems

This insidious power problem might be the most dangerous to your PC. If you work in an older home or office or in a neighborhood where the electrical grid is obsolete or overtaxed, you might run into problems. Also, if you work in an area with a lot of heavy-use electrical appliances (air conditioners, laser printers, and so on), your PC might be subject to ongoing stress that can lead to eventual failure.

To prevent cumulative damage, you need a surge protector or, even better, an uninterruptible power supply (UPS). These devices act as a firewall for your PC, stopping damaging power surges, spikes, and other over-voltages in their tracks. UPSs take an extra step and actually provide power in the case of a sudden blackout or brownout. The best UPSs constantly condition incoming power, ensuring that your PC gets a steady diet eliminating unneeded stress. These line-conditioning UPSs are the best choice for any PC owner and are a must for anyone working in a "dirty" electrical environment.

You can improve matters without spending an extra penny by simply plugging your hardware into a circuit free of other high-load bearing devices. Air conditioners, halogen lamps, and refrigerators are all appliances that will cause voltage sags and surges when turned on and off.

Static Electricity

Another form of electrical mayhem comes from static electricity. A single static discharge can fuse the submicron circuitry of a CPU or wipe clean the boot sector of a hard disk. Although the amperage from a "shuffleshock" is quite low, the voltage produced is actually very high—enough to fry a chip in an instant. Static electricity is a factor in all PC repair and upgrade jobs, so you must take precautions to avoid destroying vital components.

There are a number of ways to avoid static discharge:

- Use an antistatic mat and wristband to ground yourself during any inside-the-case procedure.

- With the PC still plugged in, touch the metal edge of the PC's chassis or another metal object to discharge static electricity before handling components. Note that if the PC is not plugged in, the grounding wire will not be able to draw off any excess static charge, making this approach ineffective.

- Outfit your office with static-reducing flooring. Sprays are available for carpeted floors, which present the most static danger. These need to be applied periodically to control static buildup. There are also low-static carpet materials, such as olefin, that can be installed.

- If you have a home office, it's probably carpeted. Make a habit of safety in regards to static danger. Ensure that your PC and printer are well-grounded, and ground yourself by touching metal that runs to the ground before touching your PC— every time.

- Avoid extremely low humidity levels, which greatly increase the danger of static shock. Use a humidifier if necessary to keep adequate moisture in the work area. Winter months in northern climates are notoriously dry.

The Electrical Landscape

Virtually all components are susceptible to damage from electric shock, be it static or otherwise. Disk drive electronics, system chipsets, adapter board chips, and every other area of your PC can suffer catastrophic damage. Most important, the damage can come in a single burst, or over months or years of silent abuse.

How do you avoid electrical damage? Here are a few guidelines:

- Always use at least a surge protector to stop sudden power spikes. Also consider a line-conditioning UPS, shown in Figure 4.3, which will smooth out the sometimes unnoticed bumps and valleys in your power stream.

- Avoid placing too many heavy-draw devices on a single circuit. PCs, laser printers, air-conditioners, and refrigerators are a few examples of devices that can strain a circuit.

- When working inside the PC, always unplug the system from the wall.

- Also be sure to discharge static electricity during internal work. An antistatic mat is best, but you can also touch any piece of metal prior to handling components to discharge yourself.

- Don't turn off the PC from the power strip or wall outlet. Shut down the operating system completely, and then use the power switch to turn the PC off.

- Make sure your power supply is rated to handle all the peripherals it powers. If your supply is rated under 200 watts, you might need to replace the supply with a more powerful model.

FIGURE 4.3.

An uninterruptible power supply (UPS) with line-conditioning capability can help eliminate the cumulative effects of poor power input. (Photo courtesy of American Power Conversion)

Unfortunately, chronic power stream problems might not be visible. Over time, under- or over-voltages can quietly stress your power supply, chipsets, drives, and adapters. Eventually, the situation can lead to intermittent problems or even wholesale motherboard failure. Here are symptoms of possible electrical problems:

- Intermittent failures, including memory parity errors, random keyboard lock-ups, system freezes, and reboots.

- Unusual power supply fan noises, or evidence of an overly hot power supply.

- Unusual behavior that occurs when another electrical appliance on the circuit is switched on. Laser printers and air-conditioners are common culprits.

- Lights flicker or dim when the PC or other appliance on the circuit is turned on.

- Sudden failure of the PC from a power spike, particularly during a lightning storm or when the lights come on after a blackout. However, power spikes can happen without visible warning.

Do It Yourself: Things You Can Repair

When it comes to PCs, *repair* usually means *replace*. Quite simply, it's less expensive to replace a damaged CD-ROM drive than it is to try to have it serviced. In the PC industry, hardware costs drop so quickly every month that, within a year, the original component might not be worth salvaging.

What's more, the nature of PC hardware doesn't lend itself to simple repair. Obviously, damaged CPUs, chipsets, and other silicon components are simply beyond recovering. Meanwhile, the sealed and calibrated drive mechanisms of hard disks and CD-ROM drives makes servicing these components complex and expensive. Finally, power supplies, floppy drives, and mice are so inexpensive that it doesn't make sense to spend money to repair them.

Easy Fixes

This doesn't mean that you can't fix problems. In fact, routine PC maintenance might demand that you occasionally play Mr. or Ms. Fixit. Many problems that look to be pocketbook nightmares actually end up requiring no more than a little attention and perhaps a $10 part. Sometimes no parts are required at all.

Getting Cable

One of the most common, and most easily addressed, breakdowns occurs with the cabling inside your PC. Wires and cables carry data and power to internal and external components. Often, these vital wires can get stretched, crimped, or twisted, leading to frayed contacts and shorted circuits. If a component ever goes down, whether a hard disk, CD-ROM drive, monitor, or printer, always be sure to check the cables first.

Another possible problem is hard disk failure. When the hard disk is down, your system is down—you can't boot, you can't run a disk scan utility, and you can't even tell for certain if your disk is the problem. Because getting a new hard disk can cost $300 and all of your data, it makes sense to exhaust other possibilities first. In fact, the problem might be limited to the hard disk cable.

This gray multiwire ribbon stretches from the IDE controller on the motherboard to the back of the PC. First, check to make sure that the connectors are firmly seated on both sides by pressing them firmly into their sockets. Also inspect the cable itself for any marks or tears. A hard fold in the cable—perhaps where it had been folded in the past—might indicate a broken wire inside. Just be sure to triple-check the cable alignment.

If reseating the cable doesn't help, try connecting the drive to the motherboard using an IDE cable that you know is working. Be sure to closely follow the drive's instructions for properly seating the cable in the sockets. If the cable was the problem, your system should boot normally.

Tip: First things first. If something is failing, you should start by reseating suspect cards and connectors to make sure that contacts are being made. You'd be shocked how often seemingly intractable problems can be fixed just by jostling a connector.

Of course, it pays to use your senses when troubleshooting. If you have doubts about a connection or about the sturdiness of a recently added component, be watchful during startup. Turn your system off and make a final check to see that all components are where you want them to be. When you turn on the power, listen for any sound that is out of the ordinary for a PC. If the system speaker begins to yelp, with a steady beep or a continuous beepbeepbeep, turn the PC off. Likewise, if you hear a crackle, smell smoke, or see a spark inside the chassis, shut the system down right away.

Apply these same techniques to cables connecting the following peripherals:

- Hard disk
- Floppy drive
- CD-ROM drive
- Monitor
- Printer
- Mouse and keyboard

You can find replacement cables for internal devices at any computer store for just a few dollars. Unfortunately, mouse and keyboard wires are built directly into the housing themselves. If straightening and tweaking the damaged cord doesn't help, you can take it to a service center for repair. Just keep a close eye on cost. Anything more than $20 should prompt you to simply replace the ailing part. The same is true of power supplies. Connectors are built-in, but PC power supplies have a number of physical configurations, so be careful. Translation: Make sure that the screw holes on your replacement match up with the holes in your chassis.

For printers, you can purchase an extra parallel cable at a computer store. These cables are pretty tough, but they can be damaged if they get squashed under a desk or other heavy object. Also check to see if the connector or the device's port have been damaged by excess stress—often a result of a hard yanking or chronic stretching of the cable.

For monitors, the data cable might or might not be able to be replaced. Some displays feature a 15-pin connector that plugs into one side of the cable, making it easy to simply replace the worn cable with a new one. However, some displays integrate the cable into the monitor housing, making such a replacement impossible.

Caution: Never attempt to work inside a monitor casing. The components inside the display can hold thousands of volts of electricity, even after the display has been shut off. The same goes for power supplies, which can also store a lot of energy even when turned off. Rely upon trained service professionals to do any troubleshooting or repair.

BUYING TIP

When buying a new monitor, look for models featuring a generic 15-pin connector on the monitor housing. These models let you easily replace a damaged cable without having to service or replace the entire display.

Viral Threats

The next time your hard disk crashes, don't be so sure it's your hard disk that is the problem. Many viruses attach to the master boot record (MBR) of hard disks, resulting in symptoms identical to a hard disk crash. Unexpected or intermittent crashes and data loss of any kind should prompt you to check for viruses. You might find that your big repair job consists of hunting and killing viruses resident on your network or hard disk.

The best way to avoid viral infections is to run an antivirus program in the background at all times. These utilities keep a constant watch on your system, looking for telltale signs of viral attack, such as .EXE files that change size. These programs take inventory at every boot-up, ensuring that a virus hasn't entered the system, before allowing you to continue. Just expect to pay a price in longer boot routines.

Note: Antivirus programs are, by definition, invasive. They must interact with the guts of your PC and operating system in order to protect against infection. Unfortunately, routines such as application installations can run afoul of antivirus trip wires. This is no surprise, since an installation might overwrite .EXE and .DLL file types, which the utility is designed to protect. When installing applications, you should always disable your antivirus program first to avoid problems.

Some games and other software might also disagree with the antivirus utility. Generally, it's a simple matter to turn off the program while running such software. Just be sure to restart it later and that it's set up to start automatically during boot time so you don't leave yourself unprotected.

How can you tell if a virus has trashed your hard disk? One clue is if—after the crash—a hard disk scan fails to turn up any flaws on the disk surface. That might indicate that the damage came from a software source, like a virus, rather than from bad hardware.

Cleaning House

As mentioned previously, accumulated dirt and grime can wreak havoc on finely tuned PC components. Dirt and dust can gum up fans and air flow, causing heat problems. They can even act as thermal insulators, leading to fried CPUs and other components. Particulates can also get between electrical contacts, rendering add-in cards and memory sockets inoperable. Dirt on exposed drive mechanisms can cloud the optics of CD-ROM drives and hinder floppy drive heads.

A Breath of Compressed Air

Before replacing a recalcitrant CD-ROM or floppy drive, try clearing the housing of dirt and dust. All you need is an inexpensive can of compressed air. A thin straw attaches to the nozzle end, allowing you to gain access to internal components and tight spaces. Release a few bursts of air into the drive mechanisms, looking for evidence of heavy dirt build-up as you do so. Often this simple operation can clear up the problem.

> **Caution:** Compressed air comes out of the can very cold, and the longer you press the trigger, the colder it gets. The sudden temperature change can crack IC chips and break the traces on circuit boards. Don't spray compressed air on hot components; let your PC cool for 30 minutes before using air on the motherboard. Also, spray in short bursts and wait a few minutes after spraying to start the PC. If the frost from a spurt of compressed air hasn't completely dissipated before you turn the power on, you can short out your motherboard.
>
> Also, keep the can upright when spraying, since the content that produces the cold burst tends to settle at the bottom of the can. Spraying upside down will tend to spray unwanted particulates onto your components.

Forced air can also help alleviate heat-related problems with the CPU, power supply, and on-board chips. Again, make sure you reach all the vital components. The power supply in particular needs periodic attention, since the internal fan naturally draws a lot of dirt into the housing. When the power supply vents and the fan gets clogged up, the unit will overheat, eventually threatening the supply of clean power to the PC. A dying power supply can have a ripple effect on your system that can lead to serious component failures, including the CPU, hard disk, and motherboard.

Making Contacts

If you seem to be suffering from problems with system memory, the L2 cache, or add-in card peripherals, you might be having problems with electrical contacts. Cards and modules hook up to motherboard electronics by way of gold or tin-plated contacts that physically touch each other to pass electrical signals. Reliable operation demands clean conductivity.

Over time, a number of things can impede the smooth flow of electrons. The most pervasive is slow corrosion of the leads, which can be a particular problem in hot and humid climates, where moisture oxidizes tin plating, resulting in rust. Dirt can also work its way between card leads and contacts in the slots. Finally, subtle expansion and contraction of components as the PC warms and cools can cause *chip creep,* a process by which contacts actually work themselves out of alignment over time.

Fortunately, all these maladies are easily addressed. If you notice problems with memory, for instance, don't be too quick to throw out the old SIMMs. Make a point to inspect the leads on the module and the pins inside the socket. The metallic surfaces should be clean and clear of debris. If you notice dust or dirt on either, use a compressed air canister to blow out the material.

If the leads are corroded, however, compressed air won't do the trick. You'll need to remove the obstructing layer of oxidized material. You can do this with a soft cloth moistened with linseed oil. Simply rub the cloth on the conductive material, brushing away from the card or module until the original tin or gold material is clearly visible.

TROUBLESHOOTING

> Corrosion of leads is a problem in hot, humid climates, where moisture and heat serve to accelerate oxidation. Another catalyst is when gold and tin leads are mixed together. This can happen when newer tin-plated memory modules, for example, are installed into older gold-plated memory sockets. The different properties of the gold and tin material cause more rapid oxidation. When possible, be sure that the contacts of all cards and modules match the material of that used in the corresponding sockets.

Note: If you live near the ocean, salt can be even more destructive. Over time, any piece of electronic equipment exposed to salty air will begin to exhibit the characteristics of a boat anchor. Tiny crystals of oxidation will grow all over the chassis, screws will corrode and stick, and connectors will short out and fail to make contact.

When Small Problems Get Big

On the other hand, simple glitches can sometimes redouble into major problems. Here are two classic examples of unexpected dangers that can strike.

Attaching a tape drive to the side of a drive bay seems simple enough, even though it requires pulling the disk drive out—a simple task. So far, so good. But when I reinstalled the disk drive, a nonstandard power supply input connector was revealed, which could be attached to the disk drive in two different ways (most power connectors attach in only one way). Failing to properly check the documentation, I took a guess, plugged in the power cord, and pressed the power button. I got quick results—a crackle and a wisp of foul-smelling smoke. The disk drive was ruined and had to be replaced.

Another example is an intermittent hard disk problem, a serious problem that could require replacing the drive. Running Windows 95 Scan Disk failed to fix the drive, and an examination of the cabling revealed clean, securely attached connectors free of crimps or folds. But when I turned the system box on its side, I heard the distinctive sound of a metal part sliding across a surface inside the box. It turned out to be a screw that had fallen out of a backplane connector for an internal modem. The screw had been lying on the motherboard, shorting out two silver traces (the electronic leads printed onto the board). Removing the screw solved the problem, but I was lucky. The shorted-out circuit could have easily cooked the motherboard.

Hard Choices

Sometimes, what seems like a disaster might actually be a minor problem. However, there will be times when you must bite the bullet and either repair or replace an expensive component. What you do depends on several factors, including the relative age and value of the damaged component, and the prospect of actually repairing it.

Most of the components inside your PC simply can't be repaired if they're damaged. All solid-state silicon components, including RAM, CPU, cache, and various controllers, are simply irreparable if damaged. Likewise, most drives are too expensive to fix. It's cheaper and more effective to replace them.

If you do need repair help, you have several choices:

- If the component came with a system that is under warranty, contact the vendor for service. Often you will be able to avoid the cost of repair, and will simply receive a new replacement part directly from the system manufacturer.
- If you bought the component separately, check its warranty. If it's still covered, contact the manufacturer.
- If you purchased a new peripheral or system and it failed to work (often called "dead on arrival," or DOA), you should be able to return it for a new part or a full refund under the money-back guarantee provided by most retailers.
- Out-of-warranty repairs can be conducted by technicians at your local computer store. These can range from single-store garage shops to regional and national chains. Best Buy, for example, provides upgrade and repair service for PCs.

Caution: Before you take your PC to a technician for repair, always make sure you know as much as possible about the problem. Provide the repair tech with a complete history of the problem, including the symptoms leading up to it and your attempts to resolve it. By being knowledgeable about the problem, you might be able save time and expense by focusing the repair effort.

If you do end up having your PC repaired by a technician, keep these tips in mind:

- Know as much about the malady as you can, and communicate what you know to the technician. Don't assume that the technician will be able to figure out the problem.

- If at all possible, make a complete backup before taking your PC in for repair. Too often, service departments of large chains assure the client that everything will be OK, and then return a system with a freshly formatted hard drive—even when the customer asked for nothing more than the installation of a modem. These are the things that get people started in home PC repair ("I can do a better job than that!").

- Don't authorize expensive part replacements until you've been given a quote on the job. You might decide to scrap the old PC altogether if the repair is too costly.

- Ask around for advice on where to go for repairs. Your local computer users group can be an excellent resource. Information about user experiences with national chain repair operations might be available via online forums.

- For big-ticket repairs, pay by credit card, not check or cash. That way, if the repair goes bad, you can dispute the payment with the credit card company and have some chance of getting your money back.

Summary

The good news is that PCs today are much more reliable than they were just 5 or 10 years ago. Hard disks and CD-ROM drives enjoy longer lives, and displays no longer suffer from annoying problems such as screen burn-in. Still, the complex electronics are sensitive. Stresses such as heat, power surges, and even dirt can all shorten the life of your PC and its components.

The best thing you can do is prevent problems before they start. Set up a PC-friendly environment. Make sure that adequate and clean power is coming to the system, even if this means spending a couple hundred dollars on a good UPS. Try to avoid computing in hot, humid environments, which invite both thermal failure and corrosion to metal leads. If you live near water, don't keep your system box or printer near a window that is always open. And keep your workplace and the PC itself clean and clear of dirt. Take time to occasionally clear out vents and sockets using compressed air, and blow out the motherboard surface to avoid overheating.

If problems do arise, rule out the easy stuff first. Check the cables and make sure a virus or software glitch isn't the cause. If your hardware has headed south, try to get it repaired under warranty. New hardware can be replaced under the purchase guarantee. Finally, if you must seek out a technician, get references, and be as knowledgeable as possible when you go in.

Think Before You Shop

Buying computer hardware is a dangerous business. Obsolescence lurks around every purchase, threatening to turn shiny new systems into worthless junk within a matter of months. As if that weren't bad enough, you have to run the gauntlet of compatibility worries, driver updates, and installation hassles. And let's not forget the usual price comparisons that need to happen.

This chapter will help you get the most hardware for your dollar. It offers the following:

- A guide to effective system configurations for various users
- Key strategies when you're deciding what peripherals and systems to buy
- What to look for in a hardware vendor

Building the Proper PC

The challenge of buying a new PC or peripheral lies in getting a handle on all the various components involved in such a decision. You can't just buy a new monitor. You must first factor in the amount of memory and other features found on the graphics board. Likewise, a new CPU upgrade needs to be undertaken with the amount of system RAM in mind.

Most important, you need to keep a steady eye on your computing priorities. Yes, faster is always better. But when it comes to spending computing dollars, faster is not always smarter. You can manage your budget by first deciding what you need in order to get your particular job done. By prioritizing your hardware needs, you can shift the money you budget to the proper area.

The following sections discuss a variety of buying profiles, providing a good system profile for each. Here are the buying profiles we'll discuss:

- A first system for a home user
- A home and office system
- A corporate desktop system
- A powerhouse multimedia PC

First-Time Buyer

First-time buyers don't want to spend $3,000 on a PC, but they also don't want to be facing another PC purchase two years down the road. In many ways, first-time buyers face the stiffest challenge. They want a low-cost PC that will enjoy a reasonable life span.

Well, there's great news. Renewed competition from CPU makers AMD and Cyrix have spurred a landslide of CPU price cuts. Combined with ever dropping prices on other components—like RAM and hard disks—buyers can now purchase a full-featured desktop PC for about $1,000. While you'll still face some tough compromises, the picture for bargain hunters has never been rosier. (See Figure 5.1.)

Service and support are a key concern for any PC buyer, but no more so than for first-time users. A helpful illustrated manual can ease setup, but there is no substitute for toll-free technical support with weekend hours. Longer warranties—three years for desktop PCs—can help reassure buyers that the company is willing to back up its products.

First-timers should look hard at software, too. A strong bundle of applications and multimedia titles can add immediate value to your new PC. Easy-to-use application suites such as Microsoft Works let you write letters, crunch numbers, and do the other workaday things a PC is so useful for. Families should look for multimedia titles. From kids' education software to useful references and mapping programs, these titles can vastly enhance the value of your new PC.

What about the hardware? Table 5.1 summarizes a good novice PC configuration. Our target price is less than $1,000.

Table 5.1. A first-time PC profile for the novice.

Component	Description
Case	Minitower
CPU	Celeron-333
	AMD K6 2-350
RAM	64MB SDRAM
L2 Cache	128 to 512KB
Hard disk	4GB-enhanced IDE
CD-ROM drive	32X-enhanced IDE
Monitor	15-inch
Graphics card	3D-capable with 4MB of graphics RAM
Sound card	Integrated audio chip with software wavetable MIDI
Modem	56Kbps

Component	Description
Network adapter	None
Inputs	Keyboard, mouse
Other	None

The most important thing with this system is convenience. The minitower case will fit nicely into tight home spaces, conveniently hidden under the desk or against the wall, while the monitor, keyboard, and mouse sit on top of the desk or workstation. The mini-tower design is spacious enough to allow easy upgrades, which might occur if you want to add a DVD-ROM drive or a Zip drive down the line.

For the most processor value, you should consider systems based on Intel's Celeron, AMD's K6-2, and Cyrix's M II CPUs. In standard business applications, these CPUs can match the performance of Pentium II processors running at the same clock speed, yet systems based on these chips cost about $1,000.

FIGURE 5.1.
The Micron Millennia C333 uses an Intel Celeron-333 processor to offer excellent perfor-mance for less than $1,500. (Photo courtesy of Micron Electronics)

I strongly suggest at least 32MB of RAM for any Windows 95 machine, and you should consider going with 64MB, if the price is right. While Windows 98 will run in 16MB and even 8MB, the demands of current applications, browsers, and multimedia titles really require at least 32MB.

Otherwise, stick to the basics. A 56Kbps modem is a must, since much of the value of today's PCs come from their Internet capability. You can go easy on the sound card—there's no need for whizbang 3D sound and realistic wavetable MIDI unless your kids want to play games and get the most realism out of their titles. You will want a 3D graphics chip, but this feature is rapidly becoming standard fare on PCs.

Home and Office System

Perhaps the most common home PC is the mixed-use workhorse that must act as a kids' machine by day and a second office by night. This system needs to run the latest multimedia games and titles while standing ready to handle large spreadsheets and complex documents. The multiuse PC will need to have many programs installed, so hard disk space will be at a premium.

This system can have a wide variety of options, but you can expect to pay about $2,000 for a well-appointed model. Keep in mind that multimedia titles—and, in particular, games—push PC hardware to the limit. You can't afford to scrimp too much and still expect to get reasonable performance.

Service and support are crucial. High-traffic systems stand a greater chance of suffering from fatal software conflicts or simple wear-and-tear problems. Babies will bang on the keyboard, while gamers will hammer at the system and possibly spill drinks in the work area. If the work you keep on your home PC is crucial—be it work documents, tax information, or your bank files—be sure to make frequent backups. Also consider keeping occasional backups in a safe place outside the home, in case you need to protect vital tax data from fire. Table 5.2 provides insight into affordable, do-everything systems costing less than $2,000.

Table 5.2. A midrange PC for home and office must be a jack of all trades.

Component	Description
Case	Midtower
CPU	Pentium II-400 or 450
RAM	64MB or 128MB of SDRAM
Cache	512KB
Hard disk	10 to 16GB-enhanced IDE
CD-ROM drive	32X CD-ROM or 2X and faster DVD-ROM
Monitor	17-inch
Graphics card	Midrange 3D-capable with 4MB RAM

Component	Description
Sound card	PCI sound card with hardware wavetable MIDI and 3D audio support
Modem	56Kbps
Network adapter	None
Inputs	Keyboard, mouse, joystick
Other	Consider tape backup

The most critical components are the CPU and motherboard. The processor must provide MMX instruction support to handle the latest games and titles. You'll want at least a 400MHz CPU, but a 450MHz Pentium II is better. Both processors work on fast 100MHz motherboards (versus 66MHz for current Celeron systems), which means the main memory runs 50 percent faster to boost virtually all aspects of performance.

You also need to beef up the audio and graphics subsystems for effective multimedia playback. A 17- or even 19-inch monitor will make for thrilling game play and comfortable spreadsheet work. This system configuration also lets you easily multitask applications, so you can run your browser next to your word processor. Make sure your system uses an AGP graphics card for optimal performance—especially for 3D graphics—and you may want to spring for a joystick for the kids' games.

Finally, a backup storage device is well worth considering, especially if you are running a home office. While a tape drive can offer lots of low-cost storage, you may be tempted by a CD-RW drive enabling you to store data to reusable discs readable on new CD-ROM drives. Another option: 100MB Iomega Zip or similar drives, which use cartridged magnetic media for fast performance.

Corporate Desktop

PCs bound for office duty have some different priorities. For one, multimedia support and flexibility aren't a big concern. Instead, compact design and easy network management are important, whether for five PCs for a small office or department, or 500 PCs for a Fortune 500 company (see Figure 5.2). Table 5.3 shows some of the unique aspects of business-bound PCs, which typically cost about $2,000.

FIGURE 5.2.
IBM's PC 350 features the space-saving slimline design best suited for tight corporate quarters. (Photo courtesy of IBM PC Co.)

Table 5.3. A first-time PC profile for the corporate desktop.

Component	Description
Case	Slimline desktop
CPU	Pentium II-350
RAM	64MB
Cache	512KB
Hard disk	6GB-enhanced IDE
CD-ROM drive	32X-enhanced IDE
Monitor	15-inch
Graphics card	2MB 3D graphics capable
Sound card	Optional
Modem	None
Network adapter	10/100MBps ethernet
Inputs	Keyboard, mouse
Other	Remote management features

In addition to compact design, corporate desktops need to be easy to maintain. Many new systems include software and motherboard hardware to enable remote management and configuration. Network administrators can update and install software and drivers from a central location—eliminating the need to trudge from PC to PC with application discs. Monitoring software also helps maintain optimal network performance, while internal monitoring devices checking for heat and case removal help reduce damage and theft of internal components.

Unfortunately, these features require dedicated motherboard hardware and up-to-date BIOSs. Microsoft's Advanced Configuration and Power Interface (ACPI), for example, provides a standard way to boot, manage, and shut down PCs over a network connection. In some cases, these management features are compelling enough that corporate buyers may need to replace their existing systems.

The Powerhouse PC

The powerhouse PC is more than a geek's fantasy. This is the kind of PC needed for top-notch game play, Web site and software development, and desktop publishing and image editing. These are different missions, certainly, but they all share requirements: lots of processing power and RAM, large storage capacities, high-resolution graphics, and fast performance.

The price tag can be steep. Expect to pay $3,000 or more for a top system. The good news is that this price will keep your initial hardware investment relevant for a longer time than a less-expensive model would. Table 5.4 provides a profile of a high-end PC suitable for demanding applications.

Table 5.4. A first-time PC profile for a multimedia powerhouse.

Component	Description
Case	Full Tower
CPU	Pentium II-450
RAM	128MB of SDRAM
Cache	512
Hard disk	16GB EIDE or SCSI
CD-ROM drive	DVD-ROM drive
Monitor	19-inch to 21-inch
Graphics card	AGP 3D-capable card with 8MB of SGRAM
Sound card	Multichannel PCI audio card with wavetable MIDI and 3D sound
Modem	56Kbps or ISDN for remote networking
Network adapter	100Mbps (if in an office network)
Inputs	Keyboard, mouse, joystick
Other	Zip drive or other 100MB or greater removable storage drive

If you need desktop power, the 450MHz Pentium II CPU (see Figure 5.3) is a good place to start. Running on a 100MHz motherboard and featuring the proven Pentium II core, this CPU provides superior performance in business, graphics, and gaming software. Outstanding floating-point processing means that computer-aided design (CAD), image editing, and 3D game play will all run at top speed. 128MB of SDRAM system memory ensures that large programs and data files can load without getting bogged down in virtual memory—even if you're multitasking several applications.

Note: On the market for some big iron? If you need to run a network or Web server, you might consider a system based on Intel's high-end Xeon CPU. These CPUs integrate 1MB or 2MB of L2 cache that runs at twice the speed of cache in Pentium II processors. Coupled with an array of large and fast SCSI hard disks, Xeon-based systems can handle tasks previously limited to RISC-workstations. The drawback? Xeon systems typically cost $5,000 to $10,000.

FIGURE 5.3.
The Micron ClientPro CS 450 MiniTower is the real deal: A 450 MHz Pentium II PC with a fast AGP graphics card, large ultra-DMA hard disk, and 128MB of fast SDRAM, and networking features. (Photo courtesy of Micron Electornics)

Consider going with an SCSI bus for storage. Although IDE peripherals offer nearly equivalent performance, you'll see differences when you multitask. SCSI can make a big difference during video capture and other very intense hard disk operations. Also consider a DVD-ROM drive, which provides access to all the latest digital movies and upcoming multimedia titles. Its 4.7GB minimum storage capacity will attract many software and title developers.

Upgrade Buying Strategies

When upgrading an existing PC, you have to keep a level head. No upgrade short of replacing the motherboard will transform the performance of an aging PC (see Figure 5.4). CPU upgrades will be hindered by the aging system bus and slow RAM. Graphics card upgrades will be limited by the lack of bus compatibility and the slower CPU.

So first things first. What do you want the upgrade to accomplish? Consider specifically the applications you want to speed up, as well as any new applications you want to gain access to through the upgrade. Often, you will find that a one-two punch (say, upgrading RAM as well as CPU) will provide a much better result than a single-component upgrade.

Turning Dollars into Hardware

There are so many upgrade options available that it can be difficult to focus on the most effective solution. One way to narrow your thinking is to set a budget. How much are you willing to pay to extend or incrementally enhance the performance and features of your existing PC? If you're willing to pour over $500 into your existing investment, you can choose from among some powerful upgrade options, such as a new motherboard or CPU replacement. If $200 is more your speed, a new 3D-capable graphics board or 16MB of RAM can add appreciable zip, depending on your existing configuration.

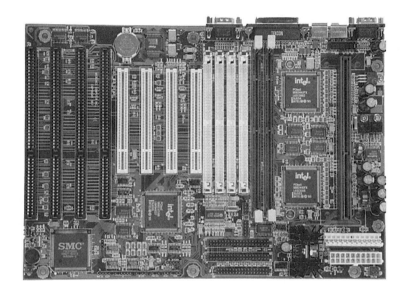

FIGURE 5.4.
A motherboard upgrade can command a stiff price and entail a lot of work, but it's the only way to break through performance choke points in older systems. (Photo courtesy of Micronics Corp.)

The following breakdowns show how general upgrade options fall with regard to price. Perhaps they can help you decide where your upgrade dollars should go.

$500 to $1,000+

Pentium II-class motherboard upgrade (CPU included)

17- or 19-inch monitor

$300 to $500

Celeron or Socket 7 motherboard upgrade (CPU included)

16GB hard disk

CD-RW drive or DVD-RAM drive

High-end 16MB 3D graphics card

$200 to $300

CPU upgrade

DVD-ROM upgrade kit

continues

$200 to $300

128MB of RAM

10-14GB hard disk

Fast CD-ROM drive (32X to 40X)

High-end 3D only 12MB graphics card

Tape backup drive

High-end sound board

$100 to $200

64MB of RAM

8GB hard disk

56Kbps modem

Zip drive, Sparq drive, or other magnetic media removable drive

4MB midrange 3D graphics card

Software Alternatives

There is also a big market for performance-enhancing software. Disk caches, memory managers, and other utilities provide tweaks and tucks able to help maximize performance. But be careful. In some cases, these packages can provide modest improvements, but in many cases they will fail to provide any noticeable benefit. Almost certainly, these packages won't live up to the best-case claims printed on the box.

Whether you should consider a performance-enhancing utility depends on your situation. Although older Windows 3.1 systems benefited from these utilities, the more-robust 32-bit code found in Windows 95 doesn't need as much help. Still, there might be times when an aging system can benefit from software utilities.

There are several types of software acceleration:

- Memory managers (so-called RAM doublers)
- Hard disk caches
- CD-ROM caches
- Web browser accelerators

Memory Managers

A few years ago, memory managers made a whole lot of sense. After all, the DOS/Windows memory scheme was a mess. Large applications had to fit under the 640KB DOS memory ceiling, and memory managers helped them do that by lifting the ceiling a bit. These products also used intricate compression schemes to make 8MB of RAM seem like more than it was. The result was that more programs could run at one time, and the system spent less time in sluggish virtual memory. With RAM costing up to $50 per megabyte, these utilities were a boon to users who couldn't afford an expensive upgrade.

The market has changed drastically over the last three years. Windows 95 fixed most of the problems that memory managers were solving. Even with additional tweaks tailored for the new operating system, the need for a fix is vastly reduced. Perhaps more importantly, RAM prices dropped through the floor. Today, a megabyte of system RAM costs about $4 or less, making it inexpensive to add memory.

So why consider a memory manager at all? Well, these programs can provide useful diagnostic features, allowing you to see how your system is using its resources. Some market tools help alleviate system crashes and other problems. Several packages also try to accelerate specific operations, such as application launches.

But the upshot remains: Memory managers today aren't a great performance buy. Although you might get some nifty widgets and controls, don't expect much in the way of an overall performance boost.

CD-ROM and Hard Disk Caches

Like memory managers, there have long been third-party disk-caching utilities. Hard disk caches use system memory to hold small amounts of data that can be accessed much more quickly than data on the hard disk. CD-ROM caches, in contrast, actually use the hard disk to store cached data, since the disk is much faster than the CD-ROM drive.

You'll get the best results from a CD-ROM drive cache. If you have an older CD-ROM drive and sufficient hard disk space to serve as a cache (say, 10 to 50MB), you might consider this option. If your hard disk space is limited, however, the caching software might fall short of your expectations.

The picture on hard disk caches is not so clear. For one thing, Windows 95 already provides an excellent disk cache, limiting the performance improvement these utilities can deliver. Some disk-caching programs also optimize application launches, shaving up to 50 percent off the launch time. (Just keep in mind that a 10-second program launch means that you save five seconds.) But if you want effective overall acceleration, you might want to look elsewhere.

Web Accelerators

These programs don't actually accelerate your PC. Instead, they pre-load Web pages so that they come up faster when you access them. They work on the theory that modems often sit idle while users read Web pages or scroll among selections. Web accelerators look at the open page and begin downloading all the linked pages right away instead of waiting around for a mouse click to the next link.

The software usually provides a performance boost. A preloaded page sits locally on your hard disk, so when you click its link, the page snaps right up on-screen. If the page hasn't been accessed, it is loaded normally over the Web.

The downside is that these caching programs pollute the Internet with lots of unnecessary traffic. You might visit a Web home page and click through just one, or even none, of the many links provided there. Yet your Web accelerator will request all the linked pages from the server. The result is a sudden and intense surge in server traffic as users employ Web-accelerating software.

> **Note:** Some Web sites have banned the use of accelerator caches because of the undue burden they put on the Web servers.

Buying Resources

If you want to buy hardware, you have a number of options, all of which have their own advantages and disadvantages:

- Retail
- Mail order/catalogs
- Web-based services

Buying Retail

The most common option is to go to the local computer or electronics store and buy the hardware. Retail shopping has a number of key advantages. For one, you know exactly who you're buying from. If the store offers a return policy—and you should buy only from stores that do—you can simply return defective products for an immediate repair, refund, or credit. Wherever possible, try to make sure you can get a 30-day unconditional return policy, otherwise you may face hassles when you try to return a product. Many computer stores also offer on-site repair services, which makes it easy to address malfunctioning parts. Of course, the local store provides the distinct advantage of immediate gratification: You can buy the hardware and bring it home.

Retail stores also have drawbacks. Prices are often higher than those of bargain mail-order firms, because of the inevitable cost of inventory and maintaining retail outlets. Likewise, the presence of retail staff can make customers think that they can get questions answered at the store. Think again. Retail staffers can be woefully unknowledgeable about the products they sell, so plan to do your research well ahead of time.

Tip: You should keep a couple of things in mind when visiting the local store. Know what you want before you go in. The sales staff won't be able to help you with in-depth questions, and the potentially large selection of products will only increase your confusion. Also be sure to inspect any product you purchase to make sure that it isn't defective or used. Make sure that boxes are shrink-wrapped and that the packaging hasn't been tampered with. If you find that products inside the box are improperly packaged, return the product immediately.

Catalog Shopping

Anyone who's ordered from an LL Bean catalog knows the drill. You browse through the pictures, check the descriptions, and dial the 800 number. Catalog shopping is convenient, fast, and often inexpensive. You can even avoid state taxes on your purchase if the company operates outside of your state.

Of course, you have to pay for shipping and then wait for the product to arrive, which can take weeks, unless you spring for a hefty shipping charge. Catalogs don't provide much in the way of product information—only the most basic specs and descriptions—so you need to do your homework before making any decisions. This is particularly important, because some catalogs are jammed with dozens of products in the same category.

One emerging trend is that of catalog showrooms. Gateway Country stores sell Gateway wares in a retail setting. Dell and Micron have followed suit with similar outlets, providing good deals on their products.

Buying Online

The fastest-growing method of commerce is over the Internet. And no industry is more poised to market to its customers using the Web than the computer industry. In fact, online buying is rapidly becoming a service offered by all retailers, whether store-front chains, mail-order catalogs, or Web-only outfits.

The Web has helped revolutionize the mail-order PC business. Today, direct-order companies such as Dell, Gateway, and Micron provide Web "configurator" services enabling you to customize preset systems using easy-to-navigate drop-down lists. Want to bump up the 32MB of standard RAM on that Pentium II 330 PC? Just click the RAM drop-down list and select the 64MB option. Usually, a price for the upgrade from the initial configuration is displayed, allowing you to make informed decisions. Once you've tweaked the configuration, the Web site usually provides an amended price.

> **Tip:** Even if you aren't comfortable buying hardware from the Web, you should consider making use of vendor Web sites. You can take your time browsing different configurations and prices, and even visit a variety of vendors, to get all the information you need. Once you're ready, you can call the 800 order line and place your order without having to face a lot of complex decisions over the phone.

The advantages of online buying largely parallel those of catalog operations. Prices can be quite low because of the lack of expensive local operations. And in some cases you might be spared the expense of state sales taxes, provided the vendor operates outside of the state from where you are ordering. Certainly Web-based buying is convenient. You simply point and click your way to the product you want, often employing useful search facilities, and place the order. If you don't want to provide a credit card number over the Internet, you can usually complete the order via a toll-free call to the sales line.

Of course, you have to wait for your purchase. Depending on inventory and shipping policies, it can take weeks for hardware to get to your door. And you'll have to foot the bill for shipping. Be aware that any idiot can put up a Web page, so you need to be careful when doing business on the Web. If you don't know the company you plan to buy from, try to get more information before you order. The local Better Business Bureau is a good place to start.

What to Look for in a Company

When you buy hardware, you're taking a risk, pure and simple. The history of the computer industry is littered with the corpses of companies that didn't make it, and they left a lot of unsupported hardware in their wake. Once-prominent names such as Media Vision, Reveal Computer Products, and Leading Edge (later revived) all failed and left the owners of their products holding the bag.

The point is, you need to thoroughly research the company you plan to buy from. Why? Because once you buy the hardware, you need to keep it up-to-date. Driver software must be updated to take advantage of the latest OS tweaks and tricks, new features are always being added, and bugs need to be squashed. If your hardware vendor bites the dust, those updates and upgrades die too.

Here are a couple of ways you can protect yourself:

- Read reviews of vendor quality and support in industry-leading publications such as *PC World*, which uses a wide survey of reader experience to assess the quality and reliability of vendor support.
- Review and post inquiries at relevant discussion groups, including USENET, CIS, and AOL. You can get a lot of valuable feedback this way.

- Check the company's Web page or online forum. Check for recent software updates and signs of active support presence.
- Search online news archives or check the library for financial details of the company.
- Call the Better Business Bureau in the company's area and inquire about any complaints outstanding with the vendor. Often companies in deep financial trouble will build a history of customer complaints.

In addition, make sure the company provides adequate support policies. A one-year parts-and-labor warranty should be a minimum, and you shouldn't buy a product without a money-back guarantee enabling you to return defective products. You'll also want toll-free technical support—with weekend hours if available—to ensure a smooth installation.

Summary

The best way to avoid buyer's remorse is to do your homework. Take the time to research the product or system you're considering. Compare prices and features, talk to current users if you can, and be sure to look for strong warranties and effective support.

Most importantly, don't expect too much from your upgrade purchases. Updating hardware is a lot like piling sandbags along a flooding river. You can delay the flood, but eventually the river will break through anything you build. Upgrades are good for adding a year or so to the life of your PC, but eventually you'll need to buy a new system or upgrade the motherboard if you intend to access the latest software and features.

PART II

Core Components

Heart and Soul: The CPU

Your PC might be made up of many different parts, but none is as important as the central processing unit. Also known as the CPU or processor, this unassuming piece of silicon is the heart and soul of any PC. In fact, the CPU is so important to the performance and pricing of systems that computer makers routinely market PCs by the processor's type and speed. Whether you're buying a new PC or upgrading an aging system, you must understand the workings of the processor in order to make good decisions.

The good news is that there are plenty of choices available if you're buying or upgrading a system. The bad news is that the sheer number of CPUs can confound the most studious buyer. Since 1997, Intel has created two new CPU brands—Celeron and Xeon—in addition to its flagship Pentium II and retired one other (Pentium MMX). Competitors AMD, Cyrix, and IDT market even more CPUs themselves. Add to that number the many upgrade-oriented processor products for 486- and Pentium-class systems, and you have a recipe for confusion.

Processor technology advances so quickly that even a system based on a high-end CPU will enjoy a useful life of, at most, five years. This might sound like a long time to your dog, but when you're talking about $2,000 or more for a new PC, it's not long at all. Behind the obsolescence freight train is something called Moore's Law, coined by Intel cofounder Gordon Moore. This law states that processor power—expressed in the number of circuits that can be packed into a given space—doubles every year.

It is possible to stay ahead of the curve. This chapter will help you understand the workings of the so-called x86-compatible CPUs. I'll discuss the broad universe of Intel processors (the 486, Pentium, Pentium Pro, Pentium MMX, Pentium II, Celeron, Xeon, and upcoming IA-64 family), which account for nearly 90 percent of the desktop market. I'll also cover x86-compatible processors from vendors such as AMD, Cyrix, and IBM. And I won't forget CPU upgrade products—such as Intel's OverDrive product line as well as upgrades from Evergreen, Kingston, and others. Although these products vary in their operation and clock speed, all share the ability to run the DOS, Windows 3.x, Windows 9x, and Windows NT operating systems and compatible applications.

This chapter covers the following topics:

- The basics of processor operation
- An overview of current CPUs and their features and advantages
- An overview of CPU upgrade products
- Step-by-step CPU upgrade instructions

Making Sense of Processors

CPUs perform their magic by doing very simple tasks very quickly. However, the many different CPU designs prove that there is more than one way to do things. The PowerPC processors found inside PowerMacs, for instance, use a small, fast, and relatively simple processor core to achieve performance. Intel's P5 and P6 CPUs, in contrast, muscle through complex x86 instructions with CPUs packing many more transistors.

Regardless of these differences, all CPUs employ innovative tricks to streamline operations and do more than one thing at a time. In addition, the same elements affecting CPU performance affect the performance of upgrade chips such as Intel's OverDrive processors.

Assessing Clock Speed

The most-recognized aspect of CPU operation is clock speed, which indicates how many millions of times per second a CPU performs its most basic tasks. For years, the general rule of thumb stated that a faster clock speed meant a faster CPU. Well, life is a bit more complicated nowadays.

First, the clock speed you see almost invariably refers to the internal operation of the CPU. Outside, most processors talk to the rest of the system at a fraction of the rate of the CPU core. The 100, 133, 166, and 200MHz Pentium CPUs all run at 66MHz on the outside, which means that the speed of L2 cache and memory access is unchanged despite the much higher clock rating on the 200MHz unit. Even the 300MHz and 333MHz Intel Pentium II and AMD K6 processors run at a pokey 66MHz externally. Intel's 350, 400, and 450MHz Pentium II CPUs, and AMD's K6-2-350, meanwhile, run at 100MHz externally.

More importantly, some CPUs get more done in one clock tick than others. That's why a 150MHz Cyrix 6x86 can match the performance of a 200MHz Pentium in business applications, and why a 233MHz Pentium II can run rings around a Pentium MMX running at the same clock speed. More confusing, a 200MHz Pentium Pro might outpace a 200MHz Pentium MMX under Windows NT but will actually lag behind under Windows 95. (The Pentium Pro is heavily optimized for 32-bit code, yielding more efficient operation under NT.) In other words, it's as much about what a processor does as how fast it does it.

With this conundrum in mind, a metric called the *P-rating* (Performance Rating) was established. Initially employed by Cyrix and AMD (but later dropped by AMD), this rating system uses publicly available benchmarks to draw a comparison to the equivalent Pentium-class processor. The intention is to enable buyers to quickly compare Intel and non-Intel x86 processors. Cyrix, for example, calls its 150MHz 6x86 the 6x86 P200+, because P-rating benchmarks show it roughly meets or exceeds the performance of a Pentium 200. The MII 300 likewise does not run at 300MHz, but offers Pentium II 300 class performance, at least when running integer-based operations.

P-ratings attempt to clear the performance issue, but they can conceal the processor's true clock speed. This can become an issue when judging MMX performance, for example. Because the benchmark fails to address MMX operation at this time, you won't be able to tell that the slower core speeds of the Cyrix M II make MMX operation much slower than that of Intel's Pentium MMX line.

For more information on the Performance Rating system, go to
`http://www.datadepo.com/prating.htm`.

What Makes a CPU Tick?

A typical CPU consists of millions of tiny transistors packed into a square or rectangular die less than two inches long on a side. On socketed CPUs such as Pentium MMX, AMD K6-2, and Cyrix M II, what you see is the ceramic casing protecting the delicate submicron transistors and pulls heat away from the CPU core (see Figure 6.1). The ceramic cover might feature silk screening to identify the CPU model and manufacturer. Recently, Intel began etching serial numbers into the casing in an effort to foil chip thieves.

Owners of systems based on Intel Pentium II, Celeron, and Xeon processors will see something quite different. These CPUs are packaged inside a black plastic module, called a single edge connector (SEC) cartridge. Like the ceramic overlayer of other CPUs, this module protects the CPU innards and provides a means for moving heat away from the CPU core. The larger casing not only improves thermal transmission, it allows Intel to include supporting circuitry in the package as well. For example, Pentium II processors include L2 cache memory and controller circuitry—running at one-half CPU core speed—inside the SEC module.

Modern processors are marvelously complex constructs featuring a number of key systems working together to drive the PC. Key among these systems are

- Data bus
- Address bus
- Primary or L1 cache
- Registers
- Instruction pipelines
- Floating-point unit
- MMX instruction

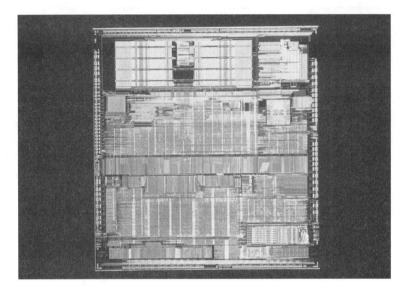

The Data Bus

The data bus is the collection of wires and circuits dedicated to moving information in and out of the CPU. Just like a highway, the wider the data bus, the more traffic able to move over it. Today's Pentium II and Pentium MMX CPUs employ 64-bit external data buses that can handle 8 bytes of data at a time, while older 486 processors use a thinner 32-bit (4-byte) data bus.

Bus width becomes particularly critical as clock rates increase and processors gain the ability to perform several operations simultaneously. With most system motherboards running at 60 or 66MHz, a wide data bus ensures that large scoops of data move into the CPU from slower main memory, keeping the processor well engaged with data and instructions despite its much faster internal clock. In addition, Pentium and Pentium Pro CPUs employ a technique called *bursting* to rapidly move chunks of data into the processor cache in a single clock tick.

Generally, the data bus width is the same both inside and outside the chip. However, some older CPUs—such as the Intel 386SX and Cyrix's 486SLX—used a narrower external data bus in order to reduce cost, running 32 bits wide inside and 16 bits wide outside. The result is similar to what happens when you close lanes on a busy highway—a slowdown in traffic. In contrast, the Pentium CPU features a pair of 32-bit pipelines internally, making them a good match for the wide 64-bit external bus, since the 64-bit bus can fill both in one operation.

If data buses are so important, why not just make them 128 or even 256 bits wide? In a word, cost. Chip designers need to dedicate CPU pins for the data bus, which enlarges the CPU die and socket and requires more connector traces on the motherboard. Case in point: The 386DX CPU had 132 pins, and the 386SX with a 16-bit external bus used only 100 pins. The 64-bit Pentium processor uses a whopping 296 pins to connect to the motherboard. Not all those pins are for data, of course, but the widening bus accounts for its share.

Bus speed also comes into play. Just as a highway might have different speed limits, the data bus in newer processors usually runs faster inside the processor than out. The compact circuitry of CPUs allows for operation at 200MHz and beyond, but the longer trace wires on motherboards can't run nearly as fast. Today, most motherboards run at 60 and 66MHz, although newer AMD K6-2 and Pentium II-350 and faster systems use a fast 100MHz bus. The result is that CPUs move data two to five times faster on the inside than they do on the outside, posing a challenge for CPU and system designers trying to keep a steady flow of data to the processor. Engineers reach into their bag of tricks to move things along. The bursting previously mentioned helps, as does the use of fast cache memory to avoid transactions over the slower motherboard bus.

The Address Bus

As the name suggests, the address bus is the set of wires carrying bits describing the location of information in system memory. The larger the number (measured in bits), the more physical memory the CPU can access. How much more? To figure this out, you simply take the number 2 and apply the number of bits as an exponent. So a 32-bit wide address bus can access 2 to the 32nd power bits of memory, or 4,294,967,296 bytes, or 4 gigabytes.

From the 386 CPU through to the Pentium, Intel chips have employed a 32-bit address bus, enabling them to access up to 4GB of system memory. The Pentium Pro and Pentium II, which often power higher-end workstations and servers, feature a 36-bit address bus to access 64GB of system memory. The forthcoming IA-64 CPU—code-named Merced—expected at the end of 1999, will employ a 64-bit address bus capable of accessing millions of *terabytes* of data.

Note: Just because a processor is able to physically address 4GB of RAM doesn't mean your motherboard will allow it. In fact, most mainstream system chipsets—a set of chips soldered to the motherboard acting as your PC's traffic cop—won't recognize more than 512MB of RAM. And many lower-end chipsets can only see 128MB or sometimes even 64MB of memory. If you need a CPU for a high-end Web or network server, make sure you look into the motherboard and chipset specifications to make sure it can handle the amount of RAM needed.

Level 1 (L1) Cache

Cache design has gotten much attention from CPU designers over the last five years, and for good reason. These small, incredibly swift pools of memory boost performance by keeping frequently used data and instructions close at hand.

There are two types of caches: the internal level 1 cache found inside processors, and the larger, (usually) external level 2 cache. Caches aren't simple. L1 caches eat up a lot of valuable on-chip space and require complex algorithms to guess what the CPU needs next, but the performance payoff is undeniable.

The concept behind caching is simple enough. A processor can grab bits internally much more quickly than it can fish them out of main system memory. Not surprisingly, the larger the cache, the greater the performance payoff. The downside is that if the necessary code or data isn't found in the cache, the processor loses time searching the cache. That's where those complex algorithms come in—helping predict what the CPU will need so that the proper data can be made available.

The first Intel CPU to use an internal cache (or L1 cache) was the 486, with an 8KB reservoir shared for both instructions and data. Each subsequent CPU generation has upped the cache amount in an effort to keep the faster engines running smoothly. The Pentium doubled the L1 cache to 16KB total, while both Pentium Pro and Pentium MMX include 32KB of L1 cache and separate 8KB instruction and data caches, while the Pentium Pro uses larger 16KB caches for data and instructions. Even bigger caches figure in the latest chips from AMD and Cyrix: The AMD K6 and K6-2 and Cyrix M II M IICPUs feature 64KB of L1 cache memory.

Floating-Point Unit

The floating-point unit (FPU) in a processor is dedicated to handling complex noninteger numbers such as 3.000001. Most PC applications don't use floating-point arithmetic, so the FPU often sits idle. However, applications that do require floating-point operations—such as photo editing, 3D design, and CAD software—rely on the FPU heavily. In addition, more and more 3D games—such as Quake II—rely on the FPU, causing it to have growing importance for a mainstream audience.

The FPU might be rarely used, but some software requires its presence in order to run. Since the Pentium processor, all Intel CPUs include an integrated FPU. Likewise all AMD CPUs since K5 and Cyrix CPUs since the 6x86 have come equipped with an FPU. And although the 486DX line of CPUs were the first Intel chips to provide built-in floating-point capability, the less-expensive 486SX left it out.

The mere presence of an FPU doesn't ensure top performance, however. Intel's Pentium II, Celeron, and Xeon CPUs, for example, enjoy a significant edge in FP performance, making them the best choice for 3D gaming and photo editing. AMD's K6 and K6-2 processors follow close behind, while Cyrix's various CPUs typically trail in FP operation.

Instruction Set Extensions

Intel's MMX instructions kicked off a flurry of instruction set extensions. The 57 MMX instructions built into virtually all CPUs introduced since 1997 boost graphics, video, and other multimedia functions. The performance boost can be big—up to 400 percent in some operations, according to Intel—but software must first be written specifically for MMX (see Figure 6.2). Many companies are developing MMX-aware applications, including UbiSoft's Pod racing game. Microsoft has already released MMX versions of its ActiveMovie playback module and DirectX game-development APIs.

FIGURE 6.2.

If you try to run an MMX title without the proper CPU, you could get stopped in your tracks.

In addition to new instructions, MMX provides a single-instruction, multiple-data scheme (called SIMD) allowing for a single operation to be conducted on a large set of data. This technique boosts performance with functions, such as image filtering, because the CPU doesn't have to reissue the same instruction for every piece of data.

Additional instruction set tweaks have occurred since the introduction of the MMX. AMD stirred the waters in May, 1998, with its 3DNow! instructions, which specifically target 3D graphics performance, critical for games and multimedia. Soon after, Cyrix and IDT both dropped their own plans for proprietary extensions and adopted 3DNow! technology for inclusion in their next-generation products. 3DNow! got a big boost from Microsoft when its DirectX 6.0 technology, which drives Windows-based multimedia software, included 3DNow! support.

Not to be outdone, Intel introduced the Katmai New Instructions (KNI)—previously called MMX2—near the end of the year. These instructions will boost 3D graphics performance and extend the reach of the MMX set, which really focused mostly on image manipulation and video. KNI will appear first in Pentium II CPUs and later (around the first-half of 1999) in Xeon-class CPUs. Celeron will not offer KNI support.

Again, while all current CPUs offer MMX capability, the actual performance can vary greatly. Intel's CPU Pentium II and derivative CPU lines deliver the best MMX performance, followed by AMD's K6 and K6-2. Cyrix's 6x86Mx and M II CPUs again fall behind, in part because its chips run at slower clock rates than its competitors.

Intelligence Inside: A Day in the Life of a CPU

In many ways, the CPU acts like a tiny bit factory, taking raw material in the form of data and instructions from system memory and turning them into usable bits on the other end. Like any factory, the CPU employs a production line to work raw bits into finished material, as well as a loading dock—called a *bus*—to move bits on and off the factory floor. The CPU even produces pollution, in the form of electromagnetic radiation and heat.

Although each operation a CPU performs is very small, the assembly line completes operations at a blistering pace—up to 500 million times per second. The newest CPUs employ more than one assembly line—a concept called *superscalar pipelining*—which allows modern PCs to keep pace with video playback and application multitasking.

> **Note:** The Pentium processor, introduced in 1993, was the first Intel CPU to employ a superscalar design. This feature was one reason that 60MHz Pentium systems often performed better than 486DX4 PCs with faster-clocking 100MHz processors.

Buying a CPU

Make no mistake—there are a lot of CPUs out there. In fact, there are so many different models and speeds that many buyers are simply overwhelmed. Blazing a trail of befuddlement is Intel, whose Pentium II, Xeon, and Celeron CPU are much more alike than they are different.

So how do you go about choosing a CPU for a new system? I'll try to answer that question in this section by providing a rundown of the various processors available. In addition to the usual specs, you'll find information about how each behaves.

You might notice that no 486-class CPUs are discussed in this section. The reason is simple: I cannot recommend 486-level processors for new systems. They simply lack the performance to address the computing needs of the coming five years.

Table 6.1 helps you focus your attention on the CPU best fitting your needs. Keep in mind that Intel competitors AMD and Cyrix have both introduced processors able to match the performance of Intel's Pentium II. These CPUs cost considerably less than Intel products, helping stretch your performance dollars considerably. But be on the lookout for "gotchas" with software such as games, which can sometimes fail to recognize non-Intel CPUs during startup.

Table 6.1. Choosing a CPU.

CPU	What It's Best For	Notes
Intel Celeron	Entry-level	300MHz Celerons can cost as little as $1,000, but the lack of L2 cache on older models really slows things down. Go with the Celeron with the integrated 128KB L2 cache.
Pentium MMX	Notebooks	Intel has ceased production on its desktop Pentium MMX CPUs, but affordable notebooks with 266-MHz CPUs can be had for under $2,000.
Pentium II	Mid-range	Intel's flagship CPU features clock rates ranging from 266MHz to 450MHz and beyond, MMX instructions, and a core optimized for both Windows 9x and NT. Prices start as low as $1,200 and go up to $3,000.
Intel Xeon	High-end Workstations/ Servers	Basically a Pentium II with 1MB or 2MB of L2 cache running at full CPU speed (up to 450MHz). You can find systems with 2, 4, or even 8 Xeon CPUs, but prices start at about $3,500 and go up to $10,000 and beyond.
AMD K6	Entry-level	This MMX-aware CPU is a terrific value for entry-level office use. You can get a system for under $1,000, but clock speeds top out at 300MHz.
AMD K6-2	Entry-level/midrange	Built on the K6 core, K6-2 adds faster clock speeds (up to 400MHz) and the 3DNow! instruction set extensions. 3DNow! is essentially MMX for 3D graphics, and is supported by Microsoft's DirectX 6.0 software. Systems cost $1,000 to $2,000.

continues

Table 6.1. Continued.

CPU	What It's Best For	Notes
Cyrix M II	Entry-level/midrange	Like K6, M II offers low-cost power for business computing. But M II has lacked 3DNow! support and offers subpar MMX performance.

> **Note:** Measuring processor performance is a tricky business. After all, no benchmark works exactly the way you do, and benchmark designers must make a lot of assumptions to address all the usage patterns in the real world. What's more, the CPU is only one ingredient in overall system performance. Finally, different manufacturers use different benchmarks and rating schemes. So where Intel will tout its iCOMP 2.0 ratings, AMD and Cyrix will tout ZD WinBench results.
>
> Intel expresses its processors using the iCOMP index, shown in Figure 6.3. This amalgam of various benchmarks helps Intel explain where CPUs fall on the performance ladder. By Intel's reckoning, a Pentium II-266 CPU is four times faster than a Pentium Classic-120.
>
> Cyrix and AMD, on the other hand, employ the WinStone 97 benchmark from Ziff-Davis, shown in Figure 6.4. Cyrix goes a step further and markets CPUs based on their equivalent performance to Pentium-class CPUs, since buyers are familiar with these processors. The 150MHz Cyrix M II CPU, for example, gets a Performance Rating of 200, allowing Cyrix to market the CPU against Pentium MMX-200 competition.

FIGURE 6.3.

Intel's iCOMP 2.0 benchmark uses a variety of tests to provide insight into CPU performance. But remember that your mileage may vary. (Figure courtesy of Intel Corp.)

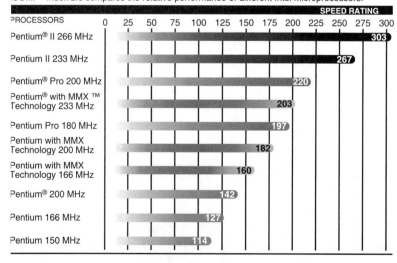

iCOMP® Index 2.0
iCOMP® Index 2.0 compares the relative performance of different Intel microprocessors.

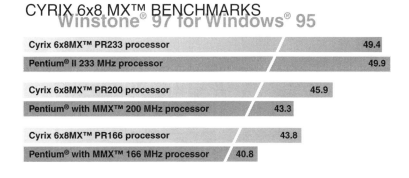

FIGURE 6.4.
Cyrix and AMD use Ziff-Davis's Winstone 97 to come up with a Performance Rating number that compares their products against Intel's Pentium line. (Figure courtesy of Cyrix Corp.)

Peter's Principle: Beware Remarked CPUs

A lot of money can be made in CPUs, and unsavory vendors know it. To turn a buck, CPUs are sometimes remarked with a clock rating higher than the part's actual performance. Similar to turning back the odometer on a used car, remarking a CPU allows unscrupulous vendors to sell cheap CPUs at a premium price. Unfortunately, users end up with performance well below their expectations (and investment!).

If you buy a loose CPU from any dealer, you should check the CPU itself to make sure all the etchings on the top and the bottom of the CPU are visible and unadulterated. If you see only a black surface on the bottom of a Pentium MMX CPU (inside the pins), that should be a tip off that something is wrong. There's should be a serial number and other information visible here. In some cases, the information may be hidden under an adhesive layer—peel it back and you may find that your Pentium MMX-233 is actually a Pentium MMX-200!

A similar problem can occur in some new systems, as well. In this case, a vendor might "push" a Pentium MMX-200 CPU to run at 233MHz. While you won't notice any difference in performance, the CPU will run hotter than intended because of the higher clock speed. Depending on the specific CPU model and your system's operating conditions, this overclocked state can shorten the life of your processor. Again, the only way to tell is to examine the chip itself to make sure the true clock speed is documented in the etchings on the CPU package.

One way to reduce your exposure to such fraud is to purchase systems from established, reliable vendors. While this won't guarantee that you'll never get a remarked CPU, these firms are much less likely to shop the gray market than small companies and garage shops.

Intel Pentium Classic: The Real Thing

When Intel shipped the first Pentium CPUs to vendors in March of 1993, it was a big deal. After all, the Pentium, shown in Figure 6.5, was the first x86 CPU to provide super-scalar pipelining, using two instruction pipes to work on more than one instruction at a time. It also broke ranks with the naming conventions of earlier 486, 386, and 286 CPUs. Intel adopted the Pentium moniker after a court ruled that Intel could not trademark-protect a number.

Figure 6.5.

Intel's Pentium CPU introduced multiple instruction pipelines for enhanced performance and established Intel's unassailable position in the market. (Photo courtesy of Intel Corp.)

The first Pentiums got off to a rocky start. The 60 and 66MHz Pentiums ran extremely hot, dissipating an incredible 16 watts during normal operation. In 1994, Intel improved things by shrinking the CPU to allow cooler operation and to push clock speeds to 75, 90, and 100MHz. These newer chips used the same clock multiplication technique found in Intel's 486 DX2 and DX4 processors, running at one-and-a-half or two times the speed of the motherboard bus. The result was significantly improved performance without the need to redesign motherboard components for higher clock speeds. Table 6.2 provides an overview of Pentium CPUs.

Table 6.2. Intel Pentium specs.

Specification	First Generation	Second Generation	Third Generation
Internal clock speed	60, 66MHz	75, 90, 100MHz	120, 133, 166MHz
L1 cache size	8KB/8KB	8KB/8KB	8KB/8KB
L2 cache clock speed	60, 66MHz	60, 66MHz	60, 66MHz
MMX support?	No	No	No
Number of pipelines	Two	Two	Two
Data bus (internal/external)	32-bit/64-bit	32-bit/64-bit	32-bit/64-bit

Specification	First Generation	Second Generation	Third Generation
Number of transistors	3.1 million	3.3 million	3.3 million
Manufacturing proces	.8 micron BiCMOS	.6 micron process BiCMOS	.35 micron CMOS
Pin count	273	296	296

Note: CMOS stands for Complimentary Metal Oxide Semiconductor, or in other words, the guts of the processor.

Intel launched speedier Pentium versions in pairs, based on the clock multiplier factor over the system bus speed. In 1995, for example, the 120 and 133MHz Pentiums ran at two times the speed of their respective 60 and 66MHz motherboards. The Pentium-150 and Pentium-166 boosted this factor to 2.5, while the last Pentium CPUs, the 200MHz and the little-used 180MHz, both run at three times the speed of the motherboard.

Note: Intel introduces CPUs in pairs because the clocks match up with the 60 and 66MHz motherboards in the market. In some cases, the faster CPU of the pair might be in short supply while Intel works the kinks out of its processors. The company tests CPUs after manufacturing and rates them for a certain clock speed based on the results. This is why, for example, 90MHz Pentium systems were so prevalent about two years ago and 100MHz PCs were not: Not enough CPUs were achieving the quality needed for 100MHz operation.

Inside the Pentium CPU

The Pentium delivered more than just faster clock speeds than the 486. These CPUs feature a 64-bit external data bus and 16KB of L1 cache (with 8KB each dedicated to instructions and data), both double that of the 486. Furthermore, the cache improves on the 486's *write-through* scheme, which stores only incoming data. The Pentium's *write-back* scheme stores outgoing data, freeing the CPU from the time-consuming process of writing data back to main system memory. (Note that the 8KB L1 instruction cache doesn't provide write-back operation, because instructions are read-only.)

The big win came from the twin pipelines, which enable the Pentium to work on two sets of instructions at once, as shown in Figure 6.6. The five-stage pipelines (pre-fetching, instruction decoding, address generation, execution, and write-back) mean that the CPU can be executing operations even as the pre-fetch stage is gathering bits for upcoming operations.

FIGURE 6.6.
The Pentium's advanced plumbing streamlines the flow of bits through the processor. (Figure courtesy of Intel Corp.)

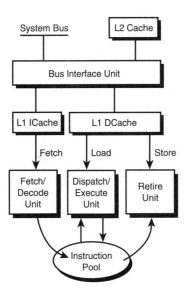

The Pentium employs a scheme called *branch prediction* to attempt to get the right bits into the right pipeline. The *branch target buffer* helps this process by looking at program code over time and making decisions based on past branches in the code.

Intel also paid attention to the Pentium's floating-point unit (FPU), essentially doubling the performance compared to the FPU inside the 486 processor. The faster FPU made the Pentium platform appropriate for the complex mathematics found in programs for image editing and computer-aided design (CAD).

Finally, Intel groomed its Pentium franchise for life on the road. The Mobile Pentium line, which started at 75MHz, uses *Tape Carrier Packaging* instead of the familiar ceramic packaging in its desktop CPUs. TCP reduced weight to less than 1 gram and thickness to less than 1 millimeter. The 3.3-volt CPU is soldered directly onto notebook motherboards so that heat can be dissipated through the bottom without fans.

The Buying Line

The Pentium might have catapulted Intel's fortunes in the PC market, but that hasn't spared this CPU from becoming a part of computing history. Intel has moved its attentions first to the Pentium MMX and now the Pentium II.

Upgrade Outlook

With more games and software requiring faster performance and making use of MMX and floating point operations, the reasonable life of Pentium-based systems is drawing to a close. Pentium users will find themselves frozen out of a big portion of the software market. The good news is that newer Pentium systems use the same Socket 7 module employed by current Pentium MMX, AMD K6-2, and Cyrix M II processors. Depending on your system's BIOS version and type, you may well be able to upgrade to a fast 300MHz MMX-class CPU without too much trouble.

If you purchased a Pentium-60 or Pentium-66, however, you are out of luck. These CPUs used a different socket type and run at a 5-volt level that is simply unsupported by any modern processor. Also, any system using a CPU based on the Intel Socket 5 plug-in may lack a viable upgrade path. The Socket 5 pinout simply won't match the layout of modern CPUs. A motherboard upgrade or new system purchase are your best options.

Intel Pentium MMX: A Good Idea Gets Better

If Pentium represented an important leap for x86 computing, Pentium MMX (shown in Figure 6.7) is a successful refinement. With Pentium MMX, Intel successfully addressed the growing multimedia demands of software ranging from games to Web browsers while maintaining affordability. The internal workings of the CPU—the dual pipelines, FPU, and data buses—remain largely unchanged from its Pentium roots and plugged right into late model Pentium motherboards.

FIGURE 6.7.
The multimedia-savvy Pentium MMX features multimedia-specific instructions and a bulked-up cache for superior all-around performance. (Photo courtesy of Intel Corp.)

The first Pentium MMX desktop CPUs were introduced at 166 and 200MHz—at the top end of the Pentium clock speed range—running three times faster than the 66MHz system bus. A 233MHz version—the last desktop Pentium MMX CPU—was introduced in June of 1997 and ran three-and-a-half times faster than its 66MHz motherboard. Notebook versions of the Pentium MMX, using the tape carrier packaging (TCP) were pushed to 266MHz.

A Look Under the MMX Hood

The most important new aspect of Pentium MMX is the extended instruction set—the first change to x86 instructions since the 386 CPU. MMX adds 57 instructions that target graphics, video compression/decompression, audio, and signal processing. The new instructions allow the Pentium MMX to do in one step what the Pentium Classic would need dozens of steps to accomplish. Tests have shown that image editing applications—such as Adobe Photoshop—gain the most from MMX technology.

Another important revision was support for so-called Single Instruction, Multiple Data (SIMD) operation. This technique allows the CPU to issue one command and to apply it to a range of data—eliminating the need to reissue the command for every piece of data that comes along. SIMD can make quick work of image-editing operations such as filtering, where wide swaths of visual data get updated with a single type of operation.

MMX doesn't come free. Software makers must write their software with the new instructions in mind, or the chip's MMX capabilities won't be accessed. Microsoft's DirectX 5.0 added MMX-awareness to Windows 95 games written to DirectX, and many applications feature built-in MMX capability.

Table 6.3 provides an overview of Pentium MMX processors.

Table 6.3. Intel Pentium MMX specs.

Spec	First Generation
Internal clock speed	166, 200, 233MHz
L1 cache size	16KB/16KB
L2 cache clock speed	66MHz
MMX support?	Yes
Number of pipelines	Two
Data bus (internal/external)	32-bit/64-bit
Number of transistors	4.4 million
Manufacturing process	.35 micron CMOS
Pin count	296

Even with non-MMX software, Pentium-MMX provides a significant boost over Pentium Classic. The new CPU doubles the L1 cache to 16KB each for data and instructions, immediately improving overall performance. Intel also tweaked its pipelining schemes, improving branch prediction to reduce costly pipeline stalls.

Note: In order to fit the new MMX instructions without expanding the transistor count, Intel overlays the eight 64-bit MMX registers over the existing FPU registers. The approach has its drawbacks: It's a little bit like setting up shop in a living/working loft. You save the expense of renting a dedicated office, but you must deal with the hassle of additional furniture, housecleaning, and the like.

The performance hit comes when applications switch between floating-point and MMX operation. The CPU needs about 100 clock ticks to reset the registers from FPU to MMX or vice versa—a long time by a processor's reckoning. However, most PC applications fail to use the FPU at all, and those that do will rarely—if ever—jump repeatedly between floating-point and MMX operation. Multitasking MMX- and FPU-intensive applications isn't a problem either, because the operating system takes much longer to switch among programs than the CPU does to reassign its registers.

The shared register scheme has been employed by Intel, AMD, and Cyrix. However, Intel's CPUs are the only ones employing multiple MMX pipelines. That gives Intel CPUs an important performance edge in handling MMX operations—one that has shown through in MMX-aware benchmarks.

Pentium MMX CPUs use a lower 2.8-volt internal operation to reduce heat dissipation while still running 3.3 volts externally to the motherboard. The split voltage requires motherboards to be outfitted with voltage regulation—something manufacturers started adding several months before the January 1997 launch of the CPU line.

Pentium MMX quickly proved to be the swiftest Windows 95 CPU you could buy, outstripping the performance of 32-bit optimized Pentium Pro-200 CPUs in most benchmarks. However, Pentium Pro at the time continued to enjoy the performance advantage in the true 32-bit Windows NT environment.

MMX-optimized operation shows even more impressive gains. Intel's boast of 400 percent improvements in some areas might be based on isolated program code (see Figure 6.8), but real-world applications such as Adobe PhotoShop and Macromedia Director still enjoy big gains on the order of 50 to 70 percent. Clearly, Pentium MMX delivered the goods.

Intel also launched a mobile version of Pentium MMX; 150 and 166MHz CPUs were available at launch time. Faster versions later pushed the mobile speed limit to 233 and 266MHz—the top rung of Pentium MMX notebook performance. Mobile CPUs are functionally identical to their desktop mates, but they use the slim and trim tape carrier packaging to reduce weight and thickness (see Figure 6.9). They also run at an even lower 2.45 volts internally.

FIGURE 6.8.

How fast is fast? Intel's MMX benchmarks show big performance gains over Pentium Classic when running MMX-optimized software. (Figure courtesy of Intel Corp.)

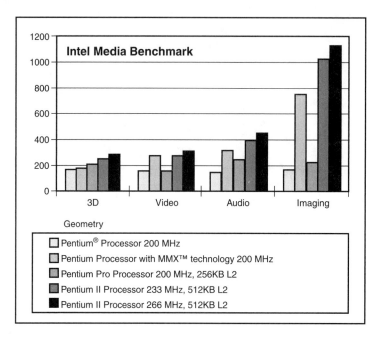

FIGURE 6.9.

The Pentium MMX for notebooks loses the bulky ceramic coating. The CPU weighs less than 1 gram and is less than 1 millimeter thick. (Photo courtesy of Intel Corp.)

The biggest challenge with mobile processors is heat. While earlier Pentium MMX CPUs suffered from high thermal output, today's Pentium MMX-266 is built on a .25 micron process that significantly reduces heat dissipation. In fact, if you want a slim notebook with a bulky fan, you are better off with a Pentium MMX-266 than with a Pentium II notebook.

Caution: In their zeal to be first with the fastest notebooks, small vendors sometimes sell systems using desktop CPUs. These notebooks are fast, no doubt about it. But short battery life combined with the risk of chronic overheating—to the point of damaging the CPU and system board—make such notebooks a risky buy. If you find a vendor selling a notebook PC at unheard-of CPU speeds, check the CPU make closely. If it isn't a notebook-specific version, walk away.

The Buying Line

Pentium MMX enjoyed an exhilarating, but very short, run. Pushed by competition from AMD and Cyrix, Intel has retired the desktop version of Pentium MMX in favor of Pentium II and its various spin-offs. The result: Pentium MMX desktops are likely to be second-run products, such as refurbished or pre-owned models.

Still, Pentium MMX may be a match for your new system purchase if you want a sub-$1,000 (or even sub-$800) desktop with decent floating point and MMX performance—something that competing AMD and Cyrix processors can't guarantee. For notebooks, the Pentium MMX-266 should be a strong bargain buy into 1999. With its decent performance and low power consumption, this CPU could be the best choice for many buyers.

Who shouldn't consider Pentium MMX? Well, anyone who wants current desktop performance should be shopping for Two—as in Pentium II, AMD K6-2, and Cyrix M II. Even notebook users should look into these higher-end processors, if only to extend the life of the notebook. Advanced chipset support for AGP and fast SDRAM memory make Pentium II more attractive than ever.

Upgrade Outlook

The upgrade outlook for Pentium MMX owners has improved with the introduction of fast, Socket 7-compatible CPUs from AMD and Cyrix. That's because Pentium MMX motherboards run at split voltage (3.3 volts on the motherboard, 2.8 volts into the CPU), use the Socket 7 module, and generally come equipped with efficient SDRAM system memory. While Intel has fled the Socket 7 market, the AMD K6-2 and Cyrix M II will work in many of these motherboards. You can upgrade your Pentium MMX-166 to a 300MHz K6-class CPU without too much trouble—BIOS permitting, of course. AMD K6-2 could further sweeten the upgrade proposition, since that CPU gives you access to the 3DNow! instructions for 3D gaming.

What you won't find is an upgrade path to Pentium II. Pentium MMX uses an entirely different bus structure from Pentium II, making system board-to-CPU communications very difficult. Last time Intel tried to upgrade across architectures, with its P24T 486-to-Pentium OverDrive, the company faced a performance and marketing boondoggle. Product arrived over a year late and failed to deliver significant performance upside.

Intel Pentium Pro: Once the Future of Mainstream Computing

January 1996 was an interesting and somewhat worrisome time for Intel. Word on the street was that the venerable x86 instruction set, with its variable instruction lengths and rigid in-order execution requirements, was too unmanageable to move forward. Simple designs such as Motorola, IBM, and Apple's PowerPC drew praise for their fresh, streamlined, and forward-looking architectures.

> **Note:** There are two philosophical camps of CPU design. Reduced Instruction Set Computing (RISC) looks to gain performance by quickly executing a stream of simple instructions, while Complex Instruction Set Computing (CISC) employs a wider set of instructions to get more done in each step. Today, most CPUs—including Intel's newest CPU—incorporate RISC technology, because it provides the best path to higher clock rates.

Pentium Pro proved a lot of folks wrong. Intel pushed the superscalar design found in the Pentium CPU, employing techniques with names such as dynamic execution and speculative branch prediction to work around the CISC bottlenecks. In essence, what Intel did was build a rapid-fire RISC core inside a fully-compatible CISC interface. Pentium Pro was retired in 1998 with the introduction of the Pentium II-based Xeon CPU line. But Pentium Pro's technologies live on in the various Pentium II CPUs.

The Pentium Pro

On the outside, Pentium Pro, shown in Figure 6.10, is an absolute monster. The processor core alone packs 5.5 million transistors. What's more, Intel moved the L2 cache—usually placed externally on the motherboard—inside a second cavity in the ceramic PGA packaging. The 256KB L2 cache uses 15.5 million transistors, and the 512KB L2 cache uses 31 million transistors. The result is a 387-pin CPU with as many as 36.5 million transistors—10 times that of the Pentium CPU! Table 6.4 provides an overview of the Pentium Pro.

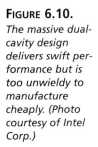

Figure 6.10.
The massive dual-cavity design delivers swift performance but is too unwieldy to manufacture cheaply. (Photo courtesy of Intel Corp.)

Table 6.4. Intel Pentium Pro specs.

Specification	First Generation	Second Generation
Internal clock speed	133MHz	150, 180, 200MHz
L1 cache size	8KB/8KB	8KB/8KB
L2 cache clock speed	133 MHz	150, 180, 200MHz
MMX support?	No	No
Number of integer pipelines	Three	Three
Data bus (internal/external)	32-bit/64-bit	32-bit/64-bit
Number of transistors	5.5 million	5.5 million
Manufacturing process	.6 micron BiCMOS	.35 micron CMOS
Pin count	387	387

The first versions of the mammoth CPU threw off tons of heat (14 watts) and cost well over $1,000, but the integrated L2 cache with its dedicated backplane bus provided an immediate performance jump. The L2 cache on other x86 CPUs runs at motherboard bus speed (60 or 66MHz), but the L2 cache inside the Pentium Pro runs at CPU speed. The 180 and 200MHz Pentium Pros, therefore, enjoy a 3x performance advantage in this critical pool of local memory. Furthermore, the Pentium Pro's L2 cache enjoys a dedicated cache bus rather than sharing time with the general frontside CPU bus as traditional caches do.

Inside the CPU core, Intel applied some nifty tricks to break out of the CISC closet. First, engineers extended the five-stage P5 pipeline to 12 stages, breaking tasks down into smaller, if more numerous, sections. The extended pipeline opened the door for still higher clock rates (now being seen in the 300MHz Pentium II, for example). More important, the CPU includes a decode unit at the front of the pipeline that breaks unwieldy x86 instructions into a series of RISC-like micro-operations. These micro-ops can move through the pipeline much more quickly and smoothly than traditional x86 code.

> **Note:** Intel went to great lengths to create a fast RISC core inside the CISC inter-
> face. Why not just go with the streamlined RISC instruction set entirely? One
> very important word: compatibility. Intel's entire market success is built on the
> simple fact that millions of programs have been written for its processors using
> the x86 instruction set. Abandon that legacy, and Intel loses the key competitive
> advantage over competitors ranging from the Motorola-IBM-Apple PowerPC
> processor to CPUs from Digital, MIPS, and Sun Microelectronics. By wrapping
> CISC compatibility around a RISC core, however, P6-class CPUs can achieve the
> performance of optimized RISC designs while still being able to run 10-year-old
> DOS applications.
>
> AMD, Cyrix, and now IDT (with its new Centaur CPU) leverage the huge market
> for Intel-compatible CPUs by designing their chips with x86 instructions in mind.
> Like Intel, all three employ streamlined RISC cores to handle translated x86
> instructions.

The RISC techniques help, but out-of-order execution is the key to the P6 design. When a CPU reaches an instruction requiring data still to come, the processor must wait. The Pentium Pro can move on to code that it can operate on by storing results in a holding area called the *instruction pool*. This buffer allows the CPU to speculatively execute instructions, holding the results until the proper data can be moved into registers in the proper order.

The addition of *symmetric multiprocessor* (SMP) support makes Pentium Pro well-suited for work inside network servers, Web servers, and high-end workstations. One challenge is keeping the data that is stored in each Pentium Pro L1 cache in sync with the others. Intel uses a protocol called MESI, which defines the four states of cache data (modified, exclusive, shared, and invalid). This scheme ensures that one processor doesn't overwrite a valid piece of data with older data stored in its cache. Up to four Pentium Pro CPUs can be set up in an SMP configuration using the built-in design.

In fact, it is this multi-processing capability that kept Pentium Pro on the shelves for as long as it did. While Pentium II offered higher clock rates, lower cost, and MMX, it could not be configured with more than two CPUs. Intel finally addressed that issue in June 1998, with the release of the Xeon CPU. And production of Pentium Pro was promptly halted.

The Buying Line

For all its technical merits, Pentium Pro carries a lot of baggage. The architecture is heavily optimized for 32-bit code. (Rumor has it that Intel expected Microsoft to transition the market to Windows NT by 1996—and we're still not there!) The 16-bit code inside Windows 95 confuses the P6's aggressive predictive techniques. As a result, Pentium Pro fails to deliver superior performance under DOS and Windows 95.

What's more, the Pentium Pro's integrated L2 cache is difficult to manufacture, with low yields keeping supply constrained. The big cache also makes it impossible to drive CPU clock speeds much above 200MHz. For all the performance of a dedicated internal L2 cache, the architecture doesn't work for a mainstream CPU that needs to be manufactured in the tens of millions of units.

Pentium Pro might not have been a mainstream hit, but the CPU did well in the niche networking and workstation markets. Pentium Pro's four-way SMP capability made it relevant even as faster and cheaper Pentium II CPUs were taking hold in the desktop market.

Upgrade Outlook

Good news greeted Pentium Pro owners in August 1998, when Intel rolled out a Pentium II-based OverDrive product for Pentium Pro systems. This upgrade turns a 150 and 166MHz Pentium Pro system into 300MHz Pentium II. Both 180 and 200MHz Pentium Pro PCs can run at 333MHz. The upgrade looks like a traditional CPU—no huge SEC cartridge here—and plugs directly into the Socket 8 module on the Pentium Pro motherboard. What's more, the 512KB L2 cache inside the Pentium II OverDrive runs at the full speed of the CPU—rather than at 1/2 speed—making this CPU upgrade something of a cross between Pentium II and Xeon. A fan and voltage converter ensure that the new CPU works in older systems.

What does an upgraded system have to gain? In addition to the higher clock rates, MMX-capability will enhance access to the latest multimedia software. In addition, Pentium II offers much improved Windows 9x and Windows 3.x performance over Pentium Pro. If you have an aging Pentium Pro server that is struggling with multimedia content or simply needs a faster clock, this OverDrive upgrade could be just the ticket.

Intel Pentium II: Revenge of the P6

Intel quieted a lot of talk about AMD and Cyrix with this blockbuster processor. Introduced in May of 1997, Pentium II offered peerless x86 and MMX performance, as well as a new system connector design that strategically altered the way Intel CPUs work with motherboards. What's more, Intel clearly plans to ride this P6 architecture into the next century. Table 6.5 provides an overview of the Pentium II.

Table 6.5. Pentium II specs.

Specification	First Generation	Second Generation
Internal clock speed	233, 266, 300MHz	333, 350, 400, 450MHz
L1 cache size	16KB/16KB	16KB/16KB
L2 cache clock speed	112, 133, 150MHz	166, 175, 200, 225MHz (333MHz, Dixon)
MMX support?	Yes	Yes
Number of pipelines	Three	Three
Data bus (internal/external)	32-bit/64-bit	32-bit/64-bit
Number of transistors	7.5 million	7.5 million
Manufacturing process	.35 micron CMOS	.25 micron CMOS
Package type	Slot 1 SEC	Slot 1 SEC

Pentium II Builds on P6 Success

Essentially, Pentium II takes the existing Pentium Pro core, with its RISC-like, out-of-order execution, and adds the same MMX support found in the Pentium MMX CPUs. This means that MMX-optimized software will enjoy a significant speed increase with Pentium II systems. Intel also doubled the L1 data and instruction caches over those in the Pentium Pro, boosting each to 16KB.

The first Pentium II CPUs were built on a .35 micron CMOS process, but that was soon moved to a tighter .25 micron process that reduces heat output and allows for higher clock speeds. All Pentium IIs offer built-in SMP support for two processors (see Figure 6.11). For 4-way or 8-way multiprocessing, you'll need to move to the considerably more expensive Xeon processor.

FIGURE 6.11.
Micronics' Dual Fortress motherboard features two massive Pentium II SEC cartridges for symmetric multiprocessing capability. (Photo courtesy of Micronics Corp.)

Bigger changes occur outside the core. Intel has adopted a cartridge carrier scheme for Pentium II that puts the processor and L2 cache inside a cigarette pack-sized module. This package, called a Single Edge Connector (SEC) cartridge, mounts vertically into the new Socket 1 slot on Pentium II motherboards. More recently, Intel tweaked the SEC package in order to enhance heat dissipation, allowing for cooler processor operation. Key to achieving 500MHz+ clock speeds, the smaller SECC2 exposes the Pentium II chip directly to the heat sink mechanism. The Slot 1 remains identical and no changes to motherboards was required.

Regardless of which type of SEC cartridge is involved, the L2 cache still sits separately from the CPU inside, connected via a dedicated backside bus that runs at half the speed of the CPU proper (see Figure 6.12). Intel calls the separated CPU system and CPU cache bus design the Dual Independent Bus (DIB) Architecture.

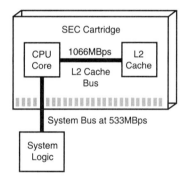

FIGURE 6.12.
Inside the cartridge, Pentium II uses an external L2 cache running at half processor speed to balance speed and affordability. Oh, and there are MMX instructions too. (Figure courtesy of Intel Corp.)

The new SEC design achieves three things:

- It separates the L2 cache from the CPU, improving production yields, lowering cost, and allowing core CPU speeds of 400MHz and higher.

- It enables fast L2 cache performance by using a dedicated backside cache bus that runs faster than motherboard-mounted designs, which are currently limited to 100MHz.

- It prevents competitors such as AMD and Cyrix from selling compatible CPUs, because they can't plug into the Intel-patented P6 bus and Socket 1 connector.

Intel introduced Pentium II at internal clock speeds of 233 and 266MHz, but current versions run at 400 and 450MHz. Clock speeds will go higher still—to 600MHz according to Intel—in 1999, as Intel shrinks the CPU to a .18 micron CMOS process. Also on tap are more instruction set extensions targeting 3D graphics performance. The Katmai New Instructions will appear in Pentium II-class CPUs running at 500MHz and above. Another compelling Pentium II variant, code-named Dixon, will put 256KB of L2 cache directly into a Pentium II core running at 333MHz. Expected in the first half of 1999, the integrated cache will run at twice the speed of the L2 cache found in previous Pentium II CPUs—a big boost to potential performance. On the mobile front, .25-micron Pentium IIs allow clock speeds of 266MHz and higher.

The Buying Line

No doubt about it: Pentium II is the focus of Intel-based computing. In an effort to stay ahead of the competition, Intel gladly killed off its own Pentium MMX CPU and has launched a variety of Pentium II spin-offs to address a variety of markets. If you want a system with maximum life span, Pentium II is your best bet.

Pentium II has its limits. The limited two-way SMP support makes the expensive Xeon processor a much better option for professional workstation and high-end server applications. And Intel's pricing structure means that you'll probably have to buy a Celeron CPU if you want a sub-$1,000 PC with Intel inside. But Pentium II will continue to appeal to a wide market for at least two more years, as the company tweaks the instruction set and advances clock speeds toward 700MHz through the year 2000. Pentium II is best for

- Mainstream business desktops
- Home systems for multimedia titles and game play
- Mixed-use home or office PCs for multimedia playback and presentations
- Power-minded notebook computers

Upgrade Outlook

If you own a Pentium II system, you may or may not be in a good position to upgrade. First, any Slot 1-based motherboard will be limited in its upgrade options, since AMD- and Cyrix-based CPUs simply won't plug into those motherboards. More of a concern, if you are an earlier Pentium II buyer, your motherboard probably won't support the higher 100MHz front bus speed required of current generation Pentium II CPUs. At the time of this writing, no Pentium II OverDrive product was planned to deliver 450MHz or higher CPU clock speeds to 66MHz motherboards.

Why can't you upgrade? The secret is in the chipsets. The earliest Pentium II systems used the venerable 440FX chipset, which was limited to 66MHz operation, lacked support for Accelerated Graphics Port (AGP) cards, and used older EDO DRAM system memory. The introduction of the 440LX chipset in the fall of 1997 added AGP graphics and faster SDRAM memory, but still left the motherboard running at 66MHz. It wasn't until Intel's 440BX chipset arrived in early 1998 that Pentium II motherboards hit their 100MHz stride.

If you have a 440BX chipset and 100MHz motherboard, you should be able to replace a 350MHz Pentium II with one running at 450MHz or faster down the road. What's more, follow-ons to the cache-integrated Dixon CPU could provide very compelling performance upsides to current owners.

Intel Celeron: A Weakling Grows Strong

No doubt about it, Pentium II is a great CPU—if you want to spend two to three thousand bucks on a computer. But the explosive portion of the market has been among systems selling for under $1,000. These PCs offer reasonable all-around performance at a price regular people can afford. With AMD and Cyrix winning customers—and significant unit sales—Intel faced a problem. Selling Pentium II at bargain prices would gut the company's earnings, yet it had committed to discontinuing Pentium MMX as part of its CPU form factor transition.

Enter Celeron. Introduced at 233 and 266MHz, this low-cost CPU uses the Pentium II processor core and plugs into the same Slot 1 motherboard connector, but lacks any fast, L2 cache. Mated with the low-cost 440EX chipset, Celeron only runs on 66MHz motherboards. Physically, Celeron lacks the large plastic SEC cartridge—rather, the CPU is mounted on an exposed PCB (partial circuit board) that plugs into the Slot 1 connector.

The first Celerons (see Figure 6.13) were much maligned for their poor performance, which trailed that of competing K6, K6-2, and M II CPUs by wide margins. The culprit: It lacks an L2 cache. Without this fast, local memory to keep things moving, the Celeron must constantly wait for slower main memory to serve up or accept data. Still, Celeron uses the same, advanced MMX and FP units found in Pentium II, making Celeron at least somewhat appealing for cash-strapped gamers. But otherwise, Celeron was stuck in low gear.

FIGURE 6.13.
The original Celeron was a slimmed down Pentium II that lacked L2 cache and shipped without the familiar black case. Later versions employed an integrated 128KB L2 cache to improve performance markedly. (Photo courtesy of Intel Corp.)

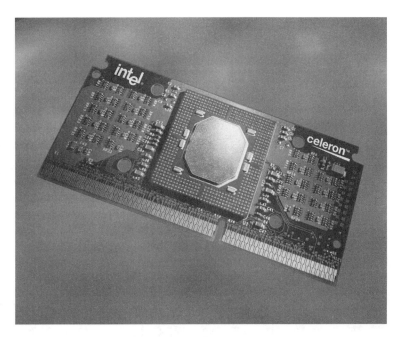

Intel fixed this problem in late 1998 by integrating a small, 128KB L2 cache inside the Celeron core. Running at the speed of the CPU itself (330 to 333MHz), the L2 cache provides an immediate benefit in all applications, and makes Celeron an effective low-cost competitor. However, the 66MHz motherboard bus continues to hold back performance.

Expect that particular wrinkle to be fixed in 1999 as Intel moves Celeron up to a 100MHz motherboard front-side bus. Combined with an integrated 128KB L2 cache and clock speeds that should head toward 400MHz, Celeron looks to be a credible low-end alternative for years to come. But Intel will surely keep a tight leash on Celeron performance, ensuring that it won't cannibalize its mainstream Pentium II sales. Table 6.6 provides an overview of specifications for Celeron.

Table 6.6. Celeron specs.

Specification	First Generation	Second Generation
Internal clock speed	233, 266, 300MHz	300, 333MHz
L1 cache size	16KB/16KB	16KB/16KB
L2 cache clock speed	N/A	300, 333MHz (128KB)
MMX support?	Yes	Yes
Number of pipelines	Three	Three
Data bus (internal/external)	32-bit/64-bit	32-bit/64-bit
Number of transistors	7.5 million	7.5 million
Manufacturing process	.25 micron CMOS	.25 micron CMOS
Package type	Slot 1 circuit board	Slot 1 circuit board

Buying Line

Make no mistake, Celeron is a fundamentally flawed CPU by design. Even with the integrated cache in the newer versions, the processor still only runs on sluggish 66MHz motherboards. Even when the motherboard speed is boosted to 100MHz, you can expect Intel's Pentium II to be providing more compelling features still. That said, the cache-integrated Celeron should provide performance equal to that of almost all Intel-competing CPUs, including the 300MHz version of AMD's heralded K6-2 CPU.

Who should buy Celeron? Well, first off, no one should even consider the cacheless Celeron CPU. It's performance is so poor compared to competing CPUs in its price range that no compelling argument exists for owning one. But the cache-integrated Celeron is a viable option, and should appeal to the low-cost consumer and business markets. If you want to keep your hardware costs below $1,000, and still want cutting edge MMX and FP performance, the newer Celeron CPUs are your best bet.

Because the Celeron circuit board ships fully exposed—not sealed in a black module, a la Pentium II—you can tell cached and cacheless Celerons apart at a glance. Cached Celeron CPUs have an enlarged CPU die bigger than that in both the Pentium II and cacheless Celeron, reflecting the significant number of circuits dedicated to the L2 cache. Of course, your best bet is to verify the CPU type before you buy. First, any Celeron running at 333MHz or faster will include 128KB of integrated L2 cache. Second, those 300MHz Celeron CPUs with integrated cache are called Celeron 300A. You should always confirm that the CPU you are buying is a Celeron 300A to ensure you are getting the proper hardware.

Upgrade Outlook

Unfortunately, the upgrade outlook for Celeron-based systems is not good. The problem is the 66MHz clock on the motherboard. At 333MHz, Celeron is running at 5X motherboard speed. Pushing that speed further becomes an exercise in diminishing returns. If you want a PC you can expect to upgrade with a processor down the line, you'll want to go to Pentium II. That said, Celeron systems based on the 100MHz front-side bus (due in 1999) could pose an interesting upgrade path, but too little is known at the time of this writing to assess the upgrade opportunities.

Intel Xeon

There are two sides to every story, and in the case of Intel, two sides to its market troubles. While the updated Celeron solved the company's low-cost travails, Intel needed something—anything—to replace the aged Pentium Pro at the high end. The Internet has created a booming market for multiprocessor network and Web servers, for example, yet Pentium Pro was stuck at 200MHz and Pentium II couldn't put together more than two CPUs for multiprocessing applications. What's more, Intel was hungry for a premium-priced (some would say overpriced) CPU it could sell to the professional market.

The new Xeon CPU takes aim at this market. Like Celeron, this CPU is a tweaked Pentium II designed to attack a different market. But unlike Celeron, Xeon boasts an improved supporting cast that turns it into a capable, high-end alternative to Digital's Alpha CPU. Table 6.7 provides an overview of Xeon CPUs.

Table 6.7. Xeon specs.

Specification	First Generation	Second Generation
Internal clock speed	400, 450MHz	500+MHz
L1 cache size	16KB/16KB	16KB/16KB
L2 cache clock speed	400, 450MHz (1MB, 2MB)	500+MHz (2MB)
MMX support?	Yes	Yes (Katmai extensions)
Number of pipelines	Three	Three

continues

Table 6.7. Continued.

Specification	First Generation	Second Generation
Data bus (internal/ external)	32-bit/64-bit	32-bit/64-bit
Number of transistors	7.5 million	7.5 million
Manufacturing process	.25 micron CMOS	.18 micron CMOS
Package type	Slot 2	Slot 2/Slot M

Xeon's main enhancement is a bigger-and-faster L2 cache that runs at the clock speed of the CPU core. See Figure 6.14. So a 450MHz Xeon CPU has an L2 cache running at 450MHz, twice the speed of a comparable Pentium II. The first Xeons feature 512KB and 1MB L2 caches, but high-end buyers can opt for a mammoth 2MB cache, which help manage large data sets encountered in network and transaction servers. The new CPU also introduces a new connector—called Slot 2—which proffers additional pins for the enlarged cache.

FIGURE 6.14.

Built for network and workstation PCs, Xeon features a bulked up module that enhances heat dissipation. (Photo courtesy of Intel Corp.)

There's more than just fast cache involved. Xeon includes diagnostic circuitry for keeping tabs on CPU temperature and other environmental factors. These diagnostics, along with a simple bus structure for moving the data to the system, allow servers to catch problems before they lead to a catastrophic crash.

No surprise, Xeon leads the feature march. The second-generation Xeon CPU will feature a tight .18 micron process, while the 500MHz Xeon CPU (code-named Tanner) is expected to be compatible with the Slot M design used by the upcoming IA-64 Merced processor. In effect, Xeon will play a transition role as Intel moves to advanced 64-bit processors designs. Finally, Xeon also plays host to Intel's new MMX 2 or Katmai instruction set extensions to add 3D graphics talents to Xeon.

Buying Line

The buying picture on Xeon is clear. This processor is for professional level workstations and network servers. With Xeon CPUs costing two to three times that of comparable Pentium II processors, the appeal is limited. So who should run Xeon? Anyone who needs a multiprocessing server for demanding applications such as Web serving, transaction serving, and database handling. Also professional 3D graphics workstations will benefit. You'll have to be running Windows NT or an x86-compatible version of Unix to get the most out of the multiple processors and large caches.

Upgrade Outlook

Xeon is still you, so you can expect clock speed enhancements to provide a window for upgrades. Early 400MHz Xeon systems may well be upgradable to 600 or 700MHz by the end of 1999. But Intel does have plans for a Slot change, moving to Slot 2 with the "Tanner" version of the Xeon line. Presumably, such a switch will spell curtains for slot compatibility and could limit upgrades.

Ultimately, the real upgrade picture revolves around Xeon's multiprocessor capability. If you buy a single-CPU Xeon system that has a spare slot for a second processor, then you have your upgrade built in. Add the second CPU, and you're off. Of course, a 4-way or even 8-way SMP motherboard provides additional upside, though the motherboards (even without CPUs installed) get quite expensive.

AMD K6: A Challenger Returns

AMD launched its latest processor, the K6 (see Figure 6.15), in April of 1997. For the first time, a non-Intel CPU stood atop the x86 performance heap, as K6 proved faster than both Pentium MMX and Pentium Pro. K6 could even keep pace with Pentium II CPUs running at the same clock speeds under Windows 95.

K6 enjoys one big advantage in the marketplace over Pentium II: AMD's processor plugs into the same Socket 7 motherboards used for Pentium and Pentium MMX CPUs. Although system vendors will have to adopt expensive new motherboards for Pentium II, K6 systems can cut costs by leveraging existing motherboard designs, though K6's lower voltage operation often requires motherboard makers to tweak their products.

FIGURE **6.15.**
AMD's K6 brings close-to-Pentium II performance, yet plugs into affordable Socket 7 motherboards. (Photo courtesy of AMD Corp.)

Tip: Because K6 plugs into Socket 7 motherboards, the CPU can serve as the core of a processor upgrade for Pentium MMX and some newer Pentium Classic PCs. Evergreen Technologies intends to offer K6 upgrade products.

A Look at K6

Socket 7 compatibility makes for good economics, but it hands the performance advantage to Pentium II and its faster L2 cache. K6 makes up some of the difference with an oversized L1 cache that, at 64KB (32KB for instruction and 32KB for data), is twice the size of that in Pentium MMX and Pentium II. The performance difference widens on Pentium IIs running at above 300MHz.

In many ways, K6 resembles the Pentium Pro and Pentium II CPUs it targets. Like these processors, K6 wraps a CISC interface around a superscalar pipelined RISC architecture. x86 instructions are decoded into fixed-length RISC86 instructions (AMD's version of Intel's micro-operations) for efficient processing in the K6's two six-stage integer pipelines. Table 6.8 provides an overview of the K6 processor.

Table 6.8. AMD K6 specs.

Specification	First Generation	Second Generation
Internal clock speed	166, 200, 233MHz	266, 300MHz+
L1 cache size	32KB/32KB	32KB/32KB
L2 cache clock speed	60, 66MHz	60, 66MHz
MMX support?	Yes	Yes

Specification	First Generation	Second Generation
Number of pipelines	Two	Two
Data bus (internal/external)	32-bit/32-bit	32-bit/32-bit
Number of transistors	8 million	8 million
Manufacturing process	.35 micron CMOS	.25 micron CMOS
Package type	Socket 7 PGA	Socket 7 PGA

You'll find other familiar tricks inside the K6. The processor supports out-of-order execution and uses branch prediction to avoid stalls in its two integer and one floating-point pipelines. The K6 also supports MMX instructions, using eight 64-bit MMX registers to process MMX instructions broken down into RISC86 operations.

The current K6 is built on a .25 micron CMOS process and runs as fast as 300MHz. Faster versions of the CPU won't be produced, however, as AMD is moving its efforts to its next-generation K6-2 processor. For more on K6-2, see the next section.

The Buying Line

AMD K6 changed everything. Finally, buyers could consider a viable competitor to Intel's top-of-the-line CPUs. The result has been healthy price competition enabling you to buy that much more PC for your dollar.

But is K6 for you? Unless you are extremely tight on cash, probably not. The CPU has already fallen under the shadow of its follow-on, K6-2, which offers faster clock rates and intriguing 3D graphics tweaks in systems costing around $1,000. But K6 does enjoy rock-solid x86 compatibility and AMD's improved manufacturing process means the K6 doesn't run overly hot. If you don't need the additional performance and can find a rock-bottom price on a K6 system, it might be worth buying.

On the performance side, K6 systems fall a bit short in MMX performance compared to Pentium II systems. Otherwise, the K6 runs neck and neck in integer performance with Pentium II PCs of the same clock speed. K6 works best for extremely low-priced desktop PCs.

Upgrade Outlook

Don't count on upgrading a K6 system, particularly if the CPU is already running at 266 or 300MHz. The K6 lines end at 300MHz, and the K6-2 won't be doubling that number anytime soon. What's more, AMD is focusing on 100MHz motherboards, which means fast K6-2 CPUs probably won't run in your existing 66MHz motherboard at all. But if you have one of the early K6 system running at 200MHz or below, you might realize a nifty gain by going to 300MHz.

AMD K6-2: The Real Deal

If K6 opened the floodgates, K6-2 is the flood. This CPU is essentially a tweaked K6 CPU that adds faster clock speeds and extended instructions for better 3D graphics performance. The CPU also sits at the center of AMD's efforts to kick-start the Super 7 initiative, which uses a 100MHz motherboard bus.

For decent Pentium II-level performance near $1,000, you can't do much better than K6-2 (shown in Figure 6.16). Starting at 266MHz, tests show integer performance in line with Pentium II CPUs of similar clock speed, while MMX performance has improved markedly over earlier models. What's more, 3D games using Microsoft DirectX 6.0 gain a big boost from AMD's 3DNow! instruction extensions found in K6-2. For gamers, K6-2 is the low-cost option.

FIGURE 6.16.
Additional 3D-specific instructions make K6-2 a viable CPU for gamers. (Photo courtesy of AMD Corp.)

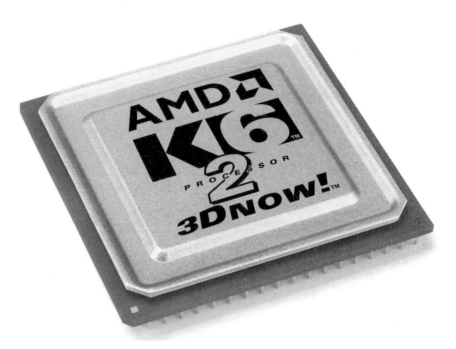

While AMD has revved its chip toward 400MHz, the real benefit comes from the K6-2 revision called "Sharptooth." This K6-2 version adds a 256KB integrated L2 cache that runs at the speed of the CPU. No surprise, the package gets big—21.3 million transistors, up from about 8 million—but performance improves significantly. What's more, the CPU supports a front-side L3 cache, allowing another 512KB to 1MB of fast tertiary memory to sit between the CPU and system RAM. Table 6.9 provides an overview of the K6-2 processor.

Table 6.9. AMD K6-2 specs.

Specification	First Generation	Second Generation
Internal clock speed	266, 300, 350MHz	350, 400MHz+
L1 cache size	32KB/32KB	32KB/32KB
L2 cache clock speed	100MHz	350, 400MHz+
MMX support?	Yes (3DNow!)	Yes (3DNow!)
Number of pipelines	Two	Two
Data bus (internal/external)	32-bit/32-bit	32-bit/32-bit
Number of transistors	8 million	21.3 million
Manufacturing process	.25 micron CMOS	.25 micron CMOS
Package type	Super 7 PGA	Super 7 PGA

Buying Line

AMD's K6-2 line presents a clear challenge to Intel's success in the low-end of the market. The K6-2-300 matches the integer performance of Pentium II-300, and unlike the earlier K6 line, keeps pace in 3D graphics operations. What's more, AMD's Sharptooth technology solves K6-2's major weakness—its reliance on L2 cache slaved to the relatively-slow 100MHz motherboard. By moving 256KB of L2 cache on-chip, future K6-2 CPUs will enjoy every performance benefit touted by Intel's latest Pentium II CPUs. The inclusion of optional 100MHz L3 (or tertiary) cache in the design adds another performance upside.

AMD has vowed to keep its CPU prices 25 percent below those of comparable Intel models, and the company has managed to keep its word despite aggressive action by Intel. The result: AMD K6-2 is a terrific bargain. Who should consider the K6-2?

- Any buyer who wants a PC for under $1,000
- Any buyer who wants general home/multimedia applications and midrange gaming
- Any buyer who wants almost any office productivity applications

Upgrade Outlook

This early in a CPU line it's hard to assess the upgrade picture, but it's clear that AMD plans to extend the Socket 7/Super 7 architecture as far as it will go. The inclusion of L2 cache in the K6-2 is good news for this market, as it eliminates one of Pentium II's key advantages. What's more, Sharptooth-class CPUs present a terrific upgrade path for those owning early 300MHz K6-2 systems. Ultimately, future Super 7 CPU announcements will determine the upgrade picture for this CPU.

Cyrix M II: The Competition Heats Up

Introduced in June 1997, Cyrix's M II has a lot in common with AMD's K6. Originally named 6x86Mx but later rebranded M II to position it directly against Pentium II, the CPU offers integer performance that is a close match for K6. And like K6, the M II uses a 64-bit external bus that plugs into existing Socket 7 motherboards. But Cyrix has priced its new CPU very aggressively, making M II PCs possibly the best bargains around.

In fact, Cyrix and AMD share many of the same prospects and problems. Both have good manufacturing capacity, strong processor designs, and sustained histories as x86-compatible CPU makers. Unfortunately, few first-tier PC makers will carry their products, making it difficult for them to break into larger markets.

M II Details

Like K6 and Pentium MMX, the early Cyrix M II CPUs were built on a .35-micron CMOS process, but current generation product has moved to a cooler .25 micron design. A pipelined, superscalar design allows M II to achieve more than one operation per clock tick. In fact, M II's P-ratings are a bit deceptive in that the actual clock speeds are actually slower than the metric indicates. An M II-300 CPU, for example, runs at 225MHz. The M II, shown in Figure 6.17, also provides full MMX instruction support—with MMX registers laid on top of the floating-point registers. Key to M II performance is the big 64KB L1 cache, which is unified so that instructions and data share space in the cache.

FIGURE 6.17.

M II offers a lower price than similar K6-2 chips, but MMX performance lags both Pentium II and K6-2. (Photo courtesy of Cyrix Corp.)

M II ran initially at 166, 200, and 225MHz, using system bus speeds of 60, 66, and 75MHz, respectively. Today, M II runs on 100MHz Super 7 motherboards and offers P-ratings of 300 to 400MHz. Actual clock rates tend to trail these figures by about 75 points. The smaller .25-micron process allows for higher speed operation.

M II gets the most out of each clock tick, using an aggressive superscalar design and large cache to help power performance. However, MMX performance doesn't enjoy this advantage. M II trails Pentium II considerably in MMX-optimized tasks, and is even a step behind K6 and K6-2 in this respect. Table 6.10 provides an overview of the M II processor.

Table 6.10. Cyrix M II specs.

Specification	First Generation	Second Generation
Internal clock speed	150, 166, 188MHz	225, 300MHz
L1 cache size	64KB unified	64KB unified
L2 cache clock speed	60, 66, 75MHz	66, 100MHz
MMX support?	Yes	Yes
Number of pipelines	Two	Two
Data bus (internal/external)	32-bit/64-bit	32-bit/64-bit
Number of transistors	8 million	8 million
Manufacturing process	.35 micron CMOS	.30/.25 micron CMOS
Package type	Socket 7 PGA	Super 7 PGA

The fastest first-generation M II CPUs offered superior performance by supporting a 75MHz motherboard that is about 15 percent faster than the 66MHz boards used by Pentium II and K6. Unfortunately, the reality was that few motherboard vendors produced these 75MHz products, limiting M II's performance. With the advent of 100MHz Super 7 designs, performance has improved considerably.

The Buying Line

Cyrix markets its CPUs using the Performance Rating scheme. In fact, you might have a hard time finding the actual core speed of the processor you're buying—an annoying bit of marketeering that makes assessing performance potential difficult. Table 6.11 shows the actual clock and bus speeds of each P-rated M II processor.

Table 6.11. Clock speeds of P-rated M II CPUs.

M II P-Rating	Internal Clock	Motherboard Clock
PR166	133MHz/150MHz	66MHz/60MHz
PR200	150MHz/166MHz	75MHz/66MHz
PR233	188MHz	75MHz
PR266	208MHz	83MHz
PR300	233MHz	66MHz
PR333	266MHz	66MHz
PR350	250MHz	100MHz
PR400	300MHz	100MHz

The buying outlook for the M II is nearly identical to that of K6. M II figures prominently in machines costing less than $1,000. The following are good applications for the M II:

- Affordable mixed-use home and office PCs that need to handle moderate multimedia, presentations, and game play
- Affordable general-purpose home PCs

Upgrade Outlook

The upgrade picture for M II is generally the same as K6 and K6-2. M II uses the Socket 7 and Super 7 motherboard architectures, which means systems based on M II CPUs should be upgradable with CPUs from AMD, Cyrix, and perhaps other vendors. However, owners of M II systems using the 75MHz bus clock may face a challenge since only Cyrix addresses this market, limiting the number of available processors.

Cyrix 6x86 and AMD K5: Better Than Pentium

Although they are now out of production, the Cyrix 6x86 and AMD K5 both helped set up the competitive processor market. Both were able to provide performance slightly ahead of Pentium CPUs running at the same clock rate, and both were significantly less expensive.

Unfortunately, neither broke out in the market. Large system makers declined to pick up the new CPUs for fear of drawing the ire of Intel, the critical supplier in the market. More important, problems plagued both lines. AMD suffered a series of delays that kept K5 a step behind the competition, while the 6x86 suffered from a series of minor glitches that impeded sales. In addition, Cyrix lacked relationships with major system vendors, a critical ingredient for marketing a CPU.

Inside the Cyrix 6x86

For all its problems, the 6x86 is a good entry-level CPU. The slimmed-down .5-micron process has allowed faster clock speeds in a smaller, cooler die. Like the Pentium, the 6x86 features 16KB of L1 cache and a superscalar core that can process multiple operations at once. To tweak performance further, Cyrix has tried to get system makers to adopt 75MHz motherboards—20 percent faster than standard 66MHz models—for its fastest 6x86 CPU.

Table 6.12 provides an overview of the 6x86 processor.

Table 6.12. Cyrix 6x86 specs.

Specification	First Generation	Second Generation
Internal clock speed	100, 100MHz	120, 133, 150MHz
L1 cache size (data/instruction)	16KB unified	16KB unified

Specification	First Generation	Second Generation
L2 cache clock speed	50, 55MHz	60, 66, 75MHz
MMX support?	No	No
Number of pipelines	Two	Two
Data bus (internal/external)	32-bit/64-bit	32-bit/32-bit
Manufacturing process	.6 micron CMOS	.5 micron CMOS
Package type	Socket 7 PGA	Socket 7 PGA

Inside the AMD K5

Table 6.13 provides an overview of the K5 processor.

Table 6.13. AMD K5 specs.

Specification	First Generation
Internal clock speed	100, 117MHz
L1 cache size (data/instruction)	16KB/8KB
L2 cache clock speed	60, 66MHz
MMX support?	No
Number of pipelines	Two
Data bus (internal/external)	32-bit/32-bit
Number of transistors	4.3 million
Manufacturing process	.35 micron CMOS
Package type	Socket 7 PGA

Behind the Pentium-beating performance is a superpipelined, superscalar core that runs more efficiently than the Pentium CPU. Like Cyrix's 6x86, the K5 can simply do more per clock tick than the Pentium CPU. However, like the 6x86, K5 lacks MMX support.

Upgrading a CPU

So you've decided that your aging system needs a faster processor to keep pace with the latest applications. This section will detail the options available when it comes to upgrading your processor. It will also guide you through an upgrade and give you strategies and tips for avoiding problems.

> **Tip:** A new processor can boost performance, but it won't resolve bottlenecks existing with memory, graphics, and other areas. Before opting for a processor upgrade, make sure you aren't overlooking other possible upgrades that might do a better job of improving performance.

How CPU Upgrades Work

No doubt about it, a processor upgrade is serious business—the PC version of a brain transplant. Although most CPU upgrades entail replacing the existing processor with a faster chip, the real payoff comes from the more-sophisticated processing features of the upgrade CPU (see Figure 6.18).

FIGURE 6.18.

Upgrade products such as Intel's OverDrive MMX can significantly boost clock rates and add new features such as MMX support. (Photo courtesy of Intel Corp.)

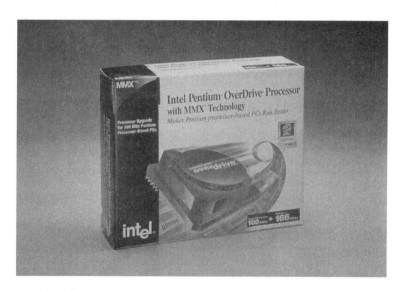

How does a CPU upgrade work? In most cases, the upgrade chip plugs into the same socket occupied by the existing CPU. The new chip communicates with the PC using the same pins employed by the original processor but adds all the talents of its more-sophisticated core. Depending on the upgrade, the new CPU might add new functions to the PC—such as floating-point math or MMX instructions—or it might simply augment existing performance with a faster internal clock, larger L1 cache, or optimized internal operation.

In general, CPU upgrades will enhance performance by doing the following:

- Boost internal CPU clock speed
- Add or improve floating-point capability for some 3D and imaging applications
- Add MMX instruction support for multimedia applications

- Provide a superscalar pipelined architecture to increase the number of operations performed per clock tick
- Add or enlarge the integrated L1 or L2 cache to reduce wait states in the processor
- Work with motherboard settings to provide faster external bus speeds

The level of benefit to your system depends on several things. The important thing is not to overestimate what a CPU upgrade can do, particularly for older 486 systems. The following bottlenecks all share one aspect: They will force a fast processor to halt operation while it waits for data to come from the system.

- Slow motherboard speed: Many 486 motherboards are limited to 33MHz operation, one-half to one-third the speed of current motherboards.
- Narrow external bus: Older systems with 32-bit memory buses will starve a fast CPU.
- Slow system RAM: Today's PCs feature enhanced RAM running at 60ns or faster, versus the 80ns RAM that you might find in a 486. The 30 percent speed difference and inefficient design can force your new CPU to wait.
- Lack of L2 cache: Because they didn't need to keep up with super-fast CPUs, older PCs might lack the ability to use a fast L2 cache. Again, your new CPU might end up waiting for data.
- Slow graphics bus: If your 486 lacks PCI or VL-bus slots, a processor upgrade can't help solve problems with graphical programs. At the very least, you'll need to consider a motherboard upgrade.
- Slow hard disk: Today's hard disks feature access times of 11 milliseconds. Four years ago, 25ms was common. This means that programs take longer to load, data crawls into RAM, and virtual memory is a swamp.

Peter's Principle: A CPU Upgrade Extends—Rather Than Renews—the Life of Your PC

If you think of a CPU upgrade as a way to extend—rather than renew—the life of your PC, you will avoid inevitable disappointment. A processor upgrade is a terrific way to wait out the arrival of The Next Big Thing while keeping your PC in useful shape.

How to Upgrade Your CPU

A processor upgrade might be PC brain surgery, but that doesn't mean it has to be difficult. In fact, compared to installing a hard disk or CD-ROM drive, upgrading the CPU can be a breeze—usually. This section will help you understand how an upgrade happens, complete with step-by-step instructions.

This section will deal specifically with Socket 7-based CPU upgrades rather than those for Slot 1-based Intel Celeron and Pentium II CPUs. Why? Slot 1 systems are still new enough that upgrades are either not required or not available for these systems. However, the same principles generally apply, and I will note when the procedures for a Slot 1 CPU varies from the Socket 7 description.

First, be warned. The complexity and diversity of the PC marketplace makes CPU upgrades a fairly uncertain proposition. There are hundreds, if not thousands, of system vendors, most of which have produced hundreds, if not thousands, of individual models. No CPU upgrade vendor can anticipate and design for this wide universe of platforms.

The leading culprit in this compatibility soup is the system BIOS (Basic Input/Output System), the code that underlies all the workings of the PC. BIOS programming can be half science and half black magic. Bugs and twitches turn up all the time in even the most up-to-date BIOS code working inside of unaltered systems. Plug in a processor purchased four or six years after your system BIOS code was written, and there's no telling how the two will interact. That's why I'll mention this piece of sage advice now (which will be repeated mercilessly throughout this book): Back up your hard disk first.

Back up to tape, to cartridge media, to floppies, or to your network. One way or another, put those valued bits someplace where they can be retrieved after disaster strikes. Also faithfully record your current BIOS settings—hard disk sectors, bus I/O, the works. If you have a flash BIOS—a BIOS that can be software-updated—store the current BIOS code onto a floppy disk and keep it handy. Also make a startup/rescue disk with the usual data.

| INSTANT REFERENCE | For more on backing up before an upgrade, see Chapter 3, "Upgrade Strategies."

Physically Installing a CPU Upgrade

Surprisingly, the physical installation of a new CPU can be quite easy. This is particularly true for systems using Socket 7 (or even Socket 5) modules, including those based on Pentium, Pentium MMX, K5, K6, 6x86, and M II processors. All these PCs include so-called Zero Insertion Force (ZIF) sockets, which use an easily accessed lever to socket and desocket the CPU. ZIF sockets eliminate the need to tenderly pull chips out of their sockets—harrowing work that can result in snapped pins and broken hearts. For newer Pentium II-class systems with Slot 1 connectors, removing and inserting a CPU is simpler still—the vertical connector is similar to that used by PCI cards.

A typical ZIF socket installation works as follows:

1. Shut off the PC, remove the power cable, and remove the system chassis. Allow the system to sit for about half an hour so the CPU is cool enough to handle.

2. Ground yourself to avoid electrostatic shock. The best method is to use a static mat with the cord attached to your wrist. Lacking that, be sure to touch the metal of the PC chassis before touching any components.

3. Place the system so the motherboard is facing the ceiling. (For tower and minitower systems, this means placing the unit on its side.)

4. Remove the upgrade CPU from its packaging, and place it pins-up on the mat.

5. Locate the system CPU. If the processor has a fan or heat sink with a wire attached, you need to detach it first. Also clear any cables or wires blocking access. If necessary, unplug cables or remove drives from their bays.

6. Find the ZIF lever (the metal lever with a plastic tip that lies next to the socket) and gently pull it up. The CPU should lift a little from the socket.

7. Making sure you're well-grounded, grasp the CPU with your thumb and forefinger and pull straight upward. Avoid raising one edge or the other, because this can result in bent or broken pins. Place the original CPU in the packaging supplied with the upgrade processor.

8. Take the upgrade CPU and orient it so that pin 1 aligns with pin 1 in the CPU socket. Usually, the pin 1 corner will have a beveled edge or will have a dot silk screened on top of the CPU in the corner, as shown in Figure 6.19. (Refer to the vendor's documentation to make sure you have properly identified pin 1.)

FIGURE 6.19.
Lining up the pin 1 position is critical to avoid damaging the CPU. You'll need to spot the subtle pin 1 clues chip makers provide, including a beveled edge, silk-screened dot, and the absence of a corner pin. (Figure courtesy of Intel Corp.)

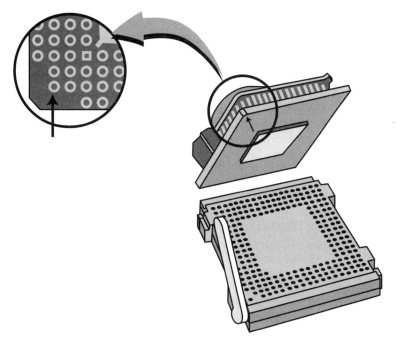

9. Slowly place the processor into the socket, taking your time to make sure the edges are aligned and that the pins seat smoothly into the socket holes. Don't force it!

10. Once you're satisfied that the CPU is properly aligned and seated, press gently on the top of the CPU to make sure all pins are in contact.

11. Lower the ZIF lever slowly. You should be able to feel some resistance as the lever brings the socket into contact with the CPU pins.

12. Make sure you haven't disturbed any wires or boards inside the chassis. Also check to make sure no tools or other objects are inside the case.

13. Before putting the case back on, plug in your PC and boot it up. You'll be in violation of FCC emissions compliance for a few minutes, but it's a good idea to see if things work before going to the trouble of screwing on the case.

14. If the machine boots up normally, congratulations! Your PC has a new brain. Go ahead and put on the case. If the machine doesn't boot normally, refer to the section "Troubleshooting: Fixing CPU Problems," later in this chapter.

Again, Slot-based CPUs—including Slot 1 Celeron, Pentium II, and Xeon—remove and install much like a typical PCI add-in card. That said, you must be sure to properly align the CPU so that pin 1 on the CPU leads matches up with the appropriate side of the motherboard slot. Also, avoid pushing one side of the edged connector deep into the socket. You should apply even force across the top of the CPU so that the leads slide in at the same time. If need be, you can work the CPU in by pushing one edge down a bit, followed by the other until the CPU fits neatly into the socket.

On most older 486 systems, you won't even have a ZIF socket, so you need to pull the chip out of the socket using a tool called a chip puller, which looks a little bit like salad tongs. The chip puller enables you to put even upward force on two sides of the CPU so that you don't end up bending pins.

Here's how to handle the physical installation of a nonZIF-socketed CPU:

1. Shut off the PC, remove the power cable, and remove the system chassis. Let the CPU cool off by leaving the system alone for about half an hour.

2. Ground yourself to avoid electrostatic shock. Use a static mat, or at least touch the metal of the PC frame before going inside the PC.

3. Place the system with the motherboard facing up toward you. (Tower and mini-tower systems go on their sides.)

4. Remove the upgrade CPU from its packaging, and place it on the static mat pins-up.

5. Locate the system CPU. If the processor has a fan or heat sink with a wire attached, you need to detach it first. Also clear any cables or wires that block access. If necessary, unplug cables or remove drives from their bays.

6. Grasp the chip puller with your thumb and forefinger, and lower the tool so that the tongs are level with the bottom of the processor. Squeeze the tongs between the CPU and socket, working them so that the tong teeth fit between the CPU pins.

7. Once you're confident that the tongs have a good grip, pull evenly and gently toward your body. To help unseat the pins, you can pull one side up slightly and then even up the opposite side. Be very careful, because tipping the CPU too far to one side will bend or break the pins!

8. If necessary, remove the chip puller and reseat the tongs on the other two sides of the CPU. Repeat step 7. Repeat this as necessary until the CPU comes up. Take your time, and work slowly.

9. Once the CPU is lifted, use your hand to slowly pull it straight up and out of the socket. Place the CPU in the packaging used by the upgrade processor.

10. Take the upgrade CPU from the mat, and lower it slowly onto the socket. Align pin 1 of the upgrade chip with pin 1 of the socket. Usually, the pin 1 corner will have a beveled edge or will have a dot silk screened on top of the CPU in the corner. (Refer to the vendor's documentation to make sure that you've properly identified pin 1.)

11. Slowly lower the processor into the socket, taking your time to ensure that the edges are aligned and that the pins fit neatly into the socket holes.

12. Once the CPU is aligned and seated, press gently on the top of the CPU, slowly adding force to lower the chip. The CPU should press flush against the socket. Don't force it!

13. Reattach any wires or drives you cleared earlier. Also make sure you haven't disturbed any boards or the inside of the chassis, and check that no tools or other objects are inside the case.

14. Plug in the PC and boot it up before sealing the case. This will enable you to see if the installation worked before you seal the case.

15. If the PC boots up normally, put on the case. If it doesn't, refer to the section "Troubleshooting: Fixing CPU Problems."

Software Needed for an Upgrade

Like almost any hardware upgrade, there's a software side to installing a CPU. Specifically, you need to determine whether the upgrade processor will work with your system. Upgrades such as Intel's OverDrive processors come with a disk to diagnose the system BIOS and to determine whether it will work with the chip. If not, you need to install a new BIOS.

If your system has a flashable BIOS—that is, if it can be upgraded from software—you can update it easily. The first step is to determine the exact model of both your PC and its motherboard. Also look for the maker and version of the current BIOS. You can find this information by watching the display during bootup. With that information, you can visit the Web site or BBS of the system manufacturer or motherboard maker to get the latest compatible BIOS version. To upgrade a BIOS, do the following:

1. Download the BIOS code from your vendor's Web site and copy the update file to a floppy disk.

2. Turn off the system and then turn it on again, pressing the appropriate command keys to enter the BIOS sequence. (In some computers, the Ctrl and Home keys must be held down during bootup.)

3. Wait for the BIOS flashing sequence to complete. The computer should automatically restart itself with the new BIOS installed.

INSTANT REFERENCE | For more information on the system BIOS, see Chapter 9, "Understanding Motherboards and Chipsets."

Older systems might be equipped with an EPROM (Electrically Programmable Read-Only Memory), which can't be readily reprogrammed. In this case, you can try to order an updated EPROM chip from your system or motherboard vendor. However, the cost and difficulty of installing the new chip can be prohibitive. In addition, the system vendor might not offer an EPROM update for older motherboards. In this case, your upgrade options might be limited.

PERFORMANCE

> Even if your CPU upgrade doesn't require a BIOS update, you should look into one anyway. Quite often, motherboard manufacturers and third-party BIOS vendors release performance-optimized updates able to deliver a big boost to existing systems. Windows 98, for example, sometimes requires a BIOS update in order to properly enable features like advanced power management and Fast BIOS operation. Other key updates include the addition of write-back cache support or streamlined memory access.

CPU Upgrade Options

So you have an older system you hope to keep around a while longer. You have plenty of options. A number of companies sell CPU upgrade kits based on Intel, AMD, and Cyrix processors.

> **Peter's Principle:** When a CPU Upgrade Turns into a Motherboard Upgrade
>
> Before you go too deep into exploring CPU upgrade alternatives, make sure you don't really want a motherboard upgrade instead. In addition to providing a fast new CPU, motherboard upgrades feature quicker system RAM, faster graphics capability, and attractive features such as Plug and Play, enhanced IDE, and USB.

The following are key points in deciding whether a CPU upgrade can really work. If any of the following points describes your current PC, you might consider upgrading the motherboard instead:

- Lack of PCI bus slots for fast graphics
- Lack of Plug and Play BIOS and chipsets for easing peripheral installations under Windows 95
- Lack of support for quick (60ns or faster) and enhanced system RAM such as EDO, DRAM, and SDRAM

Also, anyone upgrading a 486 PC should at least look into a new motherboard. The slow and narrow 486 motherboard bus alone makes any CPU upgrade problematic at best. Combined with the lack of VL bus and ISA graphics boards for these systems, a new motherboard makes sense.

For more on motherboard upgrades, see Chapter 9, "Understanding Motherboards and Chipsets."

These upgrade kits include everything you need to replace your old CPU with a faster chip. Inside the box you will usually find a CPU, a heat sink or fan, a chip puller, step-by-step documentation, and sometimes diagnostics for testing the compatibility of your PC's BIOS.

Table 6.14 lists vendors who sell CPU upgrades.

Table 6.14. Vendors who sell 486-to-Pentium upgrades.

Company	Phone Number	Web Site
Evergreen Technologies	(800) 733-0934	http://www.evertech.com
Gainbery Computer Products	(800) 825-7331	http://www.gainbery.com
Intel Corp.	(800) 538-3373 (408) 765-8080	http://www.intel.com
Kingston Technology Corp.	(800) 337-8410	http://www.kingston.com
PowerLeap	(877) 278-5327	http://www.powerleap.com

486 Upgrade Options

If you own a 486DX system, the easiest and most certain upgrade is a clock-multiplied 486-class CPU. The Intel DX4-100, for example, triples the internal clock of the 486DX-33. You might also consider even faster 486 clones from AMD, Cyrix, or IBM. AMD sells a 120MHz 486 that runs at 40MHz outside of the CPU. The downside is that these upgrades lack the architectural features of Pentium-class CPUs.

Another, potentially better, option is to use a Pentium-class upgrade using the 486 pin-out. Intel's 486-to-Pentium OverDrive chip—since discontinued—was the first such product. Although the 486-to-Pentium OverDrive boasts the same superscalar core found in the Pentium CPU, the results failed to impress in benchmark tests. What's worse, the complexity of the 486-to-Pentium upgrade caused all sorts of compatibility problems. DX4-based upgrades generally matched the performance of the 486-to-Pentium OverDrive in most applications.

Behind the poor showing was the 32-bit data bus employed by 486 motherboards, which is half the width of that of true Pentium CPUs. The narrow bus prevents the superscalar architecture from running at full tilt. Still, some applications—in particular, those employing floating-point operations—can see significant jumps.

You can find 486 upgrade products from Kingston and Evergreen that use Cyrix's 586 and AMD's K5 processors. Like P24T, these chips provide Pentium-like characteristics. And like P24T, their ability to improve the performance of an old 486 motherboard is limited.

Pentium Upgrade Options

The outlook for owners of Pentium systems is better. Pentium PCs feature a wider 64-bit motherboard bus running at 60 and 66MHz, providing four times the bandwidth of 486 systems. What's more, most Pentium PCs are outfitted with PCI add-on cards, providing superior graphics performance for both ISA and VL bus-based systems.

If you are considering a Pentium-class upgrade, make sure you get one supporting MMX instructions. This feature will ensure that your upgraded system can take advantage of MMX enhanced software. If you are sticking with Intel the OverDrive MMX product is a sensible upgrade. The addition of Pentium MMX features—the enlarged L1 cache and MMX instruction set support—make OverDrive MMX the most compelling member yet of Intel's OverDrive line.

OverDrive MMX supports Pentium PCs running from 75 to 166MHz. Clock speeds vary by model but range from 150 to 200MHz. The OverDrive upgrade includes an attached heat sink and fan, as well as a voltage regulator for allowing the 2.8-volt CPU to run on existing 3.3-volt motherboards.

Table 6.15 shows the clock-speed improvement provided by OverDrive MMX products for existing Pentium CPUs.

Table 6.15. OverDrive MMX products.

Pentium PC Clock Speed	OverDrive Clock Speed
75	150
90, 120, 150	180
100, 133	166 or 200*
166	200

*200MHz operation is available for Socket 7 motherboards. Older Socket 5 motherboards run at 166MHz.

Another upgrade entry is Evergreen Technologies' MxPro. Based on IDT's WinChip C6 processor, MxPro upgrades any compatible Socket 7 PC to speeds of 180 and 200MHz and adds MMX support. Significantly, slower Pentium-75 systems can be upgraded all the way to 200MHz. Intel's OverDrive scheme, in contrast, only allows an upgrade to 150MHz for a Pentium-75. However, tests have shown that IDT's WinChip architecture provides MMX and floating point performance significantly slower than that of Pentium MMX processors of the same clock speed.

Pentium Pro Upgrade Options

Owners of aging Pentium Pro systems will be glad to know that their processor has now joined the ranks of the upgradable. In August 1998, Intel released an OverDrive product that replaces the Pentium Pro CPU with a specially packaged Pentium II. Because Pentium Pro uses the Socket 8 architecture—essentially a larger Socket 7—the Pentium II upgrade looks like a standard CPU with pins arrayed along the bottom edge of the ceramic casing and a heat sink and fan mounted on top, as shown in Figure 6.20.

FIGURE 6.20.

It doesn't look much like a Pentium II, but this OverDrive will deliver faster clock rates, MMX capability, and a better optimized CPU core to your Pentium Pro PC. (Figure courtesy of Intel Corp.)

The Pentium II OverDrive Processor will upgrade 166 and 200MHz Pentium Pro CPUs to 333MHz clock speeds. The 150MHz and 180MHz CPUs can be boosted to 300MHz. Of course, the Pentium II core includes MMX instruction set support, while doubling Pentium Pro's L1 cache from 16KB to 32KB. 512KB of on-board L2 cache is also included. However, unlike the Pentium II, the L2 cache actually runs at the full speed of the CPU core—300 or 333MHz.

Of course, many Pentium Pro systems are dual-processor network servers or other high-end models. Pentium II OverDrive supports dual-processor configurations. Just replace both Pentium Pro CPUs with a pair of Pentium II OverDrives. Intel does not support SMP configurations beyond 2-way SMP with this product.

CPU Buying Strategies

I've said it before, and I'm going to say it again: When you buy computer hardware, you must consider what you will do with it. Many books urge you to pay for all sorts of wild-eyed technology, unmindful of the fact that all you need is something to send email and update a recipe list.

When you're buying a new PC, think about the following concerns when it comes to the CPU:

- Look for the best value.
- Think two years ahead.
- Consider upgradability.
- Know your needs.

Look for the Best Value

If you want to get the most processor for your money, buy a step or two off the cutting edge. Intel's 450MHz Pentium II processors cost $700 or more at the time this chapter was written, while the very-capable Pentium II-350 K6-2-350, and Cyrix M II-PR350 CPUs cost less than $400. You won't get the fastest system on the block, but you'll save $500 or more and have the opportunity to spend money on vital components such as RAM.

Generally you can get a better deal with an Intel-compatible processor. AMD and Cyrix price their chips very aggressively, making them a better price-performance value for most applications. AMD K6-2-based systems, for example, can sell for hundreds of dollars less than similarly configured Pentium II PCs. What's more, AMD has managed to sign on some big-hitting system vendors—including IBM, Compaq, and AST—so you don't have to take your chances with a garage-shop company.

> **Note:** Both AMD and Cyrix enjoy good compatibility records with x86 software, but problems can arise with non-Intel CPUs. For example, some games mistook Cyrix's 6x86 processor as a 486-class CPU, failing to load because they required Pentium-level processing. The problem was that there was no ID number for the 6x86 in Windows 95's CPU database. The programs simply defaulted to the Cyrix CPU they could find—an old 486SLC. Usually, these kinds of problems are more of an annoyance than anything else, and can be addressed with a simple software patch.

Think Two Years Ahead

You should also try to predict your needs a few years down the road. Will your basic email expand into heavy Web browsing and HTML editing six months or a year from now? Will your recipe lists evolve into HTML documents that incorporate photos and interactive animation? If you go with a rock-bottom processor based on your current needs, you will have no room to advance into more sophisticated work.

The key is to balance the raw power in the processor with the other components in your system. You might be able to buy a Pentium II-450 system for under $2,000 if you get it with just 32MB of RAM, a 4GB hard drive, and a 15-inch monitor—but you'll be sorely disappointed with the performance and features of such a lopsided configuration. A better choice is to step back a bit on the CPU—maybe a Pentium II-400—and boost the RAM, hard drive, and monitor to provide a better overall balance.

Consider Upgradability

Moore's Law basically states that any processor you put in your new system will be obsolete within a few years. That leaves you with two options: Buy big up front and hope to stretch the useful life of your original hardware, or spend less now and pay a premium to upgrade down the road.

The concept of a processor upgrade sounds good, but don't overvalue it in your decision. Bottlenecks in main memory, graphics, and other areas reduce the effectiveness of a faster CPU. Still, a system with an upgrade path ahead of it is better than one without.

As it looks now, the faster Pentium MMX CPUs don't offer much opportunity for upgrading. Intel doesn't plan to go beyond 233MHz with Pentium MMX, and the company has begun transitioning to its newest P6 CPU, Pentium II. Unlike previous Intel processors, Pentium II sits inside a cartridge housing equipped with a slotted connector—an approach called Single Edge Connector (SEC), as shown in Figure 6.21. This approach allows for better performance (thanks to faster L2 caching and a more sophisticated CPU bus), but the real story is that Intel competitors AMD and Cyrix lack rights to the P6 bus. That is a big incentive for Intel to push new PC buyers to the new platform.

FIGURE 6.21.
Intel lauds the performance of the SEC cartridge and its Dual Independent Bus (DIB) for optimizing the externalized L2 cache, but the real target is AMD and Cyrix. Intel hopes to shake the competition by moving the market to its patent-protected P6 bus motherboards. (Photo courtesy of Intel Corp.)

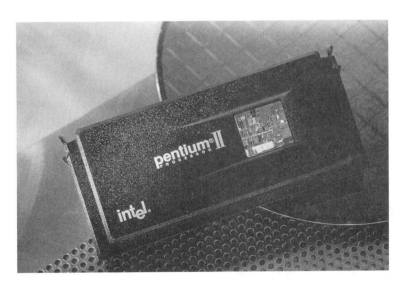

Those who bought Pentium Classic processors do have something to look forward to. Intel's MMX-enabled OverDrive upgrade chips provide a better performance boost than has been historically seen from CPUs. What's more, firms such as Evergreen sell capable upgrade chips for Pentium systems. You may also be able to plug a standard AMD K6-2 or Cyrix M II processor into your Pentium MMX system. Either of these chips should provide a nice boost in system performance over Pentium MMX CPUs running at 200MHz and below.

Know Your Needs

If you work with 3D graphics or computer-aided design (CAD), don't skimp. Make sure you get top-flight floating-point capability and aggressive pipelining in your CPU. This means Pentium II or perhaps Pentium Pro in a four-way multiprocessing system. The same goes for hardcore image editing and mathematical applications.

Home PCs for Web browsing, email, and the occasional multimedia game will do well with lower-speed Pentium II, AMD K6-2, or Cyrix M II. Bargain hunters should look at Intel Celeron (with integrated cache), as well as the lower-speed variants of K6-2 and M II.

Repair a CPU? Think Again

CPUs provide remarkable power, flexibility, and reliability, but they aren't bulletproof. The heroes of the Information Revolution can suffer any number of maladies that will render a $3,000 PC lifeless.

Here's just a short list of the bad things that can happen to good processors:

- Bent or broken pins
- Overheating
- Static discharge
- Over-voltage from a blown fuse or power spike
- Overclocking

Fortunately, these things don't happen without cause. Pins usually get broken or bent during the installation or removal of the CPU, a tricky process requiring a steady hand, a good eye, and lots of patience.

Should you accidentally break or crush a CPU (say, by stepping on it) or inherit a damaged microprocessor, you're probably out of luck. Any damage to the ceramic body will almost certainly disrupt the microscopic traces on the chip. Likewise, a snapped pin is almost certainly irreparable. But if a pin (or pins) is simply bent, you might be able to straighten it using a pair of jeweler's pliers.

Caution: Even if you manage to straighten a bent pin, you aren't out of the woods. The deformation of the metal will weaken the pin considerably, making it especially susceptible to bending or breaking in the future. If you try to install a pin that has been bent and straightened, you might run the risk of having a pin snap off inside the CPU socket itself. If this happens, you will lose both the CPU and the motherboard. So be careful!

Overheating is a common problem, particularly because some CPUs run awfully hot and leave little room for error. Many processors now rely on chip-mounted fans and a constant flow of air inside the PC chassis to stay cool. If that fan dies—and you don't notice it right away—the CPU will sit there and cook itself dead, sometimes within minutes.

A constant concern for those who tinker with their PCs is static discharge. The electronics inside a PC are very delicate, and a simple static shock can be enough to fuse submicron circuitry and wipe out bits in solid-state memory, such as the BIOS.

In the case of the processor, the stakes can be very high. A brief moment of contact can lay waste to a brand-new CPU costing hundreds or even thousands of dollars. For this reason, it's always advisable to use a static mat or other device that grounds both you and the PC when you're working inside the chassis.

Caution: Older buildings might lack grounded three-prong outlets. Be aware that your system must be properly grounded (via the round socket in the three-prong outlet) in order to avoid potentially catastrophic damage. If you do have a two-prong outlet, consult an electrician who can properly ground the wiring.

A similar situation can occur when too much voltage gets sent into the CPU. Unlike static discharge, this can occur due to user error or a power spike. Misaligning the cables to the power supply is one quick way to fry a system, as is plugging into an outlet of the wrong voltage. Everyone needs to be concerned about power spikes. Lightning strikes are a common source of crippling power surges, although the power level can fluctuate for no apparent reason as well. Also make sure that the power leads to and from the power supply don't get reversed.

Tip: When electricity comes on after a blackout, it often spikes, posing a threat to your PC. If you have a power outage, it's a good idea to unplug your PC until the power is back up.

Troubleshooting: Fixing CPU Problems

When a CPU dies, it is dead. Still, you might be able to fix some scary problems. Here are some classic symptoms of a dead or dying CPU:

- The system fails to boot.
- The system boots, but the OS fails to load.
- Erratic behavior and unexplained system crashes during startup or operation.
- Error messages indicating parity errors and other problems.
- The system locks up or dies after several minutes of operation.

If you encounter these symptoms, you should consider the possibility that the CPU is the culprit. To check the problem, do the following:

1. Perform a visual inspection of the CPU. First, turn off the PC and open the case. Let the system sit for half an hour or until the CPU is cool enough to touch.
2. Clear away any obstructing wires, cables, or bays. Check to see if any material was in direct contact with the CPU or its pins.
3. Check the heat sink and fan. Are the fan wires attached (if present)? Are the heat sink and fan properly secured to the CPU?
4. Boot up the PC with the case off. Watch the CPU fan for activity. If it doesn't rotate, the probable culprit is overheating due to a malfunctioning fan.
5. With the PC still running, place your hand near the CPU fan, and check for proper airflow. Do the same near the power supply to see if that fan is working. Check the chassis to see if any cables or other objects are blocking the air vents.
6. Turn off the PC. With your fingers, gently and evenly press along the edges of the chip. Notice if any movement occurs that might indicate that the CPU had come unseated.

Tip: If you think your PC is prone to overheating, check out a CPU temperature monitor. PC Power and Cooling's 110 Alert costs $22 and plugs into any spare drive connector, emitting an alarm when the temperature inside the chassis climbs above 110 degrees.

If everything seems in order, the problem might be with your system setup. Do the following:

1. Check your system documentation to ensure that the CPU clock jumpers are set properly for the speed and model of your processor.
2. Examine the CPU if possible. Check the silk screening on the top of the unit or the etched markings on the bottom. Does the indicated CPU speed match what you're supposed to have?

3. If possible, boot up your PC and enter the BIOS program. Look for any discrepancies in the CPU and system settings. Compare the settings against the factory defaults in your documentation.

You should also call technical support. Your system vendor might know about an issue with its PCs that could lead to apparent CPU failure.

Remember, these steps just cover CPU diagnostics. Several other problems can cause the same symptoms. Other areas to suspect are

- BIOS settings
- System RAM
- Power supply
- Graphics board and drivers
- Operating system and drivers
- Virus infection

Peter's Principle: If the CPU is the Culprit, Consider Where the Problem Came from

If you find that the CPU is the culprit, consider where the problem came from. For example, an unreliable power supply can nuke a CPU. Replace the processor without fixing the power supply, and your bad luck is likely to recur. Likewise, an overheating problem won't go away until you resolve problems such as dead CPU fans or blocked airflow.

In general, your best defense against CPU failure is prevention. Avoid overcrowding your PC's case or blocking air vents with books or papers. Also try not to jar the PC, because this can unseat the CPU or break the CPU fan.

Periodically clean out the inside of your system box with a soft brush or compressed air. Take special care to ensure that the air vents on the power supply aren't blocked by debris. That simple problem will eventually lead to overheating, followed by failure of the power supply, fan, or CPU.

TROUBLESHOOTING

You should be especially conscientious about cleaning your PC's insides if the system sits in an area with pets or where people smoke. Both tend to leave extra blocking matter in the PC's chassis. Also, if the system box sits on the floor, those vents tend to clog over time.

Also, be sure to act on problems swiftly. If you notice a lack of fan noise from your power supply, make sure you replace the unit promptly to avoid overheating. If you notice problems cropping up soon after a power outage, a power spike might have damaged the CPU.

Summary

The past two years have been hectic. Not long ago, Intel called all the shots, making routine price changes and rolling out new products at a measured pace. But with AMD and Cyrix pushing some intriguing products based on 100MHz motherboards, the chip giant has revved up its product cycles and gotten more aggressive about pricing. All this is good news for consumers.

Power users can look forward to continued improvements in the Pentium II arena, as clock speeds go past 500MHz and the new Katmai instruction set hits the streets. The integration of L2 cache directly into the CPU core will also provide a welcome boost. At the professional end, Xeon adds some intriguing talents for multiprocessor workstations running Windows NT. Further out, around 2000 or 2001, Xeon should give way to IA-64, the 64-bit CPU that breaks from the x86 architecture. Don't expect IA-64 on the desktop until 2003 or 2004, however.

In the low-end market, systems under $1,000 get multimedia-savvy MMX support and x86 performance significantly faster than that of older Pentium MMX PCs. AMD and Cyrix will both continue to push the envelope with 100MHz Super 7 motherboards, integrated L2 caches, and clock speeds pushing toward 400MHz.

Ultimately, the CPU is just one piece of the performance puzzle—albeit an important one. The motherboard bus, system RAM, and L2 cache all determine how quickly data can get to and from the CPU. If any of these poses a bottleneck, a fast CPU will simply sit idle while it waits for data to arrive from your system.

Exploring System Memory and Cache

If the CPU is the heart of your PC, system RAM is its lifeblood. Adding RAM to an aging PC can infuse new life into demanding applications and provide a greater boost than either a CPU or graphics card upgrade. Without enough memory, your PC ends up spending too much time reading data from the hard disk and starving the CPU in the process.

In addition to the megabytes of system memory, you also have to consider the small amounts of so-called cache, which helps speed processor performance. This chapter introduces you to the silicon memory—both system RAM and cache—that is at the core of your PC's operation. It also shows you how to manage upgrades. You will learn the following:

- What system RAM is and how it works
- Discussion of secondary cache and its workings
- How to shop for RAM and make sure your new memory is compatible with your system
- How to recognize and deal with RAM- and cache-related problems
- How to upgrade your system RAM and your secondary cache

Overview of System RAM

Simply put, the memory in your system makes all the compelling stuff possible. Rapid-fire CPU advancement and all the wonders of the Internet would mean little without the recent affordability of system memory. Cheap, plentiful RAM allows complex multimedia applications and robust, 32-bit operating systems such as Windows 95 and Windows NT to exist.

Just three years ago, a megabyte of RAM cost $40 to $60, limiting most systems to 8MB at the most. The tight supply put a noose around the PC industry and choked the life out of innovative software such as IBM's OS/2. Today, a megabyte of RAM costs less than

$10, and most new PCs come with 32MB or even 64MB of RAM. The result is that many old systems are begging for an upgrade, and tough decisions need to be made on new PCs.

What Is RAM?

System memory is your PC's "scratch pad." Often called *dynamic random access memory,* or DRAM, system memory is the place where the data and code the PC is working on is stored.

Consider the analogy of an office desk. When you do your taxes, you probably clear the desk of other material, pull out your files, and spread tax forms, receipts, and other documents across the desktop. To make space for this mess, you put last week's vacation planning in the file cabinet.

Your PC uses RAM much like you use your desk. Things that are being worked on are placed in system memory, where the processor can reach them quickly. Your system assigns addresses to data, specifying exactly where in system RAM the specific bits can be found. Data that isn't being worked on gets sent back to the hard disk—the PC's version of your file cabinet—or deleted, making room for the work at hand.

Let's Get Physical

System memory is easy to spot, as shown in Figure 7.1. With the PC chassis removed, look at the motherboard and look for one or more low, thin cards sitting in rows (you will probably see some empty sockets as well). Measuring just over 4 inches long by ¾-inch high, the RAM modules include a number of small black chips mounted on the cards. These chips are the physical memory itself.

FIGURE 7.1.
RAM sockets are easy to spot, as they are laid out in rows on the motherboard. (Photo courtesy of Micronics Computers)

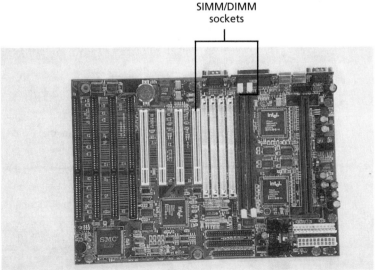

SIMM/DIMM
sockets

Inside these little black chips are thousands or millions of tiny transistors, which your PC uses to store information in the form of 0s and 1s. If a transistor has no voltage applied to it, your PC sees it as a 0. In contrast, if a transistor is charged, it is a 1. By stringing thousands of these voltage-induced 0s and 1s together, your PC—and, by extension, your operating system and software—can manipulate complex data and code.

Unlike a hard disk or CD-ROM, system memory is volatile—that is, the contents of RAM are lost when the system powers down. The reason is that system RAM must constantly be refreshed with electrical signals to prevent the charge in the transistors from bleeding away (and setting everything to 0s). That's why even a brief disruption in power forces your system to reboot. With the memory space empty, your PC "forgets" everything it knew and assumes by the empty state of memory that it has just been turned on.

The Speed Thing

If you've looked into getting a memory upgrade, you've probably seen cryptic references to the "speed" of the memory—often expressed as something like 70ns or 60ns. Actually, speed is the wrong word. What these numbers show is how quickly RAM can turn itself around (measured in nanoseconds, or billionths of a second). The faster the RAM, the more frequently it can be refreshed by your system—and the more frequently it can be updated or accessed.

Older systems frequently employ 70ns, 80ns, or even 100ns RAM, while newer Pentium-class PCs use RAM running at 60ns. Two things determine what speed of RAM your system can use—the speed of the current RAM installed, and the speed supported by your system chipset. You could buy fast 60ns RAM for the 486SX-25 machine in your office, but the chipset that plays traffic cop will strictly enforce a 100ns speed limit. You'll be wasting your money on that fast memory.

> **Tip:** Have you lost your system manuals? You can usually glean the rated speed of your RAM by reading the silk screen on the top of the chips. (Figure 7.2 shows silk-screened codes on memory chips.) Look for a dash followed by a number .−7 indicates 70ns RAM, −6 is 60ns, and so on. If you see a −10 or −12, you have a relic—that's dog-slow 100ns or 120ns RAM.

As a general rule, memory goes only as fast as the slowest chips in the system. If you have 80ns modules in your existing PC, adding 70ns or 60ns memory will do no good. It will still work, but it will refresh at the slower rate of 80ns. On the other hand, adding 80ns RAM to a system with 60ns memory is like putting a drag chute on your hot rod—your memory will run 30 percent slower.

FIGURE 7.2.

Memory speed can often be gleaned from the silk screening on the top of RAM chips. (Figure courtesy of Kingston Memory)

DRAM

MANUFACTURER	SAMPLE DRAM PART NUMBER
Fujitsu	HB 814400-80L F̲ 9445 T14
Hitachi	⊕ KOREA A107 9516 FFF HM5116100AS7
Micron	9512 C USA ⊓T 4C4007 **JDJ** −6
Mitsubishi	⟁ M5M44100AJ 222SB29–7
Motorola	MCMSL4800AJ70 Ⓜ TQQKX9236
NEC	**HEC** JAPAN D421616065 −70−7JF 943LY200
Samsung	**SEC** KOREA 522Y KH44C4100AK–6
Toshiba	TOSHIBA TCS514100FTL 70 JAPAN 9409HCK

Plug In and Turn On

Life isn't simple, and neither is RAM. There are several variations of system RAM, all of which are important to know about if you want to perform an upgrade. First, RAM usually comes in a standard format, enabling you to plug new memory into sockets on the motherboard. There are two types of memory modules you need to worry about:

- Single inline memory modules
- Dual inline memory modules

If you are upgrading an older system, you'll probably encounter SIMMs, which have been widely used in PCs for years. These modules feature either 30 or 72 connector pins with individual RAM chips mounted on either side of the card. You'll find the shorter 30-pin SIMMs in 386 and old 486 PCs, while newer 486 and most Pentium Classic PCs employ the 72-pin variety. Some Pentium MMX and early Pentium II systems also used 72-pin SIMMs. Newer systems, including Pentium MMX and Pentium II-based PCs, employ 168-pin DIMMs.

> **Note:** SIMMs plug into motherboard sockets, which are organized in banks. A *bank* is the number of sockets needed to correspond to the CPU's bus width. So the 32-bit RAM SIMMs on a 64-bit Pentium motherboard are organized in banks consisting of two sockets each. By the same token, each 64-bit DIMM socket constitutes a bank, because its data width matches that of the 64-bit external Pentium bus.

30-pin SIMMs fell out of favor because they lack capacity and performance: The fewer pins on the module limit the number of bits that the system can move in and out of the SIMM at any one time. Most 30-pin SIMMs feature capacities of 4MB and less. 72-pin SIMMs offer capacities as high as 32MB per module.

When you purchase SIMMs for Pentium or Pentium Pro PCs, you generally need to do so in pairs. To get top performance out of the 64-bit Pentium data bus, the system combines pairs of 32-bit SIMMs to yield 64-bit access. A scheme called *interleaving*—in which even bits are stored in one SIMM in a bank and odd bits in the other—enables the system to access data from one SIMM while the other is refreshing. The result is faster performance.

For example, to install 40MB of RAM into a Pentium system, you would need to pair two 16MB modules (called 2×16MB) and two 4MB modules (2×4MB) to total 40MB. No matter what the memory size, all SIMM-style RAM must be installed into banks in pairs.

Tip: You can tell if your system uses 30-pin or 72-pin SIMMs by measuring the length of the modules. 72-pin SIMMs are 4¼ inches long across the top, while 30-pin versions are shorter, measuring just over 3½ inches. Some SIMMs also put an indicator number (either 30 or 72) next to the pins themselves.

New to the scene are DIMMs, featuring a wider 168-pin connection for improved performance and higher capacities. You can find DIMMs that put 64MB of memory on a single module. Unlike 72-pin SIMMs, they can be installed singly. The reason is that DIMMs provide a 64-bit data path equal to the bit width of a single memory bank—a perfect fit for Pentium and faster CPUs. DIMMs began showing up in PCs in 1996, when PC makers introduced a new memory variant called *synchronous DRAM* (SDRAM) in Pentium-class PCs. Expect the entire PC market to move toward DIMM designs as new memory types are adopted.

You can recognize DIMM sockets from their greater length and more numerous electrical leads, as shown in Figure 7.3. DIMMs themselves are also longer than SIMMs and usually pack RAM on both sides of the module board. Many Pentium MMX motherboards provide both DIMM and SIMM sockets as manufacturers transition to the new SDRAM technology.

Not all standard DIMMs and SIMMs are identical. Some use gold-plated connectors, and others use tin-plated connectors. The main difference is cost. Tin connectors save precious pennies of manufacturing cost, which add up when you talk about tens of millions of units annually.

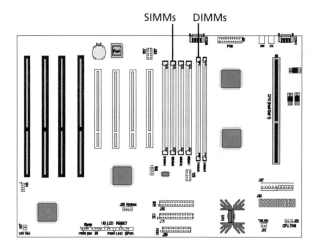

As a rule of thumb for upgrades, you should try to match the lead material with that in your PC. Check your documentation and also the original memory that shipped in the system. If the leads are silver in color, make sure you buy RAM with tin connectors; if they are gold, get gold connectors. This will avoid possible corrosion, which can lead to system crashes.

Parity and Other Religious Wars

But wait—there's more. Even if you match the speed, module format, and connector material, you have to worry about something called *parity*. When it comes to RAM, there are two schools of thought: Data security nuts want system RAM to constantly check itself for errors, and cheapskates don't want to pay for extra diagnostic chips. Don't laugh—people get upset over this stuff.

Parity RAM is PC memory that checks on itself to detect errors, using extra chips to keep count of bits. In this scheme, a ninth bit is added to every set of 8 bits (1 byte) with the sole purpose of checking up on the others. The ninth bit would perform an operation called a *checksum* to make sure that its addition matched up with the contents of the 8 bits. If the checksum failed, the system would know right away that something was amiss, before bad data got written back to the hard disk.

If you own a Pentium or Pentium MMX system, there's a pretty good chance that the memory in the system is nonparity. The reason is that, until recently, memory with additional self-checking circuitry cost more than nonparity memory. Over the past year or so, however, prices have dropped significantly, making parity memory only slightly more expensive than nonparity RAM. Also, because physical memory errors are relatively rare, vendors faced little penalty in saving money by losing this feature.

Intel played a key role in making nonparity memory prevalent when its chipsets for mainstream PCs—such as the popular 430TX found in many Pentium MMX systems—dropped parity support. On such a system, parity memory behaves exactly like nonparity RAM: The system simply ignores the ninth bit. Memory makers, anxious to trim costs and boost their manufacturing capacities, quickly moved to nonparity designs. Of course, parity remains a necessity for servers and other critical applications.

If you buy a new Pentium II system, however, you'll likely find memory that uses error-correcting code (ECC) to track and even fix errors on the fly. Where a parity SIMM simply returns the location of an error, ECC memory can actually switch the errant bit to the proper value, allowing operation to continue. ECC memory costs a bit more than parity memory and runs more slowly, but the enhanced protection is excellent for critical applications such as network servers. Intel's latest Pentium II chipsets—including the 440LX and 440BX—provide support for ECC memory.

Caution: Be careful! Parity memory will work in a nonparity system, but the reverse is not true. A system that requires parity memory will not recognize nonparity memory. If your system chipset employs parity checking, be sure to buy memory with parity.

Keeping Up with the New RAM

Not long ago, there was only one flavor of system RAM—basic fast page mode (FPM) DRAM. Those days are gone. With processor speeds pushing 300MHz, more efficient memory types are needed to keep pace. The result is an explosion of exotic memory designs. Of course, older systems won't recognize the new memory schemes, so you should purchase the type of memory documented in your PC's manuals.

If you're purchasing a new system, take note. The type of system RAM can significantly affect performance. Upgraders, meanwhile, need to gauge whether these new memory schemes make buying a new PC a better option than upgrading the existing system.

The following system memory technologies exist:

- Fast paging mode DRAM (standard DRAM)
- Extended data out DRAM (EDO DRAM)
- Synchronous DRAM (SDRAM)

Fast Paging Mode (FPM) DRAM

FPM DRAM has been around for years, but it has largely been replaced by faster EDO DRAM. Like EDO, FPM DRAM comes mounted on SIMMs. FPM DRAM gets its name from the paging scheme it employs. The memory gets broken down into a series of pages up to several kilobytes in size. Once the system accesses data within a page, subsequent accesses inside that page happen without delay.

The scheme works by first addressing the row of memory to be accessed and taking the first column address to pinpoint the address. Data in sequential columns along the selected row is accessed without wait states. If the next access occurs in a different row, a significant delay occurs while the new row is accessed and set up for multiple column reads.

Extended Data Out (EDO) DRAM

EDO DRAM became prevalent in 1994 as clock-multiplied 486 and fast Pentium CPUs started to outpace memory speeds. EDO DRAM adds circuitry to speed subsequent reads by optimizing the timing of accesses. The memory can be set up for a new access even as a read is already in progress. EDO DRAM takes just two clock ticks to perform subsequent read operations, versus three ticks for FPM DRAM.

EDO DRAM performance generally enjoys a 15 percent advantage over FPM DRAM of the same rating. However, your system's chipset and BIOS must be EDO-aware in order to work with it.

PERFORMANCE

If you upgrade a system that has an EDO-aware chipset but that contains FPM DRAM, consider dumping the old memory in favor of EDO DRAM. Not only will you get the benefit of additional memory, but you'll see improved performance as well. Note that if you mix EDO and FPM DRAM in an EDO-capable PC, all memory will be accessed as if it were FPM memory.

Note: EDO DRAM is limited by the speed of the system bus. The memory architecture really doesn't work beyond 66MHz. With 100MHz system buses now in the mainstream, memory makers have moved exclusively to SDRAM.

Synchronous DRAM

Synchronous DRAM employs the same bursting technique found in BEDO DRAM, but it adds the ability to run in sync with a 100MHz system bus. By synchronizing with the system clock, SDRAM enjoys faster and more efficient operation with the system bus. SDRAM can provide a 5 to 10 percent performance boost over EDO DRAM, depending on the application involved and the size of the L2 cache.

Unlike earlier RAM types, SDRAM comes in DIMM format, which provides a 64-bit data width matching Pentium and faster PCs. Today, SDRAM is found in most Pentium MMX and Pentium II systems. Systems using CPUs from AMD and Cyrix also employ SDRAM.

If you bought a Pentium MMX system, you may not be able to add more than 64MB of RAM. The Intel 430TX chipset can't provide L2 cache support for any more than 64MB of SDRAM, which makes upgrades beyond this point unadvisable.

More recently, the emergence of 100MHz motherboard buses has heralded the arrival of fast, 100MHz SDRAM. Called PC100 SDRAM by Intel, this memory is built to handle the tighter signal timings that occur on motherboards running 50 percent faster than earlier models. While some PC66 SDRAM modules are able to handle the higher bus speeds, most users will want to buy 100MHz-compliant SDRAM to ensure the integrity of their systems.

Table 7.1 shows the enhanced efficiency of burst-mode memory designs used by SDRAM and BEDO DRAM. As you can see, all these memory types take five clock ticks to find and return the first bit of data requested. However, the time to gather subsequent bits drops from three clock ticks per bit to just one clock tick per bit—a 300 percent improvement!

Table 7.1. Slow out of the block.

Memory Type	First Bit	Second Bit	Third Bit	Fourth Bit
FPM DRAM	5	3	3	3
EDO DRAM	5	2	2	2
BEDO DRAM	5	1	1	1
SDRAM	5	1	1	1

The SDRAM story doesn't end there. With Intel talking about 200MHz system buses and 3D graphics demanding more memory bandwidth than ever before, a new SDRAM variant promises to double the output of current memories. Called Double Data Rate SDRAM (or DDR SDRAM), this memory is tuned to sense the rising and falling edges of the motherboard clock signal—the electronic drumbeat to which all PC action is slaved. DDR SDRAM therefore can act twice per clock tick, effectively doubling performance.

You won't be able to plug DDR SDRAM into your current system. The system chipset needs to be specifically designed to handle DDR SDRAM's double-time pace. The additional expense of such chipsets, not to mention the cost of the more sophisticated memory, also poses an obstacle.

DDR SDRAM may sound like good technology, but it may never get a chance to play. Intel is committed to introducing Rambus DRAM (RDRAM) on future motherboards, so support in its chipsets for new SDRAM flavors is unlikely. RDRAM memory differs from SDRAM in that it uses an extremely fast-and-narrow serial bus to pipe large amounts of data to the CPU. RDRAM offers superior throughput for faster load times and better responsiveness in multimedia. However, RDRAM suffers from greater latency—essentially, time lost to access data—posing performance questions for RDRAM in most productivity applications.

Shopping for SIMMs (and DIMMs)

Once you've tackled compatibility questions—such as what type of memory will work in the system—buying RAM is fairly straightforward. You can take your business to a local retail store, such as CompUSA or Office Depot, or a local computer repair shop. You can also purchase memory via mail order, whether from large firms such as Micron Electronics or small memory brokers that often advertise in the classified sections of many computer magazines.

One option you might be considering is buying secondhand or used RAM from a small computer dealer or even a friend. Although RAM, being solid-state, is immune to the kind of wear and tear associated with moving components, don't jump into this trap too quickly. Over the life of a computer, system RAM is exposed to the cumulative electrical and thermal stress of thousands of hours of operation. Over time, this can cause circuits to fail, resulting in intermittent errors that occur only after hours of operation. Given that memory costs less than $10 per megabyte, the risk is high for relatively small savings.

> **Caution:** Because memory is small, valuable, and hard to trace, there exists a healthy black market for stolen memory products. Unscrupulous mail order vendors who deal in stolen goods often rip off consumers by shipping substandard DRAM or products that are rated slower than what you ordered. You should try to verify the legitimacy of an unfamiliar mail order broker before you buy.

More than any other PC component, RAM is a true commodity. As such, its price and availability can fluctuate like pork belly futures on the Chicago Board of Trade. In less than a year, the once-lucrative RAM market collapsed, as prices tumbled from over $50 per megabyte to as low as $5. Things stabilized in 1998, after RAM prices settled down around $10 to $15 per megabyte, and even began heading up again. Moves to higher-capacity chips, new memory types, and expanding memory requirements should continue to nudge prices upward.

If you want to get the best deal on RAM, keep your ear to the ground. If you hear of upcoming price hikes, it might be worth your while to move forward with a RAM upgrade sooner rather than later.

The Checklist

With so many variations of RAM available, it's important to know exactly what you need. The following checklist guides you through all the variables present in standard memory products. Use your PC's documentation and a little observation to ensure that you get RAM that is compatible with your system.

Characteristic
SIMMs or DIMMs
30-pin or 72-pin SIMMs
FPM, EDO, or SDRAM
Parity, ECC, or nonparity
Rated speed
3.3 volt or 5 volt
Gold or tin connectors

Most of these items should be apparent from your system documentation. If you've lost your documentation, the following sections will help you identify the RAM you currently have installed.

SIMMs or DIMMs

As a general rule, systems with FPM or EDO DRAM use SIMMs, and those with SDRAM employ DIMMs. Your PC's documentation will specify which type of memory you have.

Although DIMMs and SIMMs look quite similar, you can distinguish DIMMs by their slightly greater length and more tightly spaced contacts. If you're still unsure of your memory type, remove one of the modules and bring it to your retailer for examination. That person will make sure they match your existing memory.

30-Pin or 72-Pin SIMM

The visual clue is the length of the SIMM. 72-pin SIMMs are about 20 percent longer than 30-pin SIMMs and also feature more tightly spaced connector leads. If you own a Pentium PC, it's very unlikely that your memory is of the 30-pin variety.

FPM, EDO, or SDRAM

You'll need your system documentation to be sure, but you can also check your system BIOS to find out whether you have FPM, EDO, or SDRAM. During bootup, press your PC's BIOS key combination and look for the entry memory type.

Parity, ECC, or Nonparity

Look closely at the memory chips on the module. Telltale signs of a ECC or parity SIMM or DIMM include the following:

- An odd number of chips mounted on the SIMM or DIMM
- Larger memory chips accompanied by one or two smaller chips (these are the parity chips)

You can also check to see if your BIOS is set for parity or ECC operation.

Rated Speed

Most RAM chips display the nanosecond response time of memory on the top of the chip. Look for a dash followed by a number on the chip's silk screening. For example, –7 indicates 70ns RAM, and –6 indicates 60ns RAM. Remember, it's okay to match faster RAM with slower chips in your system, but not the other way around. Buy no slower than what you own now.

3.3 Volt or 5 Volt

This is an important consideration, because using the wrong voltage will result in a fried memory module (and no, your warranty probably won't cover it). System makers began to employ 3.3-volt components with the introduction of second-generation Pentium PCs. If you own a 75MHz Pentium or faster PC, look closely at your documentation to determine whether it operates at 3.3 volts.

Gold or Tin Connectors

It's not critical, but you should match the material used in your PC's SIMM or DIMM sockets. Look in an empty socket. If the leads are silver, you should buy memory with tin connectors. If the leads are gold, look for gold connectors for your SIMMs. Keep in mind that this isn't a critical issue, but it can help extend the life of your memory.

Buyer Beware

System memory might be one of the most effective upgrades you can make, but it can also be among the most dangerous. And it's not because of compatibility concerns. The problem is that it's easy to get ripped off buying system RAM, particularly when you buy from mail-order companies offering cut-rate prices.

Buying Mail Order

Despite the potential dangers, there is good reason to buy mail order—cost savings. By ordering RAM from an out-of-state vendor, you can often avoid paying sales taxes, in some cases saving up to eight or nine percent of the total purchase. With SIMMs weighing just a few ounces, it is often much less expensive to pay for shipping than it is to pay sales tax.

Because memory brokers can operate with little or no inventory, unscrupulous dealers can shut down their operations and disappear before authorities can react. Dealers who lack inventories might also encounter lengthy delays in shipping products as they wait for affordable products matching your order to become available.

There are a few things you can do to protect yourself:

- Choose a mail-order company based on a personal recommendation from someone who has had a good experience in the past.
- Check with the local Better Business Bureau for complaints outstanding against the firm.
- Make sure the company offers a money-back guarantee so that you can return flawed memory with no questions asked. Also look for a warranty, if possible.
- When your memory arrives, inspect it closely. Do the chip markings look fresh and undoctored? Does the rated speed match that of your original order? If not, notify the vendor immediately.

Playing It Safe: Going Retail

If all this makes you too nervous, you can buy RAM from a local retailer. In addition to the security of being able to see the operation, you get a chance to inspect the memory before you take it home. If something does go wrong, you can always return to the store for a refund.

Another big plus is that you might be able to get the RAM tested at the store, using a device called a SIMM tester. This device will verify the memory type, speed, and parity support, as well as detect flaws in the chips and connectors.

> **Note:** You probably won't be able to test brand-name memory sold in shrink-wrap packaging until after you've actually purchased the SIMMs. On the positive side, this memory might be easier to return under store and manufacturer policies.

Troubleshooting Memory

When it comes to problems with system memory, the news is both good and bad. The good news is that chronic memory failures are quite rare. What's more, these problems often occur in the first few days of use, which means repairs can be made under warranty. The bad news is that when something goes wrong, it is very difficult to diagnose without outside intervention. More often than not, you'll end up replacing SIMMs that display flaws.

A number of things can cause RAM to fail:

- Corrosion or cracks in the connectors due to humidity and prolonged use
- Loss of contact between the SIMM and the socket due to repeated thermal expansion and contraction of components
- Failure of solid-state components due to overheating or normal thermal stress over time
- Damage caused by a power spike or a static discharge during installation
- Temporary errors due to external radiation or overheating

Your first and best defense against any RAM-related problem is to own a PC that employs parity-checked memory. As I explained earlier, parity memory employs an extra bit as a watchdog for each byte of memory. If the parity bit expects an odd value, but main memory returns an even value, the system BIOS knows that something is amiss.

Symptoms of Memory Trouble

How do you know something is wrong with RAM rather than the CPU, cache, or some other component? Quite often, you don't. But the nature of the failure can help you pinpoint the problem. The following symptoms might indicate a RAM failure:

- Text-only parity error messages that halt system operation (on parity-equipped PCs only)
- Error message or lock-up during POST (Power On Self Test)
- Seemingly random system lock-ups or reboots
- The system fails to boot successfully and can't be booted from a floppy disk
- Lost or corrupted data, including corrupted executable files or a corrupted operating system

In fact, because memory sits at the core of nearly every transaction made inside the PC, problems with system memory can crop up anywhere. They can also vary in their character, persistence, and consistency. For example, if a certain area high in the memory space is corrupt, you might not encounter symptoms until programs and files manage to occupy all the system memory. These kinds of variables make some memory problems difficult to diagnose.

Making Sense of Parity Error Messages

If your system has parity checking and a memory problem occurs, you will generally see a message that says something like

```
Memory parity interrupt at [address]
```

When a parity error occurs, a special BIOS interrupt is invoked halting system operation. In some cases, the CPU might be halted, forcing the user to cold-boot the system. Other systems might allow the user to either reboot the system or resume operation with parity checking enabled.

Not only does parity checking provide an immediate warning of memory problems, it helps pinpoint the source of the flaw. Because the message provides address information in segment:offset format, you can take note of whether the problem occurs in a single place or happens in different places.

> **Tip:** If you get a parity error message, write down any memory address information that appears. If the problem occurs again, you will be able to tell if a certain area of memory is having trouble. Once you know that, you might be able to isolate which SIMM is having a problem by selectively removing SIMMs and seeing when the error disappears.

Isolating Memory Problems Without Parity

If you don't have parity-checked memory, getting to the bottom of a persistent memory flaw might be more difficult. If you notice unexplained failures, start observing. Take note of what sequence of actions causes the problem, and try to recreate it. Once you isolate the actions that cause a memory error, do the following:

1. Shut down your system.
2. If you haven't already, try reseating the SIMMs and boot the computer. Retrace the steps leading to the RAM failure.
3. If the failure persists, shut down the system again.
4. Remove two SIMMs and swap their positions. Restart the machine and retrace your steps.
5. If the problem recurs as before, shut down the machine.
6. If your machine has only one pair of SIMMs, the problem is probably with the SIMM socket, not with the RAM itself.
7. If there is a second pair of RAM SIMMs, swap them and restart the system. Retrace your steps as before.
8. If the error doesn't recur, the problem is probably with one of the second pair of SIMMs. If the problem recurs, one of the SIMM sockets might be flawed.

> **Note:** If you suspect a memory problem is locking up the memory exam routine during bootup, try swapping the memory as just described and see if the point of failure changes. If it does, you've isolated the problem to one of the two SIMMs. A little more swapping might help you narrow it down to a single module.

If you still can't track down the trouble or aren't willing to spend time troubleshooting, you can take your SIMMs or DIMMs to a computer store for testing. These stores often have RAM tester machines able to verify the operability of your memory. If tests don't turn up a problem, the issue could be with your SIMM sockets or other motherboard components, mandating a motherboard replacement.

Upgrade Signs

As bad as a memory failure might be, eventually you might find yourself facing an even greater enemy—obsolescence. Applications and operating systems get larger each year. In 1995, when Windows 95 first came out, most people said you needed at least 8MB and preferably 16MB. Today, the bare minimum is 16MB, but 32MB is better for anyone who multitasks two or more applications.

One thing is for sure: When your system needs more memory, it will let you know. Here are a few telltale signs of a system needing a memory upgrade:

- Constant disk activity, particularly when you're running fewer than three applications
- Slow performance, particularly when you're switching between applications or opening large files
- Sluggish screen updates

There are tools to help you track how much memory your applications and files are using. These utilities—including some that are part of Windows 95 itself—can help you determine exactly how much memory you should invest.

Windows 95/98 Memory Utilities

Your system makes it easy to determine how much physical memory you have installed. Information about your system's memory can be found at the following:

- The Power On Self Test (POST) memory diagnostic
- The Windows System Properties sheet
- The DOS-based MEM utility
- The Windows System Monitor utility
- The Microsoft System Info applet, which comes with Microsoft Office and Microsoft Windows 98

Any of these facilities can tell you how much memory is installed in your system, but they won't tell you what kind of memory it is or how fast it runs. For that kind of information, you'll need your documentation or the ability to decipher the cryptic numbering found on RAM SIMMs and DIMMs.

- POST: The most reliable way to determine the amount of memory is to simply watch your display during boot-up. As part of the POST routine, the BIOS checks system memory, counting the number of kilobytes in your system. If you have 16MB of RAM, for example, the POST will report that you have 16,384KB of memory. A 32MB system will report 32,768KB.

- System Properties sheet: If you have Windows 95 running, you can find the installed RAM amount displayed in the System Properties sheet, as shown in Figure 7.4. To view it, right-click the My Computer icon and select Properties. You will see the RAM amount displayed under both the General and Performance tabs.

FIGURE 7.4.

The Windows 95 System Properties sheet states the memory amount up front.

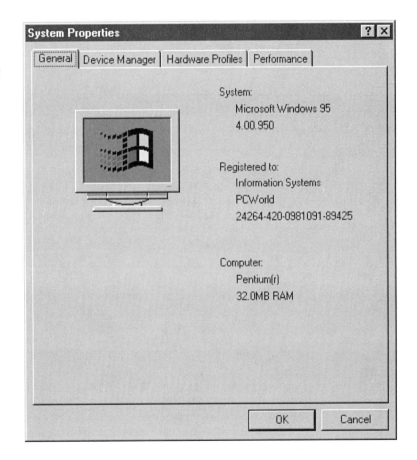

- Microsoft System Info: You can find this in the Windows 98 Start menu. Select Start, Programs, Accessories, System Tools, and click the System Information item. If you're running Microsoft Office 95 or 97, you can find the RAM amount displayed in the application's Microsoft System Info dialog box. To access it, select Help, About *Application Name*, and click the System Info button.

- MEM.EXE program: This one is familiar to DOS users. In Windows 95, click the Start button, select Run, and type mem in the Open text box in the Run dialog box. A DOS box will appear, displaying the standard text-based MEM utility output. In addition to displaying the total memory found in the system, MEM reports how much memory is available below 640KB—the once-critical area known as conventional memory.

  Despite its 16-bit history, MEM remains very useful for people running resource-intensive DOS-based software on Windows 95 machines. Game players in particular need to scrounge up conventional memory for high-performance flight simulations and other DOS games.

- Windows System Monitor: This little applet can be found under the Start menu. Select Programs, Accessories, System Tools, System Monitor. Actually, System Monitor does a lot more than snoop memory. It tracks everything from processor usage to network data packets to file accesses (see Figure 7.5).

FIGURE 7.5.

Don't be fooled by the lack of free memory reported by System Monitor. Even if you have just one application open, Windows will horde all the RAM space it can to provide disk caching and other performance-boosting services.

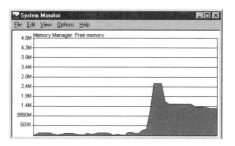

If System Monitor doesn't appear on your Start menu, you can install it by running Add/Remove Programs from the Windows 95 Control Panel. First, make sure your original Windows 95 CD-ROM is in the drive. In the Add/Remove Programs Properties dialog box, choose the Windows Setup tab and select Accessories from the list in the Components box. Click the Details button, and in the Accessories dialog box, scroll through the Components list box until you reach the entry for System Monitor. Make sure the check box on the left is checked, and click OK. Click OK again, and Windows 95 will begin installing the utility.

Third-Party Memory Utilities

A number of utilities address system memory. The most popular programs are called *RAM doublers* or *RAM enhancers*. Although these utilities played an important role under the memory limitations of DOS and Windows 3.1, the 32-bit memory scheme of Windows 95 removes much of the reason for these utilities.

What's more, the precipitous drop in RAM prices makes it more economical to buy new RAM than to purchase a software package that tries to extend your current memory. These utilities use compression techniques and other tricks to make your existing RAM look larger than it is. However, the processing and resource overhead involved can actually slow system performance.

Although I don't recommend memory-enhancing utilities, diagnostic packages can offer valuable services for users trying to determine how much memory their applications need. Programs such as Symantec's Norton Utilities and Connectix's Agent 97 give you detailed information about memory usage, virtual memory, and all other aspects of system performance.

You can also find useful third-party utilities on the World Wide Web. For instance, Tessler's Nifty Tools' SuperMonitor program snoops your system to provide snapshots of memory consumption while you work. Much like Windows 95's System Monitor, it lets you see various aspects of memory usage.

Upgrading Memory

So the plaintive thrashing of your hard disk has finally convinced you that it's time for a RAM upgrade. How do you go about it? The following sections show you.

How Much RAM Is Enough?

Before you buy new memory, you should look at your needs and your system's setup. RAM is cheap these days, but some combinations of SIMMs might force you to throw out your system's existing memory. For this reason, you should tailor your upgrade to both your applications and your motherboard.

Weighing Applications

First, you should determine what your needs are. If you have a Windows 95/98 system with 8MB of RAM, it's likely that almost any upgrade will feel like a huge improvement. Likewise, someone using large databases or multimedia applications will notice immediate improvements going from 16MB to 32MB.

So how much memory do you need? As much as possible, really. The reason is that your computing usage will probably adjust to the upgraded configuration. After an upgrade, you will feel comfortable multitasking more programs or keeping a Web browser or other application fired up all day, whereas in the past you would have shut the application down.

Software developers from Redmond to Boston are scheming to make even a hearty RAM upgrade obsolete. Microsoft talked everyone's ear off about how Windows 95 could run comfortably in 8MB of RAM (not true, by the way), yet today the company's Internet Explorer Web browser (bundled with Windows) needs 12MB just to load. Lotus Notes, meanwhile, chokes on anything less than 16MB.

The fact is, low RAM prices and the flat 32-bit memory model of Windows 95 and Windows NT have unleashed the memory hogs. There is a stampede of fat code (redolent with complex features), interactive help, and animated widgets that make conservative upgrade estimates look foolish.

So how much do you really need? Table 7.2 provides low and high RAM estimates for specific application profiles.

Table 7.2. RAM requirements by usage.

Usage Type	Low End	High End	Examples
Light office use	8MB	16MB	Minimal multitasking: word processing, email, some Web browsing
Light home use	16MB	32MB	Minimal multitasking: email, home finance software, some Web browsing, some CD-ROM titles
Heavy office use	32MB	64MB	Multitasking four to six applications: word processing, spreadsheets, presentation software, email, Web browsing, some database work
Heavy home use	32MB	128MB	Multitasking three or four applications: games, multimedia titles, heavy Web browsing, word processing, graphics design software
Design professional	64MB	256MB	Multitasking four to six applications: 3D design and CAD software, database applications, imaging
Software developer	64MB	256MB	Multitasking four to six applications: software development tools, database applications

These figures are merely estimates. You should keep a close eye on your personal usage and your system's behavior to make decisions. Still, this table can at least help guide you in your purchase.

How Much Can Your Motherboard Handle?

The tricky part is making sure the additional RAM you buy will fit in your system configuration. Motherboards are designed to recognize specific combinations of memory in the SIMM sockets. So if you want to add 64MB of RAM to your system, for example, you need to think about what combination of RAM SIMMs adding up to 64MB will work in your motherboard. It's not hard to figure out. First, here are a few ground rules:

- SIMMs should be installed into a bank in pairs. (DIMMs, however, can be installed singly.)

- SIMM pairs often must be of the same capacity and preferably come from the same manufacturer. Sometimes, particularly with 30-pin SIMMs, a bank of four must be of the same capacity and come from the same supplier.

- Most motherboards require that the first two sockets (also known as bank 0) be occupied before you install SIMMs into the next two sockets (bank 1).

For example, the documentation for the Micronics M54Hi-Plus Pentium motherboard says that it can accept RAM SIMMs of 4MB, 8MB, 16MB, and 32MB capacities. Table 7.3 shows acceptable memory configurations for the Micronics M54Hi-Plus motherboard.

Table 7.3. Typical memory combinations.

Memory	Bank 0	Bank 1
8MB	(2) 1MBx36	
16MB	(2) 1MBx36	(2) 1MBx36
16MB	(2) 2MBx36	
24MB	(2) 2MBx36	(2) 1MBx36
32MB	(2) 4MBx36	
32MB	(2) 2MBx36	(2) 2MBx36
40MB	(2) 4MBx36	(2) 1MBx36
48MB	(2) 4MBx36	(2) 2MBx36
64MB	(2) 8MBx36	
64MB	(2) 4MBx36	(2) 4MBx36
72MB	(2) 8MBx36	(2) 1MBx36
80MB	(2) 8MBx36	(2) 2MBx36
96MB	(2) 8MBx36	(2) 4MBx36
128MB	(2) 8MBx36	(2) 8MBx36

As you can see, this motherboard—like that inside many Pentium-class systems—can accept up to 128MB of RAM. However, you might not be able to get there without first removing the installed SIMMs. To handle 128MB of RAM, most motherboards employ four 32MB SIMMs, or 64MB per bank.

The problem is that this configuration demands all four sockets. So if you currently have 32MB installed in your PC (16MB apiece in the two SIMM sockets that make up bank 0), you need to yank those two 16MB SIMMs and replace them with 32MB SIMMs.

This case is a bit extreme. After all, 128MB RAM configurations are the stuff of graphics workstations and network servers—but the same problem plays itself out at more reasonable levels. For example, a 486 with 8MB of RAM might have 1MB SIMMs in each of its eight sockets (4MB per bank). To move up to 16MB or 32MB, you will have to remove at least half, and possibly all, of the existing RAM to make room for higher-density SIMMs.

What You See Is What You Get

The easiest way to assess your personal upgrade situation is to pop the top and look inside. Look for parallel SIMM modules and possibly a few empty SIMM sockets as well. If all those sockets are filled, you will have to remove some memory to effect an upgrade.

Figuring out the capacity of the individual SIMMs can be tricky. Although you can take the amount of memory, divide it by the number of SIMMs, and guess from that the capacity of each SIMM, the only way to be sure is to inspect the SIMMs themselves. Depending on where the modules are on the motherboard, you might need a flashlight or other light source to read the silk screening on the SIMM chips. You might even need to remove the SIMMs to view them.

> **Tip:** A dental mirror can help you read component markings without having to pull them out of the motherboard. You can pick one up for a cheap price at most drug stores.

You can also check your system's documentation, which might specify the SIMM configuration. Also keep in mind that some motherboards include memory laid down on the board itself, in the form of DIPs or dual-inline package.

Plugging In

This section gives you step-by-step instructions for installing new RAM SIMMs in your PC:

1. Attach yourself to a grounding mat. Turn off the PC and unplug it. Remove the case.

2. If necessary, remove the existing SIMMs. Press the tabs on the edges away from the SIMM so that the SIMM falls forward in the socket.

3. If the SIMM doesn't fall forward, simply press the back of the module while continuing to press the tabs away from the module. Pull the SIMM vertically out of the socket and place it in an antistatic bag.

Tip: If the tabs give you trouble, you can use a pair of flathead screwdrivers to loosen their grip. Slide the heads between the tabs and the card, and gently press the tabs outward.

4. Repeat as necessary.

5. Install the first SIMM. Line up the notched bottom edge of the module with the notch in the SIMM socket, as shown in Figure 7.6.

FIGURE 7.6.

The pin notch is easy to spot on a SIMM. (Figure courtesy of Micronics Computers)

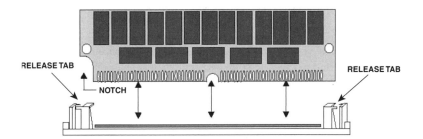

RELEASE TAB   NOTCH   RELEASE TAB

6. Insert the module into the sockets at a 45-degree angle.

7. Rotate the SIMM to an upright position until the card squeezes past the tabs and locks into place. *WRONG – JUST THE OPPOSITE!*

Caution: Take a moment to inspect the inserted SIMM, and make sure the connector is seated uniformly. A SIMM often might appear seated when it actually isn't. Make sure that the bottom edge of the SIMM module runs parallel to the socket. If you see any angle or deviation, you must reseat the SIMM.

IT MUST "CLICK"!

8. Repeat until all the SIMMs are installed.

Note: If you are working with SDRAM DIMMs, you need to vary a little from the previous steps. When working with the memory tabs, make sure they are gently pulled outward as far as they will go. Then press the DIMM straight down into the socket, making sure the key notch matches up with the key in the slot. The locking tabs will pull upwards as you insert the DIMM, and lock into place when the DIMM is properly seated.

9. Remove all tools from the inside of the PC. Plug in th
   Watch the display closely to see how much RAM is re

10. Most systems will autodetect the new memory and boo
    two beeps during bootup, try entering your CMOS setu
    saving the settings. Doing so will allow the CMOS to u
    memory amount.

11. If everything seems in order, shut down the system and

Secondary Cache: A Vital H

Unfortunately, today's microprocessors literally run too fast for
RAM. Since the introduction of the Pentium CPU in 1994 until t
1997, the clock rate of new chips has jumped from about 60 to 3;;MHz, more than a
500 percent increase. During that time, motherboard bus speed—which determines the
rate of system RAM access—has been stuck at 66MHz, an increase of exactly 0 percent.
The quickness of system RAM, meanwhile, has improved marginally, from 70 or 80
nanoseconds to 50 or 60 nanoseconds.

The result is predictable: diminishing performance returns as CPU clock speeds head up.
The problem is a recent one. Until the introduction of the 486DX2 CPU, all Intel processors ran at the same speed as the motherboard—in other words, they talked both to the
system and to themselves at the same rate. But clock-doubled CPUs such as the 486DX2
delivered significant speed-ups by running internally at twice the speed of the external
motherboard.

Today, processors run two to five times faster than the motherboard. To help the rest of
the system catch up, motherboard makers such as Intel and Micronics began putting a
small store of very fast memory between the CPU and RAM. Called *Level 2 (L2)* or
secondary cache, this fast memory is present in virtually all Pentium-class PCs.

Note: A smaller and even faster cache is found inside most CPUs. It's called the
primary, or *Level 1 (L1)*, cache.

This rest of this chapter will:

- Help you understand what L2 cache is and how it affects system performance
- Show you how to buy and add L2 cache memory to an existing system
- Help you deal with possible cache-related problems

The Workings of a Cache

The L2 cache in most Pentium and faster systems is made up of extremely fast silicon memory, called *static RAM* or *SRAM*. Running at blistering speeds of about 10 to 15 nanoseconds, SRAM is about six to eight times faster than main system memory. And unlike system memory, which must constantly receive electrical signals to keep data present, SRAM requires no refresh signal from the system. This static design cuts down access times, resulting in much faster performance.

The memory chips themselves are broken into two sections: the main data cache chips and a single tag RAM cache chip. The tag RAM stores address information for bits residing in cache. These tag bits are used by the system to determine if and where needed data resides in the L2 cache.

Not surprisingly, SRAM is expensive—about 10 times more expensive, in fact, than common EDO DRAM SIMMs. Cost is one reason why L2 caches are generally quite small. Most Pentium Classic PCs feature 256KB cache memory, while Pentium MMX and Pentium II systems use somewhat larger 512KB cache pools. But older Pentiums, sold when RAM and cache memory were exceedingly expensive, might have used cache as small as 64KB or even no cache at all.

> **Note:** Thinking about upgrading the cache on your Pentium Pro or Pentium II system? Think again. The two CPUs take different approaches to handling L2 cache, but both integrate SRAM memory into the chip packaging itself. The design optimizes performance but makes cache upgrades impossible. The only way to boost the cache is to replace the CPU or CPU module (in the case of Pentium II) with a version that has a larger cache.

What a Cache Can Do

How much does L2 cache help system performance? A lot, actually. Tests consistently show that a 256KB L2 cache can boost system performance by about 20 to 25 percent over that of a cacheless PC. And a smaller 128KB cache still delivers performance just a few percentage points shy of the larger 256K pool.

The law of diminishing returns really goes to work after the 256KB level. Under Windows 95, doubling cache size to 512KB provides only an incremental performance boost, while moving up to an extra-large 1,024KB cache fails to nudge performance higher at all. Today, most new PCs come with 512KB of cache standard.

At issue is the critical hit rate these caches achieve. Sophisticated predictive algorithms and smart access schemes let your cache wait with the proper bits 95 percent of the time. That 95 percent hit rate means your processor needs to reach into slow main memory only once every 20 transactions.

Caches can provide this efficiency because data access isn't random. Operations or data that have been accessed once will probably be called on again soon. Likewise, data located close to currently accessed bits has a good chance of being accessed in the near future. This predictable behavior makes it possible for cache to pre-load bits into fast SRAM memory before they're actually needed.

However, although a 256KB cache can achieve a 95 percent hit rate, doubling the cache yields a meager 1 percent or so improvement in efficiency. At this point, the cache has already covered most of the predictable accesses—the easy yardage has been gained.

Note: If system performance doesn't benefit that much from adding L2 cache past 256KB, why do many new Pentium MMX and Pentium II PCs ship with 512KB standard? There are a couple of reasons. First, the larger cache helps keep hit rates high even as applications get bigger and more demanding. Second, some motherboards require 512KB of installed L2 cache in order to recognize main memory in excess of 64MB.

Peter's Principle: Cache Is Critical

A system without L2 cache is not an option if you want reasonable performance in business applications. Intel's Celeron CPU, provides a stark example of what happens when you try to run a fast CPU without L2 cache. Performance of the 266MHz Celeron processor, which uses the same core found in the Pentium II, lags well behind all current CPUs of the same clock rate when running office-style applications. In fact, many key system vendors, including IBM and Compaq, have opted to sell systems based on AMD's K6 and K6-2 CPU, rather than use the cacheless Celeron. One exception is in gaming. Here, the cacheless Celeron has proven a capable CPU, primarily because of the superior FP and MMX performance. Neither AMD K6-2 nor Cyrix M II can match Celeron in these critical areas of performance.

Still, any Pentium or faster system needs L2 cache in order to keep the processor from waiting around while data makes its way out of main memory. Look for at least 512KB in Pentium II, AMD K6-2, and Cyrix M II PCs. The new Celeron's use a smaller 128KB L2 cache, but it runs at twice the speed of its Pentium II counterparts, resulting in equivalent performance. If a system you're considering lacks L2 cache, find out if it can be configured with at least a 256KB cache. Also, if you intend to use more than 64MB of RAM in your PC, make sure you find out if the motherboard can handle 512KB of L2 cache. Otherwise, any memory over 64MB will be uncached and therefore very slow.

The Hard Science Behind Cache Magic

Staying a step ahead of a processor that ticks 200 or 300 million times a second is no easy task. However, as mentioned, the predictable nature of program code makes the concept of caching possible. Two rules come into play:

- If a bit has been accessed, it is likely to get accessed again soon.
- If a bit has been accessed, bits close to it are likely to be accessed.

Knowing this, cache designers can keep recently-accessed information in the L2 cache pool and access memory addresses around the specific address being called. This is simple enough, but more sophistication is needed to wring performance out of systems. The cost of a *cache miss*, when data being called on is not found inside the cache, is very high. Not only must the CPU first check the L2 cache, it must then get data from slow main memory, resulting in wait states.

There are two major caching schemes: write-through and write-back. Write-through caches provide better performance by allowing new or changed data to be written to both the cache and to main memory simultaneously—the CPU doesn't have to take the extra step of writing to each separately. What's more, cache and memory are always in sync, eliminating the need for consistency checking. Write-through caching can boost performance 5 to 10 percent over that of write-back caches.

> **Technical Note:** In order for any cache to work, its contents must be quickly accessible. To break cache memory into manageable segments, a scheme called *set-associative caching* is used. This approach avoids address conflicts that can force the cache to be emptied. In addition, it makes it easier for the cache to decide which bits to discard when the cache is full, using a least-recently-used (LRU) policy.
>
> You'll find two-way and four-way set-associative caches. The designation defines how finely broken down the cache pool is. The smaller the segments, the faster data can be found within them—but the more time that must be spent locating the proper segment. Today, most caches use a four-way set-associative design.

The Three Faces of L2 Cache

There are three kinds of L2 cache. Older asynchronous SRAM has been largely replaced by faster synchronous burst (sync-burst) and pipeline burst SRAM designs. Table 7.4 lists the cache types and their data output cycles, expressed in number of clock ticks.

Table 7.4. Both sync-burst and pipeline burst caches achieve optimal performance, completing one transaction per clock tick after the initial setup work is complete.

Cache Memory Type	Cycle Profile
Asynchronous SRAM	4-2-2-2
Synchronous SRAM	2-1-1-1
Pipeline burst SRAM	3-1-1-1

If you're considering an upgrade, you must determine whether your motherboard supports the cache type you want to use. See the section "Upgrading Cache" for specific instructions.

Asynchronous SRAM

This cache generally operates at speeds of 20, 15, or 12 nanoseconds. The memory is called *asynchronous* because the processor must provide an address for each cache access and then wait while the cache delivers the requested data. This asynchronous operation can cause a faster processor (more than 33MHz externally) to sit idle while the information is retrieved.

The oldest and slowest cache type, asynchronous SRAM can be found in 386 and 486 systems.

Synchronous Burst SRAM

As its name implies, *synchronous burst SRAM* works in lock-step with the system clock to provide data to and accept data from the processor. By synchronizing with the clock, the SRAM eliminates the need for the processor to wait an undetermined amount of time for incoming bits.

Sync-burst SRAM uses an input buffer to store address requests, which enables the cache to receive orders even as it retrieves another piece of data for the processors—in effect, the cache does two things at once. Once the first bit in a set is retrieved, the cache can burst bits across the bus very quickly.

Although synchronous burst SRAM is the fastest cache scheme on buses operating at 66MHz and below, it's also the most expensive. For this reason, most mainstream systems don't use this scheme any longer. In addition, faster 75 and 100MHz bus speeds will outpace the ability of this cache type to deliver subsequent bits in a single clock tick.

Pipeline Burst SRAM

Affordable pipeline burst SRAM can be found in the L2 caches of most Pentium-level systems. Like synchronous burst SRAM, pipeline burst SRAM bursts data across the bus.

This allows for single-clock tick access for subsequent data bits. However, pipeline burst cache adds an output buffer to hold outgoing data at the ready for the CPU. This scheme can speed data access of sequential bits, letting the cache provide one-cycle burst mode transfers on bus speeds higher than 66MHz.

Although the pipeline scheme allows for single-clock burst operation at up to 133MHz (twice the speed of sync-burst SRAM), filling the input and output buffers takes an extra clock tick. In other words, pipeline burst SRAM is generally slightly slower than sync-burst SRAM on current 66MHz motherboards.

Finding Cache on the Motherboard

The system motherboard determines the cache type, form factor, and capacity. In fact, some motherboards might not allow an L2 cache upgrade at all. Older PCs have SRAM modules that are soldered directly onto the motherboard, while high-end Pentium Pro and Pentium II systems integrate the cache with the CPU. Even if your motherboard does feature socketed cache memory, the motherboard might not be able to accept any more than is already installed.

Generally, cache comes in two forms:

- DIP modules, which are soldered directly to the motherboard
- Socketed edge-connected modules, which are plugged into a standard SIMM-like socket

If you have socketed cache memory, it probably conforms to a standard known as COAST, which stands for "cache on a stick" (cute, huh?). The COAST format defines cache SIMMs to a length of 4.35 inches wide by 1.14 inches high. This L2 cache mini-SIMM looks very much like your RAM SIMMs. You can distinguish it from RAM SIMMs because the module is usually smaller, contains fewer chips, and is not laid next to other sockets or modules.

TROUBLESHOOTING

> Even if your system has an empty COAST socket, you might be out of luck. If L2 cache is soldered to the motherboard, you might not be able to add additional cache memory. Always check your motherboard documentation for specifics before attempting an upgrade.

Also like RAM SIMMs, a little observation can go a long way. If you see a COAST module in your PC, Table 7.5 will tell you what you probably have.

Table 7.5. When is more not better? If you see nine small chips on your cache SIMM, you probably have older (and slower) asynchronous cache memory.

What You See	What You've Got
Nine or more large chips	Asynchronous SRAM
Two big chips and one small chip on one side	256KB of sync-burst or pipeline burst SRAM
Two big chips on both sides plus a single small chip	512KB of sync-burst or pipeline burst SRAM

Whether the SRAM chips are mounted on a COAST module or on the motherboard, you can glean important information by inspecting the chips. You should see the name of the SRAM manufacturer, such as Toshiba, Micron, or NEC, silk-screened on the top of the chips. You'll also see the usual jumble of part numbers.

More importantly, though, the memory speed might be displayed on the chips. As with DRAM chips, the speed (in nanoseconds) is often displayed with a dash followed by a one- or two-digit number. –20 and –2 both indicate a 20ns SRAM chip, while –1 and –10 indicate a faster 10ns SRAM.

Cache Purchase Decisions

Buying an L2 cache upgrade is pretty simple. You can purchase COAST-format L2 cache upgrades from retail stores or from many memory brokers. You can also purchase cache memory from your system vendor. In fact, doing so might help ensure that your upgrade is successful, since the vendor can match the new SRAM with that required by your system.

Before you buy cache, you need to know the following:

- The amount of cache you can install
- The type of cache supported by the motherboard
- The speed of the SRAM (in nanoseconds)
- The speed of the tag RAM (in nanoseconds)

The amount is easy to find. Your motherboard documentation should tell you clearly. In general, most new motherboards for mainstream systems can accept up to 512KB of secondary cache, although some go as high as 1024KB. Older systems, on the other hand, might top out at 256KB or even less.

The type of cache refers to asynchronous, pipeline burst, or sync-burst. Again, you need to check your documentation for the exact type that your motherboard supports.

Tip: You can do more than merely boost the amount of cache during an upgrade—you might be able to improve cache performance as well. If the original cache in the system is the asynchronous type, don't assume that you must buy asynchronous cache. Check your motherboard or system documentation. If it can accept a pipeline-burst cache, you can realize a nifty performance boost.

The last two points regarding speed are important. Most motherboards still run at speeds of 60 or 66MHz. In order to work with these systems, the L2 cache SRAM must run at a minimum. Intel's 430TX chipset, for example, requires 10ns SRAM for 60MHz operation and 8.5ns SRAM for 66MHz operation. In both cases, the tag RAM must be 15ns. Don't buy L2 cache that runs any slower than the rate required by your motherboard.

Otherwise, when buying cache, you should follow the same guidelines you do when you buy RAM SIMMs and DIMMs. Like RAM, cache modules are small, valuable, and virtually untraceable. That makes these components good candidates for theft and resale by unscrupulous vendors. If you buy through a mail-order memory broker, you should make sure the company has a good track record, whether by getting a personal reference or by calling the local Better Business Bureau.

INSTANT REFERENCE | For more on buying advice, see Chapter 6, "Heart and Soul: The CPU."

Diagnosing/Troubleshooting Cache Problems

In most respects, you should regard L2 cache the same way you do system RAM. Together, L2 cache and RAM make up your PC's memory system, working in tandem to move data and code in and out of the CPU. They are also functionally very similar, which means that RAM and cache might suffer from some of the same problems.

Diagnosing L2 Cache Problems

If your L2 cache fails, you're probably suffering system-locking conflicts—much the way a memory error will stop a system cold. The following are possible indications of cache problems:

- Unexplained system crashes or lockups
- The system fails to boot, or it stalls during a POST routine
- Seemingly random data errors
- Unusually slow performance

Unfortunately, not many utilities can help you when it comes to L2 cache. The cache interacts with your PC's processor and main memory at the lowest level, well below the notice of the operating system or its applications.

This means that when you check CMOS, the configuration reported is the one it was set to be. The BIOS can see RAM, but it can't see cache. It treats RAM differently, testing upon POST and reporting the total it finds.

> **Caution:** Unlike system RAM, the POST messages you see during boot-up indicating cache size might not be accurate. The system doesn't poll this data the way it does RAM. Instead, it simply pulls the value from your PC's BIOS. If the BIOS setting is wrong, the POST reading will be wrong as well. If you suspect a problem, you should confirm the POST values with your system's documentation and with observations of the cache SIMM itself.

If during the POST test you see the message System Cache Error - Cache Disabled, the cache SIMM is probably bad. Although the PC will continue to run, it will do so without the benefit of L2 cache, affecting performance significantly. Although you can try the usual tricks, you might be looking at cache purchase.

You can use a low-level diagnostic program, such as AMIDiag 5.0, to check on your cache. AMIDiag 5.0 can be downloaded from the American Megatrends, Inc. Web site at http://www.ami.com.

If you're experiencing system lock-ups that don't seem related to RAM or other components, you can easily isolate the problem if it resides in COAST-format L2 cache. After you've encountered the symptom, do the following:

1. Shut down the machine, unplug the power supply, and remove the cover.
2. Making sure you're properly grounded, lift the L2 cache module from its socket. If the module won't budge, try getting it started by pulling up one edge slightly and then evening the second edge.
3. With the cache removed and placed in a safe location, plug your computer in and reboot.
4. Enter your computer's BIOS setup routine. Go to the section that controls cache settings and change the setting to 0 or No Cache.
5. Exit the BIOS setup environment, making sure to save changes.
6. Complete boot-up and use the computer normally.

If the problem fails to recur, you're probably experiencing trouble with the cache SIMM, or perhaps with the way it was seated. You should note whether you experience any noticeable degradation in performance after removing the L2 cache. If not, your cache might not have been working properly in the first place. If this is the case, replacing the module should result in a welcome 20 to 25 percent performance boost.

Troubleshooting Cache Problems

So you think your cache might be the culprit? Like RAM, the news is good and bad. If the cache memory modules themselves are bad, they're gone. There is simply no repairing 15ns static RAM chips.

The good news is that the problem could just require a software tweak or minor adjustment. Here are a couple of things you should try before heading out to buy a new cache module:

- Reseat the cache module: Press the module firmly into the COAST socket to make sure there is adequate contact between the pins.
- Check your BIOS: Go into the BIOS setting and try changing the cache settings. One possible culprit is that your BIOS is trying to conduct write-through cache operations when only write-back caching is supported.
- Check for overheating problems: If problems occur only after sustained use, make sure you have proper ventilation in the chassis and that no wires are impeding airflow around the cache SIMMs.

Upgrading Cache

Although some of the dealings with L2 cache can be arcane, the actual process of upgrading is relatively straightforward. The main thing is to be patient. Cache SIMMs aren't rugged devices. You can snap a socket pin or card connector by trying to force a SIMM where it doesn't belong. If things don't seem to fit, back away, take a breath, and try again. Of course, you need to exercise the usual precautions against static discharge.

Follow these steps to upgrade your cache:

1. Make sure you are properly grounded. Shut off and unplug the PC. Remove the case.
2. Identify the L2 cache SIMM. It should be standing alone, close to the CPU.
3. With the thumb and forefinger of each hand, grasp the cache SIMM at the top at each end. Pull it straight up and out of the socket.
4. If the SIMM doesn't budge, try pulling one edge up a little first, followed by the other. Then try pulling straight out again.
5. Pull the cache SIMM clear of the socket, and put it in a safe place.
6. Grab the new cache SIMM and lower it into the case. Align the notched corner of the SIMM with the notched corner of the socket.
7. Fit the gold edge connectors into the socket and apply gentle pressure straight down. Ease the module into the socket until it's firmly seated.
8. Make sure you remove any tools or objects from the inside of the chassis. Plug in the computer and start the system.
9. Watch the boot process closely. Make note of any odd beeps or error messages.

Most newer systems automatically detect the new cache at boot-up. However, if you notice that performance doesn't improve, or if you don't trust that little black box of code to make the adjustment, dive into the BIOS setup application to make sure the change gets recorded.

You should be able to find the cache settings in the Advanced section of the BIOS utility. Make sure that cache operation is set to Enabled. If there is a choice to select between cache memory types—such as asynchronous and pipeline burst—select the one matching your new cache module.

Summary

Cache and RAM are vital components in any PC, particularly as CPU clock speeds go beyond 300MHz. Fast and ample L2 cache allows your CPU to move along unimpeded, while large amounts of efficient RAM give you access to large applications and let you multitask programs without grinding slowdowns.

It would seem as though RAM should be an easy upgrade. But the wide variety of RAM speeds, technologies, and module combinations can make for a daunting purchase. Many new systems use SDRAM DIMMs, and older Pentium and 486 PCs use FPM or EDO DRAM in SIMM format. Before you decide what to buy, you need to check your system requirements closely.

The work is worth it. Without a doubt, system RAM is one of the most important ingredients for efficient performance. But don't overlook your L2 cache. While cache upgrades are not as simple to effect—and often are not possible at all—in some cases they can enable significant enhancements in performance. Regardless of the speed of the CPU, it takes both adequate system RAM and ample cache to keep bits flowing freely.

Power Supplies, Cases, UPSs

Personal computing is a funny thing. People get so tied up in clock speeds and standards wars that they lose sight of what makes it all possible—reliable power. After all, without juice, your Pentium II powerhouse is one very expensive doorstop. Of course, you need something to house all your components, and upgraders will find a dizzying selection of PC cases to select from.

The problem is that people pay too little attention to both the cases protecting their systems and the electrical diet their systems need to run effectively. Overtaxed circuits, old wiring, and even power-hogging neighbors can all pose problems that can lead to the early—and sometimes sudden—demise of your PC.

This chapter covers the issues related to PC power, including internal power supplies, uninterruptible power supplies (UPSs), and surge protectors. You will also find coverage of system cases, which frequently ship with power supplies included. Here are some topics this chapter covers:

- The workings of electrical systems in PCs and what is needed to make sure a system stays healthy
- Coverage of external UPSs and surge protectors, as well as mobile computing issues such as battery technologies
- Buying a new power supply or peripheral
- Buying considerations with notebook systems
- Assessing case types and options
- Installing a power supply, power peripherals, and case
- Troubleshooting power-related problems

Taking Stock of Cases and Power Supplies

Like a car's engine, your PC relies on a steady and reliable flow of fuel in order to operate. Everything from the CPU and hard disk to motherboard chip sets and RAM SIMMs requires a steady source of electricity. Unfortunately, reliable power can be elusive, particularly in older buildings. Everything from lightning strikes to air conditioners can disrupt the normal flow of power and pose a threat to both your data and your hardware.

Of course, PC makers know all this, and systems include basic protection against the power sags and surges common in day-to-day operation. Unfortunately, more severe electrical disruptions can, and will, overwhelm circuitry built into the PC's power supply and motherboard.

Trouble doesn't always come from the outside. Sometimes it's right under your nose. For example, consider your PC's power supply. The heart of your PC, the power supply is responsible for taking incoming current and turning it into the 5 volt or 3.3 volt stream your PC's components are designed to handle. It must also be able to keep up with the power demands of peripherals, which can be pretty severe on decked-out machines.

Whether your PC's power supply is on the blink or has simply become outmatched by upgrades, you might need to consider a new unit.

When it comes to PCs, there are two general categories of power components:

- Power supplies
- External power maintenance and interdiction

A Peek at Power Supplies

PC power supplies aren't marvels of submicron engineering like CPUs, RAM SIMMs, and cache modules. Nor do they improve at an astronomical rate the way hard disk capacities and CD-ROM speeds have. No, power supplies are pretty boring.

There's just one thing: Without them, nothing else works.

Your PC's power supply is easy enough to spot after you remove the case. On most systems, the power supply is a large silver box fitted into one corner of the chassis (see Figure 8.1). A number of wires, bundled in groups of four, run to various cards and peripherals or, in some cases, just hang loose in the chassis. On the outside of the case, you'll notice a fan outlet and a three-prong plug that accepts a matching female adapter.

Figure 8.1.

Even specialty dual-power supplies, such as this one from PC Power and Cooling, look alike. (Photo courtesy of PC Power and Cooling)

Note: If you own a compact desktop system from a vendor such as Hewlett-Packard, Compaq, or IBM, it might use a custom-designed power supply. These supplies are designed to maximize usable space and, often, accessibility—but at the cost of standard design. Before you buy a new supply for any system, you need to look inside the case and verify its dimensions. Obviously, custom units need to be purchased directly from the vendor or its authorized dealers.

Power supplies might look alike, but they aren't (see Table 8.1). The biggest difference is output wattage. Most desktop PCs feature a power supply able to produce 200 to 250 watts of electricity. Compact or slimline systems, however, typically use lower-rated supplies. Older systems also frequently use less-robust power plants.

Table 8.1. Typical power supplies for different PCs.

PC Type	Power Output
Slimline	100 to 150 watts
Standard desktop	150 to 200 watts
Minitower	150 to 250 watts
Full tower	250 to 300 watts

The main concern with any healthy power supply is that it be rated to handle the load being put on it. Add-in cards, additional disk drives, and other hardware upgrades all draw power from the system, placing a greater electrical load on the supply. On older PCs, or on compact models with slimline cases, this can mean the supply lacks the horsepower to push additional devices along. At some point, your hardware upgrades will demand a power supply upgrade to make them work.

Probably the most noticeable feature of any power supply is its fan. On some less-expensive models, the fan is noticeable indeed. Fan noise—that constant hum coming from the back of your PC—can be quite distracting. Many power supply models are marketed specifically on their quiet operation.

Note: Quiet operation is a target of the PC98 and Microsoft Simply Interactive PC (SIPC) specifications. The goal is to eliminate fan noise in order to make PCs a viable entertainment fixture—along with TVs and stereos. Obviously, the distracting whir of a PC fan doesn't cut it when you are trying to enjoy your favorite CD.

Fortunately, power supplies are inexpensive and easy to upgrade. If something goes wrong, you can affect a repair within a few minutes. Still, handling your PC's power source is serious business. If you run the wrong wires, you might fry the motherboard, CPU, and other expensive components—and maybe even yourself.

Surge Protection: The First Line of Defense

Power supplies might be simple devices, but they act as the interface between your PC and the electric company. That's no small task—running point when a lightning storm is raging outside, for example. Surge protectors act as armor, providing an enhanced level of protection against power surges and spikes.

These devices do their job when an over-voltage hits the power line. Most suppressors use a metal-oxide varistor (MOV), which clamps on the line and draws away excess energy. The over-voltage is sent to a ground wire to be dissipated, ensuring that your PC doesn't take the hit. More expensive units have additional circuitry to finesse their way through less-intense surges, as well as physical circuit breakers or fuses to cut the circuit entirely should a catastrophic surge hit.

However, if too much power hits a suppressor, your PC is still at risk. Surge suppressors are rated by the amount of energy—measured in joules—they can withstand. Generally, you should look for a rating of at least 240 joules.

> **Caution:** Those cheap power strips you see advertised as surge protectors often lack even rudimentary protection. Their voltage ceilings might be very low, allowing even moderate surges to get past them and into your PC. What's more, they can be so slow to react that the damage is done to your hardware before the circuit is broken. You should make sure any surge device you purchase is rated for at least 240 joules.

Some surge protectors also feature phone line inputs. These protect your modem and telephone from power surges that can occur over phone lines. Some devices also include plugs for 10BaseT ethernet wire, ensuring that a surge in your network wiring doesn't pass unimpeded into your PC. You can also find power panels that enable you to turn equipment on and off from a central location, as shown in Figure 8.2.

Uninterruptible Power Supplies (UPSs)

The next step up the electrical food chain is the uninterruptible power supply (UPS). This device provides all the amenities of a good surge suppressor and adds features such as battery backup, power conditioning, and even monitoring and management software.

FIGURE 8.2.
Monitor-base surge protectors enable you to turn devices on and off from a central location. (Photo courtesy of American Power Conversion)

The biggest advantage of a UPS is that it enables your PC to survive even a complete blackout. Depending on the size and cost of a UPS unit, you can get about 5 to 10 minutes of battery-powered operation after a complete power failure—enough time to save your documents and shut down your system. In fact, some models even include software that automatically closes your applications and shuts down the system when the power goes out. A serial cable connection allows the UPS to tell the software to shut the system down.

In addition, many UPSs condition incoming power, letting you work unimpeded through summer brownouts, power sags, and other conditions that can result in mystery lock-ups and reboots. Although many of these problems wouldn't cause a system shutdown, the conditioning of line power reduces strain on the power supply and components, thereby extending the life of the PC.

> **Caution:** If you already have a surge protector and then get a UPS, make sure you don't plug the UPS into the surge protector. Doing so can circumvent the protective circuitry of the two devices and leave your system open to damage from a power surge. Make sure you plug your UPS directly into an outlet.

The Juice

The most important feature of any UPS is its power rating. A UPS must be built to handle the load presented by your hardware. A $100 UPS box just can't meet the demands of a dual-processor Pentium II tower with a RAID disk array, CD-ROM jukebox, and 21-inch monitor.

The thing to look for is the UPS's voltage-ampere rating, or VA. Before you can buy a UPS, you need to determine the load your equipment will put on the unit. You can find a useful backup rating facility at the Web site of American Power Conversion, a leading UPS maker. Go to www.apcc.com and click the link for Workstation/PC. You simply enter the details of your PC's configuration into the online form and the site will spec out the type of UPS you need.

> **Tip:** When determining the final figure, it only helps you to be conservative with your numbers and overestimate. For one thing, it leaves room for future upgrades such as a Zip drive, second hard disk, and the like. Also, you won't have to worry about having the stated protection if you're conservative with your numbers.

Lower-end UPSs provide VA ratings of about 250 (see Figure 8.3). However, users with fully stocked PCs might want more coverage.

FIGURE 8.3.

With its compact design, modem jacks, and replaceable batteries, the APC Back-UPS Office is great for small offices. But its 250 VA rating won't do for big network servers. (Photo courtesy of American Power Conversion)

Types of UPSs

There are three types of UPS products to choose from:

- Standby UPS
- Online UPS
- Line-interactive UPS

Standby UPS

The least-expensive UPS type, standby models provide battery backup and little else. The UPS is plugged into the outlet, and power flows straight through the UPS. If a blackout or major voltage sag occurs, the standby UPS's battery kicks in, providing power to the PC. During normal operation, a small amount of power is fed to the battery to keep it charged.

The drawback is that there is a slight delay while battery power comes on after a blackout. Although most new systems can handle the transition, older models might reboot. More of a concern is the fact that these models don't actively condition power. Power sags and surges might put wear and tear on your PC's power supply.

Online UPS

Online UPSs improve on things by actively managing the incoming power stream. Voltages are monitored and adjusted to meet the PC's parameter, a process called *line conditioning*. If voltages sag, the battery makes up the difference. Power runs directly into the battery and back out through an inverter, which converts DC power to AC format. This means if power ever cuts off, the battery is already actively in the power stream. The result is a virtual elimination of transition time to battery power.

Online UPSs have their drawbacks, too. For one thing, active management and battery interdiction mean these models produce a bit of heat and fan noise. You can also expect the UPS battery to have a shorter operating life than standby models. In addition, cheaper online UPSs lack a way to provide a pass-through; if the battery dies, the UPS will no longer run power to the PC. You are better off getting a more expensive model that includes a pass-through feature that can be used until the battery is replaced.

Despite these drawbacks, online UPSs are the best way to go. Although the advantage over standby models during an actual blackout is minor, their workaday line-conditioning service can help avoid cumulative trauma to your PC's power supply and components. If your power is particularly unreliable, an online UPS is a must.

Line-Interactive UPS

A recent hybrid innovation, line-interactive UPSs provide line-conditioning services without relying on battery power (see Figure 8.4). When voltages sag—a common occurrence—these products actually work to pull more energy out of the outlet. A small amount of juice is used to keep the battery charged.

Line-interactive UPSs are less expensive than their online siblings, yet they provide line conditioning without shortening battery life. However, you'll get more robust line conditioning from an online UPS—particularly in highly variable environments.

FIGURE 8.4.
APC's Back-UPS Pro line uses line-interactive technology to maximize battery life while providing active line conditioning. (Photo courtesy of American Power Conversion)

Other Features

Some UPSs have many bells and whistles—which are important for network administrators and other pros who need to make sure their mission-critical servers are working smoothly. Among the features you'll see are these:

- Line monitoring: Provides real-time data on incoming voltages, sine wave character, and other aspects. Also provides a power-flow history, which can be useful for tracking down intermittent problems.

- Battery power status: Lets the user know how long the estimated battery charge will last if there is a shutdown.

- Automatic shutdown: In the event of a blackout, the UPS closes all open applications and shuts down the PC. The device sends a signal to a software utility over a serial cable.

- Remote management: Allows network administrators to track and manage UPS activity over a network or modem, using standard SNMP facilities.

- Pager and fax: Lets the UPS send status and power outage messages to an administrator's beeper, fax, and email.

Although these features are nice, most small-office or home users can probably do without them. However, for larger offices, these features represent an important set of tools in the administrator's troubleshooting arsenal.

> **Caution:** In most cases, it is inadvisable to run your laser printer off a UPS. The extreme electrical load limits the ability of an affordable UPS to provide even five minutes of battery run time. What's more, laser printer data isn't irreplaceable. If a print job is killed because of a blackout, you can simply reprint the document later.
>
> Also, if you have an ink jet printer connected to a UPS, be aware that these devices often have long shut-down routines in which the ink nozzles are cleaned. If you shut down your devices from the UPS switch, you'll kill this self-maintenance step.

A Word About Portables

When it comes to power, no one has more to worry about than the notebook PC owner. The batteries in these units can be capricious, losing life as they age. Depending on the notebook PC, batteries might last six hours or less than two.

There are three popular battery technologies on the market:

- Nickel metal-hydride (NiMH)
- Nickle cadmium (NiCad)
- Lithium ion (Li)

Of these, lithium ion is much preferred. These batteries can provide 30 percent more charge (or greater) than NiMH or NiCad batteries of the same size. Although supply constraints and engineering problems (remember Apple's burning PowerBook batteries?) slowed down the acceptance of lithium batteries, today you shouldn't buy a notebook without one. You will get longer battery life and more reliable operation.

> **Tip:** One of the biggest problems with nickel cadmium batteries is the so-called memory effect. If you have a battery that runs four hours at a charge, and you use it repeatedly for two hours and then charge it up again, the battery remembers the shorter cycle. Before long, it will run only two hours at a time. Your best protection is to run the battery all the way down before recharging it. Better yet, get a notebook with a lithium ion battery; these products don't suffer from memory problems.

For those who use their notebooks in hotels and want to protect them from power problems, there are even portable-oriented power-managing devices (see Figure 8.5).

FIGURE 8.5.
*APC's SurgeArrest
Notebook is a
compact module
that plugs directly
into the outlet. It
provides both
power and
modem surge
protection. (Photo
courtesy of
American Power
Conversion)*

FIGURE 8.5.
APC's SurgeArrest Notebook is a compact module that plugs directly into the outlet. It provides both power and modem surge protection. (Photo courtesy of American Power Conversion)

Buying a Juice Machine

Two purchases are covered here: internal power supplies and external power protection devices. Both are equally critical because they affect the performance of the rest of your PC. We'll deal with power supplies first.

Power to the PCs: Power Supplies

Power supply upgrades are a fairly frequent occurrence, so don't be surprised if you find yourself in the market for a new supply. Old supplies get dirty and gummed up or simply wear out after years of use and abuse. Overheating and chronic voltage sags can also bring the early demise of a power supply. And, of course, upgrades can require greater power needs than the original supply can handle.

How Much Is Enough?

Fortunately, supplies are cheap. Fifty bucks or so should get you a basic slimline power supply able to dish out about 230 watts of power—enough for a midrange desktop. That said, you're better off buying more power supply than you need. A supply that is running at or beyond capacity will produce excess heat and wear out quickly.

> **Caution:** Make sure you have enough power supply for your system. Overworked supplies produce excess heat and place unneeded thermal stress on every component inside your system. That puts expensive hard disks, CPUs, RAM, and CD-ROM drives at risk for failure or shortened operating life. It can also lead to lots of mysterious quirks such as frozen keyboards, data loss, and random reboots.

So how much power supply do you really need? As a general rule, you can estimate based on the case type of the PC. Compact systems draw a lot less power than big, rangy towers, simply because there aren't as many drives and add-in cards inside the system. Remember, external devices such as monitors, scanners, and printers can get their own power, so these usually won't factor into the supply purchase.

If the Shoe Fits

The other critical buying issue is size. Any power supply you purchase must fit into the existing space inside your PC. Before you order anything, take a close look at the power supply. Note its dimensions, measure it if you have to, and check to make sure a matching product is offered. Fortunately, the vast majority of supplies comply with a handful of size formats. Here are some of the standard sizes:

- Baby AT format: 8.35"×5.9"×5.9"
- Desktop format: 8.35"×5.5"×3.4"
- ATX or slimline format: 5.9"×5.5"×3.4"
- Tower format: 8.35"×5.9"×5.9"
- Custom format: Varies

If your machine uses a nonstandard power supply, you should contact the system vendor directly about a possible replacement. You must either purchase the supply from the vendor or get it from a third party. In either case, you will probably pay extra for the custom design.

Okay, so you've got enough juice, and the space is just right—but your work still isn't done. People often buy new power supplies in order to get away from distracting fan noise. Many companies market quiet power supplies, which might add $20 or more to the cost of a standard power supply. Often, these products cut rated noise from about 45 or 50 decibels (dB) to about 35dB.

For mission-critical systems such as network servers, you can buy redundant power supplies. These two-in-one models actually integrate a pair of power supplies into a single enlarged casing. If one supply fails, the second takes over the entire load without missing a beat. These products also feature warning lights and beeps so that you know a power supply has failed. Some high-end servers, such as IBM's 704 line, come with dual power supplies.

You can buy power supplies from any computer store or via mail order. In general, make sure you look for a money-back guarantee (you want to be able to return any DOA product) as well as a three-year or longer warranty. The warranty, in particular, says a lot about a company's confidence in the product.

Buying Protection: UPSs and Surge Protectors

Buying a surge protector or a UPS is a two-step process. One, you need to decide if you want simple surge protection or more-robust power maintenance. Two, you need to find a surge protector or UPS that meets the specific power draw and protection needs of your equipment. Features and outlet layout are considerations too.

If you have set money aside for a good surge protector, you should probably stretch for a UPS. These devices cost about twice as much, but they offer the ability to ride out even a complete power failure—something a surge protector can't do.

The Urge to Surge

For surge protectors, expect to pay anywhere from $20 to $100, depending on the level of protection (again, measured in joules) and the presence of circuit breakers and other devices. Here are things to look for:

- Adequate surge protection: At least 240 joules
- A guarantee against equipment damage
- Enough power receptacles
- RJ-11 data line surge protection

The most important issue is the level of protection. Cheap surge protectors will do little to stop a big surge or spike, leaving your power supply and components open to assault. Also, look for some form of guarantee from the surge-protection company, insuring against power-related damage to equipment hooked to the product.

Another concern is to make sure there are enough receptacles for your needs. Most protectors provide six spaces for plugs; however, you won't be able to use them all if you have many devices that use power bricks. In these cases, you might find a model that spaces out some of the receptacles to prevent lost capacity.

Also, consider a model that includes an RJ-11 telephone jack for modem hookups. But once again, be aware that you may run out of plugs. If you have two lines running from a single phone jack (as might be the case with a two-line phone) you'll need a surge protector that can pass the signals for both lines. Most protectors will only allow a single phone line to pass through its circuitry.

Buying Power Protection

When it comes to UPS, size matters. The bigger your PC and the more plentiful your peripherals, the more UPS you need to buy. The VA (voltage-ampere) rating is key.

If you can afford the extra $50 to $100, you should go for an online UPS rather than a standby model. The active line conditioning will help extend the life of both the power supply and motherboard components. Of course, all UPSs give you a few precious minutes to shut down during a power outage. Although more capacity—say, up to 15 minutes of battery run time—is always welcome, in reality, all you need is enough battery to shut your PC down.

Diagnosing/Troubleshooting

When it comes to power problems, the symptoms can be tough to read. In fact, most users fail to recognize power-related failures, attributing them to software glitches, sun spots, acts of God, and the like. There are two aspects to consider here: problems from the electrical source (that is, the line) and problems within the hardware (power supply, UPS, surge protector).

Check Your Power Line

The nature of the power your PC receives can vary widely, depending on where you live, the time of year, and the power usage habits of your neighbors. In summer, for example, the sudden load change as air conditioners click on and off is guaranteed to send surges and sags running through your electrical lines. Laser printers, refrigerators, and other power-hungry devices do the same thing. Older wiring is also a problem.

The following are common symptoms of unreliable power:

- Flickering or dimming lights
- Mysterious keyboard or system lock-ups
- Random reboots or shutdowns

If you experience any of these problems, you probably need a UPS more than a surge suppressor. Suppressors, after all, only handle over-voltages. But under-voltages from excess power draw or sudden load increases need the active management that online UPSs can provide.

Also be aware that in some cases a UPS won't help you. Older buildings might lack the ability to support a full office setup. Laser printers and large monitors in particular will add to the problem. In extreme cases, overloading these circuits can result in heating of the wire and a potential fire hazard. You should consult with an electrician to make sure that the local circuit provides enough amperage to service your PC.

A Failing Power Supply

With the exception of flickering lights, any of the symptoms previously noted can also indicate a failing power supply. However, there are a few other telltale signs to look for:

- Fan noise sounds rough or louder than usual.
- Fan noise is absent altogether.
- The power supply chassis is unusually hot to the touch.

If you note any of these symptoms, shut down the PC immediately—it's time to buy a new power supply. Although power supplies can be repaired, their low cost, coupled with the presence of dangerously high voltages inside, makes this a matter for professionals. You can also use the failure as an excuse to upgrade to a beefier model or to get one designed specifically for quiet or cool operation.

Here's one thing to keep in mind before you replace a dying unit: Make sure that you know the cause of its demise. If the supply went south soon after you loaded up on a bunch of new peripherals, you should double-check to make sure your new supply will be up to the more demanding task.

Putting in Power

Installing surge protectors and UPSs is as easy as it gets. If you can figure out which way is up on a grounded three-prong plug, you've pretty much got it licked. Installing a new power supply, however, is a bit more complex. After all, you need to fish around inside the case, unplug about a dozen cables, and unscrew a lot of screws. Still, it's hardly brain surgery. Here's how you install a power supply:

1. Shut down the PC, unplug the power supply, and open the case.
2. Disconnect the power cable connectors that attach to the motherboard and drives. Use a piece of masking tape and marker to tag each cable so you know which drive or socket each connector matches up with.

3. Disconnect the front panel switch. If the switch has terminals, disconnect the power supply from the switch. If the switch is soldered on, you must unfasten the switch from the computer chassis. Owners of newer ATX style motherboard systems won't have to worry about this step.

4. Use a Phillips screwdriver to remove the screws holding the power supply chassis to the case. Slide or lift the power supply clear. Be careful not to snag the power switch wire or assembly.

5. Get the new power supply. On some units, you need to check that the voltage selection switch (115/230 volts) is set properly.

6. Move the power supply into place, and use the provided screws to secure it to the chassis.

7. Attach the large 20-pin connector to the matching connector on the motherboard. Attach the drive connectors, making sure to align the tapered edges of both the plug and the connector as shown in Figure 8.6.

FIGURE 8.6.

Make sure you align the pins carefully.

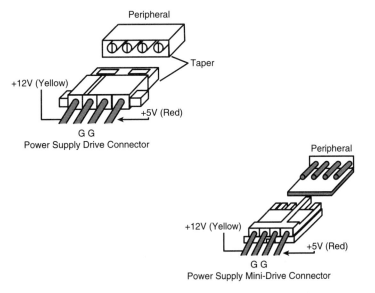

8. Connect the remote switch wires, matching the colored wires accordingly.

Tip: Most power supplies provide four sets of cables. If you're running out of power connections, you can avoid upgrading the entire supply by purchasing a Y-splitter cable from just about any electronics store. The splitter plugs into a disk drive power connector and provides two connectors for internal devices. Just be sure your power supply provides enough output to handle the additional load.

Covering Cases

Here's a subject that will warm the heart of only the most hardcore upgrader: PC cases. After the power supply, it's hard to think of a less glamorous component than the case. After all, these putty-beige products have come to symbolize everything that's wrong with the PC mentality—conservative, uninteresting, and bland.

But the fact is, the case plays a critical role in every system. Among its duties are to

- Protect internal components from dust, dirt, liquids, and other materials that can cause damage.
- Ensure adequate internal cooling by providing channeled airflow through vent placement and case structure.
- Block transmission of electromagnetic frequencies (EMF) produced by internal components. EMF can disrupt broadcast signals (TV, radio, cordless phones), while prolonged exposure may constitute a health threat.
- Provide support for monitors, drives, and other devices that may be mounted on the PC.

The case itself is typically made of sheet metal, and may have a plastic outer covering that is attached to the metal by screws or tabs. Better cases will use sturdy aluminum or steel that is not easily bent or twisted. If you plan to put a large monitor on top of a desktop PC, for example, the quality of the case becomes an important consideration.

The metal inner serves a second purpose, which is to act as a shield against EMF. All PC cases must be tested and certified by the FCC to ensure that they do not allow excess EMF to leak from the PC and possibly disrupt other devices. Often, a shielding agent may be sprayed on the inside of the case.

> **Note:** If your case is improperly seated, the shielding and possibly airflow characteristics of your system will be compromised. When you fix the case to the PC chassis you should follow the printed instructions and take care to make sure all tabs line up properly. Often, PC case operation is not obvious and a quick glance at the manual can help spare you an impromptu wrestling match.

Of course, cases come in a variety of shapes and styles. Large tower cases must encase systems are over three feet tall, while NLX form factor cases wrap around compact, slimline desktops popular with the corporate crowd. Traditionally, all cases were one-piece affairs that slid over the PC chassis, describing a shallow U shape for desktops and a deep U for towers.

More recently, we've seen multi-part cases that are essentially a set of three panels. These cases allow you to slide off just one panel to expose the interior of the system—that way you can actually remove a component without ever pulling a midtower system out from under the desk, for example. However, these panels can be tough to work with, with inscrutable tabs that allow you to release and afix the case to the PC frame.

Perhaps most welcome has been the advent of easy-open designs. If you're a frequent tinkerer—like me—you've probably been frustrated by the four or six tiny screws that hold most U-style cases in place. Not only must you use a screwdriver to access the case, but the screws themselves are easily lost. Many new cases use a single thumbscrew for tool-free tightening and loosening of the case, while others employ two or more tabs. Fortunately, you can get replacement screws and thumbscrews at most computer stores and repair shops.

Parts is Parts: What Comes with a Case

When you buy a case, you get more than a thin metal frame with a plastic outer shell and some design grillwork. Most cases ship complete with power supplies, for example, as well as a power cord and connections for the front panel switch.

Any PC you've seen has lights on the front to indicate the status of power, hard disk activity, and (until recently) turbo setting. In addition to the lights themselves, which are mounted in the front bezel, the case includes wires to connect these lights to leads on the motherboard. You'll need your motherboard manual to hook up these wires.

Other goodies include those plastic faceplates for covering empty externally-accessible drive bays, as well as metal expansion slot inserts to cover unused ISA, PCI, and AGP card slots. Both are important for maintaining the airflow integrity of the system, as well as to keep unwanted dirt off the motherboard and components. In some cases, you may also find a keylock on the front panel and a pair of small keys for the lock. The keylock is used to secure keyboard access—preventing unwanted access and tampering. Just don't lose the keys if you decide to use this feature.

Perhaps most important is the motherboard mounting hardware included with the case. This includes standoffs for attaching the motherboard to the case bottom, screws to attach the standoffs to the case, and non-metal washers to provide a layer of insulation between the screw heads and the motherboard.

Choosing a Case

What kind of case should you buy? That really depends on your existing hardware and setup. If you are fresh out of desk space, a desktop case is probably out of the question—you'll want to go with a floor-standing tower, midtower, or minitower case (see Figure 8.7). The types of cases are outlined in Table 8.2:

Table 8.2. How different case types stack up when it comes to expansion.

Case Type	Where	Expandability	External Bays
Tower	Floor	Excellent	6
Midtower	Floor	Good	5
Minitower	Floor	Fair	4
Desktop	Desk	Fair	4
Slimline	Desk	Poor	3

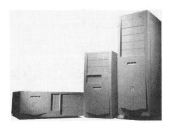

FIGURE 8.7.

As you can see, the large tower case to the right presents five externally-accessible 5-1/4" bays, versus the three such bays in the minitower and desktop cases. (Photo courtesy of American Suntek)

Expandability is typically a function of the number of available drive bays a case will present. A tower case, for example, can often hold 10 or more drives, while a slimline case is limited to perhaps four. If you intend to add multiple hard disks, CD-ROM drives, tape backup and perhaps an Iomega Zip drive to your system, you'll want to consider a tower.

Also keep in mind that externally-accessible bays are the only ones that are useful for devices other than hard disk drives. After all, you need to be able to put discs and cassettes into virtually every other bay-bound device, be it a CD-ROM drive, Zip drive, or PC Card reader.

Expandability is also impacted by the ability of the case to encourage cooling airflow over components. In this regard, bigger is always better—and towers are always best. Cramped slimline systems must be designed to exacting specifications to ensure that air does not grow stale and hot over crucial hardware like the CPU, hard disk, or RAM. With towers, this airflow is much easier to achieve, since open space is virtually assured.

Finally, towers offer superior expansion because they are typically mated with more powerful power supplies capable of driving multiple devices. The 150-watt supply in a slimline system, for example, would choke trying to get electricity to six additional drives. The 300-watt supply typically included with a tower case, however, is up to the task. If you intend to stuff your PC full of power-hungry hardware, a tower case will help protect you in every direction—power, cooling, and space.

Form Factors

Okay, so you've decided on a case size to hold your motherboard, now you need to make sure your motherboard and care are compatible. When you purchase a case, you need to look for a model that conforms to the same form factor standard used by your mother-board. See Figure 8.8. You'll want to check your motherboard documentation to confirm the form factor. The major form factors are

- AT and Baby AT: The reigning standard for PC motherboards and cases through 1995. Finally waning.

- ATX and Mini ATX: Intel-sponsored standard now employed in virtually all stan-dard-sized systems and motherboards.

- LPX and Mini LPX: Aging compact PC specification.

- NLX: Enhancements to LPX spec yield improved airflow, power management, and cooling.

FIGURE 8.8

The low-profile NLX case features a central cross bar to provide sup-port for a moni-tor. Add-in cards are mounted on a vertical riser card mounted to the bar. (Photo cour-tesy of Yeong Yang Technology)

The thing to realize is that if you use an AT motherboard, you must get an AT-style case. The form factor standards determine where critical things like I/O backplane ports are located. So if you try to use an ATX motherboard on an AT case, the serial, parallel, and other ports won't be accessible. In addition, changes to power connectors will make it impossible to use an AT power supply on an ATX case, and vice versa.

INSTANCE REFERENCE

For more on motherboard form factors, see Chapter 9, "Understanding Motherboards and Chipsets."

[handwritten margin note: DISABLE TURBO ON M/B = PULL WIRES FREE]

Back before the days of the Pentium, system vendors incorporated a turbo switch on PCs that would slow operation down. The switch fixed compatibility problems with older software (mostly games) that got confused when run at higher than expected speeds. Such problems don't exist any longer, but many systems still have that working turbo switch. The problem: If you bump that switch by accident, you may find yourself puzzling through a mysterious performance slowdown.

You can fix this problem by disabling the turbo switch entirely. To do this, do the following: Power down the PC, open the case, and find the turbo pin connector on the motherboard. You can simply follow the two wires from the turbo button to the motherboard. Once you've located the connector, pull the wires free. (You may want to label the wires detailing what pin they were attached to—just in case you need to reattach them.)

The system should now run at normal speed. However, if you notice that the system is running slowly and the turbo light is off, your work is not yet done. You'll need to seat a jumper across the two turbo pins on the motherboard. If you still find that performance does not return to normal, reattach the turbo wires to the motherboard and learn not to bump that switch.

Summary

Power is an overlooked area when it comes to troubleshooting. CPU overheating, memory parity errors, hard disk data loss, and random lock-ups and shutdowns can all be attributed to irregular power flow. Whether it's the fault of a failing power supply or of an unreliable utility, the end result is a lot of headaches.

[handwritten margin note: POWER! IS PSU up To iT?]

It's important to keep power problems in mind whenever you're sleuthing out a hardware problem. Overheating problems could be from a broken CPU fan or a dying hard disk, or they could be from a laboring power supply that's pushing too many peripherals. Likewise, old wiring or your air conditioning might cause sags and surges that create problems with your motherboard chipsets.

Ultimately, the best protection is an online UPS that provides constant line conditioning and the insurance of a 10-minute shutdown window. If you have data that you absolutely can't afford to lose, you should make room in your budget for such a device.

Cases may be nearly as boring as power hardware, but they do play an important role. That said, unless you intend to put a lot of weight on top of your case or otherwise subject it to abuse, you should be able to get buy for less than $100. The main concerns are making sure that the case fits the PC frame and matches up with openings and attachments provided on your motherboard.

Understanding Motherboards and Chipsets

If you look inside the case of your PC, you will see that almost everything inside is mounted on a single large circuit board, called the *motherboard*. This circuit board is the backbone of your PC. Everything from graphics cards and hard disks to CPUs and RAM plugs into the motherboard and communicates with the other components using the motherboard's connections.

In fact, the motherboard defines exactly what your PC can and can't do. You can make better upgrade and maintenance decisions when you understand how the motherboard works. This chapter will help you

- Learn what goes into a motherboard and how it works
- Understand how to buy a new motherboard and the role the motherboard plays in a new system purchase
- Diagnose and resolve motherboard problems

Overview

The motherboard is the foundation of your PC. Without it, CPUs, disk drives, and add-in cards are nothing but a bunch of disparate parts. The motherboard provides more than a place to plug in these devices; it determines how quickly and efficiently they can communicate and work. Most importantly, motherboard technology has entered a period of important change, as vendors boost clock rates, fiddle with memory types, and add features. This chapter will help you best assess, choose, and maintain the motherboard that drives your PC.

The Grand Tour

Motherboards are complex beasts, but they are easy to understand if you break them down into individual components. In fact, a company's motherboard models are often distinguished by incremental differences among integrated parts. This chapter will help you understand what those differences are.

Want to see for yourself? Pop the top off your PC (after shutting down and unplugging the unit, of course) and have a peek inside. If you look closely, you'll find that the components of a motherboard are easy to identify. Looking straight down into a PC, you will see the following (as shown in Figure 9.1):

1. CPU sockets or slots

2. Add-in card bus slots for ISA, PCI, AGP, and perhaps EISA or MCA

3. Memory and (usually) secondary cache sockets or chips

4. System chipsets and BIOS CMOS

5. Motherboard clock crystal and battery

6. Backplane I/O ports for serial, parallel, PS/2 mouse, keyboard, and USB

7. Pin-outs for disk drives, power, and (possibly) SCSI connectors

FIGURE 9.1.

*Micronics'
Stingray mother-
board includes all
the components
needed to make a
PC run. (Photo
courtesy of
Micronics Corp.)*

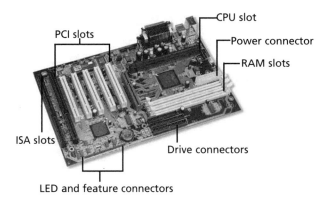

Assessing the CPU Socket

It all starts here. Motherboards must be closely tailored to the CPUs they serve, providing the correct number and types of data and address lines to the CPU. An AMD K6-2 processor, for example, uses very different connections than the dual-cavity Pentium Pro or single-edge connected Pentium II. The type of CPU socket in any motherboard directly affects its performance and upgradability.

That said, motherboards can generally host a number of different CPUs designed for their connectors. Jumpers enable you to set the motherboard to run at different speeds, allowing the same board to support both a 90MHz Pentium CPU and a 233MHz Pentium MMX CPU, for example. Intel-compatible processors from AMD and Cyrix can likewise plug into the processor socket.

In Pentium and later Pentium-class motherboards, the CPU socket is one of the most prominent features on the circuit board landscape. Pentium and Pentium Pro motherboards feature a large square or rectangle of pin holes. Often, a silver lever is positioned next to the socket. This is the zero insertion force (ZIF) lever, which allows easy insertion and removal of CPUs.

Pentium II motherboards depart from this familiar scheme: You'll see a long slot for the CPU instead of a large square, as shown Figure 9.2. The slot accepts so-called single-edge connector (SEC) cartridges, which Intel uses to house its Pentium II CPUs. Although the effect is the same—conductive gold-plated leads make contact and allow electrical signals to pass to and from the CPU—the change means that Pentium II motherboards won't accept other Intel or non-Intel processors.

FIGURE 9.2.
Notice a difference? This Pentium II motherboard doesn't feature the familiar square CPU module of past generations. The CPU goes into the dark slot near the bottom-right. (Photo courtesy of Tyan)

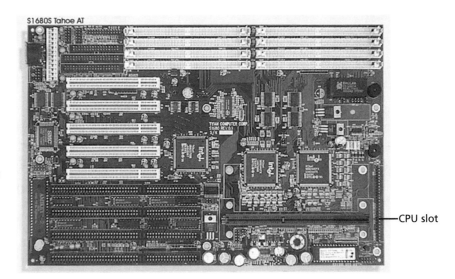

CPU slot

Intel moved to this slotted module for business reasons, pure and simple. The so-called Slot 1 design is a well-protected piece of property. Patents and trademarks surround both the P6 CPU bus and the Slot 1 design. Unlike earlier 486 and Pentium CPUs, AMD, Cyrix, and other processor makers lack access to the technology through licensing agreements. The upshot is that you won't see CPUs from competing vendors that will fit into those Slot 1 motherboards.

Ironically, Slot 1 doesn't work well for Intel's low-cost Celeron CPU line—the connector and motherboard interface are too expensive to compete against systems using AMD K6-2, Cyrix M II, and other socket based CPUs. That's why Intel has brought back the socket—the so-called Socket A—for its Celeron line. However, the 337-pin connector is not compatible with Socket 7, since Celeron uses a the next-generation P6 bus rather than the P5 bus shared by K6-2 and M II.

If you have an existing motherboard you want to upgrade, you can usually do so with the same class of processor. Table 9.1 lists your direct upgrade options.

Table 9.1. Motherboard upgrade options.

Original CPU	Socket Type	Upgrade Options
Pentium	Socket 5	Pentium MMX OverDrive, K5, 6x86, faster Pentium
Pentium or Pentium MMX	Socket 7	Pentium MMX, K6 and K6-2, M II, faster Pentium
Pentium Pro	Socket 8	Pentium Pro
Celeron	Socket A	Cache-integrated Celeron CPUs
Pentium II	Slot 1	Pentium II, cacheless Celeron
Xeon	Slot 2	Second-generation Xeon
Xeon, IA-64	Slot M	Third-generation Xeon, IA-64 Merced and later CPUs

As you can see, your upgrade options get slim once you move to a P6-bus motherboard (that is, Pentium Pro and Pentium II). The best upgrade picture exists for Socket 7 motherboards, where Pentium MMX, AMD K6, and Cyrix M II CPUs all vie for a piece of the computing market.

Tag Team: Multiprocessing Motherboards

Some motherboards can accept two or more CPUs, providing enhanced performance for computationally intense operations. Called *symmetric multiprocessing (SMP)*, these advanced PCs require a specialized operating system that can recognize and take advantage of the additional CPUs. Microsoft Windows NT Server, for example, can use up to four CPUs right out of the box, while enhanced versions can recognize even more processors. OS/2 and various UNIX operating systems also provide SMP support, but you won't find SMP inside Windows 95.

How much does SMP help, really? Not as much as you might think, although it depends mostly on the application. Often, the second CPU will yield an impressive performance boost, in the range of 70 percent. However, successive CPUs tend to deliver less and less return, diminishing to the point where additional CPUs fail to appreciably affect performance. The reason is that the CPUs are waiting for the system bus, memory, hard disk, and other components to deliver data to them. Making them faster simply increases the amount of time they sit idle.

SMP sounds good, but it isn't for everybody. Web servers, network servers, and professional workstations are the types of PCs that can make SMP pay off—particularly since SMP systems are significantly more expensive than single-processor PCs. SMP motherboards and chipsets must contain additional logic to keep the various CPU caches (L1 and L2) in sync, so that data altered by one CPU doesn't accidentally get overwritten by older data in the cache of a second CPU. The processors also need a fast connecting bus to allow them to achieve top performance.

Intel has made SMP more accessible by crafting a standard that eliminates the need for every PC maker to cook its own SMP design. Intel's Pentium II provides limited two-way SMP capability, but the newer Xeon CPU mated with the advanced 450GX chipset provides 4-way configurations starting in the first quarter of 1999 (see Figure 9.3).

FIGURE 9.3.

Tea for two: this dual-processor Pentium II motherboard is well-suited for server and workstation tasks. (Photo courtesy of Intel Corp.)

Note: If you own a Pentium Pro system, whether it's a single or dual processor, you can now upgrade it to Pentium II using Intel's latest OverDrive kit. The Pentium II OverDrive can turn a 200MHz Pentium Pro into a 333MHz Pentium II, complete with MMX instruction set support and a 512KB L2 cache running at the full speed of the CPU. If you have a dual Pentium Pro, you simply purchase two kits and you're on your way.

Get on the Bus, Gus

Another important consideration is add-in card support, which you can discern by looking at the motherboard. In most Pentium systems, you will see parallel slots lined up perpendicular to the backplane. You'll usually see two separate types of slots, corresponding to the type of bus being used by the system.

These slots are important because they determine what kind of cards you can add to your system down the road. Graphics cards, sound cards, network adapters, and other internal peripherals all plug into the add-in card buses. The number and type of slots are both key considerations.

There are six major PC buses:

- ISA: The workhorse low-speed system bus present on virtually all PCs.

- PCI: The reigning standard found on all new Pentium-class PCs sold in the last two years.

- AGP: The Accelerated Graphics Port is the new graphics-only connection for Pentium II PCs that runs at two or four times the speed of PCI and provides intriguing features for 3D graphics. The bus is fast enough to allow graphics cards to use system memory as a buffer space for speeding frame rates in games and video.

- VL bus: The first high-speed add-on card bus, it was tailored to 486 systems but never caught on with Pentium PCs. In essence, VL bus was an extension of the old 32-bit 486 bus, featuring none of the data buffering and asynchronous clock capability built into PCI. The result: VL bus was ill-suited to transition beyond the 486.

- MCA: IBM's enhanced Plug and Play add-in bus never took off in the mainstream market.

- EISA: The industry's answer to MCA, it too enjoyed only limited market share and today is found only in servers.

Note: Of these six, most new PCs incorporate the ISA, PCI, and AGP buses. You should make sure that any new system or motherboard you buy comes equipped with PCI and AGP at a bare minimum, while ISA is important if you have older peripherals you want to install into your new system. ISA buses often come with brown or black plastic slot housings. You can recognize PCI slots by their light color, shorter lengths, and closely-spaced pins. The AGP slot is usually brown in color and is slightly smaller than the PCI slots.

The bus type of a motherboard might make or break an upgrade decision. Older VL bus-based motherboards, for example, have reached the end of their useful life, as graphics board vendors have abandoned VL bus in favor of the ubiquitous PCI standard. The upshot is that if you want the latest peripherals, whether it's a sound card, network card, or SCSI controller, you'll need a PCI motherboard to plug it into. Most 486 owners need not apply. For graphics, AGP has quickly become the primary connection.

What's so special about PCI? Well, for one thing, it's fast. With a 132MBps burst transfer rate, PCI can push bits about 25 times faster than ISA. It also boasts built-in Plug and Play capability, bus mastering, and a compact slot design that shaves precious pennies off manufacturing costs.

Even as ISA devices shift over to PCI, the quintessential PCI peripheral—the graphics board—has jumped to AGP. The Accelerated Graphics Port is essentially a "PCI bus on steroids" dedicated to graphics, allowing 3D-savvy graphics adapters to use the large pool of system memory to create visuals in 3D textured scenes.

What's more, AGP can help undo bottlenecks for all graphics operations, whether 2D, 3D, or video. Most AGP graphics cards can push 528MBps (versus PCI's 132MBps) of data, a 4X improvement. Intel has pushed that number further still, to 1GBps, with its AGP 4X (or AGP Pro) specification, which is targeted at graphics workstations running the company's Xeon CPU. Regardless of which AGP specification involved, the fact that the graphics board is the only device on this user-bus means performance should benefit (see Figure 9.4).

FIGURE 9.4.

This schematic shows how AGP-based graphics boards sit above the PCI bus and gain direct access to main system memory. The result is better performance potential and more-realistic 3D texturing. But you need an AGP motherboard to get AGP. (Figure courtesy of Intel Corp.)

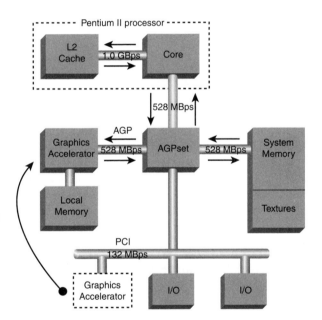

What's the catch? If you purchased an early Pentium II or a non-Intel based system, your system probably lacks AGP. Fortunately, so-called Super 7 motherboards designed for AMD K6-2 and Cyrix M II CPUs now come equipped with AGP capability. This addition is a critical factor in making these alternative CPUs and motherboards an attractive option, since it ensures compatibility with future graphics board products.

Table 9.2 helps you understand how PCI and other buses compare with each other.

Table 9.2. Buses compared.

Bus Type	Data Rate	What It's Best For	Notes
ISA	5MBps	Desktop PCs, sound cards, modems, low-bandwidth peripherals	On its way out
PCI	133MBps	Desktops and servers, graphics, network adapters, sound cards	Great hardware selection, and it's fast
AGP	264MBps/528MBps	High-end desktops, gaming PCs, and 3D workstations	Future ofPC— 3D games and titles
AGP Pro	1024MBps	Professional graphics workstations	A staple on Xeon-class systems
VL bus	120MBps	486 desktop PCs, graphics cards	Going, going, gone
EISA	33MBps	Servers	Replaced by PCI
MCA	33MBps	Servers	Never took off

Why all the worrying about those slots? Simple. The bus installed in the motherboard determines what cards you can buy for your PC. For example, people who have older VL bus systems simply can't find a wide selection of graphics cards, 10/100MBps NICs, or other high-speed peripherals. The cards that are available often lag behind their PCI counterparts by several months.

The Lowdown on System Memory

You'll also want to pay close attention to memory support in your motherboard. As with add-in cards, there are different types of memory sockets, which can affect performance and capabilities. Memory is sold in single inline memory modules (SIMMs) and in dual inline memory modules (DIMMs).

The key things to look for are

- Memory form factor: The types of RAM modules, including 30-pin SIMMs, 72-pin SIMMs, and 168-pin DIMMs.

- Memory capacity: Most motherboards support at least 128MB, although some might require a RAM upgrade in order to provide caching services to all the installed RAM.

- Memory type: The most common types, in order of increasing performance, are Fast Page Mode (FPM DRAM), Extended Data Out (EDO DRAM), and Synchronous (SDRAM).

Note: It's important to note that older Pentium, Pentium Pro and other systems can not accept the fastest memory types. For a variety of reasons, chipsets for early Pentium II and all Pentium Pro motherboards were about a half-step behind mainstream Pentium MMX chipsets—and recognition of SDRAM memory was one of the features that was lacking in these motherboards. The Introduction of the 440LX chipset added SDRAM and more to its P6 lines, but this memory failing may be a reason to upgrade an aging motherboard.

Memory vendors use a cryptic scheme to market their products. You'll see a megabyte amount (1MB, 2MB, and so on), and then an x, and then a number denoting the bit width of the module. If the second number is divisible by 8 (32, 64), the module is a nonparity-checking SIMM. If the second number is divisible by 9 (36, 72), the SIMM provides error checking. To figure out how much memory sits on a single module, divide the bit width number by either 8 or 9, and multiply the result by the number of megabytes.

For example, a SIMM marked as 1MBx32 has a capacity of 4MB. A SIMM marked as 1MBx36 also has a capacity of 4MB, but it includes error correcting. Table 9.3 shows a typical RAM configuration on a motherboard, using the number scheme previously explained.

Table 9.3. Common memory configurations.

Memory	Bank 0	Bank 1
8MB	(2) 1MBx36	
16MB	(2) 1MBx36	(2) 1MBx36
16MB	(2) 2MBx36	
24MB	(2) 2MBx36	(2) 1MBx36
32MB	(2) 4MBx36	
32MB	(2) 2MBx36	(2) 2MBx36
40MB	(2) 4MBx36	(2) 1MBx36
48MB	(2) 4MBx36	(2) 2MBx36
64MB	(2) 8MBx36	
64MB	(2) 4MBx36	(2) 4MBx36
72MB	(2) 8MBx36	(2) 1MBx36
80MB	(2) 8MBx36	(2) 2MBx36
96MB	(2) 8MBx36	(2) 4MBx36
128MB	(2) 8MBx36	(2) 8MBx36

As this table shows, motherboards can be particular about how memory is installed in the SIMM or DIMM sockets. Again, only the documentation can guide you here, but a good rule of thumb for SIMMs is to occupy the first two sockets with equal-capacity modules that should be larger or equal in capacity to any SIMMs in adjacent sockets. DIMMs, on the other hand, may be installed singly.

System Chipsets: The Key Ingredient

There are many very important components on the motherboard, but the system chipset is arguably among the most critical (see Figure 9.5). The chipset consists of a number of silicon chips soldered directly to the motherboard. These chips take care of housekeeping chores such as power management, bus activity, memory transactions, and CPU timings.

Figure 9.5.

Intel's 440BX chipset, for example, was an important advance for Pentium II systems. It introduced 100MHz motherboard bus operation, which allowed system memory to run 50 percent faster than earlier 66MHz models. (Photo courtesy of Intel Corp.)

Peter's Principle: Don't Underestimate the Chipset in Evaluating Motherboard Performance

Looking for performance? Check out the chipset first. The supporting silicon can make a big difference in performance, by streamlining data transfers and providing access to the fastest memory and bus types.

The most prevalent example was when Intel released the Triton chipset to replace the older Neptune set for Pentium motherboards. The result was that Triton-based systems running at the same clock speeds gained a 5 to 15 percent performance edge in application benchmarks. The 440BX did that and more for Pentium II motherboards, thanks to its 100MHz capability. 440BX motherboards run 50 percent faster than those based on the 440LX chipset. And while both chipsets offer support for SDRAM memory and the AGP bus slot, the speed boost makes a big performance difference.

One important thing to remember about chipsets is that they can't be upgraded. The only way to gain new features not supported in your existing system's chipset is to either replace the motherboard or purchase a new system. Before you upgrade a motherboard or buy a PC, it pays to research the chipset market first. Early buyers of Pentium II PCs, for example, missed out on the key AGP bus and enhanced SDRAM memory. The lack of these features doesn't spell doom for these buyers, but it could shorten the useful life of the PC—particularly for those wanting top 3D game play.

The chipset determines exactly what your PC can and can't do in terms of technological support and performance. Make sure you know what chipset is in a system before you buy it.

The chipset is part and parcel of the motherboard—it can't be upgraded. So when you make a motherboard or system purchase, you should consider the chipset carefully. The biggest danger is that a new chipset introduces support for enhanced buses or memory types, cutting into the long-term availability and support for components designed for the older technology.

Over the last five years, Intel has become the leading maker of both chipsets and motherboards. (This is hardly a surprise. Intel uses these businesses to ensure healthy support for its CPUs.) To acquaint you with the chipset in your motherboard, we will look at the various chipsets used in motherboards over the years.

Choosing a Chipset

Obviously, you can't buy your system chipset separately—the components are soldered permanently onto the motherboard. But you can—and should—investigate the chipset when making any system or motherboard purchase. By making the chipset a central consideration, you can guarantee that your new PC or motherboard will be compatible with the latest devices and technologies.

Among the things to consider:

- Speeds and feeds: How fast is the motherboard front side bus, the IDE interface, the PCI and AGP buses?

- Memory support: How much memory and what kind can the motherboard accept? Also make sure it can cache all the memory it says it can support (some don't).

- Bus support: It's a parade of acronyms—USB, AGP2X and AGP 4X, ATA-33 and ATA-66.

- Power management: ACPI power management enables you to save energy and enhance manageability over the network.

- Expansion: The chipset can limit the number of PCI slots and DIMM sockets on the motherboard.

So with all these variables, what should you do? Whether you are buying a new PC or upgrading your existing motherboard, make sure the chipset is at the center of your plans. The following sections describe my best suggestions, broken down by system type.

Entry-Level Systems

A single-processor aware chipset (see Figure 9.6) is fine, but you should go with no less than a 100MHz front side bus when choosing a new PC or motherboard upgrade. The speed will make a big difference and extend the life of your motherboard for a good six months to a year. Make sure you get an ATA-33 disk interface and an AGP 2X graphics support. A 64MB memory ceiling is a bit tight, but can be accepted for this range of the market—just don't complain when you find yourself stymied at your next upgrade.

FIGURE 9.6.
Intel's 440EX chipset is a slimmed down 440LX for Celeron PCs. With a 66MHz front side bus, reduced expandability, and only single-processor support, you won't find this chipset in graphics workstations. (Photo courtesy of Intel Corp.)

You may only get three PCI slots and a pair of DIMM sockets, but that should be OK. Here's a tip, though: Specify to your vendor that you want all the memory on your new system located on a single DIMM module. That'll leave a module open for upgrade later and prevent you having to discard good memory. USB will almost certainly be part of the picture, and these minimally-expandable systems will benefit from this. For example, modems, sound cards, and cable modems that might otherwise occupy a PCI or ISA slot can be run directly off the external USB bus.

Chipsets in this range include 440EX and 440ZX. The 430TX still exists in the mobile Pentium MMX market.

Midrange Systems

As previously mentioned, 100MHz bus speed is critical. You'll also want to make sure the chipset supports both AGP 2X and the ATA-33 IDE interface. You should put more emphasis on expansion—midrange chipsets need to support five or more PCI slots and four DIMM sockets. An addressable memory ceiling of 1GB should be more than sufficient, and even 256MB will do for most users. While many chipsets in this range support two processors, it is unlikely that most users will ever make use of this feature.

Chipsets in this range include 440BX and code-named Camino chipset.

High-End Systems

The rules change up high. Addressable memory should fall in the range of 1GB to 4GB, with the higher values being necessary for serious enterprise network servers. See Figure 9.7. Multiprocessing gets served with 4-way symmetric multiprocessing (SMP) capability, though the highest-end chipsets may support 8-way SMP operation. Also look for AGP 4X (also called AGP Pro) support, which doubles AGP bandwidth from 512MB to 1024MB. Other features includes fast-and-wide PCI, operating at 66MHz and along a 64-bit bus width, while newer chipsets will introduce ATA-66 IDE interface—though most systems using these chipsets will rely on fast SCSI connections for disk access.

Chipsets in this range include 450NX and the code-named Carmel chipset.

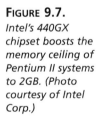

FIGURE 9.7.

Intel's 440GX chipset boosts the memory ceiling of Pentium II systems to 2GB. (Photo courtesy of Intel Corp.)

Reviewing Pentium-Class Chipsets

The Pentium years were crucial ones for Intel. Not only did this CPU allow the company to pull away from its CPU competitors, it also established Intel's dominance as a chipset—and soon after, a motherboard—manufacturer. A variety of chipsets served Pentium and Pentium MMX CPUs over the years, as Table 9.4 attests.

Table 9.4. Intel chipsets.

Chipset	Introduced	Socket Type	Description
430LX Neptune	1992	Socket 4	First Pentium
430NX Triton	1992	Socket 5	512MB FPM DRAM support
430FX	1994	Socket 7	128MB EDO DRAM, 256KB pipeline burst L2 cache
430HX	1996	Socket 7	2-way SMP, 512MB EDO RAM, USB support
430VX	1996	Socket 7	128MD SDRAM, USB support
430TX	1997	Socket 7	Improved SDRAM support, ATA-33 IDE interface, power management

Of these chips, two stood out as key market makers. The introduction in 1994 of the 440FX—the fabled Triton—helped vault the Pentium platform up and over 486 and compatible competition. The introduction of EDO DRAM support and fast pipeline-burst SRAM cache delivered a healthy performance boost across all applications. The chipset was also affordable, achieved in part by limiting memory support to 128MB.

Intel struck gold again in 1997 with the 430TX, which replaced the short-lived 430VX chipset in the consumer market. Equipped with advanced power management features, 430TX was the first chipset designed for both desktop and notebook computer designs. It also improved dramatically on the 430VX's SDRAM support, providing a more efficient memory interface that enhanced performance. The new ATA-33 IDE interface also boosted hard disk and CD-ROM drive operation, and doubled the maximum data burst rate of the bus. As it turned out, 430TX was the last Pentium-class chipset.

At least, it was the last from Intel. New systems based on AMD's fast K6-2 CPU and Cyrix's M II offering are based on advanced non-Intel chipsets offering many of the advantages of Pentium II-class offerings. 100MHz front side bus operation, AGP 2X capability, and ATA-33 IDE interfaces are all included in these new chipsets from companies like Acer Labs (ALI) and Via. See Figure 9.8. The two chipsets of note are

- ALI Aladdin V AGP Chipset
- Via Apollo MVP3

Figure 9.8.
Via's MVP3 chipset offers advanced features like 100MHz operation and AGP bus support for Socket 7 motherboards using AMD and Cyrix CPUs. (Photo courtesy of Via Technology)

While there are numerous older chipsets out there for Socket 7 motherboards, these are the only ones offering 100MHz front side bus capability. The faster motherboard not only speeds main memory, it also kicks up the speed of the L2 cache, providing an additional boost. If you buy a new AMD or Cyrix-based PC or motherboard, you should make sure an advanced chipset with AGP capability and 100MHz clock are included.

Reviewing Pentium Pro/II-Class Chipsets

The P6 class of chipsets has become Intel's stock in trade in the last year or two, and no surprise. In order to lure buyers away from its Socket 7 Pentium MMX offers (not to mention those of its competitors), Intel needed to dangle a carrot in front of the market. But most Pentium Pro chipsets offered features keyed toward networking and workstation applications—hardly the sort of cost-effective fare needed to convince mainstream buyers. That finally changed for good in 1997 as Pentium II hit stride. Today, P6-class chipsets target buyers of all types—entry level, mainstream, and power users. Table 9.5 lists Intel's P6-class chipsets.

Table 9.5. Intel's P6-class chipsets.

Chipset	Introduced	Socket Type	Description
450KX Mars	1995	Socket 8	First P6 chipset was pricey, only 2-way SMP
440FX Natoma	1996	Socket 8	Cost-effective 2-way SMP, 1GB EDO DRAM
450GX Orion	1995	Socket 8	Server-centric 4-way SMP, 4GB of EDO DRAM
440LX	1997	Slot 1	Affordable and feature-rich which supports 1GB SDRAM, AGP, USB, ATA-33, ACPI
440BX	1998	Slot 1	All that and 100MHz motherboard
440EX	1998	Slot 1	Celeron chipset runs at 66MHz, supports fewer slots, DIMMs
440ZX	1999	Socket A	100MHz Celeron motherboards
Camino	1999	Slot 1	133MHz front side bus, RDRAM, AGP 4X, ATA-66
440GX	1999	Slot 2	440BX with 2GB SDRAM
450NX	1999	Slot 2	4GB EDO DRAM, 4-way and 8-way SMP, 66MHz PCI
Carmel	1999	Slot 2	8GB RDRAM, 4-way SMP 64-bit/66MHz PCI, AGP 4X, ATA-66

When Pentium Pro first came out, it suffered from a muddled chipset message. Despite the CPU's ability to address 4GB of main memory, the first two chipsets only supported 1GB. What's more, multiprocessing was limited to 2-way SMP—minimal for the high-end server crowd. 450GB finally fixed matters by providing 4-way SMP operation, as well as introducing faster EDO DRAM that could be addressed in quantities of up to 4GB. The 440FX, meanwhile, stayed relevant as a consumer-class Pentium Pro chipset for desktops.

P6 went mainstream with the 440LX, the first real Pentium II chipset. The 440LX brought a host of technologies to bear, including the fast AGP graphics bus, Universal Serial Bus (USB) for new peripherals, and the ATA-33 IDE interface for doubling the burst rate of disk drives. ACPI power management added power-saving tweaks and remote management facilities for users and administrators alike. Most importantly from a performance standpoint, LX supported SDRAM memory (and did so quite well), allowing Pentium II users to finally use the same fast RAM used in Pentium MMX systems for nearly a year. However, the 1GB RAM ceiling and limited 2-way SMP support made this chipset inappropriate for many servers.

440BX was the P6 silver bullet. While 440LX did all the hard work of introducing new features, 440BX showed off with a 100MHz front side bus that was 50 percent faster than earlier 66MHz models. In fact, it was the first motherboard speed boost since the introduction of Pentium, back in 1992. The result: A significant performance enhancement in virtually all operations. Today, Intel has a variety of 100MHz and even faster system chipsets for its various Pentium II-related motherboards.

Around mid-1999, Intel will replace 440BX with Camino (code-name) chipset, which will appear in Katmai-class Pentium II systems. The chipset boosts AGP from 2X to 4X (for 1024MBps data rates), and updates the IDE interface to ATA-66 (double that of current motherboards). More importantly, Camino will debut Rambus DRAM (RDRAM), a system RAM using a narrow and fast bus to shuttle data to and from the CPU. It is likely that Camino will support SDRAM as well. The chipset will run the front side bus at 100MHz and possibly 133MHz.

On the low end, Intel has already rolled out the 66MHz 440EX for its Celeron systems. A single-processor chipset, the 440EX only allows three PCI slots and a pair of SDRAM DIMMs. The limited expansion, combined with slower clock speed, make this low-cost chipset appropriate only for entry level systems. It's follow-on, the 440ZX, boosts Celeron motherboard speeds to 100MHz and should be available as early as the first quarter of 1999.

Intel is bolstering the server side of the market with a series of chipsets related to its Slot 2 introductions to come in 1999. The 440GX will essentially be a 440BX chipset for Slot 2, running at 100MHz and offering all the trimmings. However, it will double SDRAM support to 2GB—critical for servers. 450NX should get serious about three months later, when it adds 4-way and even 8-way SMP operation and a 4GB memory ceiling. There will also be built-in support for a 66MHz PCI bus, which is welcome for high-bandwidth network interfaces used by servers. However, SDRAM will not be supported.

In the second half of 1999, the code-name Carmel chipset should boost memory support to a staggering 8GB, while offering both 100 and 133MHz front side bus operation. The fast-and-wide PCI bus (66MHz fast, 64 bits wide) will be offered alongside the ATA-66 IDE interface and 4X AGP graphics bus. Carmel will be the server version of the Camino chipset.

While the Pentium II chipset market has been left almost completely to Intel, competition is emerging. Acer Labs introduced its Aladdin Pro II, which provides a competitive feature set to the 440BX chipset, including a 100MHz front side bus, ATA-33 interface, AGX 2X, and power management.

Inside the BIOS

BIOS stands for Basic Input/Output System, and is the lowest level of software operating on your PC. The BIOS is responsible for all the behind-the-scenes work, configuring hard disks and parallel ports, managing bus transfers, and providing support for various memory schemes and other technologies.

But if the BIOS is the great facilitator, it can also be the source of many mysterious problems. An aging or flaky BIOS can cause all sorts of crashes and incompatibilities. Worst of all, most users fail to consider the BIOS as a potential trouble source, so they waste days going through hardware, drivers, and applications before they even consider the invisible code running their PC.

The BIOS can also determine whether your PC can accept certain upgrades, such as CPUs, video-handling hardware, and other devices. For example, an older BIOS might not be able to recognize enhanced IDE hard disks using Large Block Addressing (LBA), limiting your ability to upgrade to a hard disk with capacities as high as 8GB.

There are two types of BIOS: flash and nonflash. Most systems sold over the past two or three years use a flash BIOS, which can be easily updated using software. In contrast, older nonflash BIOSs can be updated only if you physically replace the BIOS chip itself.

> **Tip:** If you have a flash BIOS, it's a good idea to periodically update it. BIOS makers and motherboard vendors frequently update BIOS code to add support for new device types and technologies and to squash bugs and performance problems in existing code. You can easily download BIOS update modules from a vendor's Web site and then follow the installation routine's instructions to update the system. Be sure to keep a backup of the original BIOS code handy and to back up all your data. Also, consider a BIOS upgrade if you are unable to successfully install a new peripheral on your PC—the BIOS might be the culprit.

How do you know what BIOS make and version you have? When your machine first boots up, the BIOS information will be displayed briefly at the top of the screen. But unless you have a photographic memory, you won't have time to write down the information before it disappears. You can hit the Pause key during the boot phase to give yourself more time to read these updates. Another option is to enter the BIOS utility. On most machines, you do this during the initial boot—before the Windows 95 splash screen appears—by pressing the Delete key or some other key or combination. Your system documentation will specify how to launch the BIOS utility.

Once inside, the text-based utility provides choices for managing settings and capabilities. You'll be able to navigate using the keyboard's cursor and the Esc and Enter keys. You'll also see the specific BIOS make and version. Remember that system makers often tailor BIOS code for their PCs, so the AMI BIOS in a Gateway system might be different from that found in another PC.

Inside the utility, you should see controls for the following:

- Basic device settings for keyboards, mice, and display adapters
- Boot device order, which can be set to start with a floppy drive or ignore floppy drives altogether
- Cache algorithm mode for both L1 and L2 CPU caches (choose from among write-through, write-back, and disabled)
- External port configuration, including parallel port settings for enhanced parallel port (EPP), extended capabilities port (ECP), or basic bidirectional port operation
- Hard disk configuration, including auto-detection of the hard disk layout, and settings for optimized IDE data transfers
- PCI bus management, including bus mastering settings and burst mode support
- Plug and Play management, including confirmation of a PnP-aware operating system, DMA (direct memory access) resources for ISA peripherals, and reserved memory spaces for legacy cards
- Power management settings, including CPU clock slowdown, and time-out settings for devices such as displays and hard disks
- Security features, including the ability to set a BIOS-stored password
- Time and date settings

> **Caution:** As most people know, Windows 95's password facility is a farce. Anyone can get around it by simply rebooting the machine in safe mode. For true password security, use the BIOS's facility. Just don't forget your password! Otherwise, you may have to reset the CMOS contents using the BIOS reset jumper located on the motherboard. You can find information about this feature in your documentation. If no such reset is available, you may have to remove the motherboard battery to wipe clean the BIOS settings. In either case, you must rebuild BIOS settings from scratch.

If there is one technology you need in your BIOS, it is Plug and Play (PnP). In order to enjoy the automated installation and configuration talents of Windows 95 and PnP hardware, the system BIOS must be compliant with the PnP specification. A PnP BIOS plays a critical role during system startup, identifying and enumerating resources for boot devices. In effect, the BIOS sets the stage for Windows 95's ability to recognize hardware devices.

A Look at the Motherboard Clock

You can thank the PC industry for turning the word *megahertz* into a household term. A PC's MHz rating comes from the system clock, which provides the cadence for activity in both the CPU and system bus. The clock is actually a chip of quartz crystal that resonates in response to an electric charge. By adjusting the electrical input, the frequency of the resonance can be controlled.

The motherboard clock is usually visible as a black rectangle of silicon mounted near the edge of the motherboard. Most motherboards feature a clock from Dallas Semiconductor.

Most motherboards today run at 60, 66, or 100MHz, with the CPU running internally at some multiple of that rate. Why not run the motherboard at the same 300MHz or higher rate found inside the CPU? Simple physics. The submicron transistors inside can be run at much higher speeds than the long trace wires and disparate components and connectors found on motherboards. Table 9.6 shows you how the speed of different CPUs relates to the motherboard clock.

Table 9.6. Motherboard speeds and processors.

Motherboard Speed	Clock Multiplier	Speeds in MHz
60MHz	1.5, 2, 2.5, 3*	90, 120, 150, 180*
66MHz	1.5, 2, 2.5, 3, 3.5, 4, 4.5, 5	100, 133, 166, 200, 233, 266, 300, 333
75MHz (Cyrix 6x86 only)	2, 2.5	150, 185
100MHz	3.5, 4, 4.5, 5	350, 400, 450, 500

*Very few 180MHz Pentium and Pentium Pro CPUs have been sold.

If you own a Pentium or newer machine, your motherboard is probably moving as fast as any CPU can take it. The actual speed of the motherboard and the CPU can be set using jumpers found along the edge of the circuit board. These jumpers are often marked with silk screening, but you are well advised to check the documentation to confirm which jumpers control speed.

Reviewing Backplane I/O

Turn your attention to the back of the system chassis, and you'll notice a series of connectors sticking out the back. Here you will find the serial and parallel ports, as well as connectors for keyboards and mice. Pentium systems sold over the last year also often include a pair of USB ports. All these connectors run directly from the motherboard and out the back.

Serial Ports

Most PCs have two serial port connectors: a compact 9-pin connector and a larger 25-pin connector. These ports are frequently used by external peripherals, including modems, personal scanners, PDA communications, and low-end tape backup.

The serial ports use the logical COM ports to talk to the system. COM1 and COM3 service one serial port connector, and COM2 and COM4 service the second connector. Because the higher COM port addresses can change, COM1 and COM2 are the best to use, effectively limiting the number of permanent serial-based peripherals to two—one on each port. Modern serial ports can move 1.5KBps of data.

Parallel Port

On most desktops, the parallel port is used to connect to printers. Able to move up to 8MBps of data, the parallel port is fast enough for most medium-strength data transfers, including print jobs and direct-connect networking provided by Traveling Software's LapLink Pro and Windows 95's Direct Cable Connect facility. Scanners, tape backup, portable CD-ROM drives, and external near-disk storage such as Jaz and Zip drives are also designed to use the parallel port.

Not all parallel ports are created equal. Newer systems feature an enhanced capabilities port (ECP) able to provide duplex operation and higher data rates. ECP-equipped PCs can cut down print times, but not all peripherals recognize the optimized signaling.

TROUBLESHOOTING

Parallel port pass-through adapters and some peripherals won't work with ECP-enabled ports. If your parallel port devices aren't working, try setting the port back to standard bidirectional Centronics operation. You'll lose some performance, but the more standard signaling may well fix the problem. To switch parallel port modes, access your system's BIOS at boot-up and look for the parallel port entry. You should be able to toggle among EPP, ECP, and Centronics modes. Set the BIOS to Centronics, save the results, and continue with the boot process. If the problem resolves itself, a signal mismatch was probably the culprit.

Universal Serial Bus

USB ports have been appearing on PC backplanes for over two years now, yet compliant peripherals are only now hitting the market. In the years to come, expect USB to take over many of the duties served by serial and parallel port buses. Most desktop PCs include two USB connectors placed at the level of the motherboard. These compact snap-in connectors serve as the physical starting point of a network of external peripherals. Up to 127 USB peripherals can be linked.

What runs off USB? Mice, keyboards, modems, scanners, joysticks, digital cameras, and even audio speakers can function off the Plug and Play bus. USB provides 12MBps data rate, nearly three times that of the parallel port, and sufficient for a wide variety of peripherals.

Note: If you have a USB-equipped system and you plan to add USB peripherals, consider upgrading your older system to Microsoft's Windows 98 operating system. Although individual vendors will provide add-on software to enable USB on existing systems, your best bet is to get your operating system patches from Microsoft itself. Windows 98 integrates USB functionality and provides a single target for all hardware vendors to shoot for. The use of these source OS drivers and updates can help reduce incompatibilities down the road.

Mouse and Keyboard Ports

Finally, nearly every desktop PC will include PS/2 mouse and keyboard ports. These circular connectors provide compact, dedicated plug-ins for the vast majority of mice and keyboards. The biggest advantage is that these connectors don't require the use of scarce COM port resources to operate these peripherals.

There are two types of circular connectors: DIN5 and MiniDIN6. The MiniDIN6 connectors are the most common today and are preferable because they are also found on notebook PCs. Mice and keyboards designed for the smaller MiniDIN6 connector can be used by notebooks without modification.

Down the road, expect these ports to get replaced by USB. Mice and keyboards can both benefit from the emerging bus standard.

On-Board Connectors

A variety of connectors located on the motherboard handle everything from power to disk drives to the lights on the front of the computer chassis.

Power Connectors

You'll find connectors inside the case, too. Most prominent among these are the power connectors, which accept the main leads coming from the power supply. You can easily spot the connector by the raised white plastic edging surrounding the pins.

IDE Bus Connectors

Another prominent feature is the IDE connectors. On most motherboards, two of these connectors are present: one for the primary IDE bus and another for the secondary IDE bus. The boot drive must be plugged into the primary adapter and set as the master device on that primary bus. For this reason, most users will have their hard disk plugged into the primary connector, while CD-ROM drives or other internal IDE devices occupy the secondary bus slot.

SCSI Connectors

Less common are integrated SCSI bus connectors. These sockets enable the installation of internal SCSI hard disks, CD-ROM drives, and other peripherals without requiring a separate add-in card. Because of the added expense of SCSI circuitry, these connectors are more likely to be found on specialized systems aimed at higher-end applications.

Floppy Drive

Near the IDE sockets, you'll find the single connector for the floppy disk drive. A standard cable plugs into the motherboard socket and usually includes a pair of connectors for driving two devices.

Assorted Lights and Things

Along the front edge of the motherboard, you might see a number of small connectors. These serve the PC's speaker, the hard disk and power indicator lights, and the front-panel power and reset buttons. Wires from the connectors run directly to these devices. However, you'll need to check your system's documentation to be sure which connectors go where.

Battery

This unassuming device plays a critical role in the smooth operation of your PC. The battery supplies the constant electrical charge needed to maintain CMOS settings and the PC's clock. There are several types of batteries, including nickel metal hydride, lithium ion, and alkaline cells. Newer PCs use lithium batteries, which generally last 5 to 10 years before needing replacement.

Buying a Motherboard

As you can tell from what's been covered so far in this chapter, there is much to think about when you're looking at a new system or motherboard. What's more, everything from the CPU to your hard disk and graphics card is affected by the motherboard they are plugged in to. The same Pentium MMX-200 CPU will run faster on some motherboards than others.

Regardless of whether you're buying a new system or upgrading an existing one, the same buying issues apply. There are four key areas to consider:

- Compatibility/reliability
- Upgradability
- Performance
- Price

Remember that any motherboard you purchase has got to work. It must be able to make use of the processor and peripherals you own or want to buy, and it must be compatible with your software. If you are upgrading, that motherboard must also fit in the case you own.

Physical Compatibility

Your motherboard must work with your existing hardware. A variety of system cases are available, ranging from slimline and standard desktops to vertically standing minitower and midtower models to large, full-tower PCs. You'll find a number of different mother-board configurations inside each of these.

The following are common motherboard sizes:

- AT: Fits older 486 and Pentium desktops and minitowers.
- Baby AT: Fits older 486 and Pentium desktops and minitowers.
- ATX and Baby ATX: Works with Pentium and faster PCs sold in the last year and a half. Basically a Baby AT board rotated 90 degrees.
- NLX: A compact motherboard specification for slimline desktops.

ATX: The Best Board for New Systems

Most newer Pentium and faster PCs conform to the recently adopted ATX form factors. The standard motherboard specification, minted by Intel, places the processor back and to the right, in proximity with the cooling airflow produced by the power supply fan. Meanwhile, RAM sockets and cache are presented in the clear, not wedged beneath drive bays as they often are on older systems.

If you're buying a new system, you should consider one with an ATX motherboard. These boards are space-efficient and well laid out. You'll find that the tasks of installing memory, cache, and CPUs are made easier by the logical placement of components. Most ATX motherboards also feature built-in USB connectors that go alongside the familiar ports for serial, parallel, mouse, and keyboard devices. ATX motherboards usually sport seven add-in card slots—three ISA, three PCI, and a single shared space able to accept either an ISA or a PCI card.

> **Note:** If you are buying an ATX motherboard to replace your old AT model, be sure to get a new power supply and case to go with it. ATX motherboards use orientation-specific ports demanding an ATX-compliant power supply to fit with it. Also, the position of ports on the motherboard will not match with an older case. The new ports eliminate the risk of mismatching connectors, a frequent cause of fried motherboards.

AT and Baby AT: Old Standards Begin to Wane

If you're upgrading an older system, you probably have a Baby AT or an AT-style motherboard. Like ATX motherboards, these models feature as many as seven or eight add-in card slots mounted directly in the motherboard. However, the CPU is often located front and center on the board, which blocks access for full-length add-in cards. If you plan on installing peripherals for videoconferencing or other applications demanding such space-hungry boards, an AT or Baby AT motherboard might not be suited to the task.

Slimline and Custom Motherboards: Big Trouble in Small Packages

Here's where things get ugly. Many manufacturers roll their own motherboard designs for their slimline systems. The reason is simple: The tightly tailored design enables them to build a full-featured PC in a small amount of space—but your upgrade prospects will suffer for it.

One distinguishing feature of slimline motherboards is a vertical riser card in the center of the motherboard. PCI or VL bus slots are mounted on one side of the vertical riser, and ISA slots are located on the other side. The total number of slots is usually limited to about five, but that number can be deceptive. CPUs, RAM SIMMs, and drive bays can all block some of the slots. In fact, the lowest slot facing the CPU is often unusable because the CPU fan and heatsink assembly block access.

These custom motherboards can pose a number of other problems. For one, power supplies are often custom-made, which means you probably won't be able to buy an inexpensive model from a power supply vendor. Your only choice might be to purchase a tailor-made unit from the original vendor—at a premium, of course. You'll also find that the graphics and video subsystems are soldered directly to the motherboard. Although these can almost always be disabled and upgraded using add-in card products, the ability to add memory or wavetable capability to the installed subsystem itself is generally limited. My advice: Always inspect the inside of these compact systems before you buy, if possible.

NLX: Small Made Smart

Slimline motherboards are troublesome, but Intel and others are seeking to fix matters with the newly minted NLX specification (see Figure 9.9). This motherboard spec puts the expansion riser on the right edge of the motherboard, while the RAM and processor sit on the far-left edge. This layout eliminates card blockage while allowing the motherboard to fit into the low-profile PCs favored by businesses.

FIGURE 9.9.

The new NLX form factor provides a standard mother- board layout for compact PCs. (Photo courtesy of Intel Corp.)

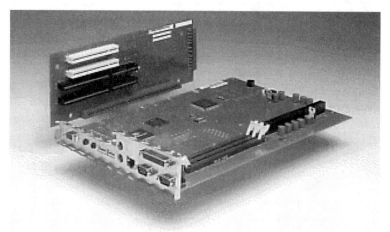

Other Compatibility Concerns

Even if the shoe fits, it might not be right for your kind of use. For example, any mother- board built before 1995 will lack Plug and Play capability. And if your BIOS lacks flash capability—that is, if it must be physically replaced in order to be updated—you might find yourself with a PC falling behind the curve. Here are some of the "gotchas":

- The system chipset lacks Plug and Play capability
- The system BIOS isn't flashable
- The motherboard uses 30-pin RAM sockets
- The system lacks PCI expansion slots, or the PCI slots lack bus-mastering facilities

If your existing PC matches any of these descriptions, you should beware of pouring too much money into upgrades. Before long, you might be forced to move to a new platform if you want access to the latest applications and hardware.

Motherboard Upgrades: Anyone for a Heart-Lung Transplant?

Of all the upgrades, replacing the motherboard is the most extreme. It is also the most expensive and most effective upgrade you can conduct. But you're talking hundreds of dollars, not to mention a lot of risky messing around with components and wires. So before you decide to embark on a motherboard upgrade, you should answer a few questions:

- Have you ruled out that a less-extreme procedure, such as a CPU, RAM, or graph- ics card upgrade, might deliver the capabilities you need?

- Have you considered purchasing a new system while keeping the monitor, keyboard, and mouse to cut down the purchase cost?
- Are you confident of your ability to successfully remove and replace the system's main board?

Buying a New System Versus a Motherboard

If the motherboard defines the character of a PC, what is the difference between buying a new motherboard and getting a new system? There are several key points.

When you buy a motherboard, you're keeping a lot of surrounding components. The result can be a nifty cost savings over a new system. Among the things you can keep are

- External devices: keyboard, mouse, monitor, and modem
- Internal disk drives: hard disk, floppy drive, and CD-ROM drive
- Add-in cards: graphics, sound, and network cards, among others
- System RAM
- Power supply

If most of these components still meet your needs, a motherboard upgrade might be a very good idea. You can move up to a new level of CPU performance and take advantage of the latest chipset innovations. You will also be able to enjoy the benefits of the PCI bus, though you'll have to pony up for a graphics card to replace that aged VL bus model.

When does buying a new system make sense? Usually, the break point is decided by the peripherals. If the new motherboard requires you to replace several drives or cards in order to get reasonable features and performance, you should consider a new system instead. Of course, you'll need to do something with your old PC, whether pressing it into limited service elsewhere in your home or office, or donating it to a charity, school, or church. (See Appendix A, "What to Do with a PC That's Beyond Recovery," for ideas.)

When does a new system make sense? Table 9.7 helps you decide when buying a new system makes sense.

Table 9.7. When a new system makes sense.

Old Motherboard	New Motherboard	The Problem
VL bus slots	PCI and AGP bus slots	You must replace all VL bus add-in cards.
30-pin SIMMs	72-pin SIMMs or 168-pin DIMMs	You must replace all system memory.
Basic IDE	Enhanced IDE (ATA-33)	You might need to replace the hard disk drive with an EIDE unit.

Making the Upgrade

So you've decided you want to take the plunge. Where do you start? Well, first, make sure all your data is safely backed up onto a medium you know you can access elsewhere. If things go bad with a motherboard upgrade, the situation can be dire. Remember the golden rule of upgrades: Plan for the worst and hope for the best.

Getting Prepared

Once you have your motherboard and all the tools you'll need to make the transfer, it's time to get started. The following steps will help you through the process, but nothing can take the place of good documentation. Make sure you review the new motherboard's documentation before you start, and keep it handy throughout the process. You'll need to refer to it in order to properly connect power and data cables and jumper settings.

First, you need to take stock of your current system configuration and prepare Windows 95 for the coming of the new one. To print a detailed record of your system configuration, Windows 95 users can turn to the Device Manager.

1. Click Start, Settings, Control Panel and open the System icon.
2. Click the Device Manager tab and click the Print button.
3. To output a complete report, click the All devices and system summary radio button. For a more concise summary, click the System summary radio button.
4. Click the OK button to print the configuration.

While Windows 98 users can also print their configuration from the Device Manager, they have an even better facility available to them in the form of the System Information utility. To use this, do the following:

1. Click Start, Settings, Applications, Accessories, System Tools and select the System Information item.
2. In the right-hand pane, click the + symbols next to the hardware, software, and resources items to see specific subcategories.
3. To view information on a category (for example, IRQ settings, shown in Figure 9.10) click the desired item. The system data will be displayed in the left-hand pane.
4. To produce a complete report of system settings, click File, Export. In the dialog box, provide a name for the text-formatted file and, if desired, point the file to a specific directory or drive.
5. Save the information to floppy, or print out the resulting files for reference. Just be warned, the output can run well over 100 pages!

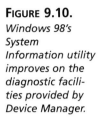

FIGURE 9.10.

Windows 98's System Information utility improves on the diagnostic facilities provided by Device Manager.

Next you'll want to remove as many components as possible from the Device Manager. This is quite easy to do. From the Device Manager sheet, click the + symbol next to each listed system item to expose the specific installed devices. Click the appropriate devices and click the Remove button for each one in turn. The following devices should be removed just before shutting down Windows for the last time:

- Sound card
- Modem
- Network card
- Any multimedia cards or devices

Just prior to shutting down for the last time, you should also change the graphics card setting so that Windows' default VGA drivers are being used. This will ensure that, no matter what graphics board you start out with in your new motherboard, Windows will be able to put graphics up on the screen.

Out with the Old

First you need to remove the existing motherboard. This is nearly as complicated as putting the new one in, so plan ahead. Use masking tape to label wires as you unplug them. That way, you can tell the difference between two identical wires leading to the hard disk activity and power-on lights. You'll thank yourself later, when you're trying to connect the new board.

Also, you'll want to have an anti-static mat and wrist strap handy to ground yourself. Just touching the PC's chassis won't ground out any accumulated static charge if the power supply is unplugged (which it should be for this operation).

1. Turn off the PC, unplug the power cord from the power supply, and remove the case.

2. Remove all external connectors, including those for the monitor, modem, keyboard, mouse, and any other external devices.

3. Unscrew the Phillips screws holding the cards in place. Then pull out the cards one by one, applying firm but gentle upward force while grasping the card by the top at each end. Put all the add-in card screws in a single place—you'll need them later. If a card seems stuck, try rocking it gently along the axis of the slot.

4. If you plan on using the existing RAM in your new motherboard, you can pull out the SIMMs or DIMMs now. For SIMMs, press the silver or plastic tabs at each end back and away from the SIMMs, then nudge the module forward with your thumb to clear the SIMMs. For DIMMs, pull the two locking tabs at each end away from the module. Make sure to place the memory in a static-free place.

> **Caution:** If your system uses SIMMs, make sure you label them to remember the original layout. Many motherboards require you to mate SIMM pairs of the same size and speed. If you had a mix of SIMMs in your old machine, you should try to install them in the new machine in the same order.

5. Find the floppy and IDE connectors on the motherboard, and find the corner of each that has the pin 1 indicator. The cables should have a red line on the pin 1 edge. If they do not, mark the appropriate edge with a felt tip marker. This enables you to correctly plug the cables in later.

6. Now unplug the IDE and floppy disk cables from the motherboard sockets, but leave them connected to the drives. Again, use firm but gentle force to ease out the connectors.

7. For AT-style motherboards, find the serial and parallel connectors. Unplug their cables from their motherboard sockets, again labeling the cables as appropriate. Unscrew the connectors themselves from the chassis's backplane. ATX motherboards have these connectors directly attached, so you won't need to worry about this step.

8. Follow the wires from the power supply to the white connector near the edge of the board. For AT-style motherboards, there should be a pair of six-wire connectors inserted edge to edge. The inside two wires of each set are black. Be sure when you re-insert these that the inside two wires are black. ATX motherboards only use a single connector.

9. If you intend to use your existing CPU in the new motherboard, you'll want to remove the CPU now. In most cases, you simply lift the Zero Insertion Force (ZIF)

lever sitting next to most Pentium and even 486 CPUs and lift the CPU clear. If your old system lacks a ZIF lever, you'll need a chip pulling tool to remove the CPU.

10. Finally, you'll need to disconnect the wires for your power and disk activity lights, on/off and reset switches, and other sundry front bezel things. The function of each wire might be noted on the motherboard. If it isn't, check the documentation. You should make a point of identifying each wire with a masking-tape label before removing it from its motherboard socket.

11. If you're lucky, you can start unfastening the motherboard. Unfortunately, most systems have a drive bay or two that must be cleared out first. Look the system over carefully and determine which drive bay or bays might need to be removed to allow egress. Use a Phillips screwdriver to remove the bays from the chassis.

12. Most motherboards are attached to the case bottom by a combination of screws and plastic fasteners. Remove all the screws and then work the motherboard to unslot the fasteners to free the motherboard. Once the motherboard is free, you'll want to keep the fasteners handy to use them for the new motherboard. When the motherboard is clear, set it to the side.

In with the New

You're halfway there. If you've managed to extricate the original motherboard, much of the hard work is done. That said, a few perils lie ahead. Among them: Making sure that the motherboard has sufficient support, and avoiding a botched power cable installation that can fry the new motherboard.

You need to be observant as you install. Check and double-check to make sure you're lining up the pin 1s of connectors, modules, and wires. When in doubt, check the documentation and look it over again. We'll start with getting the new motherboard installed.

> **Note:** If you are upgrading from an old AT-style motherboard to one built on the ATX form factor, you'll find that you must purchase a new power supply and case to handle the different connectors and back port alignments. Even if you are going from one ATX to another ATX board, you may still have to replace the power supply. ATX 2.0 motherboards use a different power connector from ATX 2.1 models. Make sure you get these details straight so you have everything you need to make things work.

1. You might have to tape those pesky cables and wires to the edge of the case to keep them out of the way. Place the motherboard carefully into the waiting chassis, being careful to align the keyboard port with the matching hole in the case. You should find that several holes in the motherboard align with those on the bottom of the case. Insert the plastic fasteners and screw down the case. You might need to provide paper or felt "washers" to be placed around the screw so the metal screw head doesn't come into contact with any circuitry.

2. What was it that the scarecrow used to sing? "If I only had a brain?" Well, it's time to give your new purchase one. For all non-Pentium II motherboards, locate the large CPU socket assembly and find the pin 1 corner (there should be a silk-screened dot on the assembly, and the corner hole will be missing). Lift the plastic ZIF lever located next to the socket. Line up the beveled edge of the CPU with pin 1 of the socket, and lower it gently into the holes. Don't force the pins. When the CPU is seated, gently lower the ZIF lever to secure the CPU and make positive contact (see Figure 9.11).

Note: In the case of Pentium II systems, the CPU actually installs vertically into the Slot 1 connector, much in the way you might plug in an add-in card.

FIGURE 9.11.

Easy does it: You need to properly align the CPU to make it fit in the socket. (Figure courtesy of Intel Corp.)

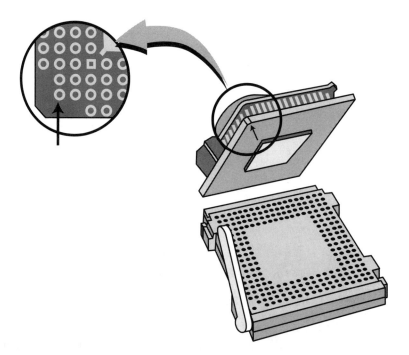

3. Next, attach the fan to the CPU as indicated by the fan's documentation. In some cases, you will need to apply a layer of thermal adhesive to ensure good contact. Plug the power wire into one of the free wires coming from the power supply.

4. If you are using your old memory, find the SIMMs or DIMMs you set aside and plug them into the open sockets on the motherboard. If you've purchased new RAM, install that as well. For SIMMs, align pin 1 of the module (the side with the bottom corner cut out) with pin 1 of the socket (see Figure 9.12). Lower the edge into the socket at a 45-degree angle, and rotate it back until the tabs click into place. For DIMMs, align the key notch with the matching key in the connector.

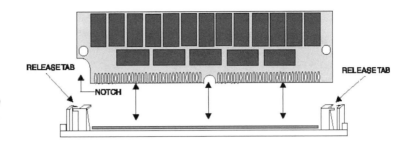

FIGURE 9.12.

Both RAM and cache modules plug/snap easily into standard tabbed sockets on the motherboard. (Figure courtesy of Micronics Corp.)

5. The most dangerous part is reconnecting the main power cables to the main board. Botch this, and you'll be serving up motherboard flambé. If you are using an AT-style motherboard, make sure the twin power cables are aligned so that the black wires are matched together in the middle. For ATX motherboards, the keyed single connector should help you avoid any surprises. Plug the cables into their respective connectors.

6. In most cases, you won't have to attach the serial and parallel port assemblies to the case—ATX motherboards build these in. However, if you need to connect them, you need to check your system documentation to determine which uses COM1 and which uses COM2. You'll want to make sure that the logical connections comply with any labeling present on the back of the PC. Once the assemblies are screwed in, plug in the connectors that came with the new board, being careful to identify pin 1 on the cables with pin 1 on the ports. Usually, the red wire orients with the connector's pin 1.

7. You'll need to check the motherboard documentation to make sure that you get all the lights and buttons on the front of the case properly connected to the sockets along the front edge of the motherboard.

8. Plug the hard disk cable into the primary IDE interface, aligning the red wire with pin 1. Do the same with the CD-ROM drive, but plug it into the secondary IDE interface. Don't mix these up, or the system will fail to recognize the hard disk as a boot device. Finally, plug the floppy cable into the dedicated floppy drive connector, being sure to align to pin 1. Attach power leads to each of these devices.

9. Reacquaint your PC with those add-in cards. If you've gone from a VL bus motherboard to PCI, you no doubt will have one or two new cards to install into the case. Secure the cards with a Phillips screwdriver.

10. Reattach the monitor, modem, keyboard, and mouse. Plug the power cord into the power supply. Make a final preflight check. Cards should be firmly seated and secure, and cables and wires should fit snugly and be properly aligned. Turn on the monitor now so that it is partially warmed up prior to bootup.

11. Take a deep breath, look sharp, and flip the switch. Note whether the CPU fan is running. If it isn't, you need to shut down and check the connection. Assuming

that the fan is OK, watch the monitor like a hawk. Observe the initial BIOS readings, POST results, and RAM count. You should also hear the single beep from a normal boot—provided that the internal speaker was properly set up. You should also hear the floppy drive being accessed.

> **Tip:** You can take control of the boot process by pressing the F8 key to invoke manual confirmation of each step. This will enable you to track the boot phase step by step, and to tell exactly where problems occur, should bad things happen.

12. Assuming all goes well, you might spend two or three reboots getting Windows to sort out the new hardware and altered settings. This is normal. But keep a close eye out for intractable problems. They might indicate a problem with your installation.

Upgrade Troubles

So what happens if things don't go smoothly? First, don't panic. There's probably a simple fix that can bring the newly upgraded system back to life.

Check the Hard Disk

If the machine fails to start, the hard disk might be the problem. Try the following:

1. Make sure the drive cables are firmly set and that power is getting to the drive. Look for any evidence of drive activity during the boot process.

2. Check that the hard drive is plugged into the primary IDE connector and that the cable orientation is correct. Also check that jumpers on the drive are correctly set to master, not slave.

3. If you're still stuck, try removing all other peripherals from the IDE channels to isolate the hard disk.

4. Still stuck? Enter the BIOS setup program during boot-up. Check the IDE hard disk settings and select automatic hard disk recognition.

5. If this doesn't work, the BIOS might be confused. You should manually enter the cylinder configuration data for your hard disk.

Card Troubles

Another possible problem comes from the add-in cards, which might conflict with the operating system or the state of the new motherboard's resources. If you suspect that peripherals are the issue, it's time to strip down the PC to isolate the problem. Do the following:

1. Shut down the PC and unplug the power.

2. Unplug any unnecessary external devices, including modems, scanners, joysticks, and printers.

3. Remove any unnecessary internal cards and devices. Sound boards, LAN cards, I/O cards, even CD-ROM drives should all be unplugged.

4. Start Windows and follow the start-up process. The operating system should recognize the lack of devices and adjust to match.

5. Reboot the system as soon as it's done changing settings, observing behavior carefully. If the problem is resolved, you can now start adding components one by one.

6. Install each device singly, allowing the operating system to configure it and run successfully. Repeat until all devices are successfully installed or the problem recurs.

7. If the problem recurs after a specific piece of hardware has been installed, you can focus on it as the likely culprit. For many devices, new driver software might do the trick. Likewise, a quick BIOS update for flash-type BIOSs is a good idea as well.

Diagnosing/Troubleshooting

What if your current motherboard is in trouble? Unfortunately, motherboards aren't terribly easy to repair. Age and handling can cause cracks in the motherboard itself, disrupting trace wires and rendering the board worthless. Among the biggest problems are

- Overheating
- Power surges
- A dead CMOS battery

Overheating

Overheating is a cumulative problem. The stress of motherboard components heating and cooling can create a great deal of wear as the material expands and contracts. Eventually, cracks can result in trace wires and the motherboard material. So-called "chip creep" can also result, in which slight movements in the motherboard gradually push electrical leads out of contact.

More than other problems, overheating can seem like a mystery. A system might boot normally in the morning, only to suffer mysterious crashes, memory failures, and other maladies later in the day. Or a system that boots fine in the morning might have trouble rebooting after several hours of operation.

Generally, heat problems will come from the power supply, from the CPU, or from problems with airflow through the chassis. The upshot is that if you replace a damaged motherboard but fail to address the ongoing thermal problem, your new investment might be at risk. (See Chapter 4, "Troubleshooting and Repair Strategies," for more information.)

Power Surges

Funny thing about power surges: You often know when they occur. In this respect, they are among the easiest motherboard problems to identify. But that's small comfort when you consider that even a mild over-voltage can destroy sensitive electronics. Here are some common sources of power surges:

- Catastrophic power surges from lightning strikes or similar events
- Power over-voltages from external peripherals or phone lines
- Intermittent problems from power sags or mild over-voltage

In most cases, a UPS or surge protector can help avoid damage to the motherboard.

Battery Problems

A common—and thankfully repairable—problem is with the motherboard's built-in battery. The CMOS battery ensures that critical configuration data is available to the BIOS at all times. Even if a system is shut down for months or years, the tiny motherboard-based battery ensures that the PC will boot properly.

But batteries die eventually, and often within five years, you might find troubling symptoms cropping up. For example, if the PC can no longer keep the proper date after being shut down, a dead battery is probably the culprit.

You can buy PC batteries from any computer store. Your first task is to determine exactly the type of battery you have and to find one to replace it. There are generally three types of motherboard batteries:

- Alkaline
- Nickel metal hydride
- Lithium

Of these, lithium lasts the longest and is common on PCs sold within the last two years. If you buy a new motherboard, a lithium CMOS battery is a good idea.

Summary

The motherboard is where it all starts and ends. Most people worry about processor speeds, RAM, and hard disks when buying a new PC, but they should pay more attention to the motherboard. These components are the *terra firma* of PCs—the foundation making performance possible.

Of all the components on motherboards, the most important is the system chipset, or PCIset, to use Intel parlance. This set of one to four chips orchestrates every data transaction occurring inside the PC. Critical features such as direct memory access (DMA), PCI bus concurrency, power management, and enhanced memory support all come from the chipset.

The upgrade picture is improving as well. Standard motherboard form factors are easing the travesty of blocked add-in card slots and buried RAM SIMMs. Still, you'll need to be very, very careful when choosing a motherboard. Keep the old carpenter's axiom in mind: Measure twice; cut once.

PART III

Basic Data Storage

Control Freaks: IDE and SCSI Controllers

Controllers work like traffic cops, managing the interface between peripheral devices (hard disks, CD-ROM drives, and more) and the PC system itself. When your CPU requests data from a disk, for example, the disk controller handles the transfer of the request to the drive and the passing back of the retrieved information over the PC's bus.

As with all PC technology, controllers have undergone significant enhancements over the years. The original PC controllers were all hardware boards inserted into slots on the motherboard and connected to disk drives via a ribbon cable. Over time, disk drive manufacturers advanced the electronics aboard the drives, allowing the drives to do more of the data management themselves, turning the controller into a fairly simple mechanism (a traffic cop with an easy job). New controllers no longer always require a large hardware board to hold the circuitry.

Manufacturers have begun integrating these simple controllers directly into the motherboard, and you'll find connectors for disk drives on the motherboards of almost all new PCs. Controller cards still exist on older machines, though, and they remain useful for adding new drives and adding other devices to new ones—they will be discussed later in this chapter.

Controllers come in several different standards and use different protocols for managing the disk drive data. The original controllers had interfaces called ST-506 and ESDI, but today these are found only on archaic PC systems. Faster, more efficient standards have stormed onto the scene. Now the two main controller types for PCs are called IDE and SCSI. This discussion will be limited to these two.

How Controllers Work

As the primary conduit between your PC's motherboard and disk drives, the controller plays a critical role in overall system performance. As programs get larger and data files grow, the need for prompt and reliable transfers between your system and your disk drives becomes critical. That's why a controller upgrade may be an important consideration for users trying to get the most out of fast hard disks, CD-ROM drives, and swift magnetic removable media drives.

Physically, a controller consists of a controller chip or chips, supporting silicon, and a standard connector for hooking to drives and devices. The controller chip provides the intelligence needed to communicate with various drives and to handle transactions without constantly haranguing the CPU for resources and permissions. The supporting logic does things like provide a ready store for holding bits so that they can be processed without risk of losing data.

As drives become faster, and more devices are able to hang off the controller, this intelligence becomes a critical factor. Smart controllers can set up transactions more quickly and with less disruption to other system activities; and once transactions are started, they can operate without the intervention of the CPU. Data can therefore flow freely from the hard disk into main system memory even while the CPU is freed up to handle a spreadsheet recalculation, for example.

Perhaps the most important transfer feature—particularly for multimedia tasks like video and audio playback—is called bursting, a transaction involving a long string of bits arrayed contiguously on the media. Because all the bits are located in the same place, the CPU and controller don't have to send specific addresses for every bit to be transferred. Rather, the address for the first bit and the last bit can be issued, and then the entire range is transferred over the interface. When you hear the maximum data rates for an IDE or SCSI interface, that rate given is almost always the burst data rate.

Of course, your hard disk or other devices need to be able to hook to the controller both physically (via a connector and cable) and logically (via a protocol). For those wanting to upgrade hard disks, this can pose a challenge, since the controller built into your system may not support the latest technologies. The result: That new hard drive may either not work at all, or may only work at the lower performance level of the existing controller.

SCSI Versus IDE

SCSI stands for Small Computer System Interface, and IDE stands for Integrated Drive Electronics. Understanding them is becoming more confusing as the two standards evolved.

SCSI's second iteration was called Fast SCSI (or SCSI-2). It provided support for several device types beyond hard disks and increased the data transfer potential. Recently, a newer version called Ultra SCSI (SCSI-3) was released, improving data transfer speeds even more. A variation on both Fast SCSI and Ultra SCSI increases the data path (and data transfer rates) from 8 to 16 bits. These are referred to as FastWide SCSI and UltraWide SCSI.

The original IDE specification evolved from the hard drives aboard IBM's PC AT, the first 16-bit personal computer. The name Integrated Drive Electronics is as literal as they come. These drives put most of the controller electronics in the drive housing itself rather than on a separate card. The resulting design cut costs, helping make it an enduring standard on the PC.

Like SCSI, the IDE standard improved over time. The newest and most popular version is called ATA-66 (Enhanced Integrated Drive Electronics). EIDE allows for primary and secondary controllers, connecting up to four devices to one controller set. It also adds support for devices other than hard disks.

See Table 10.1 for a breakdown of controller specifications.

Table 10.1. Controller specs.

Controller Type	Number of Devices Supported	Types of Devices Supported	Data Transfer Speeds
IDE	2	Only hard disks	Less than 10MBps
Enhanced IDE	4 with primary and secondary controllers	Hard disks, CD-ROM drives, tape drives, optical drives	11.1 to 16.6MBps
ATA-33	4 with primary and secondary controllers	Hard disks, CD-ROM drives, tape drives, optical drives	11.1 to 33MBps
ATA-66	4 with primary and secondary controllers	Hard disks, CD-ROM drives, tape drives, optical drives	11.1 to 66MBps
SCSI-1	8 (one of which is the host adapter card)	Hard disks, CD-ROM drives, scanners	5MBps
SCSI-2	8 (one of which is the host adapter card)	Hard disks, CD-ROM drives, scanners, removable drives, optical drives	10MBps (Fast SCSI); 20MBps (FastWide SCSI)
SCSI-3	32 (one of which is the host adapter card)	Hard disks, CD-ROM drives, scanners, removable drives, optical drives (Ultra2 SCSI)	20MBps (Ultra SCSI); 40MBps (UltraWide SCSI); 80MBps

Tip: Never consider a controller purchase or upgrade on its own. Always lump disk drives (or other peripherals) in the equation with controllers before deciding what you need. First, read Chapter 11, "Taking Hard Disks for a Spin," and determine whether you want to purchase an IDE or SCSI hard drive. Then check which type of controller you currently have in your system. Depending on your circumstances, you might not even need to upgrade your controller.

Note: Most people think of SCSI and particularly EIDE as disk drive controllers, but both standards now support control of other device types. SCSI hosts many devices and is popular for scanners and CD-ROM drives as well as disk drives. EIDE also now supports several types of devices, including CD-ROM, CD-Recordable, and tape drives in addition to hard disks.

The are some general differences you should think about when making upgrade decisions. The following is a brief look at the pros and cons of both types of controllers.

IDE: Pros and Cons

The overall technology called IDE encompasses a variety of specifications, ranging from the original IDE standard to the latest (and fastest) ATA-66 scheme. Developed from the original architecture found on IBM's first PC, IDE was closely matched to the BIOS specifications found in most systems. As a result, IDE devices have been reasonably easy to install. In fact, the vast majority of new systems come with IDE controllers already in place on the motherboard, requiring no installation at all. They are also cheaper than SCSI controller installations.

For years, IDE drives have lagged their SCSI counterparts in performance. Where SCSI-3 was pushing hard drive data rates from 40 to 80 megabytes per second (MBps), many IDE drives were still poking along at 16.6MBps. But recently, advances have helped low-cost IDE drives close the gap. Popular ATA-33 drives and controllers can push 33MBps, while a new specification—called ATA-66—is pushing that limit to 66MBps.

Despite the transfer rate parity, SCSI maintains its edge as a more efficient interface. The SCSI bus is able to handle data requests out of order, for example, so the system can prioritize transfers according to what is immediately at hand. In addition, multiple devices can coexist on an SCSI bus much more efficiently than on any IDE interface. Drives are then assured quick response times and adequate throughput, even when both a CD-ROM and hard disk drive are working simultaneously.

Recognition of large-capacity drives has also been a problem. Until a couple of years ago, IDE drives were limited in capacity to 528MB. If you owned a larger IDE drive, you had to partition the drive in order to trick the controller and the operating system into thinking it was two or more drives. Today, extensions to the PC's BIOS code have largely fixed this problem. SCSI products, by contrast, never faced the drive size limits imposed by the PC BIOS because SCSI controllers use their own BIOS to address transactions with all devices on the bus.

SCSI: Pros and Cons

SCSI got its start in the Macintosh world, where it flourished. SCSI host adapters enable you to chain several different types of devices together (hard disks, scanners, printers, and so on), running them all off a single adapter card. An SCSI-2 host adapter, for example, supplies eight different device addresses, one of which the adapter itself must use. As a result, up to seven independent devices may share one controller.

The flexibility of SCSI goes further still. Sophisticated bridge controllers can actually connect seven devices per device address. That means you can link up to 49 devices from a single SCSI adapter! Compare that to the four-device limit of EIDE controllers.

SCSI's problem is that it is difficult. SCSI controllers usually require additional setup for assigning SCSI ID numbers to devices, properly configuring termination, and to get the PC to recognize the entire chain of devices. More importantly, vendors typically charge $100 to $200 more for SCSI controllers and devices than their IDE counterparts. When an EIDE 3GB hard disk sells for just $299, that premium becomes more than the mainstream market will accept.

Purchase Decisions

In terms of buying advice, a good start is determining whether you're interested only in upgrading your hard disk drive or adding several new devices to your PC. Despite SCSI's superior technical specifications, real-world hard drive speed tests generally don't show SCSI performance to be so much better that it makes up for the added cost and hassle of SCSI format. If you don't need the biggest or fastest hard drive, go for EIDE. But if you plan to add several new devices, such as scanners and CD-ROM drives, or if you need a very large, fast drive, consider SCSI.

When should you buy SCSI? If you perform the kind of operations described in the following list, you might consider going with an SCSI controller for your hard disks and other peripherals:

- Do you anticipate adding more than one new hard disk, CD-ROM drive, CD-Recordable, or scanner to your existing system in the next three years?
- Do you aggressively multitask disk-intensive applications, such as database software or multimedia titles and tools?
- Do you want to copy CD-to-CD or handle other high bandwidth recording tasks?
- Do you plan to use your PC to capture full-motion video or audio?
- Will you incorporate one or more external hard drive, CD-ROM, scanner, or other device?

Of course, almost all motherboards support IDE. But what if you want to upgrade your IDE controller to a faster ATA-33 add-in card. Who should consider this kind of purchase? Again, if the following items describe your approach to computing, an EIDE controller might be your best bet. Keep in mind that EIDE serves the majority of desktop users very well.

- Are you unwilling to pay a premium for hard disks, CD-ROM drives, and other peripherals?
- Do you generally run classic productivity applications (word processing, spreadsheets, light desktop publishing) and titles?
- Do you plan to add two or fewer storage devices in the next two to three years?

Of course, the decision isn't entirely cut and dry. Ultimately, if you place a lot of value on maximum flexibility, performance, and upgradability, an SCSI controller is your best bet. For the majority of users, however, one of the new generation of EIDE controllers should do just fine—and save you a few bucks in the process.

Purists have argued the benefits of SCSI over IDE and EIDE for years, but there's a new variable to factor in—Universal Serial Bus (USB). Supported under Windows 98 (and a fixture on Apple's iMac), USB is taking over tasks served by those creaky old serial and parallel ports on the back of your PC. But we're also seeing USB versions of external disk drives—such as 120MB SuperDisk removable cartridge drive—and scanners.

Can you expect to throw out your SCSI card in favor of USB-based products? Not likely. For one thing, USB only pushes 12Mbps, well below the 40MBps of most SCSI controllers and the 33MBps of ATA-33–type IDE controllers. Anything more than a large-format floppy disk-type drive (think Iomega Zip) would simply choke on the narrow bus, particularly if multiple devices are hanging off it.

A more likely successor to SCSI and IDE is the IEEE 1394 specification, also called FireWire. This plug and play bus uses a fast-and-narrow connection to provide data rates of 400Mbps, 800Mbps, and later higher data rates to various devices. Like SCSI, FireWire can handle more than just disk drives—everything from multimedia devices to consumer electronics will be able to connect to your PC over this intelligent connection.

So why aren't FireWire devices out now? Well, they are. Sony makes a digital video camera with a FireWire port, and Adaptec sells PCI add-in cards that let you add a FireWire port to your PC. But Intel has put off introducing the technology on its motherboards due to its high cost. In fact, the new ATA-66 IDE specification was launched only after it became apparent that mainstream acceptance of FireWire was still a few years out. Expect FireWire to grow in importance as a mainstream PC bus around 2002.

Controllers On-Board: Finding Out What You Have

Most PCs have installed IDE or EIDE controllers, but how can you tell what you have? Fortunately, it's pretty easy once you pop the top off your system.

SCSI controllers generally inhabit hardware boards, which you will find in the PC's ISA or PCI slots (see Figure 10.1). Typically, these boards contain a number of chips, as well as a ribbon cable connector along the top edge or interior vertical edge of the board.

Look at the port sticking out the back of your PC. The dead giveaway for an SCSI adapter will be the single long, thin port (a Centronics latch style or a shielded D style connector or the 68-pin UltraWide connector). This indicates that this is an SCSI controller, because EIDE controllers don't have external connectors.

Some older computers did supply on-board SCSI controllers, but until recently almost all PC manufacturers lacked this feature. In the past year, however, there has been a resurgence of SCSI controllers built into the motherboard. Asus, Supermicro, Tyan, and even Intel now offer UltraWide and sometimes Ultra2 SCSI controllers on the motherboard.

FIGURE 10.1.

Most SCSI-equipped systems use a separate add-in card, such as the PCI-based Adaptec 3940 shown here. The fast PCI bus provides key data-handling features that enhance SCSI's multitasking capabilities. (Photo courtesy of Adaptec, Inc.)

Most newer PCs feature an on-board IDE or EIDE controller. These controllers are pretty easy to distinguish from one another. Examine the motherboard, looking for connectors laid down on the motherboard itself (you might have to push some cabling aside and use a flashlight to get a good look). You should be able to find and read labels next to the connectors that indicate IDE, Enhanced IDE, or ATA-33. Otherwise, look for a 40-pin connector sticking up from the board (20×2) with a "1" indicating pin 1 in one corner. An older Pentium-based or 486-based machine might have the EIDE or IDE interface on a circuit card occupying one of the expansion slots.

If you find only one 40-pin connector on the motherboard, you have an older IDE controller unable to support CD-ROM drives, new, larger hard disks, or EIDE-compliant media such as Iomega Zip and Jaz drives. You'll probably also notice a separate port labeled "floppy," which controls the floppy disk drive.

If you see two ports labeled "primary" and "secondary," the system is equipped with a modern EIDE controller—but whether it is ATA-33–compliant is another question. Check your motherboard documentation to see what type of controller you have. If you have an older enhanced IDE controller, and want to install a fast, ATA-33 or ATA-66 hard disk; you'll have to add a separate add-in card or upgrade the motherboard.

Note: SCSI enjoys one key advantage over EIDE: It allows for external peripherals. EIDE lacks the more robust grounding and electrical specifications required for external device operation—that's one of the reasons these devices are less expensive than their SCSI counterparts. If you want an external CD-ROM or other drive, or if your current PC is running out of drive bay space, SCSI might be your only choice—this by virtue of the fact that the IDE (and EIDE) standards allow for a maximum of only 18 inches of cabling. SCSI allows a much more flexible six feet.

Managing IDE Resources

Older IDE controllers are very limited in their capabilities. They can drive only two devices, both of which must be hard disk drives. You can't run a CD-ROM or other drive from a standard IDE connection. What's more, IDE throughput—the speed at which data passes through the bus—is limited to 10 megabytes per second. That was plenty for disk drives three or four years ago, but it's woefully inadequate today.

EIDE controllers are much improved over the older IDE type. For one thing, they now allow operation of a variety of internal devices, including hard disks, CD-ROM drives, CD-Recordables, removable media drives, and even new DVD-ROM drives. Performance has improved as well. ATA-33–compliant drives can push 33MBps, while the emerging class of ATA-66 devices double that figure.

Multiple-device support is added as well. On the typical PC with two EIDE channels, each channel (one primary and one secondary) supports up to two devices. EIDE maintains a rigid pecking order, designating one device on each channel as the *master* and the other as the slave. That means a system with a total of four EIDE devices will have two master drives (one on the primary channel, the other on the secondary channel) and two slave drives.

Each device will have jumper settings (referenced in the documentation) that configure the device to operation as either a master or a slave. When you're using more than one EIDE device, the primary channel's master device will be the boot drive of your PC.

If you set the device jumpers incorrectly, you will have difficulty booting or accessing the drives. Be sure the drive you want to boot from—that is, the one containing your operating system and start-up files—is correctly set as the primary channel's master device.

Tip: Always keep the plastic jumper connector on your device, even if the master or slave setting you're using doesn't require the plastic jumper. Just hang the plastic nub off one pin, leaving the other end unattached to a pin. That way, you won't lose it. You might need it if you change the configuration of your PC in the future.

Multiple IDE Drives

For both IDE and EIDE controllers, setting devices as master or slave is done on the devices themselves through jumper settings. The cabling on IDE controllers is fairly simple. One end of the ribbon cable connects to the 40-pin controller interface, and the two drives plug into the two other 40-pin connectors that split off further up the cable. Unlike SCSI, no terminators need be set on these IDE devices, because a termination circuit is built into the drives themselves.

Unfortunately, variations in the IDE standard over the years mean there is no guarantee that any two IDE drives will run successfully on the same IDE controller. This is particularly true if the drives come from different manufacturers. For this reason, you should try to match any hard drives intended to run off the same IDE port.

TROUBLESHOOTING

If a drive isn't recognized by your PC, first check the jumper settings to make sure that one drive is set to master and the other to slave (see Figure 10.2). Then double-check for snug fit and proper placement for all the cabling (ribbon cable and power adapter cable). If you still have difficulty, consult with the drive manufacturer's technical support.

FIGURE 10.2.

You need to properly set jumpers on EIDE hard disks to enable them as boot devices. Otherwise, your system won't see the drive at startup. (Image courtesy of Seagate)

• • / • •	Drive is Master, no Slave drive present
• • / • •	Drive is Master, Seagate Slave drive present
• • / • •	Drive is Slave to another ST9144 Family Master
• • / • •	Reserved Positions (Do Not Use)

To install the cable, you need to match the red line running along the side of the cable with the pin 1 location on the device. All ports, whether on the motherboard or an IDE interface card, include a label identifying pin 1. Make sure these match up when connecting, or the devices won't work correctly.

If your system has an on-board EIDE controller (with primary and secondary interfaces), you can add an extra EIDE drive to the secondary port if it is unused. But keep two things in mind. First, the primary controller's drive will be the boot drive of your PC. Second, even though you have two drives in this configuration, both drives' jumper settings will be set to master, because the primary and secondary ports are seen by the system as two separate controllers.

Most users won't notice any performance difference between attaching two hard drives to one controller (as master and slave) versus installing one hard drive on the primary controller (as master) and a second on the secondary controller (as master). Theoretically, drives located on the primary controller can enjoy a performance edge.

Multiple Controllers

One thing's for certain: IDE and EIDE sure don't like company. Do not try to add a second IDE or EIDE controller to your system if you plan to keep the on-board controller active. You'll probably encounter system conflicts and have difficulty accessing all the IDE devices you're trying to install. Fortunately, most motherboards let you disable the on-board IDE controller to make room for a new controller.

Adding an EIDE controller board will provide access to faster performance. Also, if you purchase a board using its own BIOS, it should coexist with the motherboard IDE controller, effectively doubling the number of disk drives you can run in your system. Promise Technology (www.promise.com) makes a variety of PCI-based IDE controllers, enabling you to run fast ATA-33 hard disk drives on older PCs.

After you've installed the new controller, you may want to disable the motherboard controller via the system BIOS (that is, if you don't intend to use it any longer). Boot your PC and hold down the key sequence that launches the system BIOS setup screen (usually the Delete key, but refer to your PC's documentation for the correct key sequence). Then look for the item that disables the on-board controller. Once you have disabled the original controller, save the new settings and exit the BIOS setup.

One way to take advantage of new technology controllers without throwing out your IDE hard drive is to add an SCSI controller to your system but keep the on-board IDE (or EIDE) controller active. While newer PCs are able to assign the boot device to the motherboard or external controller, older systems may lack this flexibility. You may have to keep your boot disk on the on-board IDE controller in these cases. Attempting to set an SCSI drive as the boot drive while your on-board IDE controller remains enabled will create headaches and won't work on most older systems.

Managing SCSI Resources

In the majority of cases, an SCSI host adapter card can be made to control any SCSI devices you add to your system. See the section "Adding an Internal Controller Card to Your PC" for instructions on installing a controller card.

SCSI-2 adapters are most prevalent in today's PCs, so they are the focus of this discussion. An SCSI-2 host adapter can drive seven different devices (while SCSI-3 can chain up to 32). As I mentioned earlier, using expensive and sophisticated bridge controllers, you can actually run several chains off one adapter. But you won't find that scenario in a typical home or office PC.

Although SCSI controllers are more flexible and powerful than their EIDE counterparts, they tend to be more difficult to work with. For example, the daisy-chaining capability making SCSI so useful also requires users to juggle device IDs and set electrical termination. These are not huge hurdles for experienced users, but novices might find themselves stopped cold by the stubborn behavior (or refusal to behave) of SCSI-based peripherals.

SCSI Software

Windows 95 users have an edge in SCSI adapter installations, because this operating system already includes drivers to run most adapters without the need for additional software. If the operating system fails to recognize your particular adapter, it will prompt you to provide the supplied drivers from a floppy or CD-ROM disk from the vendor.

Most SCSI adapter kits and devices ship with their own drivers, but some companies have tried to ease installation burden by creating general SCSI management software packages that include drivers for many peripherals. Two of the most popular are EZ-SCSI from Adaptec, Inc., and CorelSCSI Network Manager from Corel Corp.

EZ-SCSI's SCSI Explorer enables you to install, interrogate, and manage SCSI devices including hard disk spin-up, start times, power management, and other controls with a graphical representation of your SCSI chain. SCSI Tutor gives you an online tutorial of SCSI software, host adapters, and peripheral devices. SCSI Bench helps measure the data-transfer performance of your SCSI devices. You'll also find a host of utilities, including an audio CD player, a PhotoCD viewer, and a backup program. EZ-SCSI runs on Windows 95/98, Windows NT, and Windows 3.1.

Corel provides both server and workstation modules for its Network Manager, allowing you to track SCSI networked devices across a Novell Network. This package includes utilities for troubleshooting peripherals as well as CD-ROM jukeboxes, WORM, and rewritable drives.

If you have several SCSI devices on a chain and are concerned about correcting problems quickly, consider one of these packages.

SCSI IDs: Get Your Ducks in a Row

IDE has a master-slave setup, and SCSI uses unique device IDs to keep track of connected peripherals. There are seven ID numbers in all, with the SCSI controller itself usually assigned the ID number 7. Each device on the chain must be assigned a number from 0 to 6.

ID numbers are usually set using hardware control on the SCSI device itself—often a jumper device, dip switch, or pushbutton counter. External devices place this mechanism on the back of the box, and internal devices usually supply jumpers at the back of the metal casing.

When it comes to SCSI IDs, you're on your own. You may set whatever value you please (within the 0 to 7 range), but keep in mind that the IDs set the priority of the devices on the chain. Read your adapter's documentation carefully, because devices such as a bootable hard disk require a specific ID number. What's more, this requirement can differ from adapter to adapter.

Without the supporting documentation, there is no way to prevent a boot drive installation from becoming an ugly exercise in trial and error. Most SCSI adapter cards come from the factory set for SCSI ID 7, which is the highest priority SCSI ID.

Map out which ID numbers you give to each device. If you're planning to add devices in the future, keep the list around. This will save you time and hassle checking the switch settings on the devices at a later date.

Generally, SCSI adapters come with installation and configuration software listing the devices the card recognizes at each ID. You'll also find it handy for printing and keeping a record. Simply ensure that each device's ID remains unique.

> **Tip:** Better yet, write or print the SCSI IDs and their corresponding devices on a label and stick it to the back of your PC. That way, you will always know what the IDs are. In multiple user settings, you might want to place those labels on the front of the external devices.

The Terminators

Another difference between IDE and SCSI is terminating devices. With multiple devices (or even one device) running off a SCSI controller, the controller needs to know exactly where the chain ends. Under IDE, each device carries a self-terminating circuit, so users don't need to worry about telling the controller where the end of the device chain resides. SCSI devices generally don't carry these circuits, and your SCSI chain (or SCSI bus) requires manual termination at both ends.

Like SCSI ID settings, SCSI terminators come in different forms. For external devices, you'll probably find terminating resistors (see Figure 10.3)—plugs that fit into the SCSI interface socket on the back of a device. You may also have a device with terminators built in. In this case, jumper settings are used to specify whether the device marks the end of the chain.

> **Note:** The exception is with Ultra2 SCSI devices, which require no termination. They use an active terminator attached to the last connector on the low-voltage differential (LVD) cable.

FIGURE 10.3.
Terminator plugs are often used to terminate external SCSI devices. The LEDs on the SCSI Value Active Diagnostic Terminator warn you if voltage problems are affecting the connection.

External devices generally have two SCSI ports on the back—one for an incoming cable and one for an outgoing cable. This makes setting up a daisy chain simple. You just connect the outgoing cable of the previous device on the chain (or from the SCSI host adapter) to the incoming port of your new device. Then you either insert a cable on the outgoing port and attach it to the next device in the chain, or terminate the outgoing port with a terminating plug if it's the last device in the chain.

Most modern host adapters allow you to specify which ID is the boot device. However, older adapters require you to set bootable hard disks with ID number 0 in order to be recognized as a boot device.

Some external SCSI devices feature only one port on the back. In this case, a pass-through terminating plug fits between the incoming cable and the port itself. Finally, other SCSI devices, such as NEC's external CD-ROM drives, offer a self-termination feature that can be set by a dip switch. Check the product's documentation to see which method applies to your SCSI device.

TROUBLESHOOTING

> Keep in mind that both ends of any SCSI chain must be terminated. If you only have external devices, for example, you must have a terminator in place on the last device on the chain. The SCSI host adapter itself will then be served with an auto-terminating mechanism from the factory. On the other hand, if you only have internal drives, you'll have to set termination on the last drive in the chain, and again the host adapter will automatically be set. If you have both external and internal devices running off a host adapter, you'll need to make sure that termination is set for the last device inside and outside of the PC.

Internal SCSI devices will either have jumper settings or use a pass-through plug for setting termination. Check the documentation for any internal SCSI devices to determine which you'll need to use. Most SCSI devices, whether internal or external, come with terminators in the box (or use jumpers), but if yours doesn't, you can purchase one from any computer electronics store for a minimal cost.

While we're discussing terminators, I'd like to briefly mention SCSI cabling. Unlike IDE, you'll find a variety of SCSI cables. Regular SCSI uses 50-pin connectors, while Wide SCSI employs a 68-pin connector.

You'll also see variations between external SCSI connectors. If your kit, device, or SCSI card doesn't come with the cabling you need, you can pick up adapter plugs that match any of these different connections at your local computer store.

Avoiding Trouble

SCSI may be powerful, but it can be maddening as well. To avoid system crashes, conflicts, and other headaches, follow the advice in the next three sections.

Delayed Start

If you have several drives on one SCSI chain, you might want to specify that they use a *delayed start* via jumper settings on each drive. Spinning up multiple drives simultaneously upon booting your computer can drain power resources and cause mechanical failure or system crashes. If you set each device as delayed start, the host adapter sends a *start* command to one device at a time along the chain upon bootup. It's also a good idea to have all your devices start before the system, so that they are ready to be accessed when bootup occurs.

Add One Device at a Time

Don't attempt to save time by simply daisy-chaining several SCSI devices all at once. Instead, install each device, one at a time, reboot your PC, and make sure the device is recognized and accessible by the operating system. Then proceed with the next installation. You'll save time in the long run by avoiding troubleshooting problems.

Secure the Cables

With the number of cables involved in a large SCSI daisy chain, it's easy for connections to come loose. Make sure all the cable screws are tightened down and all the fittings secure. You'll save yourself the trouble of tracking down this problem later, when you can't access devices.

Adding an Internal Controller Card to Your PC

In most respects, controller cards are very similar to any other hardware card you might plug into your PC. Controller cards come with a variety of PC bus interfaces, like ISA and PCI. Keep in mind that whether a card is ISA or PCI is completely independent of the standard the controller uses (EIDE or SCSI). You need to make sure that the controller card you buy corresponds to the bus slots inside your PC.

SCSI controller cards differ from some other hardware cards in that they usually feature internal and external connectors. The internal connectors are on the card itself and are accessible only while your PC's cover is off. They provide controller interfaces for devices that will be installed inside the PC, such as an internal hard drive or an internal CD-ROM drive.

External connectors reside on the end of the card and can be found on the backplane of the PC when the card is installed. These connectors are available for plugging in cables for external devices such as scanners, external CD-ROM drives, and so forth.

Multifunction cards often include everything but the kitchen sink. Modem/sound cards are becoming common, and even an inexpensive interface card might include an EIDE and a floppy disk interface, several serial ports, a parallel port, and a game port. When you're attempting to solve a problem with a PC, it might be tempting to opt for one of these comprehensive solutions. But be careful. If the documentation is anything less than complete, clear, and accompanied by a working technical support number, don't choose this "everything card." The reason is that any option on the card that duplicates preexisting, working functions in the PC will have to be disabled by the judicious setting of interface card jumpers. Most interface cards now include a table of switch settings silkscreened on the card itself. This is an encouraging sign, but it won't replace thorough documentation, whether printed or on a disk.

TROUBLESHOOTING

> When you're upgrading a PC, whether you're working in a Plug and Play environment, Windows 3.1, Windows NT, or even plain DOS, most of your problems will be caused by resource conflicts—SCSI ID conflicts, IRQ (interrupt) conflicts, or com port or I/O addressing conflicts. It's a good idea to print or write out a record of the PC's system settings before you begin upgrading. Especially when an automated procedure promises to do everything for you, it's important to ensure that you can back out of the procedure if it fails.
>
> An example is when your PC encounters an error in reading a critical file right in the middle of an installation. You're far better off if you know in advance what you will do next if this happens. Calling the company is sometimes a less-than-optimal solution, especially when the system in question needs to be up-and-running.
>
> As you troubleshoot a problem installation, document each change to jumpers and system configuration in sequential order. Don't wait until the changes begin to accumulate—or worse, something else unexpected occurs—before you begin to lay your trail of bread crumbs to lead you back to the system you had when you began.

Controller Upgrades: Rules of the Road

With any card installation, always remember the following:

- Never remove or insert any card, tighten or loosen any screw, or remove any cables while the PC's power is on. With any installation, be sure to turn off the PC and remove the power cable from the back of the system. Some PCI cards are now *hot-pluggable,* or meant to be swapped with the power on. But these are few, expensive, and intended for very specific purposes. In the absence of clear instructions to the contrary, assume that removal from or insertion of a card to a live motherboard will result in fried circuits.

- Avoid static electricity shocks to your equipment. Wear an antistatic (grounded) wristband while installing cards. Touching the PC's grounded internal metal frame will also work, but only if the PC is plugged in.

- Systems in dusty or dirty environments often pick up grime and/or corrosion on electrical contacts. Systems operating where there are smokers, pets, or salty air are especially prone to problems with making solid connections. A fine jeweler's file can restore dubious expansion slots, but this isn't a procedure to use too often, lest the metal plating inside the slot be worn completely away. Any residue should be vacuumed up with a technician's hand-held vacuum (keeping it well away from any magnetic media) or blown away using canned compressed air.

- Determine whether your PC, operating system, and controller card are Plug and Play (PnP) compatible (see Chapter 2, "Inside Windows 95 and 98"). If all these devices comply with PnP, you won't need to concern yourself much with your cards' IRQ and DMA settings. If they aren't PnP-compatible, read the cards' documentation to determine the jumper settings required to set the cards' IRQ and DMA to avoid conflicts with devices that are already installed on your PC. If necessary, set these jumpers before installation.

> **Caution:** Even if you have soup-to-nuts PnP support, don't wander in unprepared. Take inventory of your system's IRQ and DMA settings so that you know what's free and what's not. If something goes wrong with the automated installation—and this has been known to happen—you won't be left in the dark.

- Connect any internal cables before you insert the card into the PC's slot. Once cards have been installed in the slots, the distance between cards is so small that it's impossible to connect internal ribbon cables, and so forth, after insertion. Connect cables to the cards as required and then insert the card into the slot.

- Tighten bracket screws. Unsecured cards can come loose when a PC is moved or bumped. Be sure to finish installing any card by fastening the bracket screws.

Controller Card Installation

After preparing, and after having read through your controller card's documentation for any specific instructions relating to installation, you can begin.

1. Turn off your PC and unplug the power cable.

2. Remove the PC system case using either just your hands (for thumbscrew cases) or a screwdriver (for older designs).

3. Unscrew the metal flap protecting the open slot where you'll be installing the card. Normally, this will be secured with a small Phillips screw.

4. Before you install the card, configure any on-board jumpers or switches (if present) as indicated by the card's documentation. Often getting at these tiny controls is impossible when the card is installed.

5. Connect internal cabling if necessary. For example, if you're connecting the controller to an internal drive, attach the ribbon cable (red line on cable to pin 1 on card) to the controller that will later connect to the drive.

6. Align the card with the open bus slot. Be careful to avoid catching the card's back port on the metal bracket at the back of the PC. Try easing the card's port below the top of the bracket so that, once the card is inserted, the connector will be positioned properly out the back of the PC's case (see Figure 10.4).

Figure 10.4.

Ports on the card's backplane provide cable access to external devices. Some also include internal connectors, such as those found on the Adaptec AHA-2940AU. (Photo courtesy of Adaptec, Inc.)

7. When you're sure that the card is properly aligned and that the edge connector won't bind against the plastic sides of the expansion slot, gently push the card into the slot. Using two hands, push the card down evenly at each end simultaneously until the card is fully in position in the slot. A card that isn't fully inserted won't be accessible through the operating system, and a misaligned insertion can cause smoke and a trip to the computer store when the power is turned on. Press firmly down on the card once it's in the slot to seat it correctly.

8. Ensure that the top edge of the interface card backplane is flush against the chassis, and then replace the bracket screw to secure the card.

9. Attach any external device cable and any external devices that are required.

10. Reattach the PC's power cable, and turn on the PC.

11. Test the system to ensure that the operating system at least knows that something new has been added.

12. Put the PC case cover back on, and secure the case.

Summary

Users need to pay close attention to drive interface technology when assessing overall system performance and capabilities. Older motherboards with plain vanilla IDE interfaces, for example, simply can't provide the large disk capacity and performance of new IDE ATA-33 and popular SCSI standards. Likewise, aging SCSI hard disks won't be able to take advantage of the latest SCSI2 Ultra controllers, which can push up to 80MBps of data.

For the vast majority of users, it's an IDE world. The ATA-33 specification eliminated many of IDE's worst flaws, particularly IDE's habit of tying up the CPU for every data transfer. But SCSI remains a more efficient data interface, and is clearly superior when operating multiple, high-speed drives on the same bus. Of course, SCSI also allows for external disk and device support, something IDE still doesn't do. Next up for IDE: The ATA-66 specification, which redoubles the peak data rate of the interface to 66MBps.

What lies beyond? Expect both SCSI and IDE to step aside for the IEEE 1394 FireWire specification, a Plug and Play bus able to support both internal and external devices. Intel and others had hoped to see FireWire in mainstream systems already, but delays in adoption (due in large part to FireWire's cost) prompted the company to help cook up the ATA-66 spec as an interim standard. FireWire promises to ease device installation, provide external disk support in low-cost PCs, and help reduce the number of device interface technologies resident on PCs.

But FireWire is unlikely to be a major factor until the year 2002, or so. In the meantime, users must weigh their performance and device needs against the performance advantages of SCSI and the clear cost advantages of IDE. Fortunately for users, there are plenty of good product options and add-ons for enhancing the existing drive interface on your PC.

11

Taking Hard Disks for a Spin

Along with memory and graphics cards, hard disks are probably the most often upgraded component inside the PC. The reason is obvious. Every year, programs get bulkier, file formats get more complex, and operating systems encompass more tasks. Microsoft Windows and Microsoft Office—the most popular operating system and office suite on the planet—keep disk drive companies such as Western Digital, Seagate, Maxtor, and Quantum very busy indeed. Add the explosive growth of disk-consuming files from the Internet, and it's no wonder disk capacities double every year.

Most people are probably well-acquainted with the hard disk. The central mass storage element of the PC system, it is where all your files and programs reside. Using a quick magnetic-based recording format, the disk retains information even if the power supply is shut off.

This chapter covers the hard disk and related issues. You will learn

- About the workings of hard disks and the various types of disks available for PCs
- How to troubleshoot disk-related problems and how to recover from disk crashes
- What to look for in a new hard disk purchase
- How to install a new hard disk, whether you're adding a second disk to the existing unit or replacing the original disk altogether

How Hard Drives Work

If you recall the office desk analogy from Chapter 7, "Exploring System Memory and Cache," the hard disk acts a lot like a file cabinet. When the operating system or any application is launched, its data is read from hard disk storage and loaded into RAM for processing by the CPU. The RAM acts like the top of the office desk: Papers that are being worked on sit conveniently on the desktop, and other files are stored.

When you launch a word processor application, for example, its executable program is read from the hard disk and loaded into RAM. Later, when you open a saved document, that file is also read from the hard disk and loaded into RAM. Any subsequent changes you make to that document are written back out to the hard disk as the file is saved.

Windows 95 and other operating systems also make the hard disk serve double duty, using it as an overflow reservoir for system RAM. When too many applications and files are loaded, those least recently used get stored back on the hard disk. Programs are tricked into thinking that the bits are still in RAM, but when the data is called up, the operating system goes off to the hard disk to fetch the information. Called *virtual memory*, this scheme extends the functionality of all PCs but exacts a hefty price in performance: Hard disks are 100 times slower than system RAM.

Understanding the Physical Disk Structure

So, we know what the hard disk drive does, but how does it do it? Physically, your hard disk acts like an old turntable, with a series of ceramic or aluminum platters serving the role of vinyl records holding the tunes (or in this case, the data). (See Figure 11.1.) Each *platter* is covered in a magnetic coating called *thin film*, where the data is written to and read from. A drive mechanism, called a spindle, spins the platters at speeds ranging from 5,400 to 10,000 revolutions per minute. A read/write head, similar to a turntable's record needle, floats micro-inches above each platter, reading and writing tiny magnetic charges that get interpreted into digital 1s and 0s.

In order to get data to reside on the platters, each is lined with thousands of concentric circular tracks, which themselves are broken into sectors. (For the sake of precision, realize that a vinyl record has one continuous "track," or spiraling groove, per side, while a hard disk platter has separate concentric tracks that are not connected.) The sector is the smallest geographic unit in the disk layout, with bits addressed by their position within the sector.

Figure 11.1.
Inside the sealed chamber, a hard disk drive resembles a series of vinyl records read by high-performance needles.

Remember, we have several platters stacked together, each segmented into concentric rings called tracks. The tracks that line up with each other on the various platters are collectively called a *cylinder*. This is important because when the *head actuator* guides the read-write heads to a particular track on a platter, the other read-write heads move over the same track on their respective platters. When heads move to a particular track in a stacked-platter drive, all the tracks in one cylinder are accessible at the same time.

> **Note:** Hard disk crashes are aptly named. The read/write heads of a Head Disk Assembly (HDA) float about three micro-inches above the platters on a cushion of air, never coming in direct contact with the disk during normal operation. A malfunction in the drive unit can cause the head to literally crash into the disk surface and gouge out a piece of the recording material. In a bad crash, the drive usually ceases working, and your only option is to replace the drive. Fortunately, with improved manufacturing clean-room techniques, hard drives don't crash as often as they used to.
>
> A surefire way to kill a perfectly good hard drive is to slide the system box of an up-and-running system across a desktop so that the chassis shudders against the surface. It takes only a few inches of that sort of motion to generate a resonant vibration generating substantial G-forces on the heads, causing them to come into contact with the spinning recording surface of the drive. When that happens, you're finished.
>
> Hard disks are constructed more securely today than in the past, but the data is much denser than ever before. As capacities have gotten larger, the margin of error has gotten much smaller. Larger drives also make recovering data from a dead drive more expensive than ever, if the data isn't backed up.

You won't find upgrading hard drives to be the easiest task you can perform inside your PC. (For example, upgrading RAM is much easier.) But if you follow the steps listed in the section "Installing a Hard Disk Step by Step," you can get through the process with a minimum of hassle. Hard disk vendors offer drives in different controller types (as discussed in Chapter 10, "Control Freaks: IDE and SCSI Controllers") and in an amazing range of sizes.

Hard drive problems come in two main categories: setup/format troubles and hardware failure/disk crashes. Setup/format problems can be dealt with using disk utilities or by modifying your CMOS. Hardware failure/disk crashes, on the other hand, generally mean you need to replace the unit, because the sealed Head Disk Assemblies (HDAs) of hard drives make them impossible to fix using standard home or office tools. Additionally, opening the sealed unit almost always invalidates your warranty. Fortunately, it isn't too difficult to find companies specializing in performing data recovery on failed drives, often allowing you to recoup some of your lost data—albeit at a substantial fee.

Tip: Just as it's easier to find a job when you already have one, it's easier to replace a hard drive that hasn't yet completely quit.

Understanding Disk Density

Hard disk engineers focus much of their energy on improving the density of information on a disk, called the *areal density*. Higher density means more data storage in a smaller space. Areal density is measured by multiplying the number of bits per inch (BPI) on a particular track by the number of tracks per inch (TPI) (calculated from the edge of the disk inward toward the center). High-end drives now feature areal densities of over 700 megabits per square inch, resulting in drives with 1 gigabyte (GB) on a single platter.

Recently, areal densities of more than 1 gigabit per square inch of thin film recording media have been achieved. That top limit rises by 60 percent per year, compounded, according to IBM researchers. More than capacity is at issue here. Higher densities mean that more bits are passing beneath the read/write head at a given rotational speed. The result, higher data rates and better performance.

Packing these bits on the disk requires the precise integration of different component technologies. The BPI potential depends on disk rotational speed, the read/write head technology, and the disk media type. The TPI potential depends on the read/write head technology, the disk media, and the positioning of the head actuator arm:

>**Rotational speed:** This is the number of revolutions per minute (RPM) that a platter spins. As disks have diminished in overall size from 5¼ inches to 3½ inches (even 2½ to 1.7 inches for notebooks), the linear speed of the disk has decreased.

>To understand this concept in real-world terms, think of an amusement park carousel. Suppose you're standing on the moving carousel and you want to stay even with a tree that's next to the ride. You would need to run (in the opposite direction the carousel is spinning) in order to stay in one place at the outer rim. But at the innermost point, you would only need to walk in order to stay even with the tree, due to the decrease in linear speed of the carousel surface. Unfortunately, for inductive read/write heads, the signal strength from bits decreases as the linear disk speed slows. So drive manufacturers have been increasing rotational speeds to compensate.

>Typical drives now run from 3,600 to 5,400, with faster drives running at 7,200RPM. Today's top drives now spin at 10,000RPM. Speed tests generally show that the faster the rotational speed, the better the overall performance of the drive.

>**Read/write head technology:** State-of-the-art manufacturing allows read/write heads to float about 3 micro-inches from the surface of the platter. Unfortunately, as bits get packed closer and closer together on the disk surface with improved

technology, even that tiny head-height distance reduces the ability of the read/write heads to pick up the diminished magnetic signal strength of the individual bits. Engineers are plotting how to reduce this head-height distance even more and possibly even have the heads ride on the surface of the platter itself (but this causes wear and tear on the disk and heads).

In addition, improvements in head technology continue. Inductive read/write heads, the most popular technology, simply pick up and amplify the bit's magnetic field as they pass over it. Newer Magneto-Resistive (MR) heads use a sense current that constantly runs through the head. When the head passes over a bit, the resistance changes and the amperage of the sense current fluctuates, passing on the needed data. MR heads increase areal density, because they're more precise in distinguishing between tightly-packed bits. More recently, IBM has improved on this technology with giant magnetoresistive heads able to handle up to 3.2GB of data on a single drive platter.

Disk media: Disk platters now come in aluminum alloy, ceramic, glass, and glass-ceramic combinations. The goal is to develop a platter that is strong and lightweight and doesn't expand or contract with temperature changes. See Figure 11.2. The recording media, which covers the platter and holds the magnetic data, is generally a 1 to 3 micro-inch layer of cobalt alloy. Engineers keep working to make the recording media thin, defect-free, and capable of withstanding head crashes without damage.

Looking at Logical Disk Structures

All this talk about hardware is great, but your system needs to be able to talk to the hard disk. In order to do this, your PC's BIOS, the operating system, and other low-level programs need to come to an understanding of how the disk media is organized and where they can expect to find things. The physical segmentation of the disk into cylinders, heads, and sectors certainly helps, but there is a logical aspect that needs to be understood as well.

Why? Because if you try to upgrade an older system with one of today's huge 16GB hard disk drives, there's a decent chance that your BIOS, operating system, or both will be unable to access the full store of available capacity. The problem is a limitation in a BIOS procedure called Interrupt 13h, or Int 13h, which was never designed for anything greater than 512MB drives. You may need a BIOS upgrade—or a whole new motherboard—to fix the problem.

As mentioned previously, disks are divided into tracks and segments. Your BIOS recognizes these divisions and enables programs to send or receive bits at specific points on the disk drive. However, the original Int 13h structure can only recognize 1,024 cylinders, 256 heads, and 63 sectors, limiting theoretical disk sizes to 7.86GB. To get access to additional memory, you must either run an OS like Windows 95 and NT, that goes around the BIOS using its own 32-bit disk access mechanisms, or move to a BIOS with Int 13h extensions that raise the capacity bar.

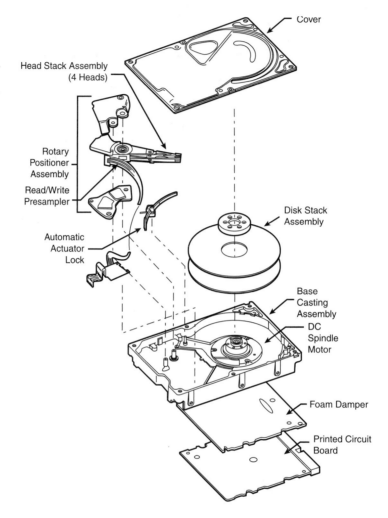

Cover

Head Stack Assembly (4 Heads)

Rotary Positioner Assembly

Read/Write Presampler

Automatic Actuator Lock

Disk Stack Assembly

Base Casting Assembly

DC Spindle Motor

Foam Damper

Printed Circuit Board

What's more, interaction with the IDE/ATA interface poses another problem. ATA can see 65,536 cylinders, 16 heads, and 256 sectors. Because your system must employ the lowest common denominator of both the BIOS's Int 13h and ATA interface, the result is a 504MB limitation. That's based on having 1,024 cylinders, 16 heads, and 63 sectors. Multiply those together and multiply by the number of bytes per sector—512—and you get 504MB.

Obviously, systems sold during the past two or three years have gotten around this onerous limitation. The trick: *Logical block addressing* (LBA) that twiddles the respective Int 13h and ATA numbers, and transforms disk addresses from a cylinder/head/sector scheme to one of linear sector numbers. This translation process divides the ATA cylinder limit by eight—from 65,536 to 6,136—and multiplies the number of heads by eight—

from 16 to 128. The resulting transformation maintains the same number of addressable bits, but better distributes resources beneath the respective ATA and BIOS Int 13h limits.

If your older system lacks LBA support, you may be able to update the BIOS, provided it is software upgradable. In the absence of a flash BIOS, you'll need to either install an IDE adapter—such as Promise Technology's Ultra33 card—or purchase a new motherboard or system. Because SCSI drives operate off host adapters with their own BIOS, they are not subject to this limit—so an SCSI hard disk upgrade is another possible solution.

Focus on File Systems

The adoption of Int 13h extensions in Windows 95 and Windows NT has largely rendered the geometry issue moot for most users. But the proliferation of different file systems is another matter. A file system is the logical structure imposed by an operating system on all disk transactions. It determines how files are stored on your disk, how much space they will consume, and what additional data travels with them. There are also key limitations with file systems, most specifically with regard to capacity. Today, there are three file systems clamoring for a place on PC hard disks, and only one is universally recognized by all. They are

- FAT16
- FAT32
- NTFS

FAT16 stands for file allocation table-16 and is the file system familiar to users of Windows 3.x, DOS, and early versions of Windows 95. Today, most computers use FAT16 to lay out their drive structures. FAT16's main advantage is that it is universally supported—Windows 3.x, Windows 95, and Windows NT can all recognize FAT16 formatted drives.

But FAT16 has a problem: It can only address disk partitions of 2GB or less. With hard disks soaring to 14GB and beyond, that meant you'd need seven partitions—and seven drive letters—just to see the entire drive! What's more, as the partition gets larger, the minimum amount of space needed to store even a 1-byte file grows alarmingly, as shown in Table 11.1.

Table 11.1. Slacker: FAT16 wastes bits as partitions grow in size.

Partition Size	FAT16 Cluster Size	FAT32 Cluster Size
16MB-128MB	2KB	4KB
128MB-256MB	4KB	4KB
256MB-512MB	8KB	8KB

continues

Table 11.1. Continued.

Partition Size	FAT16 Cluster Size	FAT32 Cluster Size
512MB-1GB	16KB	8KB
1GB-2GB	32KB	8KB
2GB-8GB	n/a	8KB
8GB-60GB	n/a	16KB
60GB-2,000GB	n/a	32KB

With Windows 95 OSR version 2.1 and later Windows 98, systems began shipping with the FAT32 file system. This scheme boosts the addressability limit to 2 *terabytes* (2,000 gigabytes). In addition, FAT32 limits lost space (called slack) by reducing the minimum size of clusters. While an extremely small drive might actually lose more capacity to slack under FAT32 than FAT16, the gain becomes significant as sizes go to 2GB. The cluster size on a 2GB partition—the maximum FAT16 can handle—is just 8KB under FAT32 versus 32KB under FAT16. That means the same one bit file will consume one-fourth the space under FAT32.

Microsoft touts FAT32 as being a more flexible and intelligent file system than FAT16. Windows 98 will dynamically update the position of frequently accessed files and code, for example, so that they reside at the outer edges of the platters, where the higher rotation speed means faster response.

Windows NT also has its own file system, called NT File System (NTFS). NTFS adds transaction logs to recover from failures as well as controls to limit access to directories and files. NTFS formatted drives can be up to 2TB (terabytes) in size. While NTFS can work with FAT16 partitions, FAT32 is not recognized. If you have Windows 9x and NT systems on a network, you'll need to consider which file system to use if you need different systems to share drives.

The compatibility landscape is something of a mess, as you can see next:

- FAT16 formatted drives and partitions: Available under DOS, Windows 3.x, Windows 9x, and Windows NT. FAT16 drives do not recognize FAT32 or NTFS structures.

- FAT32 formatted drives and partitions: Available under Windows 9x. To be added to Windows NT 5.0. Able to recognize FAT16 structures. Unable to recognize NTFS structures.

- NTFS formatted drives and partitions: Available only under Windows NT. Able to recognize FAT16 structures. Does not recognize FAT32 structures.

New Technologies

Keep your eyes open for changes in the hard disk landscape. This segment of the computer industry evolves as rapidly as any other. Four years ago, an average PC shipped with a 500MB hard drive. Now the average drive size for a new PC is about 6 to 8GB, and many mainstream systems feature 14GB drives.

The standard controller interfaces for hard drives are still SCSI and EIDE (see Figure 11.3), but both have improved recently. Today, most new drives use the ATA-33 specification (also known as ultra DMA), which can pump up to 33MBps of data. Of course, your motherboards IDE interface needs to support the fast ATA-33 specification to gain full use of these drives. Also in the works is ATA-66, which doubles throughput yet again, to 66MBps.

SCSI drives have also improved. The UltraWide Low Voltage Differential (LVD) SCSI bus can push 80MBps of data, more than enough for the most demanding applications. SCSI also offers more efficient resource management and multitasking of drive data transfers than ATA-33.

Past these specifications, drives will move to IEEE 1394, also called FireWire. FireWire offers UltraWide LVD SCSI-type data rates over a Plug and Play serial interface. But such drives are unlikely to enter the mainstream until the year 2000 or 2001.

INSTANT REFERENCE For more on disk interfaces, see Chapter 10.

FIGURE 11.3.
SCSI hard disks offer higher data rates and better multitasking performance. But many PCs need a separate SCSI add-in card, such as the Adaptec AHA 3940UW, shown here. (Photo courtesy of Adaptec)

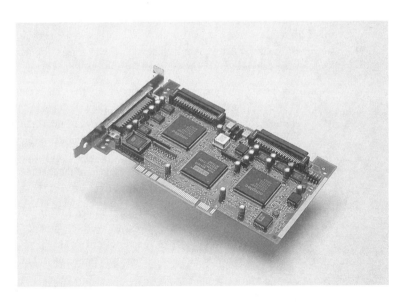

Drive manufacturers continue to come up with improved disk drive components. New PRML (Partial Response Maximum Likelihood) disks, for example, use data-detection techniques in conjunction with MR heads to improve data throughput and increase areal density. You should read the latest technology "white papers" major drive manufacturers are posting on their Web sites. For example, Quantum Corporation (www.quantum.com) and Seagate Technology (www.seagate.com) frequently provide technology papers online.

Drives featuring these technological enhancements are already available and have helped make possible affordable, large-capacity drives going to 16GB and beyond.

Drive Replacement or Add-On

You should decide whether you're simply adding a drive to your PC or replacing your current hard drive. If you've run out of room on your hard drive but you're happy with its performance, consider just adding an extra hard drive. You'll save yourself the time-consuming hassle of backing up and transferring all your data to the new drive. This also gives you the opportunity to go for the cheaper, smaller drives, and you won't have to dispose of a perfectly good drive just because it doesn't hold enough bytes. If you can use the old drive, you probably won't need 8GB of extra space.

If you do decide to add a larger, faster drive to your system, but you intend to keep the old hard drive, you should make sure the new, more efficient drive becomes your PC's boot drive. You'll gain overall performance advantages by having the disk containing the operating system and its virtual memory file be the better drive. Unfortunately, moving data from the current boot disk to the new boot disk is quite difficult. When making a purchase, consider a drive that includes a disk mirroring utility enabling you to quickly turn the new drive into a mirror image of the original boot drive.

When you're adding a drive, be aware that not all drives are compatible under EIDE's master/slave relationship (see Chapter 13, "Removable Storage for PCs"). Older IDE drives that don't support PIO (programmed I/O) modes 3 and 4 (the faster data transfer protocols) sometimes have difficulty working with another drive running on the same EIDE controller. Unfortunately, experimentation is often your only option. Generally, your boot drive should be the master drive, to take advantage of the theoretical, if not practical, performance gains.

On the other hand, if your drive is slow, deteriorating, showing an increasing number of bad sectors or intermittent errors, or altogether dead, it's time for a replacement drive. You should choose the biggest drive you can afford. After all, you'll be using it for a long time, and you'll want as much storage as your budget will allow.

What size hard drive should you buy? 3GB is the absolute minimum these days, with even 8GB drives selling for under $200. If you answer yes to at least two of the following questions, you should consider an 8GB drive or larger:

- Do you often use image, video, sound, or animation production tools on your PC?
- Do you store large video, image, or sound files on your hard disk?
- Do you store or work with large database files on your hard disk?
- Do you install five or more new applications (or application upgrades) within a six-month time frame?
- Do you regularly download new files from the Internet?

Generally, the bigger the drive, that better your ratio of dollars per megabyte. Even if the preceding questions don't necessarily apply to you, but you can afford a few more dollars for a hard drive, you can divide the disk into several logical partitions for various uses.

If you purchased your PC before 1994, your system's BIOS might not be able to handle the larger than 528MB drive capacity of new EIDE drives, due to changes in IDE's method of interpreting hard disk geometry and the newer EIDE's LBA (Logical Block Addressing) approach. If your BIOS isn't enhanced, you might be able to upgrade just your BIOS through your system vendor. In the worst case, you could upgrade the motherboard itself in order to take advantage of these high-capacity EIDE drives.

> **Tip:** Don't dwell on hard drive performance when making your purchase decisions. Comparative hard drive review test results show that performance differences between drives usually hover around five percent or less. Just make sure that any drive you're considering falls within these standard ranges of performance specifications.

Key Specs

The following hard drive specifications flow in order from most important to least important in terms of understanding and evaluating hard drive decisions:

- Average seek time: The average amount of time required to move the heads to a track, measured in milliseconds. Fast drives now offer 7.5ms average seek times. Almost all new drives are 10ms or faster. This is three times faster than the hard drives of a decade ago. The lower the number, the better.
- Transfer rate: The rate at which the drive and controller pass data back to the PC system, measured in megabytes per second. A higher number is better. This rate varies greatly, depending on the controller type. EIDE controllers and drives range from 11.1 to 16.6MBps, due to PIO (programmed I/O) modes 3 and 4, which were part of the specifications. SCSI controllers and drives now normally run from 10 to 40MBps. Don't let the differences scare you. The CPU clock speed, the amount of RAM, and even your video graphics accelerator card more clearly define your PC's overall speed.

- Disk cache: Hard drive disk caches are extra memory buffers included with many new drives. To reduce the total number of times the hard drive spends time seeking data on disk, read request information gets stored in the cache temporarily. Many times, the following read request's data can be supplied directly from the cache without accessing the hard disk again. A typical new drive can come with a 512KB drive cache. Here, a larger number is better.

- Disk rotational speed: The number of revolutions per minute (RPM) that a platter makes after spinning up to speed. Ranges normally run from 3,600 to 7,200RPM. Generally, in hard disk drive comparisons, the faster the drive's RPM, the better the overall performance of the drive during real-world operating system and software application testing.

Planning Your Purchase

With the multitude of options you have when shopping for a new hard drive, you might be confused if you don't have a plan. This section illustrates a structured way to decide on which disk you need.

> **Tip:** Before you shop for a drive, take measurements of the available drive bay. At the same time you buy your drive, make sure you will have all necessary cables, connectors, screws, and brackets to install it both physically and electronically. You'll also want to make sure you don't need custom rails to mount the drive. At the very least, you'll save yourself a trip back to the store.

- Size (capacity): Before anything else, determine the size of hard disk you need. Where only SCSI drives offered capacities above 8GB, today you can purchase 16GB drives in both IDE and SCSI versions. If you're planning to run many large applications (database, image processing, multimedia production tools), or if you store and manipulate huge files (database, image, video, sound), get the largest hard disk you can afford. The applications and data files you use in the next three years will only get larger, so plan for big storage demands. Once you've picked a drive size, calculate the cost per megabyte of different drives from different vendors, and make a short list of the cheapest.

> **Technical Note:** When it comes to hard disk capacities, your mileage will vary. First, vendors overstate capacities by marketing hard disks with the assumption that there are one million bytes in a megabyte and one billion bytes in a gigabyte. In fact, the true numbers of bytes are 1,048,576 and 1,073,741,824, respectively. So when a drive is advertised as 4.3GB, for example, the vendor often means that the drive has 4.3 billion bytes. A true 4.3GB drive would contain a little over 4.617 billion bytes. You're missing over 300MB!

What's more, formatted drives won't match the exact capacity stated on the box. And you will get different capacity readings from different utilities. All this makes accounting for disk space a fuzzy area. Don't sweat it too much. Although these phantom bits might be vexing, your drive actually loses much more data to slack in the Windows 95 filing system than to any amount of accounting weirdness.

- Controller type: If the size you choose hasn't decided the controller type for you, you must decide between an EIDE and an SCSI controller. SCSI drives theoretically supply faster data transfer and definitely provide more flexibility in adding devices, so go that way if you can afford the extra cost. Otherwise, choose EIDE for the convenience and cost savings of leveraging off your on-board controller.

- Warranty and service policies: Evaluate your short list of drives by the manufacturer's service and warranty polices. Typically, drives have warranties of about five years. Check computer publications for service records and reader complaints about vendor service.

- Performance: Finally, double-check that your potential new drive falls within the performance specs previously listed. Again, in real-world tests, the performance differences between drives isn't that significant.

Tip: Chapter 10 has a breakdown of the two different controller technologies— SCSI and IDE. Keep in mind that SCSI generally offers the largest drives available and more flexibility in adding devices in the future, but you'll pay $100 to $200 more for an SCSI drive than an EIDE drive. Additionally, an SCSI controller card costs about $150. If you don't have an on-board EIDE controller (which is free), you can pick an EIDE controller hardware card for about $50.

Diagnosing/Troubleshooting

Hard disks are much more reliable than they used to be, but that's small comfort when 3GB of your favorite data goes down with your hard disk. It can be a heart-breaker. Disks always seem to drop out at the exact moment when you've saved a substantial quantity of essential and irreplaceable data.

Fortunately, most troubleshooting consists of routine maintenance to keep the drive running smoothly or to fix minor problems. The next sections will help you identify and fix problems and give you insights into the tools available to do so.

Disk Utilities and Facilities

If you notice problems with your hard disk, you'll find two tools close at hand inside Windows 95 and Windows 98 (see Figure 11.4). Disk Defragmenter and ScanDisk both provide handy tools for assessing and fixing routine disk problems. You access these utilities from the Start button by choosing Programs, Accessories, System Tools.

FIGURE 11.4.
You'll find useful hard disk management tools in Windows 95 and 98. Simply right-click the drive and select Properties.

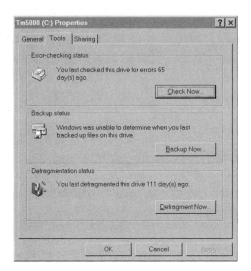

Disk Defragmenter

Windows 95 can be a real scatterbrain. When data is constantly read from and written to a hard drive, the operating system doesn't try to keep files or contiguous data together. Rather, a single large file may be scattered among many clusters, requiring the disk to work harder to retrieve information. The result: Degraded performance as the system must wait for the read/write head to find lots of individual sectors, rather than just run through a long string of contiguous sectors. This scattering of data is called fragmentation.

The Disk Defragmenter utility shuffles the bits around your hard disk, reuniting all those separated blocks by copying the useful data together into contiguous blocks. Wasted space and left-over bits are removed. Defragmenting the hard disk can often resolve vexing problems with lost files or slowed performance.

ScanDisk

When things go bad on your hard disk, Windows 95 and 98's ScanDisk comes to the rescue. This utility ScanDisk examines the entire disk surface, finding and marking mis-written data and even detecting bad sectors on the disk. To run scan disk, click Start, Programs, Accessories, System Utilities, and click the ScanDisk item.

In most cases, all you need to do is conduct a standard disk test. This routine looks for disk-related data gaffs, included cross-linked files, lost clusters, or orphaned clusters. These problems often occur when Windows loses track of a file or related cluster, and the file allocation table fails to account for data found on the disk. In most instances, no harm is done—the errant cluster or file segment was already replaced by a correctly-handled updated file or cluster. But sometimes, valuable data may be sitting in these troubled spots.

When you scan the disk, you can tell the program to discard any mislaid clusters and file segments. Or if you think you might try to recover data from the scattered bits, you can save the clusters to text formatted files saved with names like file001.chk. Unfortunately, actually dredging useful data out of these clusters is hard work, and may require the costly services of a consultant.

Another, more disturbing, problem relates to physical defects on the surface of the hard disk. These flaws make it impossible for the read/write head to read from or write to the disk. Any data located where flaws occur is lost. Once again, ScanDisk comes to the rescue. When you set its review mode to Thorough, the program takes extra time to look at the physical state of the media and mark any sectors that are bad or unusable. If possible, data on those bad sectors will be moved off, and those sectors will then be avoided for all future writes.

Additionally, Norton Utilities supplies several disk diagnostic and recovery tools. You can even handily recover erased files using the manual "unerase" utility.

If you've got a full disk on your hands, you might have some wasted space remaining from installing and uninstalling applications. Download shareware utilities such as CacheCompactor (available at CNET's www.download.com) find and delete unnecessary files hogging space on your disk.

Finally, Windows 98 delivers Disk Defragmenter Wizard, Automatic ScanDisk, and other new disk utility features.

Using FDISK to Partition a Disk Drive

Ironically, the most powerful disk utility for many users is FDISK, the old DOS-based executable that is still the only way for Windows 9x users to create and manage disk partitions. FDISK enables you to set file systems, disk partitions, and drive letters. Whether you are setting up a new drive or want to create new partitions on an existing one, FDISK is the least-expensive way to do it.

Unfortunately, FDISK won't let you shuffle partitions without nuking all the data on the affected partitions. To dynamically manage partitions systems, file system conversions, and other complex disk tasks, you should purchase PowerQuest's Partition Magic program, an outstanding utility for anyone juggling file systems and disk drives.

To wipe clean an existing drive in order to assert a new file system, do the following:

1. Back up all your data and make sure you have a Windows 9x or other system disk with boot files and the FDISK.EXE and FORMAT.EXE applications on it.

2. Restart your system with a DOS utility disk in drive A:. From the DOS prompt, type FDISK.

3. At the opening screen, hit 3 to go to Delete partition or Logical DOS Drive. This will let you clear any existing structures.

4. If you have several drive letters in your drive (say C, D, and E), press 3 to Delete Logical DOS Drive(s) in the Extended DOS Partition.

5. At the next screen, press the letter of the drive you wish to delete. Repeat steps 3 through 5 until all extended logical partitions are gone.

6. Now delete the extended partition by pressing 2 at the opening screen.

7. At the next screen, press Y to wipe out the extended partition.

> **Caution:** The primary partition includes your boot sector—you will not be able to boot from the hard drive once you wipe it out. You must have a bootable floppy with appropriate system files to format the drive as a bootable device.

8. Now delete the primary partition to completely wipe clean the drive. Press 1 at the opening screen to Delete the Primary DOS Partition. The hard disk is now clean.

To set up a drive with new partitions, and to select the file system, do the following:

1. Restart your system with the system disk in the A: drive. At the DOS prompt, type FDISK.

2. You will be prompted to select a file system for large partitions. If you want to install FAT32, press Y and continue. For FAT16, type N.

3. After the file system is set, press 1 at the opening FDISK screen to create the primary partition.

4. At the following screen, press 1 for Create Primary DOS Partition. At the next screen, press Y to set the partition as active.

5. At the next screen, set the partition size. To go to the maximum partition size, press Y (for FAT16, this means the C: drive will be 2,048MB; for FAT32, the C: drive will be the entire disk). Press N if you want to use other drive letters.

6. If you wish to create additional partitions, press 1 at the opening screen and then press 2 to select Create Extended DOS Partition.

7. Enter the size of the desired extended partition and press Enter.

8. To create additional partitions, press 1 at the opening screen and then 3 to select Create Logical DOS Drive(s) in the Extended DOS Partition.

9. Enter the size of the desired extended logical partition and press Enter. Press Esc at the information screen to return to the opening screen.

10. To create multiple extended logical partitions, repeat steps 8 and 9.

11. When you finish, exit and reboot your PC for the new partitions to take effect.

Once your partitions are set up, you can format the C: drive using the FORMAT /S toggle to make C: the boot drive. Or you can kick off a Windows 9x, NT, or other OS install routine directly from the floppy disk. Just remember, you must reboot your system for your partition work to take effect.

Going Out with a Bang: Symptoms of a Dying Disk

A hard drive on its last legs makes itself known. The key symptoms include loud noises, excessive heat, and constant data errors when you're booting or running applications. If you're concerned about the health of your hard drive, first back up the entire disk. Data is the most important part of any disk drive.

Table 11.2 is a checklist of symptoms and solutions to try before deciding whether to replace the drive. You'll have to remove your PC's cover to check some of these items.

Table 11.2. Troubleshooting hard disks.

Symptom	Solution
Constant disk errors	Run disk utilities ScanDisk and Disk Defragmenter (DOS 6.0 and higher and Windows 9x) or third-party applications such as Norton Utilities to find and correct bad sectors on your disk. Also check your PC's CMOS settings to see if the disk drive is set up properly.
Loud disk noises (whining or clicking sounds while the hard disk is booting or running)	With the PC cover off, make sure the disk is secured in the drive bay and is situated either flat or standing on end (not slanted) for proper operation. Also check that both the power supply cable and the data cable are firmly connected at both ends.
Excessive heat from the drive	Your disk drive will be warm to the touch (but not really hot) during normal operation. Make sure your PC's internal fan is working properly. Some fans have a switch disabling them while the PC cover is removed, so check for normal fan sound and air flow with the cover on. If the fan appears disabled, check its connections inside the PC.

> **Note:** Noise doesn't always equal drive failure. Some older drives have a grounding bracket on top of the drive spindle. This bracket has a bearing under it attaching to the spindle, which can wear marks in the bracket. The result: A constant whining sound that disappears once the bracket is worn smooth again.

> **Caution:** When blowing out the inside of your PC, try not to blow air and dirt through the blades of the fan, causing the blade to turn. This forces dirt in between the axle and bearing, causing squeaking and eventual failure.

If none of these solutions corrects your problem, consider upgrading your hard drive. Back up your data first, because these problems foreshadow a hardware failure.

Upgrading

The hard disk is a component you'll probably upgrade over the life of your PC. The two main reasons to upgrade are that you need more room for applications and/or data, or that your disk has crashed and you need to replace it. A third reason to upgrade, popular with people who like to improve their overall computer performance component by component, is simply to gain a faster and more responsive drive from which to run the operating system and applications. Sizes go up and prices go down continually, so this would be an affordable and effective upgrade.

When Do You Need to Upgrade?

The following is a short list of questions that will help you decide if it's time to upgrade. If you answer yes to two or more of these questions, it's time to consider a hard disk upgrade:

- Have you been unable to install a new application due to an insufficient disk space warning?
- Have you noticed unusual application slow-downs due to a reduction in temporary storage space on your hard drive?
- Have you had to search your hard drive to delete files due to insufficient disk space warnings while running applications?
- Do you continue to encounter disk errors even after performing troubleshooting operations such as checking connections and CMOS settings and running disk utilities?

Installing a Hard Disk Step by Step

If you've never installed a hard drive, try to buy a hard disk upgrade kit that includes all the necessary cables, brackets, and screws (and possibly controllers) you'll need to complete the task. It's no fun having to stop in the middle of a hard drive installation in order to make another run to the store. Once you've decided on the type of drive to install and you've made your purchase, follow the steps listed in the following sections.

Back Up Your Data

If you're replacing your drive, a full backup is critical. After you remove your old hard drive, your operating system, applications, and data files must be copied over to the new hard drive. Strongly consider a backup medium such as tape, CD-Recordable, Zip, or Jaz drives. As soon as you get over 5MB, you'll find floppies woefully inadequate as a backup medium. Let's do the math. A 1GB drive would require one billion divided by 1.4 million bytes, or about 700 disks.

Backup devices will ease your burden and allow you to easily back up your data on a regular basis. Even if you're simply adding a drive, a backup is a good idea for avoiding problems.

INSTANT REFERENCE For more on backing up your data, see Chapter 16, "Tape Backup."

> **Tip:** Whatever backup medium you use (floppies, tape, zip, and so on), you should check the data integrity of the backup once it's complete. File copy methods aren't always 100 percent accurate, and all backup devices include ways to reread the backed-up information to verify a successful copy. There is no more woebegone feeling than beginning to restore a lot of data, only to discover that it is all unexpectedly gone.

An even better solution is to use a disk partition backup utility such as DriveImage or Ghost. These applications take your current drive data and configuration and mirror it onto a new drive. You can quickly turn a new drive into a mirror image of your old drive, complete with proper boot-sector data and configuration. While these utilities can also be used to backup data, you'll need to have another drive available (and large enough) for that purpose already on line—unlikely for most users.

Choose Your Drive Bay

If you're installing an external drive, you don't need to concern yourself with drive bays (just desk space). For an internal drive, open the PC case and check for available drive bays. Check your system's documentation, because some PC designs include bay spaces that aren't obvious just by peering inside. Hard drives come in either 3½-inch or 5¼-inch (across the front of the drive) sizes. You can install a 3½-inch drive into a 5¼-inch bay with the help of mounting brackets. Also keep in mind that you'll need a bay that's close enough to the other drives to be within reach of the IDE cable.

Check Cabling

When replacing a drive without changing to a new controller, simply use the old power supply connection and controller connection for the new drive. If you're adding a drive, check for free power supply and controller connections that can reach to the drive bay you've chosen for the new drive. Power supply connections are four wide-pin sockets usually encased in white plastic, as shown in Figure 11.5.

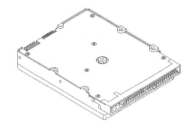

FIGURE 11.5.

The power and data connectors are positioned next to each other on the back of the disk drive. (Figure courtesy of Seagate Corp.)

Set Up the Drive

As discussed in Chapter 10, an IDE device can be either a master or a slave. Set the jumpers on an IDE device before installation. Hard drives generally come from the man-ufacturer set as the master drive for a one-drive only setup, so if that's your scenario, you won't have to modify the jumpers. If you're adding a drive, you might have to set the jumpers on both your original hard drive and the new hard drive. Ultimately, you'll want your boot drive set as master and the new drive as slave. You might have to set a jumper on the original drive to tell it that a slave is present, as shown in Figure 11.6.

::	Drive is Master, no Slave drive present
:▯	Drive is Master, Seagate Slave drive present
▮:	Drive is Slave to another ST9144 Family Master
▮▮	Reserved Positions (Do Not Use)

FIGURE 11.6.

This table from a Seagate drive manual shows the various master/slave jumper options you can choose from.

SCSI Devices Require Proper SCSI ID and Termination Settings

Set the jumpers on your hard drive to a unique SCSI ID. For the hard drive, due to faster startup and even general operating performance advantages, choose a low SCSI ID, either 0, 1, or 2 (the lower the better). Then set the termination jumpers if the drive is at the end of an SCSI chain of devices. You might need to remove termination from the SCSI controller host adapter card if you have both internal and external SCSI devices, because now the host adapter is in the middle of the chain, not at the end.

Replacing Your Hard Drive

If it's time to take out an old drive and put in a new one, follow these steps:

1. Turn off your PC and disconnect the power cable.

2. Open the PC case.

3. Remove the data cable and the power cable from the old drive. IDE data cables often include a white strap at each connector so that you don't need to grasp the ribbon cable or the connector itself. If not, you can pull on the ribbon cable, but get your fingers as close to the connector as possible. Use both hands, and pull gently but firmly until the connector detaches. The power supply cable usually requires a little extra effort. Grasp the white plastic connector on both sides (use just one hand, because it's too small for both hands to fit around it) and pull firmly.

> **Caution:** There is a reason to be careful here. The connectors used in the manufacture of ribbon cables are often cheaply made, so they pull apart easily.

4. Unscrew the mounting screws holding the old drive in place. PC case designs vary tremendously. Traditionally, drive bays are rack-like slots where you slide the drive in or out and secure it with bracket screws into the sides of the drive. But sometimes, hard drives are mounted on swing-out metal brackets. If so, remove the screws holding the swing arm in place, rotate the bay so the mounting screws are exposed, and remove them. Other times, PC designers trap the drive in the drive bay and protect it from escaping by brackets and screws on the front of the system box. If your drive is in a traditional slot-type drive bay, remove the mounting brackets on both sides of the drive. Newer systems sometimes let you attach the drive to a metal bracket (with two screws) before you slide it into a bay where the bracket just clicks into place.

5. Slide out the old drive. Drives should slide easily as soon as all the mounting screws have been removed. If you feel resistance as you try to remove the drive, you might have missed a mounting screw or may still have a cable attached.

6. Insert the new drive. If your new drive is smaller than your original drive (for example, if the new one is 3½ and the old one is 5¼), you first need to attach the mounting brackets that make the smaller box fit properly into the larger bracket frame. Then slide in your new drive.

7. Screw in the mounting screws for the new drive. Don't over-tighten the screws. (See Figure 11.7.)

FIGURE **11.7.**

Check the disk's documentation to make sure you're correctly fitting the new drive. Make sure that you don't accidentally turn the screws into the hard disk's sealed case.

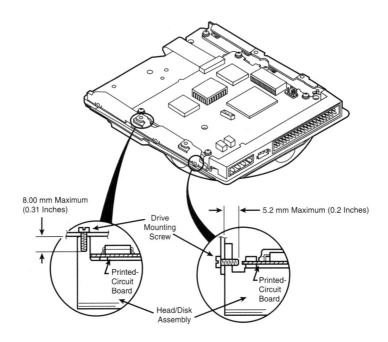

8.00 mm Maximum (0.31 Inches)

5.2 mm Maximum (0.2 Inches)

Drive Mounting Screw

Printed-Circuit Board

Printed-Circuit Board

Head/Disk Assembly

8. Reattach power and data cables. Note: Both of these attach correctly in only one way. The ribbon data cable has a red line running along the edge for pin 1 out of the cable. Your hard drive should have a small "1" marking pin 1 on the data cable connector at the back of the drive. If not, read the device's documentation to determine which device is pin 1. Make sure the red line edge of the cable and pin 1 match up, or you won't be able to access this drive.

   Your cable length (particularly in the shorter IDE cables) might determine which drive bays you need to use. Master and slave IDE drives often need to be adjacent to one another.

   The power supply cable should have a rounded edge on the top two corners of the connector. The power supply port on the back of the drive will also have these rounded edges designating the top edge of the port. Make sure the power cable is firmly secured in the correct position.

9. Close PC cover and connect the power cable.

10. Go to the section "Setting the PC's CMOS."

Adding a Second Drive

Installing a second drive into your system may be an attractive option. After all, you get all the performance and data upside of replacing the original drive, plus you can keep that old drive around for archiving data and generally boosting overall storage.

1. Turn off your PC and disconnect the power cable.

2. Open the PC case.

3. Locate the free drive bay that will hold your new drive. If your new drive is a 3½-inch unit and your bay is a 5¼-inch bay, insert and screw in the mounting brackets.

4. Mount your new drive in the bay. Slide in the new drive so that its back end ports are closest to the data and power supply cable connections. Screw in all the mounting screws, but don't over-tighten them.

5. Connect the data and power supply cables. Internal cables have several connectors running along the length of one cable. Use one of the open connectors for both the data cable (coming from your controller) and the power supply cable (coming from the power supply). Check step 8 of the preceding section to ensure that you are connecting the cables correctly.

Note: If you've already added several internal devices to your PC, it's possible that your power supply might not handle an additional drive. Check your PC's documentation regarding your power supply. The effects of an insufficient power supply would cause data errors or difficulty in accessing your new drive.

6. Close the PC case and reconnect the power cable.

7. Now follow the instructions in the following section on setting your PC's CMOS and preparing your new drive for data.

Setting the PC's CMOS

Now that you've finished the physical installation part of the hard drive upgrade process, you have to ready the system to recognize the new drive.

IDE Drives

Your PC needs to know what types of drives and ports are attached (among other things) before it boots and turns control over to the operating system (see Chapter 2, "Inside Windows 95 and 98"). Check your PC's documentation on how to adjust its CMOS settings (also called *entering setup*). Normally this involves pressing a particular key on your keyboard (such as F1 or Delete) while the PC boots.

Most modern PCs have an Auto Detection setting for IDE drives that tells the PC the drive details it needs to know, such as the number of cylinders on your disk, the number of heads, and the number of sectors per track. Once you've entered your PC's setup program, simply set your IDE drive setting to Auto. Then press the key or key combination that will reboot your PC.

If your PC doesn't have Auto Detection, you need to get the cylinder, head, and sector/track information from your drive manufacturer and enter it manually into your BIOS setup. Most drive vendors now supply this information on their Web site. You also might find it on the case of the drive unit or in the documentation that comes with the drive.

SCSI Drives

Your SCSI host adapter has its own BIOS that handles the SCSI devices attached to it. Read the part of your host adapter documentation covering installing a hard drive. Sometimes SCSI host adapters require a boot drive to be a particular SCSI ID, so check that as well.

Low-Level Hard Drive Formatting

Generally, modern hard drives come with a low-level format already performed by the hard drive manufacturer. It's best not to try to override this low-level format by performing another on your own. If you're having problems with a new drive and you've already attempted the troubleshooting procedures covered in this chapter, try a low-level format with the DOS (and Windows) FDISK command.

Partitioning Your Hard Drive

You can *partition* (divide) your new physical hard drive into several logical drives, each designated by a letter (C, D, E, and so on). The key thing to understand about drive partitions is that large ones (from 1,024MB to 2,048MB) waste an incredible amount of space due to large cluster sizes, the minimum size the operating system takes to store data on the disk. In a 2,048MB partition, for example, a small 1KB file actually takes up 32KB of disk space.

Newer versions of Windows 95 (OSR2 and later) and Windows 98 feature a file system called FAT32, which handles this problem and doesn't waste space in large partitions. Want to see if your version of Windows 95 is FAT32-savvy? Go to Control Panel, click the System icon, and check the General tab. If the System entry reads Windows 95 4.00.950 B or C, you have the OSR2 release. If you don't have this release of Windows 95, or if you're using Windows 3.x, you should choose a partition size of 512MB or less, dividing your disk into multiple logical drives and saving precious disk space.

If you've upgraded to Windows 98, and are still using FAT16, you can quickly move to the new file system. The FAT32 Converter utility will automatically migrate your existing hard disk and data to a FAT32 file format, without damaging your files.

Table 11.3 lists partition sizes and their corresponding cluster sizes.

Table 11.3. Bigger drives waste data.

Partition	FAT16 Cluster Size	FAT32 Cluster Size
16MB-128MB	2KB	4KB
128MB-256MB	4KB	4KB
256MB-512MB	8KB	8KB
512MB-1GB	16KB	8KB
1GB-2GB	32KB	8KB
2GB-8GB	n/a	8KB
8GB-60GB	n/a	16KB
60GB-2,000GB	n/a	32KB

PC experts sometimes use these logical drives to separate applications from the operating system or to simply categorize their disk like a file drawer (drive C contains business software, drive D has home software, drive E has kids' software, and so forth). Choose the number and size of partitions making the most sense for you.

Use the FDISK command (DOS and Windows 9x) to partition your drive. If you've added a second hard drive, make sure you specify the correct drive to partition, because you'll destroy any data that resides on the drive you partition.

INSTANT REFERENCE

For more on partitioning your hard drive, see "Using FDISK to Partition a Disk Drive" on page 293.

High-Level Hard Drive Formatting

Congratulations! All your hard drive installation difficulties are behind you. Simply format the partitions as you would a floppy disk (use Format.com under DOS or My Computer under Windows). If this is your boot drive, be sure to install the system files on it. Then copy your applications and data from your backup to your newly installed drive.

Repairing a Broken Drive

As I mentioned, you will deal with hard disk repairs through software utilities, correcting CMOS setup, or fixing cabling mistakes. Don't attempt to fix your hardware by opening the sealed drive box! That requires special tools that you won't find at home.

If you encounter hard disk errors, follow these steps:

- Check the power supply and data cable connections. Make sure everything is secure and properly connected regarding pin numbers. For SCSI, double-check all jumper settings and termination.

- Double-check CMOS setup. Locate the BIOS information regarding your drive and determine whether the auto-detection features have correctly recognized your drive. For SCSI, use the host adapter's BIOS settings.

- Run through the gamut of disk utilities, especially Disk Defragmenter and ScanDisk. Many a disk problem can be resolved by cleaning up and marking off bad sectors.

- Finally, if you've had a disk crash and your drive is inaccessible, consider shipping the disk to a service bureau, which can perform intensive data recovery procedures using specialized equipment. You can find these bureaus by looking in the yellow pages or searching the Web under "Computer Service and Repair." These services will likely cost several hundred dollars, so make sure you really need the missing data. Also, make regular backups to prevent needing this type of expensive service.

Summary

This chapter discussed both the current and the upcoming technologies of hard disk drives, choosing from among IDE and SCSI drives, and whether you need to add to or replace your PC's hard drive. It also provided step-by-step instructions on hard drive installation.

As performance upgrades go, a hard disk won't usually have that great an impact. However, if your hard drive is nearly filled with data, a new hard drive that increases your storage space will have a noticeable effect on your ability to get work done. A new hard disk can enable you to install and run the latest applications and operating systems, which are often twice the size of versions that came out just a few years before. A new hard disk can also save you a lot of time searching for files to delete.

CD-ROM Drives

CD-ROM (compact disc read-only memory) drives ushered in the multimedia boom in personal computing. Compact discs allowed for 650 megabytes (MB) of portable storage on a single easy-to-transport platter, which allowed software and multimedia developers to include large sound and video data in their applications and games. Consumers quickly embraced these low-cost, durable (compared to floppies), high-capacity discs. As a result, CD-ROM drives have become the most successful removable mass storage element that the PC has known to date.

Today, virtually all home PCs and over 50 percent of business PCs ship with CD-ROM drives, according to the research firm Dataquest. With CD-ROM discs virtually ubiquitous, everyone from application vendors to game companies has chosen CD-ROM discs as their delivery medium of choice. But CD-ROM technology moves fast, with drive speeds increasing by a factor of five or six in just two or three years.

This chapter will help you stay ahead of this fast-moving area. You will learn how to:

- Understand the workings of various types of CD-ROMs
- Examine CD-ROM drive buying issues that may affect your upgrade decisions
- Properly install and optimize your CD-ROM drive for your system
- Identify and resolve conflicts and problems that may arise with the drive

Overview

The first major use of CD-ROM drive technology came in the stereo component consumer market, where CDs ultimately led to the death (or at least an endangered species classification) of the vinyl LP (long-playing) record format. Their 74-minute audio capacity and ability to last for years with no quality degradation made them a hit with music consumers.

CD-ROM technology then stormed the computer market with the ability to store 650MB of data, including sound and video segments, on its shiny 4.72-inch discs. CD-ROM discs now rank as the most-used format for distributing computer software, games, and new music. Almost every new PC on the market comes with a CD-ROM drive.

Unlike magnetic-based recording formats such as hard disks or floppies, CD-ROMs use a laser light method for reading (and writing in the case of CD-Recordable drives) digital data from their discs. A laser (normally yellow) scans the rotating disc surface, and the light reflected back from the disc is interpreted as bit data. A pit (only microns deep) etched into an aluminum alloy coating indicates a binary one, and no pit indicates a binary zero. The laser light reflection only changes in the transition from no pit (called land) to pit, or from pit to land.

> **Note:** The issues of keeping CDs clean have often been overstated by computer guide books and magazines, leading to the sale of cleaning kits and paranoia among users. The truth is, if you use them properly, you won't need to clean your CDs for many years. First and foremost, avoid touching your CD's shiny recorded surface, because this tends to leave oil deposits from your skin on the surface of the CD. When you pick up a disc, touch only the edges. Adults can easily grasp a disc in one hand. Children should use two hands if they can't grasp the disc with one. When you're done using your CDs, store them in their jewel cases so that they won't collect dust or become scratched while resting on a rough surface.

The most dramatic change in CD-ROM drive technology (other than recordable media and drives, which are covered in Chapter 15, "Recordable Optical Storage") relates to speed. The initial drives had transfer rates of 150 kilobytes per second (KBps), called 1X speed. Manufacturers quickly began improving drive mechanics, and it became standard to refer to drive speed in multiples of this original transfer rate. Therefore, a 2X drive transfers at 300KBps, a 4X drive at 600KBps, and so on. In the beginning, these faster drives had premium prices.

You might have paid $800 for a 10X drive a few years ago. Over time, as more vendors jumped into this popular market and flooded stores with drives, prices dropped tremendously. Today, you can purchase an IDE 32X drive for as little as $150. Currently, CD-ROM drive transfer rates top out at 40X speed.

Innovation goes beyond simply faster spin rates. A technology developed by Zen Research and used in a new CD-ROM drive by Kenwood actually splits the laser beam into seven beams through a prism or mirror arrangement. The CLV drive spins at a modest 10x, but because multiple beams are reading up to seven adjacent tracks at once, the drive provides superlative performance. Informal tests show the difference. Using a standard CAV-type 32X CD-ROM drive, the game Unreal took 5 minutes and 47 seconds to load onto a hard drive. But the Kenwood drive performed the same operation in less than half the time, at 2 minutes 46 seconds. The technology promises to smooth out high-resolution, 640×480 video. What's more, because the drive spins at low 10X rates using a single spin speed, it never spins down, avoiding spin-up delays that occurs with fast CAV drives. You can get more information at www.zenresearch.com.

Technical Note: Manufacturers use two distinct methods to spin a CD-ROM disc: CAV (constant angular velocity) and CLV (constant linear velocity).

Hard disk drives traditionally use CAV technology, which means the speed of the platter is kept constant, no matter where the head is over the platter. As the head moves In from the outer rim of the disc toward the center, the speed of the disc moving underneath it is slower (see the nifty carousel analogy in Chapter 11, "Taking Hard Disks for a Spin"). With the magnetic-based disk/head technology of hard disk drives, this method works well.

When CD-ROMs first came out, engineers believed that a more workable method for the optical heads of CD-ROM drives was CLV, where a set speed under the head is maintained no matter where the head is. In this method, the disc itself must speed up or slow down as the head moves in and out to keep the linear velocity constant.

The CLV approach worked fine until CD-ROM drives started spinning above 12X speeds and the disc RPM (revolutions per minute) began reaching 6,300. At these speeds, speeding up and slowing down the disc would cause a slight shudder, and the optical heads needed time to settle down after a move. As the data transfer rates of CD-ROM drives have reached 20X to 40X, almost all vendors are now using CAV technology for their high-end CD-ROM drives.

Most of these CAV drives come qualified as *variable-speed* CAV technology (such as the Plextor 12/20PleX, shown in Figure 12.1), meaning that two different constant angular velocities are used when reading: one for the outer rim data, and one for the center of the disc.

FIGURE 12.1.
Plextor's 12/20PleX variable-speed drive reads data at 12X speeds near the center of the disc, and at 20X speeds at the outer edge. (Photo courtesy of Plextor Corp.)

Upgrading a CD-ROM drive is a fairly straightforward process. It's easier than replacing a hard disk, but slightly more involved than adding RAM. The most difficult part of the process is deciding which drive to buy. The options (speed, controller type, caddy or tray, internal or external) can make a drive purchase confusing, but the following section walks you through the decision.

However, repairing a CD-ROM drive, other than a simple cleaning or reconnecting of cables, is a job best left to professionals. Like hard disk drives, the technology inside the sealed unit requires special tools and environments that you won't find around your home or office. Fortunately, drives are so cheap now that replacing a drive would probably be less expensive than attempting to fix a broken one.

Peter's Principle: Buy a CD-ROM Drive Now or Wait for Cheaper, Faster, More Flexible DVD-ROMs

No discussion of CD-ROM drives can take place without making mention of DVD-ROM, the high-density optical format that promises to replace CD-ROM within the next few years. DVD drives can read discs that store 8.5GB of data per side, or as much as 17GB (compared to 650MB for CD-ROMs). One key application for DVD-ROM drives is delivery of sophisticated multimedia content that includes MPEG-2 video and Dolby AC-3 surround sound audio. But for best results, you'll need a separate add-in card to handle decoding of these complex media files.

After a troubled start, DVD-ROM drives are beginning to take off. Spin rates have jumped so that a typical DVD-ROM drive now plays CD-ROMs at an acceptable 20X spin rate, versus the slow 6X spin rates of first-generation models. And second-generation drives fixed compatibility gaps that left these drives blind to CD-RW and CD-R discs. New drives now incorporate a second yellow laser to read the green-tinted CD-R and CD-RW discs. The native red laser color of DVD-ROM drives was absorbed by the green substrate, preventing adequate reflection to pick up a signal. You will read more about DVD in Chapter 14, "DVD: The Future Arrives." For now, understand that at this time, CD-ROM drives remain an affordable and useful upgrade to consider.

Purchase Decisions

Just like hard disk drives, CD-ROM drives come in both SCSI and IDE controller types. But, unlike hard disks, the limited access speeds of the CD-ROM drives (generally 150ms for CD-ROM drives versus a typical 9ms for hard drives) don't stress the transfer rate capabilities of either standard. Both IDE and SCSI controllers can easily handle the "slower-than-hard-disk" transfer rates of even the fastest CD-ROM drives, so don't look at the IDE or SCSI decision in terms of performance. In fact, the fastest spin rates are typically offered on low-cost IDE drives, since drive makers figure they can find a much larger market among IDE-equipped systems over SCSI-equipped PCs.

If convenience is key, go with an IDE CD-ROM, which should be the easiest to install and your cheapest option, particularly if you can leverage off of your on-board IDE controller. Because all IDE drives are internal, make sure you have an available drive bay accessible via a removable space holder through the front of the machine. Of course, you'll also need an available IDE channel and power connector.

If you already have a SCSI controller (saving some of the cost) and/or your IDE controllers are full, consider a SCSI CD-ROM, where you have the option of internal or external drives. Be sure to read Chapter 10, "Control Freaks: IDE and SCSI Controllers," which covers the termination of SCSI devices.

Assessing Performance

How fast a CD-ROM drive do you need? It depends on what you plan to use it for. Multimedia producers plan their CD-ROM games and titles for play on lower-end CD-ROM drives so that they can capture a large market share. Currently, this lowest common denominator-approach has many CD titles optimized for 4X speed drives. If you have an old CD-ROM (1X or 2X speed), you might notice that some titles won't even install or play on your drive. With a 4X speed drive, you should have no trouble installing most games or titles, but you will likely notice that loading game scenes and installing applications from CD-ROM take a long time. With the cost of 32X CD-ROM drives down around $100, an upgrade from a 4X drive could make sense.

Who needs the fastest drives? If you answer yes to two or more of the following questions, you should consider a 32X or faster drive:

- Do you regularly transfer CD data (database, image, sound, or video) from discs to your PC?
- Do you install more than 10 new titles (applications, games, or reference) in a month's time?
- Do you use PhotoCDs on a regular basis?
- Do you regularly receive and install update discs from CD-ROM publishing services (legal, clip art, reference, or others)?

Keep in mind that many multimedia games and titles are currently optimized for 4X speed playback, so a faster drive will offer no significant advantage in playing back these discs. But installing applications and transferring data from your CD-ROM drive to your hard disk will run the CD-ROM drive as fast as it can go, so a faster drive will save you more time in these situations.

The following is a list of performance specifications for CD-ROM drives. Unlike with hard disk drives, performance really matters when you're shopping for CD-ROMs.

Data transfer rate: How fast the CD-ROM drive transfers data back to the PC. This is usually measured in kilobytes per second and is also referred to as an X-speed (meaning a multiple of the original CD-ROM drive transfer rate of

150KBps). A 4X drive transfers at 600KBps, a 10X drive at 1,500KBps, and a 24X drive at 3,600KBps. A larger number is better.

Average access time: The average amount of time from a CD-ROM drive's receipt of a data request until it reads the first byte of data. This is measured in milliseconds (ms). A smaller number is better. 4X drives usually have 150ms average access times. The 32X and faster drives have 90ms times.

Buffer size: CD-ROM drives also include a small amount of RAM on board to pre-store data likely to be accessed. The larger the cache, the better the impact on responsiveness. CD-ROM drives normally feature buffers that are 256KB or 512KB in size. CD-Recordable (CD-R) and CD-Rewritable (CD-RW) drives typically use larger 1MB or 2MB caches, reflecting the greater challenge involved in moving data during record operations.

To access this cache setting, do the following:

1. Select Start, Settings, Control Panel.

2. Double-click the System icon.

3. Choose the Performance tab of the System Properties dialog box, shown in Figure 12.2.

FIGURE 12.2.

You can try to squeeze a little extra performance out of the drive by tweaking the cache settings of Windows 95 and 98 from the Performance tab of the File System Properties sheet.

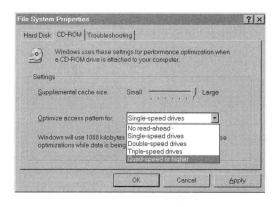

4. Click the File System button.

5. In the subsequent dialog box, choose the CD-ROM tab. In the Settings section, you'll see a slider control called "Supplemental cache size" for adjusting the cache size, as well as a drop-down box called "Optimize access pattern for," which enables you to choose a speed setting for your drive. Generally, you should set the supplemental cache size to Large (with the slider all the way to the right) and the access pattern to the speed of your CD-ROM. (The list doesn't go beyond Quad-speed or 4X, so choose Quad-speed for any drives that are faster than 4X.)

However, if you're running on very limited hard disk space—say, 10MB or less of free hard disk—you might disable this cache altogether. Do so by selecting "no read ahead" from the "Optimize access pattern for" drop-down list.

As a rule, it's more difficult to deliver faster access times than it is to improve raw data rates. Ws time will have a more profound effect on your day-to-day computing, since this spec determines how quickly the drive can find each piece of data.

Multi-Read Ensures Compatibility

Perhaps the most compelling argument for a CD-ROM upgrade is compatibility with various CD formats. Over the years, the baseline CD-ROM format has been extended to include CD-Recordable (CD-R) and CD-ReWritable (CD-RW), two formats that are becoming more common as CD-R and CD-RW prices drop below $400. Older CD-ROM drives, however, often cannot read either of these disc types, making it difficult to share files with others.

New CD-ROM drives comply with the Multi-Read specification, which defines that drives must recognize all the formats that came before. So while your current 12X CD-ROM drive may provide all the performance you need, a move to a 32X model can give you access to CD-R and CD-RW media the old drive can not recognize.

The Tray-Versus-Caddy Controversy

There are two different methods for loading and unloading discs into CD-ROM drives. A caddy mechanism encloses the disc in a removable plastic case (about the size of a jewel case). When you eject a disc, the entire caddy pops out, allowing you to switch discs without ever touching the CDs themselves (provided that you have several plastic caddies). When you're loading a disc into a tray-style CD-ROM drive, on the other hand, a plastic tray slides out from the drive but remains attached to it. You drop the disc directly onto the tray and press the close button.

In general, caddy drives aren't as fragile during loading and unloading discs as tray-style drives. Experts often suggest that caddy drives more accurately read CD-ROMs, but this might be overstated. On the downside, purchasing additional caddies adds cost, and most people never purchase additional caddies at all, eliminating the advantage of having discs pre-stored in caddies.

Tray drives are somewhat faster in loading and unloading discs and are usually cheaper to purchase. But again, trays are slightly more fragile than caddies (see Figure 12.3).

Figure 12.3.

Tray-fed CD-ROM drives, like this remote-controllable model from Creative Labs, are generally more convenient to use than caddy-fed models. (Photo courtesy of Creative Labs)

Additionally, some work environments force people to stand their desktop PC cases on end to make room for other equipment. In these scenarios, the CD-ROM player would sit vertically, not horizontally, in relation to the ground. Unfortunately, not all tray-style CD-ROMs can play discs in this way. Those that can, have plastic tabs that secure the CD in the tray even when it's situated vertically.

Unless you're particularly paranoid about banging the sliding tray, go for the tray-style drive. The extra expense and hassle of caddy drives is generally not worth it.

CD-ROM Jukeboxes: A Small Circle of Friends

The technology of CD-ROM jukeboxes (also called CD-ROM changers) has vastly improved over the years. Now jukeboxes store up to six discs at a time, run up to 10X speed, and swap discs in less than 10 seconds. If you have a small group of discs (from four to six) that you use constantly, a jukebox can save you valuable time by allowing you to keep your discs loaded and available all the time inside one drive.

Companies such as Panasonic, Pioneer, Smart and Friendly, and Nakamichi offer a variety of jukeboxes that come with the same type of options as regular single-disc drives (controller interface, internal and external, speed, buffer size, and so on), but they are differentiated by classifications such as "four-by-eight," "five-by-ten," and so forth, which describe the number of discs the unit holds by the speed the drive spins. "Four-by-eight," for example, means the drive holds four discs at one time and runs at 8X speed.

Normally, jukeboxes feature only one actual CD-ROM reader but contain slots where the other discs reside when not in use. Each disc is usually represented by a separate drive letter on your desktop. A game might be at drive E:, a reference title at drive F:, and so on. When you click a different drive letter, the jukebox quickly swaps the old disc out of the drive, inserts the new one, and spins the disc up to speed.

One feature that differs between single disc drives and their jukebox brethren is the loading mechanism. Instead of the tray-versus-caddy issue, jukeboxes have one of the following:

A slot: This is similar to car stereo CD players, where you just slip the disc through a rectangular hole in the front of the unit.

A tray: You drop the discs, usually one at a time, into a tray.

A cartridge (my favorite): You insert all the discs into a sandwiched-sized cartridge and then plug the whole cartridge into the front of the jukebox.

The beauty of cartridges is that, if you have more than one cartridge, you can keep libraries of related discs preloaded and ready to insert into the jukebox. Imagine one cartridge full of games, another full of reference CDs, and so forth.

> **Note:** Jukeboxes can be persnickety beasts. For example, if you are running an application CD-ROM, you must be sure to insert it into the same slot in the jukebox every time you use it. That's because each slot typically has its own dedicated drive letter, and the installed application won't know to look for the CD-ROM if it's not located in the expected spot.

Unfortunately, although they are ideal in concept, jukeboxes aren't for everyone. Jukebox prices currently range from about $250 to $900—far more than for a typical CD-ROM drive. Moreover, top-end jukeboxes typically spin discs at considerably lower rates than the fastest single-disc drives. The extra money and slower speeds of jukebox drives are only worth it if you have a set of discs you use frequently. Otherwise, stick with single-disc drives.

Taking It on the Road: Portable CD-ROM Drives

Due to the space restrictions and the difficulty of manufacturing, notebook CD-ROM drives can be quite expensive and can add $500 or more to a notebook purchase. If you can't afford an internal CD-ROM drive in your notebook, but you miss the convenience of playing discs while traveling, check out portable drives such as those from Sony and Panasonic.

These external drives usually connect to notebooks via a Type II PC Card (also known as PCMCIA) slot (see Figure 12.4). Available in speeds to 20X, they often use AA-size batteries, which can keep them running for about three hours without being plugged in. Expect slower access times (from 180ms to 280ms) and smaller buffers (128KB) from these lightweight, portable units.

FIGURE 12.4.
If a CD-ROM isn't built into your notebook, you might need to use a SCSI PC Card to provide the inter-face. (Photo courtesy of Adaptec)

If you plan to buy one of these portable drives, in addition to the standard price and performance features, you should look for the following features:

- Rechargeable battery options
- Rugged case designs
- Sturdy PC Card interfaces

Also, realize that many newer notebook manufacturers incorporate specially designed internal CD-ROM units that can be swapped out by extra battery packs or internal floppy drives. Unfortunately, you might be stuck with whatever speed drive the manufacturer offers and therefore won't be able to upgrade when you feel the need. You'll have no alternative company from which to choose a drive.

Troubleshooting

CD-ROM drives usually are reliable. If you're having problems, first check the Windows 95 Device Manager to see if the OS recognizes the CD-ROM as working properly. To access Device Manager, select Start, Settings, Control Panel, double-click the System icon, and choose the Device Manager tab, shown in Figure 12.5.

FIGURE 12.5.
Check Windows 95's Device Manager to make sure your CD-ROM's drivers are installed and working properly.

Dealing with Drivers

For most users, an IDE CD-ROM drive is humming along inside the PC case. But this drive needs driver software—a small program that allows the operating system and the hardware to talk. Absent a driver, the CD-ROM drive will go unrecognized and unused in your system. Windows 98 uses a file called VCDFSD.VXD, a 32-bit protected mode driver that loads Windows' CDFS (or Compact Disc File System). Like the trusty old 16-bit MSCDEX.EXE driver used in DOS and Windows 3.1, this VXD file allows Windows to talk to the drive.

Use DOS's MSCDEX.EXE to Recover from Failure

Of course, a 32-bit VXD driver won't do you much good in DOS mode, whether it's to play an old game or to recover from a devastating hard disk crash. For this reason, the Windows 98 emergency disk setup routine includes options for placing 16-bit generic CD-ROM drivers on the floppy. Your AUTOEXEC.BAT file, used to configure settings prior to Windows 98 startup, also may contain a reference to this file, called MSCDEX.EXE. The old driver allows access to the CD-ROM drive from a DOS session, critical for restoring Windows 98 from the DOS prompt, for example.

On most systems, the Windows 98 MSCDEX.EXE file can be found in the WINDOWS\COMMAND subdirectory. If your CD-ROM drive is not working under Windows 98, you can try to access it by adding a reference to this file in your CONFIG.SYS and AUTOEXEC.BAT files. Add the following lines using a text editor.

To CONFIG.SYS, add the following line (where XX corresponds to the specific name of the .SYS file used by your CD-ROM drive):

```
DEVICE=XXCDROM.SYS /D:mscd001
```

To AUTOEXEC.BAT add the following line:

```
LOAD C:\WINDOWS\COMMAND\MSCDEX.EXE /D:mscd001 /L:
```

Save the CONFIG.SYS and AUTOEXEC.BAT files. You will now have a reference to the MSCDEX.EXE driver and the CD-ROM drive that will be invoked when DOS starts up. If you proceed to Windows 98, the 32-bit driver will supercede MSCDEX.EXE. But should Windows 98 or the CDFS drive fail to load, you should still have access to the CD-ROM drive.

This 16-bit driver is also useful if you need to repartition your hard disk—say to adopt the FAT32 file system—and then reinstall Windows 95 or Windows 98. Many CD-ROM drives are unable to support the new bootable CD-ROM standard, so you may need MSCDEX.EXE on your boot disk to allow the Windows installation CD-ROM to be accessed. (Windows 98 does support bootable CD-ROM operation, which makes reinstalling Windows after a system crash much easier.) So make sure you include this file on your Windows 95 start up disk and that it is references in the AUTOEXEC.BAT file that resides there.

Tweaking AutoPlay

Windows 95 also introduced AutoPlay, a feature that monitors the CD-ROM drive and automatically launches applications or setup routines based on the AUTORUN.INF file found on the CD-ROM. This file points the AutoPlay sequence to the appropriate file to execute—often a SETUP.EXE file located on the CD-ROM disc itself. In the case of audio CDs, the AutoPlay feature will start playing the first track of the disc.

You can bypass AutoPlay by holding down the Shift key while inserting the CD-ROM disc. To turn it off altogether, do the following:

1. Click Start, Settings, Control Panel and open the System icon.
2. Click the Device Manager tab and click the plus sign next to the CDROM item.
3. Double-click the specific CD-ROM entry you want to change.
4. Click the Settings tab. Then click the Auto insert notification check box such that no check appears in the box.
5. Click OK and OK again. Restart your computer when prompted. Windows 95 will no longer monitor the CD-ROM drive for disc inserts and will not launch AUTORUN.INF files.

Even if you do disable Autoplay this way, you can still manually invoke the feature. Just right-click the CD-ROM item in Explorer and choose the Autoplay command from the context menu.

Making Sense of CD-ROM Symptoms

Table 12.1 lists potential CD-ROM related problems and their corresponding solutions.

Table 12.1. Troubleshooting CD-ROM drives.

Symptom	Solution
The CD-ROM drive is not accessible through the operating system.	The installation hasn't been successfully completed. Run through the steps in the section "Installing a CD-ROM Drive." When you've successfully completed the installation, you should see the drive referenced in the operating system. In Windows 3.1, you'll notice an icon with a drive letter for the CD-ROM (usually D or E) next to the hard and floppy disk icons in File Manager. Under Windows 95, you'll see an icon for the CD-ROM drive when you click My Computer.
The CD-ROM drive immediately ejects the disc every time you insert it.	The disc probably is mis-seated in the tray or caddy. Make sure that the disc sits firm and flat in the tray or caddy. Also, read the following Tip if you're using your drive vertically.
The CD-ROM drive makes whirring sounds while spinning a disc, and error messages pop up about difficulty accessing the CD-ROM drive.	The disc might be scratched or dirty. Clean the disc using a cleaning kit or water and a nonabrasive, lint-free cloth. Inspect the disc for scratches. You might ultimately need to replace the disc if the problem continues. You can also try cleaning the drive itself with a compressed air canister (traditionally used to clean camera equipment).
You receive constant error messages about accessing the CD-ROM, even when you use different discs.	Check all the cable connections, and make sure the drive itself is clean. If the problem continues, you might need to replace the drive.
Excessive heat emanates from the CD-ROM drive.	Check the power cable connection and the power supply specifications for your CD-ROM and the power supply output specs for your power supply. If they check out, it's likely that the CD-ROM drive needs replacing.

Tip: Not all CD-ROM drives were designed to work on their sides. Read the documentation to see if your drive supports this feature. A tray-style drive that allows vertical play will have plastic tabs embedded in the tray that snap out to secure the disc in place for proper seating of the CD disc while it's vertical.

Upgrading

Fortunately, upgrading a CD-ROM drive is a relatively cheap option. If you answer yes to two or more of the following questions, you should consider a CD-ROM upgrade:

- Is your current CD-ROM drive a 1X or 2X speed drive?
- Does your current drive have difficulty reading CD-Recordable discs?
- Does your CD-ROM still generate constant read errors, even after troubleshooting?
- Does your CD-ROM consistently make loud noises, even after troubleshooting?
- Do you often transfer data from CDs to your hard disk?
- Is your current drive incompatible with popular CD-ROM formats such as Photo-CD, multisession discs, Video CD, and so on?

Before the Installation

If you've never installed a CD-ROM drive before, consider purchasing a CD-ROM upgrade kit, because it will include all the necessary cabling, screws, and rails. If your PC doesn't already include a sound card and speakers, check into getting a full multimedia upgrade kit, which will add both to the mix. However, be warned that computer press product reviews have often found these kits to be overly expensive and of poor quality. Carefully check each component of a kit to ensure you're getting a good deal.

Once you've made your purchase, follow these preparatory steps:

1. Choose a drive bay. For internal CD-ROM drives, you need a bay that opens from the front of your PC. If your system is bulging with components, you might need to move your hard drive to a bay that doesn't abut the front of the PC. External CD-ROM drives, of course, require only desk space.

2. Check cabling. Make sure you have the necessary power cable socket (usually a white plastic molding with four large pin openings) and controller cable (IDE or SCSI). Make sure they both reach the drive bay in which you intend to install the CD-ROM drive. If the IDE cable doesn't reach, you'll need to buy a longer cable that you can either put in the place of the current cable, or connect to the second IDE channel (if available). For the power cable, you can purchase a Y-cable that will split the single connector into two connectors, adding length to the wire.

3. Set up the drive. As discussed in Chapter 10, "Control Freaks: IDE and SCSI Controllers," an IDE device can be either a master or a slave. Set the jumpers on an IDE device before installing it. CD-ROM drives generally come from the manufacturer set as the master drive, so if that's your scenario, you won't have to modify the jumpers. If you're adding a CD-ROM to an IDE controller that already has a drive attached (a hard disk, for example), you might have to set the jumpers on your CD-ROM to slave, while making sure any hard disk on the same channel is set as the master.

SCSI devices require proper SCSI ID and termination settings. Set the jumpers on your CD-ROM drive to a unique SCSI ID. Then set the termination jumpers if the drive is at the end of a SCSI chain of devices. You might need to unterminate the SCSI controller host adapter card if you have both internal and external SCSI devices, because now the host adapter is in the middle of the chain, not at the end.

Installing a CD-ROM Drive

Once you've finished the drive preparation, you can start the installation process. If at all possible, try to keep the cabling inside the PC neat and organized during your work and after you've finished the job. You'll thank yourself the next time you delve inside the PC case.

1. Turn off your PC and disconnect the power cable.

2. Open the PC case and remove the front placeholder panel, which will be taken up by the front of the CD-ROM drive unit.

3. Ensure that all jumpers and terminators are in their correct position/configuration before you put the slide in.

4. If your drive bay requires slide rails, attach them.

5. Attach the controller cable and the power cable. (With all the cabling and cramped spaces, attaching the cables after the drive is secured in the bay can be difficult.)

6. Both the controller cable and the power cable attach correctly in only one position. The ribbon data cable has a red line running along the edge for pin 1 out of the cable. Your CD-ROM drive should have a small "1" that marks pin 1 on the data cable connector at the back of the drive. If not, read the device's documentation to determine which pin is pin 1. Make sure that the red line edge of the cable and pin 1 match up, or you won't be able to access this drive.

7. The power supply cable should have a rounded edge on the top two corners of the connector. The power supply port on the back of the drive will also have these rounded edges, which designate the top edge of the port. Make sure that the power cable is firmly secured in the correct position.

8. Attach the audio cable from the CD-ROM drive to your sound card. The audio port of the CD-ROM drive is usually adjacent to the power cable port. Read your sound card's documentation to find where the connector goes on the sound card.

9. Slide the CD-ROM drive into the drive bay, as shown in Figure 12.6. Make sure that the front edge fits flush with the front of the PC case. Also make sure that the drive sits level in the bay.

10. Close the PC case and reattach the power cable.

Repairing

Checking cabling and operating system settings will fix most CD-ROM drive problems. If the drive itself isn't working properly, it must either be replaced or sent to a professional, because the internal components can't be manipulated in a home or office environment.

If you encounter problems with your drive, follow these steps:

- Double-check cabling. Mis-seated or reversed controller connectors will make your CD-ROM drive inaccessible.

- Check that your operating system correctly identifies the drive. Under Windows 95, right-click the CD-ROM drive icon under My Computer and select Properties. The resulting dialog box should correctly identify your drive. Contact the drive's technical support if this is not the case.

  In DOS (and therefore Windows 3.x) you need to check your settings in CONFIG.SYS and AUTOEXEC.BAT. The AUTOEXEC.BAT line that refers to your CD-ROM should look something like this (pathnames may vary depending on your system):

  ```
  C:\WINDOWS\MSCDEX.EXE /d:mscd001
  ```

  This is the reference for the Microsoft CD Extensions for DOS.

  Your CONFIG.SYS will have a corresponding line that specifies a device driver to match the AUTOEXEC.BAT file's mscd001 CD-ROM device name. Your drive's installation instructions will spell out the details of the CONFIG.SYS line, but it will look something like this (again, pathnames and the driver name will vary depending on your system):

  ```
  DEVICE=C:\CDDRVER\CDDRV.SYS /D:MSCD001
  ```

- Inspect the medium. It might be that the problem lies with your disc, not your drive. Make sure your discs are clean and free of scratches. If you're using CD-Recordable discs, it's possible your drive has compatibility problems with that type of CD-ROM. Check with the drive manufacturer.

- If you have recently added another SCSI or IDE device, double-check the settings of the jumpers, SCSI IDs, and terminators on all your various drives to ensure there are no conflicts.

- Clean the drive. Use compressed air to clean the tray/caddy of the drive.

Summary

CD-ROM drives are a critical piece of the PC puzzle. Not only do faster drives provide quicker response and file transfers, but they also can ease the load on your CPU. Most users opt for enhanced IDE drive models, which are affordable, quick, and easy to find. But if you do a lot of multitasking or you want a CD-ROM drive that sits externally on your desktop, you'll need to consider a SCSI device.

Of course, DVD looms on the horizon. Although this high-capacity medium comes with a lot of hype and more than a few attractive features, the technology is clearly in its infancy. Early drives lack compatibility with common media such as CD-Recordable, PhotoCD, and audio discs. They are also limited to slow 6X or 8X data rates when playing CD-ROM discs.

The ubiquity of CD-ROM discs, rapid increases in drive performance, and questions about DVD all make CD-ROM drives a viable upgrade. Combine these traits with incredibly low prices, and a CD-ROM drive upgrade might be a good way to extend the life of your PC.

Peter Norton

Removable Storage for PCs

For over 10 years, the venerable 3½-inch floppy disk has been the universal removable medium. Over that time, the format has served applications such as file sharing, data backup, and alternative boot platform. But floppy disks are showing their age—slow, small, and unreliable, they can no longer keep up with the demands of modern applications.

Change is finally in the air, and it promises to shake up the hierarchy of storage on the PC. With data coming from so many different directions—the Internet, email, and a broad universe of applications—removable media needs to be convenient enough to assist the hard disk in storage duties. Large capacities and fast performance are needed to read and write hundreds of megabytes without slowing your work to a crawl. Now a wide selection of products have arrived that can serve as a souped-up floppy drive or add themselves alongside the floppy as a new step in the storage chain.

This chapter will help you:

- Understand existing and developing removable media technologies
- Master buying issues associated with a changing market
- Troubleshoot and resolve problems with removable media and their drives
- Install new removable-media drives

An Introduction to Removable Media

As media types go, none is broader than the category of fast removable media. Often called near-disk storage—because these devices are sometimes used a secondary hard disk drives—the products use a number of different media types and drive technologies. What's more, capacities, performance, and cost vary widely. One thing's for sure, you won't see any compatibility. With few exceptions, these products hew to proprietary media formats that force you to stick with one vendor. Where groups of companies are trying to standardize a particular format, competing technologies mean that no single device has gained a dominating market foothold.

So what do these drives have in common? For one thing, all read and write data on removable rotating media, which are mounted in cartridges. The cartridge format means a single drive can access a virtually unlimited store of data, since cartridges can be swapped out at will. Media can also be moved from one drive to another without risking damage to the disk inside. The drives themselves may be either internal devices mounted in one of the PC's externally-accessible drive bays, or external units that use the parallel port or a SCSI connection. In general, internal models cost about $100 to $200 less than their external counterparts.

While these devices use different technologies to store information, most employ magnetic media similar in function to a hard disk. When the media cartridge is placed into the drive, the cartridge opens so that the media is exposed and positioned beneath the drive's read-write head. A spindle motor in the drive housing causes the media inside the cartridge to spin, while the read-write head is positioned to access desired areas of the disk as it passes underneath.

Information is written to the disk by pushing a magnetic charge out of the read-write head. This charge is picked up by the point of media directly beneath the head, such that it assumes a charged state. If that point already carries a charge—say, positive—the read-write head can toggle the media's content by pushing a negative charge.

To read data off the disk, the read-write head passively senses the magnetic charges underneath it. The magnetic fluctuations on the disk disrupt a slight electrical charge passed through the read-write head as it floats over the media. These disruptions are interpreted as bit fluctuations and indicate to the drive logic that a 1 or 0 value has been encountered.

Most of these drives operate on magnetic principles because magnetic media is much faster than optical drives such as CD-ROM. It is also much easier to write data to disk using magnetic media, since the magnetic fields can be toggled very quickly. The simplicity of magnetic media also helps contain costs, which is why a typical CD-RW drive costs two to three times more than SyQuest's magnetic-based 1GB Sparq drive.

But magnetic media is not a cure all. For one thing, the only way to get high capacities is to increase the density of magnetic fluctuations on the media. But as the individual charges get placed closer together, the charge itself must be reduced to avoid crossover between the points. This means drive heads must become more sensitive, more precise, and travel more closely to the media itself. Advanced tracking and positioning needs to be in place to make sure read-write heads don't write to or read from the wrong spot on the disk, for example.

To handle these challenges, drives often incorporate optical technologies, using a laser to help pinpoint position, for example. Lasers may also be used to prepare the underlying media to accept a new magnetic charge. By using media that must be heated prior to writing data, the drive maker is able to limit magnetic flux changes to the specifically desired point.

The Many Faces of Removable Storage

In the past, removable media could be clumped into two major categories: floppy disk drive successors and near-disk storage. Floppy successors include devices like the 100MB Iomega Zip drive and the Sony/Matsushita 120MB SuperDisk (formerly LS-120) format. A combination of low drive cost (under $200) and low media cost (about $10 per disk) meant the drives were well positioned to become the sort of commodity device that floppy drives are today.

The second class of drives—near-disk storage devices—generally provided data capacities of 1GB and higher and similarly higher prices. Drives often cost $400 or more, and media was quite expensive—on the order of $100 per disk. These devices often find a home in graphics workstations and other places where professionals are juggling data files that are hundreds of megabytes in size.

Over the past year, however, new high-capacity drives have broken through critical price barriers. Iomega's 1GB Jaz drive now costs only $250, while SyQuest's intriguing Sparq device offers 1GB capacities for just $199. The result: 1GB capacity removable media drives are now mainstream and may play a legitimate role in defining what drive format finally replaces our old friend, the 1.44MB floppy.

Floppy Disk Drives: The Old Warrior Won't Fade Away

The floppy disk drive was the first removable storage device for the PC. The term "floppy" came from the old 5¼-inch disks, which could actually bend because they had only a thin coated paper (or flexible plastic) covering, not a hard plastic shell. These floppies could hold only 360KB of data and recorded on both sides. These disks were soon followed by "high-density" versions, which increased the number of available tracks per side and could store 1.2MB of data.

The 3½-inch disks, covered in a hard plastic case, quickly converged on the PC after enjoying success on the Apple Macintosh. The first 3½-inch disk held 720KB of data, but improvements in track density lead to 1.44MB and then 2.88MB-capable drives and disks. Unfortunately, the 2.88MB format was never widely accepted, and now it's difficult to find drives that accept this format, which can be a problem when you're sharing disks.

The innards of today's floppy drive somewhat resemble the magnetic-based recording internals of the hard disk drive unit. Included are the following:

- Magnetic read/write heads: These read and write the data to and from the disk surface.

- A head actuator: This moves the heads in and out across the disk to position them over specific tracks.

- A spindle motor: This spins the disk in a circle so that the track/sector data passes underneath the heads.

Floppy drives have two spring-loaded read/write heads that actually grip the disk surface on both sides (unlike hard disk drives, which don't touch the disk surface). The direct connection between the heads and the disk surface causes wear over time, which is why it's a good idea to replace disks you use frequently.

Floppy drive capacities now seem sorely lacking when you consider the large sound, video, image, and database files that are common today. A single large TIFF image file might exceed the storage capacity of a floppy disk. Distributing applications and other software on disk has mostly vanished as the number of floppies per title needed grew past 30. Now vendors mainly use the popular CD-ROM medium for distributing software.

Manufacturers no longer attempt to increase the performance or even the potential density of these original floppy drives. What manufacturers have done is delve into research and development of new removable storage technologies such as SuperDisk and Zip-style drives, which offer much larger capacities. The goal is to replace floppy drives with these new technologies. But which medium will dominate is still up in the air.

Keep in mind that faster access and larger-capacity removable drives such as Iomega's 1GB Jaz drive do exist, although high prices will probably keep them out of the running as floppy replacements.

TROUBLESHOOTING

> If you're unexpectedly having trouble accessing a 3½-inch disk, eject the disk and try sliding the metal shutter plate back and forth with your fingers. Occasionally, the plate can become stuck, keeping the floppy drive from sliding it back to access the data.
>
> Sometimes you can fix the snag by gently but firmly sliding the plate back and forth before reinserting it into the drive. Be careful not to touch the disk surface itself with your fingers or anything else when you pull the shutter back. It's easy to damage the surface of the recording material. Also, disks are frequently damaged when shipped, so you might need to gently bend the shutter back into position to fix the problem.

SuperDisk Drives: 120MB and Floppy Compatible, Too

Compaq and other PC vendors have begun to include SuperDisk drives (formerly known as LS-120) in their new desktop products, and you can now purchase these drives separately (see Figure 13.1). O.R. Technology's a:drive and Imation's SuperDisk are being sold as upgrades.

FIGURE 13.1.
SuperDisk drives stand a good chance of being the next floppy. (Photo courtesy of O.R. Technology)

SuperDisk drives, first developed by 3M, use the same size disks and the same basic concentric track concept as standard floppy drives. However, the SuperDisk medium is specially formatted during manufacturing with a laser to contain a high-density track guide called a "servo" pattern. This pattern, which is never disturbed or removed during reads or writes, is used as an index by an optical laser head inside the drive.

The optical head precisely guides a cooperative magnetic read/write head to track locations with densities of up to 2,490 data tracks per inch (compared to just 135 tracks per inch for conventional high-density floppy disks). Higher disk rotational speed allows SuperDisk drives to transfer data about five times faster than traditional floppy drives. However, SuperDisk drives are slower than HiFD and Zip models.

Moreover, SuperDisk drives sport dual-gap read/write heads, which can read and write 1.44MB and 720KB 3½-inch floppy disks. (And no, their capacity doesn't increase just because they're used in the SuperDisk drives.) Still, the faster disk rotation means that old floppies transfer data about three times faster in SuperDisk drives than when used in floppy drives.

SuperDisk media comes with a dual-layer coating and metal particle pigment, different from the ferrite material of floppy media, which allows for the higher density. All SuperDisk disks come preformatted, although you can delete and rewrite information on the disks as you normally would with a floppy disk. SuperDisk disks can be used as boot disks for your PC as well. Internal models use the standard IDE interface, and external models use the parallel port connection.

Zip: The Front Runner

Iomega Corporation introduced an affordable removable storage drive, called the Zip drive, and it has gained tremendous popularity over the last few years. Now priced at just $99, these drives use proprietary 3½-inch disks that are twice as thick as standard 3½-inch floppies and that store 100MB of data per disk. Zip drives can't read traditional floppy disks.

Zip drives win hands down in terms of interface options. Among the various types of Zip drives are these:

- SCSI internal
- SCSI external
- Parallel port external
- Enhanced IDE (internal)

SCSI connections and IDE connections offer the fastest performance for Zip drives with 29 millisecond access times, although this speed still remains significantly slower than hard disks.

The parallel port option increases the unit's flexibility, because you can quickly connect to different computers, and it's perfect for use with notebook computers. But the parallel port becomes a performance bottleneck for data transfer and can noticeably slow drive access.

One improvement with Zip drives is that they come with bootable versions, which enable you to use a Zip disk to start up your PC. While you can launch applications directly from Zip disks, these drives are slower than many other removable media alternatives. Zip drives are better used for data storage, backup, and archiving files.

One key issue remains with floppy drives and their potential replacements—sharing data. The beauty of the floppy medium was that it was widely accepted and became a standard feature on all PCs. As the floppy's domination erodes, it might get harder to swap data to other computers using a less common medium.

Currently, Zip drives have a popularity edge over SuperDisk-style drives—Iomega Corporation has sold over 7 million units. This lead might dissolve as the larger and higher-performing SuperDisk drives and disks arrive on more desktop computers from the factory. Overall, it's difficult to determine which way the trend will go. Stay abreast of the mediums used by the people you share data with. If you all work with the same medium, you'll encounter fewer hassles down the road.

HiFD: Sony Wants to Mint a New Standard

Zip may have the early lead, but don't count out HiFD, the 200MB format being sponsored by Sony and Teac. With twice the capacity of Zip, better performance, and the ability to read and write standard 1.44MB floppy disks, HiFD seems to have what it takes to mount a credible challenge. Perhaps most important, Sony has a long record of success-fully establishing market standards—including the 3½-inch floppy disk format we are all so desperate to replace today.

Unfortunately, HiFD is the latest of the low-end crowd to appear on the market, a crucial shortcoming when it comes to earning market share. While Iomega has been putting its Zip drives in systems from Gateway, Dell, and even Compaq, HiFD has been stuck on the sidelines. And that means that HiFD is not a great option if you want a drive that you think will let you share data with other PCs.

That said, HiFD is otherwise a superior format. An extra 100MB per disk is nothing to sneeze at, particularly as growing data needs start to make Zip look just a little anemic. And the backward-compatibility allows you to use just one drive to access both floppies and HiFD media. That means you save a drive bay and the cost of that redundant floppy drive (about $50).

Syquest Sparq

Syquest's Sparq drive was perhaps the drive that helped collapse the difference between floppy disk successors and near-disk storage. For just $199, this drive delivers 1GB of storage on its magnetic-based cartridged media. The drive is available in IDE and SCSI versions, as well as a slow parallel port model for sharing with laptops and other systems. Media costs about $30, which makes the cost per megabyte exceedingly low—though the price of each disk is still rather dear.

In addition to offering a lot of storage bang for the buck, Sparq enjoys the advantage of being manufactured by a proven player in the removable storage market—SyQuest. The company's SyJet and other products have long been mainstays of graphics artists. But while Sparq may be popular, it's drives are still too expensive compared to Zip-style products to make it an imminent floppy disk replacement.

Iomega Jaz

Iomega Jaz has long been the big brother of the Zip drive. Originally a 1GB drive, the format enjoyed some success with graphics professionals, though early concerns about media reliability stunted its market. Today, Jaz has bulked up to 2GB, with newer drives and media doubling the capacity of the first models. However, drive prices are high at nearly $500 and media is expensive as well. Expect to pay $120 for a single disk, or about $300 for a three-disk pack. Fortunately, the new Jaz will work with old 1GB media, allowing you to preserve your investment in old disks.

Like Zip, Jaz is a magnetic-based media. That means it offers plenty of performance. Access times and data rates for the original Jaz were considerably faster than its Zip cousin, and the Jaz 2GB extends that advantage. If you want a drive to offer hard disk-like access to large media file, Jaz 2GB is a good option. The drive is available to work with SCSI and PC Card interfaces, but no IDE version was announced at the time of this writing.

Purchase Decisions

With such a broad market of devices, there are many purchase decisions to make. In this case, I'll break the thinking out into two categories:

- Updating or replacing an existing floppy drive
- Adding near-disk storage to your PC

For many, backing up and archiving data is an unpleasant prospect. If the only time you plan to access your backup medium is when your hard disk drive fails, you should look to a less-expensive technology, such as tape drives, to meet your needs. In this case, speed is not an issue, and the slow, sequential tape access won't drive you crazy. You'll save money with both the drive and the medium over removable disk drives.

On the other hand, if you regularly go back to your backups or data archives, retrieving and reinstalling files, these removable drives can be a cost-effective solution. In this product category, what you're really paying for is reasonable-speed random access of your stored data.

The following sections list the different factors involved in choosing from among the wide range of options. The items run from most-important to least-important for purchase decisions.

Size Matters

These products can be divided into three tiers of storage: 100 to 750MB drives, 1 to 2GB drives, and drives over 2GB.

- 230 to 750MB: Choose this when floppy-alternative drives are just a little too small for your needs but you're still mainly concerned with selective backup and transporting files between systems. These drives cost about $250 to $700, depending on the technology used. Drives in this category include the SyQuest EZ-Flyer 230, the Nomai 540 and 750.c, the Pinnacle Micro Tahoe 640MB, and others.
- 1 to 2GB: Choose this when you need to store large multimedia files for periodic access or perform regular archiving and retrieval of data. These drives can be especially useful in desktop and Web-publishing applications. Drives in this tier include the SyQuest SyJet and Iomega Jaz Drive, both of which cost about $300 to $350.
- Over 2GB: Choose this when you require regular PC or network hard drive backups. If you need an ever-expandable second hard drive, if you work in digital video production, or if you use multiple operating systems on a single PC, these drives will provide the storage you need. Drives in this tier include the

Hewlett-Packard SureStore Optical 2600fx Multifunction Disk Drive, the Pinnacle Micro Apex 4.6GB and Vertex 2.6GB (see Figure 13.2), and others. Generally, drives at this storage capacity cost about $2,000.

FIGURE 13.2.
At under $1,000, the internal Pinnacle Micro Vertex Drive provides quick performance and 2.6GB disk capacities. (Photo courtesy of Pinnacle Micro, Inc.)

Updating Your Floppy Disk Drive

Never consider upgrading a floppy drive because you need a "better" one. Your floppy drive either works or it doesn't. If it doesn't, you can consider a cheap replacement. In terms of upgrades, you might think about moving up to the new drives, which feature 100MB or more on a single removable disk. SuperDisk and Zip drives are relatively cheap, are easy to install, and might suit your needs. In this chapter, we'll discuss how to install both.

One way to go is to purchase a combination drive, which comes with different devices and includes a floppy drive. One style combines a CD-ROM drive and a floppy unit in the same drive. Another style offers both floppy and PC Card (also know as PCMCIA cards).

Your best bet with a combination drive would most likely be the floppy/PC Card combo. The CD-ROM drive that is included in such a combo might be of inferior performance, while the PC Card interface will likely be standard-issue. Keep in mind that SuperDisk drives read 1.44MB standard floppies, so you might consider that route as well.

If you already have a high-capacity portable storage device (CD-Recordable drive, tape, and so forth), you might decide on a straightforward floppy drive replacement. If you do plan to simply replace your current floppy drive with another plain-vanilla floppy, here's a quick checklist to help guide your purchase:

- Don't concern yourself with performance. Floppy drives all perform alike.
- Don't concern yourself with brand names. You'll probably just pay more for the name.
- Shop around. You shouldn't have to spend more than $50 for a new floppy drive.

Thinking about higher-capacity drives? If you answer yes to three or more of the following questions, you should consider buying a Zip drive:

- Do you plan to use your new drive mostly for data backup, archive, and temporary storage?
- Is it unlikely that you'll need to use the drive as a boot drive?
- Is fast access unimportant to you?
- Do the people you share data with use Zip drives?
- Is it unnecessary for the new drive to be able to read floppy disks?

On the other hand, if you can answer yes to two or more of the following questions, you should consider spending a little more money for an SuperDisk-style drive:

- Do you need to boot from the drive?
- Do you need to launch applications from the drive?
- Do others you share data with use the SuperDisk medium?
- Does the new drive need to be able to read floppy disks?

Table 13.1 compares floppy, Zip, and SuperDisk drives.

Table 13.1. A comparison of removable media.

	3½-Inch Floppy Drive	Zip Drive	SuperDisk Drive
Single-disk capacity	1.44MB or 2.88MB	100MB	120MB
Boot drive potential	Yes	No	Yes
Interface options	IDE	IDE, internal SCSI, external SCSI, parallel port	IDE for internal, parallel port for external
Ability to launch applications from disk	Yes	No	Yes
Price	About $50	About $99	About $149

Adding Near-Disk Storage

In many cases, you'll want to add another level of storage to your system. In this case, it makes sense to keep your floppy disk drive around, since you'll probably need it for a few more years to read the occasional 1.44MB floppy. Remember, if all you have is a Zip drive, you won't be able to read these disks, which are still being sold by the boatload.

Any drive, even those likely to replace the floppy, can act as effective near-disk storage options. An Iomega Zip drive, for example, provides reasonably quick access to 100MB cartridges. While you won't want to run executable files directly off the media, you can certainly play most video and audio files without trouble.

But if you crave the convenience of large capacity and rapid performance, the larger format drives are probably a better option. Professionals may have files that run 500MB in size or more, making them too large even for relatively-slow CD-R media (which holds 640MB). Or you may use large and fast drives as network-based storage that is readily removable, whether it's for distributed data access or network based backup.

For individual workstations, a low-cost format like SyQuest Sparq and Iomega Jaz certainly stand out. Their magnetic media format allows for fast hard disk-like access, while the 1GB and 2GB capacities reduce disk swapping and ensure adequate capacity for backing up large hard disks. After all, you'd need 160 Iomega Zip disks to backup a full 16GB hard disk drive, while a Sparq drive requires only 16 such disks. A 2GB Jaz drive cuts that number to eight.

Because compatibility with floppy disks or with the larger universe of installed near-disk drives is not so much a concern, you can focus more on other issues. The main ones:

- Cost of the drive
- Cost per megabyte of media
- Performance

Drive cost is a real concern for desktop users. You can get a 4.6GB media in the form of Pinnacle Micro's Vertex. But the fast, magnetic-based drives cost nearly $1,000, about five times more than the SyQuest Sparq. Cartridges are also quite expensive. Unless you really need this kind of multi-gigabyte capacity, such an expensive drive is probably unwarranted. Also, high media costs make the cost of losing a disk (whether to physical damage or absent mindedness) a much more serious matter. Lose a Zip disk, and it's $13 down the toilet. Misplace a Jaz 2GB cartridge, though, and you're out $125. Think about it.

In the performance real, you'll want to seek out fast random access and seek performance over all others. Fortunately, all these drives provide adequate response, largely because they rely on magnetic operation. Magneto-optical drives, which use a combination of lasers and magnetic fields, offer big capacities but sluggish performance—particularly when writing.

INSTANT REFERENCE For more on MO drives, see Chapter 15, "Recordable Optical Storage."

Backing Up Data

No matter what drive you buy, any of these options can help you back up your data. Fortunately, many of these removable disk drives come with backup software in the box. If for some reason your drive doesn't include backup software, or the software doesn't meet your backup needs, several options await you.

Windows 95 Backup

Both Windows 95 and Windows 98 offer a built-in utility called Backup, shown in Figure 13.3. You can access it by selecting Start, Accessories, System Tools. If you don't see it listed, it wasn't installed during the original operating system installation. To install it, select Start, Settings, Control Panel and double-click Add/Remove Programs. Choose the Windows Setup tab. Highlight Disk Tools and then click the Details button. Put a check next to Backup, and then click Apply. You will be asked to insert your Windows 95 installation CD-ROM.

FIGURE 13.3.
Windows 95's integrated Backup facility won't schedule your backups, but it's free with the operating system.

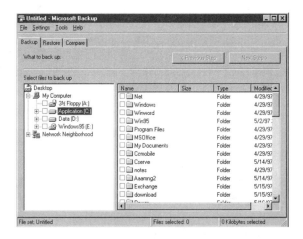

Windows 95 Backup offers only limited backup features and does not support scheduling. If you need more powerful tools, check into other options.

Free Backup Software

Backup software is a popular topic on shareware bulletin boards and Web sites. Partial-function (or limited-timed use) demos are available for free at many sites. One example is Search on Reflex Backup (from Genius Technologies) at www.download.com (CNET's shareware page). Reflex Backup supposedly works with any removable disk drive. Demos usually include information on where and how to purchase the full package.

Additionally, you can often find free applets that extend the features of your existing backup package. For example, for Iomega Jaz drives, you can add scheduling capability through a free utility called 1-Step Backup System Agent Extension (also available through www.download.com). You must have Iomega Tools and the Microsoft Plus packages in order for this applet to work.

Off-the-Shelf Backup

One of the higher-rated packages is the $149 Seagate Backup Exec for Windows 95 and Windows NT (www.seagatesoftware.com). It features full scheduling and automation of backup routines, and enables you to backup to multiple media formats. Check computer press reviews for more on the latest software.

Diagnosing/Troubleshooting

Floppy drives are notoriously flaky. Heat and cold and variations among drives and disks can cause errors. Table 13.2 is a guide to help you fix your problems.

Table 13.2. Floppy fixes.

Symptom	Solution
Disk errors while accessing a particular disk	Make sure that the disk is formatted correctly for your drive. Macintosh-formatted disks can't be read by PCs without special utilities. Also try checking the disk in another drive to see if it works. Additionally, 2.88MB formatted disks can't be read by all floppy drives. If the data isn't vital, try reformatting the disk, or simply replace it.
You're unable to access the floppy drive at all	Check data cable and power cable connections inside the PC. Make sure that the cables are aligned properly and that the fittings are snug. Try replacing the data cable. Make sure that your computer's BIOS settings have an entry for the floppy drive.

continues

Table 13.2. Continued.

Symptom	Solution
Disks frequently become stuck in the drive	The ejector arm of the drive might be broken. For $50, replacing the drive might be your best option. If you feel like tinkering, you can take the drive apart to see if you can fix the problem.
Frequent disk errors while accessing disks	Try cleaning the read/write heads with a cleaning kit, available from any computer store. Usually these kits come in wet or dry options. The wet kits cause less wear on the head. If the problem continues, consider replacing the drive.

TROUBLESHOOTING

Unlike hard disk drives and CD-ROM drives, floppy drives can be taken apart for repair. The most common reason to do this is that a floppy disk is stuck in the drive unit. Be sure to completely remove the drive from the computer before attempting to disassemble it. Getting the floppy disk out is simply a matter of unscrewing the case screws, removing the metal casing that surrounds the drive internals, and pulling the disk free. Just be careful not to bend or damage the drive's read/write heads. Before completely closing your PC case again, attach the reassembled drive to the computer with the PC case off, and determine if it works.

To extend the life of disks, follow these simple rules:

- Never expose them to extreme temperatures, hot or cold.
- Never expose them to strong magnetic fields, including resting them on audio speakers or your monitor.
- Never touch the recording surface with anything.
- Avoid spilling anything on the disk case.
- Store disks in a dust-free area or inside a case with a cover.

Upgrading

With the wide variety of drive types and models, it is simply not possible to detail every removable disk drive installation. Instead, we'll discuss installing a few specific models, ranging from a standard floppy drive and an Iomega Zip to the highly regarded SyQuest SyJet (www.syquest.com).

TROUBLESHOOTING

For any of the IDE versions of these removable drivers, users face a potential problem with drive letter assignments. Specifically, if you have an extended DOS partition on your hard drive, you may find that the new removable drive gets placed between the main (C:\) partition and the extended partition.

For example, if you have a 4GB hard disk with two partitions, the primary partition is normally assigned C: and the extended partition is assigned D: drive. But if you add a Syjet or other removable drive, the letter for the removable device may end up being D:, pushing your extended disk partition letter out to E:. Obviously, this can wreak havoc on any Windows software you installed on the D: partition. Things get even uglier if you put your Windows swap file on D:—if you have no cartridge in the removable D: drive when you boot, the hard drive extended partition is once again drive D:.

You can try to prevent this problem by tailoring your IDE master/slave disk settings. The PC BIOS automatically assigns disk drive letters at boot time, with the IDE master/slave settings playing a role in how assignments are made. If you set your removable drive as a slave on the secondary IDE channel, the BIOS is unlikely to assign that drive a letter ahead of logical partitions on the main disk.

If the problem persists, you might look into another fix. Syquest, for one, says you can actually partition the cartridge in the SyQuest drive as an extended partition. Once you reformat the cartridge, the removable drive will be seen as the last drive in the series. Of course, doing this will wipe out any data on the cartridge, so you should back it up first.

Upgrading a Floppy Drive

Because floppy drives reside alone on their own controller ports, you don't need to worry about the jumper settings that most internal device installations require. Just follow the next steps.

To replace a floppy drive, do the following:

1. Turn off the PC and disconnect the power cable.

2. Remove the PC case.

3. Remove the data and power cable from the back of the floppy disk drive, and then remove the drive itself.

4. Unscrew the mounting brackets holding the drive in place.

5. Slide the floppy drive out on its drive bay.

6. If your new drive is a 3½-inch drive and your old drive was 5¼-inch, you might need to attach mounting brackets that will hold the smaller drive in the larger bay. If so, screw in the mounting brackets now.

7. Attach the data and power cables to the back of the new floppy drive unit before inserting it into the drive bay. It might be difficult to access the ports after the drive is installed in the bay, so avoid this hassle by attaching them now. You can use the same ribbon data cable that was attached to your old floppy drive, but if you want to replace it, you can do so now.

Note: To replace the ribbon data cable, locate the floppy drive controller port on the motherboard of your PC. It should have the word "floppy" etched into the board directly underneath. It generally resides right next to the primary and secondary on-board IDE controllers.

Remove the old ribbon cable and attach the new one. Make sure the red line along the new ribbon cable aligns with pin 1 of the controller. You should also see a "1" etched into the motherboard, pointing out the proper side of the on-board floppy controller.

Now attach the ribbon data cable and the power cable to the new floppy drive. Both of these cables attach correctly in only one way. The ribbon data cable has a red line running along the edge for pin 1 out of the cable. Your floppy drive should have a small "1" marking pin 1 on the data cable connector at the back of the drive. If it doesn't, read the device's documentation to determine which pin is pin 1. Make sure the red-line edge of the cable and pin 1 match up, or you won't be able to access this drive.

The power supply cable should have a rounded edge on the top two corners of the connector. The power supply port on the back of the drive will also have these rounded edges, designating the top edge of the port. Make sure that the power cable is firmly secured in the correct position.

Note: Both ribbon cables and the power cables inside PCs usually have connectors along the length of the cables, as well as connectors at both ends of the cable. These simply let multiple devices share the same cable. There is no order to these connectors, so attach your floppy drive to whichever connectors along the floppy controller ribbon cable (and the power cable) are closest to the drive itself.

8. Slide the floppy drive into the drive bay. Make sure the front of the drive is flush with the front of the PC unit. Make sure there are no gaps between the edges of the drive and the metal frame that surrounds it.

9. Attach the screws that secure the drive in place. Do not over-tighten them.

10. Close the PC case and secure the case screws.

11. Reinsert the PC power cable.

12. If you just replaced the floppy drive with an identical unit, no BIOS adjustments should be necessary. However, if you've moved from a 5¼-inch drive to a 3½-inch drive or made some other configuration change, you should check your computer's BIOS settings to ensure that it has correctly identified the drive through auto-configuration.

Installing a Zip Drive

Currently, Iomega Corporation (www.iomega.com) offers Zip drives in parallel port and internal and external SCSI versions. At the time this chapter was written, an internal IDE version had been announced but was not yet available. Installing the parallel port version is a breeze, and you have the flexibility to quickly move the drive to another computer. But, as I mentioned, you sacrifice some performance for what you gain in flexibility.

Installing the Zip Drive on a Parallel Port

The Zip drive comes with a *pass-through* parallel port connection, which enables you to keep both the Zip drive and your printer attached to the parallel port at the same time.

1. Attach the Zip's pass-through connector to the parallel port. If you have a printer attached to the parallel port, remove your printer cable from the parallel port of your PC, and then attach the Zip drive connector to the parallel port.

2. Connect your printer cable to the back of the Zip's pass-through port. Note that you can't use the Zip drive and printer at the same time. Also, other parallel devices (and even some printers, may not work with the pass-through connection).

3. Install the Zip drive software, which will recognize your drive as the next available drive letter.

Installing an External SCSI Zip Drive

If you don't have a SCSI controller, you'll need to purchase one and install it. Read Chapter 10, "Control Freaks: IDE and SCSI Controllers," for details. The Zip drive uses a SCSI-2 thin 50-pin female, but it can attach to any SCSI controller card with the right cable adapter. If you already own a SCSI card, check which type you have. You must purchase an adapter cable if you don't have the SCSI-2 connector.

1. Connect the SCSI cable to your SCSI controller and to the back of the Zip drive.

2. Set the SCSI ID settings. If you have other SCSI devices, check them to determine if either SCSI ID 5 or 6 is free. These are the two IDs that the Zip drive can use.

You might need to set the switch (or jumpers) of another SCSI device to a different ID if both are currently being used. Choose either 5 or 6 for the Zip drive, and set the switch.

3. Set the termination of the Zip drive. The default setting is terminated for the end of the SCSI chain. If you have other SCSI devices, you might need to adjust this switch. (You can read about terminating devices in Chapter 13 "Removable Storage for PCs.") First, simply try to access the drive after you finish the installation. It's likely you won't need to adjust this switch.

4. Turn on the power for the Zip drive before turning on your PC. In order for the PC to recognize the drive, you must turn on the Zip drive first.

Installing an SuperDisk Drive

SuperDisk drives from Imation (www.imation.com) and O.R. Technology (www.ortechnology.com) come in external parallel port versions and internal IDE versions. As with Zip drives, you'll sacrifice performance for the flexibility of the parallel port versions.

Installing the Parallel Port SuperDisk Drive

Just like with the Zip drive, you can still operate your printer through the pass-through capabilities of the SuperDisk connector. Unlike Zip drives, SuperDisk drives are made by more than one manufacturer, so their installation procedures might vary. Make sure you read and follow the directions included with your drive. In general, the instructions should be similar to these steps:

1. Attach the SuperDisk's pass-through connector to the parallel port.

2. Connect your printer cable to the back of the SuperDisk's pass-through port. Again, the pass-through port may not allow some printers and most other parallel devices to work.

3. Install the SuperDisk drive software, which will recognize your drive as the next available drive letter.

Installing the Internal IDE SuperDisk Drive

Follow the manufacturer's instructions to install the internal IDE SuperDisk drive. In general, the steps are as follows:

1. Turn off your PC's power, and remove the power cable.

2. Remove the PC's case.

3. Choose your drive bay. If you're replacing your floppy drive (because the SuperDisk drive reads floppy disks in addition to SuperDisk media), remove your floppy drive and use that drive bay for your SuperDisk drive.

4. Attach the ribbon data cable and power cable. Make sure that the cables connect in the proper way. You can use any connector of your IDE controller cable.

5. In most cases you'll want to set the drive as a slave on the IDE channel. Make sure you set the jumpers to the master or slave configuration you want.

6. Insert the drive into the bay. Make sure that the front of the drive is flush with the front of the machine.

7. Secure the SuperDisk drive in its bay with screws.

8. Close the PC's case and reattach the power cable.

9. Read the manufacturer's instructions regarding your BIOS. You might need to upgrade your BIOS to recognize the SuperDisk drive as a boot drive.

Installing a SyQuest SyJet Drive

The 3½-inch SyJet uses magnetic-based recording on 1.5GB removable disks. It offers fast 12ms access times and therefore is suitable for loading files (and occasionally launching applications) from its medium. The SyJet comes in internal SCSI ($400), external SCSI ($500), and external parallel port models ($530). SyQuest has announced that an internal IDE version is under development. You can purchase individual 1.5GB disks at $125 or a three-pack for $300.

The SyJet SCSI Installation Routine

What follows are the instructions for the internal SCSI model. You'll need your own SCSI host adapter card (see Chapter 10, "Control Freaks: IDE and SCSI Controllers"), because SyQuest doesn't supply one in the box.

Before you begin, do the following:

1. Choose a drive bay: You need a bay opening to the front of your PC. If your system is bulging with components, it's conceivable that you might need to move your hard drive to a bay that doesn't abut the front of the PC. External drives, of course, require only desk space.

2. Check the cabling: Make sure that you have the necessary power cable socket (usually a white plastic molding with four large pin openings) and controller cable (SCSI). Double-check that they both reach the drive bay in which you intend to install the SyJet.

3. SCSI devices require proper SCSI ID and termination settings (again, see Chapter 10). Check the ID of your SCSI host adapter and any devices that connect to it (using your SCSI management software) before beginning this installation. You'll need to choose an unused SCSI ID for the SyJet.

4. The SyJet comes with a default SCSI ID of 4. If another device holds this ID, you must either change that device's ID or change the SyJet's ID. To alter the SyJet's ID, follow these remaining steps:

5. Remove the four screws that hold the SyJet drive into its 5¼-inch mounting boot.

6. Pull the drive out from its 5¼-inch mounting boot.

7. Turn the drive upside down.

8. Locate the JP2000 jumper on the bottom of the drive. Pin 1 is toward the center ¨ of the drive, and pin 8 is on the outer edge of the drive. Page 13 of the SyJet Installation Guide shows the jumper settings map. Using this map, move the jumpers to a new setting.

9. Before putting the drive back into the mounting boot, check the termination jumper (pin 8). If the jumper covers both pins, the drive is unterminated. If it covers only one of the two pins, it is terminated. If your SyJet is to be the last device on a SCSI chain (see Chapter 13), it must be terminated. Otherwise, leave it unterminated.

10. Reinsert the drive into the mounting boot, and screw in the mounting screws.

Installing the Internal SCSI SyJet

Follow these steps to install the internal SCSI SyJet:

1. Shut down the PC, turn off the power, and remove the PC power cable from the back of the PC unit. Open the PC case.

2. Remove the plastic cover from the front of the chosen drive bay.

3. Connect the 50-pin SCSI cable and the power adapter cable to the back of the SyJet drive.

UPGRADE ADVICE

Both of these attach correctly in only one way. The ribbon data cable has a red line running along the edge for pin 1 out of the cable. Your SyJet has a small "1" marking pin 1 on the data cable connector at the back of the drive. Make sure that the red-line edge of the cable and pin 1 match up, or you won't be able to access this drive.

The power supply cable should have a rounded edge on the top two corners of the connector. The power supply port on the back of the drive also has these rounded edges, designating the top edge of the port. Make sure that the power cable is firmly secured in the correct position.

4. Insert the SyJet into the drive bay. If it is a 3½-inch bay, first remove the SyJet mounting boot. You won't need it in this case.

5. Make sure that the front of the SyJet drive is flush with the front of your PC case and that no gaps exist between the edges of the drive and the PC.

6. Screw in the four screws that hold the SyJet into the bay. Don't over-tighten them.

7. Double-check that the cabling is correctly attached.

8. Put the PC case back on.

9. Reattach the PC power cable.

10. Insert a SyJet cartridge into the SyJet drive. This cartridge is preformatted. Make sure that the cartridge snaps into place after you push it all the way in.

11. Turn on your PC.

12. Use your SCSI diagnostics to determine whether the drive is recognized correctly. Do not reformat the cartridge.

The SyJet IDE Installation Routine

Follow the manufacturer's instructions to install the internal IDE SyJet drive. In general, the steps will be as follows:

1. Turn off your PC's power, and remove the power cable.

2. Remove the PC's case.

3. Choose your drive bay, and remove the front plate.

4. Attach the ribbon data cable and power cable. Make sure that the cables connect in the proper way. You can use any connector of your IDE controller cable. If the data or power cables don't reach, you may need to replace them with an extended data cable and a Y splitter power cable.

5. In most cases you'll want to set the drive as a slave on the secondary IDE channel. Make sure you set the jumpers to the master or slave configuration you want.

6. Insert the drive into the bay. Make sure that the front of the drive is flush with the front of the machine.

7. Secure the SyJet drive in its bay with screws.

8. Close the PC's case and reattach the power cable.

9. Read the manufacturer's instructions regarding your BIOS. You might need to upgrade your BIOS to recognize the SyJet drive as a boot drive.

Installing the SyJet Software in Windows 95

Follow these steps to install the SyJet software in Windows 95:

1. Under Windows 95, select Start, Settings, Control Panel.

2. Insert the SyJet Installation disk and click Install.

3. Follow the on-screen directions.

Repair

Unlike hard disk drives and CD-ROM drives, you can actually disassemble a floppy disk drive with standard tools. Unlike fast access drives, floppy drives are not sealed against the contaminants in the air (dust, dirt, and so on).

The problem is that you'll probably find it easier (and less expensive) to just replace the drive than to either fix it yourself or have someone else do it. Floppies currently cost $50 or less. First, though, follow these steps to determine if you can fix your drive:

1. Check cabling and power connections. Make sure that pin 1 is aligned with the red edge of your ribbon data cable and that the power cable is inserted properly.

2. Make sure that your system BIOS correctly identifies your drive.

3. Try cleaning the drive heads with a store-bought wet cleaning kit.

4. Check your disks to make sure they aren't the problem. Format new disks, copy files to them, and read and write to them. Throw out any old, beat-up disks.

Once you get past floppies however, repair simply isn't an option. SuperDisk, Zip, Sparq and other high-capacity removable drives rely on precise positioning and calibration of the media and read/write heads to operate. Opening the drive can imperil the operation of the hardware and will surely void any warranties you have in place. If you experience unresolvable problems with any of these drives, your best option is to have the drive serviced by the manufacturer.

Summary

Floppy drives should be given a lifetime achievement award by the computer industry. Due to their relatively simple technology, sufficient speed, and cheap but durable medium, floppy drives have been an integral component aboard almost every PC ever manufactured. For many years, floppy disks were the main distribution medium for software and data.

Times have changed. With the large-scale files now involved in multimedia applications, a single file can be larger than the 1.44MB capacity of the high-density floppy format.

You can easily replace your broken floppy drive with an inexpensive replacement, but for a little more money, you can extend the capacity of a single disk drive to 100MB with a Zip drive, or you can opt for floppy compatibility and larger data storage from the 200MB HiFD. For those needing big storage, the multi-gigabyte formats from Iomega, Syquest, and others are worth exploring. No matter what, you'll find a wide array of interfaces, including parallel port, external SCSI, internal SCSI, and internal IDE. There are even USB-based SuperDisk drives. Although no one yet knows whether any of these new formats will ever be as popular as floppy drives, you can take advantage of large capacities in the meantime.

DVD: The Future Arrives

Your PC has a problem. There's a burgeoning universe of cool theater-quality video, audio, and animation out there, and no way to get it into your PC. Internet connections aren't fast enough, and CD-ROM discs aren't large enough to handle sharp MPEG-2 compressed video and immersive AC-3 audio. What do you do? Why, upgrade, of course.

Digital Versatile Disk (DVD) technology is classic convergence stuff. DVD-ROM drives and DVD players promise to change the face of both computing and home theater. If you have a fast Pentium-class PC and you want access to the best and brightest content, you'll need to upgrade to a DVD-ROM drive.

This chapter covers the following:

- The workings of DVD media and drives
- Buying advice for those considering a DVD-ROM drive in a new or existing PC
- Upgrading and installation insights for a new DVD-ROM drive
- Troubleshooting and maintenance tips for DVD-ROM drives

The CD-ROM Revolution, Part II

They say necessity is the mother of invention. Well, Mom was hard at work when the DVD specification was being cooked up. It all began in the early 1990s, when it became apparent that the existing capacity of CD-ROM discs was running out of steam. The culprit was high-quality, high-bandwidth video compression schemes featured on direct satellite systems (DSS) such as DirecTV and PrimeStar.

If you're familiar with CD-ROM drives, DVD-ROM should be pretty easy to comprehend. After all, the drives themselves look identical to CD-ROM drives from the outside. And DVD-ROM drives use a similar laser-based optical mechanism to read data off of standard-sized discs. Even the discs themselves look identical, though DVD-ROM discs sport more tightly packed tracks and contours to allow vast amounts of data to be stored.

DVD-ROM drives shine a red-colored laser on the disc. The mechanism detects variations in the reflected laser light that is bounced off the media surface and interprets them as 1s and 0s. DVD-ROM drives differ from CD-ROM drives in that the laser light is more tightly focused and of a different color than that used in CD-ROM drives.

DVD-ROM and CD-ROM media also have similarities and differences. Both feature tiny pits on their surfaces that the drive's optic mechanism is able to interpret as data. But DVD-ROM drives use much more closely spaced pits and concentric tracks to pack more data on the disc.

Birth of a Spec

Several companies began investigating ways to increase the storage capacity of existing CD-ROM discs and drives. New manufacturing techniques and improved laser technology had begun to pave the way for storage potential far beyond the CD-ROM limits of 650MB per disc. Two competing organizations and design specifications quickly emerged: Super Density, from a group of companies led by Toshiba, and Multimedia CD, from Philips and Sony.

It was becoming a classic standards standoff, and one that could imperil the success of the new standard. Considering the costly '80s battle between competing videocassette standards (VHS and Betamax), the two groups decided to work together in 1996 to complete one unified standard. The result was called DVD.

Input from the movie industry added complexity to the initial designs. This group saw DVD as a terrific medium for the distribution of higher-quality home movies. To make it happen, they wanted:

- MPEG-2 video support
- Dolby AC-3 surround sound audio support
- Subtitling capability
- The capability to handle multiaspect ratios (full screen, letterbox, and wide screen)
- Encryption

Not surprisingly, hammering out these aspects took time. Hollywood studios were particularly concerned about encryption, since the digital nature of DVD invites the potential for large-scale piracy that could prove financially ruinous to these businesses. In fact, encryption remains something of a sticking point, while the advent of alternative DVD-like formats (such as Divx) threaten to obsolete many consumer purchases.

DVD readers come in two forms:

- DVD players
- DVD-ROM drives

Intended for the family room, DVD players are set-top boxes that plug directly into your television. Essentially, they are the successor to today's VCRs and Laserdisc players.

For PCs, DVD-ROM drives look and act like existing CD-ROM drives, as shown in Figure 14.1. However, they come with additional hardware—usually an add-in board—that handles the demanding tasks of video and audio processing, as well as the decryption of the disc data.

FIGURE 14.1.
DVD-ROM drives such as Creative Labs' Encore-DVD drive look like CD-ROM drives but offer up to 30 times the storage capacity. (Photo courtesy of Creative Labs)

The Four Faces of DVD

Actually, DVD is four specs in one, with separate schemes for storing anywhere from 4.7 to 17GB of data on a single disc. By taking advantage of media layering and using both sides of the disc platter, four capacity levels are supported:

- Single-sided, single-layer: 4.7GB
- Single-sided, dual-layer: 8.5GB
- Double-sided, single-layer: 9.4GB
- Double-sided, dual-layer: 17GB

All DVD discs, regardless of capacity, have the same diameter and thickness as traditional CD-ROM discs (a 12cm diameter and a 1.2mm thickness). Only the first and smallest DVD disc type—4.7GB—is currently available. Subsequent media are expected to roll out over the next year. Fortunately, all DVD players and DVD-ROM drives sold today will be able to read all the various formats.

One bit of good news is that manufacturing improvements have allowed existing CD-ROM production facilities to be refitted to generate DVD-ROMs. The major change comes in the bonding process, where two 0.6mm-thick discs (called *substrates*) must be bonded to create a single 1.2mm-thick disc. This second substrate, which is not present on CD-ROM discs, provides the "dual-layer" feature, where another level of data storage is contained. In essence, DVD discs are two discs in one.

Other DVD Details

But wait—there's more. Much more. Other DVD advances include

- Laser wavelength
- MPEG-2 video
- Dolby AC-3 surround sound audio

Laser Light

DVD-ROM drives use a red laser, as opposed to the yellow laser used in CD-ROM drives. The red laser light has a shorter wavelength than yellow lasers, which allows the
drive to focus on smaller data bits than CD-ROM drive lasers. By cramming data bits
closer together on the disc, much greater capacities (4.7GB versus 650MB) can be stored
on a single layer of disc material.

The new color also plays an important role in the layout of the dual-layered DVD disc.
The disc's underlayer is silver-colored and reflective, and the overlayer is semitransparent and gold in color. By setting the red laser to low power, the drive reads the outer
gold layer. Increase the laser power, and the drive punches through to read data on the
silver underlayer.

MPEG-2: Theater-Quality Video

By now, most PC users are familiar with MPEG-1 video, often found on existing CD-
ROM titles. This VHS-quality video compression scheme was designed to put lots of
video onto 650MB CD-ROM discs and to allow it to play back even on the slowest CD-
ROM drives. There's just one problem: The highly-compressed video lacks visual fidelity
and gets downright chunky during the fast-action sequences routinely encountered in
movies and sports broadcasts.

Enter MPEG-2. Designed by the Motion Pictures Experts Group (MPEG), MPEG-2 dramatically improves on the MPEG-1 standard while using the same basic compression
principle of storing only changes that occur between specific frames, called *key frames*.
Thus, in a talking-head sequence (such as a newscaster talking), only the movements of
the announcer's head, mouth, and eyes get stored, not the unchanging background.

That's where the similarities end: MPEG-2 delivers video quality that is superior to both
Laserdisc and Super VHS. MPEG-2 provides more than four times the resolution of
MPEG-1, making it appropriate for full-screen video and television broadcasts. It also
shoots out video at 60 fields per second—essentially 60 frames interlaced—versus
MPEG-1's 30 frame-per-second limit. Most importantly, it allows for high data rate
transfers so that enough data is available to store even action-packed sequences. Table
14.1 compares MPEG-1 and MPEG-2.

Table 14.1. MPEGs compared.

Characteristic	MPEG-1	MPEG-2
Resolution	352×240	720×480
Frame rate	30 frames per second	60 fields per second
Data rate	150Kbps	1.5MBps

The Ears Have It: Dolby AC-3 Sound

Also called 5.1 Surround Sound, AC-3 uses five separate channels of audio, plus a dedicated subwoofer channel, to produce true surround sound. The five channels designate left, right, and center in front of the listener, and left and right behind the listener. The subwoofer, which produces deep bass sounds, sits front and low.

More importantly for PC users, AC-3 can be used in traditional two-speaker setups. Algorithms are applied to produce the illusion of surround sound from two speakers, although you'll get more realistic results with all five speakers in place. In order to decode AC-3 data, DVD kits require a special chipset on the DVD add-in boards (see Figure 14.2).

Figure 14.2.
DVD-ROM kits require a separate AC-3 board to handle the demands of surround sound audio.

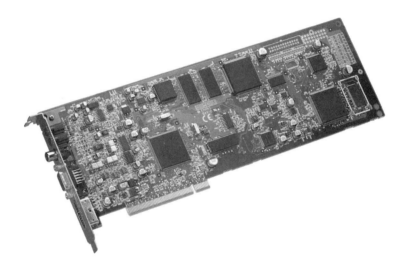

Peter's Principle: DVD-ROM Software Might Be Recycled CD-ROM Software

After more than a year with DVD-ROM drives on the market, only DVD-ROM titles are still relatively hard to find. While there is a growing selection of DVD movies and live music concert discs from companies such as Warner and Columbia, computer-related games, reference, and entertainment titles are taking a bit longer to arrive in mass.

Some vendors have begun porting CD-ROM titles that came in multidisc sets into single-disc DVD packages. Unfortunately, there are two key issues involved in porting CD-ROM to DVD-ROMs consumers should be aware of.

First, games that were created for CD-ROM might not include the superior MPEG-2 video or Dolby AC-3 sound that DVD offers without having undergone significant and expensive rework. The main advantage of a ported game would be that you would no longer need to swap discs in and out of your ROM drive

continues

continued

as you progress through the game. Don't expect stunning sound and video on a CD-ROM ported game unless the improvement is specifically mentioned on the box or in a computer press review.

Second, reference titles that were originally designed to reside on a series of CD-ROM discs will have a different indexing system (used for searches) than titles that were specifically designed to reside on one large DVD disc. Thus, don't expect fast searches on a DVD reference title that was ported from CD-ROM without an indexing overhaul. Again, computer publications would be your best source for information about particular titles.

All that said, game vendors such as Electronic Arts have announced their intention to ship DVD-specific titles in 1999. While the future looks promising for DVD, you should still carefully check any DVD title you suspect might have been ported from CD-ROM multidisc sets. It might not include the stellar attributes that original DVD titles offer.

A Better Future: DVD-ROM Improves

Early DVD-ROM drives had a problem. While they can read most CD-ROM formats, they can't read CD-Recordable discs. (The greenish tint of CD-R media conflicts with the red laser of DVD.) Moreover, the performance of first-generation DVD-ROM drives playing CD-ROM media left something to be desired, with spin rates confined to 8X, or 1,200KBps.

Second-generation drives, which arrived about six months after the first products, solved both of these problems. These drives use a second laser to read CD-ROMs, which doesn't conflict with CD-R. Additionally, the spindle motors spin CD-ROMs at 20X speed, so that performance is close to that of contemporary CD-ROM drives.

But DVD is not done yet. Third-generation drives are pushing spin rates further still, even as recordable versions emerge.

Note: One shadow on the DVD scene is the Divx standard backed by retailer Circuit City and others. Intended for the movie rental market, Divx drives and media are similar to DVD-ROM but allow retailers to charge users for each use of the disc. Divx players are equipped with a modem that can dial into a billing center to charge for additional viewings. While Divx players can read DVD format media, current DVD-ROM and DVD player devices can not recognize Divx discs.

> The problem is that Divx has already slowed acceptance of DVD players, and if the standard does take off, it will probably mean that future DVD-ROM drives must incorporate Divx features. That means added cost and the specter of incompatibilities with future DVD titles.
>
> And now the good news. The shine on Divx seems to be fading, as the format's backers reevaluate their options. One reason for the change: Widespread and organized opposition to the format have helped stall its acceptance.

In addition, DVD kits are getting needed improvements in video quality and compatibility. Some first-generation kits lacked full compatibility with Windows 95's Media Control Interface, resulting in crashes and scrambled video. In addition, more-sophisticated MPEG-2 decode chips on second-generation products deliver sharper MPEG-2 video playback.

Getting Dense: Higher-Capacity DVD-ROM

To steal a line from the Rolling Stones, DVD capacities are going up, up, up, up, up. Those first 4.7GB DVD discs will be peanuts compared to the 17GB capacity medium that uses a dual-layer, double-sided design. Fortunately, you don't face a huge decision here. All DVD drives now come with multipowered lasers, so they can read both the translucent outer data layer and the reflective inner data layer. However, expect some pricier drives and players to be able to automatically read both sides of a double-sided disc. Otherwise, you would have to manually flip the medium over in order to read data found on the other side.

For the Record: DVD-R and DVD-RAM

Over the next year, expect to see recordable DVD drives (DVD-R) emerge on the market. Basically, these are CD-Recordable discs on steroids. They are excellent for data archiving and document distribution.

However, many vendors plan to skip the write-once, read-many style drives altogether and move directly to a rewritable DVD spec called DVD-RAM. The first DVD-RAM drives will be able to write and rewrite on 2.6GB discs, which means that they won't offer the full capacity of professionally produced media. However, they will be readable on standard second-generation DVD-ROM drives.

INSTANT REFERENCE | For more on DVD-RAM, see Chapter 15, "Recordable Optical Storage."

Purchase Decisions

Given that DVD-ROM titles are not yet crowding store shelves, most users won't want to pay a lot of extra money for a DVD-ROM drive. After all, most folks will be using the drives just to play CD-ROMs. Fortunately, DVD-ROM drive prices have dropped markedly, and now cost little more than top-flight CD-ROM drives. Also, more and more systems are including DVD-ROM drives as standard equipment.

So who should consider buying a DVD-ROM drive? Certainly home entertainment enthusiasts who own systems like the Gateway Destination, which use big TV-like screens for playing back movies. However, game players will want to consider these drives as well, since more and more titles are taking advantage of the large-capacity data storage and ability to play back superior digital video. Reference titles are also moving to the DVD format.

The message here is that DVD will take a while to make an impact on the business and reference market. Most publishers aren't willing to add the expense of a new media type until the installed base of DVD drives runs into the millions or even tens of millions.

On the other hand, if you're looking for the latest and greatest in computer entertainment, you'll find it in DVD. Games and other titles that have been designed specifically for DVD's strengths feature stunning sound and video and hours of interaction without the need to switch discs. Here are some things to keep in mind when you shop:

- Planned use
- Drive technology
- Graphics card compatibility

Planned Use

If you're interested mainly in DVD's superior movie technology, consider a DVD player (which hooks directly to your television) instead of a DVD-ROM computer drive. Although most DVD-ROM kits provide TV-out ports on the back of the DVD decoder boards, you still need to control the movie from your computer (pause, play, stop, rewind, fast-forward, show subtitles, and so on). If you're using a PC/TV system such as Gateway Destination, this won't be a problem. But if your TV and computer are separate, the hassle involved will be frustrating. Gamers have only one way to go—DVD-ROM drives.

Which Generation?

If you do decide on a DVD-ROM drive, make sure you get at least a second-generation model. It will be able to read CD-R discs and run CD-ROMs at speeds of at least 20X. Third-generation products add even faster disc spin rates. If you plan to use the DVD-ROM drive as a CD-ROM drive replacement, you absolutely need this capability.

Graphics Card Compatibility

At the moment, DVD-ROM kits use video overlay techniques to incorporate the MPEG-2 video stream into your graphics card's output. The MPEG-2 video is literally laid on top of your desktop's graphics as a separate video element. However, not all kits do this the same way, and the result can be problems with video playback.

DynaTek's DVD471TII kit, for example, requires your PC to have a graphics chipset that supports *linear memory addressing* over the PCI bus. This means that the DVD decoder board writes in bursts directly to the graphics card's memory. It's a fast and efficient way of doing things, but compatibility is limited. At the time this was written, the DynaTek kit had been tested successfully with only eight different graphics chipsets.

> **Tip:** Before you purchase a DVD drive, check your existing hardware. Make note of your graphics card's chip. Also make sure your PC's PCI bus slots support bus mastering—you'll need it to move the mass of video information that DVD titles employ. Also take a look at your BIOS version and sound card model. Once that's done, check with the kit maker to ensure your hardware will work with the product you want to buy.

The other approach is a simple pass-through method, which is used by kits such as Diamond Multimedia's Maximum DVD Kit. In this setup, after the installation procedure, you attach a cable (known as a VGA loopback cable) from the back of your graphics card's VGA port to the back of the DVD decoder board. The analog video signal from your graphics card is then passed through the cable to the DVD board, which handles the overlay process and outputs the result to your monitor. With this style of kit, your monitor is attached to the DVD board instead of your graphics card.

Which overlay method is best? It's hard to say. Theoretically, the linear memory addressing approach has a performance edge over the pass-through approach. In my testing of DVD kits, though, the difference (to my eyes) seems negligible. Additionally, the pass-through method can work with almost any video card, whereas the linear addressing method can be a compatibility issue for many PC systems. As a general recommendation, the pass-through method seems the most trouble-free.

Minimum System Requirements

Make sure you check the system requirements of these kits carefully. Most require at least a 133MHz Pentium or equivalent processor with 16MB of RAM. There might also be video graphics card and sound card requirements. All the kits available thus far require a free PCI-bus slot for the DVD decoder board and must be run on a Windows 95 system. You won't be upgrading a low-end PC with a DVD-ROM drive.

Tip: Some kits don't include mounting rails with the DVD drive. If your PC's drive bays lack mounting rails, you'll need to make a second trip to the computer store to get all the hardware you need to install these railless kits. Therefore, before you buy, check to see if your PC has drive rails in place. If it doesn't, either make sure the kit provides them, or pick up a pair from the computer store at the time of purchase.

Price

Don't rush to buy the least-expensive DVD-ROM drive. As is sometimes the case with other computer equipment, with DVD-ROM drives, a higher price might mean a better product. Check computer publication reviews that feature round-ups of several kits, and look carefully at the pros and cons. The good news is that prices have dropped rapidly. You can purchase a DVD-ROM drive for as little as $200.

Moving Up to DVD

If you've upgraded a CD-ROM or hard disk drive, you'll be well-prepared to handle the physical issues involved with a DVD installation. That said, DVD upgrades are among the most challenging you'll find. Why? Because a new DVD drive affects so many areas of your system, including:

- Disk drive
- Graphics subsystem
- Audio subsystem

For this reason, you need to be aware of what is inside your system before you upgrade. Many graphics subsystems, for example, are incompatible with the linear addressing scheme used by the highest-performance DVD kits. Older Pentium PCs might also lack bus mastering PC add-in slots necessary to stream video and audio from the drive to your display and sound system.

See You Later, CD-ROM?

Not if you can help it. If you have an extra drive bay and your PC is not otherwise loaded with components, I advise you not to replace your CD-ROM drive with a DVD-ROM drive. You will always find occasions when more than one ROM drive is beneficial.

You should consider a DVD drive as your lone optical media reader when at least one of the following is true:

- The new DVD drive plays CD-ROM discs significantly faster than your existing CD-ROM drive.

- The new DVD drive can read CD-R media, or you never use CD-R discs.
- Your PC lacks an open externally accessible drive bay for both CD-ROM and DVD drives.
- Your PC's power supply lacks the output to support two optical drives in addition to the existing power load.

Before You Go

Prior to installation, decide whether your DVD-ROM drive will operate as a master or a slave on the enhanced IDE bus. If another faster drive (such as a hard disk) resides on the same IDE controller cable, you should set the DVD-ROM drive to slave via a jumper on the back of the drive. If the DVD-ROM drive alone connects to the IDE controller, it must be set as master.

Caution: Unlike CD-ROM drives, which invariably come from the factory set as master, I've seen DVD-ROM drives come set both ways. Make sure you examine the drive before you begin the installation. Otherwise, you're asking for serious conflicts that could knock out your boot drive and add hours to your installation.

Note: Have you been unable to find a DVD drive for your SCSI setup? Good news. Pioneer sells a second-generation DVD-ROM drive that uses the SCSI-2 interface. Early DVD-ROM offerings were strictly IDE-based, and IDE users will find a wider selection still. But SCSI options do exist.

Just so you understand the big picture, Windows 95 recognizes a DVD-ROM drive as a regular CD-ROM drive. So don't be alarmed if you run across the properties of your DVD-ROM drive listed as "CD-ROM" under My Computer. When you place a regular CD-ROM in the drive, the DVD-ROM device plays it as a CD-ROM drive would normally play a disc. When you insert a DVD-ROM disc, your kit's included DVD player software (the last step of the installation) will kick in to play the disc.

Windows 98 fixes this situation. DVD-ROM drives will be accurately identified from the OS interface, and Windows 98 includes a DVD applet for playing media specific content such as MPEG-2 movies. Windows 98 also includes drivers for many DVD-ROM drives, though any kit you buy will include drivers for Windows 95, as well as application software for running DVD content.

Installing the DVD-ROM Drive

Okay, enough talk. Let's install the kit:

1. Turn off your PC, disconnect the power cable, and remove the PC's case.

2. On the front of the PC, locate an available 5¼-inch drive bay (one of the wide ones). Remove the plastic placeholder from the front of the bay.

3. If your computer requires mounting rails, check to see whether they are present in the bay. Some DVD kits don't include the rails, so you might have to purchase them separately at a computer store. If you do need them, install them now.

4. Slide the DVD drive in from the front of the PC. Make sure that the front of the drive is flush with the front of your PC case and that there are no gaps between the edges of the drive and the borders of the front PC panel.

5. Connect the IDE controller cable and the power cable.

> **Caution:** Both of these cables attach correctly in only one way. The ribbon data cable has a red line running along the edge for pin 1 out of the cable. Your DVD-ROM drive should have a small "1" marking pin 1 on the data cable connector at the back of the drive. If it doesn't, read the device's documentation to determine which pin is pin 1. Make sure the red-line edge of the cable and pin 1 match up, or you won't be able to access this drive.
>
> The power supply cable should have a rounded edge on the top two corners of the connector. The power supply port on the back of the drive will also have these rounded edges, designating the top edge of the port. Make sure that the power cable is firmly secured in the correct position.

6. Here's the step many DVD-ROM kit installation guides leave out: Before you insert the DVD decoder card, you should boot up your system and verify that your PC recognizes this drive properly. This step will save you troubleshooting headaches (or tech support calls) later if you've made a mistake or there is a problem with your DVD-ROM drive unit.

7. Don't close the PC's case just yet. Make sure you've removed all the tools you've used and that cables are firmly connected, and then reattach your PC's power cable and power up the system.

8. After Windows 95/98 comes up, double-click the My Computer icon and look for a new drive letter corresponding to the DVD-ROM drive. (You can also highlight the drive, right-click, and select Properties to find the "CD-ROM" entry mentioned a moment ago.)

9. Insert your favorite CD-ROM disc and make sure it plays properly.

> **Note:** Don't insert one of the DVD-ROM discs that came with the kit! You haven't yet finished the DVD installation, so these discs won't play.

If there's a problem, step back through the instructions and make sure you haven't missed anything. Contact the kit vendor's tech support if a problem remains. Your DVD-ROM drive should be acting like a CD-ROM drive at the moment.

Once you've resolved any problems (or if you haven't had any), shut down Windows 95, power off your PC, and disconnect the power cable before continuing to the DVD board installation.

Installing the DVD Decoder Board

Installing a DVD board is much like any card installation, except, perhaps, for the final stage, in which you attach cables to your video graphics card. Even if you've never attempted a card installation, the following steps will walk you through the process:

1. Locate an available PCI-bus slot, preferably one with clearance for a full-length board.

> **Note:** Sometimes CPUs, RAM SIMMs, and other components stick up from the motherboard and prevent a full-length card from being pushed all the way down and secured in the slot. If this is the case, you must find another PCI slot to install the board into.
>
> A full-length card insertion can be tricky due to the fact that you have several things to watch at the same time: The card connector fitting into the slot on the motherboard, the ports fitting through the opening out the back of the PC, and the opposite end of the card fitting into the plastic guide.

2. Unscrew the screw keeping the slot's metal placeholder bracket in place, and slide the bracket out of its slot.

3. Insert the DVD decoder board into the slot. If the DVD card is full-length, the card edge that doesn't contain the output ports must slide into a plastic guide slot, which you'll find inside your PC case, opposite the bracket you just removed. Using two hands, position the card carefully, and then press down gently yet firmly until the card is seated in the slot.

4. Screw in the mounting screw that holds the card in place.

5. You might need to attach a cable from the DVD board to your sound card. This differs from kit to kit, depending on whether this cable is internal or external. Read your kit's documentation and connect the internal sound cable if required.

6. Next, check the graphics card setup. If your DVD board uses linear memory addressing (explained in the earlier section "Graphics Card Compatibility"), you won't need to make a connection between your DVD board and your graphics card, because the PCI bus handles the data, so you can skip to step 9. If your kit uses a pass-through approach, disconnect the monitor cable from the graphics card.

7. Now connect the provided pass-through cable to the "VGA in" port on the back of the DVD board, and plug it into the graphics card's VGA port.

8. Connect the monitor cable to the back of the DVD board's "VGA out" port. Check you kit's documentation, and make the connections your kit requires.

9. Now attach your two-speaker cables, TV out cables, or surround sound speakers to the back of the DVD board as needed.

10. Replace the PC case.

11. Reattach the power cable.

Installing the DVD Player Software

You'll need to install software. In addition to the usual device drivers, these kits need a DVD player module installed because Windows 95 doesn't yet recognize DVD drives. You'll also need software for handling MPEG-2 video and AC-3 audio.

1. Power up the PC. After Windows 95 starts, you'll see the New Hardware Found dialog box, which asks you to insert the manufacturer's disk.

2. Insert the kit's DVD driver disk into the A: drive, and click OK. Windows should find the drivers and install them. Now check your kit's documentation on loading the DVD player software. You might need to take another step in which you run SETUP.EXE for the player software.

3. Congratulations! You're now ready to enjoy DVD.

Repair

Here's the good news about DVD-ROM repair: Unless you found this book sitting in a used-book store, your DVD-ROM drive probably is still under warranty. Therefore, you should contact your kit vendor's tech support with any problems.

As with CD-ROM drives, DVD-ROM drives are sealed devices not intended for home repair. Working inside the unit requires special "clean room" environments to maintain the precision of the mechanics.

That said, gremlins can plague your DVD device, causing it to seem to fail when nothing serious is wrong. Before calling the vendor, run through this list of fixes:

- Make sure all cables are properly connected and secure.
- Make sure your DVD-ROM drive is recognized under My Computer as a CD-ROM drive under Windows 95. If it isn't, there was a mistake in the installation, or the unit has a hardware problem.
- If you own an older PC, make sure you installed the PCI board into a bus-mastering PCI slot. Also ensure the PCI slot you're using is active. You can check both in the PC's BIOS.
- Ensure the CD-ROM and DVD-ROM discs you use in the drive are clean. You should clean DVD-ROM discs just as you would CD-ROM discs—usually with a cleaning kit or water and a scratch-free, lint-free cloth.
- Double-check that the drive itself is clean. Use canned compressed air products to blow dust and debris off the disc tray and inside compartment.

Summary

As upgrades go, DVD is a big deal. These new drives provide access to a whole new level of content and software, including theater-quality video and audio. And with storage capacities of up to 17GB, you'll eventually see comprehensive encyclopedia titles packed with hours of broadcast-quality video.

Just be cautious, particularly if you own an older system. DVD applications will be written for cutting-edge PCs, which means that adding DVD to slower PCs might make for problematic performance. In addition, there are pesky graphics compatibility issues to contend with. You'll need to do a little sleuthing to ensure that you buy what you need.

Of course, the biggest concern with DVD is that it is still a market in its formative stages. Drives for DVD-R and DVD-RAM have yet to arrive, which means that compatibility for these upcoming media types can't be ensured with existing DVD-ROM drives. Even if compatibility works out, the performance, capabilities, and prices of these drives will improve. So be careful.

PART IV

Advanced Data Storage

Recordable Optical Storage

Optical recorders let PC users create (or *master*) their own optical discs, such as CD-ROMs and DVDs without needing to send data to a service bureau for processing. Although they're not the easiest products to use, optical recorders do allow for relatively cheap and fast mass storage that can easily be distributed to others.

This area is becoming increasingly important. The universal installed base of CD-ROM drives, for instance, makes CD recordable and rewritable drives a terrific tool for archiving and distributing large amounts of data for playback on any machine. The emergence of DVD promises to make similar drives for high-density media important as well. This chapter will help you

- Learn about the major types of optical recorded media and how they work
- Understand key buying issues associated with optical recording devices in general and with certain types in specific
- Recognize and resolve problems associated with optical recording drives and media

Overview

Optical recorders serve a growing number of applications, ranging from casual home use to publishing and data management. Table 15.1 lists some of the most important applications.

Table 15.1. Applications served by optical recording media.

Task	Examples
Home entertainment	Creating custom audio discs, PhotoCDs, multimedia productions
Publishing	Mastering copies of critical data, software publishing

continues

Table 15.1. Continued.

Task	Examples
Data backup and archiving	Saving important files, such as email archives, to permanent media in case of system failure; saving data and storing off-site in case of flood, fire, or other catastrophe
Data distribution	Forwarding database updates to colleagues and businesses; software distribution within companies

All these drives use lasers to read changes in the surface of the disk media, which the on-board controller interprets into digital 1s and 0s. In this respect, they act just like their read-only CD-ROM and DVD-ROM counterparts. But these devices also include the ability to shine a more powerful laser pulse onto special media enabling them to write data to disc.

In all cases, these drives can read earlier media formats. So a DVD-RAM drive can read CD-ROM, CD-R, CD-RW, and DVD-ROM discs. A CD-RW drive, meanwhile, can read CD-ROM and read and write CD-R and CD-RW discs. But no CD-format drive can read DVD media, and DVD-RAM drives can not write to CD-R or CD-RW.

> **Note:** The Trouble With Audio: A lot of folks buy CD-R drives hoping to record their favorite audio CD tunes to custom discs. While CD-R drives are capable of creating discs readable by your audio CD player, many products fall victims to limitations of their IDE bus. The problem? Drives trying to record a stream of audio data over the IDE bus often fall victim to delays in the transmission. This is caused by the fact that the IDE bus is trying to send data from a CD player (the source) and get it to the receiver (the target), even as hard disk activity crowds the channel at the same time.
>
> If you want to record your own audio CDs, you should consider getting a SCSI-based CD-R or CD-RW drive that is able to handle this kind of critical transaction.

Not all recording drives are best suited for each of these uses, so I'll break down which drive does what as we go along. Additionally, not all disc formats can be read by all drives—a critical point when you're making a purchase. We will cover all these points in this chapter.

There are several flavors of recordable optical media spanning the CD and DVD media spectra. We will cover the four most important and widespread optical formats and drives:

- CD-Recordable (CD-R)
- CD-Rewritable (CD-RW)

- DVD-Recordable (DVD-R)
- DVD-Rewritable (DVD-RAM: DVD Random Access Memory)

CD-R: First Out

The first mainstream recordable laser-based medium now enjoys the greatest market share. You will find CD-R drives under a number of different names, including:

- CD-WO: CD-Write Once
- CD-WORM: CD-Write Once Read Many
- CD-R: CD-Recordable

These labels call attention to a key element of CD-R technology: Any given portion of the medium can be recorded to only once. Although the data can be read back from the disc as long as the disc remains intact, you can never again record over a track after it has been "burned" by a CD-R drive.

The biggest advantage of CD-R discs and drives is that this medium can be read by almost any CD-ROM drive—an important point given that CD-ROM drives are ubiquitous on today's PCs. The installed base of CD-ROM drives makes CD-R particularly useful for distributing data to others.

> **Note:** Unfortunately, first-generation DVD-ROM drives can't read CD-R discs. The green tint of the CD-R medium's coating conflicts with the frequency of DVD drives' red lasers, making the medium unreadable. Second-generation DVD-ROM drives resolve this problem by using a second, yellow laser head to read CD-R media.

Burn, Baby, Burn

How does CD-R work? Basically, these drives replicate the professional CD-ROM creation process through the use of chemicals. With a professionally recorded CD-ROM disc, data is stored on the medium by using a laser to create pits and rises along the concentric spiral track. At playback, the reading laser of the CD-ROM drive detects changes in the reflection between a pit and a nonpit (called a *land*). A microprocessor in the drive makes sense of the varying returns and converts this into bits, which can be sent to the PC and interpreted as data.

CD-R recording differs somewhat, mainly because the equipment on your desktop can't easily burn pits into waiting media. Rather, CD-R drives employ a special medium that provides a chemical interaction to create the illusion of burned pits and lands. A polycarbonate substrate with prestamped grooves (used to align the data-bearing "pits") is layered with a reactive, photosensitive dye and a reflective layer.

The action occurs in the photosensitive layer of dye, which reacts when exposed to the specific frequency of the write head's laser. When the recording laser heats a point on the disc, that point becomes less reflective than the unburned areas around it, producing the same effect as a physical pit in a regular CD-ROM. Because the dye composition is altered by the laser, each point on a CD-R disc may only be written to once.

CD-R and CD-ROM

Back in 1994, CD-R units could cost as much as $6,000—limiting them to corporations that had a real need to quickly produce limited runs of CD-ROM discs. But, as with all computer technology, competition has lead to steady and significant drops in price. Today, CD-R drives are affordable enough for desktop use.

That said, you can expect to always pay a premium for optical recorders over CD-ROM players or reader drives because of the extra hardware involved in the mastering technology. Although CD-R drives can read CD-ROM media like a standard drive, they might not be appropriate as the primary reading drive. That's because CD-R read speeds lag considerably behind that of standard CD-ROM drives. Whereas CD-ROM drives today read at up to 40X speeds, CD-Rs don't run faster than 20X.

Also, CD-R drives record at a different rate than they play back. Typically, a drive capable of 20X read performance will manage write speeds of 8X. More typical are 12X read and 8X write spin rates. The main advantage of faster recording spin rates is the time it takes to burn a disc. Depending on your CD-R software, your PC system, and the method of recording, a typical CD-R drive with a 2X record speed can burn one 650MB disc in about 40 minutes. 4X drives don't halve that number (the drive won't always reach peak spin rates since it must wait for data and verify operation), but it can shave 10 minutes off that time.

Note: The usability of your CD-R software makes a big difference when you prepare to burn (or premaster) a CD. In fact, many people believe a CD-R drive is only as good as the software that drives it.

The best premastering software features automated wizards that walk you through the format of the disc you'll be creating (audio CD, PhotoCD, data CD, and so on) and enable you to drag and drop files you want to record. This software also determines whether your PC is powerful enough to successfully make it through the planned recording session. Finally, an effective help system can get you through jobs without too much pain.

One of the better packages is Adaptec's Easy CD Creator, shown in Figure 15.1, but you should check reviews in computer publications for the latest information on CD-R software products. Almost every CD-R drive includes CD-R software in the box, but if you find yours to be ineffective, you can purchase off-the-shelf CD-R software for about $100.

FIGURE **15.1.**
Adaptec's Easy CD Creator software provides packet-writing capability for drives that support it, but you'll still want a powerful PC to avoid problems during recording. (Photo courtesy of Adaptec Inc.)

Performance Matters in Recording

The process of mastering CDs can be fraught with frustration and errors. First-time users of CD-R drives often fail at their first few attempts at recording discs and have to throw out the partially recorded blank discs ruined in the process. Fortunately, CD-R discs now cost about $1 apiece, cutting the cost of a lost disc.

Recording to CD is done in "sessions." You can record an entire CD in one session or add to a partially recorded disk with additional sessions on CD-R drives that support this multisession technique. In traditional CD-R drives, a successful recording session requires your entire PC system to keep a continuous stream of data flowing from your hard disk to your CD-R drive. The CD-R drive must record an entire track of the disc without stopping. If your CD-R drive ends up waiting on data when it's in the middle of recording a track, it fails to correctly record that track, and the resulting disc becomes unreadable and worthless. This is called a *buffer underrun* error.

Fairly recently, a technique called *variable-packet writing* emerged. It eliminates the need to record an entire track at once. The software and drive can record a single file at a time and leave the disk ready for additional recording in later sessions. Unfortunately, many manufacturers only include this technology in their CD-RW (CD-Rewritable) products (which we'll discuss later), so many current CD-R drives still suffer from troubling buffer underrun problems.

How do you avoid underruns? Here's a list of hardware factors that can help ensure a successful burn:

- CPU: When it comes to CD-R recording, the more powerful the processor, the better. Experts recommend at least a Pentium 133MHz processor or the equivalent for trouble-free recording.

- RAM: Have at least 16MB of RAM for recording. 32MB or higher will greatly decrease your chances of buffer underruns.

- CD-R buffer size: The bigger the buffer of your CD-R drive, the better. If your PC can feed data to a large CD-R drive buffer, the chances of buffer underrun will be minimal. Many CD-R devices come with only 512KB buffers, but this seems adequate. If you can afford one with a 1MB or larger buffer, you'll be increasing your chances of error-free recording.

- Large hard disk: CD-R software usually gives you the option of creating a physical or virtual image of your data to set up a recording (we'll discuss this in a moment). A physical image is the most effective for a successful burn, but this requires large amounts of spare hard disk space, because the software will literally create a 650MB premaster copy of your data on your hard drive before writing the data to the CD-R disc. Only you know how much hard disk space you need on a regular basis, but having a spare 650MB for recording will probably demand a 2.5GB or larger disk.

- Fast hard disk: A fast SCSI hard drive will lessen the chances of buffer underrun. Also, be sure to defragment the drive (see Chapter 11, "Taking Hard Disks for a Spin") and uninstall any hard disk compression you're using before recording.

- SCSI versus IDE: Just like CD-ROM drives, CD-R drives come in SCSI and IDE interface drives. While both IDE and SCSI offer high throughputs (up to 33MBps for IDE and 40 or even 80MBps for SCSI), the real advantage comes with SCSI's efficient interface. SCSI ensures more consistent data delivery and lower CPU utilization. In fact, some applications—such as duplicating audio CDs to CD-R media—require that the CD-R device run on the SCSI bus. That said, basic recording operations on Pentium class systems will generally run without flaw over IDE.

- Internal versus external: Some columnists in computer publications claim the electromagnetic fields generated by your other computer equipment (monitors, PCs, and so on) can negatively affect an external CD-R drive during recording, causing an unsuccessful write session. This might be overstated, because many people (including myself) have recorded using external CD-R drives without difficulty. The shielded casings on most drives are quite adequate for blocking out any EMF interference. Still, if your environment is rife with electronic equipment, consider going with an internal drive, which will have extra EMF protection from your PC case.

Note: Most CD-R software enables you to set up either a physical or virtual image of the data you want to record to disc. The physical image approach builds a complete disc image on your hard drive (complete with indexes required by your chosen CD-ROM format) before the recording begins. During recording, the physical image is simply copied bit-by-bit to the CD-R disc. A virtual image approach, on the other hand, performs an on-the-fly recording. You build a template of all the data you want to record in the session, but no full disc image is constructed on your hard drive. The software copies the data file-by-file during the recording session and builds the indexes on-the-fly.

The physical image approach greatly increases the chances of a successful recording session, because the only processing left to do is copying files. The downside is that it can require up to 650MB of free hard disk space. The virtual image method doesn't require massive free hard disk space, but it can lead to buffer underrun problems during the on-the-fly recording due to processing overhead.

Fortunately, your decision here is actually a simple one. If you have the free disk space, always go with the physical image method. It's much safer, and the CD-R software usually cleans up the physical image from your hard disk once the burn completes. If you're pressed for space, go with the virtual approach, but first run the premaster test (almost all CD-R software provides one), which performs a "dry run" with your data to see if the whole PC system can maintain the necessary data transfer rate. The test will return either a high-confidence result or a low-confidence result on your chances of success before writing any data to the CD-R disc.

CD-RW: Most Versatile Option

Over the past year, CD-RW (CD-Rewritable) drives have become an important recordable option. These drives use a combination of the variable-packet writing scheme and a phase-change disc medium (first developed by Panasonic-Matsushita) to allow writing and rewriting on CD-RW discs. CD-RW drives can also write to affordable CD-R media, making them an extremely versatile option for those wanting the ability to publish multimedia data, exchange files, and backup files. CD-RW drives (see Figure 15.2) bridge the gap between CD-R discs (which can't be rewritten) and DVD-RAM discs (which can only be read by a tiny portion of optical drives).

As discussed earlier, variable-packet writing negates the problems of buffer underrun because the CD-RW drive doesn't need to write an entire track at once. In fact, even if the CD-RW buffer does underrun, the laser can mark off that section of the CD-RW disc as unusable and continue writing, much like a hard disk drive would.

The phase-change medium, on the other hand, departs from the usual CD-ROM approach. Here, a tiny dot of the crystalline medium is subjected to a laser pulse to write bits. The energy alters the crystal structure of the medium, causing the substance to toggle from absorbing light to reflecting light. A drive can then determine the value of a bit based on whether the read laser light bounces back to the detector or is absorbed by the medium. Each portion of the medium can be toggled up to 1,000 times.

Unfortunately, CD-RW forces a number of minor compromises that can make them hard to recommend. For one thing, discs can't be read by older CD-ROM or CD-R drives—you'll need a newer drive conforming to the Multi-Read specification to be able to read CD-RW media. CD-R compatibility, by contrast, is already well-supported in CD-ROM drives sold over the past few years.

CD-RW drives are also pricier and slower than their CD-R cousins. Playback speeds top out around 24X (on the newest models), while CD-RW recording is often limited to a sluggish 2X rate. CD-R recording generally occurs at 4X speeds, however. Also, while CD-R discs hold a 650MB, CD-RW discs only hold 480MB of data. The reason: The file system tables required to enable multiple recordings consumes over 100MB of space on each CD-RW disc.

Perhaps the biggest issue with CD-RW media is the fact that many CD-ROM and CD players are unable to read CD-RW discs. Older drives are unable to discern the smaller reflective change in the CD-RW phase-change materials. For this reason, CD-RW is a better format for data backup rather than for distributing files to a broad audience.

No surprise, CD-RW drives cost more than their CD-R cousins. CD-RW discs likewise run at a premium, costing about $10 per disc, versus just $1 for CD-R discs.

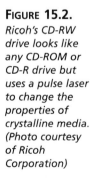

FIGURE 15.2.
Ricoh's CD-RW drive looks like any CD-ROM or CD-R drive but uses a pulse laser to change the properties of crystalline media. (Photo courtesy of Ricoh Corporation)

DVD-R and DVD-RAM: Poised for the Future

With DVD-ROM set to all but replace CD-ROM in the PC marketplace, it's no surprise to see similar recordable devices planned for the DVD format. After all, the prospect of multigigabyte storage, accessible from millions of mainstream desktop PCs, is appealing. Just don't get ahead of yourself. While DVD-R (DVD-Recordable) and DVD-RAM (DVD-Random Access Memory) drives are available, their appeal is limited by their relatively-high cost and inability to write to a media format supported on most PCs. After all, DVD is just getting started.

DVD-R drives are able to record once on 3.8GB discs (single-layer, single-side)—almost 1GB less than the capacity of DVD-ROM discs, which hold 4.7GB single-layer, single-side. DVD-RAM drives, by contrast, handle even less data—2.6GB on a single-layer, single-side disc—but will allow multiple rewrites. Why the lower capacities for these recordable media? The phase-change medium used in these discs is difficult to manage at very high densities.

In fact, most manufacturers have gone right past DVD-R and offer DVD-RAM drives as their only recordable solution. DVD-RAM is much more flexible than DVD-R and will appeal to a larger mainstream market that will use DVD-RAM as a super-duper floppy drive. Creative Labs began selling a $500 DVD-RAM drive kit in August of 1998, achieving a price comparable to many CD-RW kits. Bundled with a SCSI-2 card, the kit can transfer data at 1.38MBps.

The good news is that these drives can read all the earlier optical media, including CD-ROM, CD-R, CD-RW, and DVD-ROM discs. (The exceptions are first-generation DVD-ROM drives, which could only read DVD-ROM and CD-ROM media.) The drawback? At $30 per disc, DVD-RAM is a little expensive for general distribution.

DVD-RAM has a significant challenger in the form of DVD+RW, which has been championed by Sony, Phillips, and Hewlett-Packard. The format offers a higher 3GB per side data capacity, and does not require the use of a cartridge for read or write operation. DVD+RW drives are now shipping.

Hey, MO!: Near-Disk Storage Serves a Niche

Magneto-optical drives (or MO drives), on the other hand, use a combination of laser and magnetic heads to read and write data on cartridge media. When reading data from disks, the drive head reads the magnetic charge of points on the medium, just like a hard disk or other magnetic drive.

These drives are used primarily by graphics professionals and others needing to back up, access, and save multi-megabyte files. Unlike magnetic media, such as Iomega Jaz, MO offers shelf lives on the order of CD and DVD discs, since the optical media is not susceptible to corruption from stray magnetic fields. The cartridged MO media is also better protected than CD-RW discs.

To write data, the MO drive head first heats the media surface with a laser, causing the desired area of the disk to achieve its curie temperature—the point at which it can be affected by a magnetic field. At this point, the head writes data to the magnetic surface—generally during the second pass of the disc—switching the polarity of the heated medium. As the medium cools, the magnetic value of that point is locked in.

MO drive's main advantage over DVD and CD formats is its hard disk-like read performance. When reading, MO drives only use the magnetic portion of its read-write mechanism, allowing it to access data more quickly than CD-ROM or DVD-ROM drives. Write operations, however, are impaired by the two-step process. But for backup and archive operations, this concern is not overwhelming. And performance is at least comparable to that of DVD-RAM writers.

Purchase Decisions

With all the choices in optical recorders, how do you decide which one to buy? First, you should determine your needs. What's more, patience might be the key. If you can afford to wait six months, DVD-RAM and CD-RW drives should get more affordable still. But if you must buy now, you might be limited to write-once technologies—unless you have the money to spend for early technology.

In all cases, you should consider optical recording media over magnetic media for the following applications:

- Permanent or long-term data archiving and backup
- Software or data distribution and publishing (CD-R only)
- Multimedia production and distribution

Peter's Principle: Speed: Optical Storage Versus Magnetic Storage

When do optical technologies not make sense? Most often when very fast, responsive performance is needed. Magnetic technologies, such as the Iomega Zip and Jaz drives, operate on the same principles as hard disk drives. Here, focused magnetic fields are used to switch bits on and off a magnetic medium. This process is much quicker than laser-based drives. The magnetic polarity can be switched instantly, whereas optical media must be heated before the bit switch can occur.

Generally, access times for hard disks can be as low as 7ms, while Iomega's Jaz drive provides 12ms access times. Optical CD and DVD media, on the other hand, feature access times of about 150ms and above. The faster access times make magnetic media great for running applications from a removable platform. For example, you could run Word or Excel off a Jaz drive.

The price you pay for the speed is reduced durability. Magnetic media can be easily corrupted. In other words, on bits can easily be switched to off bits. When that happens, files get lost. For example, any household magnet can corrupt magnetic media.

To help you make sense of the media, I've provided a list of pros and cons for each type.

CD-R: Mainstream Media

CD-R is the most prevalent recordable optical medium, and it's also the most affordable. If you want to produce finished content for distribution or you want permanent data archives, CD-R is the most economical choice.

Pros

- Records all the popular CD formats (audio discs, video discs, PhotoCDs, data CDs) except CD-RW.
- Lower drive cost than CD-RW and faster record and playback speeds.
- Least expensive optical recording platform.
- Great for home use, data distribution, creating masters of software titles, and archiving data.
- Blank CD-R discs are economical, at about $1 per disc in bulk.

Cons

- Can't read DVD and often cannot read CD-RW media.
- Slow playback speeds make CD-R drives ineffective as your sole CD-ROM drive.
- Writes only once on a track.
- Ineffective for data backup due to the write-once restriction.

CD-RW: Floppy of the Future?

CD-RW is a good option for people who want more flexibility than the write-once character CD-R provides. CD-RW discs can act as super-floppy discs, for example, provided that the CD-ROM drives in your organization can recognize the phase-change medium. And despite their write-many character, the optical medium is quite robust—a stray magnetic field won't corrupt the data. These drives are also faster and can read more formats than their CD-R cousins.

Pros

- Records all the popular CD-ROM formats, including CD-R and CD-RW.
- Can rewrite on CD-RW media as well as record to inexpensive CD-R media.
- Variable-packet writing and phase-change media solve buffer underrun recording problems.
- Great for home use, data distribution, creating master CDs, backup, and archiving.

Cons

- CD-RW media isn't cheap; it costs about $10 per disc.
- Record and playback speeds lag behind CD-R and drive prices are somewhat higher.
- CD-RW discs can only hold 480MB because of the way the file allocation table is created.
- Can't read DVD discs.

DVD-R: The Lost Generation

DVD-R has real promise. In an age of 7GB hard disks, the viability of 650MB CD-ROM media for mass storage backup is in question. DVD-R lets you burn to 3.8GB discs and enjoy the enhanced bandwidth of DVD-ROM playback. In addition to reading DVD-ROM and DVD-R discs, these drives can handle all the CD varieties.

Pros

- Can read all CD-ROM and DVD-ROM media, as well as CD-RW and CD-R.
- Fast CD-ROM playback.
- Useful for home use, data distribution, mastering DVD titles, and archiving.

Cons

- Most manufacturers passing on DVD-R to offer DVD-RAM products.
- Not effective as an incremental backup device due to its write-once restriction.
- Might become obsolete if DVD-RAM drives succeed.
- Expensive media at almost $80 per disc.
- Only writes 3.8GB single-layer, single-side, as opposed to DVD-ROM's 4.7GB single-layer, single side.

DVD-RAM: Now This Is Cool

DVD-RAM is tempting technology, and it's available now. No, DVD-RAM is not perfect—its 2.6GB capacity is less than that of DVD-R, for example—but these drives let you read virtually every CD and DVD format there is. In addition, DVD-RAM approaches the appeal of near-disk magnetic storage devices such as Iomega Jaz and magneto-optical devices such as Syquest. If CD-RW is a super-floppy, DVD-RAM is a super-duper floppy.

Pros

- Reading-compatible with all ROM formats, including CD-ROM, CD-R, CD-RW, and DVD.
- Can write and rewrite at 2.6GB single-layer, single-side.

- Great for home use, data distribution, master DVD titles, backup, and archiving.
- Supports high-speed CD-ROM playback (24X).

Cons

- DVD-RAM media is only readable by the small market of DVD-RAM drives and late-model DVD-ROM drives.
- Can't write full DVD-ROM capacity (only 2.6GB single-layer, single-side, as opposed to DVD-ROM 4.7GB single-layer, single-side).
- Media costs $30 per disc in five-unit quantities.

MO Drives: Limited Appeal

Unlike the other optical options presented here, MO drives are more appropriate to vertical applications. Jukebox MO drives can back up vast amounts of data, and MO remains popular among graphics artists and others who must access and store very large media files.

Pros

- Large capacity formats range up to 7GB per disc.
- Quick magnetic read-only operation makes for fast file loading and transfer.
- Optical write media protects against data loss due to stray magnetic fields.

Cons

- Drives often cost hundreds of dollars more than typical CD-RW drives.
- Write operation is much slower than reads, though competitive with other optical recordable formats.
- Lack of format standards means an MO drive from one vendor will not read discs that came from the drive of another vendor.

Optical Media Buyer's Wrap-Up

The best deal going in optical recorders is the CD-RW drive. At about $400, these drives are affordable for recorders and worth the extra $100 over a CD-R drive because of their added backup and temporary storage capabilities. The CD-RW medium costs more than CD-R but significantly less than the initial DVD-RAM discs. Even if the CD-RW format becomes obsolete after DVD-RAM emerges, it will still cut CD-R discs, which will be useful for years to come.

Who can use DVD-RAM, then? Well, if you're not concerned about distributing or sharing your media with others, then DVD-RAM may work for you. Prices are competitive at around $500 and up, and the drives will read DVD-ROM and all CD and CD recordable formats. And you can't beat the 2.6GB per side capacity. DVD+RW may become an option in early 1999, but DVD-RAM clearly enjoys a market lead. Just don't expect a wide audience for your DVD-compatible discs until well into the next century—say 2002, or so.

Upgrading

If you use your PC for multimedia production work, an optical upgrade might be in your future. You might also want to opt for one of these technologies for your backup needs instead of using a less-flexible tape drive or lower-capacity Zip or LS-120 drive.

Should I Stay or Should I Go?

One question is whether you should keep the existing CD-ROM drive in your system when you upgrade. That depends. IDE CD-ROM drives could be forced out of the mix if you already have a pair of IDE hard disks and an IDE Zip drive, for example. Remember that you're limited to four IDE devices. Regardless of the system mix, slower CD-ROM drives are probably best retired in favor of faster-moving recorders.

If you're going with a CD-R drive, it's unlikely that it will outperform your CD-ROM drive for playback (unless your CD-ROM drive is 4X speed or slower). For this reason, it makes sense to add a CD-R drive to the CD-ROM drive in your system rather than swapping it out. CD-RW, on the other hand, might spin CD-ROMs faster than your existing CD-ROM drive, in which case replacing the CD-ROM drive with the CD-RW drive is a reasonable option.

For DVD media, performance goes up a notch. DVD-RAM drives run CD-ROMs at high speeds. This, combined with the drive's ability to read all existing CD-based formats, makes it attractive to replace the older CD-ROM drive with a DVD-RAM drive.

The following section steps you through adding a CD-R drive to your PC. Except for the final software installation, the process is identical to adding a CD-ROM drive to your system.

> **Tip:** For SCSI CD-R drives, it's a good idea to consider installing the CD-R drive on its own SCSI controller card instead of adding the CD-R to a SCSI controller with other devices already attached. Multiple devices riding on the same SCSI controller can slow data transfer speeds. In recording, the required data rate to avoid buffer underruns demands all the performance advantages you can muster. Another, less expensive solution is to simply not power on your other SCSI devices when you're entering into a recording session. If you're using a SCSI hard drive, however, this won't be an option.

Preparing a CD-R Drive Installation

If you've never installed a CD-ROM or CD-R drive before, consider purchasing a CD-R upgrade kit, because it will include all the necessary cabling, screws, and rails. Once you've made your purchase, follow these preparatory steps:

1. Choose a drive bay: For internal CD-R drives, you need a bay that opens onto the front of your PC. If your system is bulging with components, it's conceivable that you might need to move your hard drive to a bay that doesn't abut the front of the PC. External CD-R drives require only desk space.

2. Check the cabling: Make sure you have the necessary power cable socket (usually a white plastic molding with four large pin openings) and controller cable (IDE or SCSI). Make sure they both reach the drive bay in which you intend to install the CD-R drive.

3. Set up the drive: As discussed in Chapter 10, "Control Freaks: IDE and SCSI Controllers," IDE devices can be either a master or a slave. Set the jumpers on an IDE device before installation. CD-R drives generally come from the manufacturer set as the master drive, so if that's your scenario, you won't have to modify the jumpers. If you're adding a CD-R to an IDE controller that already has a drive attached (such as a hard disk), you might have to set the jumpers on both your CD-R and the hard drive.

SCSI devices require proper SCSI ID and termination settings. Set the jumpers on your CD-R drive to a unique SCSI ID. Then set the termination jumpers if the drive is at the end of a SCSI chain of devices. You might need to unterminate the SCSI controller host adapter card if you have both internal and external SCSI devices, because now the host adapter is in the middle of the chain, not at the end.

Installing the CD-R Drive

To install a CD-R drive, do the following:

1. Turn off your PC and disconnect the power cable.

2. Open the PC case and remove the front placeholder panel, which will be taken up by the front of the CD-R drive unit.

3. If your drive bay requires slide rails, attach them now.

4. Attach the controller cable and the power cable. With all the cabling and cramped spaces, attaching the cables after the drive is secured in the bay can be difficult.

Tip: Both of these cables attach correctly in only one way. The ribbon data cable has a red line running along the edge for pin 1 out of the cable. Your CD-R drive should have a small "1" marking pin 1 on the data cable connector at the back of the drive. If it doesn't, read the device's documentation to determine which pin is pin 1. Make sure that pin 1 and the red-line edge of the cable match up, or you won't be able to access this drive.

The power supply cable should have a rounded edge on the top two corners of the connector. The power supply port on the back of the drive will also have these rounded edges, designating the top edge of the port. Make sure that the power cable is firmly secured in the correct position.

5. If you are using the CD-R drive as your primary CD-ROM reader, attach the audio cable from the CD-R drive to your sound card. The audio port of the CD-R drive is usually adjacent to the power cable port. Read your sound card's documentation to find out where the connector goes on the sound card.

6. Slide the CD-R drive into the drive bay. Make sure that the front edge fits flush with the front of the PC case. Also make sure that the drive sits level in the bay.

7. Close the PC case and reattach the power cable.

8. Congratulations! The only step remaining is to install the CD-R software that came with the drive. Follow the instructions included with the software. The first time you launch the software, it will scan your PC system for your CD-R drive. From there, you're ready to begin recording.

Repair

Checking cabling and operating system settings will fix most CD-R drive problems. If the drive itself isn't working properly, it must either be replaced or sent to a professional, because the internal components can't be manipulated in a home or office environment.

Troubleshooting

If you're encountering problems with your drive, step through these procedures:

- Double-check cabling. Mis-seated or reversed controller connectors will make your CD-R drive inaccessible.

- Check that your operating system correctly identifies the drive. Under Windows 95, right-click the CD-R drive icon under My Computer and select Properties from the list of choices. The resulting dialog box should correctly identify your drive. Contact the drive's technical support if this is not the case.

> **Note:** In DOS (and therefore Windows 3.x), you need to check your settings in CONFIG.SYS and AUTOEXEC.BAT. The AUTOEXEC.BAT line that refers to your CD-ROM should look something like this:
>
> ```
> C:\WINDOWS\MSCDEX.EXE /d:mscd001
> ```
>
> This is the reference for the Microsoft CD Extensions for DOS.
>
> Your drive's installation instructions should include information about the matching CONFIG.SYS line, but it should look like this:
>
> ```
> DEVICE=C:\MYDRIVER\MYDRVR.SYS /d:mscd001
> ```

- Inspect the medium. It might be that the problem lies with your disc and not your drive. Make sure that your discs are clean and scratch-free.
- Clean the drive. Used compressed air to clean the drive's tray or caddy.

Recording Tips

In addition to the tips mentioned throughout this chapter, keep the following in mind when you're setting up a recording session:

- Always start with clean discs. Make sure there are no scratches or marks on your blank CDs.
- Have your CD-R software perform a test before the recording to check the system throughput. This can alert you to a problem before you end up ruining a blank disc.
- Try not to perform any other PC tasks during your recording. For CD-R recording, this is vital to keep up the necessary transfer rate. It's a good idea for CD-RW or DVD-RAM recording as well.
- Verify the integrity of the session after recording. All CD-R software includes an error message window that lists any problems encountered during a session. Be sure to check this window before distributing the disc.

Summary

The PC platform is changing rapidly, and the area of recordable optical media is one of the fastest-moving technologies. In just over a year, the recordable storage available to mainstream users has increased five times over. And with DVD-RAM and CD-RW, optical media is now taking over many applications heretofore limited to fast, magnetic technologies.

My advice is to buy for your needs. If you need a drive that can record to a broad audience, a CD-R or CD-RW drive is your only real option. These drives both write to the nearly-universally recognized CD-R media, while CD-RW adds the ability to use CD-RW media for backup and other applications. But if you need large amounts of capacity and want to get access to DVD-ROM titles to boot, then a low-cost DVD-RAM kit makes sense. Just keep in mind that others probably won't be able to read what you write.

Ultimately, the good news is that all these choices represent opportunities that simply didn't exist a couple of years ago.

Tape Backup

When it comes to computing, nothing is more important than your data. Quite simply, data is the currency of personal computing, whether it is in the form of word processing and spreadsheet documents, email archives, or complex page and Web layouts. And with the expanding role of PCs in everyone's lives, there is more data to protect than ever before.

Unfortunately, most users don't adequately protect this valuable resource. This chapter discusses tape backup drives, the most common device used to archive large amounts of data. With hard disks pushing 7GB in size, it's no longer possible to archive data on 1.44MB floppy disks, and even products such as Iomega Zip drives (100MB) or even CD-R drives (650MB) are unable to cleanly archive today's 16GB hard disks.

This chapter introduces you to tape drives. It covers the following topics:

- How tape backup drives work and what they're useful for
- How to install a tape drive
- Troubleshooting tape drives

The Tale of Tape

If you've browsed through this book, you've already read about affordable 7GB hard disks, 17GB DVD-ROM drives, and fast magneto-optical drives that can hold nearly 5GB. So why would anyone want to use cassette tapes, a technology used on desktop PCs back in the early '80s? Three words: cost per megabyte. Cassette tape drives remain the preferred means of backing up large amounts of data because data cassettes are much less expensive than removable disks such as Syquest, Jaz, and Apex. How much less? Table 16.1 shows the relative prices of various types of media.

Table 16.1. Cost per megabyte.

Drive Type	Capacity	Cost	Cost Per Megabyte
Tape (Travan TR-4)	4GB	$35	0.9 cents
CD-ROM	640MB	$12	1.5 cents
Pinnacle Micro Apex	4,710.4MB	$99	2.1 cents
Pinnacle Micro Vertex	2,662.4MB	$79	3 cents
Iomega Jaz	1,024MB	$79	7.7 cents
Hard disk	7,168MB	$350	4.9 cents

In addition to its low cost, tape can be rewritten freely, a feature normal CD-ROM drives can't offer. But tape isn't appropriate for general data handling because of the linear nature of the medium. In other words, the drive can't simply jump to the desired place on the medium to access data the way hard disks and CD-ROM drives do. Instead, it must scroll to a spot on the tape, which can take tens of seconds. That kind of delay— hundreds of times slower than CD-ROM drives or hard disks—means that tape drives are too slow to act as general data storage.

How Tape Backup Works

If you're familiar with how an old eight-track tape works, you already have a good idea of how tape drives store data. To write data to tape, a drive head changes the magnetic charge on the tape medium as it passes beneath it. To read data, the head simply senses the charge of the medium, which the drive interprets as a binary 1 or 0.

Like eight-track tapes, tape backup media are divided into tracks, each of which runs the length of the tape. The tracks run one into another, forming a long chain of tracks. When the drive reaches the end of one track, it simply reverses the direction of tape motion and picks up the next track. On a 740-foot-long tape, 72 tracks yields a total of 53,000 feet of recording surface.

> **Note:** The side-by-side tracks used in data cassettes help shorten the length of the tape. After all, a 72-track tape measuring 740 feet in length would be over 53,000 feet long if the tracks were all laid end-to-end. These tracks allow the drive to access data on the tape more quickly.

But how does the drive know where one bit starts and the next ends? Like other media, the tape is segmented into defined spaces called *bit cells* within which the drive knows to look for a magnetic charge. If the drive detects a change in charge between two bit cells, it interprets a digital 1. If the bit cells are of the same charge, a 0 is identified. These bit cells are contained within larger sectors, which may be called *sectors* or *frames*. They contain both data and error-correction bits to ensure precision.

These sectors or frames also include *slack space*, providing enough travel for the drive head to start and stop the medium without overrunning data on the tape. This is important, because sometimes the PC can't maintain a continuous data stream to the tape, requiring the drive to pause while the processor catches up. Without gaps in the sectors, any pause in the data stream could result in lost data, much like CD-R recording sessions can be undone by a buffer underrun.

Compression is an important part of tape drive operation, but it can be a source of confusion as well. Tape drive vendors often quote capacities based on compressed data, usually assuming a 2-to-1 compression ratio. But the effectiveness of compression can vary widely, depending on the type of data being compressed. If you need to back up JPEG images and MPEG movies—both already heavily compressed—the vendor's 2-to-1 compression assumption won't pan out. Always rely on the uncompressed capacity when you're considering storage.

Types of Backup Media

A few years ago, the tape backup market was a mess. Tapes for one manufacturer's drive wouldn't work in another, leading to incompatibilities and limiting data-recovery options. If you switched to a different tape drive, you had to purchase all-new media to go with it.

Today, there are several types of tape backup media, including

- DAT: Digital Audio Tape
- DLT: Digital Linear Tape
- LTO: Linear Tape-Open
- 8mm cartridge
- QIC-format Travan

Of these, only the QIC-format Travan tape is designed for use on single desktops. The others are priced for larger network duty and can handle capacities of 25 to 35GB or more (see Figure 16.1).

Travan: The Desktop Choice

Established in 1987, the QIC standard gets its name from its quarter-inch cassette, which defines the width of the tape. The QIC standard started at 400MB with the QIC-40 specification and has moved up as hard disk capacities have increased. Today, new QIC media provides 2GB and greater capacities of uncompressed data.

Behind the higher capacities is a technology called Travan, which was established by 3M and several hardware makers in 1992. Key to the new standard is the relative density of magnetic charge changes that can occur on each inch of tape, called *flux transitions*. The more flux transitions per inch (ftpi), the more data the tape can store.

FIGURE **16.1.**
With its auto-
loading cassette
mechanism, fast
performance, and
large capacities,
this DAT backup
drive is ready-
made for net-
work servers and
other demanding
backup environ-
ments. (Photo
courtesy of
Seagate Corp.)

Table 16.2 lists four variations of the Travan specification.

Table 16.2. Travan flavors defined.

Travan Type	Capacity	Flux Transitions Per Inch
TR-1	400MB	14,700
TR-2	800MB	22,125
TR-3	1.6GB	44,250
TR-4	4GB	50,800
NS-20	10GB	79,800

In fact, ftpi determines the capacity of a Travan tape (see Figure 16.2), because all Travan media employ the same amount of physical surface area. All tapes are a quarter-inch wide and measure 740 feet in length. Greater ftpi densities mean that more bits are stored per inch and also allow for more tracks to be packed into the medium. The TR-1 spec, for example, provides 14,700 flux transitions per inch, resulting in 400MB of data stored in 36 tracks. In comparison, the 4GB TR-4 spec employs 50,800 flux transitions per inch on 72 tracks. The NS-20 media boosts both ftpi (79,800) and the track density (108 tracks) to achieve 10GB uncompressed data capacity.

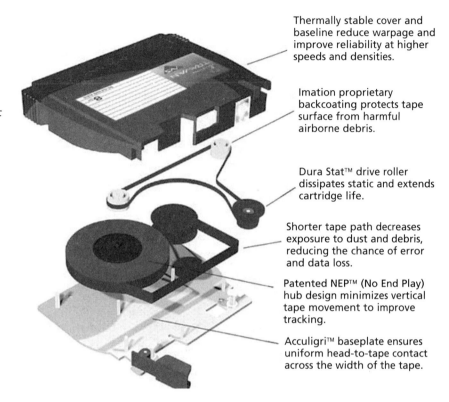

Thermally stable cover and baseline reduce warpage and improve reliability at higher speeds and densities.

Imation proprietary backcoating protects tape surface from harmful airborne debris.

Dura Stat™ drive roller dissipates static and extends cartridge life.

Shorter tape path decreases exposure to dust and debris, reducing the chance of error and data loss.

Patented NEP™ (No End Play) hub design minimizes vertical tape movement to improve tracking.

Acculigri™ baseplate ensures uniform head-to-tape contact across the width of the tape.

FIGURE 16.2.
This exploded view of a Travan cartridge shows how the magnetic media travels inside the plastic casing. (Photo courtesy of Seagate Corp.)

DAT: Cheap Media, Pricey Drives

Derived from the same media and architecture used in digital audio tape (DAT) cassettes, these drives are best for large-capacity data storage. The DDS-3 specification, for example, can store 12GB of uncompressed data on a single cartridge.

The DAT scheme employs a helical scan approach that lays bits down diagonally along each track. The helican scan technology gets its name from the fact that the head describes the shape of a helix as it travels along the tape. The diagonally laid tracks allow much higher data densities, but the more complex drive design results in much higher drive prices.

On the other hand, DAT cassettes are cheap—making DAT a terrific option if you tend to purchase a lot of tapes and use them on just a few drives. The secret? DAT tapes lack tracking controls found in other media, including DLT and Travan, relying on logic and controls inside the drives themselves. However, DAT drives can cost $2,000 or more—exhorbitant by Travan standards.

DLT: Big Data

If you need mass storage, and lots of it, on a single cassette, considering Digital Linear Tape (DLT). See Figure 16.3. With uncompressed tape capacities of 35GB available, you won't find a better way to back up disk-laden network servers and other data hogs. DLT delivers performance to match, with transfer rates of 5MBps. Compare that to the 600KBps top transfer rate of Seagate's TST8000R line of 8GB Travan format tape drives. The fast transfer rate allows network administrators to get backups done quickly and efficiently—without monopolizing network resources for hours on end.

Unlike other tape formats, DLT is able to read and write data at the same time. By allowing data to be verified (read) even as it is being written, DLT drives are able to cut down on the time-consuming step of verifying the integrity of a backup. But if you thought DAT drives were pricey, DLT will shock you. Prices can run $5,000 or more for a DLT drive able to read 35GB media. For network applications, a 6-drive DLT switcher makes an excellent option, since you can automatically backup hundreds of gigabytes without having to stop everything to load a new tape.

FIGURE 16.3.
The integrated tape reel inside DLT drives allow enhanced tape control and faster performance.

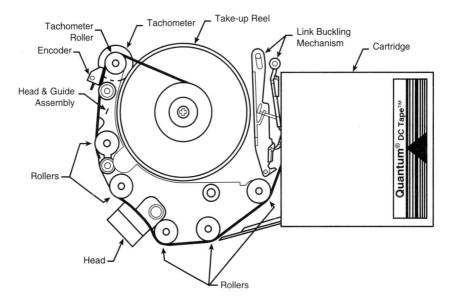

LTO: New Technology, New Standard?

The problem with tape backup is that there are way too many incompatible formats. Your Travan TR-4 cartridges won't work in older Travan drives, much less in DAT or DLT drives. As a result, buyers are forced to make scary decisions that may lock them into a particular tape technology for a decade or more. If the technology you choose fails to keep up with higher data capacities and lowering costs, you'll face the possible expense of an early switch.

Linear Tape-Open technology was minted by IBM, HP, and Seagate to provide an open industry standard that would also ensure adequate capacity growth down the road. LTO supports 8 concurrent-channels (later to go to 16) with recording densities of 100MB per square inch.

LTO is actually broken into two formats:

- Accelis: Lower densities and high read performance
- Ultrium: Very high densities and better write performance

Accelis tapes offer 25GB of data storage to nearly match that of DLT media. With 128 data tracks on 216 meters of 8mm tape, the Accelis format is slated to eventually pack 200GB of data on a single cartridge. Initial data rates run 10MBps, but are slated to go as high as 180MBps in later generations. The media is optimized for rapid data access, making Accelis appropriate for near-online storage of media files and other extremely large files. Access cartridges use two reels.

The Ultrium format, by contrast, favors capacity over playback. Starting at 100GB, Ultrium cassettes contain 660 meters of ½-inch media containing 384 data tracks. Future generations of Ultrium tape will pack 800GB of data with 80MBps data transfer rates. Unlike Accelis, Ultrium tapes only contain a single reel, with the media being taken up on a reel integrated into the Ultrium-class drive itself.

Making Backups

Advancements in tape drives have vastly improved performance—a good thing considering the amount of time it would take to move gigabytes of data otherwise. Today, fast tape drives can move data at up to 500KBps, enough for video playback directly from tape media. The problem is that accessing specific data will always take an unacceptably long time with tape drives since the drive must scroll the tape to the appropriate section to read the data—a process that can take several minutes. For this reason, tape backup can't compete with spinning-disk media, which provide access times in milliseconds.

One of the most critical elements of any backup drive is the software making it work (see Figure 16.4). Backup software varies widely, so it makes sense to look for software providing the features you need. Virtually all these packages enable you to select the files to be backed up.

Better software provides powerful options to tailor backup routines. Scheduling features enables you to back up data every day, every week, or at any other specified interval. In addition, backups can be tailored to save all the selected data on the disk, or only data that has been changed since the last backup. There are three categories of backups:

- Full backup: Writes everything on the disk to tape
- Incremental backup: Writes to tape anything that has changed since the last incremental backup
- Differential backup: Writes to tape anything that has changed since the last full backup

FIGURE 16.4.
Microsoft Backup provides the ability to selectively back up files and filter them by date. But you'll want a more sophisticated program for automated scheduling of backups.

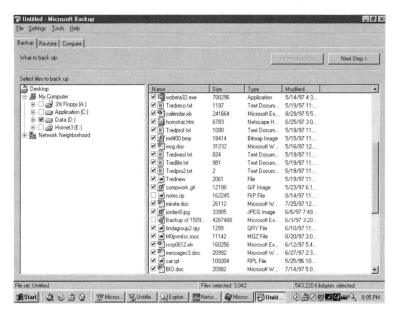

Full backups take the longest time and chew up the most media, but they also provide the most surefire security. With a full backup, you know everything you need is on the tape. Incremental backups are the most problematic, because only altered data appears on the tape. You need to make sure that you have both the original full backup and all subsequent incremental backups on hand in order to restore all the data to its most current form. However, incremental backups are the most economical in terms of media space and time.

In between are differential backups. These backups save all the changed data since the last full backup. Although you repeat the work of earlier incremental or differential backups, you need to keep only two tapes handy at any time—the first full backup and the latest differential backup.

Caution: Backups can go bad. Media can fail, or the drive might simply fail to write to the medium properly. You can reduce data loss by setting the backup software to conduct a full verification after the backup is complete. This feature causes the drive to review the entire tape, comparing what was written to the original data. Although this process significantly increases the time it takes to complete a backup, it can catch flaws before they become a problem. Be aware that on-the-fly verification can sometimes fail because some file contents may change between the backup and verification steps.

Also be sure to do test restores of your data on a regular basis. This will let you verify the integrity of your data backups before you find yourself in a do-or-die situation.

INSTANT REFERENCE For more on backup tactics, see page 394, "Establishing a Smart Backup Scheme."

Even if you have your data backed up to tape or other media, the data is only as safe as the media itself. Calamities like a fire or flood, for example, will wipe out the benefits of even the most disciplined backup regimen. Theft is also a concern, since backup media may contain confidential data.

For this reason, you should consider keeping a fully executable set of backup media in a separate and secure location. Moving the data out of the immediate vicinity should ensure that physical damage to your property doesn't also destroy all your data. You can even contract with a backup service to automatically transmit your files to a remote server. Of course, if you are dealing with confidential data, you may want to carefully consider your options, particularly if a vendor intends to use the public Internet to handle transfers.

Buying Backups

When it comes to buying a tape backup, you need to make sure the drive you purchase can meet your needs. A computer that has a stuffed 8.4GB hard disk simply can't be backed up with an 800MB Iomega Ditto drive. You'll also need to think about the interface type and compatibility with other tape formats if you have older media around that you need to access.

Capacity Concerns

The biggest challenge in buying a tape drive is figuring out the maximum data capacity it supports. Often, manufacturers market their drives based on compressed data capacities, usually based on a 2-to-1 compression ratio. The result is that you might think the drive can handle more data than it really can.

In fact, 2-to-1 is an optimistic estimate. In general, you can expect data compression ratios to fall around 1.7-to-1 overall, with document files enjoying higher capacities. If you're compressing a lot of previously compressed data—Internet images, video, or program files—scale down your expectations.

Today, the highest-capacity tape drives can store 4GB of data before compression. If you have a large hard disk over 4GB in size, you'll need to consider a higher-end tape drive.

> **Tip:** If you already own a tape drive and are upgrading to a larger hard disk, consider your new backup needs. Odds are you might have to update the tape drive as well, in order to handle the expanded data capacity of the new hard disk.

Interface Options

Another critical concern is the device interface. You'll also want to consider whether you want an internal or external model, because this might determine which interface you use. Tape drives are sold with interfaces for the following bus types:

- SCSI
- Parallel port
- Enhanced IDE
- Floppy controller
- Proprietary controllers
- USB

The last two options represent technologies in flux. The advent of inexpensive IDE and SCSI interfaces has made proprietary controller types a dying breed. That's good news, since today's drives will now plug into the existing controllers on most PCs and saving money as a result. USB-based backup, meanwhile, is becoming more popular as PCs equipped to handle the new bus emerge. If you have a Windows 98 system, you may find a USB drive to be the easiest option, since it enables you to use an external drive offering full Plug and Play operation.

For the fastest and most trouble-free backups, SCSI drives are the way to go (see Figure 16.5). You'll spend more money for the fast SCSI bus and interface, but you won't have to share ports the way you must with parallel port drives. In addition, higher-speed tape drives can move data at their full 500KBps data rate. SCSI also provides superior multi-tasking, allowing the system to perform other activities more efficiently during backup routines.

Figure 16.5.
The fast SCSI connection employed by the internal Seagate TapeStor 8000 helps speed backup jobs to the 4GB TR-4 medium. (Photo courtesy of Seagate Corp.)

Tip: If you already have external SCSI peripherals installed, go with an SCSI tape drive. After all, you already have the SCSI host controller in place, so you can simply add the tape drive to the daisy chain. Otherwise, the SCSI decision will rest on your usage. If you make frequent and large backups, you'll enjoy quicker backups on an SCSI drive. This is particularly true if you tend to conduct backups while working with the PC, because SCSI is able to handle multiple tasks better than IDE.

Parallel port tape drives are an option if you need portable, light-duty backup facilities. Home and home-office PCs might do well with parallel port drives. In addition to being very simple to install, parallel port models are much less expensive than their SCSI counterparts. They can also be shared easily among several PCs, making them a great option for people with a desktop and notebook PC, for example.

That said, these drives must often share the parallel port with the printer, which can invite conflicts and prompt a lot of annoying port swapping. Drive throughput can also be limited by the parallel port.

Another common option is for floppy controller-based drives. Often, if you have two floppy drives already installed, you might need to install a separate controller card. Of course, floppy-based drives need to be internal models, but the floppy interface provides faster performance than low-cost parallel port models.

You might also be on the lookout for tape backup devices based on the Universal Serial Bus (USB). USB provides 12MBps throughput that is much faster than parallel port connections while avoiding the expense and complexity of SCSI. That said, storage devices based on USB have been slow to emerge, and users will need to be running Windows 98 to ensure that USB devices work on their systems. But if you find a USB version of a desired product, the Plug and Play features and one-size-fits-all connector are very tempting.

And what about the choice of external versus internal? Generally internal drives are less expensive and more convenient than external models. Not only do internal models conserve desktop space, but they also avoid adding yet another power cord (and sometimes an enormous adapter module) to the tangle behind the PC. Of course, if you want to use an IDE interface, you must go with an internal drive. Of course, external models (see Figure 16.6) are excellent for PCs that don't have drive bays, as well as for offices in which a tape drive is shared among more than one system.

On the downside, internal drives consume drive bay space and require internal connections for power. If you own a slimline system or a PC with a paucity of bays, you might want to pay a little more for an external device.

FIGURE 16.6.
Form and function: The Seagate TapeStor 3200 uses 1.6GB TR-3 media and sports a stylish, vertically mounted design. (Photo courtesy of Seagate Corp.)

Compatibility

Another critical concern is compatibility. In general, tape drives with larger capacities can at least read tapes made for smaller capacities. In many cases, these drives can both read from and write to smaller media.

Of course, if you have one drive that you use on your system, compatibility might not be a huge concern. But if you need to read tapes from a previous drive or share tapes from other systems, this ability to read and write different media is a valuable one.

Installing a Tape Backup Drive

Installing a tape backup device is very similar to installing a CD-ROM or other drive. Windows 95/98's Plug and Play facility will guide you through the routine, automatically detecting the new device. Or you can decide to identify the device to the OS yourself. The biggest difference among drives is between internal and external devices.

Physical Installation

It's far more complicated to install an internal backup drive. To install the unit, do the following:

1. Shut down the PC, remove the power cord, and remove the case.

2. Make sure you're well-grounded (an antistatic wrist strap is a good idea) before reaching into the case. Find an open externally accessible drive bay, and pry off the front cover.

3. Connect the drive cable to the drive, being sure to match pin 1 of the cable to pin 1 of the connector.

4. Slide the drive into the bay, and align the screw holes with those in the mount.

5. Use the screws provided with the drive to affix the drive to the bay. Be sure to follow the instructions that came with the drive to make sure that it is properly mounted.

6. Attach the data cable to the appropriate SCSI, EIDE, or floppy connector, as determined by your drive's interface (see Figure 16.7).

FIGURE 16.7.
For floppy-based drives, the presence of two floppy drives will require a third cable to split off of the existing leads. Often, this cable will be provided. (Figure courtesy of Seagate Corp.)

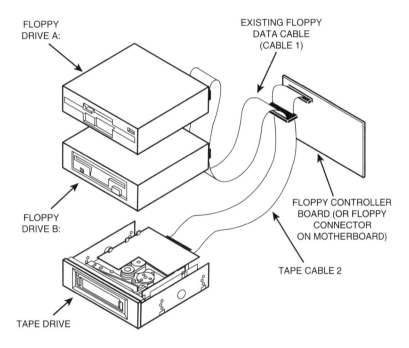

7. Attach one of the free power leads from the supply to the power connector on the drive. Make sure you properly align the connector.

8. In some cases, you might need to set jumpers found near the back of the drive to match the settings on your motherboard and configuration of other drives. Consult your documentation for specific information.

If you have an external drive, you simply need to plug the drive into the appropriate cables. If it's an SCSI drive, you'll need to make sure you have the proper cable connectors to mate with your SCSI card or the connector on other daisy-chained SCSI devices.

Also check the device's documentation on how to terminate and enumerate SCSI devices.

Parallel port drives might include a printer pass-through port. If so, you might need to check your system BIOS and set it to standard Centronics operation. ECP- and EPP-enabled parallel port configurations might get confused by the pass-through port.

To install the drivers for the device, do the following:

1. Plug in the PC and power it up.
2. Windows 95 and 98 will detect the new hardware during bootup and prompt you to install the new device.
3. Click through the Add New Hardware Wizard. When Windows prompts you to detect the new device, click No.
4. Select the Other Device item and click Next. Insert the tape drive's driver disk into the floppy drive.
5. In the next dialog box, click Have Disk and select the .INF file from the appropriate drive and directory.
6. Windows will update the new driver information. When you're prompted to restart the system, click Yes.
7. Your tape drive should now be installed.

You'll also need to install the backup program that comes with the device (or a third-party program of your choosing). Once this is done, you can test the drive and make sure it works.

Tape Management: Handling with Care

Dealing with backup drives can get tricky. The cassettes themselves are sensitive to environmental stress, and the physical logistics of juggling backup media can be complicated. In both cases, it makes sense to have a strategy to avoid trouble down the road.

Establishing a Smart Backup Scheme

Before you get started backing up data, establish a routine. Decide how often you need to back up your data and how thorough you want to be. Usually, you can avoid burning too much time (and money on tapes) by establishing a set of incremental backups between full backups. Good backup programs, such as Adaptec's Backup Exec, will often enable you to choose from a number of schemes for optimizing your tape management.

Imation Corp., the 3M spinoff that invented the Travan tape medium, provides the following guidelines for scenarios using three or six cartridges a week.

Three-Cartridge Weekly Backup

This backup principle requires daily backups and a single weekly off-site backup copy to provide a data history of up to two weeks. Friday backups are full backups. Monday-through-Thursday backups are incremental (all on the same tape). Note that restoring incremental changes might be more difficult using the three-cartridge principle.

- Start the cycle on a Friday, and back up your entire hard disk to a cartridge labeled Friday 1. This is a full backup of your system. Store this data cartridge off-site.

- On Monday, back up only the files that have been created or updated since the last backup (Friday 1); use a cartridge labeled Daily for this. Store this cartridge on-site.

- On Tuesday, Wednesday, and Thursday, use the same Daily cartridge to back up files that have been created or updated since the preceding day. Store this cartridge on-site.

- On Friday, do a full backup using a cartridge labeled Friday 2. Store this cartridge off-site.

- Continue the weekly routine of incremental backups for Monday through Thursday using the same Daily data cartridge. On Fridays, alternate the Friday 1 and Friday 2 cartridges.

Six-Cartridge Weekly Backup

This backup principle requires daily backups and a single weekly off-site backup copy to provide a data history of up to two weeks. Friday backups are full backups. Monday through Thursday backups are incremental.

- Start the cycle on a Friday, and back up your entire hard disk to a cartridge labeled Friday 1. This is a full backup of your system. Store this data cartridge off-site.

- On Monday, back up only the files that have been created or updated since the last backup (Friday 1); use a cartridge labeled Monday for this. (Or, for easier restoring, do a full backup.) Store this cartridge on-site.

- On the appropriate days, use cartridges labeled Tuesday, Wednesday, and Thursday to back up files that have been created or updated since the previous day. (Or, for easier restoring, do a full backup.) Store these on-site.

- On Friday, do a full backup using a cartridge labeled Friday 2. Store this cartridge off-site.

- Once you get this far, you continue the weekly incremental backups for Monday through Thursday using the same Monday-through-Thursday data cartridges. On Fridays, alternate the Friday 1 and Friday 2 cartridges.

Caring for Cassettes

Cassette tape media can be tricky. The flexible tape can suffer from exposure to dirt, humidity, and temperature. Over time, tape can stretch as it is pulled time and again through the drive mechanism. For this reason, it's a good idea to stay on top of potential problems.

Watch the Environment

Give your new tape cartridges time to acclimate. The media material expands and contracts in relation to room temperature. So when you bring new tapes in from outside— say a delivery truck—you should give them at least eight hours or so to adjust to the temperature of the room in which you will use them. In fact, for this reason, it's a good idea to keep your tapes close to where they will be used.

Of course, it's a good idea to avoid constant temperature and humidity fluctuations, because this can stress the medium and shorten its useful life.

Cleaning Up

Tape drives aren't sealed like hard disks, so dirt can be a problem. Dust gathered on tape heads can end up on the medium, impairing the drive's ability to read and write. The problem is that the head must be in contact with the medium in order to function. If dust or other particulates block this contact, the device can't operate properly.

The best approach to this problem is to keep your work space reasonably clean to avoid exposure. In addition, you should periodically clean the drive heads and motor assembly using a cleaning media tape. This cassette fits into the drive like any other data cassette, but it's designed to clear the internal components of dirt.

Get Tense

Over time, environmental stress and normal operation can loosen the medium in its spools. The result is lost precision as the tape slips with each drive movement. You can avoid this problem by periodically running the tape from beginning to end in a single run. Some backup software includes a retension command that performs this operation automatically. If a tape is subject to extreme temperature changes, the tape should be run. In fact, it's a good idea to do this every time a tape is loaded.

Take Care of Media

You'll get longer life out of your media—and, consequently, better data protection—if you take care of your cassettes. Keep in mind the following points when handling cassettes:

- Remove cassettes from the tape drive when they're not in use.
- When you're finished using a tape, reset it to the very beginning or the very end.

- Store cassettes in the same room where they will be used, and keep them in their protective covers.
- Keep tapes away from destructive exposures such as magnetic fields and sunlight.
- Keep critical backups (usually the full backups) offsite, just in case.

Summary

Surprisingly, tape backup drives are more important than ever. These slow devices provide affordable, flexible data storage for everything from home PCs to network servers. Although cassette technology has been around almost forever, the buying landscape can get tricky. Tape capacity, compatibility, and interface choices are all part of any buying decision.

Don't overlook the importance of software, either. Yes, Windows 95 does include a backup utility able to get the job done. But if you want to make consistent and effective backups, you'll want the automated scheduling capability provided by third-party products. When buying a backup drive, look for the quality of the software.

Tape backup drives aren't sexy, but they can really be lifesavers. After all, with more and more of our personal and working data on PCs, the effects of loss or damage to the system can be disastrous. Tape backup drives are the best way to avoid losing your investment.

PART V

Multimedia

New Dimensions: Graphics Accelerators

When it comes to performance upgrades intended to make systems faster, people think of two things: CPUs and graphics boards. To a large extent, the arrival of Windows 3.0 in 1990 helped develop this belief that graphics boards are important to performance. The upgrade picture these days is a bit more complex—RAM and cache upgrades are now just as important to consider as CPUs and graphics—but the basic truth still holds.

In fact, graphics board upgrades take on renewed importance these days. The emergence of 3D graphics standards has created a new class of software, written to display realistic and smooth 3D images (see Figure 17.1). Every kind of software, from arcade-style games to business presentation packages, can make use of complex 3D graphics to boost visual impact.

FIGURE 17.1.
Diamond Multimedia's Viper 550 is typical of today's affordable graphics accelerators. It packs 2D, video, and outstanding 3D graphics acceleration into a low-cost PCI or AGP add-in card. (Photo courtesy Diamond Multimedia)

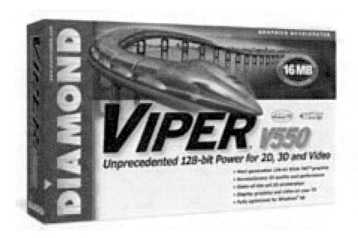

If you have a 486 system, you'll need to replace the motherboard or buy a new system if you want to enjoy the exciting 3D and video features of the latest software. Board makers have already abandoned the older ISA and VL-bus slots, and most cards now are built for PCI and the Accelerated Graphics Port (AGP) bus. In fact, if you want to play the best 3D games and titles, you'll want to purchase a system with an AGP slot because AGP cards offer key advantages in 3D graphics performance and imagery.

You'll also need a graphics card capable of 3D imaging to keep up with advanced multimedia, gaming, and Web software. With 3D rapidly becoming standard issue on even the least expensive PCs, many productivity applications are starting to take advantage of the 3D acceleration features offered in affordable graphics cards. This chapter shows you how to move into the third dimension and covers the following topics:

- How graphics cards speed up and enhance 2D and 3D graphics and video
- What to look for when buying a new graphics card for games, business, and other applications
- How to diagnose and troubleshoot common graphics problems
- How to upgrade your system with a new graphics card, including complete installation instructions

Packin' Pixels: How Graphics Boards Speed Performance

Graphics boards speed up system performance in two ways: They free the system CPU from the mundane chores of displaying and updating graphics information, and they accomplish these chores many times faster than a general CPU ever could. The result is rapid-fire screen updates that make possible wonderful things such as Deathmatch Quake II, super-scrolling spreadsheets, and really smooth animated text in PowerPoint presentations.

To understand how graphics boards do their tricks, you need to know how Windows works. Windows made the graphics accelerator board market possible by providing a standard way to draw text, graphics, and other elements onscreen. Under DOS, most applications wrote to the display in a custom way that confounded graphics board makers and demanded a different driver for each application. DOS programs also displayed information to the screen in their own way, working directly with hardware to display graphics, fonts, and other information.

Windows provides a standard interface for display interaction. Under DOS, programs each displayed information to the screen in their own way, working directly with hardware to display graphics, fonts, and other information.

Windows provides a standard interface for display interaction, however, by putting several layers of software between your applications and graphics hardware. This new scheme, shown in Figure 17.2, establishes a standard set of rules for graphics work and enables graphics boards to use hardware to speed up common graphics operations that used to fall under the responsibility of the host CPU. The result is improved overall performance.

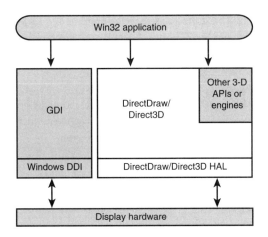

FIGURE 17.2.
Microsoft employs a series of function-specific software layers to address graphics capabilities such as 2D, 3D, and video. (Figure courtesy Microsoft Corp.)

2D Graphics Acceleration

The rule book for 2D graphics, established firmly with the release of Windows 3.0, is called the *Graphics Device Interface* (*GDI*). Applications send GDI calls to Windows to do everything from moving blocks of graphics, to scrolling text, to displaying color.

Software on the other side—the graphics board driver—talks to the GDI and handles the information that results. Depending on the capabilities of a graphics board, the driver directs the flow of work to the dedicated graphics chip on the board or to the host CPU. If no acceleration hardware is in place, all the GDI calls are handled by the processor.

> **Note:** Watch out for cards that use a scheme called *GDI bypass* to boost performance. These boards have drivers that intercept inbound GDI graphics calls and replace them with custom code that is designed to perform the same operation more quickly. Although performance might get a boost—GDI is a very slow component of Windows 95—the prospect of incompatibilities in the vital graphics-handling area of the OS is a real concern. Microsoft has stated that GDI bypass isn't an acceptable solution, and you won't find any drivers with Microsoft's WHQL certification using this tweak.

Graphics boards handle several key 2D operations:

- Bit block transfer: Perhaps the most important function of a graphics board is the *bit block transfer,* also called a *bit blit.* A bit blit moves rectangular chunks of graphics data from one place in graphics memory (and onscreen) to another. Scrolling text and dragging a graphic across the screen are both examples of bit blits.

- Line drawing: This technique speeds the drawing of lines by defining the beginning and end point and filling in the pixels in between. This approach is faster than operating on each pixel individually. Similar approaches are used for drawing arcs and polygons.

- Color and pattern fill: This refers to the method of applying color and patterns to an area of the screen—usually a polygon, circle, or other geometric shape. Instead of updating each pixel individually, the card can identify a range on the screen to update in one step. Gradients are supported as well.

- Clipping: This process provides for the quick display of items that obscure other items, such as a drop-down menu that covers part of a spreadsheet.

- Offscreen memory caching: This technique employs unused graphics memory to store frequently needed graphical information, such as fonts and application menus. Caching eliminates the need to go to main system memory for updates.

In the past, some graphics boards provided a greater range of acceleration features than others. Today, almost all graphics boards deliver similar capabilities, with performance differences coming from the type of memory. The result is that demanding multimedia titles, such as mapping software (shown in Figure 17.3), enjoy much-improved performance.

FIGURE 17.3.

DeLorme's Map'n'Go street map software is an excellent example of graphics-heavy software that benefits from 2D acceleration.

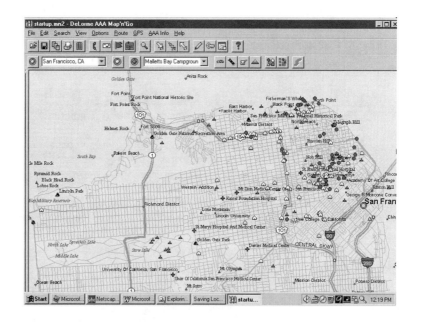

Video Acceleration

Around 1994, software such as Apple's QuickTime and Microsoft's Video for Windows helped introduce digital video playback to PCs. The new software enabled Windows-based PCs to recognize compressed video files and play them back onscreen.

Even today's fastest Pentium II PCs, however, struggle to display video of a quality approaching that of a standard VHS tape. As with the reels in a movie, digital video consists of a series of individual images, or frames, played in swift succession to create the illusion of motion.

The amount of data involved is tremendous: To display 30 frames of uncompressed digital video, a PC would have to move nearly 200Mbps. To make digital video possible, that number would be cut down to as little as 150Kbps. To do this, video is stored in compressed format so that it can be moved more quickly and efficiently until it reaches the processor.

The problem with compression is that it takes a lot of work from the processor to decode the video stream. So much processing must occur that video frame rates can drop from a smooth 30 frames per second (fps) to a jerky 5fps or less. Not surprisingly, the responsiveness of other applications suffers as well.

Video-capable graphics boards help improve things by easing the burden on the CPU and by improving the quality of stretched video windows. Although compression schemes such as MPEG-1, MPEG-2, Indeo, and Cinepak might do things in different ways, they all share characteristics that enable standard video-accelerating hardware to boost performance.

DirectDraw: Crucial Shortcuts

Before any hardware could help video playback, Microsoft had to provide an efficient path for video data under Windows. GDI might be a useful standard for static images and simple animations, but it spells a slow-moving death for consumer applications such as video playback and game play.

To this end, three years ago Microsoft began working on a set of standards called *DirectX,* which provides programming tools and pathways for efficiently moving multimedia data and handling complex controls. On the graphics side, the DirectDraw application programming interface (API) enables hardware and software makers to move multimedia graphics more quickly and efficiently. DirectDraw also provides the crucial programming hooks that enable video clips to access video-accelerating hardware.

As with any peripherals, you need the proper drivers to gain access to all the features in the operating system and the peripheral's hardware. You might have a video-capable graphics card, but unless you install DirectDraw drivers, those features will go unnoticed by your applications.

INSTANT REFERENCE For more on installing drivers, see the section "Installing a Graphics Board."

> **Tip:** The best place to get drivers is online, from the vendor's Web site or from a forum on CompuServe, AOL, or another online service. Make a point to visit these sites every few months to see if a significant upgrade or feature release is available. You might be able to extend and enhance the life of your graphics card with these occasional downloads.

The DirectDraw API provides the following key features:

- Direct frame buffer access
- Double buffering
- Color space conversion
- Pixel interpolation

Direct Frame Buffer Access

As the essential shortcut that makes video and game play possible under Windows 95, direct frame buffer access enables programs to cut through layers of GDI code to call up bits onscreen quickly. Under GDI, software sends commands to Windows 95, which interprets them and turns them into specific graphics commands. The extra layer ensures compatibility but exacts a penalty in performance.

Direct frame buffer access cuts through the thick levels of code, replacing them with a thin layer that provides direct access to memory without inviting all sorts of incompatibility shenanigans. Even on a card that doesn't have video-acceleration features, direct frame buffer access can speed video frame rates and the display of 2D and 3D graphics.

Double Buffering

As with direct frame buffer access, double buffering has applications outside of video. This scheme enables the graphics controller to store two pictures in its memory: the current image and the image that is next to come up. By staying ahead of the game by constantly storing an image of what's to come, graphics boards can avoid distracting flaws such as frame dropping, slow screen updates, and image shearing (in which the image onscreen splits in half as part of it fails to update quickly).

Double buffering is particularly important in video and 3D graphics, in which up to 30fps are needed to maintain the illusion of smooth motion. By splitting graphics memory with this efficient scheme, the graphics card can stay ahead of the game.

Color Space Conversion

To save space, the color information in video clips is stored in a format called YUV. This format, which is the same as the one used by your TV, breaks video data into separate color and brightness components. The U and V represent the color signals, and the Y represents the relative brightness.

In contrast, your PC's monitor uses a red-green-blue (RGB) color scheme, in which colors are created by mixing varying levels of the three colors within each pixel. Because of this, the YUV color information in a video clip must be converted to the standard RGB format recognized by the display.

The problem with color space conversion is that it takes a lot of processor power. In fact, about 30 percent of the video playback workload consists of changing YUV into RGB. Video-accelerating hardware immediately boosts the performance of all video playback by freeing the CPU from this task.

Pixel Interpolation

Pixel interpolation improves the visual quality of video clips that are stored at lower resolutions than they are played back. This feature is needed because many clips are stored at resolutions of 320×240 pixels but are played back full-screen on systems running at 640×480 or 800×600 pixels. Although you can instruct the host CPU to double up pixels to fill the extra space, the results can be very unattractive.

Pixel interpolation makes expanded video look more realistic by averaging color information when pixels are added. Instead of breaking smooth curves into jagged boundaries the color averaging keeps the illusion of smoothness.

> **Note:** One downside of pixel interpolation is that sharply contrasting areas—such as what is found on a checkerboard kitchen floor—can be averaged into softer grays. This can make the original image look hazy or undefined.

The color interpolation feature on graphics boards can vary. Some less-sophisticated graphics chips average information only between pixels running horizontally—this is called an *x filter*. Most chips today provide both x and y filters; in other words, they average going up and down as well as side to side.

In addition, some chips take more pixels into account when doing their work. Older or less-sophisticated chips compute averages using two pixels: the pixel in question and the one adjacent to it (called a *2-tap filter*). Today, most graphics chips average color values among 4 pixels (a *4-tap filter*), enabling the hardware to come up with a better approximation of reality when it expands the video image. Often, the higher pixel count can smooth out the distracting stair-stepping of colors, known as *banding*.

> **Peter's Principle:** How to Discern Video Quality
>
> If you look closely, you can tell the difference in the way video accelerators affect playback. Although all video-compression schemes introduce some degradation, often the lack of proper video-accelerating hardware makes a bad situation worse.

Look for telltale signs, such as banded or blotchy colors. Skin tones, in particular, are a challenge for video chips. Also check for stair-stepped or jagged effects on diagonal lines (see Figure 17.4). Bicycle spokes are a classic example of an interpolation challenge, although nearly any angled surface will do. In addition, look for high-contrast points, where very different colors meet head-on. You might be able to see some hazing as the hardware unintentionally wipes out detail.

Figure 17.4.

Look closely at the wing and tail edges of this dogfighting F/A-18 Falcon, and you'll note stair-stepped edges. Banded colors also appear on the fuselage.

Hardware-based interpolation does more than enhance image quality—it boosts performance as well. Think about it: During video playback, your CPU is busy enough just pushing out the video stream. Double the size of the video window, and you're asking it to take time out to calculate additional pixels in up to 30 frames every second. What's more, the considerably larger video stream must be ushered across the bus and to the graphics card.

With hardware interpolation, the driver software can tell the system CPU to handle just the decompression tasks and to route the native resolution (and still YUV-encoded) video stream to the graphics board. Once there, the video-savvy chip handles interpolation in hardware, and the CPU gets busy with succeeding frames. Because video isn't expanded until after it has reached the card, the system bus carries less data.

Motion Estimation

More recently, some graphics cards have begun adding a feature called *motion estimation.* Targeted for the high-quality MPEG-2 video found in DVD titles, motion estimation enables high-end PCs to play back MPEG-2 video without requiring a dedicated decompression card. Performance won't match that provided by dedicated MPEG-2 hardware, but this feature opens up the next level of video playback at a very affordable price.

With motion estimation, the graphics card can ease the processing burden of determining what information is redundant in a video frame. In clips where little action is taking place—say, a video of someone giving a speech—these cards can simply keep all the unchanged visual information already in graphics memory and send it to the screen. Only changed pixels need to be processed.

Peter's Principle: Understanding Video Performance

When it comes to general-purpose video-acceleration hardware, don't expect too much. The most demanding component of video playback—decompression—still falls entirely on the CPU, which is also busy with other system tasks. Video acceleration can ease the load and extend the quality of video, but it won't fix it outright.

Nowhere is this more true than with the coming generation of MPEG-2 clips used in DVD-based titles. The MPEG-2 compression scheme is extremely complex and data-heavy. Even the most effective general-purpose video hardware can't do enough to make MPEG-2 playback entirely effective.

PCs that use MMX-enhanced processors enjoy a big advantage when it comes to video playback. MMX extends processors' instruction sets to enable them to handle multimedia tasks such as video playback and decompression. Although a video-savvy graphics card already handles many of the tasks for which MMX is tailored, these enhanced CPUs still provide added performance for video play-back. If you expect to play a lot of digital video, consider getting a system that has an MMX processor.

By the same token, this hardware won't make poorly captured or compressed video look better than it is. A Cinepak-compressed clip captured at low 160×120 resolution in 8-bit color and at 10fps will look awful and jerky on the most sophisticated hardware (see Figures 17.5 and 17.6).

FIGURE 17.5.

Video hardware won't help low-resolution video, such as that found on many Web sites.

FIGURE 17.6.

Lots of motion forces compression schemes to throw out more visual data to keep the data rate low; the result is degraded image quality.

3D Acceleration

If the introduction of video playback to PCs was important, it pales in comparison to the impact that 3D graphics have on personal computing. From rapid-fire gaming to immersive Web browsing, the emergence of 3D standards and acceleration hardware promises to redefine the visual experience.

It's no surprise that popular 3D programming standards form the basis of accelerated 3D applications. It's less surprising that Microsoft put the standard in place. As with DirectDraw before it, the Direct3D API gives hardware and software vendors a single interface to hook into 3D-accelerated features. Most important, everyone who creates a 3D game or graphics card knows that Direct3D will be part and parcel of the Windows 95 operating system, helping create a large audience for compatible products.

Peter's Principle: 3D Standards Cleanup

The 3D standard landscape is finally settling down. Microsoft's Direct3D technology, which is vastly improved after years of revisions, has finally begun to attract significant attention from game makers. What's more, graphics chips such as Nvidia's Riva 128 TNT and Intel's i740 are optimized for Direct3D rather than a scheme specific to the chip itself. That contrasts starkly to just a year or two prior, when it seemed that every board was tailored to its own 3D API.

The picture isn't completely clear yet. One of the most powerful 3D graphics chips—3Dfx'2 Voodoo 2—uses the proprietary Glide API. Likewise, Rendition's Verite uses its own RRedline and Speedy3D APIs. However, both chips support Direct3D as well.

You'll also want to look for effective support for OpenGL, a workstation-class technology that is moving into the mainstream. OpenGL doesn't compete directly with Direct3D for developers' attention, but more games are taking advantage of OpenGL's highly detailed and flexible environment. Of particular note, Microsoft plans to merge Direct3D and OpenGL into a single 3-D API, code-named Fahrenheit.

Part of the reason that 3D graphics are so compelling is that they consist of virtual models of reality, called *scenes*. In general, your PC uses thousands of small triangles to build objects such as buildings, people, clouds, or whatever else populates the space. For example, with the frame of a house, the PC first creates a wireframe model, on top of which materials, colors, and textures can be applied.

A lot of complex math is involved here. Every face of every object in a 3D scene must be computed, positioned, and visually described. Variables such as lighting, atmospheric effects (fog), and camera angles all add to the workload. Finally, the PC even has to contend with objects in the scene that can't be seen from the current camera angle—a challenging process that can chew up processing time, memory, or both.

Let's say you're displaying a 3D scene in a flight simulator program, one of the most common 3D applications. Here is a typical chain of events:

- Geometry: The PC determines where triangles need to be to form desired objects—in this case, airplanes and clouds. All this work occurs on your host CPU.

- Transform and lighting: The PC computes the position of triangle vertices and sketches a wireframe model in system memory. At this stage, lighting calculations are also made to provide realistic source and reflective lighting effects. Generally, this work occurs on your host CPU.

- Rendering : Finally, the graphics are drawn using the graphics board's accelerator chip. To provide realistic appearance, bitmap patterns are draped over the wireframe objects. An enemy plane gets matte black treatment with a few embellishments, such as tail and wing markings. For maximum effect, the interior cockpit is rendered, showing the pilot and controls. Clouds are draped in white. Accelerated graphics cards can boost these operations.

> **Note:** When buying a 3D graphics board for game play, you should look for one with dual-texture mapping units. This feature, which adds to the cost of the graphics chip, enables the board to quickly apply multiple levels of textures to games that accommodate this efficient process. The result is enhanced realism at high frame rates, as both texture maps and complex alpha, lighting, and blending effects are handled in a single pass. Most boards need a second pass to stack these visual effects on a scene, slowing performance.

- Bilinear or trilinear filtering: Further realism can be attained by smoothing blockiness in texture-mapped graphics. Filtering averages pixel color information to smooth bitmaps. Trilinear filtering provides better results by averaging over a wider range of pixels than bilinear filtering does. Filtering can be applied to virtually any 3D scene to provide the effect of greater realism.

- Double buffering: Graphics cards speed frame rates by working on one scene even as they display another. By using additional graphics memory to hold two sets of images, double buffering enables smooth updates of complex scenes.

- Flat or gouraud shading: For nontexture-mapped polygons, gouraud shading blends color values of triangles to further provide the illusion of smoothness. Less-sophisticated flat shading, often seen in unaccelerated games such as Falcon Gold and Hornet, yields a cartoonish look. Both games and 3D design applications employ gouraud-shaded scenes.

- Mipmapping: This term describes the use of multiple versions of a texture to be displayed based on the distance between the viewer and the displayed object. Using mipmap details on a wall, for example, can increase in size and clarity as the user approaches it. Without mipmapping, texture images blocky as pixels are expanded. With mipmapping, a close-up, detailed version of the texture is swapped in to maintain realism.

- Atmospheric effects: If your dogfight occurs on a hot, muggy day, your PC might wrap the scene in a slight haze. A translucent effect can also be used on the enemy plane's canopy to provide a glassy effect. The same process creates a semitransparent missile contrail. Newer accelerated graphics cards can boost these operations.

- Lighting: Your PC computes one or more light sources, revising surface appearances based on the type, angle, and brightness of the light. Secondary sources—say, the flame from a missile's firing—might also affect the appearance of a nearby craft as the reflection of the light source is computed. Most graphics cards accelerate light effects, though to different extents.

- Z-buffering: Much happens on a busy battlefield. Planes can be hidden behind clouds or mountains, or even behind other planes. Your graphics card can avoid drawing these obscured objects and pixels using a scheme called *z-buffering*, which keeps positional data in memory to decide whether a particular object is visible. The payoff is improved performance, although many graphics cards require an additional 2MB or more of memory to handle the z-axis data. Newer graphics cards offer z-buffering capability.

Note: The preceding list might read like a vocabulary test, but it's important to at least become familiar with the terms of 3D acceleration. Graphics card vendors are slapping these and other terms onto their boxes and making claims about how their product is better than the next because it supports certain features. However, be aware that although a graphics card might support some high-falutin' features, much of the software you now own might fail to take advantage of them. Still, a more feature-rich 3D graphics card stands a better chance of keeping pace with upcoming software.

All that said, the feature list is only the beginning. Even a card with all the hot items can choke when called upon to do several advanced tasks simultaneously. You should make a point to refer to the most recent product round-ups to assess performance, particularly because there are so many performance-related issues to puzzle through with these products.

When your system processes 3D graphics, a lot of work is involved. First, your CPU must set up the scene, performing geometry and lighting calculations. Then the work is passed to the graphics card, which gets busy supplying textures, shading, and other elements. Figure 17.7 shows the 3D graphics processing pipeline.

FIGURE 17.7.

The geometry portion of the graphics pipeline heavily stresses floating point performance, which is why a fast Pentium II-class CPU is so important to performance, regardless of the graphics card you use. (Illustration courtesy Diamond Multimedia)

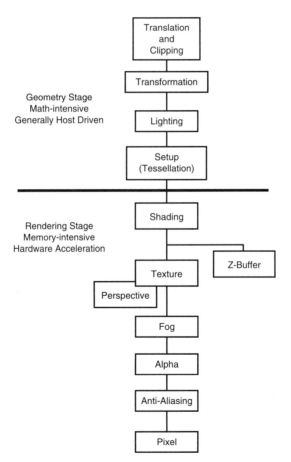

What's in a Graphics Board?

In a sense, graphics boards are like a miniature PC inside your PC. As with your system, graphics boards have a single CPU that calls the shots and determines performance. Also similar to your PC, graphics boards contain memory—called a *frame buffer*—and an internal bus for moving bits from memory to the processor and back. As with systems, there has been an improvement in price and performance with graphics boards.

What goes into a graphics board? The following systems help determine a board's features, performance, and cost:

- Graphics coprocessor
- Bus
- Memory
- RAMDAC (the card's digital-to-analog converter and color manager)
- Software drivers

Together, these components help determine the relative performance of your PC's graphics. The amount of memory determines the maximum resolution and color depth that your PC can support. The more memory you have, the more colors and pixels you can potentially display on your monitor. The type of memory can also make a big difference in graphics performance.

The speed of the RAMDAC, as shown in Figure 17.8, determines the maximum refresh rate, which is the number of times per second that the graphics hardware sends an update to the monitor. Finally, driver software enables the operating system and programs to talk to your graphics hardware, keeping everything working together.

The following sections run through these various systems so that you can understand how graphics boards accomplish their magic.

Inside the Graphics Coprocessor

This chip is the heart of any graphics board and, as such, determines exactly what the board can and can't do. Key features for accelerating 2D and 3D graphics and video playback are all designed into the square of silicon sitting in the center of the board.

Today, most new graphics chips provide video and 3D graphics capabilities, as just described. One key factor in predicting chip and card performance is the data width of the graphics chip, measured in bits. Most coprocessors feature 64-bit data paths. This is the minimum that you should consider for any graphics upgrade; anything narrower invites performance-sapping data bottlenecks.

A few graphics cards use chips that are 128 bits wide. Number Nine's Imagine 128 and Nvidia's Riva 128 TNT chips employ wide 128-bit data paths. While these chips can move much more data smoothly, other bottlenecks—including the system bus and graphics memory—mean that 64-bit chips are often capable of providing equivalent performance.

Figure 17.8.

The Matrox Millennium II uses a fast 220MHz RAMDAC to provide fast refresh rates at high resolutions. Note the chip at the upper-left corner. This is an external RAM-DAC that most lower-cost boards usually integrate into the main chip. (Photo courtesy Matrox Graphics)

Typically, graphics chips are designed for one or more memory types. For example, Intel's i740 chipset is usually mated with SGRAM memory, while older S3 Virge DX chips use EDO DRAM.

The Bus

One key element of graphics performance is the bus. With the introduction of Pentium systems, most graphics boards have been designed for the PCI bus, which runs 32 bits wide at 33MHz. Capable of pushing 132MBps of data, PCI proved a valuable performance boost to PCs. Its predecessor—the ISA bus—could move only 5MBps.

The arrival of the Pentium II processor and Intel's 440LX chipset introduced a new graphics-only bus, called Accelerated Graphics Port. This bus, which is essentially a souped-up PCI bus, can push up to 526MBps of data over a 32-bit, 66MHz connection. The fine timings of AGP limit PCs to a single AGP slot, which is dedicated to graphics.

Despite the higher bandwidth, the impact on 2D and video performance is generally negligible compared to PCI. That's because PCI's 132MBps already can handle most tasks. But AGP brings intriguing 3D-specific talents, including the capability of enabling your graphics card to use your system's main memory to enhance 3D scene realism. Called direct memory execute (DIME) mode, or AGP texturing, this feature enables game makers to use tens of megabytes in system memory to construct highly realistic scenes in games and titles. The fast AGP bus is used to pipe textures stored in system memory directly to the graphics chip.

If your system has an AGP bus, you should definitely purchase an AGP card because it will open the path to better performance. Going with AGP will also help open PCI slots for other devices.

Inside Graphics Memory

Two considerations are important with memory—how much you have and what type it is. The more graphics memory, the more pixels and colors you can display on the monitor. 3D graphics and image and photo editing are examples of applications that require 4MB or more of graphics memory.

Most boards today come with 4MB or more of memory, although some come with as much as 8MB or even 16MB. Some boards also provide for memory upgrades, making it possible to boost the maximum colors and resolution without actually installing a new graphics card.

To determine how much memory is needed to display an 800×600 image at 24-bit color, you need to do a little math. Multiply 800 by 600 to determine how many pixels (in this case, 480,000) the graphics memory must track. Then multiply that number by the color depth (24 bits), which is the number of bits used to store color data for each pixel. Divide the result by 8 to get the number of bytes required. In this case, you need 1,440,000 bytes, or just under 1.4MB, of memory to display true-color graphics at 800×600 resolution.

Keep in mind that 3D graphics always needs more memory than you think. Double buffering means that the card must be capable of holding two sets of scenes in its memory, while z-buffering requires more memory still to store information about where objects are located in the scene. Finally, texture images must also be stored in graphics memory, and these can take up several megabytes. In a word, more memory is always better when it comes to 3D graphics.

Note: Future games will demand still more memory by using triple-buffering to further boost frame rates. Today, if a double-buffered game can't get in sync with the monitor's refresh rate, it will typically run at half the refresh rate. That means game frame rates could drop to 40fps on a monitor running at 80Hz. Triple-buffering removes this limitation, enabling frame rates that match the full refresh rate of the monitor.

The type of memory is also an important consideration. Your graphics card uses memory very similar to that in your system. In fact, some cards use the same type of memory as that found in many PCs. The following memory types are common:

- EDO DRAM (extended data out dynamic RAM)
- VRAM (video RAM)
- SDRAM (synchronous DRAM)

- SGRAM (synchronous graphics RAM)
- WRAM (Windows RAM)
- RDRAM (Rambus DRAM)
- MODRAM

In general, memory can be divided into two categories: single-ported and dual-ported. As with standard system memory, EDO DRAM, SDRAM, and SGRAM are single-ported memory architectures. These memories use a single door to move data in and out of the frame buffer. These memories enjoy an advantage in that they are cheap to manufacture (and enable cards to carry more memory affordably), but the single data port limits bandwidth at the high end.

New memories get around the single-port limitation by doing things more efficiently. EDO DRAM and SDRAM, both discussed in Chapter 7, "Exploring System Memory and Cache," cut down the amount of time it takes for each bit to be accessed. SGRAM adds graphics-specific tweaks to the optimized SDRAM interface, boosting common graphics operations such as bit blits.

One overriding problem is refresh rates. Because the same port must be used to both accept incoming data from the controller and send data to the monitor, a bottleneck exists. At higher resolutions, color depths, and refresh rates, this bottleneck can restrict and slow performance. For more on refresh rates, see the next section.

Dual-ported memory, although more expensive, enables boards to break through the refresh-rate bottleneck. VRAM and WRAM architectures use two doors—one going in, the other going out—to improve the flow of data through the frame buffer. The difference is that WRAM adds some graphics-specific tweaks to the memory design that can help squeeze additional performance out of some 2D graphics operations.

Note: Dual-ported memory might enjoy higher data throughput, but the difference isn't always important in day-to-day use. People running applications at 800×600 resolution and below 24-bit color will find that single-ported memories can keep pace with their graphics demands. Graphics professionals and anyone running at 1024×768 and 24-bit color should consider VRAM or WRAM memory for their next card purchase. At these higher settings, the additional data ports can make a difference—particularly if you run your monitor at high refresh rates of 75Hz or more.

An important newcomer to the graphics memory fray, Rambus DRAM (or RDRAM), is also worth mentioning. New boards based on Cirrus Logic's Laguna chip employ this memory type. RDRAM works by moving bits very, very quickly along a narrow path. In fact, the RDRAM bus runs at an astounding 500MHz (versus 80–100MHz for other memory types) but is only 8 bits wide (versus 32 bits for other memories).

Recent drops in Rambus DRAM pricing and expected enhancements that will improve responsiveness have made RDRAM an attractive option.

RAMDACs and Refresh Rates

RAMDAC determines how frequently the graphics card can refresh the image on the monitor. The faster the RAMDAC, the more quickly the board can update things, and the more stable the images that appear onscreen.

Most affordable graphics boards don't have separate RAMDACs at all. Instead, this component is built directly into the graphics chip, enabling board vendors to cut costs.

RAMDACs generally run at speeds of 135MHz, 170MHz, 185MHz, 220MHz, or 250MHz. On larger monitors, the difference between these speeds can mean a lot.

At 1,024×768 resolution and 16-bit color, a 135MHz RAMDAC can manage a refresh rate of only 60Hz. The same graphics card with a 220MHz RAMDAC can refresh the screen at twice that rate—120MHz—at the same setting.

Driver Software: The Secret Ingredient

Drivers aren't actually part of the board per se, but in many ways this software plays the most critical role of all. In general, drivers are the sophisticated chunks of code that enable peripherals (such as graphics cards) to talk to and take orders from the operating system and its applications. Without driver software, your 1-2-3 for Windows spreadsheet wouldn't be capable of putting its numbers and interface on the display because Windows 95 would have no idea that the card is there.

Although the board vendor itself is the main source of driver code, the following parties might write drivers for products:

- The board vendor
- Microsoft (as the operating system vendor)
- The graphics chip vendor
- The third-party driver vendor

Generally, hardware vendors write drivers for their products, and this is where you should look first for updates. The board maker has the greatest vested interest in adding value and performance to its products and is usually responsible for providing service and support for the card.

Microsoft gets involved in driver development mainly to ensure support for its operating systems. When Windows 95 came out, few hardware makers had adequate programming experience in the new driver scheme to have drivers ready for the August 1995 launch, so Microsoft helped write drivers for the most popular existing peripherals and included these drivers on the CD-ROM disc.

One overlooked source is the graphics chip vendor. Because board makers often carry a wide variety of graphics chips on their various lines, they don't build drivers from scratch. Instead, they enhance the base-level chip code provided from the maker of the graphics coprocessors, such as S3 or Cirrus Logic. In fact, the basic drivers provided on the Windows 95 disc might come directly from the graphics chip company.

> **Tip:** Although it's always best to get your drivers from the board maker, it might sometimes be advisable to check with the chip vendor for a driver update when something in the operating architecture changes. Often, the maker of the graphics chip is on the front lines of driver development, building in the baseline features required to access new capabilities. In these situations, a visit to the maker's Web site might be in order.

All drivers are the same in that they access the standard graphics interfaces (GDI, DirectX) of Windows 95 and 98. This provides support for virtually every Windows 9x-compatible application. However, the quality of driver software does vary. Often, larger vendors have the resources to keep a software development staff on hand to fine-tune drivers, while the smallest no-name vendors must use the base-level drivers provided by Microsoft or the builder of the graphics chip. Be warned: Company size is not a real predictor of driver quality, and no one can predict how much a vendor will stress driver development in the future.

> **Peter's Principle:** Keep Your Drivers Up-to-Date
>
> Graphics performance is critical to overall system operation, and driver software plays a big role. Whether you want the best performance or enhanced features and reliability, your best bet is to periodically check for updated driver software.
>
> The best way to get new graphics drivers is from your board vendor's Web site. Typically, vendor Web sites provide several drivers for each board, serving different operating systems such as Windows 3.1, Windows 95 and 98, Windows NT, and OS/2. Always look for driver version numbers that are higher and driver dates that are newer than those of your current driver.

Purchase Decisions

When you buy a graphics card, the decisions you make depend on both your existing system and your application needs. Sometimes these two things might be at odds. Before you decide to spend money on a graphics board upgrade, consider whether the system you're upgrading can accomplish the tasks you want to accomplish.

Suppose that you have a 486DX-33 PC and you want to buy a VL bus graphics card so you can play the latest 3D games. Although that graphics board might support some 3D features, chances are that your old warhorse PC isn't up to the task. The lack of L2 cache and effective floating-point capability in the processor, as well as a slower system board bus, combine to hinder performance. Even the fastest graphics board can't overcome these odds. What's more, you'll find a very limited selection of VL bus-compatible 3D graphics cards, possibly making a move to a PCI-equipped motherboard a necessity.

That same 486 might be eligible for an upgrade for different purposes. The original graphics board might have only 1MB or even just 512KB of RAM, but you need to be able to view spreadsheets on a large 17-inch monitor. An affordable $150 card can get you 2MB or even 4MB of graphics RAM, as well as additional video and 3D acceleration functions.

System Considerations

The easy (but very critical) part is buying a board that works in your existing system. By far, the most important issue is the system bus. The vast majority of Pentium-based PCs employ the Peripheral Component Interconnect bus, better known as PCI. Most 486 systems, on the other hand, use the VL bus add-in card standard—although older PCs might lack a high-speed bus. The newest systems—whether Pentium II-class or based on AMD K6 CPUs—use the Accelerated Graphics Port (AGP).

Why all the talk about buses? The bus inside your PC determines what type of card you can buy and the extent of your selection. It also affects performance. Whenever possible, purchase an AGP graphics card, which provides key advantages in 3D games and titles.

Also consider the size of your PC's monitor when you're buying a new graphics board. It doesn't make much sense to spend extra money on a card that has 8MB of RAM and can display 1600×1200 pixels when all you have is a 14-inch monitor.

What if you already have a top-flight 2D graphics board and want to add superior 3D graphics? You best bet is probably a dedicated 3D card, such as the Diamond Monster 3D II or Creative Labs 3D Blaster Voodoo2. This option is also attractive for those without an AGP graphics slot because the dedicated card provides onboard features that offset the advantage of the faster bus.

Of course, your board needs to work with your operating system. Virtually all boards now come with drivers for Windows 9x, and most provide Windows NT support as well. However, the existence of drivers doesn't mean that a board is appropriate for your environment. For example, 3D gaming cards such as Creative Labs' GameBlaster might offer 2D graphics acceleration under Windows NT, but their advanced 3D and video features might be tailored specifically for Windows 9x. Be sure to ask the vendor about the operating system for which the graphics card is tuned.

If you have a Windows 98 system, you can even plug in a pair of graphics boards so you can drive a second monitor. The only requirement: The boards must be plugged into an AGP or PCI slot (no ISA support). What's the point? With dual monitors, you can view your email or Web browser while the second screen displays Quake II, for example.

Usage Considerations

It's no surprise that what you buy depends on what you expect to do with it. A graphics card intended for basic office use—word processing and spreadsheets, for example—differs greatly from a board for 3D games and multimedia.

What should you buy? Table 17.1 gives you some ideas.

Table 17.1. A graphics board buying guide.

Applications	Memory	Features	Price
Office applications	2MB SDRAM	2D graphics	$120
Office applications and presentations	2MB SDRAM	2D graphics/ video	$120
Mixed home/office use	4MB SDRAM	2D and 3D graphics/video	$120-$200
Gaming and multimedia	8MB SGRAM, RDRAM, WRAM	2D and 3D graphics/video	$200-$300
Photo editing	8MB or 16MB WRAM or VRAM	2D graphics	$400+
Professional 3D design	8MB to 16MB SGRAM or VRAM	2D and 3D graphics	$500-$1,000

For many home gamers, 3D graphics capability is a must. Games and titles make heavy use of 3D graphics, and although many will play without 3D hardware, a good accelerator delivers markedly smoother and more realistic performance. Best of all, 3D graphics technologies are starting to level off. Microsoft's Direct3D is the most popular target for software developers—so your board should support it—but 3Dfx's Glide API remains a key player, thanks to the popularity of the company's Voodoo 2 chipset (see Figure 17.9).

If you're buying a 3D card, consider one that has at least 4MB of RAM. The 3D applications use this memory for z-buffering, speeding the display of 3D scenes by telling the coprocessor not to draw obscured objects. In the last year, more cards come equipped with 8MB of RAM, enabling greater texture detail.

FIGURE 17.9.
Creative Lab's 3D Blaster Voodoo2 is dedicated to 3D graphics—you need a separate board for 2D and video acceleration. (Photo courtesy Creative Labs)

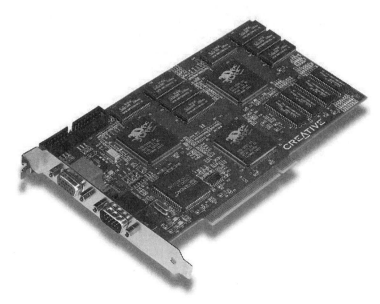

Where to Buy

Graphics boards can be purchased almost anywhere computer hardware is sold, from the local consumer electronics chain or superstore to mail-order catalogs and even vendor Web sites. The wide availability makes price comparisons easy, allowing you to get the best deal.

> **Tip:** Vendors cycle through graphics board products quickly, and cut-rate pricing of aging boards is common. Be careful if you find a certain board or chip being widely sold at discount prices. This might be a signal that the board is on its way out, which means that driver support will wane, and its features and performance will lag behind more current products.

Certainly, price is an important consideration, and you can often find lower prices from mail-order companies than you will at retail outlets. But more important than a $10 or $20 savings in the short term is the quality of a board vendor's software drivers and commitment to supporting its products.

> **Tip:** Some companies, such as Diamond Multimedia and Number Nine, offer trade-ins on older boards when you buy a new model. Before you simply replace a graphics card, it makes sense to check with the manufacturer of your existing card to see whether you might be able to get credit toward a new purchase.

You will probably own the graphics board you buy for two, three, or even five years. During that time, the vendor will likely refresh its drivers a dozen times or more, introducing new features, fixing bugs, and playing catch-up with operating system modifications. These driver updates can also squeeze more performance out of your existing hardware.

Tracking driver quality and support is a tricky thing, and the quality of a certain vendor's work can wax and wane depending on existing management, the number of products in its lines, and other variables. Your best bet is to visit online forums (such as CompuServe and AOL) or Internet newsgroups and find out what others recommend. Look for a history of behavior from the company, and ask people about their experiences. If possible, try to find people who are using the product you're looking to buy. Also look for real-time online support, which can be found on some vendors' CompuServe or AOL forums. On the Internet, you can often get immediate replies to your questions through IRC-based (Internet Relay Chat) services. Consulting vendor's forums, Web sites, and your software documentation can help you find the best and most compatible board in your price range.

Also visit the vendor's Web site before you buy. See if there is any late information about the product, and check for evidence of recent driver updates. Driver updates can be a two-edged sword: On the one hand, frequent updates indicate a commitment by the vendor to improve the product. On the other hand, too-frequent updates can indicate a "driver *du jour*" policy in which half-cooked bug or feature fixes get rushed to the market and then fixed incrementally after the fact. That kind of approach can invite a lot of vexing compatibility problems for users.

Tip: The first thing you should do after bringing home a new graphics board is download the latest drivers from the vendor's Web site or other forum. Chances are the drivers in the box are up to six months old, which means that they might be one or more versions old. Depending on how the board's installation routine works, you can avoid installing the older drivers altogether and simply install the downloaded software during the standard Windows 95 installation routine.

Diagnosing/Troubleshooting

Under Windows 3.1, graphics-related problems were nearly an epidemic. Buggy driver software caused inexplicable crashes and problems, and could even cause problems that seemed unrelated to the graphics card altogether. Fortunately, Windows 95 has improved this situation. Vendors have much less leeway in how they write their code, and the operating system's 32-bit architecture resolves most of the memory space conflicts that caused so many problems. In addition, graphical utilities—such as Number Nine's HawkEye suite, shown in Figure 17.10—help you avoid inadvertent driver setting mismatches that can lead to trouble with your monitor and applications.

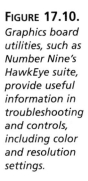

Figure 17.10.
Graphics board utilities, such as Number Nine's HawkEye suite, provide useful information in troubleshooting and controls, including color and resolution settings.

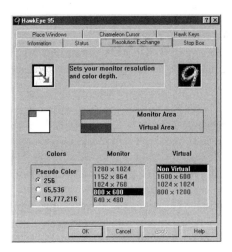

That said, graphics remain a lightning rod for problems, particularly on the driver side. When incompatibilities crop up with a new software program, it's always a good idea to suspect your driver software.

Other problems can present themselves. For instance, a mismatch in the refresh rate or graphic settings between your board and monitor can cause the display to distort or even fail to appear. Older driver software might lack the capability of supporting certain titles (specifically, DirectX-optimized games), causing them to fail when launched.

Problems Caused by Graphics Settings

One of the most common problems is a mismatch between the signals going out of your graphics board and the signals your monitor can recognize. This is particularly true during a graphics board upgrade because the enhanced board might dangle advanced capabilities beyond the reach of your aging monitor. Typically, your board sends signals at a higher frequency than your monitor can handle.

> **Caution:** A mismatch in signal frequency represents one of the gravest dangers to your PC's hardware. When your graphics board sends more than your monitor can handle—known as *overdriving* the monitor—this can cook the internal components and damage or even ruin the display. Overdriving can even pose a fire hazard.

Three settings can cause your card to overdrive the monitor:

- Refresh rates
- The resolution setting
- The color-depth setting

Symptoms of Overdriving

How can you tell when your graphics board is too much for your display to handle? The symptoms can vary, but typically you will observe the following on the monitor:

- A scrambled or distorted image
- Shrunken or multiple instances of an image
- A blank screen or other unusual display activity
- A high-pitched whine from the display

If you encounter any of these symptoms, the graphics board might be talking too fast for your monitor to understand. Unfortunately, the display isn't equipped to just ignore out-of-match incoming signals, so it tries to handle the signal and display what it can.

The important thing is not to panic. Actual monitor damage is unlikely, except in the most extreme cases. However, you do need to stop the overdriving as quickly as possible because the longer you stress the monitor circuitry, the greater the chance of permanent damage.

Fixing an Overdriven Display

When does overdriving happen? Typically, this problem occurs after you have changed the resolution, color, or refresh rate settings of your graphics board. Fortunately, Windows 95 provides a facility for backing out of a signal mismatch. The following steps detail how to change your resolution and color depth and back out of the problem.

> **Note:** When Windows 95 first came out, it lacked the capability of changing color depths without rebooting the computer. Although later versions of Windows 95 and a software patch called PowerToys added these *on-the-fly* color changes, your configuration might require you to restart.

1. Right-click the Windows 95/98 desktop and select Properties from the context menu that appears.
2. Choose the Settings tab. A drop-down list called Color palette appears on the left, and a slider bar called Desktop area appears on the right.
3. Adjust the slider bar to the desired resolution, and then select the desired color depth from the Color palette list. Click OK or Apply to make the settings take effect.
4. Windows 95/98 displays a box that tells you that it will test the display for 15 seconds. Click OK.
5. If the display looks normal after the screen updates, click Yes. If you notice any problems with the display but can still make out the control buttons, click No to return to the previous settings. If you do nothing, the display returns to its previous settings after 15 seconds (good for when a blank or very garbled screen makes clicking No impossible).

Not all settings get changed on-the-fly from the Properties dialog box. Many Windows 95 systems lack the capability of changing colors without a restart. In addition, refresh rates are generally controlled by vendor-specific utilities that also might require you to restart. In these situations, you won't get a friendly notice that offers you a chance to back out.

In such cases, you must go through the steps required to change color depths or refresh rates. Windows 95 prompts you to restart the computer before new settings can take effect. Before you restart, make sure that all open documents are saved and that your applications are closed.

When the system reboots, look for any signs of trouble. If the screen looks badly garbled or distorted, you should try to return to your old settings. If the distortion is too severe to navigate, do the following:

1. Press Ctrl-Esc.

2. Press the U key to select Start, Shut Down.

3. Press the R key to tell Windows 95 to restart.

4. Watch the display closely. When you see the message Starting Windows 95, press the F8 key.

5. In response to the text list of choices, select 3, Restart in Safe Mode.

6. From the safe mode of Windows 95, restore your graphics settings and restart the PC normally. You should now have your display back.

Better yet, try to avoid these situations by first checking the specifications on your graphics board and monitor before changing the settings. Your monitor documentation should state the maximum resolutions and refresh rates it can handle.

Dealing with Driver Problems

More problematic are driver-related problems. In fact, graphics driver-related problems can cause problems that seem unrelated to video performance. Symptoms of driver conflicts include the following:

- Windows fails to start

- Application and system crash or lock up

- Onscreen distortion occurs

- Certain applications (such as games) fail to launch

- Slow performance or poor video display occurs

How do you know if a driver conflict is at issue? Usually it's a matter of timing. If the problem occurs immediately after you installed a driver update, you might have an older driver that is incapable of handling the latest software demands. Look into restoring the old driver or finding an updated version that might resolve the problem.

Unfortunately, troubleshooting driver problems can involve a lot of trial and error. You might need to go through a couple different driver versions, installing and uninstalling them before you find the one that works properly.

The DirectX Dilemma

On a related note, the introduction of DirectX gaming APIs has introduced a new facet of Windows graphic driver development. Windows games and multimedia titles often require DirectX software components to be installed in the operating system before they will run. Often, this means getting a driver update.

How do you know whether the lack of DirectX capability is holding you back? Usually, games will fail to launch, displaying a dialog box saying that DirectX version 5.0 or some other version is needed to run the game. What's more, upon installation the title should offer to add the necessary code and update your drivers.

Caution: By default, Microsoft's DirectX installation routine found in games checks your driver software to see whether it is certified. Ironically, older versions of DirectX may actually downgrade your drivers from the latest version to an earlier "certified" version of the drivers. During the DirectX installation, if the routine finds uncertified drivers, it tells you that the driver software is not certified and recommends that you replace the existing driver set with the generic one provided in the DirectX routine.

If you know your drivers are a recent version with proper DirectX support (for example, if you downloaded them from the vendor's Web site just weeks ago), click No at the dialog box. The routine installs all the proper DirectX components into the operating system while leaving your graphics board alone. If you experience problems with the game that seem related to the DirectX functionality, you can always reinstall the generic code later—or, better yet, seek a tailored fix directly from the board vendor.

Note that knocking out your drivers for Microsoft's not only affects performance, but it could also nuke all the enhanced features in your current board. You will lose custom graphics controls, such as Number Nine's HawkEye utilities and Diamond's InControl Tools, as well as enhanced refresh-rate settings for specific boards. Worse, boards that provide TV broadcasts or video capture will lose all these enhanced features. In other words, Microsoft's "fix" will kill your hardware until you reinstall the original drivers.

Note that DirectX 5 and 6 provide more intelligent queries to help avoid accidental overwriting of valid drivers. You'll also find a Restore old driver button in the DirectX setup routine that enables you to return to the old settings.

You can tell whether DirectX is installed on your system by searching for a few key files in your Windows System directory. If you find the file ddraw.dll, your card has some level of DirectX support in place.

Upgrading the Graphics Board

One of the most frequent upgrades, the task of installing a new graphics board, got considerably simpler with the advent of the PCI bus and Windows 95 plug-and-play support. Under DOS, ISA-based cards required DIP switch changes to set memory exclusion areas and other settings. Today, all this is handled automatically with new cards.

When Does Upgrading Make Sense?

First of all, when does an upgrade make sense? The following scenarios make an upgrade worthwhile:

- The new hardware can significantly improve system performance, particularly with video playback and 3D graphics display.

- You want access to higher resolutions and color depth settings—crucial for getting the most out of 17-inch and larger monitors. If you're upgrading to a larger monitor, you might want to consider a new graphics board at the same time.

- You want to access hybrid features such as video capture or TV broadcast reception on the PC. Some boards build in these features.

- Chronic hardware conflicts or lack of driver support make your aging board a liability. A new model will fix this situation.

- You need more graphics memory for high-resolution operation, but the current board doesn't accept memory module upgrades.

In all these cases, a less-drastic software driver upgrade won't solve the problem. What's more, a proper upgrade can add new applications and functions to your PC, ranging from video capture and TV reception to cutting-edge support for 3D graphics.

However, at times a graphics board update doesn't make sense. Any systems limited to ISA or EISA add-in card slots won't be capable of taking advantage of current-generation hardware. For one thing, graphics board companies have stopped supporting these bus types entirely (because of PCIs); for another, the slower buses will completely bottleneck even the most advanced graphics chip architecture.

Unfortunately, owners of VL bus systems are falling into the same trap. Despite the bus performance, board makers have largely moved away from the VL bus architecture in favor of PCI. With the next-generation AGP specification now appearing in systems, you can bet that what meager resources were going to old VL bus machines will be shifted to other tasks.

Installing a Graphics Board

Windows 95/98 makes upgrading add-in cards easier than ever. Although Plug and Play is hardly perfect, the scheme does a good job of sniffing out new components and guiding you through the installation. To install a new PCI-based graphics adapter, you'll want to do a couple housecleaning chores first to avoid unnecessary conflicts.

First, change your graphics settings to VGA:

1. Right-click the My Computer icon on your desktop, then select Properties, and click the Device Manager tab on the System Properties dialog box.

2. Double-click the Display Adapters category, and then double-click your display adapter's listing to display its properties.

3. Click the Drivers tab, and then follow step 4 for Windows 95 or steps 5 and 6 for Windows 98.

4. In Windows 95, click the Change Driver button. When the Select Device dialog appears, click the Show all devices radio button and select Standard Display Adapter (VGA) from the Standard Display Types category. Click OK, and provide the Windows 95 CD or disks if prompted.

5. In Windows 98, click the Update Driver button to start the Update Device Driver Wizard. Click Next, select the Display all… radio button, and click Next. When the Select Device dialog appears, click the Show all hardware radio button and select Standard Display Adapter (VGA) from the Standard Display Types category. Click OK, and provide the Windows 98 CD if prompted.

Next, uninstall any third-party graphics control panels or utilities. Vendors such as Diamond, Number Nine, and Matrox routinely include graphics utilities with their cards. If these are running, you may experience problems when you try to install the new adapter. Do the following:

1. Click Start, Settings, Control Panel.

2. Open the Add/Remove Programs icon, and scroll through the list of installed programs until you find the graphics utility.

3. Select the utility, and click the Add/Remove button. Follow any dialog box instructions.

Finally, you are ready to make the upgrade. Do the following:

1. Shut down the PC, remove the power cord, and open the case.

2. Making sure you are well-grounded, use a Phillips screwdriver to free the existing graphics adapter from the backplane.

3. Grasp the card at the top at each end, and apply even upward force. If the card doesn't budge, try rocking out the back end a bit first, and then raise the front end.

4. Set the existing card aside, and fit the new card in the slot. When placing it, make sure there is adequate clearance for the entire card. (Some multifunction graphics cards can be full-length, limiting the slots into which they can fit.)

5. Inspect the expansion slot for debris, dust, or obstacles that might prevent the card from seating properly. After the card is seated in the slot, press down firmly to make sure you have good contact.

6. Plug in the power cord and start the PC. Keep a close eye on the monitor. (You might see a new video BIOS text message appear at the very beginning of booting.)

7. Wait while Windows starts. The New Hardware Detected dialog box should appear. Click Yes to detect the new hardware.

8. Place the floppy or CD-ROM disc from the packaging into the drive. When Windows asks where to look for drivers, click Get drivers from disk, and select the proper drive location.

> **Tip:** If you downloaded the latest drivers from the Internet prior to installation (always a good idea), you can simply tell Windows to install this driver from its existing location. The best thing to do is to download the driver code and expand the compressed files into a temporary directory dedicated to the new driver. When you are navigating Windows' Add New Hardware wizard, click the Have Disk button to install the drivers from a specific directory.

9. A dialog box tells you when the driver installation is complete. At this point, you can restart Windows and access the new functions.

10. If all is working properly, turn off the PC and screw the backplane down to avoid possible problems with the connector. Seal the case and restart.

11. If your board has custom utilities or software controls that were not installed during the driver setup, you can install them now. Check the board's documentation to determine where the setup files for any included software are located.

Adding Memory to an Existing Graphics Board

Some graphics boards use socketed memory, memory modules, or even standard SIMMs (in rare cases) to enable upgrades down the line. If you have a graphics board that meets your acceleration needs but lacks the capability of displaying the highest color and resolution settings, a memory upgrade might save you money over buying a new board outright. In addition, some feature upgrade modules, such as for MPEG playback for video capture, might include additional memory as part of the package.

Your best bet when buying new memory is to go directly to your board vendor because the company will know the proper memory type, capacity, and form factor for your board. Otherwise, peruse the documentation carefully. If you have a board with two 1MB EDO DRAM modules, for instance, you must be sure to purchase a second pair of 1MB EDO DRAM modules for your upgrade. As with systems, upgrades generally must happen in paired increments because the graphics controller might not recognize odd memory configurations such as 3MB or 6MB.

If the board uses SIMM-style memory, you might be able to buy the new RAM the way you would system memory. Again, you must match memory type, speeds, form factors, and capacities. Review the documentation carefully, and check the SIMMs themselves for clues as to their specifications.

Installing new memory is easy. Follow these steps:

1. Shut down the PC, remove the power cord, and open the case.

2. Making sure you are well-grounded, use a Phillips screwdriver to free the existing graphics adapter from the backplane.

3. Remove the board. Grasp the card at the top at each end, and apply even upward pressure. Don't force it. If the card doesn't budge, try rocking out the back end a bit first, and then raise the front end.

4. Fit the new memory modules into the open sockets, being sure to orient them properly, as shown in your documentation. With the board lying face-up on a flat, hard surface, place the modules so that they sit even in the sockets.

5. After the module is fitted to the socket, apply even downward pressure on each end using your thumb and forefinger. The module should press into the socket and lock into place. Don't force the module; if it fails to seat, try lifting the module and reseating it.

6. Repeat this step for the other module or modules, and then put the card back in its original slot.

7. Restart the PC. If everything is working properly, turn off the PC and screw the backplane down to avoid possible problems with the connector. Seal the case and restart.

> **Note:** Now you can check your new configuration. Just right-click the desktop, select Properties, and choose the Settings tab. Check the Color palette and Desktop Area controls. You should notice additional resolution and color depth options that were not available before the upgrade.

Summary

For the last several years, graphics boards have waned as a prime performance-boosting upgrade. Most boards provide closely matched 2D graphics capabilities, and video play-back features affect only a minority of graphics operations. In addition, the advent of the PCI bus in 1993 widened the data pipes to the graphics card enough to ease much of the bottleneck.

Now it's time for users to pay attention again. New graphics boards are now designed first for the fast AGP bus found on virtually all new PCs. Meanwhile, 3D graphics standards are finally shaking out and creating a wave of software and games that graphics cards can accelerate. The impact that 3D acceleration can have on these programs is remarkable. Everything from Quake to AutoCAD looks better, runs faster, and becomes more compelling. The visual impact that the best boards and software create help turn ho-hum blocks and triangles into stunning virtual worlds.

Before long, even common Web browsing might benefit from 3D acceleration. The VRML (virtual reality modeling language) standard promises to bring fully navigable 3D worlds to your desktop. Furthermore, 3D graphics can do wonders for everything from business presentations to school reports. If you have a Pentium-class PC, a 3D graphics board should be on your short list of upgrades.

18

Audio

For a long time, personal computers were to be seen and not heard. Despite the runaway appeal of the built-in audio found on Macintosh computers, most early IBM-compatible PCs demonstrated few audio talents beyond first the occasional monotone beep from the built-in speaker, and later the obnoxious repetition of oversimplified Bach fugues.

We've come a long way. A little company called Creative Labs helped give PCs a voice with its Sound Blaster audio card. Since then, progressive generations of Sound Blaster and competing boards have helped bring the entire range of digital audio recording, editing, and playback functions to the PC. In the process, they've helped transform the buttoned-down old business box into a creative medium and an entertaining center for the home.

This chapter covers PC-based sound, including the following topics:

- The workings of PC-based audio under Windows 95, including the emergence of new PCI-based sound boards
- Shopping for a sound board for Windows 95 and DOS-based applications
- Diagnosing and resolving audio problems
- Upgrading your system with a new sound board
- Choosing PC-based speaker systems and microphones

The Ins and Outs of PC Audio

In the last few years, sound has become as important to many PC applications as graphics. Games need engaging sound effects and music scores, multimedia titles employ audio and video clips, and business presentations and even Web sites gain impact from music and sound. More recently, 3D audio has become big in both titles and games—a feature you'll find in newer sound cards.

Today, any multimedia PC worth its salt is capable of handling CD-quality digital audio playback and recording, as well as playing back realistic-sounding scores from Musical Instrument Digital Interface (MIDI) files. For best results, though, you'll want multichannel audio (to play several independent sounds simultaneously) and polyphonic MIDI (to play MIDI scores that incorporate dozens of instrument sounds). Don't let the dizzying array of specs and terms overshadow the most important issue: compatibility. Whether you want to record music under Windows 9x or hear realistic sounds in your DOS-based flight-simulation game, you need to make sure that your audio hardware can handle the task.

Sound on Board

If you look inside almost any multimedia PC sold prior to 1997, you'll see an ISA sound card sitting inside the case. In most instances, that card is a Creative Labs Sound Blaster of one sort or another. Newer systems might not have a sound board, but a tiny chip on the motherboard serves the same function—turning digital files into analog electrical impulses that your speaker can transform into sound.

But sound boards didn't introduce the capability of handling digital audio to PCs. After all, the first IBM PC could play musical tones, after a fashion, over its crude speaker by sending electrical impulses corresponding to the frequency and amplitude of the desired sound. What sound boards did was introduce the first tools needed in the evolution toward handling sophisticated sound transactions. Digital-to-analog converters transform digital signals into analog waves for waiting speakers. In the other direction, analog-to-digital converters (ADCs) take incoming sounds from a microphone or line input and convert them into 1s and 0s for storage on disk.

Most sound boards consist of the following components:

- Digital-to-analog converter.
- Analog-to-digital converter.
- Audio-processing chip or digital signal processor (DSP).
- Amplifier chip for boosting outbound signals for unpowered speakers. Fewer cards include an amplifier because almost all PC speakers now amplify incoming signals.
- Analog input ports for microphone, line-level signals, CD audio, and MIDI devices.
- Analog output ports for speakers, line-level signals, and joysticks.

Some boards also add a MIDI controller chip and dedicated memory (either RAM or ROM) for storing wavetable MIDI sounds.

Sound boards handle several types of sound. The most common is wave audio, or the Windows .WAV files that your system plays back. Another audio file type, MIDI audio (.MID), has seen much activity in the past few years as an effective way to play back musical scores. More recently, though, big advances (and even bigger hype) have been

made in 3D audio technologies, as well as the emergence of full-duplex boards for telephony and videoconferencing. The following sections explain these file types and how
sound boards work with them.

Wave Audio

The most common sound type is wave audio—essentially, a digital reproduction of
real-world sounds. The frequency and amplitude of analog sound—which is essentially
vibrations in the air or some other medium—is represented as a series of 1s and 0s. The
digital-to-analog converter (DAC) recognizes and converts these bits into familiar
sounds, such as musical instruments and people's voices.

> **Technical Note:** The waveform character of audio is where the Windows
> audio format, called a *wave file* (.WAV), gets its name. Wavetable MIDI, dis-
> cussed a little later in this chapter, refers specifically to the use of waveform rep-
> resentations of sounds from musical instruments.

The problem with wave audio is that the files get big—really big. To represent an analog
wave form, your PC slices up the analog curve into lots of small portions—as many as
44,100 separate slices for each second of audio. Each slice is then given a digital value
corresponding to its audio character, up to 16 bits per slice.

If you do the math, you'll see that 44,100 slices—each needing 16 bits of data—consume
more than 700,000bps. Stereo audio uses two independent channels, doubling this total
to 1,400,000bps. To store a single minute of audio, your PC might need more than 10MB
of storage space. A 10-minute uncompressed .WAV file will fill a 100MB Zip disk.

The highest range of audio fidelity is 44.1KHz 16-bit audio, corresponding to the fidelity
of audio CDs and the limits of human hearing. Doubling the size of already-large files by
pushing them to 88.2KHz, for example, adds nothing to the experience. Although older
boards were limited to 8-bit audio (the original Sound Blaster and Sound Blaster Pro, for
example), today virtually all sound boards can record and play back 44.1KHz 16-bit
wave audio.

Sampling at lower rates can save a lot of disk space, though at the expense of audio quality, as shown in Table 18.1.

Table 18.1. Wave audio settings and capacities.

Quality Level	Audio Setting	Size of One Minute of Uncompressed Audio
CD quality	16-bit 44.1KHz stereo	10MB
Radio quality	8-bit 22.05KHz mono	1.25MB
Telephone quality	8-bit 11.025KHz mono	.6MB

Sound boards sample the incoming analog wave form, taking thousands of snapshots each second (up to 44,100 snapshots, to be precise) and using up to 16 bits of data to store the snapshot or sample in memory (see Figure 18.1). The resulting wave audio file can be played back on any compatible PC.

FIGURE 18.1.
Using a lower sampling rate loses much of the analog data that is contained within the curve of the audio waveform. (Figure courtesy of Microsoft Corp.)

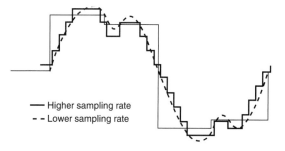

—— Higher sampling rate
- - Lower sampling rate

MIDI Audio

Another audio file type got an early start in the world of professional music. The Musical Instrument Digital Interface (MIDI) is a standard for enabling electronic instruments and synthesizers to work together. Jazz keyboardist Herbie Hancock was one pioneer willing to experiment with the new medium by hooking it up to his Apple II. Rock musician Todd Rundgren was so impressed by the potential of the new technology that he essentially changed careers. The MIDI standard defined an index of instrument types and provided instructions corresponding to musical notes and other parameters. The standard also defined communications and control—so a user could send instructions to a MIDI device and always get the same results—as well as protocols for interpreting the output of old-fashioned acoustic instruments.

Note: The standard instrument library, known as General MIDI, provides 128 standard instruments. General MIDI-compliant sound cards work with any MIDI file, producing the score using the proper instruments. Virtually all PC sound cards conform to the General MIDI standard, although some might offer extended sounds and capabilities.

MIDI is a perfect fit for the PC. Not only does the established specification spare everyone the usual standards battle, but it also solves many of the thorniest problems with PC-based wave audio. Most notably, MIDI files are very small. A minute of MIDI music often requires just 10KB of disk space. What's more, MIDI files are easy to edit, so users can change instruments or invent new ones, alter the composition, and change the relative amplitude and pitch of instruments using software tools.

The appeal of MIDI is growing still, thanks to a feature called DirectMusic that Microsoft has included in its DirectX 6.0 multimedia facility. DirectMusic enables software developers—and, in particular, game developers—to create dynamic MIDI scores that change based on events in the game. If you jump into a firefight, for instance, the music picks up tempo and intensity. What's more, you won't hear a simple loop; rather, the score varies as you play to keep the experience dynamic. Of course, to make this work, you must have DirectX 6.0 installed, and the software must be written to take advantage of the DirectMusic feature.

> **Note:** MIDI is good only for playing and creating musical scores. To reproduce voices, animal sounds, or most other sounds, you need to digitize the sound into a wave audio file.

Two types of MIDI exist:

- FM MIDI synthesis
- Wavetable MIDI synthesis

Both are discussed in the following sections.

FM MIDI

Until about three or four years ago, most affordable sound boards provided so-called FM MIDI synthesis. This scheme emulates the sound of instruments by mixing sine wave signals. This approach is inexpensive, but, acoustically, the results are horrendous. Rich orchestral scores sound cheap and thin on an FM MIDI card. The subtle nuances created by 10 or more simultaneously playing instruments get cut down to a synthetic-sounding baseline. You can recognize the tune, but the richness of the original score is lost. Still, FM synthesis MIDI cards can play any general MIDI score—they just won't do it well.

Wavetable MIDI

Wavetable MIDI synthesis provides realistic music playback by using actual recorded instrument sounds during playback. During MIDI playback, sound samples of French horns, oboes, violins, and other instruments are accessed from memory and played. Not every variation of every note is stored, so the card does a little math on the digital sample to create the desired instrument note and aspect from the original sample. Although the results aren't perfect, they're much better than those produced by FM synthesis.

Wavetable MIDI became prevalent when the cost of silicon memory dropped. Most boards use anywhere from 512KB to 8MB of onboard ROM or RAM to store instrument sounds, with more memory providing a greater selection of instrument notes and samples. Creative Labs' Sound Blaster AWE 32, for example, comes with 2MB of MIDI sounds in ROM and even enables you add up to 32MB of RAM SIMMs for storing custom MIDI sounds.

For the most realism, a wavetable MIDI card must be capable of playing multiple instrument sounds at one time—critical for orchestral sound. Called *polyphony,* this multi-instrument capability is described in terms of the number of simultaneous instruments (or voices) that can be played. The new Sound Blaster AWE 64, for example, can output 64 separate instrument sounds at once—more than enough for even the most demanding scores. A good baseline for most boards is 20- or 24-note polyphony.

> **Note:** Many low-cost cards today provide *software-based wavetable MIDI.* With this approach, no onboard storage is needed for instrument sounds. Instead, sound samples held permanently on the hard disk are moved to system RAM and then are played as needed. PCI-based sound boards, such as the Ensoniq Audio PCI, employ this approach.
>
> Software-based MIDI reduces hardware costs on the board and accommodates a much greater variety of potential sounds, including custom sounds—such as weapons and sound effects—that might be loaded by games and titles. The drawback is that software wavetable MIDI takes CPU power, which can degrade performance on older Pentium PCs. In addition, these cards can't provide MIDI playback for DOS-only games, because they rely on Windows 95 resources to move MIDI sounds from system memory to the sound card.
>
> Creative Labs' Sound Blaster AWE 64 actually handles both hardware and software wavetable MIDI. This board includes 1MB of onboard MIDI samples and has the capability of playing 32 instrument sounds simultaneously (32-voice polyphony). This card can also juggle an additional 32 voices in software, providing 64-voice polyphony for software running under Windows 9x or a Windows 9x DOS window.

Wave Guide MIDI

Another MIDI variant is *wave guide MIDI,* which actually produces sounds based on mathematical models of the instrument produced by the host CPU. Although the computation involved is quite complex, wave guide takes MIDI scores beyond the stilted stitching together of individual notes. You can create scores that have the individual flavor and dynamics of a real composition.

Don't expect wave guide MIDI to push wavetable MIDI aside. Many instruments, such as pianos, present so many variables that current PCs can't effectively render them in real time. Some sound boards, such as Creative Labs' Sound Blaster AWE 64 Gold, use a mixture of wavetable and wave guide, depending on the instrument being played.

Positional 3D Audio

Positional 3D audio first appeared on the scene about three years ago, when competing technologies such as SRS (Sound Retrieval System) and Q Sound hit the market. All 3D audio schemes try to improve the immersive quality of PC-based sound, giving the illusion of depth and direction to sounds coming from a pair of stereo speakers.

Unfortunately, 3D audio has been more about market confusion than innovation. The same term—3D audio—describes the general sound-enhancement scheme used by SRS and the specific positional audio features of DirectSound3D. With its roots in home theater systems, AC3 gets tagged as 3D audio technology as well.

Note: DirectSound is one component of Microsoft's multimedia initiative, called *DirectX*. DirectX is a collection of programming tools, Windows 95/98 components, and driver software that provides enhanced multimedia performance under Windows 95/98. This technology addresses everything from graphics and audio to network game play and input devices. For sound cards, DirectSound and DirectSound3D provide a standard way for software titles to access your sound hardware. DirectX updates are often provided as part of CD-ROM-based games, but they can also be downloaded from Microsoft's Web site.

Stereo-Enhancing 3D

The least-relevant of these is stereo-enhancing sound, which attempts to add depth by restoring spatial information captured by stereo microphones during the recording process. SRS and Spatializer are the two leading stereo-enhancing technologies, and both can be found in sound boards and some speakers. Both schemes use algorithms to add the spatial information to a two-channel analog stereo.

Surprisingly, stereo-enhancers can be effective. Depending on how audio was captured initially, instruments in a song can sound as though they are coming from places other than the speakers. However, they also tend to use a brute-force approach, boosting volume and adding distortion to the original signal—potentially making it more distracting than useful.

Programmatic Positional Audio (DirectSound3D)

More relevant to PC users is the emerging generation of games and titles that support positional 3D audio. Technologies such as Microsoft's DirectSound3D and Aureal's A3D help programmers pinpoint individual sounds in three-dimensional space.

The illusion can have a huge impact on gaming. With stereo speakers properly spaced on the desktop, players can hear the footsteps of approaching enemies. They can also hear chopper blades move from left to right as an enemy dashes across the screen. But positional 3D audio won't happen overnight. Software makers must retool their games for DirectSound3D, and PCs must have the DirectSound3D components installed into the operating system. Finally, a hardware interface component—those pesky drivers again—is needed so that compatible sound cards can accelerate the process of positioning sound on a two-speaker system.

Home Theater 3D Audio (AC-3)

A third type of 3D audio makes its debut courtesy of the DVD (digital versatile disc) standard. Dolby's AC-3 digital audio specification is used in DVD-equipped home theater systems and with MPEG-2 broadcasts over digital satellite systems (DSS), such as DirecTV and PrimeStar. As a home theater-based technology, AC3 applies mostly to the playback of digitized linear content such as films and music.

Unlike DirectSound3D and A3D, AC-3 audio is pre-processed. The digital audio stream contains information telling AC-3-compliant hardware exactly how to play the sounds over a six-speaker set that includes four corner speakers, a forward speaker, and a subwoofer. Needless to say, AC-3 can't provide the dynamic, interactive results delivered by real-time 3D audio-processing technologies.

AC3 brings a couple of important talents to the PC. For one, it's identical to the scheme implemented on high-end consumer electronics and upcoming HDTV systems—a key convergence point. In addition, PCs will be capable of reproducing AC3 3D audio in a two-speaker setup. A key point for reducing system cost, two-speaker capability mimics the rich surround sound accomplished using the 5.1 setup of home theater systems, in which four corner speakers, a center speaker, and a subwoofer combine to provide surround sound (see Figure 18.2).

FIGURE 18.2.
Home theater-oriented AC3 audio employs six speakers strategically placed to produce true surround sound. (Figure courtesy Microsoft Corp.)

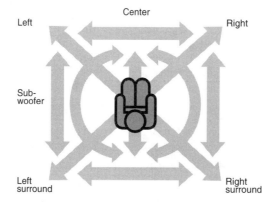

The New Face of Sound Boards

The next year is an important one in the sound board business—and a hectic one for upgraders. New PCI-based sound boards are supplanting ISA products based on the age-old Sound Blaster standard and are offering enhanced talents and lower-than-ever prices. The new standard is Microsoft's DirectSound, which is supported in Windows 95, 98, and NT 4.0.

DirectSound: The Emergent Standard

Under DOS, software needed direct access to hardware to access its features. Because of Sound Blaster's enormous market share, harried software developers—and, in particular, game companies—focused their efforts first on the Sound Blaster architecture from Creative Labs. To this day, titles that run exclusively in a dedicated DOS session (as opposed to a DOS box within Windows 95) require compatibility with a Sound Blaster or other supported sound card model.

Windows 95 changed all that. The operating system puts a level of software between hardware and applications—called a hardware abstraction layer, or HAL—to preserve stability and compatibility in the face of changing hardware. As long as sound cards and other peripherals comply with the standards put into place by Windows 95, any Windows 95-compatible application or game can make use of any sound device. Individual game makers no longer need to write separate interfaces for a dozen or more sound boards.

The real catalyst is DirectX—and, more specifically, the DirectSound API that addresses audio within DirectX. Under DirectSound, audio is treated much like graphics under DirectDraw and Direct3D (see Figure 18.3). Audio features ranging from MIDI playback and reverb effects to 3D positional audio can be handled by either the host CPU or by logic on the sound board. In addition, as with graphics cards, DirectSound-compliant sound boards can boost the performance of these functions by applying dedicated hardware.

FIGURE 18.3.
DirectSound abstracts audio functions from the hardware, enabling either the host CPU or customized audio hardware to handle audio functions. (Figure courtesy Microsoft Corp.)

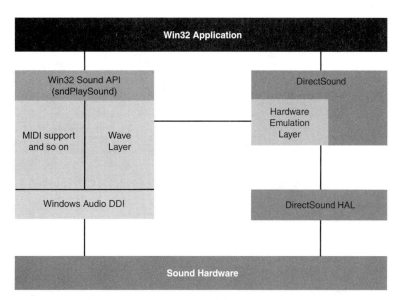

How do you get DirectSound? As with the rest of the DirectX components, DirectSound drivers and software are included with Windows 95/98 multimedia titles and games. You can also download the latest version of DirectSound from the Microsoft Web site.

Sound Blaster-Compatible: Fading Star

For more than 10 years, Creative Labs' Sound Blaster standard has been the target of DOS and Windows software developers. Today, millions of compatible sound boards are installed in PCs. These boards run on the ISA bus and provide wave audio and MIDI sound capability.

Unfortunately, new PCI sound cards can't ensure full Sound Blaster compatibility, particularly when you play games in a dedicated DOS-only session. If you have a number of games or applications that you want to make sure continue to work—but you still want access to PCI features—you may have to install a PCI sound card next to your existing ISA one. Of course, not many machines have enough IRQs to support two sound cards.

As shown in Figure 18.4, line and microphone inputs are available for recording analog sound to digital files. Speaker and line-out ports send analog sound to speakers or external recording devices. These boards also include a MIDI port for controlling external MIDI devices, such as musical (and even acoustic) keyboards.

FIGURE 18.4.
The input and output ports for the Sound Blaster AWE 64 Gold are available on the PC's backplane. Note the gold-plated line-in and line-out ports, which Creative Labs says produce higher-quality audio. (Figure courtesy Creative Labs)

RAM board connectors   CD in audio

Line in
Microphone in
L/R RCA jacks (line out)
Joystick/MIDI

Depending on the board, MIDI support might be simple FM synthesis or more-realistic wavetable synthesis. Refer to your sound board factory documentation. Often, the type of MIDI can be determined by the chipset found on the board. A Yamaha OPL-3 chip indicates a board with FM MIDI, while a Yamaha OPL-4 indicates wavetable MIDI capability.

Most wavetable MIDI cards come with 512KB to 4MB of MIDI instrument sounds in RAM or ROM. The more memory dedicated to MIDI instruments, the better the potential range of instrument sounds. The quality of the algorithms used to create musical notes from the samples and the compression applied to the sample sounds themselves can also have an impact.

Many sound boards also include EIDE or SCSI interfaces for connecting to CD-ROM drives. Older sound boards might include proprietary interfaces for CD-ROM drives from Panasonic, Mitsumi, and other vendors.

Sound Boards Go PCI

With the Sound Blaster standard no longer a mandate, vendors are moving sound cards off the troublesome ISA bus and onto the same PCI bus used by graphics cards. This not only eases often-painful installations, but it also opens enhanced applications to these peripherals. For example, PCI's high bandwidth provides for the use of 20 or more independent channels of audio to be handled simultaneously (see Figure 18.5). The capability of playing back many audio sources at once means that rich soundtracks can play even as dialog and 3D positional sound effects are output. What's more, each channel can react differently to user input, so one sound can grow louder as a person moves through an environment while another sound (on another channel) becomes fainter. With their limited bandwidth, ISA cards can't support this sophisticated interaction.

FIGURE 18.5.
Diamond Multimedia's Monster Sound board is among the first of many PCI-based sound boards designed according to the Microsoft DirectSound specification. (Figure courtesy Diamond Multimedia)

Why the change now, years after PCI became an industry standard? Again, the answer is compatibility. The Sound Blaster standard requires that IRQ and DMA settings remain fixed. PCI, however, may change these settings dynamically as part of the Plug and Play specification. PCI-based sound boards forgo compatibility with Sound Blaster cards to provide optimized performance under Windows 95 and DirectSound.

Buying a Sound Board in a Changing Market

Buying a sound board is very much like buying a graphics card or a modem: You can safely purchase these products from mail order or retail vendors. You can usually find lower prices through mail order, but you'll lose the security of being able to return the product directly to the store if something goes wrong. Just be sure that the mail-order vendor honors returns with a 30-day money-back guarantee, and ask about restocking fees before you purchase. These fees can cost you up to 15 percent of the purchase price if you need to return the product.

Key Buying Considerations

Before you purchase a new sound board, you should decide what you hope to do with the upgrade. The following are good reasons to upgrade a sound board:

- Enhanced wave audio fidelity (16-bit 44.1KHz sound)
- Enhanced wavetable MIDI capability, to provide greater realism than FM synthesis as well as 32-voice or better polyphony for orchestral scores
- 3D audio capabilities for games and multimedia titles
- Better compatibility with games and software
- Full-duplex audio for telephony and videoconferencing
- Digital studio functions, including multichannel recording and effects generation, such as reverb and chorus effects

Even if you find a sound board that meets your needs, some characteristics might make it unsuitable for your system. For example, many systems (in particular, compact desktop PCs), such as those that have been manufactured by Compaq and Packard Bell, lack the space for full-size add-in cards. You should check whether the card you want to buy will fit in the available space inside your PC.

> **Note:** You might find the best sound board in the world, but it's worthless if it doesn't fit inside your PC's chassis. Keep in mind that some sophisticated sound boards are full-length or three-quarter-length add-in cards. The circuitry required for wavetable effects processing, drive connectivity, and wavetable MIDI memory might be getting smaller, but these modern-day miracles often require the greater space found on a full-length card.

In general, expect to pay anywhere from $60 to $250 for a sound board. That's quite a range, but it's easy to narrow down. Table 18.2 provides general price ranges for boards required for specific types of uses. Of course, peripheral prices are volatile, so it pays to shop around.

Table 18.2. Choosing a sound board.

Application	Type of Sound Board	Cost
Business audio	PCI audio	$60-$100
Mixed-use home office	PCI or Sound Blaster audio	$100-$250
Home and gaming	Sound Blaster audio	$100-$200
Professional audio and production	PCI or Sound Blaster audio	$200-$250

Compatibility Improves

The PC audio market has finally transitioned. Windows 95/98 and DirectSound have helped redefine sound boards, enabling PCI-based sound boards to deliver exciting 3D audio and accelerated performance. Best of all, compatibility concerns are finally on the wane as DOS-based titles give way to popular DirectX games and titles.

The changing market means that you may want to make an upgrade to that old ISA sound card of yours. If you run Windows 9x and use DirectX software, a PCI-based sound board can offer more features and better system performance than can ISA boards such as Creative Labs' Sound Blaster 64, shown in Figure 18.6.

FIGURE 18.6.
Creative Labs' Sound Blaster 64 improves on previous models with better audio fidelity and enhanced MIDI capability, yet it maintains compatibility with Sound Blaster-compatible software. (Figure courtesy Creative Labs)

Still hanging onto those old DOS games? If your games will run only in a DOS-only session—that is, they won't run in a Windows 9x DOS box—then you may still need to consider a Sound Blaster-compatible ISA-based sound card. In most cases, however, even these games can run with PCI sound cards. If your software runs in a Windows 9x

DOS box, go ahead and jump to PCI, because this software can access your board using Windows 9x drivers.

If you are buying a Sound Blaster-compatible card, make sure that it supports wavetable MIDI audio. For Sound Blaster and compatible boards, this usually means that a wavetable MIDI controller chip or DSP will be on board, as will dedicated memory. Without wavetable MIDI, MIDI playback sounds unrealistic.

In most cases, however, you'll be looking at a PCI audio card. These products are less expensive than Sound Blaster-compatible boards. The least expensive products still provide realistic-sounding wavetable MIDI by using the fast PCI bus to pass MIDI sounds between system memory and the card, eliminating the need for onboard ROM or RAM.

> **Tip:** If you have a Sound Blaster-compatible board for your DOS games, you might consider upgrading to a PCI board while keeping the existing board in the system. The older board will provide support for DOS games while the new board provides advanced features under Windows 95. Of course, you'll need a free IRQ for the new board—hardly a given on today's multimedia PCs. You'll also want to buy a short mini-jack extender that enables you to plug the output from your ISA sound card into the input of your PCI sound card.

Sound Card Fidelity: Lower Your Expectations

As the PC begins to look and act like a consumer electronics device, many previously hidden weaknesses will be revealed. Chief among them is audio fidelity. Although virtually every major sound board maker claims that its products produce CD-quality audio, the actual quality of wave audio produced by sound boards falls significantly below that of consumer audio equipment. The problem is that electromagnetic interference inside the PC's case introduces noise to the original signal. Creative Labs' Sound Blaster AWE64 Gold tries to reduce this problem by using digital output and gold connectors for speakers and other devices. Ultimately, the digital-to-analog conversion step must move outside the PC case—something that the upcoming generation of USB speakers might provide.

How do sound board companies justify their claim? CD quality means that the boards can handle the same bit depth and sampling rate employed in audio CDs (16 bits, 44.1KHz); by this definition, nearly all sound cards are indeed of CD quality. However, actual tests of signal quality indicate that sound boards consistently perform more poorly than audio equipment, producing lower signal-to-noise ratios, higher total harmonic distortion levels, and greater channel crosstalk.

Several characteristics go into audio fidelity. Some boards include specifications on the side of the box defining performance, and others provide no information at all. However, the lack of benchmark standards in the PC audio industry makes it difficult to know how printed specs were produced. Here are the primary specs to look for:

- Signal to noise (S/N) ratio: The level of desired signal compared to the level of unwanted noise, expressed in decibels. The higher the number, the better. Consumer audio equipment produces S/N ratios of 80–90dB, while tape recorders produce about 60dB. S/N ratios below 70dB can be perceived as an audible hiss.

- Frequency response: The precision with which the board reproduces a signal across the 20Hz–20KHz frequency range of human hearing. Most boards suffer at least moderate degradation at the highest and lowest ends of the range. This degradation can impair the quality of sound by reducing the impact of low bass and high treble sounds.

- Crosstalk: Leakage that occurs between the two stereo channels. Severe crosstalk can eliminate the effectiveness of stereo altogether.

- Total Harmonic Distortion (THD): Changes that occur to the original signal due to distortion produced by the amplifier. At peak volumes, THD levels increase considerably.

> **Tip:** If you want to get the best fidelity out of your sound board, do not use the speaker-out port or make use of the internal amplifier. The amplifier on the sound board is of low quality and introduces significant levels of noise and distortion to the original audio signal. For best results, use amplified speakers plugged into the line-out port. Better still, disable the amplifier—most cards have jumpers or software to do this.

Unfortunately, assessing audio quality isn't easy. To measure the electrical characteristics of a sound board, you need specialized audio testing equipment, such as the Audio Precision System Two, which costs $100,000 or more. Of course, your ears are the ultimate judge. Listen to your new board, and test its range of performance on different audio clips that run the gamut of high and low frequencies. Listen for distortion.

Full-Duplex Audio

The Internet has helped transform PCs into a vital communications tool, but your sound board might not be up to the task. Applications such as Internet telephony and videoconferencing work best when both parties in a conversation can speak and hear each other at the same time. Known as *full-duplex audio,* this capability requires that a sound board be capable of juggling inbound and outbound audio data simultaneously.

Many older sound boards lack duplex audio functionality. Although you can still run many telephony or conferencing applications, you will be unable to speak simultaneously. The abrupt cut-outs produced by these older boards make natural conversation difficult. In addition, some software requires full-duplex capability on the sound board.

Diagnosing/Troubleshooting

Under Windows 3.1, sound boards earned a deserved reputation for being a pain to install. The problems start with the heavy resource demands of Sound Blaster-compatible devices. These boards require dedicated IRQ, DMA, and port address settings to operate, which invites conflicts with other devices. In addition, many problems arise due to spotty Sound Blaster compatibility.

TROUBLESHOOTING

> The inside of your PC is polluted with electromagnetic signals—the kind of stuff that can wreak havoc with analog audio signals. If you aren't satisfied with your sound quality, try moving the board away from electromagnetic field (EMF) sources such as disk and CD-ROM drives and the system CPU, as shown in Figure 18.7. Also make sure that speaker and microphone wires aren't draped over power cords or other EMF sources.

FIGURE 18.7.

Install your sound board as far away as possible from components that produce interference, such as hard disks, CD-ROM drives, and processors. Also note how the hands grip only the top edge of the board, pressing evenly in a straight-down motion to avoid damaging any onboard components. (Photo courtesyof Creative Labs)

With all these problems to contend with, it's fortunate that hardware breakdowns with sound boards are rare. Still, little mistakes can cause vexation. Speaker and microphone cords attached incorrectly can seem like serious breakdowns. Likewise, a slipped audio cable to an internal CD-ROM drive can disable audio CD playback. What's more, running from store to store trying to find connectors not included with the hardware can hold you up for days, especially if the performance of your sound card isn't the only important thing in your life right now.

Managing Resources

To function, Sound Blaster-compatible boards must have access to the following system resources:

- Interrupt Request (IRQ)
- Direct Memory Access (DMA)
- Memory address

IRQs, DMAs, and memory addresses provide the vital data pathways between your sound board and your PC. IRQs are the dedicated resources that enable sound boards and other peripherals to get the CPU's attention, while DMA provides a shortcut to your system's memory. Meanwhile, the memory address reserves a section of your PC's memory for the sound board, ensuring that no other peripheral or program attempts to grab it.

The Plug and Play Solution

The problem is that these resources are limited. Any PC loaded with multimedia peripherals will have, at most, one or two available IRQ addresses, which can lead to hardware conflicts and system crashes. DMA ports can also become scarce.

Windows 95 Plug and Play tries to resolve this problem by keeping tabs on each peripheral's resource needs. The operating system works with the motherboard BIOS to set the IRQs, DMAs, and other resources of peripherals, including sound boards. This scheme ensures that all peripherals get the resources they need.

There's just one problem: Older systems lack PnP capability, leaving you to figure out which resource settings are available when you upgrade your sound board. If you're replacing an old sound board, make a point to write down all the original settings so that you can simply point the new board at these freed resources when you install it.

> **Tip:** If you have a Sound Blaster-compatible board that includes DOS-compatible drivers for games, you can find key information in your AUTOEXEC.BAT file. Use a text editor, such as Windows' NOTEPAD.EXE, and find the line that starts with the phrase Set Blaster =. The number following the letter I indicates IRQ, the number after the D indicates the DMA settings, and the number after the H indicates the High DMA setting. Windows 95 records this information under Device Manager, of course, but sometimes the operating system changes these on-the-fly as part of the PnP specification. To ensure operation under DOS, you'll want to know these numbers.

Using Windows 9x to Manage Sound Board Settings

Regardless of whether you have a Plug and Play system, the built-in facilities in Windows 95 and 98 make it easy to determine your sound board settings. You can adjust your sound board's IRQ, DMA, and address port settings from the Hardware Device Manager. If your sound board is experiencing problems, this is a good place to start. To access the Hardware Device Manager, do the following:

1. Select Start, Settings, Control Panel.

2. Double-click the System icon to launch the System Properties dialog box, and choose the Device Manager tab, as shown in Figure 18.8.

FIGURE 18.8.

Check your sound board's resource settings from the Windows 95 or 98 Hardware Device Manager.

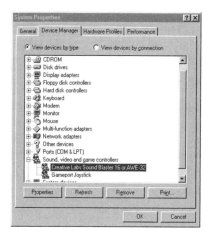

3. Click the plus sign (+) next to the Sound, video and game controllers item.

4. Double-click the sound card item that appears. The sound adapter's properties sheet appears.

5. Choose the Resources tab, shown in Figure 18.9, to view the settings in the Resource settings list box.

6. Select the resource you want to edit. To change settings, click the Use automatic settings check box, and then click the Change Setting button.

7. In the Edit Interrupt Request dialog box, shown in Figure 18.10, you can change the existing settings by using the spin control.

8. Click OK to save the new settings, and then click OK in the other two dialog boxes to return to the Control Panel.

Figure 18.9.

Prior to setup, Windows 95 gives you an inventory of your new card's resource settings. Take a moment to print these.

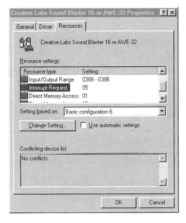

Figure 18.10.

From the Edit Interrupt Request dialog box, you can edit IRQ settings for your sound board.

TROUBLESHOOTING

Scratchy-sounding wave file playback can result from DMA conflicts. Use the Hardware Device Manager, as just explained, to reassign the existing DMA setting. If the original DMA is 1, your card might be conflicting with an enhanced-capabilities parallel port (provided that your system has one). If the original DMA setting is 5 or higher, your card might have problems working with a 16-bit DMA channel. Try reassigning it to a low DMA setting of 1, 2, or 3.

Upgrading a Sound Card

Despite all the horror stories, upgrading a sound card can be a painless experience. Plugging in a single add-in card, after all, is a lot less complicated than squeezing a new hard disk into an internal drive bay. Still, the possibility of a catastrophic conflict means that you should proceed carefully.

Who Needs to Upgrade?

First, figure out whether you need to upgrade. If your sound board lacks any of the following, you might consider an upgrade:

- Wavetable MIDI playback
- 3D positional audio
- 16-bit 44.1KHz wave audio processing
- Sound Blaster compatibility

Although any of these situations can motivate a sound board upgrade, you might consider a more incremental approach. Some sound boards feature connectors for accepting wavetable MIDI add-on cards; these are called *daughtercards*. You can also purchase separate ISA boards that add functionality to your existing Sound Blaster-compatible card.

These are some of your audio upgrade options:

- Upgrade the sound board.
- Install a wavetable MIDI daughtercard.
- Install a wavetable MIDI ISA card.
- Add RAM for wavetable MIDI instrument sounds.

Installing a New Sound Board

The following steps describe how to install a new Sound Blaster-compatible sound board into a Windows 95 PC:

1. If you have an installed sound board, remove its software first. In the Windows Control Panel, double-click the System icon and choose the Device Manager tab.

2. Select Sound, video and game ports, and click Properties. Click the Remove button.

3. When the removal process is finished, exit Control Panel, shut down your applications, and turn off the PC. Unplug the power cable and remove the system case.

4. Remove all plugs, such as those for speakers and a microphone, from the backplane. Also remove any joystick or MIDI device connectors from the MIDI/game port.

5. After grounding yourself, remove the backplane screw using a Phillips screwdriver.

6. Disconnect any cords or cables connected to the sound card, including the CD audio cable that runs from the CD-ROM drive to the top edge of the sound card.

7. Grasp the card by the top edge at each end and pull directly upward. If the board doesn't budge, pull the inside end up a bit and then rock the backplane end upward.

8. Seat the new card into the add-in slot. Apply even downward pressure until the card fits firmly in the slot. If the card won't seat completely, try rocking it in by pushing the interior edge down first.

9. Reconnect the original wires. Read the port ID markings first and attach devices for the bottom-most port. Then work your way up. This will enable you to read ID markings for subsequent ports.

10. Make sure that the speakers are plugged in and powered up.

11. Boot the system and watch for any changes. After Windows boots, your PC should detect new hardware, and the Add New Hardware dialog box should prompt you to search for the new driver.

12. You will probably see a box called Building Driver Information database. After this operation completes, the Add New Hardware Wizard box enables you select your board from a list of manufacturers and models.

13. Select the appropriate item from the Manufacturers scrolling list box. Then select the desired item from the Models scrolling list box. If the board you're installing isn't shown, click the Have Disk button.

14. In the Install From Disk dialog box, enter the drive and subdirectory containing the installation and driver files for your sound board. Usually these files are located on a floppy disk included with the packaging.

15. After the new hardware is selected, a dialog box shows you the new settings for your peripherals.

> **Note:** You might need to change the configuration of your hardware to match that assigned by Windows. You should check your documentation for the factory defaults set by the vendor. You can try changing the settings used by Windows to the board's default settings by going to Control Panel and using Device Manager to switch assigned IRQs, DMAs, and addresses. Or, you might need to refer to your board's documentation to determine how to change its settings to match that of Windows. Of course, PnP-compliant cards and systems don't require this intervention.

16. Test the new sound board under Windows by selecting Sounds from Control Panel. In the Sounds Properties dialog box, select one of the sound files shown in the Events scrolldown list box. Click the play button (the right-pointing arrow).

17. If you hear the sound, your wave audio configuration is correct. If you don't, make sure that your speakers are on and that all cables are properly set up. If the problem persists, you'll need to troubleshoot the installation.

Installing a Daughtercard Upgrade

The following steps describe how to install a Wave Blaster or similar daughtercard upgrade to sound boards that have the proper connectors. These daughtercards can add wavetable MIDI capability to older boards.

1. Shut down the PC, unplug the power cable, and remove the system case.

2. Remove all plugs, such as those for speakers and a microphone, from the sound card backplane. Also remove any joystick or MIDI device connectors from the MIDI/game port.

3. After grounding yourself, remove the backplane screw using a Phillips screwdriver.

4. Disconnect any cords or cables connected to the sound card, including the CD audio cable that runs from the CD-ROM drive to the top edge of the sound card.

5. Grasp the card by the top edge at each end, and pull directly upward. If the board doesn't budge, pull the inside end up a bit, and then rock the backplane end upward.

6. Install the daughtercard. Place the sound board face-up in one palm, and align the daughtercard so that its rows of sockets line up with the parallel rows of pins.

7. Seat the daughtercard on the pins and apply even downward pressure until you feel the card seat firmly.

8. Replace the upgraded sound card. Grasping the card by the top edge at each end, align the board with the original add-in card slot, and apply even downward pressure to fit the card firmly in the slot. If the card won't seat completely, try rocking it in by pushing the interior edge down further.

9. Reconnect the original wires. Read the port ID markings first, and then attach devices for the bottom-most port and work your way up. This enables you to read ID markings for subsequent ports.

10. Make sure that speakers are plugged in and powered up.

11. Boot the system and watch for any changes. After Windows boots, your PC should detect new hardware, and the Add New Hardware dialog box should prompt you to search for devices.

Installing Wavetable MIDI RAM SIMMs

Some wavetable MIDI-capable sound cards, such as the Sound Blaster AWE 32 and AWE 64 Gold, enable you to add more RAM beyond the ROM soldered to the board itself. To do so, follow these steps:

1. Shut down the PC, unplug the power cable, and remove the system case.

2. If sufficient room exists on the component face of the sound board to readily access the empty SIMM sockets, you can try to install the SIMMs with the board installed. If you can do this, proceed to step 7.

3. Remove all plugs, such as those for speakers and a microphone, from the sound card backplane. Also remove any joystick or MIDI device connectors from the MIDI/game port.

4. After grounding yourself, remove the backplane screw using a Phillips screwdriver.

5. Disconnect any cords or cables connected to the sound card, including the CD audio cable that runs from the CD-ROM drive to the top edge of the sound card.

6. Grasp the card by the top edge at each end and pull directly upward. If the board doesn't budge, pull the inside end up a bit, and then rock the backplane end upward.

7. Install the RAM SIMMs. Place the sound board face-up in one palm, and seat one SIMM into the lower socket at a 90-degree angle to the board face. Be sure to align pin 1 of the SIMM (the notched edge) with pin 1 of the socket.

8. Rotate the SIMM in the socket toward the top edge of the board. The SIMM socket clips should click into place on the small holes in the module.

9. Repeat steps 7 and 8 as necessary.

10. Replace the upgraded sound card. Grasping the card by the top edge at each end, align the board with the original add-in card slot, and apply even downward pressure to fit the card firmly in the slot. If the card won't seat completely, try rocking it in by pushing the interior edge down further first.

11. Reconnect the original wires. Read the port ID markings first, and then attach devices for the bottom-most port and work your way up. This enables you to read ID markings for subsequent ports.

12. Make sure that speakers are plugged in and powered up.

The Ins and Outs of Microphones and Speakers

A sound board isn't much good without speakers. Although most new PCs that have a built-in sound board do sell with speakers, boards sold individually lack them. Many boards also include microphones for recording voice snippets, telephony, and voice recognition.

PC Speakers

Speakers might be the most important part of your new sound system. If you have an older system, upgrading the speakers might be a good idea (see Figure 18.11). Many older PCs came with cheap, low-end speakers that produce less than five watts of output and fare very poorly when reproducing deep bass sounds.

Figure 18.11.
Altec Lansing's ADA305 speakers can add oomph to tinny PC speakers. A pair of shielded satellite speakers and a central subwoofer provide effective audio across a wide range of frequencies. (Photo courtesy of Altec Lansing)

Technical Note: Don't expect to use standard stereo speakers on your desktop. All speakers produce magnetic radiation that interferes with the operation of PC monitors and that can wipe floppy disks and other magnetic media clean of their data. For this reason, PC speakers incorporate shielding to limit magnetic emissions.

Caution: PC speakers might be shielded, but radiation still emits from the front of the speaker. In addition, some speakers leak more magnetic radiation than others (they have very strong magnets inside), so it's always a good idea to keep magnetic media a safe distance away.

Also, if you notice waviness or distortion in your monitor's image, magnetic fields from your speakers may be the culprit. Try moving them away from the monitor. Also make sure the speakers are not pointed at monitor housing, either, as magnetic fields tend to be stronger toward the front of the speaker than on the sides.

When you shop for speakers, you face the same spec game common with sound boards. For example, speaker vendors tend to trumpet wattage figures based on maximum output (often called *peak power output*, or PPO), as opposed to the *root-mean square output* (RMS) figures generally quoted by consumer audio companies.

RMS wattage figures are based on operation at low distortion levels—typically below one percent—and indicate wattage per channel. PPO figures, in contrast, provide inflated wattage outputs that are achieved only when the amplifier introduces significant distortion to the sound. Sometimes vendors also add the wattage of each channel together, calling a 40-watt speaker system 80 watts because two 40-watt speakers exist in the set.

Today, many PC speakers include a subwoofer to provide enhanced performance for low-end bass audio. Particularly effective for adding impact to the sound effects in combat-oriented games, a subwoofer also enhances music and other content.

Not everyone needs the same kind of speakers. After all, that thumping subwoofer might get a tad disruptive in the office. Business-oriented setups can get by with a standard two-speaker set with power output under 10 watts. Game players and people who put on presentations should consider a little more muscle—20–40 watts per channel, with a subwoofer if you need the punch for low-end audio. Stereo speaker companies such as Bose and Cambridge Soundworks produce high-quality PC speakers and subwoofers.

USB Speakers

A new class of speakers have arrived with the advent of Windows 98 and its support for the Universal Serial Bus. USB speakers don't plug into a sound board at all. Rather, a digital connector plugs into a USB port on the back of properly equipped PCs, with the digital audio stream being decoded into analog format at the speaker housing itself.

A couple advantages make USB appealing for audio. One, the digital-to-analog conversion occurs outside the electromagnetic bombardment that takes place in the PC chassis, enabling potentially higher audio quality. Two, you can ditch your sound board to cut down on resource hassles and possibly save a few bucks.

So, is USB for real? Well, yes—mostly. If you run Windows 98 on a USB-equipped system, USB speakers can and will play all sorts of audio under Windows. From business presentations to games using DirectSound3D, you'll hear everything. What's more, these speakers can be controlled by software—after all, that USB wire can handle both commands and data—so you can do things such as apply audio presets that crank bass for games and enhance the mid-range for speech.

But while the 12MBps data rate of USB is higher than that of parallel or serial ports, it falls short with the most demanding 3D positional audio found in new games and titles. To make multiple channels of audio fit within USB's bandwidth, sounds must be compressed into one or two channels, impacting fidelity. In addition, MIDI sounds output over USB require that your system render the MIDI sounds itself—no hardware assist from a sound board is forthcoming. That can put a crimp on your CPU.

Ultimately, USB speakers are best for business users who won't be playing demanding, multichannel audio that is being incorporated into the latest games. If you have USB-equipped desktops and notebooks, you'll be able to share the speakers easily, and you'll find generally better audio quality from USB speakers than from low-cost notebook audio speaker and chips. What's more, those speakers will free up a slot in your system, not to mention some IRQs and DMAs. But if you play demanding games, steer clear of USB and invest in a good PCI audio card.

Microphones

Most sound boards come with a microphone for recording voices and sounds. Microphones generally plug into the microphone in-port on the back of your sound card, and they may stand on your desktop, mount onto your monitor, or even be packaged as a lapel microphone.

Many microphones feature unidirectional designs to avoid picking up extraneous noise common in work environments. However, microphone input quality on PC sound boards tends to be poor. Although a higher-end microphone might help, the real problem is often with the sound board's microphone input line. The line might lack the capability of handling the input signal strength, resulting in lost audio data.

Microphones also play a key role in voice recognition. Many boards include basic recognition tools for navigation and interface controls. In addition, third-party recognition programs from Dragon Systems, Kurzweil, and IBM enable your computer to recognize spoken dictation.

In addition, some monitors and even keyboards now come equipped with speakers and microphones. However, the microphones on these devices might lack the tight focus of some unidirectional models, and their placement might make them unsuitable for precise tasks such as voice recognition.

Summary

People often underappreciate the importance of audio quality in a multimedia PC. Everything from games to presentations to educational titles gets a big boost from a good sound board and speakers. Even the mundane beeps from Windows 95 get richer with a better sound system.

Expect the importance of audio to grow as the PC becomes more of an entertainment and education device. DVD will bring AC3-encoded surround sound to the desktop, and Windows 95 games will employ 3D positional audio to make it sound like the bad guys are right behind you. Meanwhile, Web pages and presentations will leverage the realistic playback produced by wavetable MIDI-capable sound cards. And with Windows 95 Plug and Play, sound boards can finally claim to provide easy listening.

Displays

How important is the PC's display? The monitor accompanying a new PC can represent up to 25 percent of the total cost of the computer. What's more, the display acts as the computer's primary output device—a device you might be looking at for eight hours or more each day.

Recent price drops have made 15-, 17-, and even 19-inch monitors (measured diagonally) more affordable than ever. Also, Windows 95's multitasking talents, combined with the visual demands of multimedia applications and Web browsing, make screen real estate extremely valuable.

This chapter discusses the workings of CRT displays and their role in your system's operation. You will learn

- How displays work
- How to buy a new display
- How to recognize and resolve display problems
- The best way to upgrade to a new monitor

Making Sense of Monitors

If you're like most office workers, you probably spend hours reading text from a PC's monitor. This makes your monitor the most critical element of your system. A poor display can decrease productivity and potentially affect performance more than any CPU or memory upgrade. Small screens limit productivity, and low refresh rates and lack of tight focus can cause eye strain and headaches.

Despite the importance of the display in any computing environment, many users tend to skimp when they buy a new system. Buyers often try to get the fastest processor or the largest hard disk possible, anticipating that upcoming software will outstrip their existing PC. Retail systems are at fault as well: In an effort to attain attractive price points, vendors use smaller, older displays that can shave $200 to $400 off the cost of a new PC.

Peter's Principle: Choosing the Right Monitor Size

Generally, monitor sizes match up with standard resolutions used by Windows 95. Older 14-inch monitors, for example, are useful mainly at 640×480 pixel-per-inch resolution. Any higher, and the text gets too small to read.

A 15-inch monitor will do well at 800×600 and 640×480 resolutions. A 17-inch model can push up to 1,024×768 pixels comfortably, while a 19- or 21-inch display is needed to make 1,280×1,024 resolution readable (see Figure 19.1).

Keep in mind the resolution you might like to work in when buying a new monitor. If you want to see large swaths of financial spreadsheets or view several open programs, a 17-inch or larger display running at least 1,024×768 is your best bet.

FIGURE 19.1.

Larger 17-inch models allow crisp 1,024×768 resolutions, great for multitasking and graphics work. (Photo courtesy of ViewSonic)

More Than Television: How Monitors Work

The monitor on your desktop has a lot in common with the television in your family room. Both are cathode ray tube (CRT) displays using a beam of focused electrons to excite phosphors on the surface of a large glass vacuum tube. But your PC's monitor might have a lot less in common with your TV than you think.

For one thing, PC monitors are much more sophisticated than TVs, which is why a 17-inch monitor can cost about the same as a 32-inch TV. Your monitor provides much crisper output than a TV, up to 1,280×1,024 or even 1,600×1,200 pixels. In contrast, TV resolutions in North America are limited to about 525×700 pixels, as defined by the NTSC (North American Television Standards Commission) standard. What's more, PC monitors provide a more stable display, making it possible to read small text and view detail without eye strain.

A Picture Is Worth a Thousand Pixels

How do graphics, text, video, and animation get to your screen? The process starts with a device in the back of your monitor called an *electron gun*, which sprays a focused beam of electrons toward the surface of the glass vacuum tube. The inside of the glass screen you look at is layered with phosphorescent material, which, when excited by electrons, glows a specific color.

If you look at a monitor closely enough, or hold a magnifying glass to one, you'll see lots of tiny red, green, and blue dots. These dots are the individual color elements making up pixels (which stands for "picture elements"). Each pixel gets its color from the combination of the three color dots.

The electron gun firing away in the back of the monitor determines what those dots look like. If it lays a big electron charge on the red color dot and then sprays no electrons on the green and blue dots, that pixel will appear pure red. Often, all three dots will get varying strengths of electron charges to produce literally millions of colors. The dots are defined by the monitor's *shadow mask* or *aperture grill*, a thin layer of material with tiny spaces for allowing through electrons. This mask focuses electrons on precise points, ensuring sharp images and precise color positioning.

The electron gun is one busy worker. It paints every dot of every pixel approximately 70 times per second. The reason is that the phosphors on your screen fade quickly and require a constant stream of electrons to remain lit. Keeping up with the demands of refreshing high-resolution displays is one of the things that distinguishes high-end monitors from less-expensive products.

In fact, the way PC monitors refresh also distinguishes them from TVs. Your TV set only refreshes every other line for each screen pass. The even rows are refreshed and then on the next pass, the odd rows are refreshed. That eases demands on the electronics, but results in a display that appears to flicker, causing eye strain when viewed at close range.

Firing Line: Refresh Rates Explained

The process of updating the screen is called the *refresh rate*. It's a key ergonomic concern with any CRT display. A refresh rate of 75 updates per second (or 75Hz) is recommended. Lower refresh rates can result in perceptible flicker in the display, causing eye strain and headaches.

UPGRADE ADVICE

Older monitors, even those capable of resolutions as high as 1,280×1,024, lack the advanced electronics to handle higher refresh rates. If you experience discomfort or eye strain from frequent use of your monitor, you might need to upgrade to one that can support 75 hertz (Hz) or higher operation at the resolutions you use.

Here's how refresh works: The electron gun shoots its beam of electrons at the topmost pixel on the left side of the screen and then works its way across to the right side. The beam turns off and the gun moves to the leftmost pixel on the second row and begins painting the screen again from left to right. This operation is repeated for every row on the screen. On a 15-inch monitor running at 800×600 resolution, this means that 600 rows (each containing 800 pixels) are painted in each screen pass.

To keep the phosphors properly lit, this process must be repeated 70 or more times per second. When the gun reaches the bottom-rightmost pixel, the beam is again turned off, and the gun then shoots at the top-leftmost pixel to start the whole process again.

To update the screen 70, 80, or even 100 times per second, the electron beam must be targeted quickly. Rather than having a moving gun, which could never keep up with the task, magnetic fields are used to quickly and precisely target the beam to the desired location.

Tip: Your monitor's refresh rate capabilities are documented in its manual, but you can figure this out yourself. Look for the monitor's maximum vertical frequency, which is expressed in kilohertz (kHz). (Hint: It's often printed on the back of the monitor.)

To determine if your monitor can handle a certain refresh rate at a specific resolution, just multiply the number of rows (for example, there are 768 rows in a resolution of 1,024×768) by the refresh rate (say, 75Hz). Now, multiply that number by 1.04, which is a fudge factor that accounts for time lost reorienting the beam between rows.

In our example, 768 times 75 equals 57,600. Multiply that by the 1.04 fudge factor, and you get 59,904Hz (or 59.904kHz). So your monitor must be able to support a vertical frequency of 60kHz or higher in order to produce a 75Hz refresh rate at a 1,024×768 resolution.

UPGRADE ADVICE

Remember, your graphics boards must be able to produce the refresh rates and resolutions that end up on your monitor. A new 21-inch monitor able to display 1,600×1,200 resolution at a rock-solid 100Hz refresh rate will be wasted on an old 2MB graphics board with a 135MHz RAMDAC that limits refresh rates to about 75Hz.

Screen Types

The display quality of a monitor is directly affected by the type of shadow mask being used. Most monitors use an Invar shadow mask, made of a special composite that resists expansion when heated. Shadow masks like these feature tiny holes for the electron beam to shoot through.

Some monitors use Sony's Trinitron aperture grill technology and have names such as Diamondtron and SonicTron. The Trinitron tube produces brighter and sharper images but typically costs $100 or more than similar shadow-mask monitors. Behind the enhanced display is a grill with thousands of tiny rectangular openings rather than the round openings in standard tubes. However, pixels are slightly malformed due to the rectangular holes in the mask. In addition to several of Sony's displays, Gateway's Vivitron line of monitors uses this scheme.

> **Note:** You can identify a Trinitron-style screen by one or two faint horizontal bands appearing about one-third of the way from the top and bottom of the glass. These are wires that hold the Trinitron mask in place, helping provide exceptional precision. However, some users might find the band distracting, particularly on bright white backgrounds, where the contrast of the wire is most evident.

In either case, the potential image fidelity of a monitor can be measured in the *dot pitch* (or *aperture grill pitch*) of the shadow mask. The pitch defines how far apart the centers of contiguous pixels are from each other. The smaller the number, the better the precision of the tube and the sharper the images.

Most 15-inch monitors today feature .28 or .26 millimeter dot pitches. Older 14-inch displays often had wider .39 or .41mm dot pitch measurements, which translated into fuzzy text and lack of fine detail. The larger the monitor, the lower the dot pitch number needs to be, since pixels must be much more precise at higher resolutions (see Table 19.1).

Table 19.1. Recommended dot pitches for monitors.

Tube Size	Maximum Recommended Dot Pitch
14 inches	.39mm
15 inches	.28mm
17 inches	.26mm
19 inches and larger	.21mm

Features to Look For

Beyond pixels and refresh rates, there are several other key issues to consider, including

- Electromagnetic shielding
- Power consumption
- Display controls
- Speakers

Most newer monitors feature shielding that blunts the leakage of electromagnetic radiation from the display. Most monitors comply with the MPR-II specification, and others comply with the more rigorous TCO standard. Both specifications originate from Swedish government standards that have since been adopted internationally.

Tip: If you suspect that your monitor is a health hazard, you can easily protect yourself. Just sit further back from the display. Electromagnetic energy dissipates at an exponential rate based on its distance from the source. By setting the monitor back by about two feet, you can drastically cut your exposure.

Power consumption is another critical area. Larger 17-inch displays, for example, can run at 700 watts of power. So-called *green monitors* can reduce your electric bill, minimize heat output, and extend the useful life of the monitor tube by shutting down display components. Look for an Energy Star-compliant display.

When it comes to power consumption, most displays support two levels of low-power operation: stand-by and sleep modes.

- Stand-by mode: The electron beam and the electron gun are shut down, blanking the screen. This mode reduces stress on the gun and relieves wear and tear on the phosphor material. Energy consumption can be cut by about 74 percent over normal operation. Return to operation is immediate.
- Sleep mode: Monitor components are shut down to the point that the gun and components will cool off. Power savings are significant. Power draw can drop to nearly 0 watts, but returning to operation can take several seconds or more.

Tip: Whether or not you have a shielded monitor, the display will leak electromagnetic radiation. If you're concerned about EMF exposure, avoid working with your face close to the display. The level of electromagnetic radiation decreases exponentially as the distance from the monitor increases.

Displays are persnickety things and can fall out of alignment over time. To help keep things in order, most monitors feature controls for straightening, resizing, and unbending images that have gotten out of whack. Among the controls, you will find the following:

- Vertical size and position: Moves and sizes the display area to fit the viewable area of the screen.

- Horizontal size and position: Moves and sizes the display area to fit the viewable area of the screen.

- Trapezoid: Adjusts the vertical aspect of the display so that the top and bottom are both the same width.

- Pincushion: Adjusts the corners of the display area to resolve bowing that can distort images.

- Rotate: Untilts the display area.

- Degauss: Refreshes the display and clears distortion by reasserting magnetic field controlling display.

Finally, you might consider a monitor with integrated speakers (refer back to Figure 19.1). The advantage here is space savings. If you have a crowded desktop, a multimedia monitor can decrease clutter. However, the magnetic output of the speakers puts display fidelity at risk, and monitor-bound speakers invariably provide poor audio quality. Unless your space situation is dire, I recommend sticking with desktop speakers.

Flat-Screen Displays: A View of the Future

Larger displays are a good thing. They enable you to comfortably multitask several applications without losing sight of their interfaces. And they're a boon to anyone involved with graphics, whether designing Web pages and brochures or playing games and multimedia titles. Anyone buying a PC should consider a 17-inch display.

But large monitors have big problems. For one thing, 17-inch and larger CRTs are huge, hogging all sorts of valuable desk space and making it difficult to maintain an ergonomic layout. While new short-neck versions of these products ease the space crunch, they still suck a lot of juice when running and produce plenty of heat.

Enter flat panel displays. Anyone who has used a notebook computer is familiar with LCD screens. Ranging in size from 12.1 to 14.1 inches, today's notebook displays are now approaching the viewable area of 14- and 15-inch CRTs. Now an emerging class of LCD displays for desktop computers offer 15-inch viewable areas at prices below $1,000—about 50 percent less than just one year earlier.

Still, $1,000 is a lot to pay for the equivalent of a 17-inch CRT monitor, which typically offers 15.8 inches of viewable area at prices as low as $400. But LCD screens offer key advantages. For one, an LCD screen consumes a fraction of the space and power of its CRT cousins. LCDs also don't throw off a ton of heat, reducing air conditioning requirements, and emit no electromagnetic radiation, eliminating health concerns.

But perhaps most compelling is the fact that the display quality of these new LCD screens is superior to that of virtually all CRT monitors. Unlike CRTs, which refresh the image 70 or 80 times each second, pixels on an LCD screen remain constantly lit. That means less eyestrain and fewer headaches, even after long hours of viewing. LCDs can also offer better clarity and sharpness because each pixel is individually addressed by its own circuit.

How LCD Displays Work

Flat displays take an entirely different tack from CRTs when it comes to putting images on-screen. Instead of shooting a beam of electrons at phosphorescent material stuck to the glass, most flat displays use an electrical charge to excite liquid crystals suspended between two layers of glass.

There are two main types of LCD screens:

- Passive-matrix
- Active-matrix

Unlike CRT monitors, which are analog devices, LCD monitors are digital technology. Pixels are set on or off and to a specific value based on digital inputs. That makes today's graphics cards, with their analog VGA out ports, a poor match for LCD monitors. In order to work with a standard graphics card, a desktop LCD monitor must convert the incoming analog signal back to digital format. The result is added cost to the monitor and degraded image quality.

New LCD monitors are employing digital connections. Because no formal LCD graphics interface standard has been adopted, these connections are proprietary. In fact, many LCD monitors are bundled with a compatible digital graphics board, such as ATI's Rage Pro LCD.

Passive-Matrix: The Low-End Leader

Passive-matrix screens enjoy the advantage of being cheap to produce. However, display quality is unacceptable for many applications. Brightness and contrast are both limited, and passive-matrix screens can't be viewed from some angles. Today, passive-matrix screens are hard to find on notebooks, as vendors move to the much-improved quality of active-matrix displays.

Passive screens light individual liquid crystals by sending intersecting charges from the horizontal and vertical edges of the display. The level of the charge determines the relative color value of red, green, and blue emitting crystals found in each pixel element. However, because charges are sent across the screen to each pixel, individual pixels can't be refreshed quickly enough to produce exceptional brightness or contrast.

Dual-scan passive screens improve on the original idea by splitting the display into top and bottom halves. This way, two sets of intersecting charges come into play—one set lighting the top half of the screen, and the second set lighting the bottom half. The quicker response makes for a brighter display.

Note: You can spot a dual-scan passive-matrix screen easily. The split point between the two halves is usually easily visible, particularly with white backgrounds when the screen brightness is pushed up.

Active-Matrix: High Price, High Fidelity

If you buy a new notebook or desktop LCD screen, chances are it's an active-matrix model. Also known as TFT (twisted film transistor) displays, these screens provide very bright, high-contrast images—nearly matching those of desktop CRTs. The secret is that each pixel in the display is activated by a charge provided from its own transistor. The one-to-one pixel-to-charging device ratio solves many problems, but the complexity of these screens makes them expensive.

Perhaps more of a concern is when a transistor goes dead, a pixel on the screen goes out. With so many thousands of transistors on each display, manufacturers run into so-called *yield problems*, where a high percentage of screens coming off the production line are unacceptable. Wear and tear during ownership can also lead to dead pixels—a distracting flaw.

That said, 12.1-, 13.3-, and even 14.1-inch TFT displays have become standard equipment on high-end notebooks. The cost of displays is dropping as manufacturers improve production techniques and yields. In general, LCD screens bound for desktop use will be active-matrix models.

Flat-Panel Applications

Flat-panel technology is intriguing, to be sure. After all, large, bright, flat-panel displays could dramatically cut the space and power requirements of desktop PCs. And advances in this area have already transformed portable computing.

Portable Computing

Of course, you won't be upgrading your display on an existing notebook. In fact, the fact that you can't change a notebook screen down the road makes the display decision all the more critical. If you choose the wrong display type, your entire investment might go south. For general-purpose computing, consider getting an active-matrix screen of 12.1 inches or larger.

Table 19.2 will help determine display needs when buying a new notebook.

Table 19.2. Choosing a notebook display.

Application	Display Type
General-purpose/business portable	12.1-inch active-matrix or passive-matrix
Desktop replacement (without separate CRT)	13.3- or 14.1-inch active-matrix
Multimedia sales presentations	13.3-inch active-matrix
Low-end general purpose/business portable	12.1-inch active-matrix or 12.1-inch dual-scan passive-matrix
Lightweight notebook	12.1-inch dual-scan passive-matrix

Peter's Principle: Wide Notebook Screens Are Vulnerable to Damage

Do you travel a lot, or subject your notebook to abuse? If so, you should stay away from the new, larger displays. Wide 14.1- and even 15-inch screens are appearing on notebooks, but they are subject to much more torque and twisting force than more-compact models using 12.1-inch screens. Similarly, an impact on larger screens is more likely to result in damage, because the reinforcing frame material is located further from the center. Even if you don't abuse your notebook, keep in mind that, historically, the largest displays generally produce more problems than more-established, easier-to-manufacture screens.

Desktop Computing: Flat Panels

After years of promise and ridiculously high prices, the buzz on desktop LCD displays has gotten loud. In 1998, the prices on 15-inch LCD screens finally cracked the $1,000 barrier, and will continue to fall as volumes increase and manufacturing yields improve. While LCDs will remain much more expensive than CRT monitors offering the same viewable area, the days of $5,000 screens limited to corporate buyers is ending.

Should you consider buying one of these displays for your desktop PC? Perhaps. While businesses have long seen a benefit in the small footprint and low energy draw of these screens—perfect for crowded stock brokerage stations, for example—end users will appreciate the sharper picture and better ergonomics. Unlike CRT monitors, LCD images do not degrade at the far corners of the screen and pixels don't fuzz out (focus) or overlap (bloom) because of vagaries in the electron beam.

In addition to crisp visual precision, LCDs can help relieve eyestrain and headaches resulting from hours of looking at a screen. Larger CRT monitors actually exacerbate this problem, as the subtle flicker of the display takes up a wider field of view on large 19-inch monitors, for example. LCDs images, by contrast, do not flicker. If you stare at a display for hours on end—and suffer recurring eyestrain and headaches—you should look into a desktop LCD screen as a possible solution.

One thing to consider when buying a desktop LCD monitor is the graphics connection. While early LCD screens used a typical analog 15-pin VGA connector—the same as on a CRT monitor—newer models employ more efficient digital connections. The issue is this: While CRTs rely on analog signals to produce timings for the electron beam, LCDs need digital 1s and 0s to tell them which pixels to turn on and what color they should be. But because no such digital graphics connection existed on desktop PCs, LCD screens included componentry to turn analog VGA signals into digital commands for the LCD display. That componentry costs money, but ensures that the LCD screen will work with any graphics card.

Newer displays actually forego the VGA-compatible connection and are instead designed to work with graphics cards offering a digital output next to the VGA port. ATI's Xpert LCD board (Figure 19.2), a popular graphics board, includes the digital output for LCD screens. Of course, using the digital connection limits your graphics card options.

FIGURE 19.2.

ATI's Xpert LCD features two outputs—a VGA port for CRT monitors and a digital flat panel (DFP) connector for new LCD screens. (Photo courtesy of ATI Technologies)

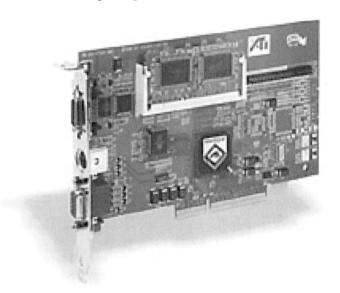

The emergence of a Digital Flat Panel Monitor (DFPM) standard means that future graphics cards and LCD displays can all conform to a single specification. With the LCD market expected to grow rapidly, expect to see more popular graphics boards offered in flavors customized for flat panel operation. See Figure 19.3.

FIGURE 19.3.

Expect to see more of the 20-pin DFP connector on graphics boards as flat panel displays enter the mainstream.

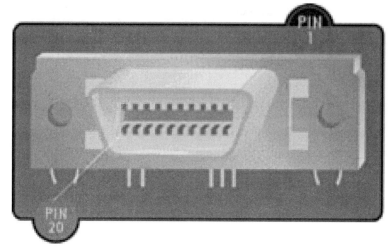

If you are looking for a desktop display, don't consider anything less than an active-matrix LCD for desktop use. Light from windows or other sources can wipe out a passive-matrix screen. In addition, these screens update more slowly than TFT models, making them unsuitable for animation or video playback—a particular concern for presentations and multimedia.

Other Visions: LCD Panels, Head-Mounted Displays, and More

Beyond desktop displays, you'll find all sorts of things to hook up to PCs. There are inexpensive LCD panels that sit atop projection machines, enabling multimedia presentations. For brighter output, a PC projector lets you pump your VGA output directly to the screen, as shown in Figure 19.4.

FIGURE 19.4.

ViewSonic's PJ800 projector enables you to put your PC's graphics up on the big screen.

Gamers have been tempted by head-mounted displays, but these products have failed to take off. 3D eyeglasses, meanwhile, provide the illusion of depth to images displayed on a CRT monitor. The glasses synchronize with the refresh rate on the monitor, alternating what is displayed to each eye.

> **Note:** The immersive quality of head-mounted displays can be so effective that it can lead to nausea and neck strain. It pays to be careful.

Purchase Decisions

Buying a new monitor isn't as tough as it might seem—despite all the specs and technical jargon previously covered. For one thing, compatibility is almost a nonissue with displays, unlike virtually every other component of your system. With a few exceptions, any new monitor you purchase will work with existing systems bought during the last five years. Problems usually only crop up with older displays, which might lack the capacity for the high-resolution, high-refresh operation provided by today's graphics boards.

The key decisions you need to make boil down to the following:

- Price
- Tube size
- Refresh rate support
- Control and management features
- Image quality

Price

In general, price is a direct function of the size and quality of the monitor you want to buy. The larger tube and more-complex electronics inside a 17-inch display generally make it more expensive—by about $150 to $300—than a 15-inch CRT. However, there are enough variations that prices differ widely among products.

Tube Size

Tube size defines the distance from one corner of the tube to another, measured diagonally across the screen. A 17-inch monitor, therefore, measures 17 inches from corner to corner. The vast majority of monitors use a standard 3×4 aspect ratio (three units tall for every four units wide), so the shape of the screen is constant among products. There are even a few models that turn the monitor screen on its end, allowing for high-resolution display of documents in full screen (see Figure 19.5).

FIGURE 19.5.
The ViewSonic VP140 caters to document imaging with its vertically-oriented screen.

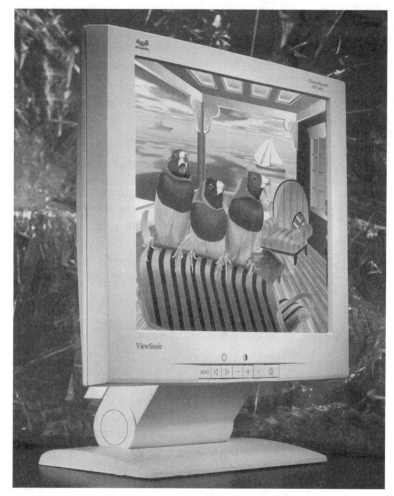

Peter's Principle: Specs Do Lie: Check the Viewable Screen Measurement, Not the Physical Dimensions of the Tube

In 1996, several major monitor vendors settled a suit brought against them by the California Attorney General's Office. The suit claimed that display makers falsely advertised the size of their monitor screens.

At issue was the common computer industry practice of using the CRT glass measurement to describe the size of the monitor. Since the bezel of the monitor (the plastic material around the edges) obscures part of the visible screen, the actual viewable area of a display is always less than the stated tube size. In fact, a so-called 17-inch monitor can have 16 inches or less of viewable area.

Today, monitor makers are compelled to prominently display the actual viewable area of their products. This practice puts manufacturers in line with practices in the consumer electronics field, where television makers have long used viewable area exclusively. You should make a point of checking the viewable screen measurement, since the usable size of some monitors can be up to a half inch or more larger than others.

17-inch displays have become the sweet spot product for new PCs, thanks to Windows 95's graphical interface and the multitasking it promotes. Compared to 15-inch monitors, a 17-inch monitor adds about 30 percent more viewable area, making it possible to multitask a spreadsheet on one side of the screen while a Web browser updates on the other. At the high end of the consumer market, 19-inch monitors have become popular.

The larger size doesn't come without cost. You need to consider your workspace when upgrading to a new monitor. 17-inch and larger monitors need a lot of desk space, and they can weigh 40 pounds or more. Make sure that you have enough room and a strong-enough desk to handle the load of a larger monitor. Another consideration is power consumption. Operating wattage for 17-inch models runs about 70 watts, up from 40 watts for a typical 14-inch display. Larger tubes, of course, will consume even more power.

In general, expect to pay about $200 to $250 for a 15-inch monitor. Because high-resolution operation (1,024×768 and higher) is unnecessary on these smaller screens, 15-inch monitors can get by with less-sophisticated electronics and a coarser shadow mask dot pitch.

Caution: Be careful not to run your display at higher color and resolution settings than it was designed for. Your graphics board can damage or destroy your display by sending frequencies outside its range. If you hear a whining noise, or the display looks all rattled or squished, you're probably overdriving the monitor. Try to shut down Windows 95 immediately by pressing Alt-F4. If that doesn't work, simply turn off the PC. When you reboot, press F5 when you see Starting Windows 9x appear on the screen, and then select Safe Mode to go into straight VGA operation. You can choose a safe graphics mode from there.

Which size of display is best for you? That depends on your needs. Unless your needs are particularly modest or demanding, a 17-inch display is your safest bet. It provides great viewing for nearly all applications and gives you room to grow. Table 19.3 can help guide your decision.

Table 19.3. Size matters: Which monitor do you need?

Tube Size	Price Range	System Type	Applications
14-inch	$150-$200	Not generally recommended.	Only for the most basic text-based recommended. applications.
15-inch	$150-$300	Budget-oriented home PCs	Low-demand office applications such as email or word processing.
17-inch	$200-$500	Mainstream PCs	Spreadsheets, light-to-heavy multitasking, general-purpose graphics, multimedia.
19-inch	$700-$1,000	High-end mainstream PCs	Heavy multitasking, very large spreadsheets, moderate-to-heavy graphics use. Great for intensive game play and multimedia.
21-inch and larger	$1,000-$3,000	Workstation-level PCs	Professional graphics, computer-aided design, application development.

While LCD screens offer sharper and more comfortable viewing than CRTs, the basic rules of resolution hold true. A 15-inch flat panel display will deliver a viewable area just shy of most 17-inch monitors. So you can probably run comfortably at 1,024×768 resolution on a 15-inch LCD. Larger sizes remain prohibitively expensive, however.

Refresh Rate Support

As with dot pitch, refresh rate demands change with monitor size. The industry group VESA (Video Electronics Standards Association) recommends a 75Hz refresh rate for ergonomic operation. However, 17-inch and larger monitors running at high resolution will benefit from even higher refresh rates. The real breakpoint occurs at 1,280×1,024 resolution, where most bargain displays are unable to manage more than 75Hz at this setting.

Tip: Perceived flicker is much greater on a white background than on a darker, more subdued background. If you can't shell out $700 for a hot new monitor, you'll be glad to know that you can ease eye strain and discomfort for free. Just adjust your application backgrounds to a neutral color like gray. To do this, right-click the Windows 95 desktop, choose Properties, and select the Appearance tab. Click the area labeled Window Text and choose the Color drop-down item. Choose the desired color (a light gray might work) and click OK. Now the white background on your word processor, spreadsheet, and other programs will appear in a subtler shade.

Keep in mind when purchasing that your graphics board must be up to the task. If you have an old graphics card with 2MB of graphics RAM, it simply won't be able to deliver the goods to a flashy 17-inch CRT. In these cases, you might need to consider a double upgrade of the graphics card and display.

If you can afford it, flat panel displays effectively solve the refresh rate problem. If you suffer from chronic discomfort even at higher refresh rates, an LCD display may be the best way to reduce the problem.

Control and Management Features

Monitor control features such as degauss and pincushion (discussed in the earlier section "Features to Look For") can help ease the frustration caused by a display that just doesn't look right. But keep in mind that these settings can be tough to get exactly right, and monitor controls—even onscreen ones—tend to be hard to use.

Graphics professionals need exacting display controls, including color matching and calibration, to ensure utmost precision. These features can boost monitor price by as much as $500 to $1,000, so they're not for everybody. Most people can get by with a minimum of screen resize and position controls, manual degauss, tilt, trapezoid, and pincushion controls.

Often, your best bet with a new monitor is to get one with DDC compliance, a Plug and Play technology enabling your monitor talk to your graphics board. Under the DDC-2b specification, for example, the monitor and graphics board can actually negotiate an optimal setting, boosting refresh rates to their best level for the selected resolution.

The expense associated with this scheme (because it requires separate wiring) keeps DDC-2b on the sidelines. But DDC-2a is common. This spec helps your graphics board recognize the monitor and send the best preprogrammed signal to the display. In order for this to work properly, Windows 95 must recognize the display.

Improper display information can cause mismatched signals. Squished or distorted screens are a common symptom of this failure. Most new monitors come with a driver disk for placing the display's exact preferences into the operating system. This way, your graphics card will know what to do.

Image Quality

Ultimately, you must decide what looks good to you. Keep in mind that not all displays are right for all people. NEC's mid- to high-end monitors, for instance, tend to be bright, sharp, and clear—perfect for most business applications and, in particular, multimedia presentations. MAG Innovision's displays, on the other hand, produce more subdued— but equally sharp—images.

Which do you need? Look for yourself. If possible, arrange to use a monitor for some time before purchasing it. Often, the quirks of a particular model won't make themselves known until you've used it for several hours. Also consider your environment. Bright lights overhead or behind could lead to a lot of glare, so consider a screen with an antiglare coating.

You can also use a monitor test program to ferret out hard-to-see flaws. Sonera Technologies' DisplayMate, for example, is almost universally accepted as a visual benchmark for monitors (see Figure 19.6).

FIGURE 19.6.

The intricate patterns of DisplayMate's various test visuals let you detect hidden flaws that might annoy you over time.

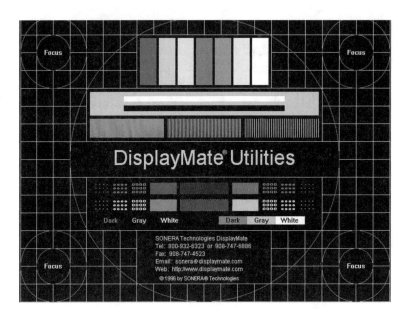

In general, subdued monitors are best for long hours spent reading text or figures. However, these displays might not compete well with other light sources in a brightly-lit environment. Brighter displays are excellent for full-motion video, animation, and graphics. Much like your TV, the heightened brightness adds impact to moving images.

Discerning image quality doesn't take much—just a pair of good eyes and a little patience. Remember that a simple control tweak might fix what looks like a serious problem, so don't be afraid to twist a few knobs and push a few buttons during this process.

- Pay special attention to details in the far corners of the screen. Many monitors produce hazy images at these extremes, reducing the usable visual area of the display. Precise display is very difficult at the screen corners because of the sharp angle required for the electron gun to paint these regions. The result is that round pixels might distort to an oval shape and lose their sharp edges.

- Turn the monitor brightness up as far as it can go, and look closely for spreading pixel colors. Called *blooming*, this occurs when pixel edges bleed into each other, reducing contrast and sharpness.

- Look at the lit area of the display. Does it appear perfectly rectangular, or does it have a trapezoid look in which one horizontal edge is wider than the other? Also check to see if the display area looks slightly tilted or askew. If the monitor you're looking at lacks controls for these imperfections, walk away.

- Display an image with straight, thin vertical lines along the outer edges of the screen. (The scrollbars and application window frames of any word processor or spreadsheet will do.) Look for any curvature or bending along the line.

Diagnosing Display Ailments

Things can and do go wrong with monitors. Magnetic interference can warp displays, and a power surge can blow fuses or cook sensitive electronics. Even daily wear and tear adds up to perceptible loss of fidelity.

Fortunately, you won't find yourself worrying about monitor software going bad. In contrast to other PC components, monitor compatibility is very good. However, you might find yourself chasing what looks like a monitor problem, only to find that the culprit is your graphics board. Table 19.4 lists some common maladies.

Table 19.4. Common monitor maladies.

Problem	Symptoms
Frequency mismatch	Squished or distorted display, blank display, rolling display, high-pitched whine
Loose or overlong cable	Intermittent image loss, incorrect colors, poor focus, and image fidelity
Blown monitor fuse	Black screen
Power supply problems	Intermittent clicking on and off, incorrect colors, brightness changes

TROUBLESHOOTING

As a rule, always keep the graphics board and its drivers on your short list of suspects when it comes to display problems. A squished or distorted display might result from a frequency mismatch, which can be best addressed by changing the refresh rate or resolution of the graphics board.

You might notice that your monitor clicks and snaps a lot when switching on or going into DOS mode to display. What you're seeing are the electronics of the monitor struggling to synchronize with the new frequency being put out by the graphics board. Often this process—which was described by one product manager as a mating dance between the graphics board and the monitor—can take several seconds to complete.

Utilities and Facilities

For monitors, the best weapons in your troubleshooting arsenal are your eyes. Close attention to detail can help you discern simple vagaries in display quality, allowing you to avoid needless driver updates or graphics board installations.

Windows 95 provides a few useful tools for managing monitor quality. As with graphics boards, most of the action occurs in the Display Properties sheet under the Settings tab. To access your monitor's profile, do the following:

1. Right-click the Windows 95 desktop, and then choose Properties from the context menu.

2. In the Display Properties dialog box, choose the Settings tab.

3. Click the Change Display Type button to bring up the Change Display Type dialog box.

4. Under Monitor Type, you should see the brand and model of the monitor installed under Windows 95.

5. Click the Change button to access the Select Device dialog box for changing or updating the monitor profile.

There are several instances when this control can come in handy. For example, you might find that after moving up to a new resolution or color setting, your display looks wrong. A squished or distorted image is a common symptom of a frequency mismatch— basically, a breakdown in communication between the graphics board and the monitor. This can occur because Windows 95 doesn't know the exact model of monitor installed, so it prompts the graphics card to pump signals at a frequency that is slightly off spec. If you need to update the monitor profile from a floppy, simply click the Have Disk button and select the appropriate .INF file from the dialog box.

Dealing with Interference

More than drivers or other software, monitor problems arise because of outside interference or issues with the incoming signal. Many factors can lead to display problems, including

- Uneven electrical current
- Interference from speakers, fans, or telephones
- Poorly connected or overlong cabling

Power Problems

Monitors need a lot of juice, particularly larger 17-inch models. The hefty draw can outstrip older wiring found in aging buildings. Problems can also arise when several devices are running off the same circuit.

This problem is particularly acute in home offices. Laser printers, fax machines, and televisions can all draw significant amounts of power. Although a blown fuse or tripped circuit breaker is a common result of such a situation, other problems can arise short of a power shutdown.

If your monitor clicks on and off spontaneously, uneven power flow might be the culprit. This kind of oscillation can damage the monitor, causing blown fuses or fried circuitry. An air conditioner, laser printer, or other heavy-drawing device can cause this kind of problem.

There are two ways to resolve this problem: Make sure that the monitor is running off a circuit free of unwanted oscillation, or purchase an uninterruptible power supply (UPS). A UPS ensures that incoming electrical flow is consistent, and it employs a battery to supplement power should there be a loss of electricity.

Interference from Other Devices

As everyone knows, a home office can be a pretty crowded place. Phones, radios, printers, fax machines, and other devices all compete for space on your desktop. In addition to drawing power, all these devices produce electromagnetic fields that can interfere with your display's normal operation.

Magnetic interference usually appears as a visible discoloration or distortion of the screen. Often, the area of the display closest to the magnetic source will show greater change, making it easy to determine the source of the interference.

If you're having trouble, look around the vicinity of the monitor and identify electric devices. Try removing them one by one from the area of the monitor until you see the problem go away. This way, you can isolate the culprit, rearranging your setup.

> **Tip:** Just because your PC speakers are shielded, don't ignore them as a possible source of interference. All speakers produce some amount of magnetic radiation, particularly toward the front of the speaker, where sound is produced. Imperfections in the speaker casing, due to poor manufacture or cracks from an impact, can nullify the benefits of shielding. If you encounter interference problems, make sure that your speakers aren't the culprit.

Cabling Problems

Another suspect when things go awry is your monitor's cable. Analog signals traveling along the 15-pin VGA cable are subject to interference from outside sources, as well as from degradation as signals are pushed over longer distances.

Most monitors use cables less than five feet long, ensuring that the length of the connection won't affect the signal quality. Cable extenders—additional cable lengths enabling you to place the monitor further away from the PC—add convenience but also increase the possibility of signal problems. If you want to buy a cable extender, get one that is shielded to eliminate external interference. If you experience trouble, you should consider removing the extra cabling to eliminate the problem.

> The analog signals traveling through your monitor's cable are especially suscep- tible to outside interference. Make sure that power cords and other potential sources of trouble aren't draped across the cable. If you notice problems, inter- ference introduced at the cable might be the culprit.

Upgrading

Monitor upgrades are among the least-difficult of any PC upgrade. However, they don't come cheap. A new 17-inch monitor can cost anywhere from $200 to $700—more than virtually any other upgrade short of a full motherboard purchase. Still, the impact it can have on your computing experience makes a new upgrade well worth the price.

> **Tip:** When you purchase a monitor, make sure you get one with a replaceable VGA cable. That way, if the cable fails or is flawed, all you have to do is unplug the cable and replace it with a new one. A monitor with an embedded cable will need to be professionally serviced.

Who Needs to Upgrade

Almost any PC can benefit immediately from a larger monitor. Although a new display won't make your PC any faster, the extra viewing area can significantly improve your productivity. Because a 17-inch monitor provides nearly 40 percent more viewing area than a 15-inch display, you can cut down on the time you spend scrolling through documents or switching among various applications.

A monitor upgrade makes particular sense if you often multitask several applications. A 17-inch or larger display enables you to run two, three, or more applications and keep them visible on-screen. A wide view can also come in handy when you're browsing the Web, because you might have two or more browser windows open at a time.

A monitor upgrade might not make sense on older systems, particularly those with graphics boards with 1MB of RAM or less. If you own a 486 PC with 8MB of RAM, for example, your system probably won't be able to effectively multitask applications, thus reducing the usefulness of the larger monitor.

Upgrading Your Monitor

Follow these steps to upgrade your existing monitor:

1. Set Windows 95 to VGA resolution by right-clicking the Windows 95 desktop and choosing Properties. Click the Settings tab.
2. Click the Color palette drop-down list and select 256 Color.
3. Click the slider bar in the Desktop area control, moving the control to the left until it reads 640 by 480 pixels. Click OK to make the new settings take effect.
4. When prompted to restart the PC, click No. Then shut down the PC.
5. Locate the monitor connector that plugs into the back of the graphics board. Unscrew the two securing screws, and pull the connector clear of the adapter board.
6. Remove the old monitor from the desktop, and place it out of the way.
7. Place the new monitor on the desktop and plug the cable into the back of the graphics adapter.
8. Secure the cable connector by twisting the two screws clockwise.
9. Boot up the PC and turn on the monitor.
10. Install the new monitor driver software. Place the floppy disk from the monitor package into your PC's A: drive.
11. Right-click the Windows 95 desktop, choose Properties, and click the Settings tab. Click the Change Display Type button.
12. Click the Change button. In the dialog box that appears, click the Have Disk button.
13. Use the dialog box to locate the .INF file, and click OK.

Once installation is complete, you can change the graphics settings to suit your desired resolution and color depth.

Repair

Repairing a monitor is an unlikely scenario. In fact, attempting to open a monitor to repair it can result in fatal injury, because thousands of volts of electricity can be stored inside. Even after the display has been unplugged, a lethal charge can reside inside the monitor.

Caution: At the risk of sounding redundant, I'm going to say it again: Do not tinker with the inside of your CRT monitor. CRT displays produce thousands of volts of electricity in order to create the focused electron beam lighting up your monitor screen. This energy can remain in the electron gun assembly well after the monitor has been turned off and unplugged. You are risking fatal injury by prying open the case. And if that's not enough, you're also voiding the warranty.

Summary

Ultimately, the monitor is your window to the digital world inside your PC. If you spend long hours working at the computer, a large, high-resolution display can make all the difference. Additional screen real estate will cut down on time-consuming scrolling and hunting through windows, while high refresh rates and sharp images will reduce eye strain and headaches.

As with so many other purchases, choosing a monitor is a subjective decision. Some people like the bright, TV-like output of NEC and Sony displays, and others opt for the subdued tone of monitors from MAG Innovision. Still, no matter what your preference, one rule holds firm: Bigger is better. You should buy as much monitor as you can afford.

Digital Video Capture

About five years ago, the marketing whizzes at Intel figured the PC buying public needed a good reason to keep spending money for faster and faster processors. Word processors and spreadsheets, they figured, had all the horsepower they needed (this was before the release of Office 97). Intel's solution was to push PC-based digital video as a productivity application.

This effort had an impact that can be seen throughout this book. PC-based videoconferencing received early attention from Intel through its ISDN-based ProShare product, and Intel successfully positioned its Indeo compression scheme (known as a *codec*) as a standard for delivering software-based video clips.

Today, several years after Intel's first efforts, video enjoys an expanding role in PC communications and interaction. The Internet provides a standard transport for low-cost videoconferencing, while the growing availability of digital ISDN phone lines, emerging cable and ADSL service, and 56KBps modems enable home- and business-oriented videoconferencing applications. Sophisticated editing software, low-cost video capture hardware, and the emergence of cheap, multigigabyte hard disks have all contributed to the availability of video as a mainstream endeavor.

Add Intel's video-savvy MMX processor enhancements, and most mainstream PCs now possess the horsepower and storage capacity to handle video playback and editing. All that's needed is a single-card video-capable upgrade to fill in the last pieces of the puzzle.

This chapter covers the following:

- The basics of PC-based video and key issues such as compression and file formats
- Videoconferencing hardware and applications
- Installing video hardware
- Troubleshooting and repair for video capture hardware

Video Capture Comes Home

Until very recently, the only reliable way to get video into your PC was by way of a video capture card. Unfortunately, capture boards are both pricey and somewhat difficult to install, though they remain the best option for those seeking to capture high-quality video. For consumer-level video, external adapters such as the Play Inc.'s Snappy let you grab clips from your camcorder or other device for less than $300. Finally, videoconferencing gets a boost from affordable, monitor-top cameras that plug into your USB or parallel port.

When capturing video, the capture card or module receives the analog video signal from an input device, such as a VCR or television. The signals, which are transported over an S-Video, composite video, or other connector, are processed in real time as they reach the capture hardware. Each individual frame of video is converted—including the synched audio—to digital format, and is written to your PC's hard disk.

Capturing video is difficult work, since your PC's processor must often play a critical role in moving and processing the incoming data. In addition, a fast hard disk, plentiful RAM, and speedy interface all help to improve results. Parallel port-based capture devices, for example, can not offer the video quality and flexibility PCI-based video capture boards provide. These modules must crunch video down to a highly-compressed digital format before the data is sent over the parallel port interface to your PC's hard disk drive.

The lack of bandwidth on the parallel port means that resolutions, frame rates, and image quality must all be compromised to keep data rates low enough. PCI-based video capture boards, on the other hand, can easily move 5MBps of data or more, enabling users to capture video to formats at high resolution, high quality, and fast frame rates.

This section will describe the various video capture hardware devices available and how they work. The primary options are:

- Video capture boards: Corporate or professional grade video creation and editing
- Combination graphics card/video capture: Consumer grade video creation and editing
- External video capture modules: Corporate or consumer grade video creation and editing
- Monitor-top cameras: PC-based videoconferencing

Video Capture Applications

Video capture might seem like a neat application, but who really needs it? After all, capturing video takes a fast Pentium system with a large and fast hard disk and plenty of RAM. In other words, you need a cutting-edge setup to do video capture, right?

Recent market advances, however, make professional-quality video capture available to most new systems. A Pentium II-400 PC with 64MB of RAM and an 8GB EIDE hard disk costs about $1,800. Throw in a $999 video capture card, and this mainstream desktop PC can support all but the most demanding video compression. Of course, people who have older systems might have to lower their expectations.

Still, not all video input is about producing professional-looking clips. Videoconferencing, for example, employs low-bandwidth (and low-quality) video along with audio and data communications. Other products, such as Play, Inc.'s Snappy, can produce brief clips and high-quality snapshots from an analog source.

Videoconferencing

Probably the fastest-growing video application, videoconferencing enables PC users make video calls over standard or digital ISDN phone lines. Unlike traditional video capture, videoconferencing melds modem-based communications, video capture, and real-time video playback into a single application. Although videoconferencing requires much less video fidelity than traditional capture applications, the need to juggle other sundry tasks makes it an extremely demanding application.

You need the following components in order to make videoconferencing happen on your PC:

- A monitor-top camera
- A video-enabled v.80 modem (33.6 or 56KBps) or ISDN adapter
- A video input for the camera (a video input card, parallel port, or other device)
- Recommended: A video-accelerating graphics card and an MMX-enhanced processor
- Videoconferencing software
- Someone on the other end with a similar setup to receive your video call

Most of these components are provided in videoconferencing upgrade kits. Upgrade kits from companies such as Intel, Creative Labs, and Diamond Multimedia cost anywhere from $199 to $599 and give you everything you need to make video calls over standard analog phone lines (see Figure 20.1). ISDN-based videoconferencing systems, which generally cost $200 to $500 more than analog systems, provide higher-quality communications due to the 128-bit potential data rate provided by the digital connection. If you purchase a new system, you can have it preconfigured for videoconferencing.

INSTANT REFERENCE | For more on ISDN, see Chapter 21, "Modems."

FIGURE 20.1.

Diamond's Video Phone Kit includes a video-capable modem and parallel port monitor-top camera to let Pentium-class PCs handle video calls over standard phone lines. (Photo courtesy of Diamond Multimedia)

Note: Have you seen those AT&T commercials showing a doctor teleconferencing with a patient? If so, strike it from your memory—that isn't reality. The simple truth is that any video that happens over a phone line (even a digital ISDN line) will look terrible. Small video windows, blurry graphics, lost frames, and poor lip-synching all plague desktop videoconferencing. The problem is bandwidth.

Analog calls produce frame rates between 1 and 10 frames per second, depending on the quality of the hardware, noise in the connection, and the nature of the video. Motion in the camera's viewing area will drop frame rates drastically as the codec throws out visual bits in an effort to keep the video data stream within the requirements of a 33.6KBps connection. Audio and video synching will also suffer under these conditions. Even ISDN-based videoconferencing won't provide professional-quality results, although it can pass muster for one-on-one business conferences.

Low-End Video Capture

Another video capture application is the use of inexpensive cameras and devices to capture short clips or still images. Play's $99 Snappy adapter, for example, plugs into a parallel port and grabs high-resolution still images from an analog video source. The Connectix QuickCam camera also uses the parallel or USB port. Available in both black-and-white and color versions, this small camera can capture video up to 15 frames per second and at resolutions of 320×240 pixels.

Note: If you have a Windows 98 PC with USB ports, definitely consider a USB camera rather than a parallel port model. USB offers much higher data rates and easier installation.

Another affordable option is graphics cards which include video inputs. ATI's Expert@Play and Diamond Multimedia's DTV 2000 (shown in Figure 20.2) both let you capture video from an external camera, TV, or VCR.

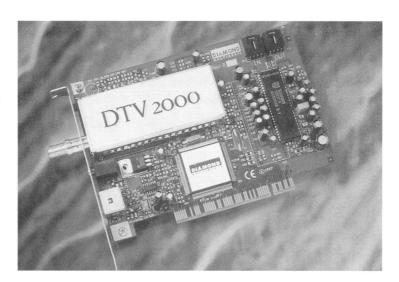

FIGURE 20.2.
Diamond's DTV 2000 captures video from broadcast or cable TV and displays it on your monitor. (Photo courtesy of Diamond Multimedia)

These applications are appropriate for spot capture duty and low-resolution video production. The QuickCam even comes in a videoconferencing package, although the quality of the call falls below that of dedicated conferencing products. Still, for spot work, the QuickCam and similar products are versatile options.

Video Capture Card: The Professional's Choice

To capture reasonable-quality digital video, you'll need a dedicated video capture board specializing in turning analog video into digital format. These boards include hardware to compress incoming signals into popular compressed video formats, easing the load on your system and enhancing the quality of the compressed video. Just as important, your PC needs to be up to the task of handling video capture.

Video capture boards can range widely in price and features. For example, low-cost hybrid boards such as ATI's PC2TV provide inputs for a VCR or TV in addition to functioning as a graphics and video accelerator. True video capture cards, on the other hand, limit themselves to capturing and compressing incoming analog video. Even these products can range widely in price and features, from $199 to $2,000 and more. Among the affordable products in this range is the Pinnacle MicroVideo DC-20 Plus.

You'll generally find the following components and functions on a typical video capture board:

- Analog video inputs
- Analog video outputs (to a TV or VCR)
- Analog-to-digital converter (ADC) and filtering hardware
- Digital video compression hardware
- Effects acceleration hardware
- System bus connection

All these features typically reside on a single add-in card, as shown in Figure 20.3. When the board is installed in a PC, the backplate contains a number of ports for moving data in and out of the PC. Video and audio inputs and outputs let you move video to and from TVs and VCRs.

FIGURE 20.3.
Data Translation's Broadway 2.5 MPEG capture card includes a chip for encoding analog video to MPEG format in real time. (Photo courtesy of Data Translation)

Analog Input

Needless to say, video capture boards are all about input. In order to capture video, you need to send an analog signal from a source such as a TV or VCR. The input ports on the board determine what quality the board can produce. There are three types of input: S-Video, Composite, and Component.

- Composite: The least expensive video connection, composite video mixes all the elements of the video signal into a single port. Although it's useful for saving space and reducing cost, bundling the video signal together results in lost fidelity and limits its usefulness for high-quality video clips.

- S-Video: These ports are found on almost all capture boards. They represent the best input choice for budget-minded home and business video capture. Most VCRs and camcorders, for example, use S-Video connections to move video out to other devices. S-Video splits the signal into two parts: One part has color information, and the other has brightness information.

- Component: Professionals will want to look for component video inputs for their capture boards. This scheme splits the video signal into three parts—brightness, color, and hue. Component video is more precise than S-Video. Expect boards with component video inputs, such as Truevision's Targa 1000 Pro board, to cost $2,000 or more. Of course, your analog device—whether a camera or VCR tape deck—must provide component video outputs.

In addition, better capture boards provide audio inputs. Although the audio capture components probably duplicate what is present on your sound board, the added cost yields better playback quality. The reason is that integrated audio capture allows for much more precise timing when stitching sounds and images into a video clip. When audio is handled on a separate board, several clocks get involved in determining which audio bits are matched with which image bits. When this process happens on one board, a single clock is used to synchronize audio and images.

Analog Video Output

Although many video capture boards might be intended for producing digital video to other PCs, the most common distribution format remains the familiar VHS cassette tape. Analog output ports enable you to move edited video clips to tape as well as review your work on a television monitor before saving. The output ports used by video boards (just described) generally match up with those provided for input.

Analog-to-Digital Converter (ADC) and Filtering Hardware

Once analog video signals get onto the board, they must be converted to 1s and 0s. As just mentioned, some boards accept both audio and image streams, and others allow the existing sound card to do the work of digitizing audio for incorporation into the video stream later. In either case, a dedicated audio cable delivers the analog signal to an analog-to-digital converter (ADC) for conversion.

In either case, both audio and video signals are filtered to remove extraneous noise and interference that can impair quality. All boards provide this service, although the quality of filtering varies. Generally, expect to pay more for better filtering.

Audio sampling takes place as it does with any sound board. The incoming waveform is sampled up to 44,100 times per second, with as many as 16 bits of data dedicated to each sample. The resulting digital version of the audio stream is kept in lockstep with the video so that it can be stitched together with it later.

Like audio, inbound video is sampled from an analog signal. The board takes snapshots of the incoming series of images—called *frames*—taking up to 60 snapshots each second. The video is then interleaved with the digital audio signal to create a digital video stream.

Digital Video Compression Hardware

Turning an analog video stream into digital bits is tough, but compressing these bits is the real challenge. Until a few years ago, only boards costing $2,000 or more featured on-board compression hardware that let you capture directly to a compressed video format. Most boards captured to an intermediate format featuring only modest compression, putting a lot of strain on the system CPU, bus, and hard disk. The result was that frame rates and fidelity suffered.

The professional compression standard for video capture is a scheme called Motion JPEG (Joint Photographic Experts Group). This codec compresses data within each frame—a process called *intraframe compression*—to squeeze video down by a factor of 5 to 100. By keeping each frame intact, authors can use editing software such as Adobe Premiere to conduct precise frame-by-frame edits of the digital video file. Some boards offer different on-the-fly compression schemes, such as MPEG and Indeo Video Interactive.

Peter's Principle: Which Video Compression Scheme Do You Need?

Capturing video is all about compression. Raw digital video files are simply too huge to be managed by desktop PCs. Thirty frames of true-color video at a modest 320×240 resolution adds up to over 6.5MB of data per second. That's over 395MB each minute before you add in sound.

All compression schemes, called codecs, cut video down to size by doing two things: coding blocks of redundant information in each frame into a space-saving format, and selectively filtering visual data to reduce the amount of data in the video stream. In addition, many video codecs identify and discard redundant data between frames. Called *interframe compression*, this scheme demands much processing work on both the compression and playback side, since several frames must be assessed at one time.

If you want to be able to edit captured video, you should use an intraframe compression scheme, such as Motion JPEG. The file will be a little larger than it needs to be, but each frame contains all the data used to display the video image to enable frame-accurate editing.

On the other hand, if you want to simply convert analog video to digital format, an interframe codec such as MPEG or Indeo 4.0 is your best bet. These produce more compact files than intraframe codecs and enjoy a wider installed base of playback drivers on mainstream PCs. Of course, interframe compression will limit your editing options down the road.

> **Note:** Compression schemes that throw out unneeded data are called *lossy*, meaning that they lose some of the original data. Those that strictly crunch existing bits (such as PK Zip) are called *lossless*. Obviously, lossy schemes won't work on data and executable files, which must remain intact in order to work. This is one reason why PK Zip and disk compression systems attain top compression ratios of about 2 to 1, while the lossy Motion JPEG codec reaches 100 to 1. The M-JPEG scheme can discard reams of visual data without incapacitating the video file—although the quality of the clip suffers as more data is discarded.

Digital Video Formats

Compression is a key consideration when it comes to video capture and editing. When you handle compressed video, it is saved to a specific format which other devices and applications can understand. Apple's QuickTime is the most popular mainstream video format, having become very popular among CD-ROM title makers who want to be able to provide reasonable-quality video able to play back on a wide range of Pentium-class PCs. Microsoft's AVI file format—for audio-video interleave—is also quite popular. Both formats are able to support multiple compression schemes. So an AVI file can be encoded with either Indeo or Cinepak.

QuickTime and AVI are the most popular formats now, but more powerful PCs are pushing video quality to new heights. The MPEG (Motion Picture Experts Group) format provides adequate quality video that can play back on even a modest CD-ROM drive. The highly-compact format and compression scheme allows up to 70 minutes of video to be stored on a 650MB CD-ROM disc. MPEG has become popular for Web-distributed video files.

The emergence of DVD-ROM drives has brought the first broadcast-quality video format to PCs—MPEG-2. A 4.7GB DVD-ROM drive can typically hold two hours of MPEG-2 video, enough for a feature film. The visual quality of MPEG-2 is stunning—in fact, it's the same format used by direct broadcast satellite providers such as DirecTV and PrimeStar. However, MPEG-2 is difficult to decode without dedicated hardware. If you try to playback an MPEG-2 video file on a Pentium II-400 system, you will likely experience some dropped frames, particularly if you try to do anything else while the video plays.

Perhaps the hottest video format arena is in so-called streaming video. These Web-centric formats allow video to play on a remote PC even as the rest of the file is still being transferred over a network. The most popular streaming video format is RealVideo.

System Bus Connection

When it comes to video capture, there really is no question—the PCI bus is the one and only option. Even with on-board, on-the-fly compression to squish video streams down to size, the amount of data is enormous. Heavily compressed MPEG-1 video might require only 150KBps of data, but higher-quality clips will go much higher. A good Motion JPEG-compressed video can run at 5MBps or higher.

The PCI bus brings a couple of key talents to the capture game. For one, a capture board can take advantage of the 132MBps peak sustained throughput of the PCI bus (versus just 5MBps for ISA). Furthermore, PCI bus mastering capability means the board can send digitized video directly to an SCSI hard disk without the intervention of the system processor. Both characteristics enable high-quality digital video capture at high frame rates.

External Capture Modules: Best for Home

A video capture board is great if you need to capture and edit high-quality video. But if all you want to do is grab still frames from your TV or camcorder, and maybe put together a short video, an internal board is probably overkill. After all, capture cards require a PCI slot and attendant IRQ and DMA resources—many of which can be in short supply. And hardware conflicts with these devices aren't unheard of.

For modest work, therefore, an external module is a great idea. No, you won't get stunning, 800 by 600 clips captured to frame-editable Motion JPEG format. But you can get serviceable digital video at a low cost and a minimum of hassle. Best of all, you can share the external device with other desktop and notebook PCs.

Generally, there are two classes of products:

- Single-frame capture only
- Frame and video capture

Single frame products can only capture still images from a video source. These are useful if you want to grab images from your home movies to use as digital photographs, for example, or maybe want to built a montage of still from a video. These products can be quite affordable.

The market-leader is the $100 Snappy device, from Play, Inc. (see Figure 20.4). This handy little device captures stunning 1,500×1,125 pixel images over the PC's parallel port. The AIMS Labs GrabIT II costs just $50 and offers even higher 2,400×1,800 resolution—though this does not ultimately determine overall picture quality. The tiny yellow adapter attaches to the parallel port and lets you capture single images at resolutions.

Video capture over an external module can be a bit dicey on low-cost hardware, but is a nice added feature if you don't expect too much. Connectix's QuickClip USB attaches to a PC's USB port and can capture color video at 15 frames per second at resolutions as high as 320 by 240. Of course, it also grabs still images.

If you are willing to spend $200 or so, you can get an external adapter that compresses video before it gets to your PC. The compressed data stream can provide 30 frame per second video without overworking slow parallel ports. The Iomega Buz and Pinnacle Studio 400 both offer this capability.

Figure 20.4.
The Play Snappy enables you to capture vivid still images from a source video such as a VHS tape or camcorder. (Photo courtesy of Play, Inc.)

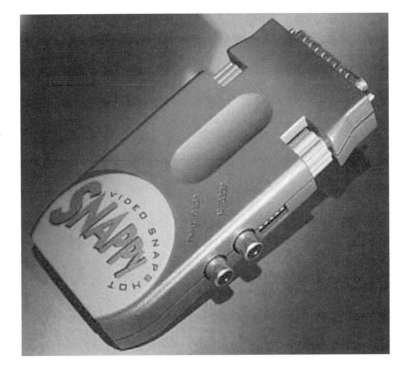

Monitor-Top Cameras

This class of product was among the first to move over to the USB bus, and if you are running Windows 98 on a USB-equipped system, I recommend you go with a USB version of a camera. The bus is fast enough to handle the low-resolution video needed for videoconferencing, and eliminates many of the installation hassles.

Just be sure you know what you are getting. Unlike capture modules, you won't be able to use these cameras to grab video from a source tape or device. And because the camera must be physically attached to your PC to grab video or stills, you can't use it as a stand-alone camera. But if you want to be able to conduct video conferences and perhaps capture still images of objects in the office, these cameras make a nice addition.

The Connectix QuickCam (see Figure 20.5) practically invented this market, but a variety of other products are also available. Intel's Create & Share bundle offers excellent software for videoconferencing, image capture, and image management. And if you don't have a USB port on your system, you can get the PCI version, which uses a dedicated board to capture video and audio.

Figure 20.5.
The Connectix QuickCam USB is compact, effective, and easy to install, thanks to its USB interface. (Photo courtesy of Connectix)

Purchase Decisions

If you're in the market for a video capture board, you need to consider what you expect to do. A video capture board appropriate for producing low-bandwidth MPEG video for playback on a CD-ROM drive won't fit the bill for producing high-resolution output bound for super-VHS tape.

Types of Capture Boards

There is a wide range of video capture boards. When you're looking, the following points should guide your buying decision:

- Video source: VHS, 8mm; super-VHS, super-8; Beta 1
- Video target: CD-ROM, hard disk, VHS, or super-VHS tape
- Editing goals: Precise editing, no editing
- Compression scheme: MPEG-1, Motion JPEG, Indeo, or Cinepak

The most versatile video boards use Motion JPEG compression, which enables you to save to an editable format and then recompress to a more compact scheme such as MPEG-1, or output to VHS or another tape format for analog playback. Less-expensive models lack M-JPEG editing.

Generally, capture boards fall into three categories:

- Under $500: Low-cost boards that use the system CPU to compress video to Indeo or Cinepak format.

- $800 to $1,400: Midrange boards with hardware for compressing to Motion JPEG, Indeo Video Interactive, or MPEG-1 formats.
- $2,000 and over: High-end boards with hardware for compressing to Motion JPEG or MPEG-1 formats. Also includes composite video inputs and outputs and accelerated effects generation.

The midrange boards provide the best combination of features and price. These products offer professional-looking results for less than $1,000. These products can help you whether you want to move your home videos to CD-ROM or edit hours of footage down to a few minutes and then record it back to VHS tape.

Otherwise, if all you need is something to nab still images from your VHS tapes, an external module, such as the Play Snappy is your best bet. For videoconferencing, look to a monitor top camera such as Intel's Create and Share or Connectix's QuickCam USB.

Compatibility Concerns

Before you buy, be certain that the board you purchase will work in your system. Some products are optimized for the Windows NT operating system and might lack drivers for Windows 95. Even if a capture board does have Windows 95 drivers, it might be optimized for NT. As a result, performance under Windows 95 might be disappointing.

Of course, you need to match the board with the add-in card bus in your system. Today, you'll have a hard time finding a video capture card for ISA or VL bus slots. Also be sure that the board you buy can fit inside the space available in your PC. Often, capture boards are full-length affairs, requiring more space than many compact systems provide.

Also make sure the capture card you buy will work with your existing graphics hardware. Although most PCI-based capture cards will work with most graphics boards, some products still might want things their own way. This is particularly true of ISA-based capture boards, which often provide a dedicated graphics card connection (or even force you to throw out your graphics card) in order to work. Also make sure your system supports bus mastering PCI—while current motherboards do offer this streamlined data transfer feature, older Pentium systems may not.

The Big Picture

If you want to purchase a capture board, you need to think big—not big bucks, big picture. To snap a few shots of your newborn, a $99 QuickCam will do the trick, while Play's Snappy lets you nab quick snapshots from a TV broadcast. Alternatively, you could invest in a graphics board that includes capture capability. Expect resolutions to be limited to 320×240 and compression to be handled by the host CPU.

If you want to convert hours of camcorder video to digital format—whether for edited output to tape or archived to CD-ROM—your investment gets more substantial. Here you'll need the talents of a true video capture board.

In order to get at least VHS-quality results, you'll need to spend about $800 to $1,200 on a Motion-JPEG capture card. Other alternatives exist as well. Data Translation's Broadway will capture your tapes straight to MPEG-1 format—perfect for moving your clips to CD-ROM while preserving video quality. Digital Video Arts' WakeBoard Multimedia Pro uses Intel's Indeo 4.0 codec to provide a similar level of quality. Both provide interim formats allowing for frame-accurate editing.

Beyond this price, you enter the level of video production products. Better input filtering, enhanced special effects handling, and multichannel audio all set these products apart.

In all cases, you can expect to get some software in the deal. For true video capture boards, look for applications such as Adobe's Premiere 4.2 or Ulead Video Studio. Unfortunately, you are very likely to only get a limited version of the software with the board bundle. These slimmed down editions typically leave out important features. You may be able to purchase a full-featured package at a bargain price, however, if vendors offer upgrade pricing for users of existing video editing products.

Diagnosing/Troubleshooting

Video capture is a complex task involving many of the components of your PC. Problems that arise might reside in the video capture card itself, or they might come from the hard disk, sound card, operating system, capture software, or even the analog source device. One thing to keep in mind is that it often takes several passes to get things right. A healthy respect for trial and error will help you solve most glitches and obtain the best results.

Capture Setup

Getting ready to capture video is as important as—if not more important than—the actual act of capturing itself. Before you can begin pulling in a video stream, you need to define many parameters, from the name of the file to be created to the video's frame rate and format. Often, neglecting to pay attention to one of these details can yield subpar video or result in unexpected trouble.

Because the software used to capture video varies from product to product, I can't give you precise step-by-step instructions. However, I can tell you what you probably need to be aware of. From there, it should be a simple matter of making the proper settings in your capture software. Of course, you should make sure to check the software documentation and online help system for specific information and tips.

Preparing the System

Before you start capturing, you need to make sure your system is ready for the task. Here are a few tips that can help boost the quality of your captured video:

- Check your specs: You'll need a fast Pentium CPU and a large 2GB or more hard disk to ensure reasonable capture. Although you can get by on 32MB of RAM and an EIDE hard disk, you're better off with 64MB of RAM and a fast SCSI hard disk.

- Defragment the hard disk: During capture, digitized video is laid down on the hard disk as it's captured, making the disk a potential bottleneck that can result in lost frames. Before you start, defragment the hard disk using Windows 95 Defrag or another utility. It's also a good idea to do a surface scan of the disk once in a while. These steps will allow video data to be laid down contiguously, speeding performance.

- Shut down software: Turn off any unnecessary background utilities or applications. These consume valuable system memory and CPU resources. Network software, in particular, chews up a lot of CPU time as it prompts your system to keep a constant eye out for traffic.

- Work with the latest: Make sure that the compression software you use is up-to-date. Current versions can provide more attractive results and demand less horsepower.

Lights, Camera, Action

Once your system is up to snuff, you can get ready to capture video. There's a good deal of setup involved, and neglecting any part of it will result in problems. Before you start capturing, make sure you have done the following:

- Watch those wires: Make sure your cables are properly set up. Make sure the red and yellow S-Video leads match up with the same-colored connectors on both the output device (camcorder, VCR, and so on) and the capture board. Also, you may have to connect an internal CD-Audio link wire from the capture card to your sound card.

- Set your source: Make sure you set your capture program to recognize the inbound analog signal. Most U.S. users will select NTSC. Likewise, you'll need to set the source device from among selections such as S-Video, Composite Video, and Component Video.

- Define your target: Before capturing, you need to tell the program how to save the inbound video. Set the compression type (Motion JPEG is typical for digital editing jobs) as well as the pixel resolution and color depth. You can also set the frame rate to as high as 60 fields per second. You'll also need to provide a filename and location for the video file.

Technical Note: When people talk about units of video, they speak of frames. *Frames* are the atomic unit of digital video—the individual snapshots that, when played in rapid succession, create the illusion of motion. Your TV displays video at 30 frames per second (fps), the same pace considered optimal for PC-based video. Movies actually run at 24fps. For PCs, 15fps is considered the acceptable minimum frame rate before playback becomes noticeably jerky.

Although 30fps is considered the optimal video frame rate, some capture boards actually go higher. The best boards provide the ability to capture 60 *fields* per second. At this level, each frame of video consists of two fields. The additional captured information provides incrementally improved playback.

Symptoms and Solutions

In case you're having trouble with your video capture, the following is a short list of things you can look into.

Distorted Video Picture

- Confirm that the input video source matches the incoming NTSC, PAL, or SECAM signal.
- Make sure the source tape and playback device are in good working order.
- Try replacing the video cable.

Sound and Video Both Fail to Work

- Make sure that all cables are properly installed.
- Check the IRQ and DMA settings of your sound and video capture boards. A resource conflict will cause these peripherals to fail.
- Check your sources. Remember, the output source of your VCR, camcorder or other device must be properly selected in order for a signal to be sent to your capture card.
- Test the output on another display device. If you don't seem to be getting anything from your camcorder, for example, try plugging the camcorder into your TV and see if anything is displayed. If nothing turns up, the problem is likely with the camcorder or its settings, not the capture card.

Video Fails to Display

If there is no video, try changing the video input source to the correct setting. If you aren't sure which is correct, try different settings among S-Video, Composite video, and Component video.

Sound Fails to Work

- Make sure that the capture program is set to record audio.
- If there is no sound with an S-Video configuration, make sure that a separate audio cable has been set up, because S-Video doesn't carry audio signals.
- Check the sound level on the analog source device.
- Check the sound level on your sound board. Also make sure that speakers are properly plugged in and turned on.

Upgrading for Video Capture

Unfortunately, installing a video capture board ranks right up there with installing a sound board as a surefire way to ruin a weekend. For this reason alone, you should think carefully about a video capture upgrade before you jump into it.

The following section will step you through installing two major video input-related upgrades—a videoconferencing system and a video capture board.

Upgrading to a Videoconferencing System

Adding videoconferencing to a PC is difficult because so many subsystems are involved. Assuming that you have an older modem, you might need to install a new modem and sound card. The following components might be involved:

- Video capture card
- 33.6 or 56KBps modem with v.80 video handling capability, or ISDN adapter
- Monitor-top camera
- Microphone and speakers (integrated into a headset or separate)
- Full-duplex sound card
- Video-aware graphics accelerator

> **Caution:** If you're attempting to upgrade a networked PC, think hard about what you're about to do. Videoconferencing upgrades are tough under normal circumstances, but they get brutal when you try to put these components on top of a networked system. If you're in an office environment, you should make sure that your IS staff does the upgrade. For home or small office networks, consider removing the network card and drivers, turning the PC into a stand-alone desktop. Once you've successfully installed the video capture board, you can try to reinstall the network hardware.

> **Tip:** Many kits include everything listed except the sound and graphics cards. However, PCs purchased within the last year or two probably include the proper graphics and sound hardware. Check your system documentation to see if full-duplex audio and video-accelerated graphics are supported. You might even be able to avoid buying an upgrade kit if all you need is a single upgrade for, say, the video input and camera.

Because videoconferencing systems incorporate so many features, installation routines will vary widely. As a rule, it's a good idea to proceed with caution. Before you start, make a point to record all your current hardware settings—IRQs, DMAs, address ranges, and the like. Also record any free resources that might be available. That way, you'll have a ready inventory of available resources that you can apply to the new hardware.

> **Caution:** To their credit, vendors try to ease upgrades by using software to automatically find free resources for the new hardware to use. However, these resources can fail and can even result in system crashes and aborted installation routines. Don't leave this to chance. Make sure you record your system's resource profile before you start, so that you can take control if the need arises.

Video Capture Hardware

Depending on the package, a separate video capture board might be included in the box. Higher-end ISDN-based conferencing products, in particular, employ dedicated video capture hardware to receive analog signals from the camera and compress them into digital format for transmission.

Less-expensive systems, such as those that work over analog phone lines, often lack hardware-assisted compression and decompression. These products call on the system CPU to do the hard work of crunching in- and out-bound video data into manageable sizes. This scheme puts a lot of pressure on the CPU and limits video quality, but it can save $100 to $300. In either case, the video capture capabilities might be combined with communications hardware on a single card, saving valuable add-in slots.

Communications Hardware

There are two classes of videoconferencing products: those that work over standard analog phone lines, and those that work over fast ISDN phone lines. Generally, ISDN-based products are appropriate for business applications, and standard phone line packages will work for consumers. The primary difference is video quality. The 128KBps data rate of an ISDN connection is nearly four times that of the optimal 33.6KBps connection possible over analog modems.

> **Note:** ISDN has many advantages when it comes to videoconferencing. In addition to the 4X data rate advantage, the all-digital ISDN communication scheme avoids the vagaries involved in working with analog tones to transmit data. Line noise and drop-outs, which sap bandwidth and unceremoniously end connections on standard modem calls, are simply not a problem with ISDN. Call connection is also much quicker, since the digital link doesn't require the time-consuming handshake process needed by modems.
>
> The drawback is that a very small percentage of homes and businesses have ISDN lines installed. Your ability to use ISDN videoconferencing will be limited to the small universe of fellow ISDN customers who have videoconferencing systems installed. In contrast, analog phone lines are universal.

INSTANT REFERENCE For more information on ISDN and communications, see Chapter 21, "Modems."

Today, most users will consider an analog setup, if only to enjoy the widespread compatibility that a modem-based package delivers. The modem in these packages should be a 56Kbps model that complies with the v.90 specification. While these modems don't transfer upstream data any faster than earlier 33.6Kbps models, the newer circuitry in these models can help you attain higher sustained transfer rates even under difficult line conditions. These modems also include support for a standard called v.80 that enables efficient handling of video over analog phone lines.

> **Technical Note:** You can't use any old 28.8KBps modem for videoconferencing. In order for the modem to work with the H.324 video standard employed in analog videoconferencing packages, it must support an industry protocol known as v.80. This protocol determines how videoconferencing software runs on analog modems, providing a streamlined path for video and audio coming over the wire. Before buying a modem, make sure that v.80 support is built in so that you can take advantage of software-based videoconferencing packages in the future.

As with the video hardware, the modem may be combined with video and audio handling onto a single card. This integration might help avoid space constraints, but it won't reduce system resource requirements. Whether on a single card or scattered among three separate cards, the video, communication, and audio hardware needs the same system resources in order to function.

Full-Duplex Sound

One area that gets overlooked is audio hardware. With all the excitement over being able to see other people during a video phone call, it's probably not surprising that speech gets short shrift. After all, we're already used to gabbing on the phone. But PCs aren't designed to be telephones. The sound hardware in your system might lack even the rudimentary features that make your $9 phone such a useful device.

You'll need the following features in your sound card or hardware in order to make videoconferencing effective:

- Full-duplex audio
- Noise cancellation
- Microphone and speakers (or, better yet, a headset)

Full-Duplex Audio

By far, the most important feature is full-duplex audio operation. *Full-duplex* means that your sound card can simultaneously accept both sound input and output. Consider a speakerphone. Better speakerphones enable both you and the other party to talk at the same time, while cheaper models cut off the incoming audio when you speak. In much the same way, full-duplex sound boards allow you to both speak and hear at the same time.

The problem is that most older cards provide only half-duplex capability. If the card is accepting sound, it can't produce audio output. If the card is playing sound, it can't accept incoming audio. In the case of videoconferencing, this means that one person's speech gets cut off when someone else decides to speak. If you own a Creative Labs Sound Blaster card, however, you may be able to upgrade your hardware by way of a device driver. The result: Your half-duplex card becomes a full-duplex model.

Noise Cancellation

Noise cancellation is critical to full-duplex operation. If you use desktop speakers, the sound from them will reach the microphone. The result is that your audio card ends up listening to the same sound input from both ends, making it impossible to use the microphone for speech.

Noise cancellation knocks out duplicate input by filtering the analog wave signals. Noise-cancelling microphones also eliminate extraneous sounds that come from the periphery—such as office noises. So-called unidirectional microphones help focus on the speaker's input only.

Microphone and Speakers

For best videoconferencing results, you might consider using a headset microphone. The proximity of the microphone to your face will cut down on extraneous sounds being picked up, while the headset speakers reduce interference and desk clutter. A headset with a nice long cord also allows for better hands-free operation, since the microphone always moves with you.

Many kits also use lapel microphones that clip onto your shirt or collar. Like a headset, these microphones stay with you when you move in your chair or walk around. However, they require external speakers. One advantage is that a compact lapel microphone won't mess up your hair.

Finally, desktop microphones keep you free of entangling wires. Just make sure that the unit provides unidirectional operation so that it won't pick up every sound in your home or office. Also make a point to keep it away from your desktop speakers to avoid feedback.

Graphics Accelerator

A graphics card won't usually be part of a videoconferencing upgrade kit, but you might need to invest in a new one nevertheless. To get reasonable results from video playback, you'll need a graphics card that can take some of the processing burden off your CPU.

INSTANT REFERENCE   For more on graphics boards, see Chapter 17, "New Dimensions: Graphics Accelerators."

Fortunately, nearly every mainstream graphics board now includes a strong suite of video-handling features. Color space conversion lets your graphics board turn video data into a format recognized by your display, while pixel interpolation lets you zoom up tiny video windows without producing horrendous blockiness.

Not even a video-savvy graphics card can turn spotty modem-based video into VHS-quality fare, but it can help improve a bad situation. More importantly, it lets your system do a better job at other tasks, which is critical for sharing applications and data.

Video Capture Card Upgrade

So you want to turn your home or office PC into a desktop video studio. The good news is that a couple hundred bucks and a weekend's worth of work can actually make this happen. The bad news is that it could be a very, very long weekend.

An Ounce of Prevention

The fact is, videoconferencing products remain notoriously difficult to install and use. As with any upgrade, you should note your PC's hardware resources, including IRQ, DMA, and address range resources consumed by components such as your graphics card, sound card, and modem. Also make note of which specific settings are free. Often, adapters will have preferred configurations—Creative's Sound Blaster sound boards, for instance, always want to grab IRQs 5 and 9—so knowing these preferences ahead of time can help avoid problems later.

Once that's done, back up your existing data. Back up both data and system files, because an installation can conceivably wreck key Windows 95 or 98 executable files. Make sure you also have a Windows startup disc handy (including CD-ROM drivers!) so that you can start from scratch if necessary.

Finally, check out the video capture card vendor's Web site for possible driver or installation utility updates. Newer software might eliminate conflict problems with other hardware and even improve capture performance. You might also find online documentation that reveals common problems and solutions—information not available when the manual was put together several months before the release of the software.

Step-by-Step Installation

Installing a video capture card is similar to installing a sound card in that the hardware requires a number of specific IRQ, DMA, and base address resources. For this reason, I can't stress enough how important Plug and Play is to making a video upgrade work.

To install a new video capture card, follow these steps:

1. Shut down the PC, unplug the power cord, and remove the case.

2. Make sure you're properly grounded. Identify an appropriate PCI card for the installation—preferably one that has enough room for a full-length card.

TROUBLESHOOTING

> Older PCI systems might not have PCI bus mastering available in all slots. You might need to refer to system documentation to check which slots are busmaster-enabled. Without bus mastering, your capture card will be unable to achieve maximum performance.
>
> Likewise, some systems don't activate all the PCI slots. You might have to go into the system BIOS (accessed during the boot sequence) to actually turn on PCI bus slots. Again, your system documentation will provide the necessary information.

3. Use a Phillips screwdriver to remove the backplate that lines up with the slot you want to use.

4. Install the video capture card into the PCI slot. Make sure that it is firmly seated.

5. Power up the PC. Windows 95 will detect the new hardware.

6. Insert the video capture card's driver disk into the A: drive.

7. Click the radio button labeled Driver from disk provided by hardware manufacturer, and then click OK.

8. Windows 95 will read the driver information from the disk and attempt to configure the card to match your system. At this time, the setup routine may also begin installing bundled application software.

9. Shut down the PC, screw in the capture card's backplate, and reattach the case.

10. Reboot the system and install the card's application software, which probably can be found on CD-ROM.

Upgrading to External Devices

Fortunately, installing external video capture devices is a lot easier than installing a video capture board. There are no pesky cards to install, and you won't even have to mess with IRQs or DMAs. Of course, you won't be getting that studio-level video quality either, but you knew that before you spent your money, right?

To install a USB monitor top camera or module under Windows 98, all you really need to do is plug in the hardware and wait to be prompted for the driver disc. Often, Windows 98 will find a default driver on the hard disk or the Windows 98 CD-ROM. Once you have things working, you might consider updating the device driver with a later version downloaded from the vendor's Web site. This will help ensure you enjoy the best performance and smooth out any bugs that were found in the earlier software.

If you are running Windows 95, however, things can get a bit more complex. That's because Windows 95 lacks full USB support, so product installations need a bit more hand holding. Before moving to installing the device, you need to make sure USB is running under Windows 95.

For your system to be USB aware, you must be running the most recent version of Windows 95—called OSR 2.1—and have the USB components installed. To see if USB is enabled on your PC, check the Device Manager (click Start, Settings, Control Panel, open the System icon and click the Devices tab). If you see any entries that reference USB in the scrolling list box, you should be set.

If no such reference exists, you may be able to install the drivers from your Windows 95 CD-ROM. Look for the file usbsupp.exe in the other\usb folder on the Windows 95 disc. Launch this file and follow the dialog box instructions to enable USB on your Windows 95 system. If this file is not present, you are out of luck. Your version of Windows 95 is likely too old to accept the upgrade, and Microsoft does not distribute the USB upgrade to consumers.

> **Caution:** Even if you have USB setup on your Windows 95 PC, it may not help. Many product vendors are passing Windows 95 by and only offering USB for Windows 98 PCs. The reason: There have been wide reports of problems with USB device compatibility under Windows 95. In fact, Microsoft itself tells manufacturers to "reconsider" offering USB products for Windows 95, urging them to concentrate on Windows 98 and NT 5.0. If you intend to use USB peripherals, you should consider upgrading to Windows 98 first.

As previously mentioned, installing a USB device under Windows 95 tends to be a bit more involved than under Windows 98. Windows 98 will typically detect a new device when it is plugged in and automatically launch the setup routine. Under Windows 95's less-robust USB model, however, such an assumption simply won't play out.

You should check your documentation and follow its instruction precisely. Below is a typical Windows 95-based USB device installation.

1. Quit all your Windows applications and insert the product setup CD-ROM disc into the CD-ROM drive.

2. Launch the installation routine. You can use the Add New Software facility in the Windows 95 Control Panel, or simply double-click SETUP.EXE on the disc.

3. Follow the instructions in the setup interface. You may be prompted to select the specific product model and bus type (parallel or USB), as well as specify a destination folder for the product's application software.

4. Windows 95-based USB devices should include Microsoft's USB Supplement software to enable the bus under your operating system. The system should be restarted after this supplement is installed (if the program doesn't reboot automatically).

5. Plug the camera or module into a USB port on the back of the computer. Windows 95 should detect the new hardware and install the drivers from the CD-ROM disc in the drive.

6. The device should operate normally.

Summary

Is video capture for you? It might be. Streaming video software for Web sites makes it possible to post your digitized home movies on the Internet. Video capture boards also provide a great way to boil down hours of agonizing video into an entertaining, edited final product. The cards let you distribute to other PCs, or you can play to VHS tape to send to others.

Whether you want it or not, video capture will join the PC platform. Video phone initiatives from Intel and others are pushing things forward, making ubiquitous videoconferencing a possibility in the next few years. Whether you want to try your directorial hand or want to place video calls to Grandma, you should keep an eye on this changing field.

PART VI

Connectivity

Modems

The entire Internet revolution—you know, the one that's changing the face of communications and commerce—comes down to a single, inexpensive device: the modem. Five years ago, modems were just another option on desktop PCs. Today, they are nearly ubiquitous on non-networked PCs.

It's no surprise that modem technology has advanced along with all other aspects of the PC. These advances have improved the speed of transmission over phone lines and added useful capabilities while reducing costs enough to make modems standard issue on even entry-level systems. With PC users making even greater use of the Internet, new modems can have a greater impact on your productivity and experience than any processor or RAM upgrade. In addition, nifty features such as simultaneous voice and data (SVD) and distinctive ring recognition that can route voice, fax, and data calls can help make the most of a single phone line.

This chapter covers

- The workings of PC modem hardware, including analog modems, digital ISDN modems, and new xDSL and cable modems
- How to purchase a new modem that is right for your phone line and needs
- Dealing with and resolving modem problems
- Installing a new modem

Making Sense of Modems

As you probably already know, modems enable PCs to communicate with each other over telephone lines. The word *modem* is a contraction of the term *modulate-demodulate*, which effectively describes how the device turns binary bits into an analog screeching and back again.

It's easy to overlook the hard work modems undertake. Unlike most other PC components, modems straddle the difficult line between the digital universe inside PCs and the analog world we occupy. What's more, these devices must ply bits over a ragged telephone network that is fraught with limited bandwidth, noise, and interference.

Actually, analog modems are only the most common wide-area communications hardware for PCs. People who have digital phone lines—such as Integrated Services Digital Network (ISDN) or the emerging xDSL (digital subscriber line) service—can use all-digital interface devices that support superior performance. Because the vast majority of PCs connect to each other via standard phone lines, we will focus on analog modems.

INSTANT REFERENCE   For more information on ISDN. xDSL, cable modems and other digital connectivity options, see Chapter 22, "Digital Connectivity."

Modem Characteristics

Although all modems essentially do the same thing—provide an interface to the analog phone network—they vary in performance and capabilities. Here are some of the varying capabilities:

- Data rate: The number of bits per second (bps) a modem can send or receive.
- Protocol compliance: Compatibility with international standards to achieve specific data rates and other characteristics.
- Fax: Allows fax transmission and receipt using the PC.
- Error correction: Ensures that data arrives uncorrupted at the other end.
- Compression: Reduces the number of bits in a transmission.
- Telephony support: Combination of hardware and software allowing the modem to act as an answering machine and to provide services such as call forwarding, faxback, and multiple voice mailboxes.
- Distinctive ring: Allows the modem to recognize incoming calls as voice, fax, or data, and to respond accordingly.
- Simultaneous voice and data: Allows voice and data to be carried over the same line on the same call.

A lot of technical stuff goes into making modems work. Generally, you don't need to be up to speed on the very latest International Telecommunication Union (ITU) compliance and other issues, but this can help.

Modem Magic

How do modems communicate? Essentially, they use agreed-upon standard methods to express digital 1s and 0s as analog tones. However, unlike the digital domain, in which the lack of a charge indicates a 0 bit and the presence of a charge indicates a 1 bit, working with analog sound is more troublesome.

Turning Bits into Tones

In order to send and receive 1s and 0s over phone lines, modems must code and decode bits into waveform audio. To do this, modems employ a variety of modulation techniques. At the core of this approach is *frequency key shifting*, which uses standard analog frequencies (or tones) to denote a binary 1 or 0. Table 21.1 lists the frequencies that indicate a 1 or a 0 to a modem.

Table 21.1. Frequency key shifting standards.

Modem Side and Value	Frequency
Sending 0	1,070Hz
Sending 1	1,270Hz
Receiving 0	2,025Hz
Receiving 1	2,225Hz

Imagine two piano players suffering from laryngitis. They can't speak, but they can use their keyboards to respond to yes-or-no questions. Player 1 agrees to use the note A to signify no, while a C note signifies yes. Player 2, in order to avoid confusion with his partner's playing, uses an E to signify no and a high G to signify yes.

While our mute musicians are able to use this code to pass information, the approach runs out of gas fast. Modems take up to three cycles to lock onto a note change, limiting maximum data rates to just 300 bits per second—the rate achieved with the old Bell 103 standard that was the first modem standard.

To squeeze more bits into a transmission, new modems use a method called phase *key modulation*, in which transitions in waveform timing designate a 1 or a 0. By managing and accelerating frequency transitions, modems moved up to speeds of 9,600bps.

Current schemes add volume to the mix, using changing amplitudes to designate additional bit transitions. The result is modems that can reach data rates of 28.8 and 33.6Kbps—more than 100 times faster than the original Bell 103 specification.

Setting Standards

In order for these ambitious modulation schemes to work, however, everybody needs to agree to work the same way. Modems must be able to assume specific frequencies, timings, and amplitudes in the analog signal. They must also be able to tell other modems in some standard way exactly what their capabilities are.

Setting the standards is the International Telecommunications Union (ITU). The ITU provides the forum for developing and ratifying modem communication standards, ensuring that a US Robotics modem you buy at CompUSA will be able to talk to the Hayes modem installed on your friend's PC.

Table 21.2 shows the series of ITU standards employed in the PC modem market.

Table 21.2. Modem standards.

ITU Standard	Data Rate
V.32	4,800 and 9,600bps
V.32bis	14.4Kbps
V.34	28.8Kbps
V.42bis	36.6Kbps
V.90	56Kbps

Note: The V.90 56Kbps specification replaces competing, proprietary technologies known as K56Flex and x2. By the time you read this, virtually all Internet service providers (ISPs) and many private companies should have moved to V.90-compliant hardware. If you own an x2 or K56Flex modem, you may be able to download a free software upgrade that turns the hardware into a V.90 device.

56K Modems: The Last Stop

Today, the fastest modems are so-called 56K products. Unlike earlier modems, which move data at the same speed in both directions, 56K modems only provide their maximum benefit when downloading information. By specification, these modems can receive data at speeds of 56,000 bits per second—or 56Kbps—and send data at a rate of 33.6Kbps. See Figure 21.1.

The asymmetric data rate is a problem for videoconferencing, where you need two-way, high-speed communications. But for most applications, downstream data rates are more valuable than upstream. That's because most of us download a lot more data than we send. Consider, during an hour-long Web browsing session, you may access megabytes of images, text, and data; yet the only thing you may upload are simple mouse clicks and text commands.

FIGURE 21.1.
Diamond Multimedia's SupraExpress 56E provides both V.90 and K56Flex 56Kbps capability in a convenient external design. (Photo courtesy of Diamond Multimedia)

If you were paying attention back when 33.6Kbps modems were introduced, you might remember that people were saying the devices couldn't get any faster. As it turns out, 56Kbps modems work around the bandwidth limitation by taking advantage of the digital phone connections often employed by larger organizations such as ISPs. The secret is the fact that much of the phone network is already digital.

When you make an analog call, it travels over copper wires to the local phone-switching station. In most newer facilities, the call is converted to digital format and routed over the phone network to the switching station on the other end. Here, the call is converted back to analog form and sent over copper wires to the other phone. Similarly, signals coming to you from the far end are converted to digital format and back again.

But if your ISP connects to the phone system via a digital T1, T3, or even an ISDN connection, there is no need to convert analog impulses at all. Instead, everything travels as straight bits from the outbound connection all the way to your local switching station. It is only here, perhaps a few thousand yards from your home or office, that any analog signals get involved at all. The result is a much cleaner, sounder analog signal than one that has been converted twice.

> **Note:** 56K modems ought to be renamed "53K modems" because 56Kbps signaling actually violates FCC frequency limits, adopted in 1976, which are set to prevent unacceptable levels of crosstalk in the phone network. When operated within FCC-approved specifications, these modems are capable of 53Kbps downstream transfers. The FCC is reconsidering the 53Kbps limitation, however, as phone lines have improved since 1976.

56K modems take advantage of the enhanced quality of these digitally originated connections. However, like any modem, the quality of your local line and switching station, as well as your distance from the station itself, will determine whether you get anything close to 56Kbps downstream operation. What's more, upstream communication occurs at only 33.6Kbps maximum.

> **Note:** The good news is that even if you are hooking up to a slower device, all 56K modems provide compliance with earlier ITU standards. So if your V.90 modem calls into a 33.6Kbps V.34 modem, the call will take place at a symmetric 33.6Kbps data rate—phone lines willing, of course.

Double Your Data with Duplex Modems

56Kbps may be the end of the line for ubiquitous, analog-based modem access, but wily vendors are touting another solution—use two modems. That's right. Diamond's SupraSonic II board actually puts two modem controllers, data pumps, and RJ-11 jacks on a single ISA card. When you need to move a lot of data in a short time, the modem dials in to your ISP over two phone lines and aggregates the bandwidth (as shown in Figure 21.2). The result: Up to 112Kbps of bandwidth that nearly matches that of ISDN access.

Figure 21.2.

Duplex modems use software to stitch two dial-up sessions together, allowing you to combine their bandwidth for large file downloads and the like. (Image courtesy of Diamond Multimedia)

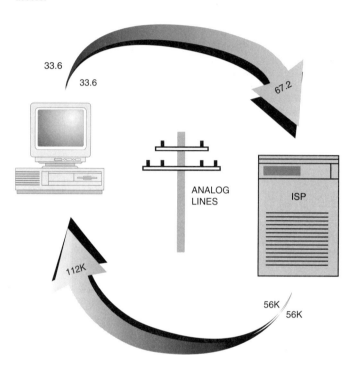

Of course, you need two phone lines to make this scheme work, and your ISP must also provide support for modem duplexing. If you intend to use a duplex modem setup to improve bandwidth, call your current and competing ISPs to see which are supporting the technology. Be aware that you may end up paying more for a duplex-capable account, or you may simply be charged an additional amount when you log on over two lines. You'll need to work out the rate details with your ISP—just be aware that you probably won't get 2X bandwidth for free. Netcom, for example, charges $10 extra per month for the duplexing capability.

What's more, you may need to worry about clogging up both your main and secondary phone line. Diamond's ShotGun technology, which drives its SupraSonic II product, includes the ability to automatically avoid these tie ups. For example, the software will only dial the second line when a large transaction is in progress—after all, extra bandwidth won't really speed up compact, text-based page updates. In addition, if you have call waiting on your phone service, the software will detect an incoming call on the secondary line and release it for the call to ring through. The current Web transaction will continue uninterrupted on the primary data line, though at the lower 56Kbps rate.

Of course, you're also able to take control. You can lock down the second line when you really need it—say, to download the latest 20MB Web browser update. You can also manually release a line when someone in the house needs to make a phone call. Simply click a button and your connection is moved to the single line.

Modem Reality

Advances in modem speeds have been nothing short of remarkable. In fact, engineers have repeatedly predicted the demise of modem speed increases. Modem data rates, they said, could go no faster than 14.4Kbps, and then 28.8Kbps, and finally 33.6Kbps. If you had told a modem engineer in 1990 that 56Kbps modems would be all the rage by 1997, he would have said you were crazy.

But it's not all that easy. The specified data rates often have little to do with reality. Line noise, modem design quality, and system resources all combine to drag actual performance below the line set by the standard. In fact, most 28.8Kbps modem calls occur at rates of 20 to 26Kbps. What's more, modems send and receive additional start and stop bits, as well as bits for error correction. These consume part of the bandwidth pie, further reducing the actual data being sent each second.

Driving the Dirt Road

Al Gore and others might like to go on about the Information Superhighway, but in reality, the public telephone network is a rutted dirt road. Aging telephone switching hardware introduces noise and crosstalk to the phone signal, while exposed phone lines stretch for miles in proximity to power lines that emit electric fields. Meanwhile, some second phone lines might be installed using a multiplexer box tricking a single line into doing double duty, thus reducing performance.

The result is an infrastructure that is hostile to reliable data communications. Generally, those in metropolitan areas can expect the best level of service. Growing communities and new neighborhoods often enjoy new, all-digital telephone switches. Older neighborhoods and rural areas, however, might have to make due on aging analog equipment. Even the newest equipment, such as Diamond's 56Kbps-capable PC Card modem, shown in Figure 21.3, can't overcome poor line quality.

FIGURE 21.3.

The 3Com Megahertz 56K PC Card can deliver 56Kbps capability to your notebook. But you'll be hard-pressed to predict line quality while on the road. (Photo courtesy of 3Com)

Peter's Principle: Check the State of the Local Phone Network Before You Set Up Shop

Modem communications and real estate sales operate under the same catch phrase: Location, location, location. If you plan to set up shop and you rely heavily on modem-based communications, make sure you investigate the state of the local phone network first. If you have a short list of locations you're thinking about moving to, inquire with the local telephone service provider about the state of the switching hardware servicing the areas. Try to find out when the infrastructure was installed and whether any upgrades are planned.

You also might be able to get the phone company to conduct a loop qualification test. This routine provides critical signal data that defines the quality of the line. It can also tell you how far you are from a switching station—often a predictor of relative performance. You need an active line to conduct this test, so you might have to ask someone in the area to request the service for you.

Beyond analog communications, access to digital services such as ISDN, xDSL, and enhanced cable service are all very much geographic issues. Again, new neighborhoods in metropolitan areas stand the best chance of having access to these services. You'll need to contact the local phone and cable companies to determine what services are available.

Tip: Don't be surprised if you can't get straight answers about digital services from the phone company. You might have better luck talking to a local Internet service provider (ISP). These folks often know the local communications landscape better than some call-center rep and might even be able to steer you to the right people inside the phone company to answer your questions.

Compression and Correction

To work around the potholes and cracks in the phone network, modems use data compression and error correction. The data compression process isn't hard to understand. Hardware in the modem takes groups of bits and crunches them into a more efficient format.

The Compression Question

The process of communications data compression is similar to what happens with compression programs such as PK Zip or hard disk compression. Data is compressed on-the-fly by the modem before it is sent out. On the receiving end, compressed data is expanded in the modem and sent to the system over the standard COM port bus.

Of course, both modems need to use the same compression scheme, or the squeezed bits will be unintelligible to the receiving hardware. That's where ITU standards come in. In addition to setting communications protocols, the international body defines compression formats. Backward compatibility ensures that the newest 33.6Kbps modem will recognize the compression of both new and older models.

Note: Depending on the types of files being moved, compression might not have a significant impact. Many of the largest files are already compressed, meaning that modem-based compression is unable to find efficiencies in the data stream. Graphics files such as .GIF, .JPG, and .TIF are already compressed, as are files with .ZIP and .ARC extensions. Video files (.AVI, .MPG) are also cut down to size. Modem compression does help with text-based documents, including those ubiquitous HTML pages, and most uncompressed application files. If a modem maker says that compression provides 2X performance over the rated speed, be sure to take that figure with a grain of salt.

When two modems connect, they generally try to use the most efficient compression scheme supported by both. The ITU-established V.42bis protocol is preferred, because it offers better compression rates than MNP-5. If the modems fail to establish V.42bis compression, they will move to MNP-5.

Understanding Error Correction

Far more important is error correction, which ensures that data gets to the receiving modem intact. Problems arise when noise in the phone line interferes with the signal, impairing the receiving modem's ability to detect the inbound signal. When this happens, the modem might guess wrong, putting 1s where there should be 0s, and vice versa. Without a scheme to detect and correct such mistakes, most modem transmissions would end up as gibberish.

Two kinds of error correction are built into modems today: forward error correction and data-level error correction. Forward error correction consists of redundant bits built into the data stream that can be used to rebuild lost or mangled data on-the-fly. This scheme reduces the bandwidth available for usable data but avoids time-consuming retransmission when minor errors occur. It is the first line of data defense for modems.

Data-level error correction uses a checksum scheme to compare chunks of data against expected results in a small header field. To do this, the sending modem breaks the data stream into standard-sized blocks, which are bookended by information about the data itself. In front of the block, a header provides information on where the data inside the block must go with respect to other blocks. This allows blocks of data to be sent out of order and reconstituted on the receiving end.

On the back end of the data block, the sending modem uses a standard algorithm to compute a series of error correction bits. Based on the data inside the block, these bits allow the receiving modem to distinguish errors in the transmission. The receiving modem uses the same algorithm to determine the appropriate error correction data. If the result matches that sent by the other end, the block is assumed to be whole. If the result doesn't match that of the other end, the receiving modem tells the other side to resend the corrupted block of data.

There have been several standard error correction schemes over the years, but only V.42 and MNP-4 remain important to modem users. Compliant modems can negotiate among themselves to come up with the optimal scheme for each transmission. Typically, two modems will first attempt to use V.42 and then move down to MNP-4.

Other Talents

Of course, modems do more than just screech bits at each other. For years, most modems have included fax send and receive capability, and many new models provide voice and data capability. Many are also telephony mavens, providing services such as voice mailboxes and messaging, distinctive ring capability, and so on.

PC-Based Faxing

Today, virtually all new modems provide fax capability. This enables your PC to send and receive fax transmissions, whether from another PC or from a standard fax machine. What's more, the advent of power Pentium-class systems and the multitasking talents of

Windows 9x have made the PC a much more attractive fax platform than before, when such operations would slow system operation to a crawl.

It's no surprise that standards lie behind the fax capability. Most modems comply with the Class 1 specification, which places most of the fax processing burden on the system CPU. Windows' fax facilities are tailored to Class 1 operation. Class 2 products add some modem commands and intelligence to offload the work from the CPU to the modem itself, but the lack of support in Windows 95 makes it a less attractive option for most users.

In general, fax transmission may occur at data rates as high as 14.4Kbps. However, older fax machines and modems might not be able to support anything beyond 9,600bps. Given that long-distance fax calls can add up to hefty phone bills, the higher fax data rate might make an upgrade worthwhile in and of itself.

> **Note:** If you have an Internet connection, you can use an Internet-based fax service to help trim the cost of long-distance faxing. A wide variety of free and pay services use different methods to handle your transmissions. Some turn simple email messages into fax transmissions, and others, such as FaxStorm, take document files and transmit them as fax output. In addition to possibly cutting down long-distance charges, useful features such as fax broadcasting and transmission status updates can help people who send many faxes. You can find a wealth of information and useful links on Yahoo!'s Internet Fax page:
>
> ```
> http://www.yahoo.com/Computers_and_Internet/Internet/Internet_Fax_
> Server/
> ```

Voice and Data Handling

Many modems allow simultaneous voice and data communications over a single line. This feature is useful for everything from online technical support to online gaming (in which gamers can follow through on their burning need to mock their opponents). The voice-data capability was originally launched using two approaches:

- Radish VoiceView: The modem switches rapidly between voice and data operation, suspending data briefly while analog voice signals are carried through.
- DSVD (digital simultaneous voice and data): The modem parses out a section of the 28.8 or 33.6Kbps bandwidth to transmit digitized voice.

Today, DSVD is firmly entrenched as the standard technology for putting voice and data into a single call. This scheme is useful for allowing voice communications, but it does have a cost. Data throughput drops, because as much as 9.6Kbps of the available bandwidth gets handed over for voice operation. Also, neither DSVD nor Radish VoiceView technology is suitable for use over the Internet, since they assume a direct connection. Still, if you plan to use your modem for head-to-head online gaming or direct PC-to-PC collaboration, a DSVD modem might provide very useful capabilities. Of course, both parties need DSVD-capable modems to make this work.

Digital Domains: Modems for the New World

Analog modems top out at 33.6Kbps for symmetric data rates and about 56Kbps for downloads. These speeds are impressive given the challenges of the phone network, but they are woefully inadequate for the burgeoning demand presented by Web browsing, telecommuting, and other applications. To get better performance, some form of digital network needs to be put into place.

Note: The telephone companies have a strong vested interest in changing the current data-carrying landscape. The phone system is what is called a *circuit-switched network*: When you initiate a call, you grab a line and keep it until you hang up the phone. This is fine, until a lot of people want to use the network at the same time—say, following an earthquake. At that time, the network simply runs out of circuits. The result is circuit-busy messages and even the lack of a dial tone altogether.

Enter the Internet. Phone companies install switching capacity according to well-researched historical usage patterns. For example, the phone company knows that the average phone call lasts about two or three minutes. Given that fact, they can assume that a reserved circuit will probably come free within minutes of being engaged. But the average data call (faxes aside) lasts 45 minutes or more. And often circuits are engaged for hours because users simply forget to log off. The result is the equivalent of a small natural disaster every evening as millions flock to their modems and tie up circuits to browse the Web.

The answer is the use of so-called *packet-switched systems*, which are similar to that of Ethernet networks, in which a fixed amount of bandwidth is shared among users. Although an overstressed packet-switched network will bog down, it won't deny service during periods of heavy usage. Asymmetric Digital Subscriber Line (ADSL) and cable-based Internet access both use a packet-switched scheme to split the bandwidth pie among consumers.

There are a variety of digital technologies in deployment able to offer higher bandwidth and better response. These technologies are covered in detail in Chapter 22. The short list includes:

- ISDN: Integrated Services Digital Network
- ADSL: Asymmetric Digital Subscriber Line
- Cable modem
- DSS: Digital Satellite Service
- T1/T3

It may read like alphabet soup, but these technologies are already enjoying a broad deployment nationwide—particularly in metropolitan areas. Data rates range from 128Kbps (for ISDN) to as high as 50Mbps (for cable, theoretically). And because the connection is digital, issues like line noise, interference, and modulation delays simply go away. In effect, these technologies can put you on the equivalent of a local area network connection.

INSTANT REFERENCE | For more on these technologies, see Chapter 22.

Probing Ping Rates

There's more than bandwidth separating digital and analog connections. Online gamers crave the instant response needed to stay competitive in a deathmatch melee. The problem is that analog modems are notoriously slow. Modems must translate bits into tones and tones into bits, while poor line quality can require data to be resent. The result? Delays in receiving information that in a heated firefight can spell the difference between online life and death.

How much delay are we talking about? When it comes to Internet responsiveness, the ping rate is key. Ping rate measures how long it takes, in milliseconds, for a server to respond to a request. A fast digital connection can offer ping rates as low as 10ms, while many analog modems are saddled with sluggish ping rates of 200ms or even higher. If you are trying to play online games with a 250ms ping rate, you are basically reacting to enemies a quarter of a second too late.

More than the modem is to blame for high ping rates. The responsiveness of the target net server, for example, is critical. An overloaded server can bog down responsiveness even on a local area network or fast cable modem. At the same time, the directness of your Internet connection plays a role. If your connection to a remote Internet server follows a circuitous route, moving through many routers and jumping across several networks, your ping rates will again suffer. The more direct path you can take to your target server, the better your chances for fast response.

All things being equal, however, modems are a poor option for online gaming. Too many skilled gamers are riding fast, digital cable modems or digital ISDN modems. But you could do worse. Satellite-based Internet access—such as Hughes' DirecPC—is rife with performance sapping delays on the order of 500ms or more. That's more than half a second! The problem: The geosynchronous orbit of the DirecPC satellite is so far up (22,000 miles, to be exact) that it takes light nearly half a second to make the round trip from earth. There's plenty of bandwidth—about 400KBps—but responsiveness is poor. Low earth orbit (LEO) satellites like Teledisc, due to launch in 2003, will alleviate this problem eventually.

Buying Bandwidth: Shopping for Modems and Other Devices

So you want fast Internet access, do you? Today more connectivity options are open to PC users than ever before. Modems of varying speeds and talents can fire bits over standard phone lines and even turn your PC into an answering machine. Real bandwidth jockeys might consider one of the several digital infrastructures available, from ISDN to direct satellite systems. While I cover digital options in more length in Chapter 22, Table 21.3 will help you focus your thinking.

Table 21.3. Bandwidth options at a glance.

Type	Data Rate	Cost of Installation	Monthly Cost	What It's Best For
33.6Kbps	33.6/33.6Kbps	$70	N/A	Casual Web modem browsing and email, home and small office. This type of modem is ubiquitous.
56K modem	56/33.6Kbps	$120	N/A	Casual and heavy Web browsing and email, home and small office, server access. Best overall choice.
ISDN	128/128Kbps	$200	$36-$100	Heavy Web browsing, small office, videoconferencing and data-conferencing, Web publishing uploads. Limited availability.
Satellite	400/33.6Kbps	$500	$20-$120	Heavy Web browsing and email, small office, server access. This is the best option for rural locations.

Type	Data Rate	Cost of Installation	Monthly Cost	What It's Best For
Cable modem	4MBps/ 33.6Kbps	$400	$40-$60	Heavy Web browsing and email, home and small office, server access. This is still in trials.
ADSL modem	1.6MBps/ 128Kbps	$400	$60-$120	Heavy Web browsing and email, home and small office, server access, Web publishing FTP uploads, videoconferencing and dataconferencing. This is still in trials.

It's worth noting here that the pricing for online access can vary widely depending on the service provider, the connection technology, and the region you are in. ISDN service in Denver can be downright economical, yet remains exorbitant in northern New England. Likewise, per-minute charges are not reflected in this chart.

The vast majority of users will remain with analog modems for years to come. Digital technologies are either too expensive, too complex, or too limited in their availability to make them worth buying. In the meantime, expect 56K modem technology to fill the gap while the phone companies, cable companies, and others lay down the infrastructure needed to make higher-bandwidth connections ubiquitous.

A new modem is a smart upgrade if your PC is more than a year old or so. Even if you access the Internet with a relatively-recent 33.6Kbps modem, you should consider an upgrade to a V.90-compliant K56Flex model. The same goes for anyone using a modem for email, file downloads from a remote server, and other time-consuming pursuits.

The economics of modem upgrades are among the best in the PC marketplace. For one, modems are cheap. A 33.6Kbps modem from a top-flight manufacturer can cost $70 or less. Depending on your usage and the billing patterns of your ISP, you could recoup that entire amount within a year. If you make long-distance calls to transfer files to and from a remote server, the upgrade will probably pay for itself sooner than that.

Still, there are plenty of questions. We'll try to answer them one by one in the following sections.

56K or 33.6Kbps?

The 56K format wars are over, and that means you should buy nothing less than a v.90 modem running at 56Kbps downstream. ISPs and information providers are rapidly moving to the international standard, and many users are able to update their older proprietary 56K modems with a simple software upgrade.

That said, there may be some people who need to make their modem work with proprietary technology. Your employer, for instance, may have invested in a lot of 3Com modems using the x2 56Kbps standard, and may not be able to upgrade them. If that's the case, you'll want to get an x2-compliant modem that is also able to handle V.90 operation. This will ensure compatibility with the broad universe of 56K modems while still giving you optimal access to the location using the x2 technology.

The good news is that all 56K products provide complete compatibility with existing V.42bis modems operating at 33.6Kbps. For this reason alone, a 56K modem is worth considering if you use your PC for Web access. Before you decide, call your ISP and find out which 56K standard it intends to support. If it's not V.90, find out if the ISP intends to move to the standard soon—you may want to buy a V.90 modem and live with the lower 33.6Kbps data rate for the short time until the ISP upgrades its hardware.

> **Tip:** While 3Com and other vendors have offered free upgrades to the ITU V.90 standard, you should be careful. Some users have reported problems with the upgrade software, which, in the worst case, can actually destroy critical circuitry. The good news: By the time you read this, problems with the upgrade should be understood and resolved. Still, you should at least be ready for the possibility of losing the modem, just in case.

Internal or External?

Personally, I prefer external modems. They cost about $20 more than internal ISA cards and add yet another cable to the rat's nest behind the PC, but the convenience of the external device is terrific. External modems can be easily moved and shared among systems (including notebooks), and their visible status lights come in handy when things go wrong.

> **Peter's Principle:** The Advantages of External Versus Internal Modems
>
> One reason I've come to value external modems is that they come in handy when things go wrong. Occasionally I run into situations in which the modem stops responding to commands and just sits there, screeching nonsensically into the phone. I can shut down communications apps, try killing the connection from software, and even issue hang-up command codes from the Windows

Terminal applet. But the modem won't let go of the line. At this point, if you had an internal modem, you would need to reboot your PC to get your phone line back. An external modem, however, can be powered down from a toggle switch on the unit, freeing the line. After you turn it back on, you're ready to go.

An external modem also gives you visual clues when something is wrong, unlike an internal. If I'm in the middle of a lengthy download and data stops coming, it helps to be able to see the SD (send data) and RD (receive data) LEDs. If the RD light never comes on while the modem polls periodically, you know that the connection might be kaput. On the other hand, if the RD LED stays on but your software says no data is arriving, the PC itself, or the connection between the modem and the PC, becomes suspect.

So why do people buy internal modems? For one thing, they don't consume any desk space and don't require serial and power cables, which both add to the wire pollution at the back of the PC. Internal modems typically sell for $20 less than their external counterparts—an additional advantage. Finally, an internal modem is the best choice for older PCs without a fast 16550 UART chip, since new modems will overmatch the aging UART.

Internal modems are worth considering, though. For one thing, far too many devices want to use the same serial port that your modem connects to. PDA connectors, sheet-fed scanners, and who-knows-how-many-other peripherals make their living off scarce serial port space. An internal modem frees that connector, eliminating the hassle of plugging in and unplugging devices. Of course, you still must deal with IRQ and I/O assignments for the internal device.

In addition, an internal unit might be a must for older systems, because old PCs can't accept serial port data quickly enough to keep pace with 14.4Kbps and faster modems. The culprit is an obscure chip called the UART (universal asynchronous receiver-transmitter) that acts as a middleman between the modem and the CPU. The old UART lacks a memory buffer to store incoming data, so it must constantly pester the CPU every time bits are received. Not only does this bog down the entire system, but the lack of buffer means that faster modems simply overrun the UART's ability to get data to the CPU. The result is lost data.

Internal modems provide their own UART—the 16550—which provides a 16-character buffer for inbound and outbound data (see Figure 21.4). This buffer allows the serial port to keep pace with the fastest analog modems, providing data rate services of up to 115Kbps.

Note: Not all 16550 UARTs are the same. Early 16550 UARTs suffered from a flawed buffer. Two updated versions, the 16550A and 16550AF have fixed the buffer problem. You should check with your system or motherboard manufacturer to see which UART version is in your PC. If you have a troublesome 16550 UART, you may want to go with an internal modem upgrade.

FIGURE 21.4.
Diamond Multimedia's SupraExpress 56i internal modem packs its own fast UART chip, allowing older systems to deal with fast data downloads. (Photo courtesy of Diamond Multimedia)

Tip: If your PC has a slow UART but you want to upgrade to an external modem, you still can. You'll just need to shell out a few more bucks for an I/O upgrade card providing backplane connectors for serial and parallel port connectors. This card will include the 16550 UART, allowing mainstream modems to operate normally.

The USB Advantage

An external modem may in fact be your best choice thanks to the arrival of modems using the USB bus. USB modems (shown in Figure 21.5) offer all the advantages of external modems—status lights, the ability to toggle power, easy sharing—with some welcome improvements. Among the advantages, a USB modem provides over a typical serial modem:

- No power cord: Power is supplied over the USB wire, so the external modem has no extra power line or space-hogging power converter module.

- Shareable port: Not only does a USB modem free your serial port for other devices—like a personal digital assistant (PDA)—but USB enables you to plug other devices into USB ports while using the modem. No more port logjams.

- Higher performance: While faster UARTS can handle the load of even 56Kbps downloads, USB offers a more efficient design that will streamline overall system performance. And if you have a duplexed modem or ISDN adapter that pushes over 115Kbps (the limit for the serial port), you'll notice a lift in performance since USB doesn't have to cut down on your connection speed.

- Plug and Play: USB detects the modem when it is plugged into a port and is ready to go right away. Serial port modems, on the other hand, demand you to manually install the modem or use the Add New Hardware facility to kick off a detection routine.

FIGURE 21.5.
3Com's US Robotics' 56K Voice Faxmodem Pro uses a USB connection to provide easier setup and greater convenience. (Photo courtesy of 3Com)

All this sounds great, but there are a few caveats. One, USB modems are not as common as serial port products, so prices may be a bit higher and the selection more limited. In addition, you may not be able to use a USB modem on older desktop and notebook PCs lacking USB support. A serial modem is guaranteed to work on just about any system.

Other Choices

If you need maximum bandwidth and can't afford or access ISDN, cable modems, ADSL or other service, consider a duplex modem product. Intelligent software can stitch together the work of two modems, effectively doubling data rates, particularly on big downloads and uploads. However, your ISP will need to offer duplex access—likely at extra cost—and you will need two phone lines to make this solution work.

If you need a new modem and want to go the duplex route, check out products that put two modems on a single card, as shown in Figure 21.6. You'll save system resources, card slots, and money by going with an integrated two-in-one device.

FIGURE 21.6.

Diamond Multimedia's SupraSonic II puts two modems on a single ISA card to effectively double data rates. However, you'll need two phone lines and an ISP who offers duplex service to get the added performance. (Photo courtesy of Diamond Multimedia)

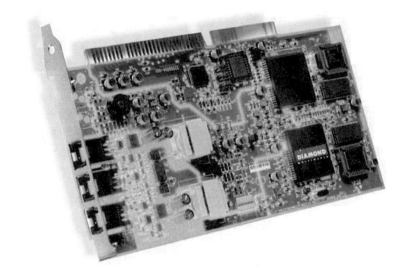

Once you've decided on modem speed and location, you can start looking in earnest. That said, many folks might consider paying extra for DSVD modems (assuming that there is someone on the other end with compliant hardware). Game players will get a kick out of the gratuitous verbal sparring (at the expense of a suitable response), while office users can use the modem to combine audioconferencing and dataconferencing.

You might be tempted to consider a so-called Win modem, but I'd advise against it. These modems rely on the system CPU to handle the job of juggling bits instead of relying on an internal chipset. The name Win modem comes from the fact that these products work only under Windows (they won't work with DOS-based games) because special driver software is needed to shuttle the modem duties to the system CPU.

Win modems are less expensive than regular modems, but not by much anymore. What's more, they saddle your CPU with extra work, which can be a problem if you multitask Web browsing with the latest cycle-sucking software. Most distressing is the spotty compatibility record these products have. Unless you are severely strapped for cash, I'd avoid these controller-less modem products.

Moving on Up: Upgrading a Modem

Once you've decided what kind of modem you want, upgrading should be fairly painless. External modems operate over a serial port, which means they use the IRQ and base I/O address of the serial port itself. That will help ease setup, but you still have to deal with the PC's COM port weirdness.

Understanding COM Ports

Your PC has four COM ports, numbered 1 through 4. While there are four distinct I/O addresses for these COM ports, there are only two IRQs. That limits your options to using two external serial devices at any one time, particularly since your PC will have at most two physical serial connectors on the back. Because of the way COM port addresses work, you can only be certain that the lower two COM ports—numbers 1 and 2—will always be available for your modem.

Before you install a new modem, check the Hardware Device Manager in Windows 95 or 98. This useful facility can give you detailed information on COM port status. To check for available COM ports, do the following:

1. Select Start, Settings, Control Panel.
2. Double-click the System icon. In the System Properties dialog box, choose the Device Manager tab.
3. Click the plus sign (+) next to the item Ports (COM & LPT).

Tip: If a red X or yellow exclamation point appears next to either of the COM port items, a conflict of some sort is preventing normal operation of the indicated ports. For more information on how to troubleshoot COM ports, see the section "Troubleshooting COM Ports."

4. Double-click the COM port you want to examine. (On most PCs, you should see two COM port entries and one LPT port entry.)
5. In the Communications Port (COMx) Properties dialog box, choose the Resources tab to view the IRQ and address range settings for the COM port.
6. If both COM ports are without conflicts, you should be able to make use of either of them for your modem.

Installing Modem Hardware

If you spent the extra money for an external modem, you'll get some return on your investment when you install the hardware. External devices are easier to install, if only because you don't have to open the case to do so.

External Modem Installation

The following steps illustrate how to install your modem hardware. First you will need to find the appropriate serial port on the back of your system. Most PCs have two serial ports, which usually appear as a pair of nine-pin connectors, or as one nine-pin and one 25-pin connector on older machines. Depending on the cable provided with the external modem, you'll plug into either the nine-pin or the 25-pin serial connector. The other end plugs into the 25-pin connector on the modem itself.

Likewise, you will see two phone jacks (known as RJ-11 connectors) on the modem. One of these must be connected to the phone jack on the wall, and the other may be attached to a telephone. The second line acts as a passthrough, letting you use the same phone jack for both your phone and modem.

1. Attach the modem cable to the 25-pin connector on the back of the modem.

2. Attach the other end to the appropriate nine-pin or 25-pin serial port connector on the back of the PC.

3. Plug the phone cord into the wall jack and the other end into the RJ-11 jack on the modem. Make sure you plug this line into the connector on the modem that is intended to be hooked to the wall.

4. If you want to connect a telephone or fax machine to the modem, attach a phone cord from the device to the second RJ-11 jack.

5. Plug the power cord into an outlet and attach the round connector component into the modem's power input jack.

Internal Modem Installation

Installing the hardware for an internal modem is in many ways similar to doing so for external hardware. For example, cable setup is the same. Likewise, internal modems often provide two RJ-11 jacks like their external counterparts.

Otherwise, you need to follow the same steps as those for an internal card installation:

1. Shut off the PC, unplug the power cord, and remove the case.

2. Make sure you ground yourself by touching a metal portion of the PC chassis. Better yet, use a grounding mat and wrist strap.

3. Use a screwdriver to unscrew the backplate of a free ISA card slot. Pull out the backplate connector.

4. Seat the card into the ISA slot. You might need to rock the card slightly from back to front to ease it into the connector.

5. Plug in the serial cable and phone cords.

6. Power up the PC, and then follow the steps for setting up the new modem hardware under Windows.

7. Once you've determined that the modem is working properly, shut down the PC, secure the ISA board backplane with a screwdriver, and reattach the case.

Setting Up a New Modem

Installing a modem should go quickly. Generally, your biggest worries come from possible mouse conflicts, because many pointing devices use a serial port to hook to the PC. You can check your mouse settings from the Mouse icon in Control Panel. If you have a PS/2-style mouse, you should be in the clear.

Once you've installed the hardware and decided which COM port you want to use, do the following to set up the new device:

1. Start up the PC. If your system auto-detects the modem, follow Windows Plug and Play routine. If it doesn't, skip to step 4.

2. Go to Control Panel (select Start, Settings, Control Panel) and double-click the Modems icon.

3. Click the Add button. Click Next to proceed.

4. In the next dialog box, select the Don't select my modem check box. This will allow you to identify the modem yourself.

5. In the Manufacturers scroll-down list box, select the name of the vendor that made your modem. The Models list box should list product names specific to the company you selected.

6. In the Models scroll-down list box, select the specific model you're using, and click Next.

7. If the specific model isn't listed, insert the floppy disk containing the modem's installation files into your A: drive. Click the Have Disk button, and then double-click the .INF file that appears in the dialog box. Click Next.

8. In the next dialog box, select the COM port to use. You must click one of the choices in the box called Select the port to use with this modem.

9. Windows will take a little while to install the driver software and update its records.

10. Click the Finish button to return to the Modem Properties page. You should see the newly installed modem listed in the text box.

Once you get the modem up and running, it's a good idea to pay a visit to the manufacturer's Web site to see if an updated driver is available. Owners of 33.6Kbps modems, or those with 56Kbps modems using x2 or K56Flex can often upgrade to industry standard V.90 56Kbps via a software upgrade.

Note: One welcome bit of news is that it is unlikely that you will find yourself messing with jumper switches during this routine. New modems do all their stuff in software, allowing you to change port settings without fishing around inside the case.

Dealing with Modem Trouble

As is the case with so many other PC components, you won't find yourself doing a lot of true repair jobs. Modems are solid-state devices that resemble sound and graphics boards in their make-up. When a chip or other component gets damaged on the modem card or inside the case, it is often most economical to have the unit replaced. In any case, it takes professional tools to fix major damage to modem components.

That said, a lot can go wrong. Modems must be installed around the PC's sometimes-elusive COM ports, and they can be dragged off-line by conflicting hardware such as mice. In addition, the interface to the public phone network opens all sorts of possible problems.

Troubleshooting COM Ports

Many modem troubles are caused by conflicts with mice, because both modems and mice want to use COM ports to connect to the PC. However, other devices can muscle in on your modem's territory, grabbing the IRQ or port address that your COM port has reserved. If you do not have a PnP-compliant modem and are experiencing port problems, you can use your system's BIOS setup program or the Windows Device Manager to disable the conflicting port.

> **Tip:** If you experience chronic or intermittent mouse problems you can't figure out, you should check your modem. You might be experiencing a COM port conflict, in which both the mouse and the modem want to use the same port. Because many users make use of the modem only occasionally, the perceived mouse problem might not crop up enough to warrant an aggressive look.

If you can't get your modem to respond, try changing its COM port setting. The second port might be free, allowing reliable operation. Do the following:

1. Double-click the Modems icon in Control Panel.
2. In the Modems Properties dialog box, select the device you want to adjust, and click the Properties button.
3. Click the Port drop-down control, and select a COM port setting other than the one that is active.
4. Click OK, and then click Close in the next dialog box in order for the changes to take effect.

Dealing with Dialing

Often, what seems like a modem problem is nothing more than a glitch in your modem's dialing properties. Windows 95/98 enables you to assign permanent dialing routines to access outside lines, disable call waiting, and use a telephone billing card.

If the modem begins dialing but can't seem to connect with another line, do the following:

1. In Windows, from Control Panel, double-click the Modems icon.
2. Click the Dialing Properties button.

3. Check to make sure that the area code item matches the area code you're calling from.

4. In the How I dial from this location area, make sure that the settings for accessing an outside line, using a phone card, and disabling call waiting are set properly.

5. Also make sure that the phone is set to tone operation.

Modem Problems with Windows 3.1/3.11

Under Windows 3.1 or 3.11 (Windows for Workgroups), modem installation and trouble-shooting can be more difficult. It's important to keep track of IRQ assignments, COM port assignments, and I/O assignments, because the earlier versions of Windows won't do this for you. A common mistake is assigning the same value to the port address and the modem address, in the case of an internal modem. The two are not the same, so setting them to the same value will result in a resource conflict producing unusual and confusing symptoms, such as having a modem that will go off-hook but not dial, or dial but not detect a carrier signal.

When you're troubleshooting modem difficulties under Windows 3.1 or 3.11, take care to write down the system settings as they are before you begin, and then document each change made until the system works and the modem responds correctly. Here are the most important parameters:

The COM port to be assigned to the modem

The IRQ to assign to the port and modem

The I/O address of the modem

The I/O address of the COM port

Modems are often misidentified, especially by telecom software running under Windows 3.1 and 3.11. Also, sometimes hardware-specific default values are incorrectly stored. For this reason, your software might fail to identify the make and model of your modem. Software like that used to install America Online, for example, might misidentify your modem, even sometimes getting a very well-known model wrong, or it might not see your modem at all. If this happens and you're quite sure that the jumpers (if any), ports, and addresses are set correctly, try running Windows' dumb terminal program, found in the Accessories program group. If you can type AT (which means "Attention!" in modem-speak) and then press Enter and see the modem respond with OK, and then you can dial ATDT 12345 and press Enter and hear the modem dial, the fault can be placed on the tele-com or application software that's attempting to identify your modem. Go back into that software and opt to manually specify the modem type instead of asking the software to do so. Select the most generic option on the list, usually "Hayes-compatible generic modem." If that selection doesn't work, try choosing a generic US Robotics modem of the correct maximum speed.

Summary

The Internet has made the modem one of the most critical components of any PC. Yet many older systems came without a modem, or with one that operates at 28.8Kbps or slower data rates.

Fortunately, modems are affordable, often costing less than $100 for some cutting-edge 56Kbps models. Meanwhile, Windows 95's improved communications facilities have helped take much of the sting out of modem setup and configuration. Given that a faster modem can enhance your Web browsing, cut your ISP bills, and save you time, it's clear that a modem upgrade is well worth considering.

Of course, the rapid growth of the Internet has prompted many developments in the digital realm. ISDN, ADSL, cable modems, and satellite systems are all competing to provide much greater bandwidth and reliability to your connections. All these options still suffer from key drawbacks, particularly in the areas of pricing and availability; but if you need fast access, you may want to explore these options in depth in the following chapter. For the rest of us, low-cost and ubiquitous 56Kbps modem access is your best bet.

Digital Connectivity

Two or three years ago, if you were looking for a fast connection to the Internet, you had one clear choice—ISDN. Standing for *Integrated Services Digital Network*, ISDN is the digital equivalent of dial-up phone service. Compared to the 28.8Kbps modems of the day, the 128Kbps data rate of ISDN adapters—typically called modems—was downright blazing. And ISDN offered advantages no analog modem could boast—like reliable connections, lines free of performance-sapping noise, and lightning quick log-ons.

There was just one problem. The phone companies, by all accounts, weren't terribly interested in deploying ISDN. In fact, if you look at the way phone companies have typically begged their local governing boards to allow them to raise ISDN rates, you'd think they were trying to kill off the service entirely. And while ISDN service continues to exist to this day, the technology has, in fact, ceased to be at the center of attention for high-speed connections.

The explosive growth of Internet traffic and the ever-increasing demand for bandwidth has helped give birth to a variety of solutions. For most of us, that means 33.6Kbps modems being supplanted by 56Kbps products. But as demand grows, it is clear that an analog connection will not be able to keep pace with the growing class of streaming video, two-way conferencing, and large graphics and database traffic.

This chapter covers a number of important, digital connectivity technologies now available for home and office users. It explains how they work, why they provide the level of performance they do, and why some services are better than others. Most of all, you'll read about the limitations, particularly when it comes to getting access to these technologies outside of major metropolitan areas.

Key aspects of coverage include:

- The workings of digital communication hardware, including ISDN, cable modems, satellite, and asymmetric digital subscriber line (ADSL)
- How to choose a particular technology, given your access needs, location, and budget
- Dealing with and resolving problems with hardware
- Installing new comm hardware

An Overview of Digital Connectivity

Remote access technology has entered a transition period. Even v.90 56Kbps modems can't keep up with the pace set by many new Web-based applications. Streaming video, PC-based audio and videoconferencing, and remote control software all demand more performance than modems and phone lines can produce. Anyone who has tried to download the latest version of Internet Explorer or Netscape Navigator can tell you that.

Enter a foursome of intriguing, promising, and as-yet-flawed digital technologies that may help break the modem bottleneck.

- DSL: Digital Subscriber Line
- Cable modems
- DSS: Digital Satellite Service
- ISDN: Integrated Services Digital Network

Each of these approaches has their advantages and disadvantages. And in fact, what's good for a user in Seattle, Washington, may be completely inappropriate (or rather, unavailable) for someone in Burlington, Vermont. In all cases, performance is superior to that of analog modems, with higher data rates, enhanced reliability, and quicker logon times.

To better understand how these technologies impact you, the following sections will examine each one in order.

ISDN: The Fading Digital Star

The first stop on the digital odyssey is ISDN (see Figure 22.1), because it has been around for well over 10 years now and is the most widely deployed. ISDN stands for Integrated Service Digital Network, and the telephone companies' efforts to roll out this service have been almost as clumsy as the name itself. For over 10 years, ISDN has been projected as the new face of phone service, providing an intriguing mix of voice services, digital controls, and high bandwidth to millions of subscribers. Today, ISDN is becoming a telecommunications footnote, as faster and potentially less-expensive options reach market.

The ISDN phone line—which is different from the analog phone lines found in virtually all homes—can carry up to 128Kbps of data—more than twice the maximum data rate of today's v.90 modems. What's more, ISDN provides 128Kbps in both directions, making the service excellent for videoconferencing, remote network access, and other applications demanding good upstream performance.

ISDN actually consists of three separate channels: a 16KBps D (data) channel that carries commands and control data, and a pair of 64KBps B (bearer) channels that carry the data itself. Of course, you need communications hardware that is tailored to plug into an ISDN phone line, using an RJ45 plug that is slightly larger than the typical RJ11 jack found on phones today.

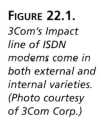

FIGURE 22.1.
*3Com's Impact
line of ISDN
modems come in
both external and
internal varieties.
(Photo courtesy
of 3Com Corp.)*

ISDN is digital, so the term *modem* is actually a misnomer since no modulation or demodulation takes place. ISDN adapters provide an interface between your system and the digital ISDN network. The advantage over analog communications is significant: Digital connections can be initiated much more quickly than their analog counterparts and are not plagued by performance-sapping line noise. Once you start an ISDN connection, you can rely on its staying put—unlike analog calls, which can drop off unexpectedly.

If you get ISDN service, you should make sure your ISP or company provides bonded ISDN service. In some cases, only one of the two ISDN B channels is recognized by the server hardware, limiting you to 64Kbps data rates. While you may not always need the higher performance, the two-channel capability is critical for videoconferencing and large file and application downloads.

> **Note:** While almost all carriers now charge a flat rate for ISDN service, some phone companies may charge 1 to 10 cents per minute of use of each ISDN channel. If this is the case, you can save money by only using a single B channel for most of your communications. If you need to videoconference or download a multimegabyte file, you can engage the second channel (at the appropriately higher per-minute rate) to boost performance. Of course, your usual ISP connect-time fees would apply.

ISDN service is actually quite flexible, as well. The Basic Rate Interface (BRI) ISDN service consists of a single ISDN line (with its three channels) that provides 128Kbps of bandwidth. This is the most popular single-user form of ISDN service, and the most affordable. That said, pricing varies widely based on your location—you should check with your local telephone company to find out the latest rates.

Primary Rate Interface (PRI) ISDN bundles up to 23 ISDN B channels (and one D channel for command and control) into a single service. The result is a 1.544Mbps data rate. PRI ISDN is typically used by corporations and information service providers for high-speed access to the Internet, wide area networks, and other resources. PRI ISDN is typically delivered via a T1 line. Individual ISDN lines can often be purchased using a fractional T1 service, enabling companies to tailor their setup to specific needs. For example, room-based video often requires a 384Kbps data rate that is equal to six ISDN B channels (or three BRI ISDN lines). Fractional T1 service is often used for these devices.

Unfortunately, ISDN access can be limited. Outside of metropolitan areas, expect distances to be too great to support ISDN's line loop limit (some 18,000 feet, or just over three miles). Still, the access picture for ISDN is better than for the relatively new DSL technology.

Even if you're within a service area, ISDN can be maddeningly complex to set up. Despite the fact that the service is well over a decade old, setting up ISDN often requires users to exercise extra care. You need to make sure you purchase communication hardware compatible with the local switching hardware, as well as keep track of additional account information such as the service provider ID number (SPID). If you don't already have ISDN lines pulled into your office or home, you'll need to arrange for the physical installation as well, since ISDN will not work over standard phone lines.

As if that weren't enough, getting service and support from the telephone company can be all but impossible. As a result, you may have a very hard time getting even the most basic information needed to make your hardware work with the ISDN line.

DSL: The New Grail or Just Another ISDN?

If ISDN is fading, DSL is a rising star. *Digital Subscriber Line (DSL)* technology promises not only big bandwidth to end users, it works over standard copper phone wire. The fact that DSL can work with the existing wire drawn into many homes and offices is critical. The costs involved in laying a wire infrastructure is enormous, and is part of the reason that ISDN failed to take off. While DSL does require a lot of new switching hardware and expensive infrastructure updates by the telcos, it is less of a task than that presented by ISDN.

DSL can work on existing copper wire because the digital information is sent in the high-frequency area of the phone lines, above the 4KHz band used for voice and modem signals. In essence, DSL signals run along free lanes available in the phone lines. In fact, voice and DSL transmissions can occupy phone lines at the same time. What DSL does require are new switches to manage the digital signals, as well as a new class of adapters to hook the PC into the ADSL network.

Like 56K modems, however, the most popular forms of DSL are asymmetric technology. That means data coming down to your PC moves more quickly than data that is sent out. Again, because the vast majority of Internet-based transactions involve significantly more downstream activity than upstream, the asymmetric approach appeals to a large audience. What's more, DSL is fast, really fast. Most home users will see data rates on the order of 1.5Mbps downstream, and 640Kbps upstream.

The Many Faces of DSL

One thing DSL is not, is simple. In fact, there are many varieties of digital subscriber line service, ranging from low-cost, low-speed consumer grade DSL to industrial strength versions that provide symmetric megabit-range data rates. (See Figure 22.2.)

FIGURE 22.2.

DSL technology provides a broad range of symmetric and asymmetric data rates to consumers and corporations alike. (Graphic courtesy of Westell Technologies)

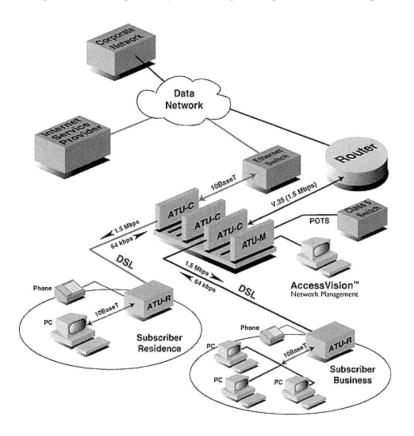

The most prevalent form of DSL is asymmetric DSL (or ADSL). Also known as DSL.Lite, this service provides data rates starting as low as 16Kbps to 64Kbps for upstream communications, and 1.5Mbps to 8Mbps for downstream transfers. However, there is a veritable alphabet soup of DSL variants targeting various markets. They include:

High bit rate DSL (HDSL): Running at the same speed up and down stream, this high-performance link requires a shorter loop and two or three copper twisted pair wires.

ISDN DSL (IDSL): This is a hybrid ISDN-DSL technology that provides data rates as high as 768Kbps.

Single line DSL (SDLS): Like HDSL, this runs at the same up and down stream data rate, and matches HDSL's high performance. But the loop distance is even shorter because SDSL only uses a single twisted pair wire.

Very high bit rate DSL (VDSL): A very short loop enables extremely fast downstream and fast upstream performance; but availability is limited.

Rate adaptive DSL (R-ADSL): This variable service can be changed to handle the specific demands of the user. Data rates can be symmetric or asymmetric.

Table 22.1 illustrates the features of various DSL technologies.

Table 22.1. A confusing parade of DSL technologies offer varying upstream and downstream data rates.

Type	Upstream	Downstream	Loop Distance
ADSL	1.5-8Mbps	16-64Kbps	12,000-18,000 feet
HDSL	1.544Mbps	1.544Mbps	15,000 feet
SDSL	1.544Mbps	1.544Mbps	10,000 feet
VDSL	13-52Mbps	1.5-2.3Mbps	1,000-4,500 feet
RADSL	varies	varies	varies

There may be a lot of DSL flavors out there, but one thing is for sure, they all provide more bandwidth than was previously available. The fastest downstream DSL connection runs about 100 times faster than a 56K modem and 50 times faster than ISDN. Even consumer-grade DSL, with its lower costs, will move 1.5Mbps downstream—a figure that is more than 10 times faster than ISDN.

Strengths and Weaknesses

One key advantage to the lower data rate DSL service is the fact that it requires no extra hardware aside from an ADSL modem to run in your home or office. With faster DSL variants, you need a splitter to break out the DSL and voice segments of your wiring. But ADSL can work with both voice and DSL signals running throughout the line. You can set up your phones and DSL adapters where you want, and you avoid the added expense and hassle of installing additional hardware.

DSL is good technology, no doubt about it, but it's not free. For one thing, the telcos must upgrade much of their switching hardware to suit the new service—a challenge that will delay rollout of the service for years in many parts of the country. And while ADSL will work over existing copper wire, the lines in many older homes may not be up to grade. That means a significant fraction of customers will need to replace their phone wiring in order to enjoy DSL service.

Ultimately, what limits ADSL is the short range of the service. In order to get ADSL, you must not live more than 18,000 feet—or three miles—from the DSL-equipped phone switch. For those in rural areas, such proximity is unlikely, and telcos are not going to rush to upgrade switches lacking a ready base of nearby customers. In many instances, ADSL may not be an option for years. It's worth noting that higher-speed DSL services require even shorter line lengths, on the order of 10,000 or even less.

Okay, so you can get ADSL service and your wiring is up to snuff. What do you need to get the service? Obviously, your current modem won't do (though you can use it normally for dial-up service over your ADSL-enabled line). You'll need a DSL adapter (shown in Figure 22.3), often called a DSL modem, to translate your PC's data into the packeted format recognized by the DSL network. The adapter will also monitor the DSL line, plucking out packets addressed to your PC while letting all others pass. In effect, your DSL modem works a lot like an Ethernet network interface card (NIC).

FIGURE 22.3.
The Westell ATU-R external ADSL adapter provides 1.544Mbps down-stream and 64Kbps upstream data rates. (Photo courtesy of Westell Technologies)

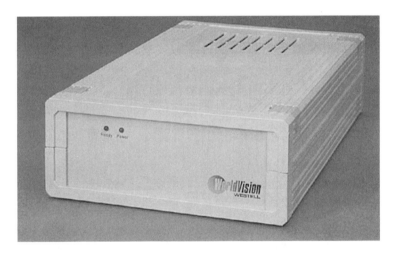

While DSL modem prices are quite high, they should drop quickly as the service becomes more widespread. Vendors such as 3Com, Cisco, and Westell are marketing DSL adapters. Of course, you'll need the service to reach your region before you invest in hardware.

Cable Modems: The Future of Home Browsing?

Another emerging option comes in the form of cable modems, which connect to the thick coaxial cable used to supply cable TV transmissions. Coax is a bandwidth hero, able to shove 6MBbps or more to the receiving PC. Unfortunately, because the cable network was laid with only TV broadcasts in mind, upstream facilities are limited in all but a small portion of installations. Without modification, there is no way to direct that bandwidth for applications such as Web browsing.

Like DSL, cable already enjoys a large installed infrastructure, with coax cable running to over 60 million homes. But unlike DSL, cable is generally unavailable in corporate districts—offices don't use cable TV, but they do use telephones. For this reason, cable modems are an attractive option in the home Web access market, while businesses must look elsewhere.

The compelling thing about cable is its potential raw performance. Downstream data rates can run at 42Mbps—about four times faster than a typical Ethernet network—while upstream rates can go to 10Mbps. Based on an industry standard called DOCSIS (for Data Over Cable Service Interface Specifications), this performance makes even advanced DSL services pale in comparison.

But wait, there's more. Unlike DSL and its cousins, cable service is actually deployed and working in large segments of the market. And the cable modems themselves (such as that shown in Figure 22.4) are less expensive than DSL adapters.

FIGURE 22.4.
The 3Com VPC Plus internal cable modem plugs into a PCI slot and includes the telltale coax con-nector. (Photo courtesy of 3Com)

Coax connector

So cable is fast, cheap, and available. Why isn't it the slam dunk choice for speedy Web access? A couple issues. For one thing, many cable networks need to be reworked to handle two-way communications. For many current customers, a cable Web connection demands that you dial up to a service provider and send all upstream data via a modem. The added cost and slow upstream performance both water down cable's appeal. And even with two-way networks, upstream bandwidth is limited to about 64Kbps (as shown in Figure 22.5).

Cable providers are also struggling to establish standards that will allow a cable modem designed for one provider's service to work with another. Today, that issue is generally handled by renting the modem hardware to users, so when the user moves to a new ser-vice, he or she simply rents the adapter from their new provider.

Bigger problems come from cable's broadcast roots. Bits on the cable network are broad-cast, with the box detecting packets intended for your desktop. But because all data is broadcast to all customers, others are able to snoop your data. Also, bandwidth over cable is shared. So if there's 50Mbps of bandwidth coming from the cable head end in your neighborhood, you must split that amongst your neighbors. At 6 o'clock in the morning, therefore, you may enjoy 50Mbps downloads, while at 7 o'clock at night your service could degrade significantly—particularly if your provider isn't keen on updating hardware.

FIGURE 22.5.
This graphic shows how cable services handle the upstream data. (Graphic courtesy of 3Com)

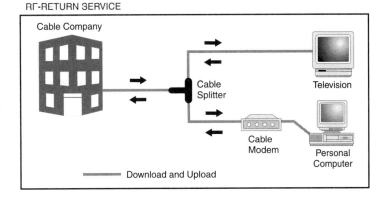

Satellite Systems

OK, so what if you don't have DSL being deployed to your doorstep? Or maybe your cable provider is a decade away from even considering Web services. Does that mean you have to live in a digital dark age, crawling about at 56Kbps while your friends count their megabits?

Not necessarily. Today, the most widely available high-bandwidth Internet access option is via *direct satellite system (DSS)*, such as DirecPC from Hughes Networks. (Check out the Web site at www.DirecPC.com.) A compact 18- to 21-inch dish, identical to those used for satellite TV services, receives downstream data from the Internet. With up to 400KBps data rates, and access from even the most remote locations in the continental U.S., satellite service is the most widely available high-bandwidth option around.

Inside DSS

Here's how it works. The DSS dish is mounted on your house or other structure where it can get a line-of-site view of the satellite, which is typically positioned in the southern portion of the sky. The dish connects to your PC via a coax cable and an add-in card. The final piece of the puzzle is an analog modem, which you need to dial into the Internet to send commands and data upstream.

When you dial into your service provider, your upstream commands and data are routed to the Hughes Network, where connections are then made to the resources you are accessing. Responses to the Hughes Network are then routed to Hughes' transmitters, which bounce the signal off the geosynchronous satellite. Your dish receives the signal and sends the broadcast bits to your adapter card for processing. The card parses out the packets with your name on them, and produces the results in the form of displayed Web pages, downloaded files, and the like.

While downstream data rates are quite fast—400Kbps is more than three times faster than ISDN—upstream is limited to the 33.6Kbps ceiling of your modem. What's more, satellite communications introduce noticeable delay into your transactions. While large files and Web pages download quickly, rapid-fire updates—such as those required in online gaming—are delayed by the time it takes the signal to travel from Earth to the satellite (22,000 miles up) and back again (as shown in Figure 22.6). While ground-based digital connections may enjoy a 10 millisecond or briefer response time (called ping rate), DSS customers will experience 500ms response. That half-second delay on every transaction makes Deathmatch Quake II impossible to play.

Of course, beggars can't be choosers, and if you live in a rural community, DSS may be your only high bandwidth option. What's more, the digital downstream connection helps improve the reliability of Internet access with drop-outs becoming less frequent.

Problems Abound

Before you rush out for a dish, consider the challenges involved. First, the hardware involved gets expensive. The dish, cable, and adapter card will run you upwards of $400 to $600—though you can get a break on that by signing up for the service at the same time. The service can also be pricey, running $120 a month for all-you-can-use access. With increased competition from cable and DSL providers, however, these rates are coming down. Of course, you'll also need to pay for a standard analog ISP account in addition to the satellite service.

Installation is probably the biggest challenge. Lining up the dish to receive transmissions is an exacting process. Unless you are a serious do-it-yourselfer, the challenge of orienting and mounting the dish on a steep roof may require professional installation. Figure another $200 for installation costs.

FIGURE 22.6.

What comes around, goes around—eventually. Satellite services describe a circuitous data path. (Photo courtesy of Hughes Network Systems)

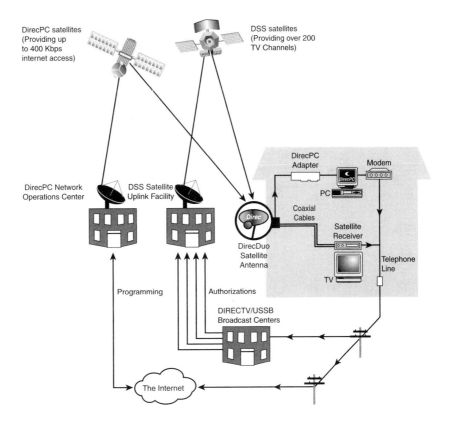

Of course, you need line of site to make DSS work, and that can be an issue in areas with tall trees, buildings, and other obstructions. Those living far to the north will have a rougher time, since most users will need to line up with a satellite orbiting over the southern United States. Northerners will find their dishes pointed rather close to the horizon rather than overhead. Not only does this make trees and buildings a problem, it also increases the distance to the satellite and the amount of atmosphere between you and it. The result: Weaker signal strengths in far northern climes that can lead to lower data rates and even lost service.

Weather also plays a factor. Heavy rains and snowfall can impede the Ku band signal most of these satellites transmit, though noticeable degradations are generally limited to severe weather. Likewise, icing on the dish can prevent signal capture. Finally, gamers will want to avoid this technology all together, as the latency of satellite transmissions is very poor. It can take over ½ a second for signals to travel out to the ISP and then back from the geosynchronous satellite.

Buying Bandwidth: Shopping for Digital Modems and Other Devices

So you want fast Internet access, do you? Today more connectivity options are open to PC users than ever before. Modems of varying speeds and talents can fire bits over standard phone lines and even turn your PC into an answering machine. Real bandwidth jockeys might consider one of the several digital infrastructures available, from ISDN to direct satellite systems. Table 22.2 will help you decide.

Table 22.2. Bandwidth options at a glance.

Type	Data Rate	Cost of Installation	Monthly Cost	What It's Best For
33.6KBps modem	33.6/33.6KBps	$100	N/A	Casual Web browsing and email, home and small office. This type of modem is ubiquitous.
56K modem	56/33.6KBps	$189	N/A	Casual and heavy Web browsing and email, home and small office, server access. The lack of a single 56K standard could make some products obsolete.
ISDN	128/128KBps	$400	$36-$100	Heavy Web browsing, small office, video-conferencing and dataconferencing, Web publishing uploads, Internet gaming. Limited availability.
Satellite	400/33.6KBps	$500	$40	Heavy Web browsing and email, small office, and server access. This is the best option for rural locations.

Type	Data Rate	Cost of Installation	Monthly Cost	What It's Best For
Cable modem	4MBps/ 33.6KBps	$800	$60	Heavy Web browsing and email, home and small office, server access, Internet gaming. This is still in trials.
DSL modem	1.6MBps/ 128KBps	$800	TBD	Heavy Web browsing and email, home and small office, server access, Web publishing FTP uploads, videoconferencing and dataconferencing, Internet gaming. This is still in trials.

The vast majority of users will remain with analog modems for years to come. Digital technologies are either too expensive, too complex, or too limited in their availability to make them worth buying. In the meantime, expect 56K modem technology to fill the gap while the phone companies, cable companies, and others lay down the infrastructure needed to make higher-bandwidth connections ubiquitous.

Location, Location, Location

Once you start shopping for fast access, you need to worry about where you live. Those living in suburban metropolitan areas will generally fare best, as will those in well-serviced urban areas. Poorer neighborhoods, however, will find the modern switching equipment and lines needed for DSL and ISDN hard to come by. Of course, rural areas are often not served by these new technologies, and even the basic POTS phone lines are of substandard quality.

It's not hard to understand why this happens. Telcos and ISPs want to make money like anyone else, and they stand the best chance of doing that if they update their infrastructures in affluent and densely populated areas. This is particularly important since services like ISDN and DSL require that the subscriber be located anywhere from 10,000 to 18,000 feet from the switch (a distance of about 2 to 3.5 miles). Greater distances result in signal degradation making advanced services untenable.

For home users, cable service is a big driver and is likely to be the only high-bandwidth option for a year or more. Also keep in mind that large cities with numerous ISPs are more likely to provide a variety of options spanning analog, ISDN, DSL, and cable modem service. Rural areas, by contrast, simply lack the necessary infrastructure.

Assessing Performance

So you need your bits and you need them fast. What's the best option? If you live in a well-served area, you may actually be able to choose among ISDN, DSL, cable, and satellite service. If that's the case, you'll want to weigh the relative performance.

Unfortunately, there are few straight answers. Services like cable and DSL both feature variable data rates that can be quite different depending on the provider, the service tier, and (for cable, at least) the time of day. Still, any digital solution is going to make your analog modem look pretty sorry in comparison. You'll see an end to annoying drop-outs and noise-induced slow downs. Logging onto the Internet will go much more quickly as well, since you no longer have to wait for the noisy handshake routine modems must go through.

Table 22.3 compares the specified data transfer rates for the most prevalent technologies.

Table 22.3. Digital options provide more than just faster speeds, they also deliver quick response.

Type	Upload	Download	Responsiveness
POTS	33.6Kbps	53Kbps	Slow
ISDN	128Kbps	128Kbps	Quick
Cable	33.6Kbps	10-40Mbps	Slow
DSL	16-640Kbps	1.5-6Mbps	Quick
Satellite	33.6Kbps	400KBps	Slow

Of course, no matter what service you use, you'll be affected by the speed of the Web. If the Web server you are contacting is overloaded, you'll see the same slowdowns that your friends using 56Kbps modems do—you'll just be paying more for the privilege. Also, the specifications provided don't always match with the reality of the specific service you might have available to you. And just as poor phone lines can prevent optimal analog operation, weather can degrade satellite performance.

You should also do some research before signing on with a service. A cable service may provide Web access, but that's no assurance it's any good. You need to find out if you'll need a separate modem for upstream connections, and you'll also want to know how many users are sharing the available head end bandwidth in your area. Without this kind of information, you won't be able to assess the level of performance you will get.

Internal or External Adapters

In many cases, the adapters you buy will have to run internally in your PC. That's because, unlike analog modems, the data flow coming through the adapter is much higher than what your serial port can handle. A typical 115Kbps serial port will be completely outmatched by a 400Kbps satellite service, much less a 6Mbps DSL connection.

So you'll have to make sure your PC has what it takes to host the adapter. Expect to need a free PCI slot, since many external DSL and cable modems connect to your PC via a network interface card (NIC). Internal adapters do away with the separate box and offer lower cost, but you may need room for a full-length card, something many compact PCs won't have. You should check to make sure you have a full-length PCI card slot open before you decide on an internal adapter.

One growing option for Windows 98 users is a USB connected external adapter. USB provides 12Mbps of bandwidth and offers superior Plug and Play. What's more, USB's power handling capability eliminates the need for a separate power cord for your cable or DSL modem, helping reduce the amount of wires behind the PC. The main drawback is the lack of USB product. Vendors are just now moving aggressively into USB, in part because only a portion (albeit a growing one) of PCs support this bus.

Installing Advanced Hardware

There are so many different types of hardware involved that it is impossible to cover every scenario here. That said, in most cases you'll end up installing an internal adapter. For cable modems, the setup actually involves installing an ethernet card, while others use internal cards specific to their function. You should follow the documentation provided by your vendor when installing hardware.

The good news is that all the internal devices currently being sold comply with the Plug and Play specification. That means Windows 95/98 will be able to detect the new card, assign it resources, and kick off the appropriate driver installation routine. In most cases, you'll need to have the driver disc handy, since drivers for these devices will not be present on the standard Windows 95/98 disc.

To install an internal adapter card, do the following:

1. Shut off the PC, unplug the power cord, and remove the case.

2. Make sure you ground yourself by touching a metal portion of the PC chassis, or use a grounding mat and wrist strap.

3. Unscrew the backplate of a free ISA card slot and pull out the backplate connector.

4. Seat the card into the appropriate ISA or PCI slot. You might need to rock the card slightly from back to front to ease it into the connector.

5. Affix the backplate using the screw you just removed. Plug in the phone cord or coax cable.

6. Power up the PC, and then follow the steps for setting up the new modem hardware.

7. Once you've determined that the adapter is working properly, shut down the PC, secure the board backplane with a screwdriver, and reattach the case.

> **Tip:** You should always make a point to check the vendor's Web site for the latest drivers and firmware after you've completed the installation.

Summary

For better or for worse, there is a universe of connectivity options out there. Before you start doing heavy duty research, however, you'll need to assess what services are available where you are. You'll also need to find out if new or enhanced services are imminent in your area. After all, you'd be pretty disappointed about your new satellite dish if, four weeks later, the local cable company rolled out 10Mbps cable modem access.

Keep in mind that in many instances, high-bandwidth equals high-cost and high anxiety. Unless you really need to speed data transfers, enhance online reliability, and establish LAN-like service, these technologies may simply remain too expensive and difficult to consider. And if you generally send a lot more data than you receive—typical of Web site developers, for instance—be sure to look at options that will improve your upstream performance.

Ultimately, many of us will be forced to wait while services like cable and DSL work their way into our neighborhoods and price ranges. In the meantime, fast modems and duplex modem products may be the best option.

I/O Add-Ons

Processors get faster, hard disks get bigger, and RAM gets less expensive. If all this seems woefully predictable, you can take heart in the vagaries of new, enhanced input/output technologies. Although improvements in the capabilities of SCSI and IDE bus technologies have been welcome, a spate of new buses are helping extend the capabilities of desktop and notebook PCs.

From wireless infrared communications to daisy-chained Universal Serial Bus, these technologies make it easier than ever to move data among systems and peripherals. This chapter covers the following:

- The various types of enhanced I/O systems and devices, and the means of adding their capabilities to existing PCs
- Advice and information to help you decide which I/O technologies are worth purchasing
- Upgrade instructions for various I/O peripherals
- Troubleshooting and repairing strategies for I/O products

I/O Upgrades: Let's Get Serial

Some of the most exciting upgrade opportunities for your PC might be components that enable advanced I/O capabilities. Behind these devices are a flurry of industry standards and improving technologies. From enhanced printing to easy remote file access, these upgrades might be worth a look—particularly if you want to make use of new peripherals that take advantage of these I/O technologies.

The technologies involved are

- Universal Serial Bus (USB)
- IEEE 1394 FireWire
- PC Card (or PCMCIA) and CardBus
- IrDA-compliant infrared communications

Note: In an effort to push the PC platform forward, market-makers Intel and Microsoft have published the PC99 specification. PC99 provides a blueprint for acceptable system designs in 1999, and attempts to do things like woo system makers away from ISA card slots and toward Plug and Play designs. Expansion buses like USB, FireWire, and PC Card/CardBus are make-or-break issues for PC makers trying to move their products into the consumer electronics mainstream.

Infrared communications, meanwhile, provide a critical wireless data on-ramp for devices. Remote controls, keyboards, and controllers running over a standard IR bus allow the creation of effective home-entertainment PCs. The ability to set up inexpensive ad hoc IR networks will be critical as more and more homes own multiple PCs.

One thing happening is the adoption of streamlined serial bus architectures. Buses such as SCSI, enhanced IDE, and even PCI and ISA are all parallel bus technologies. In other words, they move groups of bits across many wires in lockstep. This approach works: PCI can push 132MBps by running 32 bits across at 33MHz. Vendors Compaq and HP have combined to augment that bus with the PCI-x specification, which runs at 66MHz on a 32-bit bus to provide a transfer rate of 264MBps. A fast-and-wide PCI—64 bits and 64MHz—has also been talked about for high-end servers.

But parallel schemes have problems, particularly when it comes to external buses. Getting lots of bits to cross wires in lockstep isn't easy, and timing issues get more and more difficult as speeds move up through 33MHz and beyond. This is particularly true of external bus architectures, in which electrical signals must travel lengthy cables, braving external interference and crosstalk from other wires within the cable to deliver bits safely. Parallel schemes also get expensive, because the number of wires and pins needed for multiple data lanes adds cost to peripherals and systems.

Serial approaches, in contrast, use a single lane moving very quickly to meet or beat the performance of parallel buses. Again, the absence of complex timing interaction among multiple wires allows for much higher clock speed operation, even across a cable running several meters in length. Better yet, those speeds can be packaged into affordable, space-saving designs—making them potentially appropriate for desktop and mobile use.

Not that these old standbys have stood still over the years. Early serial ports, for example, could not even match the output of 14.4Kbps modems. The answer: Improved UART chips enabled the port to efficiently capture more data. The serial ports found on today's machines can easily handle 56Kbps operation, and typically offer transfer rates of 115Kbps. If you have an old 486 with a fast external modem, you might consider an inexpensive I/O upgrade card—typically for ISA slots—offering enhanced serial and parallel ports.

The parallel port has seen even greater revisions, albeit at the cost of compatibility. Today's fastest bi-directional parallel ports—called Extended Capabilities Parallel (or

ECP Port)—can move as much as 1MBps of data. Not only can the fast port improve print times and other data-intensive transfers, the bi-directional capability enables interaction between the PC and devices. Unfortunately, older cables and most parallel pass-through modules don't recognize the extended capabilities, often leading to perplexing failures. What's more, your system BIOS must be set for ECP operation to make this capability work. For compatibility reasons, this feature may be turned off by default.

> **Note:** While serial and parallel port technology has advanced, both are approaching the end of the line. Unlike USB, neither port offers the ability to detect and dynamically load and unload device software—a critical ease of use feature. What's more, USB can juggle 127 devices off a single port—using hubs to interconnect devices—while serial and USB get confused when more than one device sits on the port. If you use Windows 98 and have working USB ports on your PC, you should look to USB versions of peripherals rather than their serial/parallel counterparts. This will ensure that the devices work on future PCs you own.

Universal Serial Bus: First Among Equals

Of all the new I/O schemes, USB has had the most impact. For the past two years, systems have shipped with a pair of USB ports on the back, helping build a ready-made installed base for USB peripherals. What's more, the arrival of Windows 98 delivered trouble-free USB support to millions of desktops and notebooks.

Perhaps most important, USB solves a critical problem—the lack of serial and parallel ports to handle all the gadgets hooked to your PC. Everything from printers and scanners, to speakers, microphones, joysticks, and PDAs can hook into this standard port on the back of your PC. You already have enough ports, you say? Consider this: USB brings several critical talents to the PC that the serial and parallel port lack:

- 12Mbps throughput
- Plug and Play
- Hot swapping of devices (allows swapping without restarting the PC)
- Daisy-chaining or the operation of more than one device on a single cable or bus
- Autotermination and detection

What It's For

More than the other new I/O technology, USB solves problems that are present right now. Both the parallel and serial ports are seriously overworked, forcing users to juggle peripherals competing for scarce connector space. Things can get ugly fast. Anyone who has fished around among the tangle of cables at the back of a PC knows how difficult it can be to keep things straight.

USB solves this problem by using a standard port to serve all sorts of peripherals. With a data rate of 12Mbps, USB is 10 times faster than the current serial bus and about 50 percent faster than the most advanced parallel port. That makes the bus appropriate for uses ranging from keyboards and mice to scanners, printers, and even telephones.

More important, USB is Plug and Play. With the proper device drivers and operating system support, devices plugged into the USB port are automatically detected and enabled by the system. Windows 98's virtual device drivers (known as VxDs) allow for dynamic loading and unloading of device capabilities. Unlike SCSI, in which each device must often be manually terminated and identified via SCSI IDs, USB does all the work automatically.

Here are some of the peripherals that can employ USB for enhanced operation:

- Basic input (mouse, keyboard)
- Game controllers (joysticks, gamepads, head-mounted displays)
- Digital USB cameras for videoconferencing
- Digital audio speakers
- Modems
- Scanners
- Printers

How It Works

USB frees up the connector logjam by allowing peripherals to hook to the USB bus through other peripherals (see Figure 23.1). Like SCSI, a peripheral such as a scanner or printer can have more than one USB connector, enabling the device to hook to the system and to serve as a conduit for other devices downstream. Unfortunately, most devices lack a second USB connector for daisy chaining, which means you may have to invest in a USB hub that provides additional ports for your devices. Some peripherals, such as monitors, actually offer built-in hubs to help alleviate the port crunch.

FIGURE 23.1.

USB hubs can be found on monitors, scanners, or dedicated devices serving as data centers for your USB peripherals.

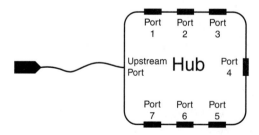

Data moves up and down the four-wire USB cable. Devices can sit up to 50 feet from the host PC, and a maximum of 127 devices can run off the PC's USB controller.

Higher-bandwidth devices such as scanners, printers, and sound hardware can run at up to 12Mbps, while less-demanding mice and joysticks run at a low-bandwidth mode of 1.5MBps.

> **Note:** USB capability is part and parcel of the PC99 specification, and it's on Microsoft's menu for its Simply Interactive PC (SIPC) initiative. The reason is that USB eliminates the need for ornery parallel and serial ports and provides Plug and Play outside of the box. If you purchase a new system or motherboard, make sure that USB ports are provided. Often you'll see twin connectors placed low in the chassis, just off the motherboard plane.

Unlike the chaining SCSI specification, USB works using a star topology scheme, as shown in Figure 23.2. In this design, all devices operate downstream from a single USB controller—you can't install a second USB controller in a PC. Most desktop PCs have two USB ports coming from the central controller. Devices hanging off these ports might serve up to three other devices. A maximum of 127 devices may be installed on the USB bus.

FIGURE 23.2.

USB allows a wide variety of peripherals to connect to each other, all answering back to a single host USB hub on the system. (Figure courtesy of the USB Organization)

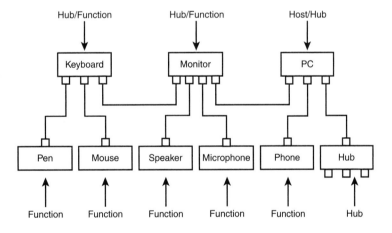

USB also allows low-power devices to run without an external power supply. Modems, scanners, and force feedback joysticks are good examples of peripherals able to forego a power cord in their USB incarnation.

IEEE 1394 FireWire: Convergence Cabling

If USB has already enhanced the PC platform, the IEEE 1394 bus—more memorably known by its Apple-trademarked name, FireWire—could revolutionize it. This fast and furious serial bus takes aim at high-bandwidth peripherals such as video cameras and hard disks. In fact, there is speculation that FireWire could transform into a general-purpose system bus, supplanting PCI as the backbone of system communications (just don't hold your breath).

FireWire provides the following capabilities:

- Data throughput rates of 200Mbps, with future versions providing 400, 800, and 1,200Mbps
- Plug and Play
- Hot swapping of devices
- Daisy-chaining
- Autotermination and detection

As you can see, FireWire has many of the same attributes as USB, with one prominent exception—speed. Expect to pay for the added performance, because FireWire-enabled peripherals and adapters must use more sophisticated electronics and chipsets to manage the higher data rates.

What It's For

Where USB solves current problems, FireWire does more to open new opportunities. Video capture, for example, can take place over a general-purpose FireWire bus rather than a dedicated capture card. FireWire is already being used by consumer electronics companies such as Sony to connect new digital camcorders to PCs. Similarly, FireWire looks like a good bet to play a key role in PC convergence, connecting the PC to TVs, stereos, and other general-purpose devices (see Figure 23.3). Finally, Microsoft and Intel hope to eventually move hard disks, DVD-ROM drives, and other storage devices onto FireWire, using the Device Bay standard that specs out external bays for future PCs.

FIGURE 23.3.

FireWire covers some of the same ground as USB but weighs heavily on consumer electronics and multimedia. (Figure courtesy of Texas Instruments and the 1394 Trade Association)

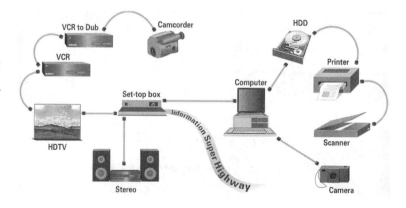

Among the applications FireWire addresses are these:

- Digital camcorders and VCRs
- Videoconferencing
- Direct-to-home (DTH) satellite video and audio MPEG-2 data streams
- Musical synthesizers with MIDI and digital audio capabilities
- High-speed printers
- Hard disk drives
- Networking—in particular, home networks
- Cable TV and MMDS ("wireless cable") set-top boxes
- External DVD drives

How It Works

Like USB, FireWire is a self-terminating Plug and Play serial bus that can automatically detect devices as they are installed and removed. Again, dynamic device driver management is the key. 32-bit OSs such as Windows 95/98 and NT can load and unload device system software on-the-fly without requiring a reboot.

FireWire is described as a noncyclic network that has finite branches. *Noncyclic* means that peripherals can't be set up to create loops, while a maximum of 16 devices may be strung together, daisy-chain fashion, between nodes (the *finite branch* part). The maximum distance between each device is 4.5 meters (although bridging hardware can extend this distance), allowing a daisy chain of 16 peripherals to extend up to 72 meters. FireWire can support up to 63 peripherals in this manner (see Figure 23.4).

Although FireWire supports up to 400MBps operation right now, not all configurations take advantage of it. Most FireWire adapters, such as Adaptec's FireCard, provide 200MBps operation. FireWire-compliant peripherals, meanwhile, are generally tuned for 200 or 400MBps operation, with future products supporting data rates as high as 1.2Gbps.

Tip: A 200MBps FireWire peripheral will work on a 400MBps FireWire adapter, but the reverse isn't true. If you plan on using FireWire for demanding, professional video-capture applications or the like, consider getting a FireWire adapter set for 400MBps data rates. This will ensure that you have headroom for optimal performance.

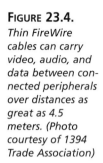

Figure 23.4.
Thin FireWire cables can carry video, audio, and data between connected peripherals over distances as great as 4.5 meters. (Photo courtesy of 1394 Trade Association)

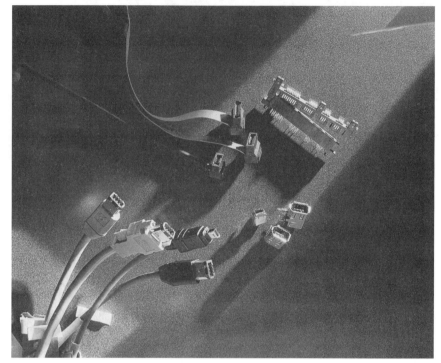

Already, Sony has adopted FireWire (using the trade name I_LINK) in some of its desktop and notebook PCs, while Compaq has introduced FireWire in some of its Presario desktops. But it will be a while before FireWire ports are built into all mainstream PCs. Intel has backed off putting FireWire support into its system chipsets—a critical prerequisite for widespread adoption. What's more, FireWire's added cost makes it difficult to incorporate into the PC platform. In the meantime, add-in adapter cards and manufacturers' driver software enable upgraders to turn their PCs into FireWire-capable systems. When FireWire does become ubiquitous, it stands to obsolete the IDE interface on most motherboards, making it the drive interface of choice in the next century.

Infrared Device Association: IrDA Beams Onto the Desktop

USB and FireWire are welcome technologies, to be sure. They're fast, they're convenient, and they bring Plug and Play technology to peripherals sorely in need of its benefits. What they won't do is alleviate the nasty tangle of wires and cables that plague virtually every desktop PC. These technologies cut down on the clutter by using a single cable standard, but the cables are there nonetheless.

Enter infrared communications. By managing the timing of invisible light pulses, infrared light can be used to pass bits back and forth between devices, without the use of connecting wires. All that is needed are an IR emitter and receiver for each device and a standard way to interpret the light signals.

The Infrared Device Association (IrDA) got things moving by establishing a standard specification for IR communications. Although IrDA hardware is most frequently found on notebook PCs, a wide range of systems and peripherals can benefit from IR facilities.

What It's For

Obviously, IrDA is about communications. But more precisely, it is about convenient, cable-free connectivity, allowing PCs to access external devices or other systems without clumsy cables.

The following devices benefit from IR capability:

- Notebook PCs
- Handheld PCs, or Personal Digital Assistants (PDAs)
- Networked systems
- Ink jet printers and black-and-white laser printers
- Cordless mice and keyboards

Today, IR ports can be found on almost all notebooks and a good many handheld PCs. Many personal printers include IR ports as well. The benefit is obvious to anyone who has taken a notebook into a remote office and who needs to print documents. IrDA lets you simply beam your print job across the desk to a waiting printer. You don't need to hunt up a parallel cable or—worse yet—haul your own cable along to do print jobs on the road.

Even more promising is the ability to share files between notebook and desktop PCs. You can get your notebook on the network using a PC Card network interface card, but they tend to be pricey and prone to loss. Parallel or serial port communications over Windows 95's Direct Cable Connection facility or Traveling Software's LapLink are clumsy, requiring users to fish around behind the overcrowded backsides of PCs to hook up cables.

Unfortunately, desktop IR never took off. You won't find many PCs with IrDA ports on their front bezels. However, you can purchase IR ports that hook into a dedicated IR card. The small module hooks to the back of your PC using a cable (ironic, isn't it?), allowing it to be placed for maximum convenience. These ports can be used to talk to notebooks, printers, or other IrDA-compliant devices.

How It Works

The first IrDA peripherals ran at a relatively pokey 115.2KBps. That's fast enough for simple file transfers and print jobs, but not enough for more-demanding uses.

Reconciling the contents of a notebook and a desktop hard disk, for example, can involve hundreds of megabytes. Likewise, complex print jobs can be several megabytes in size.

The Fast IrDA specification, called FIR, addresses this problem by boosting maximum bandwidth to 4Mbps. Although this isn't as fast as the USB specification, it's more than enough for the vast majority of IR-based transactions. After all, you probably won't have to run real-time video over a wireless connection. More important, FIR peripherals can talk to older IrDA devices.

IrDA has its drawbacks. For one thing, most desktop PC users must go to the expense of adding an external IR module (shown in Figure 23.5) to receive and send signals. Also, the infrared signal requires a direct line of sight. You need to line up the IR ports and make sure no obstructions are present to make transfers work. Older modules will require you to dedicate a serial port to the IR device, which really limits your options for other devices if you already have an external modem. Windows 98 users, however, can find USB-based modules, which eases the port resource crunch.

FIGURE 23.5.
You'll need an external IR transceiver, like this ActiSys model, to share data between your desktop and IR-equipped notebooks. It can handle up to 4MBps. (Photo courtesy of ActiSys)

Mobile Marvels: PC Card and CardBus

In 1990, a group called Personal Computer and Memory Card International Association (PCMCIA) ratified a standard for credit card-sized peripherals that plug into tiny slots. Designed specifically for notebooks, this standard has helped create a market of tiny modems, LAN cards, and even multimedia peripherals. Today, any notebook you purchase will probably have one or more slots for the PCMCIA specification—known as PC Card.

The original PC Card specification has since been improved. Driving the move was the need for faster data rates and more direct access to system resources in order to support a wider range of peripherals. The enhanced bus, called CardBus, promises to deliver PCI-like bus performance over a modular, externally accessible bus architecture.

PC Card

There are actually several varieties of PC Card peripherals, demarcated by the height of the card. Right now, three official categories exist, and a fourth is under review. All three existing categories use the same 68-pin design. Table 23.1 outlines the categories and their intended markets.

Table 23.1. PC Card types.

PC Card Type	Card Height	Products
Type I	3.3mm	Flash memory
Type II	5mm	Modems, LAN adapters audio/game cards, SCSI interface
Type III	10.5mm	Hard disks
Type IV	To be determined	To be determined

The PC Card bus uses a 16-bit wide interface, running at 16MHz. The resulting through-put is roughly equivalent to that of an ISA bus card. This is more than enough speed for most communication and even mass-storage peripherals. Even fast 100MBps LAN cards will run acceptably on the PC Card interface, although the faster CardBus scheme allows greater performance in some applications.

Perhaps most importantly, PC Card was Plug and Play before Microsoft's Windows 95 turned it into a catch phrase. Thanks to a complex system of BIOS updates and PC Card drivers, these devices can be plugged in and taken out at will. Device drivers load and unload automatically, a process known as *hot-swapping*. You can complete a dial-up ses-sion with a PC Card modem, yank the card, install a LAN adapter, and be ready to log on to the network within a few seconds.

However, PC Card lacks direct memory access (DMA) and bus mastering, thus limiting performance for multimedia data transfers. The lack of DMA capability means that Sound Blaster-compatible PC Card products are impossible to build, because the stan-dard demands a DMA address. PC Card also lacks power management features, which means that PC Card modems, for example, draw power even when they're not in use.

CardBus: The Second Coming

CardBus builds on the success of PC Card while addressing its most glaring problems. What's more, CardBus is intended to serve as a true, modular, general-purpose bus, just as PCI does for desktops. The difference is that you don't need to come face-to-face with intimidating circuit boards and silicon chips in order to install a device.

It's no surprise that performance gets a big boost. CardBus beefs up the data pathways to a hefty 32 bits running at a fast 33MHz. The result is a bus that is as fast and wide as PCI, matching its impressive 132MBps bursting data throughput. CardBus also moves to a 3.3-volt design that reduces power draw and heat dissipation.

If you buy a new notebook, it probably includes 32-bit CardBus slots. Desktop PCs, meanwhile, can be outfitted with a PC Card reader, as shown in Figure 23.6. If you have a new CardBus-equipped notebook, definitely look to peripherals that can take advantage of it, but you'll also be able to use most older, 16-bit PC Card devices.

Figure 23.6.

If you want to share PC Card peripherals with your desktop, you'll need to buy an adapter such as Card Dock to do so. (Photo courtesy of Adaptec Corp.)

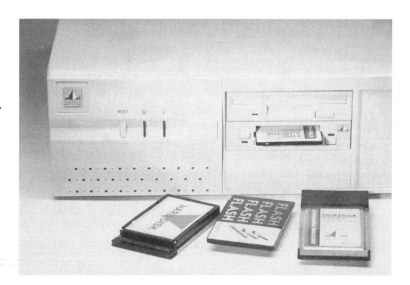

Note: In addition, CardBus will probably adopt some implementation of a proprietary Toshiba technology called Zoomed Port Video (ZPV) or Zoom Video (ZV), depending on who's doing the marketing. Zoom Video specifically addresses video capture and playback on notebook PCs, allowing video data to be transferred directly to the graphics adapter frame buffer without going first to the host CPU or memory. At the same time, audio data is streamed directly to the digital-to-analog converter.

ZV allows for high-performance video capture on notebook PCs. By setting up direct data pathways to sound and graphics hardware, the system CPU can stay out of time-consuming transactions and focus on other tasks. ZV peripherals plugged into enhanced CardBus slots will be able to grab video streams, perform compression or decompression, and move the data to sound and graphics hardware on-the-fly.

Buying Bandwidth: A Guide to the New I/O

So you want to add I/O capability to your new or existing PC. What's the best option? It depends on what you need to do. Although USB, FireWire, and IrDA all boast intriguing capabilities, they all serve very different needs.

That said, even the best technology won't go far without support. For example, FireWire may be 50 times faster than USB, but USB is much more useful simply because both hardware makers and Microsoft have built USB support into their products. FireWire, meanwhile, will likely remain relegated to roll into 2001. At the very least, check to make sure that peripherals are available to work with any technology you choose, otherwise, you will end up buying the digital equivalent of an exercise machine—perfectly good technology that never gets used.

> **Note:** In many cases, none of your existing peripherals will be set up for USB or FireWire. This means that you should factor in the potential cost of upgrading these peripheral devices alongside the cost of adding a bus adapter. More important, you must make sure that USB-compatible products are available for the types of peripherals you're considering.

When Do Upgrades Make Sense?

Upgrading to a bus is like buying a house: It's not serving its purpose until you furnish it. In the case of USB and FireWire, actually furnishing your bus upgrade might be tougher than you think. New peripherals can take a long time to emerge, because vendors move cautiously before adding the cost of new connectors and drivers to their existing products.

USB is a case in point. After more than two years on the market, products have finally arrived to fit into the USB ports found on the backs of almost every PC. The holdup: Windows 98. While later versions of Windows 95 offer partial USB support, Windows 98 makes things much easier for hardware makers. And since peripherals makers were not anxious to develop—and support—special software for their USB products, everyone just waited. The lesson is that you need to be patient. No multibillion-dollar industry changes overnight, and the potential risk for vendors moving to a new standard too soon is enormous.

More importantly, you should time an upgrade with a peripheral purchase. For example, if you're thinking about buying a new scanner, you might want to look into available USB-compatible models. If you find something you like, this might be a good time to start the switch by purchasing a USB adapter card (assuming you need one) and a USB-compatible scanner to run off it (see Figure 23.7). Future peripheral purchases, whether joysticks or mice, could also take advantage of the new hardware.

FIGURE 23.7.
Older PCs can get access to USB peripherals by way of an inexpensive adapter card. The PCI-based CSA 6700 from CMD costs $59. (Photo courtesy of CMD)

> **Tip:** Keep your wits about you. A USB scanner might sound cool, but if it's the only external device you use (aside from a keyboard or mouse), USB probably isn't worth the added expense. You can save more than a few bucks by getting a low-cost parallel port scanner (such as Visioneer's PaperPort). Without other peripherals to contend with, you will never run across the port-shortage problems that plague many users.

The following sections discuss three general application areas:

- Mainstream home and office
- Video capture and connection to consumer electronics
- Mobile computing

Mainstream Home and Office

If you have a PC that you use for office-centric productivity applications and multimedia games and titles, USB will provide the most value. With its 12Mbps data rate, USB promises to become the workhorse external data bus of mainstream PCs. Best of all,

USB is as close to a sure thing as you will find in the sometimes-slippery arena of PC standards.

Just take a look at the devices USB is tailored to service: scanner, printers, mice, keyboards, digital cameras, PDAs, joysticks—even speakers (see Figure 23.8). We're not talking about rocket science here. Although USB's Plug and Play and dynamic device loading are neat features, the bus itself basically shoulders the unglamorous work now performed by serial and parallel ports.

FIGURE 23.8.

The Storm Technology PageScan USB scanner does away with a bulky power cord thanks to its power-carrying USB interface. (Photo courtesy of Storm Technology)

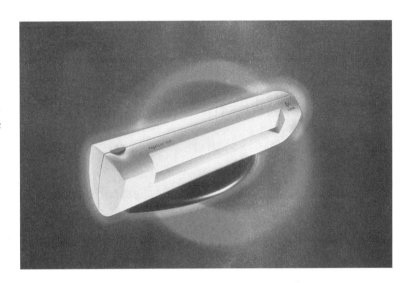

Here's my advice: If you're buying a new PC for a home office, make sure that USB is part of the picture. If possible, get started now by configuring your new PC with USB peripherals whenever possible.

Note: Gamers in particular should check into USB for joysticks, gamepads, head-mounted displays, and other devices. For joysticks, the digital USB connection significantly improves the precision and efficiency of joystick performance over that of standard analog models. Your system must constantly poll analog joysticks for positional data, tying up the processor and affecting performance by as much as 10 or 15 percent. A digital USB joystick, on the other hand, could use a standard software interface—such as Microsoft DirectInput—to send data to the CPU without requiring constant hand-holding. The result is a more up-to-date joystick data gathered at a fraction of the cost in system resources.

> **Note:** If you are on the market for a new monitor, you have a terrific opportunity to jump start your USB setup. You can find a wide selection of monitors with built-in USB ports on the front bezel or in the back of the chassis. While these displays use the standard VGA connector for their video signals, they also connect to your PC over a USB wire. Several USB ports are conveniently embedded into the monitor then connect to your PC over this wire. The setup makes it easy to hook mice, keyboards, and joysticks into a single hub rather than daisy-chaining them awkwardly around your desktop.

Small and home offices might benefit from IR communications as well, particularly if notebooks are being used as either primary or travel PCs. IR makes great sense if you want to share a printer among two or three PCs but you don't want to set up a formal network. Each user can simply beam his or her print jobs directly to the printer.

Likewise, an office that has a mix of desktop and notebook PCs might benefit from the use of IR adapters on desktop systems. People who travel can quickly replicate files on their notebook PCs, eliminating the need to swap disks or use external Zip drives or other media.

Digital Consumer Electronics and Video

If USB is for the computer crowd, FireWire is the stuff of home theaters and video studios. Although the high-bandwidth FireWire bus won't get the mass market support that USB is wrapping up, the architecture serves its niche extremely well.

Who needs FireWire? If you do any video capture or editing, consider this technology. Vendors such as Sony, Matsushita, and Panasonic all sell FireWire-enabled digital video products, such as camcorders and VCRs. The bus allows for easy transfer of digital video to your PC, without the use of bulky and difficult video capture cards. You'll need to add FireWire to your system, however (see Figure 23.9).

FIGURE 23.9.
Adaptec's AHA-8945 card is a combination FireWire and SCSI PCI adapter. (Photo courtesy of Adaptec Corp.)

Likewise, FireWire might become the common currency between PCs and consumer electronics. Hitachi, for example, plans to introduce FireWire to its DVD players in 1998, which should allow them to be used both as DVD-ROM drives for the PC and as DVD players for the TV. Likewise, Sony and others expect to add FireWire connections to upcoming consumer audio components.

Another possible area is for home networks. PC makers such as Compaq and IBM see a future for home-based networks, where a single server PC might work in conjunction with other devices. FireWire plays a key role in many of these plans. The Plug and Play technology, high bandwidth, and prospects for adoption by both computer and consumer electronics companies position it as a superior bus for this application. Certainly it beats trying to foist cantankerous Ethernet network interface cards and cabling on the home market.

Mobile Computing

With powerful MMX-capable notebooks providing nearly all the power of cutting-edge desktops, the need for effective notebook buses is vital. Here, a combination of enhanced performance and wireless capability is in demand. Notebooks now need to be able to do everything that desktops do—including video capture and playback—as well as provide easy data-sharing capabilities.

For high-performance peripherals, the CardBus architecture is the way to go. On notebooks that have CardBus slots built in, credit card-sized peripherals can provide data rates of up to 132MBps, matching the performance of the desktop PCI bus. Of course, you'll need to have a CardBus-capable notebook.

On the connectivity side, IrDA-compliant infrared communications make it easy to share data. This standard allows printers, scanners, PDAs, and notebook systems to share data without using bulky cables or wires.

Anyone who travels with a notebook computer appreciates the importance of a wireless bus. Each additional device and wire represent yet another valuable component to be lost or damaged. Additional components quickly become a huge nuisance as they join the unruly pile of batteries, power cords, external power supplies, PC Card modems, phone cords, and external floppy drives that are already stuffed into many PC carrying cases.

There's one problem. If you have a notebook PC lacking IrDA, you won't be able to add it without actually buying a separate IR port. If you've purchased a notebook in the last two years, however, it should come equipped with an IrDA port.

Tip: If you're thinking about buying a new notebook, look for an IrDA port before you make your purchase. Usually the port appears as a flat, smoke-colored, rectangular panel on the side or back of the notebook chassis. This panel must face the other IR port in order for communications to work. This is one reason why notebooks that have a rear-mounted port, or that have two separate ports, are preferable to those that have a single side or front-mounted IR port.

USB: Working with a New Bus

If your PC doesn't have one of these buses already built in, you'll need to upgrade. In general, the best way to do so is to install a multi-I/O card into an add-in card slot. The ports for the newly added bus will be available on the backplane of the card.

When Not to Upgrade

Before you rush out and buy hardware, take an inventory of your system. You might find that your PC is already outfitted with the connectors you need, and that an upgrade is really just a matter of handling drivers. You might also be able to get by with an external device, avoiding the hassle of installing an add-in card.

> **Note:** Be aware that some older Pentium MMX systems are shipped with USB ports but use chipsets lacking USB capability. The ports on these systems are not operational. Also, some systems may have working USB ports and chipset support, but will have USB capability switched off in the BIOS—for possible compatibility reasons. You can switch on the USB feature in the BIOS setup program to see if this feature will work. In any case, it pays to check the documentation to see if USB is supported or enabled.

Older 486 PCs might lack the facilities to support some I/O upgrades. For example, an old 486 PC outfitted with only ISA bus slots won't have what it takes to support the fast-moving FireWire bus. It might also lack key Plug and Play BIOS facilities. Likewise, if all the fast PCI slots on your PC are taken, you'll have to find a way to free one up before you can install a FireWire upgrade card.

Also, keep your wits about you. A 400MBps FireWire connector might sound really cool, but do you need that kind of bandwidth? If you're slinging mice and keyboards instead of high-quality video, you should stick with more mundane technologies like USB. Likewise, if your setup works well with existing parallel and serial ports, you can't go wrong by waiting. All this stuff will only get cheaper.

So you've decided to upgrade to one of the new I/O technologies, and your system has what it takes to do the deed. Now it's time to roll up your sleeves and get to work. The following sections give you brief insights into installing each of the four buses.

Working with USB

The most likely upgrade you face is to USB, since it's gaining the most support among peripheral product makers and is reasonably affordable. Although there were very few USB upgrade cards at the time this chapter was written, CMD Technology of Irvine, California was marketing an upgrade card for PCI-based systems. The following steps are based on their product:

1. Shut down the PC, unplug the power supply, and remove the case.

2. After grounding yourself, find a free PCI bus slot and remove the protective back-plane cover.

3. Install the USB controller card, being careful to press it firmly but carefully into the open slot.

4. Plug in the USB cable and hook it to a USB-compliant device, such as a mouse, keyboard, joystick, or monitor-top camera.

5. Start the PC. Windows 95/98 will detect the new hardware and will launch the Add New Hardware wizard.

6. Insert the driver disk that came with the USB add-in card. Click the Next button to start the installation routine.

7. When you're asked to detect hardware, click the No radio button, and then click Next.

8. In the Device Type scroll-down list box, select Unknown Device and click Next.

9. In the next dialog box, click the Have Disk button, and then double-click the appropriate .INF file on the file menu that appears.

10. Windows will load the new driver and inform you when it is done.

11. Restart the PC. Your USB card will now be active.

Note: While USB is only natively supported in Windows 98 and (when it arrives, Windows NT 5.0), there is a way for NT 4.0 users to gain access to USB's benefits. Inside Out Networks' EdgePort/4 USB hub includes drivers and software for enabling a complete USB bus on NT 4.0 systems. The card itself includes four bus-powered USB ports, and costs $399.

In some cases, you may have trouble getting USB peripherals recognized. There are a number of issues that can get in the way. First, your PC's BIOS must be USB-enabled. Older PCs, for example, may not have any knowledge of USB in their BIOS—only a BIOS update can enable the motherboard-based ports. Even BIOSes with USB support may fail to see your USB ports because that feature has not been switched on.

You should check the documentation closely to see if your BIOS version supports USB. If no mention appears in the documentation, check with the system, motherboard, or BIOS vendor. You can also check to see if a USB item is provided in your BIOS' setup interface by pressing the setup keystroke combination during boot up. If a USB item appears in the interface and is disabled, toggle the item to enable USB operation. Save the settings, exit the BIOS setup applet, and continue with bootup.

Even if your BIOS sees the USB ports, you won't go far if Windows has gone blind. To see if USB is enabled, do the following:

1. Click Start, Settings, Control Panel and launch the System icon.

2. Click the Device Manager tab and click the plus (+) sign next to the Universal Serial Bus item. You should see two items called something like Host Controller and USB Root Hub (as shown in Figure 23.10).

3. If these items don't appear, check to see if an item called Other Devices appears in the Device Manager list. If so, click on the + next to it.

4. If the USB entries appear there, click each one and click the Remove button.

5. Next, press Refresh to try correctly reinstall the USB components. If the USB components fail to appear, you'll need to check with the system vendor.

FireWire: Now We're Talking Hot

For high-performance peripherals and convergence-oriented electronics, FireWire is the way to go. You'll need to be careful about your selection of products, though, because Microsoft isn't rushing to get FireWire drivers and support built into its operating system. Still, a reliable vendor should be able to provide a card delivering the attractive promise of FireWire.

In many ways, a FireWire add-in card upgrade is almost identical to that of a USB peripheral. Here are the steps to follow:

1. Shut down the PC, unplug the power supply, and remove the case.

2. After grounding yourself, find a free PCI bus slot and remove the protective back-plane cover.

3. Install the FireWire controller card, being careful to press it firmly but carefully into the open slot.

4. Plug in the FireWire cable and hook it to a FireWire-compliant device, such as a mouse, keyboard, joystick, or monitor-top camera.

5. Start the PC. Windows 95/98 will detect the new hardware and will launch the Add New Hardware Wizard.

6. Insert the driver disk that came with the FireWire add-in card. Click the Next button to start the installation routine.

7. When you're asked to detect hardware, click the No radio button, and then click Next.

8. In the Device Type scroll-down list box, select Unknown Device and click Next.

9. In the next dialog box, click the Have Disk button, and then double-click the appropriate .INF file in the file menu that appears.

10. Windows will load the new driver and inform you when it is done.

11. Restart the PC. Your FireWire card will now be active.

PC Card: Convenience Upgrades for Frequent Swappers

A PC Card adapter might not be an obvious upgrade choice for desktops unless you need to do things like swap hard disks (or store them off-site for security). However, many new digital cameras use PC Card Flash memory to store images. Image transfers over the PC Card interface are much faster than over the typical serial connection. Also, a PC Card adapter is a terrific way to share peripherals and data with notebooks.

Unlike the previous two installations, installing a PC Card adapter and reader means digging into drive bays. An adapter card interfaces with the system, while a PC Card reader gets mounted into one of the externally accessible drive bays, allowing you to add and remove cards conveniently.

Here's what to do:

1. Shut down the PC, unplug the power supply, and remove the case.

2. After grounding yourself, find a free PCI bus slot and remove the protective back-plane cover.

3. Install the PC Card controller card, being careful to press it firmly but carefully into the open slot.

4. Install the PC Card reader. Find an open externally accessible drive bay (preferably a 3½-inch bay) and pry off the bezel cover that conceals it.

5. Fit the power and data cables into the appropriate sockets on the reader, being careful to match up the pin 1 orientation. Thread the wires through the front of the drive bay so that they hang loose onto the motherboard.

6. Slide in the PC Card reader module, lining it up with the mounting brackets.

7. Line up the mounting screw holes in the drive with the spaces in the drive brackets. Hold the drive in place and screw in the supplied screws.

8. Once the reader is in place, connect the data cable to the matching port on the adapter card. Again, be careful with connector alignments.

9. Now connect the power cable to the device.

10. Start the PC. Windows 95/98 will detect new hardware and will launch the Add New Hardware Wizard.

11. Insert the driver disk that came with the PC Card or CardBus add-in card. Click the Next button to start the installation routine.

12. When you're asked to detect hardware, click the No radio button, and then click Next.

13. In the Device Type scroll-down list box, select Unknown Device and click Next.

14. In the next dialog box, click the Have Disk button, and then double-click the appropriate .INF file in the file menu that appears.

15. Windows will load the new driver and inform you when it is done.

16. Restart the PC. Your PC Card reader will now be active.

Infrared: Blinded by the Light

An infrared adapter upgrade is the easiest of the group from a hardware standpoint, because it doesn't involve cracking open the case. Newer motherboards include a dedicated IrDA connector that you can plug into. USB-based transeivers are also an option. For older motherboards, you'll need to run off the serial or parallel ports—although you can also find ISA-based adapter cards.

The bigger challenge is software. IrDA ports need to access those elusive COM resources, inviting potential conflicts with modems, mice, and other peripherals. Before you start, make sure you take a good hard look at your COM port resources. Figure out who's using what. Check the Modem icon in Windows 95/98's Device Manager to see what COM port it's using. Also make sure that your mouse isn't riding the other COM port. (It won't be if it's a PS/2-style unit.)

If you have a COM port to spare, you're ready to roll. Here's what you need to do:

1. Shut down the PC.

2. Plug in the IrDA-compliant transmitter/receiver device.

3. Start the PC. Windows 95/98 will detect new hardware and will launch the Add New Hardware Wizard.

4. Insert the driver disk that came with the IR module. Click the Next button to start the installation routine.

5. When you're asked to detect hardware, click the No radio button, and then click Next.

6. In the Device Type scroll-down list box, select Unknown Device and click Next.

7. In the next dialog box, click the Have Disk button, and then double-click the appropriate .INF file in the file menu that appears.

8. Windows will load the new driver and inform you when it is done.

9. Restart the PC. Your IR module will now be active.

Summary

Some of the coolest things in the evolution of the PC architecture are happening among buses. USB and FireWire represent the first mature external buses for PC users since the introduction of SCSI. And if things go well, they will boast greater ease of use and affordability than their predecessors. Now the wait is on to see how large a market exists for these peripherals and their drivers.

Meanwhile, IR and PC Card technologies significantly enhance notebook computing. They also might play a growing roll on desktop PCs as more and more users seek ways to juggle files among multiple computers. If you find yourself struggling with floppy disks or Windows 95's less-than-perfect Direct Cable Connection facility, an IR port or PC Card drive could be a terrific addition.

Networks

The explosive growth of the Internet has transformed the PC into a vital communications device. But anyone working in a corporate office probably saw the revolution coming 5 or 10 years ago, in the form of PC-based networks. Email, shared files, and network-based applications and services have long been critical tools for corporate PC users.

Today, networks are pervasive. Everyone from Fortune 100 businesses to the local coffee shop run connected PCs to share data and handle communication. And now networks are poised to enter the home. For instance, you might be contemplating hooking your work laptop to your home PC. With many home users buying their second and even third PC, a network makes it possible to get further use out of aging systems.

In fact, a new class of network products, designed to work without clumsy cabling, is helping to invite home and small office users to enter the networked age. We'll cover both standard Ethernet networks and examine new "cableless" network products.

In this chapter, you will learn to

- Understand how networks work, including the functioning of individual network components such as interface cards and cabling
- Make proper buying decisions for network hardware and software
- Recognize and troubleshoot common network problems
- Set up and maintain a Windows 95-based local area network, using Ethernet network interface cards and 10-BaseT wiring

Get to Know Networks

The basic mission of any network is to move information from point A to point B quickly, efficiently, and inexpensively. Networks enable you to distribute information and services, whether between two computers sharing a printer or among the millions of computers that make up the world's largest network, the Internet.

The *local area network*, or LAN, is just one of many tools enabling a computer to communicate with other devices. LANs let one computer share information and resources with other computers that have a need for this information (or resources).

When most people think of networks, they think of PCs connected to a central device via cables. While the cost of all these components has dropped dramatically over the past three years, the hassle of running wires is a daunting prospect to many users. In fact, many home users can't afford to run wires through walls. We'll cover home-specific networking products later in this chapter in the section titled "Networks Come Home," on page 582.

The Classic Network Explained

The pieces of a local area network seem simple when viewed from a distance. If you look more closely, you'll see that each piece constitutes a complex system of its own. Perhaps most critical is that all the components of a network—whether network interface cards (NICs), cables, routers, or drivers—must work in conjunction with all the other networking components, often from a wide variety of vendors. With that in mind, we will start with the "big picture" and move in.

The following components make up a network:

- Server and client/workstation computers
- Network interface cards (NICs)
- Cabling
- The network operating system

Servers and Clients

Like love, war, and the tango, it takes at least two to make a network. In its simplest form, a network might be just two PCs, one being the server that shares its resources with other computers on the network. The resources can be anything from peripherals such as printers and modems to application software such as spreadsheets and databases.

The second computer in our novice network is the client, or workstation. This is the computer that needs to use the resources the server makes available. In an office, clients are the systems sitting on each employee's desk. If you're browsing the Web, client machines are those being used to view data (while servers "serve it up"). Note that you will often hear the term *peer-to-peer network*. What this means is that all computers on the network fill the role of server and workstation. In essence, a peer-to-peer network is when no single computer maintains the dedicated server role. Basically, it is a peer of the rest of the computers on the network.

> **Technical Note:** In general, there are two types of networks: peer-to-peer and server networks. A peer-to-peer network is generally a small network in which the individual PCs tend to be more powerful (although this isn't a requirement) and the access of shared resources is fairly small. This is ideal for a startup network. You'll make a smaller investment in money and time, and you won't need dedicated network specialists.

A server network has a computer or computers dedicated to the network that do nothing but service workstation requests. In addition, they tend to manage the logical network. This means that, among other services, they provide a central point for logging on to the network by maintaining a user database of sorts. This model is used for larger networks that have specific needs beyond basic file sharing.

Note: In actuality, any computer can be a server or a workstation. It's just that we tend to designate the role of a computer based on which role it fills most of the time.

Network Interface Cards

Networked PCs need to connect to each other somehow, which is where the network interface card, or NIC as it is known in the industry, comes in. The physical workhorse of your network connection, it translates information moving over the network into standard-sized "packets" of data. These packets are translated into electrical signals, which are passed onto the cable.

On the receiving side, a network card receives the electrical signal and then decodes and reassembles the individual packets for delivery to your computer. As part of its job, the NIC checks incoming packets to make sure all the packets were received correctly—a function called *error checking*.

NICs plug into the add-in card slots of PCs and are available for ISA, PCI, and EISA bus slots. Although, in the past, most clients used ISA-based NICs, the higher bandwidth, faster processing (bus mastering and so on), and Plug and Play convenience of the PCI bus have made PCI NICs a growing market. The act of upgrading your network speed will definitely benefit from the fast PCI bus connection. Companies such as 3Com, Intel, and Adaptec sell NICs.

Network Card Considerations

There are a multitude of NIC cards on the market today, manufactured by companies big and small. In my experience, one thing holds true: You get what you pay for. If you buy on a budget, you might have to put up with some tough compromises. For example, Windows 95/98 Plug and Play capabilities—an important consideration—might be lacking, or the drivers might lack full compatibility with your software and hardware. Unless you've had extensive experience with NIC cards, I suggest you buy a NIC from a well-known manufacturer such as Intel, IBM, or 3Com.

Note: A NIC can cost anywhere from $30 on the low end to $300 for the top of the line. You must weigh the monetary savings against the amount of time it takes to install a NIC. How much is your time worth?

Once your NIC is physically installed in the PC, you need to hook it to the network cable. If you're using an Ethernet network, you'll find yourself looking at two possible connectors on the back of your PC. The first will be a small circle that looks similar to the cable TV connector on your television; it services a coaxial BNC connector. The other connection, which looks like a common phone jack—although it's a bit larger—is for twisted-pair wiring. You will use only one of these connectors, and you'll know which one after you've gotten through configuring the card (see Figure 24.1).

FIGURE 24.1.

Not all NICs are created equal. Here, one card provides both coaxial and RJ-45 network connections. (Photo courtesy of Adaptec, Inc.)

You also need to configure Windows to use the NIC. If you're willing to shell out a little extra money, it would be worth your while to get a NIC that is Plug and Play. It can make building your network much less complicated.

Cabling

Not to understate the issue, but networks are really about plumbing. Exchange bits for drips and packet sniffers for adjustable wrenches, and suddenly you're a plumber. It's no surprise, then, that the physical media or cable used by networked PCs to communicate plays much the same role as a water pipe running from one area in a house to another.

Of course, your pipes need to fit and be appropriate for the job. The type of cable you choose depends on the environment in which you build the network, as well as other mitigating factors such as cost and availability. The most common cable you will hear of is unshielded twisted pair, or UTP. There are others as well, such as coaxial and fiber optic.

Down to the Wire: A Critical Choice

Networked PCs must have some sort of connection, whether via physical cable, radio, or infrared transmission. But there are serious repercussions in choosing cabling. You must balance cost against efficiency and usability. If you buy cheap cable and your LAN grows, you might end up having to rewire the entire network—a potentially costly and disruptive process with larger networks.

For the purposes of this chapter, we will discuss physical cables. Three common types of cable get used in most networks:

- Coaxial cable: Similar to the cable found in your cable TV hookup, network-based coaxial cabling comes in two varieties: thinnet and thicknet. The difference boils down to the distance these cables can support before signals degrade. Thicknet can carry a signal about twice as far as thinnet can. However, thicknet is physically less flexible than thinnet, making it difficult to wire, and it is more expensive. Both types provide good resistance to interference, which reduces transmission problems.

- Twisted pair: The most common network cable, twisted pair also comes in two types: shielded (STP) and unshielded (UTP). STP provides better shielding from electromagnetic interference, improving signal quality and allowing for greater distances. Twisted pair is commonly found in the phone system wiring of office buildings. If the phone cabling is of good-enough quality (say, category 5), it can be used to carry network traffic. Category 5 unshielded twisted pair cable is the most commonly used cabling.

- Fiber optic: Fiber optic deserves passing mention as an upcoming transport of network traffic. Limited to professional installations for networks requiring high speed and reliability, fiber optic cable often serves as backbone wiring for large LANs or other data networks. It is 10 times faster than twisted pair, immune to electromagnetic interference, and can run longer distances without signal degradation. The problem is that this miracle wire is much more expensive than the other cabling. Of course, we can hope that one day all cabling will be fiber optic!

If you're building a small network in your home or in a small office, the best thing to do is grab some precut lengths of UTP (unshielded twisted pair) cable and set up your network that way. If you're designing a bigger LAN, I suggest that you get help. In all the corporate environments I have been in, outside contractors have always handled the cabling. This is because cabling an office is difficult and time-consuming and must be done right the first time. Having your LAN administrator or office manager test cables with a voltmeter is not a productive use of that person's time.

Note: Not only is wiring an office expensive and time-consuming, but it's extremely disruptive as well. Employees often need to vacate their work spaces during the wiring process, and network service can be disrupted as well. For this reason, most corporate wiring jobs occur over the weekend—but even then, the complexity of the task can spill over into the work week. Your best bet is to spend a lot of time planning and preparing for problems.

The Network Operating System

The network operating system—or, more precisely, an operating system designed to control and operate a network—is needed to optimize the sharing of resources among machines across a distance. Novell NetWare (or, more recently, IntranetWare) and Microsoft Windows NT Server are just two examples of network operating systems. These are usually installed on server PCs, or they can be added to the existing operating system.

Client PCs, meanwhile, run standard desktop operating systems but require tweaks to talk to the server and its OS. Windows 95, for example, comes with drivers and protocols for the more mainstream networks such as NetWare and NT Server.

In addition to the network operating system, you will need to choose the protocol the network will use. This is kind of like air traffic controllers all agreeing to speak English, whether the airport is in Osaka or Omaha. You might have heard terms such as TCP/IP, IPX, and NetBEUI mentioned before. These are the three most common transport protocols used today. We will examine each of these protocols to help you decide which one is right for you.

NetBEUI

NetBEUI is an extremely fast network protocol. Unfortunately, it can be used only on small local area networks. This is because NetBEUI lacks any real "addressing" overhead other protocols carry. It is designed to operate on small to medium-sized LANs. You can liken this to a small cocktail party where all the people know everybody's names. You don't need name tags, so there are no awkward introductions or "addressing" that can slow a conversation.

This is a Microsoft-designed protocol and therefore is limited to Microsoft networking—which is ideal if you're going to connect three or four Windows workstations and you want an easy implementation.

IPX/SPX

IPX/SPX is a Novell network protocol that is designed specifically to work with Novell's NOS (NetWare). However, it will work with Windows NT and Windows 95/98. (Microsoft calls its version of IPX/SPX NWLink or NetWare Link.) Small, fast, and relatively efficient, IPX/SPX is only slightly slower than NetBEUI. IPX/SPX is a *routable* protocol, which means that the "addressing" is more specific than with NetBeEUI.

The postal system works as an analogy here, since it is essentially a network in its simplest form. If I lived in a very small town that had its own post office, I could write a letter to another local person and address the envelope (or the packet in the case of a network) using the recipient's name and nothing else. The mail carrier, as well as everybody else in town, knows where each person lives and doesn't need a street address or zip code. The mail carrier will look at the recipient's name and put the letter in that person's box.

NetBEUI is like that. You want to send a file to computer1. The file is broken into packets by the NIC and sent to the network. Since there is only one computer1 on the LAN and the LAN is limited in size, only one box will receive these packets.

With IPX/SPX, the system changes. The network expects more address information and also expects that not every computer is on the LAN or in the same "town." Therefore, IPX carries more addressing information in its packets. This allows the information to be routed, or sent to another LAN that is attached to your LAN with a router. (Think of a router as a post office that sorts by zip code and then sends the mail to the "local" post office.)

Using this example, think of the extra addressing information (in IPX/SPX) as the city, state, and zip code of a mailing address. Now, when you want to send mail (or a network packet) to a friend in another city (or another computer on another LAN attached to your local network by a router), the mail carrier reads the zip code and knows to forward it to the post office at that zip code. Then the second mail carrier will deliver the mail. That way, your carrier doesn't have to know everyone in the entire world in order to deliver mail.

Perhaps you're thinking, "That's great, but how does it affect me?" Well, the truth is, probably not much. If you're building a small network, the extra addressing information that the IPX has is just overhead slowing down your network. That said, many multiplayer games use IPX to communicate, though a few use TCP/IP.

TCP/IP

TCP/IP (transmission control protocol/Internet protocol) was developed to allow dissimilar machines to talk to one another. The Department of Defense wanted their computers to be able to communicate with other machines of different types, so they built this suite of protocols to deal with the problem. Since then, TCP/IP has grown into the protocol used by the Internet. It lets all sorts of computers share information across the world's largest network.

Like IPX, TCP/IP (IP for short) is a routable protocol. It is meant to be passed through the router on its way to its destination. You might have had some experience with TCP/IP if you have an Internet connection on your PC. The downside of TCP/IP is its addressing scheme. Each PC or node on the network must have a specific address assigned to it.

Networks Come Home

Networks can be intimidating, but with more and more homes and small offices using two or more PCs, they are a vital tool. What's more, they can help reduce costs by letting you use a single modem and printer shared among multiple systems. And everything from data sharing to backup becomes much easier and quicker when happening over a network.

But most home and many small office users can't afford to tear up walls and ceilings to run 10BaseT cable. Now, a new generation of products can link up your systems without dedicated wiring. While these products use the same networking concepts and facilities discussed in the section above, they use innovative means to move data. The three product classes move data over the following media:

- Existing phone line
- Existing power grid
- Radio waves

Phone and power line networking products are particularly attractive since they piggy back data over an existing network in virtually every home or office—the phone or power wiring. Signals are simply laid atop the existing wiring, at a frequency that does not conflict with the primary use of the wiring.

Radio-based networks, by contrast, use transmitters and receivers at each PC to send data by radio. The radio waves can typically pass through walls and other obstructions, but distances may be limited by intervening materials.

Phone Line Networks

The Home Phone Networking Alliance (HomePNA) serves as the advocate and standards body for devices designed to move data over phone lines (see Figure 24.2). Based on existing Ethernet technology, current phone networking products can move 1Mbps of data. What's more, this technology employs the same driver model and facilities used by network cards under Windows 95, making installation identical to that of current network cards.

Phone-based networks offer a number of advantages that may make them the most attractive to home and small office users. First, the 1Mbps data rate is three times faster than that of competing powerline networks, and the HomePNA says that 10Mbps performance is planned over the next few years. Phone line networks are less expensive than radio-based network products, and don't pose the problem of broadcasting data that you may want to make sure is not tapped.

Of course, this technology wouldn't be of much use if it blocked your ability to make phone calls. In fact, the specification allows for both phone calls and data operation to take place simultaneously, without any impact on performance (see Figure 24.3). This is done by having the data stream occupy a much higher frequency range on the phone line, well above the 4Khz band of voice communications. What's more, future ADSL transmissions will be able to work alongside phone networking transmissions as well.

FIGURE 24.2.
*This schematic
shows how a
phone-based PC
network coexists
with your tele-
phones. (Graphic
courtesy of
HomePNA)*

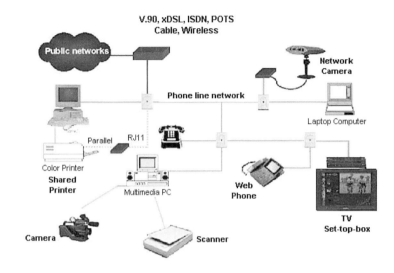

FIGURE 24.3.
*HomePNA's phone
networking
technology
enables the phone
line to handle
both voice and
data simultane-
ously by using a
higher frequency
range for data
handling. (Photo
courtesy of
Adaptec, Inc.)*

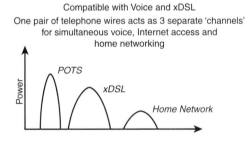

Compatible with Voice and xDSL
One pair of telephone wires acts as 3 separate 'channels'
for simultaneous voice, Internet access and
home networking

Powerline Networks

A company called Intelogis takes a different tack to the same goal. Its PassPort Plug-In Network kits allow users to network PCs over the power wires in your house. That means any PC outfitted with the technology can connect with another equipped PC just by plugging into a power outlet. As with phone line products, data is transmitted by using a frequency outside the range of the electrical stream.

The PassPort Plug-In technology runs at 350Kbps, about one-third the speed of phone line products. That speed gap is offset by easier setup, since the PassPort Plug-In Network kit uses external, parallel-port modules rather than internal add-in cards. The kit also comes with a printer plug-in, that lets you hook your printer directly to the network for access from any networked PC.

> **Caution:** PassPort has a major flaw: Security. The data you share among your PassPort-networked systems is accessible by other PassPort users connected to the same section of your transformer hub. In other words: If you share power with your neighbors, you may also be sharing data.

While the speed of the network is slower than that of home phone line products, Intelogis expects to produce a 1.5Mbps version that will boost performance by more than 400 percent. In addition, the technology provides more flexibility, since homes typically have power outlets in every room, while access to phone jacks may be limited.

Radio Networks

The final option for users who want to connect PCs without stringing wire is a radio-based network. These products use radio waves in place of Ethernet cable or your home's existing wiring to move data among PCs. The network itself acts just like any Ethernet network, allowing PCs to share printers, modems, and other devices, and providing convenient file sharing, backup, and email features.

Diamond's HomeFree wireless network kit is fairly typical for the breed. It offers 1Mbps data rates (about one-tenth of typical Ethernet and equal to home phone line networks) and can operate over distances of 150 feet. In order to avoid conflicting with 900MHz cordless phones, the transmitter modules operate at 2.4GHz, well above the spectrum used by phones, intercoms, and other home radio appliances (see Figure 24.4).

FIGURE 24.4.
Radio-based networks avoid conflicting with cordless telephones by operating at a much higher frequency. (Graphic courtesy of Diamond Multimedia)

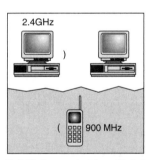

2.4GHz

(900 MHz

Reliable home network unaffected
by other wireless devices

One real concern with radio-based networks is security. By definition, data broadcast by the network module is accessible to any receiver within range. To ensure security, products use frequency-shifting, rapidly hopping from one frequency to the next, to foil attempts to listen in. If you are considering a radio network kit, you should make sure frequency-hopping is part of the package.

One key obstacle to radio-based networking has been price, since each network card must also include a radio transceiver (see Figure 24.5). The extra cost of this component has typically driven the price to about $300 per PC. Diamond's HomeFree product, however, provides radio-based network for under $100 per system.

FIGURE 24.5.
Diamond's HomeFree upgrade kit includes a network card with a radio transmitter/receiver built into the back end. (Photo courtesy of Diamond Multimedia)

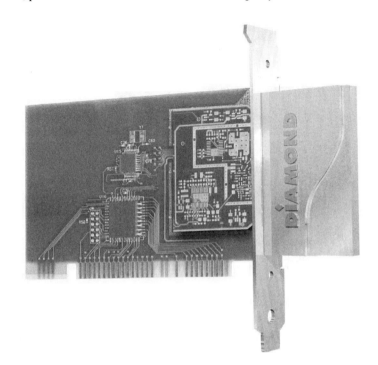

Building a Network

The following sections outline the construction of a very simple network. They describe an environment with one machine acting as a server and two machines acting as workstations.

In order to build a network, the following parts are needed:

- Three computers
- Three pieces of cabling (UTP CAT 5, with RJ-45 connectors)
- One hub
- Three NIC cards
- A protocol (NetBEUI, TCP/IP, or IPX/SPX)

Note: A *hub* is a networking device to which multiple computers can connect. It functions as a type of large intersection, where the hub acts as the traffic cop, directing network traffic to and from the correct port. It allows computers in a network to be arranged in a star rather than a continuous ring (see Figure 24.6). Small hubs are relatively cheap, costing about $100 for a five-port hub. This is a good investment when you're building a network.

FIGURE 24.6.
An inexpensive hub lets your networked PCs pass data back and forth freely.

Building the Infrastructure

In order for the three computers to talk to each other, the cabling needs to be in place. First, place the hub somewhere central to all three computers. Connect one side of each cable to the first three ports available on the hub. The other end of each cable goes into the matching port on the back of your NIC, which we will now install on your PC. (Make sure to plug the hub into an AC power source!)

Installing the NIC

Installing the physical NIC card is the same for each of the computers. You open the back of your PC and choose an available slot that fits the bus type of your card (PCI, ISA, and so on).

Note: As I mentioned, using a NIC that is Plug and Play is an excellent way to avoid configuration conflicts.

It is important to ensure that the NIC card is seated properly. I have seen many NIC cards get fried because they weren't inserted correctly. Once you have your NIC card securely installed, close the computer and start Windows 95/98.

If your NIC is Plug and Play, Windows will recognize it and add it to your configuration. If your NIC is not Plug and Play, you need to follow these steps:

1. Select Start, Settings, Control Panel.

2. Double-click the Network icon. In the Configuration window that appears, click the Add button.

3. From the list of choices, shown in Figure 24.7, choose Adapter and click Add. (The network interface card is also referred to as the network adapter.)

FIGURE 24.7.
Tell Windows what type of network hardware you have installed.

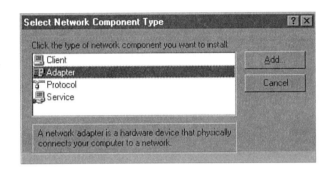

4. Windows might build the driver database needed to present you with the list of choices for network cards. After a short wait, the list will appear.

5. You will see a scrollable list of card choices, as shown in Figure 24.8. Selecting one of these will install Windows 9x's default drivers. You are probably better off with the drivers supplied with your NIC. Insert the disk or CD and click the Have Disk button.

FIGURE 24.8.
Windows 95/98 gives you a handy list of applicable NICs from which to choose. But you are probably better off loading the drivers that came in the product box, since the Windows drivers can be quite dated and limited in functionality.

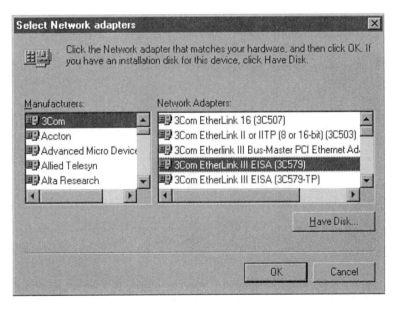

6. You will be asked for a path to the files. Type in the correct drive and click OK. Windows will search the specified drive and begin copying files.

7. After you have chosen your NIC and clicked OK, you will return to the screen at which you started. Your new NIC and a couple of lines referring to protocols and client software will have been added.

The default for Windows 95/98 to install is the adapter (which you already chose), Client for Microsoft Networks, Client for NetWare Networks, IPX/SPX, and NetBEUI. Depending on how you want to configure your network, not all of these items are needed. The next section covers choosing a protocol.

Speaking the Right Language

As soon as the NIC card appears in your network list (in the Configuration tab window), you will see a number of other items listed as well. By default, Windows installs IPX/SPX, NetBEUI, Client for Microsoft Networks, and Client for NetWare Networks into your network configuration. Here is where you have a choice of which protocol or protocols you want to use. For our example, we will use Microsoft's NetBEUI because it is fast, easy to install, and very common among small networks.

This means that we want to remove IPX/SPX from our list, as well as its accompanying Client for NetWare Networks. Do the following:

1. Highlight IPX/SPX (or another item if you aren't following the example).

2. Click the Remove button.

3. Click OK.

Options in the Network

Before you click OK (in the Network window) to install your network card, there are a few options you might want to check out.

Identification

Click the Identification tab. This information can be configured only if you use the Client for Microsoft or Novell Networks.

The Computer name enables you to uniquely identify your computer, as shown in Figure 24.9. This name must be unique to allow efficient resource sharing. For example, imagine that two of your neighbors are named Bob Smith, and your spouse tells you to go over to Bob Smith's and borrow his weed whacker. You get the picture.

The Workgroup is the name you will give your small network. It might be something like BobNet or Network1. You want to have all the computers on your network join the same workgroup.

The Description is just a small comment field that helps identify your computer when you see it in Network Neighborhood or another browser. This field is optional.

FIGURE 24.9.

What's in a name? A lot, if you're a network. You need to uniquely identify your systems and networks in order to ensure correct operation.

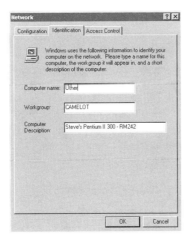

Access Control

The last tab is called Access Control. In a workgroup environment, you will want to specify how a resource from your computer can be accessed (that is, who can read a file). You can specify either share-level access or user access. This option can be changed at any time, so it isn't important to set it now. Leave it at share level; you will discover how it affects you later. Go back to the Configuration tab to get back to where you started.

File and Print Sharing

Note that in the middle of the Network Configuration window is a button labeled File and Print Sharing. This button is where you allow your resources (files and printers are resources) to be shared with others on the network. This is why you wanted a network in the first place. When you click this button, a small dialog box appears giving you the option of sharing your files and printer on the network.

Check the boxes to share your resources with others on the network. (You don't have to check the second option "printers" if you don't have a printer attached to your computer.)

Primary Logon

One other option, Primary Logon, decides how Windows 95 will start itself—whether it should look for the network first or log you into Windows first. If you're going to be working with a network, choose Client for *X* Network (whether Microsoft or NetWare).

You're Finished (Well, Not Yet)

When you click the OK button at the bottom of the Network window, several things will happen. Windows will attempt to begin loading the files and drivers necessary to control your NIC card. Depending on your computer, it might ask you for the Windows

CD-ROM. You should have this available. Once the appropriate files have been copied, Windows will want to restart the computer so that it can load the new NIC and the new protocol so that the computer can be networkable.

Before you click Yes, you might want to check a couple of things, perhaps to avoid the mistakes that plague even the best networking specialists:

- Is your network cable plugged into both the port in your NIC card and the wall jack (or hub)? (Check the back of the NIC and see if it has the connectivity lights. If it does, check that they are green.)

- Is your hub plugged in?

- Have you enabled shares for all your networked resources? Remember, you need to designate shared drives and other resources to make them visible to the network.

- Did you give your computer a unique name? For TCP/IP networking, did you give each computer a unique ID?

> **Note:** It's worth noting the TCP/IP addresses have some rules that you should try to adhere to. Specifically, there are IP addresses dedicated to internal use only— that is, the addresses won't appear as part of the public network for accessing a Web site or other resources. 192.168.0.xxx, for example, defines a range of IP addresses for internal use.
>
> The danger is that you might randomly assign an IP address to a system on your network that is the same as one on the Internet. Not a problem yet, but if you ever place that system onto the Internet, a conflict arises. After all, your desktop and ESPN.COM may be sharing the same IP address range!

Any one of these things can lead to hair-pulling and teeth-gnashing, but these problems can be avoided if you double-check. Now click Yes. At this point, if all went well, your computer should be up and talking on the network. Now you can set up the other two computers.

Troubleshooting

In a perfect world, you wouldn't have to bother with this section. However, because computers want everything to be just so, sometimes things don't go as planned. So we will begin this section with some basic troubleshooting techniques for networking. The first step is to identify the problem. Problems can be broken into these categories:

- Resource conflict: Somewhere at the hardware level, two pieces of the computer's hardware are competing for resources.

- Connectivity: The NIC isn't receiving, sending, or translating data correctly.

- Configuration: Something about the configuration of the network or protocols is interrupting or preventing communication.

- Physical: There is some sort of physical (hardware) problem that can't be corrected through configuration.

Resource Conflicts

Pieces of hardware in your computer need specific memory allocations and interrupt requests (IRQs) in order to function. Generally, different types of cards will by default take certain I/O ports and IRQs. It isn't important to know the function of these settings, but it is important to know what the values of these settings are in case you need to change them. Again, Plug and Play will minimize or even eliminate a great deal of frustration.

IRQ

IRQ stands for Interrupt Request Line. When your network card (or any other card) wants to send a signal or an interrupt to the CPU, it must have its own distinct line on which to send. That way, the computer knows which card the interrupt is coming from. Network cards generally use IRQ 3 or 5. Check your NIC's documentation to discover the default value.

Table 24.1 is a general guideline to IRQ settings. Your system might very well be different.

Table 24.1. IRQ preferences.

IRQ Setting	Preferred Hardware
2	Video Graphics Adapter
3	Available (unless you have a second com port)
4	COM1, COM3
5	Available (unless LPT2 exists)
6	Floppy disk controller
7	LPT1
8	System clock
10	Available
11	Available
12	Mouse (PS/2 systems)
13	Math coprocessor (if applicable)
14	Hard drive controller
15	Available

A classic network "gotcha" occurs with sound cards. Sound Blaster-compatible boards like to grab IRQ 5 by default, which happens to be one of the preferred IRQs for many network cards. If you're installing a network card on a machine with an installed sound board, be sure to check on the status of IRQ 5 first. You might even want to nudge the sound board to another IRQ (perhaps 9) to avoid problems. Just remember to also change any references to the sound board found in your AUTOEXEC.BAT file, or the change might not take hold.

I/O Port

Base input/output indicates through which path data flows between the card (NIC or otherwise) and the CPU. As with the IRQ, all cards must have a different I/O port through which to communicate. Network adapters generally use 300 to 30F or 310 to 31F.

If your NIC has caused a conflict in one of these two settings, it is fairly simple to discover the problem:

1. Go to the Start menu, select Settings, and go to Control Panel.

2. Double-click the System icon.

3. Choose the Device Manager tab.

4. If Windows 95/98 has a problem with your NIC, under the Network Adapters section your network adapter will have a yellow exclamation point next to it (see Figure 24.10).

FIGURE 24.10.
Windows Device Manager provides instant insight into the operation of network hardware.

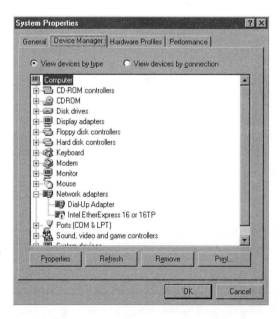

5. Highlight the item that has the exclamation point, and click the Properties button.

6. The Device Manager will bring you to the properties screen of your NIC. It is here where we will try to discover the problem.

7. If under the Device Status you see Device failure, you know there is a problem. Click the Resources tab to find out more.

8. You might be given a choice to set the configuration manually, or you might see the screen shown in Figure 24.11. If you do see the button for setting the configuration manually, go ahead and click it.

FIGURE 24.11.
Windows keeps track of hardware settings, enabling you to quickly diagnose conflicts and make changes.

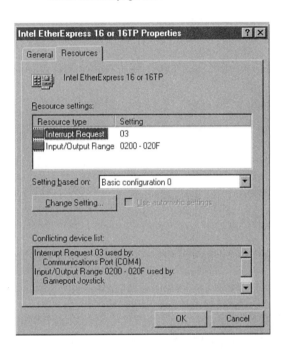

9. Check out the conflicting device list. This will tell you if there is a problem. In this case, it is saying that both the IRQ and I/O port are in use. These values must be changed to ones that are not in use.

10. Highlight the resource type item in question (for example, Interrupt Request or I/O Port) and click the Change Setting button. When a box appears, scroll through the available choices until the conflict information box says that no devices are conflicting.

11. Click OK and repeat step 10 for any others.

12. Click OK.

13. The system will want to reboot, so go ahead and shut down.

Connectivity

In its simplest terms, connectivity boils down to a clear-cut question: Is there a clean connection from the computer to the network? If your phone doesn't work, the first thing you check is the phone cord. The same applies to your PC network. Symptoms of connectivity problems include Windows not recognizing the card, and an inability to browse the network. Here is a list of items that you can check to see if you are connected:

- Ensure that the NIC card is seated properly. If the card is even a little misaligned, it won't initialize.
- Look at the back of the NIC. If it has lights on it, are they on? Are they green? Usually this indicates that the card is functioning correctly. Check the NIC documentation for more details.
- Check your cable connections. Is the cable plugged into the NIC securely? Is it plugged into the hub securely?
- Is the hub on? Try switching ports on the hub.

Note: I once had a coworker who had gone through all the configuring of his brand-new PC. He spent two hours trying to troubleshoot a problem to no avail. In the end, it was discovered that the hub was unplugged. This is an example of the importance of looking for the obvious first, because it's often the answer.

One important thing to remember about connectivity is electricity. Connectivity involves getting an electronic signal from one place to another intact. If there is a broken piece in the chain, the signal won't get transmitted, so check all your physical connections.

Configuration

Configuring your network settings can be tricky and confusing. You have to go back through each piece and recheck each entry. Here are some common problems and solutions:

- Did you enter the correct protocol? IPX won't talk on a network running NetBEUI. It will look like it's running correctly, but the components won't be speaking the same language.
- Did you enable File and Print Sharing? This is important. Others on the network won't be able to see you unless you enable this setting.
- Check the identification for the computer. If the computer's name is the same as one already on the network, your PC won't be allowed to join the network.
- Did you install the correct NIC card software for your NIC? (Check the Network icon in Control Panel.) Manufacturers tend to name NICs with numbers that can cause two cards to look alike. However, Windows 95 won't raise a flag. Because the cards are so similar, Windows will assume that you know which one you're installing. Be sure to choose the right NIC when installing!

Physical

I saved physical for last because it tends to be the most expensive problem and the most uncommon one during installation. However, physical problems aren't out of the realm of possibility. You must realize that, outside of technical professionals, very few people can really tell when a piece of hardware has gone bad.

The surest means of checking is one of two ways:

1. Replace the item in question with one that works.
2. Put the item into a working environment and see if it functions.

I prefer the second method because of the certainty involved. If I suspect a NIC is bad, I will pull it out and place it in a system that works. If it doesn't work, I know it's broken. If it does work, I have considerably narrowed down the possibilities. Here are some problems that might be plaguing you:

- Bad NIC: Generally, when a NIC card goes south, the green activity lights won't activate. Also, Windows won't be able to find your card. Your best bet is to swap the card out with another one and try again. Unless it is the exact same model of NIC card, you will have to reinstall the card.

- Bad cable: This is the easiest and cheapest problem to fix. If you suspect a cable is bad, swap it out with one that you know works. Look for fraying, or, if the connectors on the ends of the cable are clear, check to make sure that the wires inside aren't loose. Sometimes I swap out the cable just to be sure. Since the only thing you have to do to your computer is reboot, this is a no-hassle fix to try.

- Bad hub: This problem is the most infrequent, but it can happen. Check to make sure that all the lights are on. Also, try moving your cable around to different ports. If one PC works on the hub and another doesn't, you can be pretty sure that the problem is not with the hub.

- Bad slot: It's possible that the slot in which your card is in is bad. However, this is highly unlikely. Try switching slots and rebooting your PC. Windows doesn't care in which slot the card rests.

TROUBLESHOOTING

On some computers, it is necessary to "activate" a PCI slot. If your NIC card is PCI and isn't responding in any way, check your computer's documentation regarding the installation of PCI expansion cards. If you're a little more comfortable in a computer's BIOS, check the settings and ensure that your slot is active or not thought to be in use by a piece of hardware you might have removed earlier.

Most troubleshooting involves using your head and following logic. Windows 95/98 also includes a troubleshooter facility that can help puzzle through some network card difficulties. Select Start, Help, and then search in the index for "troubleshooting network cards." This can point you in the right direction, but the information is probably too general to resolve many issues. Just be methodical in your approach, and check your documentation. Usually that is good enough to solve any problem.

Sharing Your Network

Here is something you might want to remember as your budding network takes form: If you want to share some files or even your entire hard drive, you must create a share "point" from which the rest of the network will access (assuming, of course, that you enabled File and Print Sharing back in the Network icon in Control Panel). To share a directory or drive, follow these steps:

1. Bring up My Computer or Explorer.

2. Highlight the item or drive you want to make available to others. (Only directories or drives can be shared, not individual files.)

3. Once the directory or drive is highlighted, right-click it to get the menu shown in Figure 24.12.

FIGURE 24.12.

The Sharing sheet of your drive's Properties dialog box enables you to assign and control access to your data.

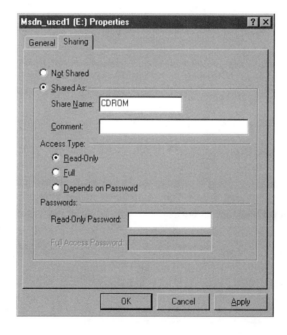

4. Choose the Sharing option. A dialog will appear, asking for information about how you want to share this resource.

5. Click the Share As button. The Share Name field will become active.

6. Type a name that you want the rest of the network to see. This is how other computers in the network will identify this resource.

7. Choose the type of access you want to grant. You can choose Read-Only or Full Access or set it according to a password.

8. When you click OK, you will notice that the directory or drive you chose to share now has a small hand icon next to it. This indicates that the resource has been shared.

9. Double-click Network Neighborhood, and watch as the list of computers in your network appears. Then double-click your computer. (The computers are listed according to the names you gave them in the Computer Description field earlier.)

10. You will see the names you gave your resources (share points) earlier. Double-click a resource to view its contents.

11. Alternatively, you can map a drive to that resource. Click the Resource name (for example, CD-ROM), and then right-click. This will bring up the option to map a network drive. Choose to do so.

12. A dialog box will appear. Choose the drive letter you want to represent this resource. Then decide if you want to reconnect to this resource when you next log in. (I recommend doing so unless you're going to use this resource only once.)

13. Click OK. Now you have utilized your first network drive! (For fun, check My Computer to see the new drive listed there.)

Summary

Networking is becoming an essential tool in our everyday lives. Some people even think that the appliances in our homes will be networked. The alarm clock will contact the coffee maker 15 minutes before it is set to go off so that the coffee can get started. Don't laugh. The technology already exists—it's just a matter of time.

Speaking of the home, the recent rush of cable-free networking kits and products really open the field to small office and home users. While performance lags behind 10Mbps Ethernet, most light-duty networks won't notice the difference. And it sure beats tearing open walls and ceiling to run 10BaseT cable throughout the house.

If you plan on building a small network, I can give you a few words of advice. Plan ahead! Once the people in your office or organization get a taste of it, the demand will be extreme. As far as troubleshooting goes, use your head and go with your instincts. They are usually right. Good luck!

PART VII

Input and Output

Printers

When it comes to PC upgrades, it might seem out of place to talk about printers. After all, these devices aren't actually part of the PC. Instead, they are independent devices packed with enough silicon and electronics to make them qualify as computers in their own right.

But printers do, in fact, contribute a great deal to the overall value and effectiveness of any PC. For all the benefits of digital technology and ubiquitous Internet-based communications, sometimes you just gotta have it on paper. A good printer can help you produce incredibly professional-looking output, whether it's a million-dollar sales presentation or a birthday card for your 8-year-old.

This chapter will help you understand what's involved in buying, using, and maintaining a printer. Here are some of the things you'll learn:

- How the various types of monochrome and color printers work, be they laser, ink jet, dye sublimation, or some other process
- What is involved in purchasing a new printer, with specific advice for home, office, and specialty buyers
- How to diagnose and resolve common printer problems
- Tips on routine maintenance of print engines and print media such as toner and ink
- How to upgrade your PC with a new printer
- What repair opportunities are available for printers that have problems, helping you avoid expensive servicing or even the replacement of the unit

Printers Are Improving

The great thing about PCs is that everything gets better, faster, and cheaper. Printers are no exception to the rule. In fact, they often seem to deliver the most telling examples of runaway advancement, as clever engineers and designers learn to squeeze more dots into ever-tighter spaces.

It all started back in 1984, when Hewlett-Packard released the HP LaserJet Series I. This 300dpi laser printer, and the HP LaserJet Series II that followed in 1986, helped usher in the desktop publishing revolution, transforming small offices into self-sufficient publishing operations. It also pushed noisy and slow daisy-wheel printers right off the mainstream market.

Today, over a dozen years later, PC-based printing has moved again—this time into color. Although it's not appropriate for everyone, inexpensive color ink jets provide an incredible range of talent, producing near-laser-quality text and rich, color images that approach photo quality. Whether you work in a home office or a huge office or just have a PC for your home, the latest printers can help turn the bits and bytes inside your PC into attractive, compelling output (see Figure 25.1).

Desktop printers fall into three main categories, each of which employs a unique method for putting information on paper:

- Monochrome laser printers
- Monochrome and color ink jet printers
- Advanced color printers

No matter what printing technology is involved, all these devices do about the same thing. They take a digital description of an image—usually a printed page—and turn it into something we can see. In the case of printers, the digital 1s and 0s are rendered as analog dots on a paper medium, with the precise placement, shading, and coloration of the dots forming a recognizable image.

In order to make this digital-to-analog conversion, if you will, most printers contain memory to hold and process image data and internal mechanisms for transferring the print media (toner, ink, or dye) onto the page. A series of rollers moves the paper at a controlled rate while the printing mechanism applies the media to the paper. What we see at the other end of this process is text, graphics, and color.

Laser Printers

Laser printers use fine black toner—nearly identical to that used in copiers—to produce sharp text and graphics on the page. The toner is made from magnetic iron compounds, plastic, and pigment, which allow it to be shaped, applied, and melted onto the page. Laser printers get their name from the laser light that is used as part of the process.

Here's how it works: An optical photoconducting (OPC) drum is used to transfer toner to paper. First, the OPC drum is charged with static electricity, causing it to repel the toner. Then a very thin laser beam strafes across the OPC drum, strobing at a rate of 300 pulses per horizontal inch (in the case of a 300dpi print job). Each strobe of the laser represents a single microscopic printed dot. The laser strobe removes the static charge from the drum, allowing toner to adhere to the point where it impacts.

The OPC drum turns beneath the laser as the paper moves, advancing each printed line into position beneath the laser. The now-uncharged point attracts and holds a bit of toner, so a magnetic roller covered with toner is brought into the proximity of the OPC drum. Toner then transfers to the magnetic roller, where it is then exposed to a strong static charge called a *corona*, which is situated beneath the moving paper. The corona draws the toner off the turning OPC drum and onto the paper. An instant later, the plastic toner is melted onto the page by the heated Teflon fuser roller.

> **Note:** Some printers use an array of tiny LEDs (light emitting diodes) instead of a laser to dispel the charge from the OPC drum. Exactly 8½ inches wide, this array flashes light onto appropriate points on the turning drum below to achieve the same effect delivered by lasers. LED mechanisms can also be less prone to breakdowns, because there is no moving laser gun. The drawback is that LED resolutions are limited to the number of diodes that can be physically placed across the width of the page.

A printer's resolution is determined by how finely the printer's laser can describe charged areas on the drum. A 300dpi printer puts as many as 120,000 black toner dots on each printed square inch. A 600dpi printer lays down four times as many pixels in each inch. Print enhancement technologies further enhance the image by laying down gray half-toned dots.

Most laser printers employ their own pool of memory to store pages being processed. However, all these dots can demand a lot of space. Although a 300dpi printout needs less than 1MB of memory to print, a 600dpi page requires nearly 4MB. This number goes up further still if enhancement technology is used, because each dot must now store more than simple black-and-white data.

The process is quite versatile: Laser printers present a wider range of print speeds and resolutions than any other printing technology. Small personal laser printers, for example, print four to eight pages per minute (ppm), and larger network models can push 30 to 40ppm or more. Likewise, resolutions stretch from 300dpi to 1,200dpi or more. Often, higher resolutions have extreme memory requirements. A full 8½×11-inch page printed at 1,200dpi can require 32MB of printer memory.

In general, laser printers are very easy to maintain and care for. They use modular toner cartridges that ease the replacement of consumables. Most cartridges integrate the print drum and toner, although some models use separate cartridges for each, allowing slightly less expensive operation by extending the life of the drum.

One drawback of lasers is their prodigious power consumption. These printers consume a tremendous amount of energy in order to produce charges for the drum and, to a lesser degree, to melt the toner onto the page. The previously mentioned corona is created by passing a 10,000-volt current through a wire near the paper. In fact, there are actually two coronas, called the *primary corona* and the *transfer corona*. Even when the printer is idle, power draw is significant. You might even notice that the lights dim when the laser printer in your home office begins to print a page.

> **Caution:** For obvious reasons, it is important that your laser printer be well-grounded. Not only can unanticipated capacitance kill you, it can also kill your printer.

> **Tip:** Whatever you do, make sure you get an Energy Star-approved laser printer. These devices provide sleep modes that kick in after adjustable periods of inactivity, reducing power draw tremendously. That way, you can leave your printer on all day to occasionally print documents without pouring money down the electrical outlet.

Ink Jets: Squirting Pages

Ink jet printers have become the most popular option for home printing, thanks to very low prices, improved print quality, and the ability to cheaply produce color output. Some color Canon printers and HP DeskJets, for example, can be purchased for about $100. They offer 300dpi color printing, perhaps not too fast or very brilliant, but quick and brilliant enough for the cost. For better color printing results, you have to spend $200 or more.

They are also compact and consume little power. In the past, buyers had to choose between monochrome and color models, although both work on the same principle. Today, most personal ink jet printers are color, because this capability costs little more than straight monochrome while adding significant value.

Ink jets work by spitting tiny dots of colored ink onto the page. In this sense, they are similar to older impact printers, which repeatedly struck a ribbon of ink placed in front of the paper to form letters and graphics. The ink is stored in a reservoir, which often consists of replaceable cartridges that are swapped out when the ink is consumed. In the case of color ink jets, there are separate ink cartridges for red, green, blue, and black ink.

> **Tip:** Some color ink jets—particularly older models—omit the black ink cartridge. To create black (say, for text), the printer shoots all three other colors to form a dark dot. The result, however, is usually closer to brown or gray than true black—a real problem for anyone who prints any amount of straight text. In addition, the use of three ink cartridges for each black dot increases the rate of ink consumption.
>
> You'll also find ink jets that use a dedicated black cartridge and a single removable cartridge for the three ink colors. While this simplifies installing the cartridges, you'll end up spending more because the entire color cartridge must be replaced when the first color of the three goes dry. In other words, you throw out perfectly good ink. You most economical choice is a printer with four separate cartridges—one for black, and one each for cyan, magenta, and yellow.

The printing action happens at the nozzles, which place the ink on the page. Behind the nozzles, an interface circuit applies charges to a series of impulse drivers, corresponding to the appropriate color of ink. These drivers push a tiny drop of ink through the nozzle in one of two ways:

- A charge is applied to a pizoelectric driver (an electronic crystal often made of synthetic quartz), which causes it to expand. The controlled expansion pushes a known amount of ink through the nozzle and onto the page.

- A charge is used to heat a small amount of ink, producing a ball of vapor that pushes the ink onto the page.

In both cases, a print head positions the nozzles by moving across the paper as it is fed through the printer. Often, you can hear the operation of the print head moving back and forth as a print job is underway. Through the exact positioning of the print head, resolutions of 720dpi and higher are possible on the most sophisticated ink jet products.

Unlike laser printers, most low-end ink jets don't employ their own memory to store the entire image of the page to be printed. Instead, they accept data from your PC in real time, placing it on the page as the bits arrive. To do this, most ink jets employ a small buffer (from 128 to 512KB) to hold incoming data. The lack of dedicated memory is one reason why ink jets can cost hundreds of dollars less than laser printers. That said, some higher-end ink jet printers do include a CPU and memory.

Note: The memoryless design of ink jets can save you a few bucks—but not without a cost. Ink jet printers put a greater load on your computer's CPU, in part because it must finesse the data flow to avoid sending too much or too little data at one time. Unlike laser printers, in which your PC can fire off and forget about print jobs handed off to the laser printer, the system stays engaged in ink jet print jobs until the very end.

Ink jet printers can get by without memory because documents don't have to move through the printer at a constant rate of speed. If your PC falls behind the ink jet's output, the printer merely waits for the data flow to catch up and starts laying down dots where it left off. Laser printers, in contrast, are committed to a set output speed when the print job begins. Because the paper is in precise physical contact with drums and rollers, stopping the mechanism will result in slippage, and the output will be distorted. For this reason, laser printers ensure that the page will run smoothly through its mechanisms by first assembling the entire print job in printer memory before starting to print.

Although ink jet resolutions have improved, they still lag behind their laser counterparts in print speed on longer documents. The reason for this is that once a page has been assembled in a laser printer's memory (some laser printers have more sophisticated motherboards than their host computers), the printer can then print as many copies as you want without any significant amount of further processing. Every page a lower-end ink jet prints must be reassembled and sent to the printer by the CPU. Ink jets also can't produce black-and-white text that is as sharp as that of good laser printers.

Note: You can usually tell ink jet output by the lower-contrast text. Letters might not appear truly black, even on ink jets that have a true black ink cartridge, and edges can look less than smooth. Still, top ink jets can produce text results that mirror lasers under casual observation. (Just don't let the ink get wet!)

In the past, ink jets were notoriously persnickety. Nozzles could gum up and jam, impairing output quality. Even today, you'll need to recalibrate your printer after replacing ink cartridges—a simple process in which you tell the printer which test pattern looks best. However, ink jets are very much affected by the paper stock they print on, because the absorptive properties of the stock determine how the dots look on the page.

Note: Recently, a new category of personal printers has emerged—true-color photo printers, designed to produce near-photo-quality snapshots from digital image files. As digital cameras become less expensive and more popular, photo printers provide a convenient and inexpensive way to view digital snapshots.

Most of these products are small, printing onto specially coated 5×7-inch paper that provides outstanding quality. They also use advanced color printing processes such as thermal dye transfer or dye sublimation. These parallel-port printers are compact and easy to install, but the coated paper makes them expensive to operate. However, at least one printer, the Panasonic ColorShot, actually produces images by heating chemically receptive paper stock. Instead of laying ink or wax onto paper, the paper itself changes to reveal the desired image. And unlike other printers, the ColorShot (see Figure 25.2) uses the USB bus to connect to your PC, making it easy to run alongside a traditional laser or ink jet printer.

FIGURE 25.2.
Polaroid's compact ColorShot printer doesn't lay any ink or toner at all. Rather, it heats a chemically-receptive media to bring out photo-quality color and sharpness. (Photo courtesy of Polaroid Corporation)

Advanced Color Printers

Most PC users have been working with ever-improving laser and ink jet printers, but a small portion of graphics professionals need more. Enter high-end color printers, which employ a number of different processes to produce precise color documents.

Although physical approaches vary, all these printers share two key qualities: They are very expensive (from $2,500 to $10,000 or more), and the cost of printing each page is much higher than it is for standard laser or ink jet printers. Both of these issues are enough to make advanced color printers a niche for people who need better fidelity, whether to proof documents before they go to press or to produce professional-quality color output for distribution.

There are three main areas of high-resolution color printers:

- Color laser
- Solid ink

- Thermal dye transfer
- Thermal wax transfer

Color Laser Printers

Costing $3,000 to $10,000, color lasers use the same toner and drum process employed by their monochrome cousins (see Figure 25.3). Instead of just black toner, four separate toner colors (cyan, magenta, yellow, and black) are employed. But unlike other color printers (including ink jets), color lasers can produce top results on regular copier paper—a potential huge savings in consumable costs over the life of the printer.

FIGURE 25.3.
Hewlett-Packard's Color LaserJet 5 provides attractive, versatile color and monochrome output. Falling prices have made color lasers a growing market segment. (Photo courtesy of Hewlett-Packard)

Output is very good. Monochrome text handling and speed are identical to standard lasers, making color lasers the only advanced color printer appropriate for monochrome output. Color quality has improved markedly over the last two years as well, and prices have come down to the point where many small departments or offices can afford to consider one for their pre-press work.

Solid Ink Printers

Costing about $3,000 to $4,000, solid ink printers can be thought of as thermal wax transfer printers. These models melt solid sticks of colored wax and spray the resulting liquid onto the page, much like an ink jet printer does. Some newer models actually apply the melted wax to a rotating drum, which then transfers the material to the page—similar to the operation of laser printers.

Because solid ink models can use plain copier paper for output, these printers reduce cost per page and are appropriate for mixed text and graphics output. However, resolutions are low enough that image quality might fall behind that of other models.

Thermal Dye Transfer Printers

The most expensive color printers at $7,000 to $15,000, thermal dye transfer models also produce the best overall quality. This is stuff for true professionals. Printing is agonizingly slow, and it must be done on custom polyester-coated paper that can push costs per page to an astounding $10.

The process works by rolling a dye-saturated ribbon across the page. The ribbon is heated to transfer the dye to the page, with separate passes for each color. Thermal dye models are one of the few printers to provide continuous tone printing, producing 16.7 million separate colors to eliminate dithering patterns.

Thermal Wax Transfer Printers

Costing $3,000 to $4,000, thermal wax transfer printers might be on their way out. These printers work much like their pricier dye transfer siblings, in that they heat a wax-coated ribbon as it rolls against the paper. The melted wax is laid on specially coated paper, which makes this sort of printer expensive to operate. They also produce dithering patterns, which detract from their high contrast and excellent color production.

The Software Behind the Scenes: Languages and Drivers

Like any device, hardware is just a bunch of well-engineered parts until some software comes around to make it do something. Such is the case with printers, which require two things to operate—a device driver to access printer capabilities, and a page-description language to render pages into a format that is intelligible to the print controller.

Page-Description Languages

Until recently, Adobe's PostScript was the only printer language that enabled printers to do neat things like produce adjustable-size fonts, white-on-black text, and rotated or scaled images. With its roots in the Apple Macintosh arena, PostScript has been the exclusive language of publishing, with almost all service bureaus using PostScript devices to produce physical output.

A more recent version of PostScript, PostScript Level 2, is optimized for color output. PostScript 2 provides complex color-handling and color-matching capabilities and is used almost universally among high-end color printers as their page-description language.

Over the past four years, Hewlett-Packard's PCL language (now at PCL 6) has matched PostScript's monochrome capabilities. Powered by the market juggernaut of its LaserJet line of printers, PCL has become the PC standard for print-based output, although PostScript continues to enjoy a niche among people who produce proofs for professional output. Today, many non-HP printers provide PCL emulation, allowing them to use the standard HP drivers supplied with Windows 95 to operate.

Drivers

Printer drivers act like any other hardware device driver. This segment of code acts as the emissary between your system and the printer hardware, telling it what it needs to do in a form it understands. Windows 95 provides a standard minidriver that addresses most of the base printer functions for all models, while an enhanced driver component provides access to custom features.

Custom drivers address features such as bidirectional communication, PC-based printer controls, resolution-specific operation, and the like. These drivers are critical to the optimal operation of your printer and can affect both features and quality of output.

> **Tip:** Stay on top of driver updates. Vendors often update their driver software to provide enhanced features or better output quality and speed. New drivers might also fix inevitable bugs that crop up when the code interacts with system-level stuff such as the graphics device interface (GDI). Usually you can get the latest driver versions from your vendor's Web site. In fact, you should make a point of checking for updated drivers when you first install your printer, because the driver disks in the box might be up to six months (and several revisions) old.

Making Connections

Of course, your printer needs to get bits from the PC somehow. The most common transport is your PC's parallel port. For one thing, the parallel port is ubiquitous: Printer vendors don't need to worry about including an interface card or other hardware to ensure that PCs can send jobs to the printer. For another, it's the fastest ubiquitous external bus. Parallel ports run at speeds of 120 to 500KBps, depending on the type of parallel port involved.

Table 25.1 lists the three styles of parallel ports on PCs.

Table 25.1. The three types of parallel ports.

Parallel Port Type	Throughput	Description
Centronics	40–300KBps	Standard issue on PCs through the early '90s. Highest level of compatibility with all devices.
Enhanced Parallel Port (EPP)	2MBps	Better performance and allows bidirectional communication, but EPP mode might preclude the use of other peripherals.

Parallel Port Type	Throughput	Description
Enhanced Capability Port (ECP)	2MBps	Provides multitasking tweaks to the EPP specification.

You'll need an EPP or ECP port in order to take full advantage of Plug and Play capability. The new specs convert four of the parallel port's data lines into a two-way data bus that allows for more complex configuration and control.

> **Note:** Before you get worked up over promises made by vendor advertisements, check your PC's hardware. If you lack an EPP or ECP configuration, your machine might not be able to make use of those features. If this is the case, you'll need to add an I/O card that includes the new features (see Chapter 23, "I/O Add-Ons").

A printer shared among users might employ an Ethernet network connection, often residing as a node on the network. Network connections can significantly improve the speed of print jobs with faster printers, because the throughput of the network—when not congested—might be 100 times that of a parallel port. Printers can often be upgraded with a network access card that fits into a slot in a printer's side panel.

If your printer lacks an ethernet slot, you can still hook it to the network by way of a dedicated network print server box. This device hooks to the ethernet-based network and to the printer via a standard parallel port. The one limitation: Controller-less printers such as ink jets or GDI laser printers can not work off a print server box.

Another emerging option for printers is USB. Polaroid's ColorShot photo printer uses this bus in part because the designers expect it to sit alongside a workhorse laser or ink jet printer installed on the parallel port. But USB offers advantages for mainstream printers, including better performance and more intuitive setup. You should inquire about the availability of USB versions of printers if you run Windows 98 on a USB-equipped PC.

Finally, some high-end printers feature an SCSI connection to connect to an individual PC (which might itself reside as a network print server). SCSI provides fast transfer and also allows the use of a local hard disk inside the printer to store frequently accessed graphics such as fonts, forms, and bitmaps. Although a printer hard disk adds expense, it can save hours of time by eliminating the need to pipe repetitive graphics and fonts over congested connections.

Purchasing a Printer

Since the LaserJet Series II, monochrome laser printers have become indispensable tools for offices large and small. And no wonder: They can produce sharp black-and-white documents that are nearly indistinguishable from professionally printed materials. Today, your options are much more varied. You can choose from among monochrome or color; laser, ink jet, or dye/wax transfer; personal or workgroup; and a variety of other options.

How do you decide what to buy? Ultimately, no printer can cover everything. That fast, inexpensive, razor-sharp text output of most lasers will let you down when you want to create a fun color invitation for a party. Likewise, ink jets can make you wait around while that 80-page document gets painted oh-so-slowly by overworked nozzles. And if high-end color printers don't bankrupt you, they will probably let you down when it comes to workday monochrome documents.

So you need to decide what kind of printer will cover the most ground for you. Table 25.2 should help you focus on a specific printer class. Then you can move on to more specific breakdowns to determine the type of printer that suits you in each class.

Table 25.2. Choosing a class of printer.

Printer Type	Cost	What It's Best For
Monochrome laser	$150–$3,000	Business documents, newsletters, fast printing of large documents, workgroup printing, fast personal printing
Color ink jet	$150–$700	Home and small office, simple design work, personal home or office printing
Advanced color	$3,000–$15,000	Prepress output for professional design, professional presentations

Laserpalooza: Monochrome Laser Printers

Laser printers helped launch the desktop publishing revolution, and their value is still evident today. You won't find a wider variety of printers within a class than with lasers. These versatile machines run the gamut from inexpensive, light-duty, personal printers to monstrous 40ppm workhorses that churn out the workload for an entire network.

Laser printers fall into the three broad categories listed in Table 25.3.

Table 25.3. Main laser printer categories.

Printer Type	Printing Speed	What It's Best For
Personal	4–8ppm	Small and home office, private office printer
Workgroup	8–16ppm	Small office, departmental printer
Network	16–40ppm	Medium and large departments

Regardless of the type of laser you select, you'll need to decide if you want to pay a little extra for a PostScript-capable printer or one that uses HP's PCL language. As explained earlier, the decision really boils down to compatibility with service bureaus and Macs.

> **Tip:** When you're buying a new laser printer, it's a good idea to look for models using standard RAM SIMMs for their on-board memory. Many printers use proprietary memory cards, which vendors might sell at a stiff premium. By using a printer with SIMM-based memory, you will be able to shop around for the best price when you upgrade down the road.

Printers with Personality

If you're reading this book for advice on how to stock your home office or your personal space at work, you should consider a personal laser or LED printer (see Figure 25.4). These mighty mites provide an impressive blend of speed, affordability, high resolution, and reliable operation. With resolutions of up to 600dpi, you can produce professional-looking monochrome documents from your desktop.

FIGURE 25.4.
The EPL-N1200 from Epson is small, quick, and inexpensive. It features Energy Star operation but lacks the paper-handling capacities of larger workgroup models. (Photo courtesy of Epson America)

In particular, personal lasers are great for office workers who need to output confidential documents. They can churn out up to eight pages per minute, and most models take a good deal of the printing burden off your PC, allowing you to get back to work quickly when you're printing large documents. However, personal models run at speeds one-half that of workgroup-capable printers and often lack paper-handling capabilities. For instance, the compact form can result in circuitous paper paths that make it inadvisable to use some personal lasers for printing adhesive labels and transparencies. Paper trays might be limited to just 100 pages, requiring frequent reloads, and output trays might be nonexistent, causing finished pages to spill onto the desk or floor.

> **Peter's Principle:** If You're Running Windows 95/98 or NT, Now's the Time to Consider a GDI Printer
>
> Over the past three years, a new class of personal laser printers, called *GDI printers* or Windows printers, have emerged. These printers cost significantly less than traditional models using HP's PCL or Adobe's PostScript language. They produce output based on the raw GDI graphics data sent from the PC. Because the printer doesn't interpret the incoming data, there is much less need for intelligent (read: expensive) controllers and on-board RAM. By the same token, these printers must make use of processing power and RAM on the PC itself, which can slow overall performance significantly.
>
> GDI printers were actually introduced several years ago but failed to take hold because they suffered from slow performance and failed to work with DOS and OS/2 applications. Since then, Windows 95, 98, and NT have reduced the importance of the OS question, while low-cost RAM has reduced the performance hit on host systems. The emergence of fast Pentium CPUs didn't hurt either.
>
> Is a GDI printer for you? If you use and print from Windows-based applications exclusively, you're certainly a candidate. However, you should also make sure that you have enough processing power—a Pentium MMX or faster PC is a good idea if you multitask applications—and plenty of RAM, on the order of 32MB or more. Note that 16MB RAM systems will run into trouble, because Windows itself grabs 12MB, leaving little RAM for running applications and print jobs side by side. Also, you might want to avoid a GDI printer if you print a lot of long documents. These will hobble your PC during the length of the print job—and, for an 80-page manuscript, that can be a while.

Workgroup Printers

Workgroup printers run at speeds of 8 to 16ppm and provide the best mix of performance, resolution, and affordability. LexMark's Optra L, for example, can produce stunning 1,200dpi output that is almost indistinguishable from professional linotype prints. Likewise, Hewlett-Packard's Si line of network printers can produce crisp 1,200dpi pages 24 hours a day if asked to. In addition to parallel port connections, you can expect to see network and possibly SCSI connectors on these printers.

Workgroup printers are best for departments and offices that have 10 to 50 people, depending on how much printing goes on. Often these models are highly flexible. Memory might range from 2 to 40MB, and paper trays can be bulked up to handle 500 pages or more at a time. Some models also provide duplex printing add-ons that allow the printer to run pages through twice—once on each side—before depositing them in the output tray.

These models might also suit single users who either need to print at very high resolutions or who frequently output many longer documents. You'll pay for this privilege, however. Although workgroup models can be had for about $1,000, prices quickly move up as you add memory for high-resolution operation. A well-appointed workgroup laser can cost $1,600 to $1,800.

Network Lasers: The Big Time

Finally, a word about network laser printers (see Figure 25.5). These behemoths are best for big offices and departments that want to share a printer on an Ethernet or Token Ring network. With paper capacities in the thousands of sheets and the ability to push 30 pages or more per minute, network laser printers can quickly recoup their big $4,000 or higher price tags.

FIGURE 25.5.

Fully decked out with paper-handling options, Hewlett-Packard's LaserJet 5Si can meet the printing needs of a large department. (Photo courtesy of Hewlett-Packard)

Although many network lasers offer 600dpi and higher operation, they usually run at a more pedestrian 300dpi. The lower resolution allows quicker, more efficient printing while still producing good results.

Affordable Color: Ink Jets

Ink jets are best for home and small office users who want versatility and low cost. What's more, an emerging class of workgroup ink jet printers is providing an affordable option to pricey color laser printers. Although the text quality won't match that of top lasers, it's good enough for everything short of business proposals. And the ability to add a splash of color to any document can be a real boon for both home and business users alike.

Expect to pay $150 to $400 for an ink jet, with the higher-priced models pushing resolutions up to 600dpi or even 720dpi (some products even push all the way to 1,440dpi). Although all these models work on standard paper, you'll get much better color output on special coated paper (often customized for the specific printer model). Coated paper will run you up to 10 cents per sheet, about seven to eight times the cost of standard stock.

Of course, speed can be a problem. A quick ink jet hooked to a fast PC can spit out a single page nearly as fast as a personal laser can. However, subsequent pages take longer. New workgroup-class ink jet printers, such as the HP 2000 Professional Series Color Printer, offer near-laser speeds and affordable color output. However, lasers generally offer the most economical black-and-white output.

Artistic License: Dye Sublimation and Thermal Wax

If you're looking for professional color output to proof materials headed for press or to produce professional-quality output for distribution, the stakes get much higher. Still, $4,000 or less will get you a good color laser printer—about one-half to one-third the cost of such hardware just three years ago.

In this area, you need to decide what level of output you need. For drop-dead-gorgeous color, thermal dye transfer is the best choice. But the $10,000 and over price point might make you drop dead yourself. A solid ink printer might be the best choice for dedicated, high-quality color output. With a price of $3,000 to $4,000, it is certainly a competitive option.

For mixed use of color and monochrome, you have two choices: a color laser printer or a high-quality ink jet printer. The best ink jet printers can produce 720dpi resolution that, on specially coated paper, approaches the quality of other processes. However, they also give you the option of decent black-and-white output. Particularly useful are large-format ink jets, which can produce magazine-spread-sized print-outs.

Note: Epson now offers ink jets capable of 1,440×720 resolution, including the wide-format Stylus Color 1520 (see Figure 25.6) and Stylus Color 3000 (see Figure 25.7). These printers bridge the gap between advanced color and standard ink jet processes.

FIGURE 25.6.

Epson's Stylus Color 1520 has 1,440×720 resolution color output. (Photo courtesy of Epson America)

FIGURE 25.7.

Epson's Stylus Color 3000 also has 1,440×720 resolution color output. In addition, it has Adobe PostScript Level 2 and faster page output. (Photo courtesy of Epson America)

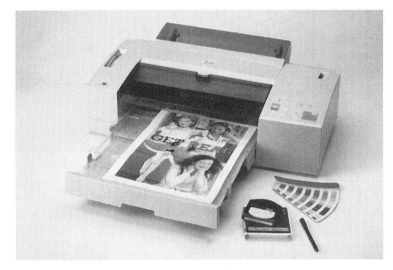

Diagnosing/Troubleshooting

Unlike many of the components inside a PC, printers are complex beasts with a lot of moving parts. Problems can occur with the printer's gearing or head motor, for example. Toner and ink can get dirty or old, causing nozzle jams, uneven distribution, smearing, and other problems. And printer memory is just as likely to fail as a PC's main memory. Of course, you also have software to worry about.

Clearly, we can't cover every problem for every type of printer. The best advice is to keep your eyes open. If you suspect a problem with print quality, try closely examining a variety of different types of print-outs. Do problems occur with color or monochrome jobs? Does the problem occur throughout the print-out, or only along the far edges? By looking closely at anomalous behavior, you can cut down the number of suspects.

Dirty Old Laser

Laser printers are particularly susceptible to dirt because toner is already dirt of a sort. Loaded with iron oxide, it is, naturally enough, abrasive. And the strong static charges involved in the printing process attract airborne dust. The result is that, over time, a machine will become quite grimy inside, and the dirt can eventually wear down and break internal parts.

The most common part destroyed by dirt is the Teflon upper roller in the heated fuser assembly. Parts inside that heated assembly attract partially melted toner, which forms into spikes and stalactites that are significant enough to dig through the microscopically thin Teflon coating on that upper roller. The next thing you know, every printed page has ugly vertical streaks.

It's much easier and less expensive to avoid a broken fuser than it is to replace one. You can use a clean, dry paint brush, a can of compressed air, and a few QTips to thoroughly clean the insides. Many printers also come with their own brushes for sweeping out toner particles and dust.

> **Caution:** Never, ever use any liquid or liquid solvent to clean the insides of a laser printer. Also never use water to clean up a toner spill—you'll only make things worse. And avoid getting toner onto your clothes.
>
> If you work around laser printers (and toner) often, consider keeping a low-cost vacuum handy to pick up spills. Adding a soft brush attachment can allow you to periodically clean the inside of the printer as well.

With proper care and maintenance, your laser printer can serve you faithfully for years. Many 8ppm HP LaserJet Series II printers are still alive and printing, with page counts in excess of one million.

> **Tip:** If you have a heavy-use office printer that you rely on, it's a good idea to have a knowledgeable printer or copier professional clean the machine regularly. Check your manual for suggested maintenance routines, which can vary depending on the amount of documents you tend to print. Not only will this keep your office workhorse online, but it can also ensure that the fan (if there is one) continues to circulate air. A working fan is needed to make sure that ionized or "fried" air passes out of the printer before it begins to corrode plastic parts.

Easy Outs

Whether you've just installed a new printer or have an old war horse, things can go wrong. If your printer refuses to print, don't panic. Because printers are external devices with their own power and internal settings, you should check a few simple items before you go fishing around for deeper issues in the printer or your operating system:

- Check the cable: Is it fitted tightly into both the PC and the printer? Also make sure that the cable is a proper 25-pin parallel cable, not a 25-pin serial cable (they look a lot alike!).

- Get online: Make sure that the printer panel indicates the unit is online and ready to accept data.

- Check paper, toner, and ink: Make sure that there is paper in the input trays, because print jobs will fail otherwise. Also make sure that there isn't a paper jam holding up the works. Toner or ink cartridges need to be properly installed as well. Be sure that you have removed the plastic tab and the tape seal from the toner cartridge.

- Try a print test: There is often a test button on the front panel of the printer. If pressing this button produces a printout, but the printer won't work otherwise, the problem doesn't reside within the printer itself.

TROUBLESHOOTING

> There is an exception to the preceding point: If the I/O port hardware on the printer has failed, the print test will work despite the fact that something is amiss with the printer itself. Many laser printers have a small circuit board containing the Centronics connector and perhaps a UART. If one of the few chips on this board burns up, your printer is an orphan.

- Check the power: Don't laugh. Many personal printers and ink jets make almost no noise when they are on. Worse, some vendors have all but eliminated front panel lights and panels, making it hard to tell if the printer is actually on.

- Check your printer settings: Are you printing to the right device? From your application, select File, Print, and then choose the Name scroll box to view the available printers, as shown in Figure 25.8.

- Be suspicious of printer pass-through devices: If you have multiple devices working off a single parallel port, you might be using a pass-through port to let both work without having to swap connectors. Unfortunately, pass-throughs don't always work. Try printing without the pass-through hardware in place.

FIGURE 25.8.
Windows 95 and 98 both enable you to set up multiple printers. They also treat PC faxing and a few other electronic output applications as print jobs. Check the Print properties dialog box to make sure you're printing to the intended device.

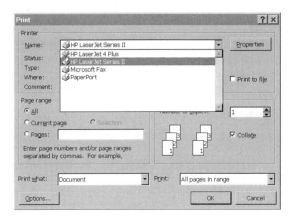

Pop Goes the Port

One common problem occurs when your applications or operating system can no longer find the port leading to the printer. This can happen due to a classic hardware conflict, in which another device grabs the resources reserved for your parallel port.

A hardware or software installation might cause this problem. If several devices are sharing your LPT port, make sure that none of them redirected the address information for the device.

The parallel port leading to the printer is usually referred to as LPT1. To check if you printer is properly installed, do the following:

1. Go to Control Panel (select Start, Settings, Control Panel) and double-click the Printers icon.

2. Select the installed printer, and then select File, Properties.

3. In the printer's Properties page, choose the Details tab, shown in Figure 25.9.

4. Check the Print to the following port drop-down list control. If it says LPT1: (Printer Port), your printer is probably properly installed. If it doesn't, select the LPT1 port from the list and click OK.

If the printer is properly installed on the LPT1 port, the problem might be with a port conflict. Use Windows 95's Device Manager to ferret out conflicts here:

1. Open Control Panel (select Start, Settings, Control Panel) and double-click the System icon.

2. In the System Properties sheet, choose the Device Manager tab.

3. Click the View devices by connection radio button.

4. Click the plus sign (+) next to the Ports (COM & LPT) item.

FIGURE 25.9.
Most local printers use the LPT1 parallel port. However, some printers might use a network connection or other special port. Make sure you have yours set up correctly.

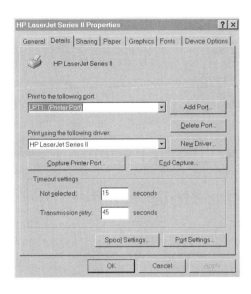

5. Look at the Printer Port (LPT) item that appears below it. If you see a red exclamation point or a yellow question mark next to the item, some sort of conflict is occurring. Double-click the item to access its properties sheet.

6. In the Printer Port (LPT1) Properties dialog box, choose the Resources tab and look at the information in the Resource settings box.

7. If a conflict exists, uncheck the Use automatic settings item and click the Change Setting button.

8. In the next dialog box, use the spinner control to change either the IRQ or base address setting to one that doesn't conflict with the other hardware on your system. Click OK on several sheets until the changes take effect.

At this point you must also change the port settings at the system BIOS. Do the following:

1. Reboot your PC and press the key sequence during boot phase to enter your CMOS setup program.

2. Go to the entry for parallel port operation and open the IRQ or base address settings.

3. Change the settings to match what you entered in the Windows Device Manager.

4. Use Esc or other prompted key combinations to exit the BIOS setup routine. Make sure you save the new settings.

5. When Windows finishes launching, check the Device Manager for a parallel port conflict. Also try sending a test print job to the printer.

Language Barriers

Another frequent problem can be language mismatches between your PC and printer. If your PC is speaking PostScript but your printer understands only PCL, the result will be unintelligible pages of PostScript code.

Most new laser printers can automatically detect incoming PostScript and PCL data, switching to the proper mode on-the-fly. But if the printer has been set to specifically receive either stream, the auto-detect feature won't work. (This might have been done to speed up print jobs or because the auto-detect feature wasn't working properly.)

Installing a New Printer

So you bought a new laser or ink jet printer and you need to install it. Fortunately, printers are among the easiest devices to install. There are no pesky add-in cards to deal with and, as long as your LPT addresses are OK, no IRQ weirdness to deal with either.

First, get the physical stuff set up:

1. Place the printer on a flat, stable surface where it will be used.

> **Tip:** A flat, stable surface is key to getting acceptable printing results. The calibration of ink jet nozzles and lasers can be affected by less-than-level surfaces. Over time, an unlevel setup will cause toner and ink to distribute unevenly in their cartridges, affecting the even distribution of media onto the paper.

2. Connect the 25-pin parallel port cable to the printer and the parallel port on the PC. The PC side parallel connector is often a pinch type, and the PC side uses pins.
3. Plug the printer's power cable into a grounded outlet.

> **Caution:** Printers can draw a lot of power, so failing to ground them can pose a potential fire hazard. Make sure you plug into grounded, three-pronged outlets. You should also make sure that the electrical circuit you are running off of can handle enough amperage to support the printer and any other equipment on the circuit (including your PC and monitor).

4. Open the printer chassis and install the toner or ink cartridge as shown in your printer's documentation.
5. Power up the printer and wait until it has initiated.
6. Conduct a print test routine (usually from a test button found on the outside of the printer).

7. If the print test completes successfully, your printer is working properly. Proceed to install the software.

Now install the printer into Windows 95 using the steps below. All your Windows applications will take their cue from the settings you apply during the Windows 95 installation. If you set the new printer as your default, all these applications will print to the new device unless told otherwise.

1. Turn on the printer and the PC.

2. When Windows 95 starts up, double-click the Add New Hardware icon in Control Panel.

3. Click Next to start the installation. If you trust Plug and Play, you can let the OS try to recognize the printer. Otherwise, click the No radio button to control the installation yourself.

4. In the Hardware types scroll box, select the Printers item and click Next.

5. In the next dialog box, click the Local Printer radio button.

6. In the next dialog box, you can select the printer from the lists of Manufacturers and Models. However, doing this will use Windows 95's bundled drivers. A better option is to click the Have Disk button.

7. Place the printer's driver disk in the A: drive. Then click OK in the Install from Disk dialog box.

8. If the install routine doesn't begin, you can use the Browse button to search for the proper .INF file on the floppy disk.

9. Once the installation routine is complete, you can check your printer's settings from Control Panel in Windows 95. Double-click the Printers icon. If the new printer icon appears in the Printers window, the printer has been properly installed.

10. To make sure the new printer is set as the default, click the printer icon and then select the File menu. If the Set as Default menu item has a check next to it, your new printer is the active default printer.

Note: For many newer ink jet and personal laser printers, you'll want to configure your parallel port for bi-directional operation, whether its EPP or ECP. Without it, you'll lose many of the performance and feature benefits that these printers provide.

Tip: You might be able to get better results from your existing hardware by using high-quality toner. The finer granularity of enhanced toner can provide more precise dot placement and better contrast. On the other hand, you should avoid using recycled toner cartridges. Many vendors fail to properly refurbish cartridges, leaving the rollers pockmarked and using improper toner.

Adding Memory to Your Existing Laser Printer

If you want to take full advantage of your current printer, you might need to add RAM. After all, a 600dpi printout needs about 4MB, and even more if any gray-scale enhancements are involved.

You can usually easily install RAM in the back of a printer. Although access varies among different models, most printers have a liftable panel that exposes memory sockets and sometimes slots for Ethernet or other cards. Simply install the memory modules as instructed by the printer's manuals. The printer will automatically detect the larger memory pool at startup, allowing you to process larger print jobs more quickly.

Installing a USB to Parallel Port Cable

You can turn your existing parallel port printer into a USB device simply by adding a converter cable (see Figure 25.10). With a parallel connector on one end and a USB connector on the other, this cable can hook your existing printer to your USB port. Doing so can free up your PC's parallel port for other devices—say, a scanner, second printer, or external Zip drive—and even improve performance.

FIGURE 25.10.
The Belkin USB Parallel Adapter lets you hook existing printers to your USB ports. Multiple printers can be run using these cables. (Photo courtesy of Belkin Components)

To install a USB-to-parallel port cable, do the following:

1. Insert the installation disk into drive A:
2. Plug the USB Parallel Adapter into the PC's USB port and into the desired printer.
3. From Windows Explorer, double click the SETUP.EXE file and follow the setup instructions.

4. When installation is complete, you should see a new printing output device in the Details view of your printer's setup. Click Start, Settings, Printers.

5. Right-click the icon for the printer you've set up on the USB cable and click Properties from the context menu.

6. Click the Details tab.

7. Click the arrow next to the drop-down list box labeled Print to the following port. Select the entry LPTUSB1.

8. Click OK. Your printer will now print over the USB-to-parallel cable. The LPT1 output is available for any device you wish to place on your parallel port.

Note: The USB Parallel Adapter is only intended for use with printers. Multifunction devices, scanners, Zip drives, and other parallel port devices will not work with this product.

Summary

Low-cost desktop printing was one of the great drivers of the PC revolution. Once people could produce professional-looking output using their PCs, the value of these machines grew immensely. Today, businesses large and small rely on the faithful operation of these devices. Just as the fax machine changed the way people do business, the printer helped transform the business document.

The wide array of printers provides terrific options for anyone who has a PC. Home users can find outstanding low-cost ink jet printers that can produce party invitations and family newsletters and even crank out great-looking digital photos. Small and swift laser printers serve home and small offices alike, while midrange and network printers provide output for busy departments. Finally, high-resolution color printers improve the ability of designers to quickly and effectively proof their work before sending it to press.

Keyboards

The most important peripheral connected to your computer isn't your graphics card, your printer, or even your monitor. The single most critical piece of hardware aside from the CPU is the keyboard. It's not high-tech, and when it works, it doesn't get noticed at all. But the PC's keyboard is absolutely critical to your productivity, comfort, and health.

You need look no further than the ever-expanding number of repetitive strain injury (RSI) cases plaguing corporate America. As people spend more time at their computers and work longer hours, the likelihood that a poor or malfunctioning keyboard can cause permanent injury grows.

This chapter will address the topic of keyboards and accomplish these aims:

- Help you understand how keyboards work and explain the differences among keyboards
- Introduce buying alternatives for keyboards
- Help you install and maintain a PC keyboard, and show you how to fix ergonomic dangers

Overview

Many reasons exist to consider a keyboard upgrade, not the least of which is *ergonomics*. Ergonomic devices such as keyboards, office chairs, and desks are designed to minimize strain on the human body, which can lead to painful injury over time. Although numerous factors go into a friendly environment, your choice of keyboard is extremely important. In addition, you can find compact keyboards that save desk space, remote keyboards that use infrared or radio signals, and multimedia keyboards that integrate speakers, microphone, and audio controls. Some keyboards even contain embedded scanners.

For all the variety—and a little weirdness—the devices we'll look at here perform similar tasks.

How Keyboards Work

Believe it or not, there's actually a spark of intelligence within your keyboard. A small microchip inside the keyboard recognizes key presses and transforms them into recognizable scan codes, which are read by the keyboard controller on the motherboard.

The process works like this: The keyboard keys are arranged above a sensor grid that detects key impacts. The keyboard controller constantly checks the state of each point on the grid, corresponding to each key on the keyboard. It does this by sending intersecting signals from the top and sides of the grid.

Of course, this polling happens very quickly. When the integrated keyboard chip detects keyboard contact, it sends a signal to the motherboard keyboard controller, which then issues an *interrupt* that tells the system which key was pressed. By checking the keyboard thousands of times each second, the controller can "see" every keyboard event.

Physically, the keyboard is a rectangular circuit board encased in a plastic housing. The keyboard keys rest atop a base plate over the circuit board, which itself is protected by a plastic surface, or shield. The shield does two things: It prevents dirt, water, coffee, donut crumbs, and other assorted trouble from getting into the keyboard electronics and stopping up the works. It also provides a backstop for heavy-hitting typists who might otherwise damage the contact between the key and the circuit board.

Two types of keyboards exist: mechanical and membrane. Mechanical keyboards, which mount the keypads on a post and spring, are used in almost all keyboards because they're cheap, reliable, and easy to maintain. Membrane keyboards are often used in industrial environments or areas where sparks must be prevented. In this case, a conductive membrane is used in place of a mechanical switch. When contact is made with the membrane, the keyboard controller detects it and passes a signal to the PC.

Most keyboards plug into one of two types of connectors: a DIN5 keyboard connector or a smaller MiniDIN6 keyboard connector. The two look similar—both are round plugs with oriented pinouts—but the MiniDIN6 connector is much smaller.

> **Tip:** You'll do better with a MiniDIN6 keyboard if you have the port for it. The compact connector is identical to that used on almost all notebooks, which means that you can use your keyboard on a notebook system, should the need ever arise. The larger DIN5 connector requires a separate adapter.

Different Types of Keyboards

If you're like most people, you think a keyboard is a keyboard—it's not. Keyboard makers have been busy cooking up models of every size, shape, and function. Ergonomics has driven much of the design innovation: Split keyboards, sloped keyboards, and keyboards with non-QWERTY layouts or radical one-hand designs have all been tried.

On the feature side, keyboard manufacturers have added everything from sheet-fed scanners and mouse pads to multimedia sound systems. The common thread is that every desktop PC comes with a keyboard, so the desk space is already being used. Why not make it work for you?

The following sections give a rundown of the types of keyboards you might select.

Standard Keyboards

You know the type: 101 keys aligned horizontally in five or six rows, with a classic QWERTY layout and function keys arrayed along the top, the left side, or perhaps both (see Figure 26.1). You might also find an extra *macro key* or two tucked in a corner. These macro keys can assign complex actions to simple keystrokes, enabling you, for example, to fire up your Web browser with a single click, or shut down your PC in one step. Gateway's AnyKey keyboards have long included macro capabilities.

FIGURE 26.1.

The classic design of the NMB keyboard is familiar to anyone who has used a PC. (Photo courtesy of NMB Technologies)

Caution: Keyboard macros are nice, but they have their drawbacks. For one thing, the macro keys you assign might conflict with the key combinations assumed by applications—you won't know which operation will be executed until you actually press the keys. Worse, programmable keyboards can get horribly confused. Gateway's talented AnyKey keyboards carry a Tech Note sticker telling people how to cease macro operation, should they inadvertently invoke a macro mode that knocks out the keyboard's functionality.

Otherwise, the picture is pretty basic. For any keyboard, you'll want to select a style based on comfort. For many people, this boils down to "clicky" versus "mushy." Another concern is the amount of key travel, which determines how far down the keys can be pressed—a critical concern for notebooks. You might also want to go with a keyboard that offers an expanded cursor key set (set up in a square with diagonal cursors, as opposed to the up-down/left-right arrangement on most keyboards). If you do much data entry, a dedicated numerical keypad is a must.

> **Tip:** When it comes to keyboards, comfort is key. Your best chance of getting a product you like is to go to a store and try out the various keyboards on display. This is particularly useful for judging nonconventional designs, such as split-face ergonomic models from Microsoft.

Split-Fingered Fastballs

The last couple of years have seen a flood of split-design keyboards intended to improve ergonomic typing. These products, such as Microsoft's Natural Keyboard and Cirque's Wave Keyboard 2, split the keyboard roughly down the center—between the G and H keys on a QWERTY layout—and slope the two sides down from the midpoint (see Figure 26.2). You'll also find adjustable split keyboards, which enable you to customize the angle and width of the split.

FIGURE 26.2.
Microsoft's Natural Keyboard features the same split-and-sloped design seen on many ergonomic keyboards. (Photo courtesy of Microsoft Corp.)

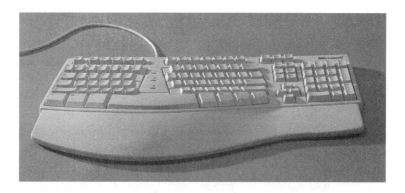

The idea is to eliminate the unnatural positioning of your wrists, elbows, and shoulders required by traditional keyboards. When you type on a traditional keyboard, your palms are set flat, with your hands close together on the home row—a situation called *pronation*. Pronation can bind tendons, cut circulation, and crimp nerve bundles. Irritation leads to chronic inflammation of soft tissue, which can soon lead to irresolvable RSI symptoms. This problem can show up in the wrists, hands, elbows, shoulders, and even the upper and lower back.

The sloped keyboard does two things. It turns your palms inward—a more natural position that doesn't require any twisting or flexing—and it sets your hands further apart. When you place your hands closer to shoulder width, you are again assuming a more comfortable position.

Although these products might look very different from your usual keyboard, their physical operation works the same. You'll need to give yourself time to master the new orientation, however. In fact, some users might find that the unfamiliar layout can actually aggravate things because they strain against the altered positioning. In addition, accomplished typists find themselves initially poking at the unused space in the middle of the keyboard and generally fighting against the angled surface.

> **Note:** Give that ergonomic keyboard a chance. While it may take a few days to get used to the new format, you may find yourself quite comfortable with it. In fact, you may have a hard time returning to a standard, flat-style keyboard.

Multifunction Keyboards

Just as printer vendors have transmogrified some of their products into printers/scanners/fax machines, keyboard vendors offer multiple-personality products of their own. Not surprisingly, some of the components built into keyboards fail to match the performance of the best standalone peripherals. An integrated black-and-white sheet-fed scanner, for example, won't do for high-resolution color work, and keyboard speakers lack the power of their desktop siblings. You might also have to contend with extra wires attached to the keyboard, which can complicate your desk space. Among the variations you'll see are these:

- Multimedia keyboards: NMB Technologies' ConcertMaster Multimedia Keyboard, shown in Figure 26.3, adds stereo speakers, a built-in microphone, and even SRS surround sound capability to a standard keyboard. It also includes useful audio controls.

- Scanner/keyboards: Visioneer sells a $250 keyboard with its popular PaperPort monochrome sheet-fed scanner attached to the back (see Figure 26.4).

- Keyboards that point: Any number of products integrate a trackball, trackpad, or even IBM TrackPoint devices into the design (see Figure 26.5). The advantage is that they save space consumed by mice and other roaming rodents.

- USB keyboards: USB-equipped keyboards can act as a peripheral hub for other USB devices, turning them into command central for your USB peripherals.

FIGURE 26.3.

NMB Technologies' ConcertMaster Multimedia Keyboard is an attractive alternative to monitor-mounted speakers, which can cause interference with the display. (Photo courtesy of NMB Technologies)

FIGURE 26.4.

NMB Technologies also offers a keyboard that integrates a sheet-fed scanner. (Photo courtesy of NMB Technologies)

FIGURE 26.5.

The Cirque
WaveBoard2
features a built-in
trackpad for
pointing, eliminat-
ing the need for a
separate mouse.
(Photo courtesy
 of Cirque
Corporation)

FIGURE 26.5.

*The Cirque
WaveBoard2
features a built-in
trackpad for
pointing, eliminat-
ing the need for a
separate mouse.
(Photo courtesy
 of Cirque
Corporation)*

Wireless Keyboards

Wireless keyboards enable you to work more flexibly by untethering you from the PC (see Figure 26.6). These products typically include the keyboard and a separate receiving device that plugs into the standard PS/2 keyboard port on the back of your PC. With a length of cord, you can place the receiver where you need it.

FIGURE 26.6.

*The Logitech
Cordless Desktop
set includes an RF
keyboard and
Logitech Wheel
Mouse. (Photo
courtesy of
Logitech Corp.)*

Two types of wireless technologies exist: *infrared* (IR) and *radio frequency* (RF). Until recently, IR models offered a distinct cost advantage, but price drops on RF technology have helped make these a more attractive technology. Unlike IR keyboards, you do not need a line of site link between the keyboard transmitter and the PC-based receiver. Regardless of the wireless technology, you must worry about the incremental expense of batteries needed to power the small transmitter and keyboard controller.

A Lesson in Ergonomics

PC keyboards have been at the center of the ongoing controversy over RSI and other repetitive strain ailments. And no wonder: Keyboard-related health care costs are rising rapidly among corporations, forcing everyone from Fortune 500 corporations to home-based business owners to think about their working habits and environment.

The problem is that you use the keyboard so much. If you spend most of your work day in front of a computer, the keyboard is your primary means of communication with the device. Sure, you click the mouse now and then—inviting an injury to your arm and shoulder, by the way—but the keyboard acts as the bridge between your analog self and the digital guts of the PC.

What's more, you probably use the keyboard more than ever. Web browsing, email, and corporate networks have all eliminated the need to do things away from your desk. No more penning a letter and licking stamps—you just pound out an email message and fire it off. And who goes to the library anymore to look up back issues of magazines? You just search a publisher's archives on the Web.

There's one problem: Way too many people think that a sloped or split keyboard will solve their problems. The theory behind the designs sounds good, but there is no conclusive data that shows that alternative keyboard designs actually help. I've even heard stories of healthy workers who, upon switching to a split keyboard, promptly developed RSI symptoms.

Ultimately, ergonomics is about work habits. A split keyboard won't help if you're slouched over your desk or plagued by a chair that completely lacks lumbar support. Below is a checklist of considerations to be aware of when assessing ergonomics.

- Posture: Keep your back straight, shoulders back, and eyes looking at the monitor at a slight downward angle. Both legs and forearms should be parallel to the ground. A keyboard tray eliminates bending up at the elbows, while a foot rest or a good thick book (like this one!) ensures that your thighs won't press down against the chair and cut off ciruculation.

- Chair: You need a firm-backed chair that keeps you sitting upright, not tilted back or spilling forward. Lumbar support is key—you should be able to feel the chair press into the lower part of your back (not painfully, mind you). Armrests are a no-no: They force your shoulders up when you type, aggravating pronation and introducing neck strain.

- Monitor: The monitor should sit on the desk to ensure the proper viewing angle. If it's up on a computer case, you'll invite neck strain and headaches from looking up all the time. Here's a separate but related point: You'll want fast 80Hz and higher refresh rates to eliminate perceived flicker in the image.

> **Note:** Small 14-inch monitors invite RSI injuries by requiring substantially more keyboard and mouse activity than do spacious 17-inch displays. The need to constantly click scrollbars and press cursor keys also slows productivity.

- Keyboard: A split-and-sloped design is worth trying. Remember that the keyboard should be low to keep your forearms parallel to the floor—otherwise, the alternative design won't help much. If your desk is too high, consider getting a slide-out keyboard tray, or try adjusting your chair height so that you are over the keyboard.

- Lifestyle: This is the last and most critical piece of the puzzle. No ergonomic setup will relieve symptoms unless you take frequent breaks from work—stretch, go get a cup of coffee, talk to people. Computer work is unique in that it tends to lock people into unhealthy positions. For example, studies have shown that people blink much less often than usual while working in front of a PC monitor. You should arrange to get up from your chair at least two or three times an hour, and make a point to look away from the screen and focus on a distant object once every few minutes.

Purchase Decisions

The keyboard is a very personal purchase, and one that can have a real impact on your productivity. In addition to personal preference, you'll need to consider issues such as your work space, ergonomic needs, and the possibility of springing for a multifunction keyboard.

First Impressions: Try Before You Buy

The funny thing about keyboards is that either you like one or you don't. Prices, specs, and slick advertising won't change that. For this reason, it's a good idea to actually use a keyboard before you buy it. Try out several keyboards at a local retail store, if possible, or sample keyboards on different systems at the office.

Look for a level of firmness and feedback that works for you. Heavy-handed typists might want the tactile click and pop of IBM-style keyboards, while less exuberant typists might opt for smoother travel. The following are points to consider. Remember to go with your preferences.

- Tactile feedback: Are the keys firm or mushy? Do they provide a confirming click or a silent rebound?

- Key tops: Pay attention to the tops of the keys: Are they indented to aid precision? Do they feel slick and slippery, or do they provide a little grab during impact?

- Sound: Do you want the keys to be silent or clicky? Does the keyboard rattle against the desk when you type?

- Construction: Heavy or light? Do the keyboard feet provide a stable platform, or does the unit shimmy and rattle during use? Is there unwanted flex or bend in the keyboard?

- Cord: Look for a long one. Too many keyboards skimp on a short cord that won't give you enough leeway to properly set up your desk space.

Features and Fun

If you're upgrading your existing keyboard, you might be tempted by the neat capabilities offered on some products—but be cautious. If you are running Windows 98 and have USB ports on your system, you might consider a keyboard that plugs into your USB ports. But consider this: If you want to use that keyboard at some point on an older system or perhaps on a non-USB equipped notebook, you will be out of luck. Furthermore, just two USB ports exist on the back of most PCs. Using a USB port for something such as a keyboard—which doesn't compete with other devices for space on the Mini-DIN6 port—means you could end up spending $100 for a USB hub to add ports for other devices more capable of taking advantage of USB's talents.

Also err on the side of caution where multifunction is concerned. Keyboard-based speakers won't match the quality and power of traditional desktop-based models—and you certainly won't get a subwoofer with them. Likewise, integrated scanners offer fewer capabilities than their standalone counterparts and might be restricted by your setup. After all, you won't be able to scan cardboard stock if your keyboard is set straight against the monitor—the paper will get jammed against the display bezel on its way out.

However, an integrated pointing device might be worth considering. Mice are a source of back and shoulder strain as well as desk clutter. The Cirque Wave Keyboard 2 keyboard puts a trackpad directly on the split-style keyboard, and IBM sells a keyboard with a TrackPoint device positioned in the middle of the keys.

Keeping Keyboards Alive

More than any other component, keyboards are subject to abuse. Hard disks and CD-ROM drives are tucked away safe inside the PC's case, while your monitor sits back from the action. But the keyboard is front and center, sharing space with—and sometimes the contents of—coffee cups, Coke cans, and Chinese food containers.

Fortunately, keyboards are built to take the pounding. The plunger-and-switch mechanisms used by the keyboard keys are simple and hardy. In addition, most keyboards feature a plastic shield that keeps dirt, food, and liquids from striking the key contacts or underlying circuitry. This shield is constructed so that the plastic pops up beneath each key, providing a dam against foreign invaders.

Things do go wrong, though. The following sections contain a couple of tips for when the worst happens.

Waterlogged Keyboards

Perhaps the most common problem comes from spilled liquids getting into the keyboard. Depending on what you spilled, you might have a good shot at recovering your hardware. If you spill something, do the following:

1. Power down the system (using the power button directly), and unplug the keyboard immediately. Don't wait! You need to cut power to the device to avoid a possible short circuit that will fry the electronics.

2. Turn off your PC using the mouse.

3. Tip the keyboard upside down and drain out as much of the liquid as you can.

4. Remove the keycaps and use a slightly damp cloth to remove liquid from beneath the keys. Use distilled bottled water rather than water from the tap to eliminate mineral deposits on the components.

5. If it's a water spill, use a blow dryer or fan to run air over the keyboard face. Make sure to set the blow dryer air to cool—you don't want to cook the keyboard, just dry it out.

6. Let the keyboard sit for 12 hours, preferably in a dry spot under direct sunlight.

7. Reattach the keyboard and boot up the PC. Keep your fingers crossed....

To fully dry out the keyboard, you may actually have to disassemble the chassis. This is easy to do, as keyboards usually use two formed plastic halves to form their body. Use a Philips or appropriate screwdriver to undo the screws, and then pull the component apart. Be careful to set it down and allow air to access all the internal components.

If possible, try to use distilled water rather than water from the tap. Tap water contains residue and minerals that can adhere to components and actually damage the keyboard.

Other Liquid Assaults

The preceding approach will work well for water, but the situation is more grave if you spilled soda or milk into the keyboard well. Once dried, these liquids leave a residue of sugar and other sticky stuff that coats contacts and electronics, stops conduction, and renders the keys inoperable. You'll also have problems with stuck keys and plungers.

You can try to rinse out the gook by, ironically, plunging the keyboard into water immediately after the accident (unplug the keyboard first!). Be sure to work the water thoroughly so that the other substance is washed out of the well. Then follow the procedure just mentioned for drying the keyboard. You'll probably need to leave more time to dry— up to 24 hours. As before, you may have to pull the keyboard apart to get sufficient access to internal components, both to get water to them and to allow them to dry.

Keep in mind that this is for severe spills. If you spill a little liquid on the keyboard, you should simply mop it up with a rag or paper towel and see if the keyboard continues to work normally. Your keyboard should contain minor spills well, so dousing the unit will probably do more harm than good. If you do end up dunking the keyboard, don't get your hopes up. There's no guarantee that the water will remove all the residue—particularly if you're using tap water, which contains residues and minerals that can compound the problem. Still, it's worth a shot—you know that the keyboard will definitely be doomed otherwise.

If you're at this point, you might want to keep in mind that keyboards are cheap and easy to replace. In fact, a crippled keyboard could be just the excuse you need to upgrade to an ergonomic model or perhaps get a keyboard that uses USB to connect to your PC.

Cleaning the Keys

Keyboards are made to get dirty, and most are made to get cleaned as well. If lots of gunk is jamming your keys, or if you need to fish around for some loose change, you can clear matters by popping off the keys. Do the following:

1. Turn off your PC.
2. Select the key you want to remove. Using a small screwdriver, gently pry the key up from each side, being careful not to damage the other keys. Even better, use a keyboard cap remover, available at many computer stores, to evenly apply pressure to opposite sides of the cap.
3. On most keyboards, the key should click off its plunger, revealing the layer below.
4. To reattach the key, press it on top of the plunger and push down until it clicks into place.
5. If you remove multiple keys, be sure to return them to their proper spots!

Easy Money: Keyboard Upgrades

Installing a keyboard might be the easiest upgrade possible. In fact, the hardest part of the whole thing might be prying the keyboard out of the box. However, you need to check the port on your system first to make sure that you buy a keyboard that matches it. The smaller MiniDIN6 connector is now used on virtually all new systems and is often called a PS/2 keyboard port. Even if you end up with a mismatch, you can buy a simple converter at any computer store that enables you to plug larger keyboard connectors into MiniDIN6 system ports, and vice versa.

Keyboards access dedicated system resources, which remove the uncertainty of resource conflicts found with sound boards, modems, and the like. Although USB-type keyboards change the rules a bit, the Plug and Play facilities of the USB bus should keep installation equally simple.

The only place where you can expect trouble is with multifunction keyboards that have scanners and sound systems. In these cases, you'll have separate wires leading to their respective ports. In the case of the scanner, you'll have to locate the resources for the included serial or parallel port scanner. Of course, such a device will also have specialized drivers for integrated functions, such as scanners or pointers. You'll want to make sure you have those drivers handy and are using up-to-date versions to avoid trouble.

Summary

A quality keyboard can make a huge difference in your productivity, comfort, and work environment. If you bought a PC a couple of years ago with a chintzy, small-form-factor keyboard—you know, the cheapest the vendor could find—you would do well to consider an upgrade. Basic keyboards are cheap, at around $100, while snazzy enhanced models can be had for $150 or less.

Ultimately, it's about your comfort. If you're fine with what you have, then by all means, stick with it. But if you feel you need to make a change, give yourself enough time to make an informed decision. If possible, try out a new keyboard before buying it—or at least test-drive a model by using a coworker's system for a couple of hours. Your body will thank you for the extra consideration.

Point and Shoot: Of Mice, Joysticks, and Other Controllers

If you buy a PC today, you absolutely must have a pointing device. On the vast majority of PCs, that means a mouse. With these versatile little creatures, you can point and click your way around your PC's interface.

As with keyboards, mice are relatively simple devices that are easy to install. Still, not all pointing devices are equal. You'll find a variety of mouse designs and styles, as well as alternative pointing devices. And let's not leave out some of the most sophisticated controller devices—gaming peripherals such as joysticks, gamepads, steering wheels, and even foot pedals.

This chapter covers the serious business of pointing under Windows 95, including these topics:

- How mice and other pointing devices work
- What to look for in a pointing device or game controller
- How to install pointing devices and deal with problems that can arise

Pointing Places

Many PC users will never buy a mouse or other pointing device. Nearly all PCs now come equipped with a mouse, which, if cared for properly, can last the life of the PC and beyond. That said, there are some pretty pathetic mice out there; some users might need to explore options beyond the traditional pointer.

Several types of pointing devices exist for PCs:

- Mice
- Trackballs, trackpads, and IBM TrackPoint devices
- Joysticks and gamepads
- Other gaming devices

Inside Mice

Along with the keyboard, the mouse is one of two primary input devices found on most PCs. The workings are simple enough: A rubbery little ball inside the mouse housing rolls against the surface of your desktop or mouse pad as you move the mouse. Usually, this ball is nudged up against a pair of perpendicular roller bars inside the mouse housing so that when the ball moves, the roller bars move in lockstep. Moving the mouse forward or back causes the vertical (or y) roller to spin with the ball; moving it left or right causes the horizontal (or x) roller to do its thing.

How the Mouse Works

A motion digitizer reads the turning of the two bars, interpreting them as increments of travel (measured in hundredths of an inch). The controller then sends digitized signals telling your PC that the mouse has been pushed forward half an inch and left three-quarters of an inch. Keep in mind that the mouse sensor has no idea where the mouse cursor is on the screen—it simply reports relative positions over known periods of time.

Most mice can detect motion to as little as 1/400th of an inch—more precision than most users will ever need. This level of precision is up almost four times since about five years ago, when a typical mouse provided precision to 1/100th of an inch.

You'll also find two or more buttons on the top of most mice, as shown in Figure 27.1. As with the roller bars, these buttons have sensors that send a signal each time a button is pressed or released. Your PC's operating system and applications keep track of where the cursor is onscreen, interpreting movement and clicks based on the small bits of data sent by the reliable rodent.

FIGURE 27.1.
The Microsoft IntelliMouse may feature a nifty wheel for scrolling, but it otherwise uses the same ball-and-roller mechanism found in almost all mice. (Photo courtesy Microsoft Corp.)

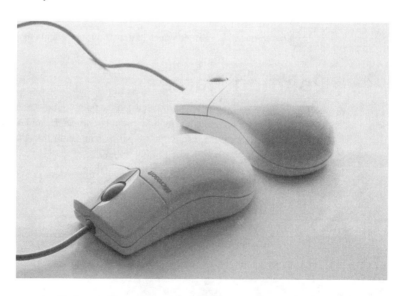

> **Note:** A few mice actually use an optical system in which positional information is determined by bouncing laser light off a reflective mouse pad. Although these mice don't have moving parts—and therefore don't succumb to dirt in the works—they do require the mouse pad to be clean and in good shape. Dents or nicks in the reflective pad can return spurious positional data, causing cursor fits.

Mice don't live on clicks alone. A small amount of electrical power must be available to the mouse for the sensors to work. In the past, this power requirement meant that mice needed a dedicated adapter card to operate. Today, low-voltage designs enable mice to operate over the serial port or dedicated PS/2 mouse port.

As with all hardware peripherals, mice talk to the system by way of a software driver. Windows 9x comes with a variety of standard mouse drivers, including those for Microsoft, Kensington, Logitech, and others. You can also go with the plain-vanilla PS/2 mouse driver, which lacks product-specific features. For most users, this driver will suffice (it's just pointing, after all) and stands the best chance of avoiding compatibility conflicts.

Issues and Problems

Mice aren't perfect. They have moving parts, so they need maintenance, and their innards can get gummed up because they spend all day shuffling around dusty and dirty desktops. You'll need to do routine maintenance every few months or so, depending on the state of your work area.

In addition, mice have a bad rap as an ergonomic troublemaker. Users tend to lean into their mice, causing shoulder, arm, and back pain over time. The act of moving the mouse around aggravates things because your shoulder and elbow are moving and straining. These two drawbacks are enough to fuel a market for alternative general-purpose pointing products (now that's a lot of alliteration!).

Rodent Alternatives: Inside an Un-Mouse

Most desktops are equipped with mice, but not all of them. Tight work spaces, specific ergonomic needs, and sometimes just plain old preference make alternative pointing devices desirable. Among these are trackballs, trackpads, and eraserheads (such as IBM's TrackPoint). You'll also find some truly goofy and innovative stuff out there, such as Diamond Multimedia's gyroscope-driven GyroMouse.

We're Talking Trackballs

The most popular mouse alternative, trackballs, are simply mice turned on their backs. They employ the same roller bar and button design found in mice, except that the roller ball is positioned on the top of the device for the user to move (see Figure 27.2). When you spin the ball forward with your thumb or finger, the trackball's y-roller bar goes into action, signaling the motion detector to send updated positional data to the PC.

FIGURE 27.2.

*The Logitech
TrackMan Marble
is one of the most
popular trackball
products. (Photo
courtesy of
Logitech)*

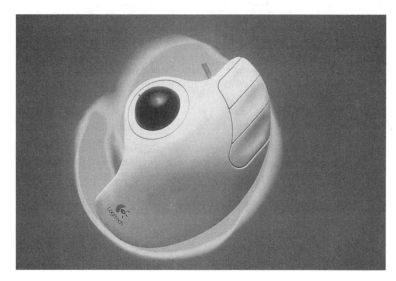

Trackballs come in many shapes and sizes, ranging from tiny notebook-oriented dealies with a ball the size of a BB, to large, colorful desktop jobs designed for the kiddies to slap around (see Figure 27.3). In between, you'll find products such as Logitech's TrackMan Marble, which features a marble-size ball and three buttons along the right-front edge (refer back to Figure 27.2).

FIGURE 27.3.

*The Microsoft
Easyball is tailored
for kids, with an
oversize roller ball
and big, colorful
buttons. (Photo
courtesy of
Microsoft Corp.)*

Trackballs address the two major drawbacks of mice: their tendency to get gummed up with dirt, and the ergonomic problems associated with pushing the mouse all day long. Because the trackball roller never touches the surface of the desk, the only dirt that gets into the mechanism comes from your thumb or airborne particles. Likewise, trackballs enable you to remain stationary while pointing—no more leaning into those mouse clicks—which can reduce cumulative strain.

Unfortunately, trackballs bring their own baggage. For one, the thumb is the least-dexterous finger, which means that many trackball designs make it difficult to precisely manage the cursor. What's more, simple operations such as clicking and dragging become difficult with a trackball because you must apply pressure on a button with one finger while using another to roll the ball.

Mouse Innovations

It's no surprise that 3D mice also are beginning to emerge. Applications ranging from first-person shooting games, such as Quake, to VRML browsing environments and low-cost 3D authoring demand a whole new dimension in pointing. These products often depart from the slip-and-slide mouse design and are used in the air or manipulated on a base.

The Diamond GyroMouse, for example, is mounted on a base and recognizes pressure going from side to side, front to back, and up and down (see Figure 27.4). The result is that you can tell your application to move the cursor upward in a 3D environment simply by pulling up on the mouse device.

FIGURE 27.4.
Diamond's GyroMouse provides six degrees of freedom and a whole new way to point. (Photo courtesy of Diamond Multimedia)

Road Pointers

For a while, trackballs were also a fixture on notebook PCs. Apple's PowerBooks really got the proverbial ball rolling with its front-and-center trackball and handy wrist-rest design. But as with mice, trackballs are prone to sticking over time as particles get inside the housing. And unlike desktop trackballs, no convenient way exists to pop open the notebook pointing device and scrape out the insides.

IBM's TrackPoint

Enter IBM's innovative TrackPoint pointing device, shown in Figure 27.5. This eraser-head-size nub sits in the middle of the keyboard and provides good pointing control without forcing your hands to leave the home row. The device is pressure-sensitive: Resistors at the base of the nub sense contact pressure, speeding or slowing the motion of the cursor to suit. Depending on which contact or contacts are pressed, the device sends positional information in the desired direction.

FIGURE 27.5.

IBM's innovative TrackPoint pointer found on the IBM ThinkPad line of notebook computers makes road pointing much more reliable. (Photo courtesy of IBM Corp.)

TrackPoint

Because the TrackPoint doesn't roll, no furious spinning needs to occur. Better yet, dirt has no way to enter the device, so the TrackPoint won't gum up over time. However, the pointing experience is very different from mice and trackballs—enough so that many users find it difficult, and the presence of the device among the keyboard's keys can invite unintended key clicks.

You won't find eraserheads on many desktop systems. IBM sells a keyboard with a TrackPoint II pointer built in, but that's about it. But you might see TrackPoint-like devices on notebooks from IBM, Acer, Toshiba, and others.

Trackpads: The Notebook Standard

Over the past two years, many notebooks have adopted the trackpad as their pointing device. First seen on Apple PowerBooks, this device appears as a simple black square embedded into the notebook's wrist rest. Their biggest advantage is that trackpads use the most natural of interfaces—your finger.

Trackpads use conductive material to sense where your finger is on the square. A steady, if small, current runs through the square. When you drag your finger across the square, it disrupts the signal. The trackpad's sensors can follow the direction and speed of the disruption by identifying which sensors have changed state (see Figure 27.6).

FIGURE 27.6.
Cirque's desktop-based Easy Cat trackpad device uses the same technology employed in many notebooks. (Photo courtesy Cirque Corporation)

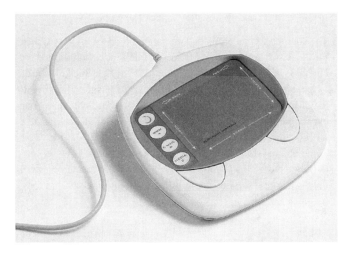

The big advantage is that the trackpad has no moving parts. It is also sealed against dirt and grime. Still, the finger is a pretty blunt instrument. If you change the angle of your fingertip as you drag along, the onscreen cursor might jump left or right as different sensors get triggered.

Again, you won't find many of these on desktops, although companies such as Cirque sell keyboards with embedded trackpads. You can also buy a separate desktop trackpad module that plugs into the standard mouse port.

Who's Game?

Nowhere will you find more innovation, ambition, and engineering effort than in game controllers. Gamers are notoriously serious about their pointing devices. After all, a good controller can literally mean the difference between life and death.

Joy to the World

The joystick is the quintessential gaming peripheral. Appropriate for flight simulations and many other PC games, these devices work like the control stick in a fighter plane. The user pushes the stick left to right and forward to back to initiate motion, while 2–20 or more buttons provide weapons control and other features.

Joysticks work by placing four resistors in the base of the stick. When the stick is pushed forward, an electric charge is moved into the resistor. The further forward you push, the greater the rate of charge. Sensors check the resistance and report changes in the attitude of the stick. Driver software turns the signals into program-specific commands for down, up, left, right, and so on.

The problem with most joysticks is that they need constant attention. Your CPU must continually poll the joystick port (usually the game port found on the sound card) to get the latest stick status. When your CPU is busy displaying rich 3D scenes, the extra work-load can considerably slow frame rates and responsiveness.

The solution to this problem comes in the form of digital joysticks, which have been sold for the past two years. The Microsoft SideWinder Precision Pro, Logitech Wingman Digital (see Figure 27.7), and CH Force/FX FlightStick all speak in your PC's native tongue—those ubiquitous 1s and 0s—to pipe positional information directly to the system. Most of these products plug into the standard gameport found on most sound cards, but they use digital internal electronics to send digital signals to the PC. The result: lower CPU overhead and higher sampling rates than available with traditional analog devices. Some older systems and dedicated game port cards, however, may not be capable of supporting the digital signaling over the game/MIDI port. In these cases, you may want to opt for a digital joystick that uses a USB connector.

FIGURE 27.7.

Logitech's Wingman Extreme Digital maximizes your survival skills with enhanced precision and less CPU overhead than analog joysticks. (Photo courtesy of Logitech)

Gamepads and Other Gear

Outside of joysticks, you'll find other sundry pointers. Gamepads are identical to the controllers you find with Nintendo or Sega game consoles (see Figure 27.8). These two-hand devices usually have a directional pointer on one side and a number of function buttons on the other. The functions each button performs can often be customized.

FIGURE 27.8.

*Creative Labs'
Blaster Gamepad
gives you all the
controls you need
to jump, kick, run,
and otherwise
fight your way
out of trouble.
(Photo courtesy of
Creative Labs)*

Other input devices include steering columns, such as the ThrustMaster NASCAR racing wheel. This two-piece set includes a full steering wheel with shifter, which attaches to the desk and includes a small clamp to keep you from twisting it into the air. A foot pedal unit includes accelerator and brake pedals. Most recently, Microsoft has introduced a force-feedback steering wheel—the Sidewinder Force Feedback Wheel—that resists during sharp turns and rumbles when you veer off the road. Expect similar products from leading vendors over the year.

Another device that's very handy for flying games is a separate throttle control. Available from companies such as Thrustmaster, CH Products, and Suncom, these are usually programmable devices that enable you to assign keystrokes to various buttons and knobs. This helps you keep your hands on the controller, rather than hunting for keys on the keyboard. This is known as "HOTAS"—hands on throttle and stick.

For the ultimate in verisimilitude, you can also add rudder pedals to round out the flying experience.

Pointer Purchases

As with keyboards, you'll want to buy mice and other devices with comfort in mind. For example, a small child wouldn't do well with the relatively large Microsoft Mouse 2.0, and lefties might want to avoid the right-sided buttons found on the TrackMan Marble. Likewise, a flight-sim junky wouldn't know what to do with a gamepad. Table 27.1 will help you figure out what to purchase.

Table 27.1. Choosing pointers.

Device	What It's Best For
Mouse	General-purpose home and business desktop computing, multimedia, and Internet applications
Trackball	Same as mouse, but optimal for space-limited environments and for users with mouse-related repetitive strain injuries (RSI); also notebooks
Trackpad	Space-limited and dirty/dusty environments; users with mouse-related RSI; notebooks
TrackPoint	Same as trackpad; easier keyboard access
Joystick	Flight simulations and other flying games; also some racing and water games, as well as first-person shooters such as Descent
Gamepad	Best for side-scrolling games (Mario), shooters (Quake), and fighting games (Mortal Kombat)
Steering wheels and foot pedals	Driving/racing simulations; some flight simulations

At the Pet Store: Shopping for a Mouse

You can choose from several types of mice, including these:

- Standard serial port or PS/2 mice
- Wireless mice (infrared or radio frequency)
- Two- or three-button mice
- Enhanced functionality mice (such as the Microsoft IntelliMouse)

The variety is by no means as staggering as what you'll see with keyboards, but it is there nonetheless. For the vast majority of users, a trusty wired, serial, or PS/2 mouse will do the trick. These mice are proven, don't require batteries, and provide access to all the standard features in Windows 95 applications.

When it comes to ports, you might look into a USB mouse—if your system has the ports and drivers to support it. However, you'll be choosing from a limited selection of mice.

Otherwise, a PS/2 mouse works best, plugging into the dedicated round mouse port (found next to the keyboard port) on the back of the PC. Best of all, it keeps your serial ports free for other devices, such as modems and PDAs.

> **Note:** If you use anything other than Windows 98, you should probably avoid USB for your input and other devices. Windows NT won't support USB until version 5.0, and many USB peripherals lack drivers for Windows 95.

In general, expect to pay $20–$100 for a new mouse or trackball. Although most people can certainly get by with a basic mouse, you can choose from the advanced features that many products offer. Programmable button and keyboard combinations enable you to create nifty shortcuts to programs and OS features.

For mice, you might consider something like Microsoft's IntelliMouse, which puts a small daisy wheel between the left and right buttons (refer back to Figure 27.1). On applications that recognize IntelliMouse, turning the wheel with your finger causes programs such as Web browsers to scroll up and down. When you press the wheel down, you can scroll up and down by moving the mouse back and forth.

Some mice feature three buttons. Although Windows 95 and most applications don't recognize the third button by default, your mouse's software can assign a universal function to it—for example, double-clicking or pasting from the Clipboard. Usually you can set these capabilities to suit your needs in software, as shown in Figure 27.9. (In Windows 95, go to Control Panel by selecting Start, Settings, Control Panel, and then double-click the Mouse icon.) In general, neither of these enhancements is enough to lure me away from a comfortable mouse design (although Microsoft has gotten it right with the Mouse 2.0 design used in the newer IntelliMouse product).

FIGURE 27.9.
Visual utilities make it easy to customize mouse settings.

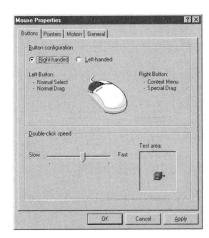

Buying Game Gear

It's 1 a.m. You've been up half the night trying to get an urgent report in by the deadline. Your spouse and kids have been asleep for hours, but you're too keyed up to go to bed just yet. Looks like a splendid opportunity to fly a loaded A-10 "Warthog" attack jet low into North Korean territory and give the business to some invading infantry.

Or, it would be—if you had the tools to fly the mission. Imagine trying to drive your morning commute with nothing but four cursor keys to control steering and speed. Or imagine that you're an airline pilot taking a stab at a cross-wind landing using only a keyboard. You can be sure that both will be very short rides.

What Devices Are Best

Considering that top-notch PC games cost upward of $50, it makes sense to own a game controller that helps you get your money's worth. Still, price is a problem. You can buy a perfectly compatible four-button joystick for $30, but it might not last long. A joystick I was once given as a gift worked for about two and a half hours before I destroyed it while playing F14 Fleet Defender.

If you're buying a joystick, seriously consider a digital model. Microsoft's SideWinder Precision Pro and CH's Force Flightstick are two outstanding devices. The SideWinder, for instance, offers a neat yaw feature (you twist the stick) for rudder control or rotation. At $70, the SideWinder Precision Pro is among the better buys.

More intriguing are the Force Flightstick and SideWinder Force Feedback Pro (see Figure 27.10), both of which actually buffet and resist your hand as you play. These force feedback joysticks use small motors in the base to make you feel, as well as see, the effects of a high G turn. You have to fight the stick during a dive, or try to keep it level as turbulence or enemy fire buffets your plane. If you're serious about gaming, you simply must try one of these new joysticks.

Nonflyers might consider a gamepad or similar device. With these compact controllers, you can conduct complex maneuvers in a wide variety of games. You'll want a device that provides comfortable spacing of buttons and controls and that feels sturdy enough to handle the relentless pounding that gameplay invites. Also consider buying controllers in pairs, if you think you'll be playing against human competitors.

Accessories for Better Gaming

While you're out looking for great devices to improve your games, don't forget about accessories that can help you take full advantage of your hardware. With the CH Products Y Cable, for example, you can hook two joysticks into your MIDI/game port so you can play head-to-head games. Just be aware that your joystick or other game controls will be limited to the most basic controls because the game port lacks the wiring to provide extended controls to multiple devices.

FIGURE 27.10.

The Microsoft SideWinder Force Feedback Pro helps you feel the buffet of heavy AA fire as you make your bombing runs. Best of all, it works off the standard MIDI/game port found on almost all sound cards. (Photo courtesy of Microsoft Corp.)

Perhaps a better option is the GameCard 3, also from CH Products, which puts a pair of game ports on an ISA add-in card. The multiple ports enable you to play head-to-head and take full advantage of your advanced joysticks or gamepads. Other accessories include extension cables for increasing your reach and switch boxes that enable you to select from among a variety of devices without having to reach around the back of the PC to unplug and connect wires.

Installing and Caring for Pointers

In general, installing a new pointing device is quite easy. PS/2 mice and trackballs, for instance, use the dedicated IRQ 12 resource—which means that every system, OS, and pointing device manufacturer knows exactly where to put its resources.

Serial mice are a bit trickier because they must grab one of four available COM port addresses (which share two interrupts between them). The biggest danger with serial mice comes from modem conflicts. You should check your modem settings to make sure you don't disable your modem when you install a new serial mouse. To do this, follow these steps:

1. Click Start, Settings, Control Panel.

2. Open the Modem icon, and click the Properties button. Note the COM port that is being used.

3. Click Cancel and then Close to exit the Modem Properties box.

Now when you install the serial mouse, make sure you specify a COM port address that is distinct from the one being used by the modem. In most cases, your best choice is COM1 or COM2.

Trapping a Better Mouse

Windows 95 makes installing a mouse simple. In fact, virtually any PS/2 mouse will function just fine using the default mouse driver in Windows 9x. Your best bet to switch mice is to set up for generic operation before installing the new pointing device, and then move to any extended drivers, such as for the Microsoft Intellimouse. To do this, follow these steps:

1. With your original mouse still installed, open the Windows 95 Control Panel (select Start, Settings, Control Panel).

2. Double-click the Mouse icon.

3. In the Mouse Properties dialog box, choose the General tab.

4. Your current mouse will be listed in the Name text box. If this listing is not for the standard PS/2 mouse, click the Change button.

5. Click the Show all devices radio button.

6. Select Standard mouse types under Manufacturers list box, and then click the Standard PS/2 Port Mouse entry under Models.

7. Click OK to load the new driver and exit the Mouse properties box.

8. Shut down Windows and power down the PC.

9. Install the new PS/2 mouse and boot up the machine. Verify that the mouse is working by trying to move the cursor after bootup.

10. Now install the enhanced drivers (if needed) by launching the Mouse properties dialog box (select Start, Settings, Control Panel, and open the Mouse icon).

11. Place the driver disk for your new mouse in drive A:, and click the Have Disk button.

12. Select the new device's appropriate .INF file. The device will be installed.

13. The new mouse driver should be enabled. You may have to restart your PC so the new settings take effect.

The routine for installing new trackballs and other pointing devices is identical. In general, these devices behave very much the same and use similar system resources.

Setting Up a Joystick

Joystick installation is similar as well because it uses the same Windows 95 installation facility. Here, the thing to remember is that joysticks come with customizable functionality. Your hot new joystick has many buttons that won't really do anything until you tell them what to do in the joystick's setup. (You can reach this dialog box by selecting Start, Settings, Control Panel, and then double-clicking the Joystick or Game Controllers icons.)

TROUBLESHOOTING

> Before you get too involved with installing that new joystick, check the Windows 95 Control Panel (select Start, Settings, Control Panel) and make sure that a Joystick icon is present. If it isn't, you might have a problem with the game port on your sound card, and the system won't detect your gaming device. Refer to your sound board's documentation to explore the problem further.

To install a new joystick, follow these steps:

1. Open the Windows 95 Control Panel (select Start, Settings, Control Panel).

2. Double-click the Add New Hardware icon.

3. In the dialog box that appears, click the Next button to start the process.

4. In the dialog box that appears, you will be prompted to have the system automatically check for new hardware. Select the No radio button and click Next.

5. In the Hardware Types scroll box, scroll down to the listing for Sound, Video, and Game Controllers, and double-click it.

6. Insert the driver disk for your new mouse into drive A:. In the Select Device dialog box, click Have Disk.

7. Select the new device's appropriate .INF file. The device will be installed.

8. Shut down the PC.

9. Plug the new joystick or other device into the game port of your PC (most likely the sound board's combination MIDI/game port). Your new joystick or device should be active in Windows 95.

If your joystick is of the vanilla, four-button, two-axis variety, Windows 9x will recognize its capabilities by default. You won't even need to bother with drivers.

Note: Keep in mind that games played in DOS mode won't have access to Windows 95 drivers or capabilities. These games must provide direct support for your joystick for it to work. Failing that, your joystick should provide emulation for one or more popular models—similar to the way many sound boards make software think they are Sound Blaster cards. Even under Windows 95, you might find that you get the best results when using emulation mode. Check your device's documentation for details on setting and working with emulation.

Caring for Mice

Pointing and gaming devices do wear out. Button contacts get worn, springs give way, and roller mechanisms can eventually jam or stick chronically. Crimped and pulled wire leads can also decapitate your mouse or joystick, cutting it off from the system altogether or resulting in maddeningly intermittent operation.

An Ounce of Prevention

Your best weapon is prevention. The following points will extend the life of your mouse:

- Clean out the interior of the mouse periodically to keep too much dirt and gunk from accumulating inside the mouse housing.

- Keep the mouse pad or desk area where the mouse resides clean and clear of dust and dirt.

- Avoid pulling the mouse wire taut or otherwise straining the leads to the device. Also try not to crimp or crush the wire.

- Go easy on the buttons—there's no need to smash them. Repeated heavy blows will only shorten the life of the springs.

- For joysticks, avoid slamming the stick to the wall. Heavy-handed use won't help you pull any extra Gs, but it will wear out or even snap the metal contacts at the base. Keep it up, and you'll be flying a keyboard.

Mouse Cleaning

One thing you will have to do periodically is clean out the insides of your mouse. The ball that pops out the bottom is designed to be tacky enough to grip the surface and provide friction to move the roller bars inside the mouse. Unfortunately, that same characteristic also ensures that dirt and particles on the desktop will stick to the ball and end up inside. Over time, the cumulative hovering of grime will cause the cursor to stick annoyingly.

If you notice the mouse sticking, it's easy enough to clear up the problem. Follow these steps:

1. Shut down the PC. (You don't want to send all sorts of accidental mouse clicks to your waiting system!)

2. Turn the mouse on its back and look for the circular ball plate.

3. Press down on opposite ends of the plate with your thumb and forefinger. Twist the housing in the direction indicated (usually counterclockwise).

4. Hold your hand over the mouse and turn it over. The housing and ball will spill into your palm.

5. Clean the ball in gentle soap and water, making sure that you rub or scrape off any matter that is stuck to it.

6. Now clean the inside of the mouse housing using a lint-free swab dabbed in alcohol. Work along the two perpendicular bars to make sure all the accumulated dirt is removed.

7. Make sure to turn both roller bars and scrape along the entire length. Shake out the mouse to ensure that the dirt doesn't end up right back in the mouse.

8. Turn the mouse on its back, plop in the mouse ball, and place the ball plate back into the mouse. Twist the plate clockwise to tighten it into position.

9. Turn on your PC and start mousing around.

Summary

Windows 95 and the emergence of USB support will change the input marketplace. Over the next 6–12 months, expect more products to support the fledgling USB bus. Although USB should ease installations and cable clutter, it won't radically change the way you use these devices. Most importantly, comfort will remain the key decision point with any of these devices.

For serious gamers, the future is definitely digital. If you can, purchase a digital joystick with USB support. You'll enjoy better overall system performance, quicker and more precise response, and more advanced features and flexibility. Most importantly, you'll kill more bad guys.

Digital Cameras

Digital cameras are one of the coolest things born of the PC revolution. These nifty gadgets enable you to snap photos that can be instantly downloaded to your PC. No going to the corner store to develop rolls of film, or scanning photos late at night. You just snap the picture and download it to your PC.

Digital cameras aren't new; in fact, they've been around for several years. What is new are lower prices and improved image quality, which finally makes these cameras a reasonable alternative to traditional silver-film photography. In fact, even camcorders have gone digital. Falling prices and the adoption of media and interface standards have helped make these high-fidelity video devices a consumer favorite.

This chapter helps you understand the following:

- How digital cameras work
- Whether a digital camera purchase makes sense for you, and which is best for your needs
- How to operate a digital camera, including bus issuesThis chapter limits itself to the coverage of standalone digital cameras and related devices. For coverage of videoconferencing hardware, including monitor-top cameras, and video-capture products, see Chapter 20, "Digital Video Capture."

INSTANT REFERENCE This chapter limits itself to the coverage of standalone digital cameras and related devices. For coverage of videoconferencing hardware, including monitor-top cameras, and video-capture products, see Chapter 20, "Digital Video Capture."

The Photo Revolution

Ten years ago, computers were for geeks. Today, my mom sends me more email than snail mail, and many television commercials include Web site addresses. With more than 100 million Web pages out there, and near-photo quality ink jet printers costing less than $300, digital cameras play to a ready audience.

Most importantly, digital cameras are finally affordable. You can buy many models for under $250, and $1,000 gets you unprecedented image quality and features. Today's midrange cameras offer true color at so-called megapixel resolutions, with more than one million pixels in their 1,024×768 snapshots. The best cameras push resolutions as high as 1,280×1,024 and higher (see Figure 28.1).

FIGURE 28.1.

The Epson PhotoPC 700 looks a lot like a standard 35mm camera and provides 1,280×960 pixel images. The built-in two-inch LCD viewer allows in-camera viewing. (Photo courtesy of Epson America)

The attraction of these products is obvious. Digital cameras can readily move images to Web pages and color printers. Many people need to quickly move photos to the digital domain, and digital cameras are the fastest way to do so. In addition, a growing number of niche markets benefit from all-digital photography, including

- Real estate agents
- Insurance adjusters
- Newsletter publishers and online media organizations
- Law enforcement
- Home and small businesses

Peter's Principle: Digital Cameras: Expect Less, Get More

Digital photography is intriguing technology, but don't sell your Kodak stock just yet. Digital cameras still cost much more than their 35mm counterparts and fail to match the resolution of analog film. In fact, if you want the best possible digital output, you should use a high-resolution color scanner to capture images from 35mm slides or prints. Printing photo-quality pictures gets expensive as well. The cost of a good ink jet or photo printer, combined with expensive coated paper, can make digital output more expensive than traditional film processing.

That said, digital cameras excel at convenience and flexibility. These products eliminate troublesome scanning and can save you precious days or hours of processing time when you're in a hurry. The best cameras, which now push up to about 1,280×1,024 pixels, even come close to matching analog output under casual scrutiny. The lesson here is that if you don't expect too much of these much-publicized products, you'll probably be more satisfied with them.

How Digital Cameras Work

Digital cameras are similar to scanners in that they employ thousands of tiny light sensors to turn reflected light into electrical impulses. The challenge is greater with digital cameras, however, because they must capture all the information in a single instant, whereas scanners can take 30 seconds or more to pass over a page, and then make several passes.

Taking a Picture

When you take a digital photograph, the camera's lens snaps open just like a normal camera. But instead of silver-halide-based film waiting in the back of the chassis to receive a dose of reflected light, a microchip with thousands of light-sensitive transistors is there. These transistors, known as *charge-coupled devices* (or CCDs), turn light into electrical pulses. The brighter the light, the greater the charge.

CCDs can discern levels of brightness, but they don't recognize color. As with all digital devices, these products create natural-looking colors by compositing three building-block colors and mixing them into each pixel. To do this, digital cameras must take three snapshots to complete a single color picture.

Digital cameras use three colored filters to deliver the proper light to the CCDs: one each for red, green, and blue. For each color pass, the camera stores eight bits of color information per pixel, or 256 colors per pixel. Add up the bits per pixel for each of the three passes, and you end up with 24 bits of color information for each pixel. That equals 16.7 million colors—more than the human eye can discern.

The precision of the CCDs determines the top resolution, an important consideration in any digital camera purchase. That said, lens quality and image processing techniques can affect the end result significantly.

Managing Images

After the lens and CCDs have done their work, the resulting color image is stored to memory in a compressed image format. A dedicated compression chip—often tailored to the standard JPEG compression scheme—squeezes the original bitmap image down by a factor of 10 to 100 times. The bits are then moved to the camera's memory buffer, a non-volatile store of silicon memory.

Most cameras enable the user to set image quality to at least two settings—high and low quality. High-quality snapshots often come in at 1,024×640 pixels and go easy on the compression to maintain visual fidelity (see Figure 28.2). Cameras can store only a limited number of high-quality images—often about 20 to 30.

FIGURE 28.2.

This 1,280×960 resolution JPEG image was snapped by a $300 digital camera. Not bad, huh? (Photo courtesy of Epson America)

The low-quality setting usually employs a lower 320×240 resolution and more aggressive compression. It's no surprise that image quality suffers, with perceptible graininess and loss of detail. That said, you can often pack 100 snapshots into the installed memory of a digital camera when using the lower-resolution setting. Low-res images also download to your PC more quickly and use less hard disk space.

Today, most cameras use integrated silicon memory. However, Intel, Kodak, and others are pushing a specification for PC Card-based memory to be a digital camera standard. The main advantage is modularity. When your camera runs out of memory, you simply snap in another PC Card, the way you would snap in a new roll of film. To take additional pictures with an integrated memory camera, you must go to a PC, download the photos, and clear the memory—hardly an option when you're at the Grand Canyon, for example.

Moving Pictures

Your pictures aren't worth much if you can't get them into your PC. There are several ways to get images from the camera to the PC:

- Serial cable
- USB cable

- Flash memory cards
- Floppies

Today, most cameras use a standard serial port cable. The serial port connection means that virtually any desktop or notebook PC can communicate with the camera (provided that it has the right software, of course). However, the serial connection itself is slow and invites conflicts and clumsy cable swaps.

Expect newer cameras to begin offering USB bus capabilities. The faster 12Mbps throughput will be a welcome relief: Serial-based downloads can take much time. The daisy-chaining USB bus also means that you won't have to unplug a modem or other serial device to free up a port for the camera.

Another burgeoning option is the use of the standard-factor PC Card modules just mentioned. These Flash memory cards, shown in Figure 28.3, can store up to 10MB or more of data, and they enable you to swap cards if the memory gets full. This option is key when you're on the road and you don't have a PC around to download your full memory buffer to. They can also move images to your hard disk very quickly.

Figure 28.3.

Flash memory cards from Intel and others can put megabytes of swappable storage in your wallet. Flash memory is the best solution for taking pictures far from your PC. (Photo courtesy of Intel Corp.)

Both the USB and Flash memory implementation suffer a basic drawback—most PCs aren't equipped to deal with them. This means that you might face an I/O upgrade to make use of newer cameras.

To help resolve this issue, Olympus came out with a floppy adapter for Flash memory cards. To transfer images from the camera, simply take the Flash card out of the camera, place it in the adapter, and then insert the adapter into your PC's floppy disk drive. The adapter allows the floppy drive to pull data off the Flash memory and into your hard disk. Since then, several other manufacturers have released similar solutions.

Sony, meanwhile, has shaken things up with its Digital Mavica camera line. The hook: The Mavica uses a standard 1.44MB floppy disk to store images for transfer to the PC. Although the floppy is no speed demon, the media is dirt cheap and literally every PC has a drive to read the disks. If you want guaranteed access to your digital photos—whether your on the road or at home—a floppy-based storage scheme may be your best bet (see Figure 28.4).

Figure 28.4.

The Sony Digital Mavica gets its boxy shape in part from the standard floppy disks it uses to store digital images. (Photo courtesy of Sony)

Floppy drive

Sundry Concerns

Although everyone is legitimately excited about digital cameras, there are many drawbacks. First, you won't get the level of quality you see with regular cameras, so you won't want to throw out your 35mm camera anytime soon. Second, although digital cameras do away with film, they'll have you buying batteries by the palette.

What's more, digital camera owners face challenges with their image archives. Everyone is used to buying new photo albums to hold their growing collection of pictures—and the same holds true for digital snapshots. If you plan on taking a lot of photos, you'll need to find a place to archive them before they completely overrun your hard disk. The best solution is a CD-R or DVD-ROM drive that can write the files to a CD-ROM disc.

All that said, these cameras get a boost from the emergence of cheap, photo-quality ink jet printers. Printers such as the HP PhotoSmart and Epson Stylus Photo can produce true-color output at resolutions of 1,200 to 1,400 dots per inch (dpi). The result is instant print-outs that look nearly as good as their Fotomat counterparts (see Figure 28.5).

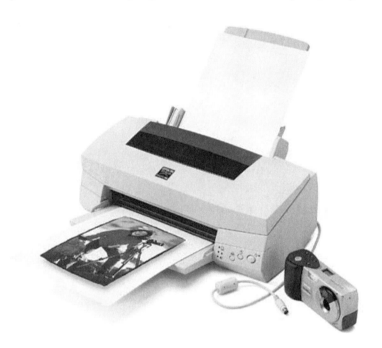

FIGURE 28.5.
With resolutions up to 1,440dpi, the Epson Stylus Photo 700 is optimized to produce photo-quality prints on specially coated paper. (Photo courtesy of Epson America)

Other Cameras

There's more to this market than digital Instamatic cameras. Sony has been selling a consumer-minded digital video camera for more than a year, and others are expected. As low-cost videoconferencing and Web video become mainstream, more and more PCs also sport small, monitor-top video cameras. The following sections tell you what to look for.

Direct to Video

Digital video cameras work in much the same manner as their still-photo counterparts, except that they must function much more quickly (see Figure 28.6). As with digital cameras, CCDs capture light and convert it into analog electrical impulses, which are then converted into digital 1s and 0s. Again, three color-specific passes are needed to enable the digital video camera to build a true-color composite.

There's just one problem. Digital video cameras must take up to 30 snapshots each second, converting light into electricity into binary bits so that the individual images can be strung together into a coherent video. What's more, these cameras must also capture analog sound, sampling the waveforms and converting them to binary as well.

If this sounds like a lot to do, it is. For this reason, digital video cameras cost thousands—not hundreds—of dollars. In addition, these cameras use a digital tape-based medium or small hard disks rather than the solid-state memory found in digital cameras. The reason is that video files are too large to store economically in silicon.

Digital video cameras also present challenges for moving data to PCs. Even USB's 12MBps data rate is insufficient to conveniently move enormous video files. For this reason, many vendors look to the IEEE 1394 bus standard, known as FireWire, to provide fast downloads to the PC. FireWire can move data at rates of 200 to 800MBps, and it also provides easy Plug and Play installation. However, few PCs feature FireWire ports (most now come with USB ports), adding to the expense of these peripherals.

Purchase Decisions

When it comes to buying a digital camera, you have plenty of choices. Price remains a big issue. Generally, cameras with higher resolutions and attractive storage and image control features command a premium. That said, you can find excellent products for as little as $300.

Here are the main issues to watch for when buying:

- Color depth: Accept no less than 24-bit color.
- Resolution: 640×480 is a good minimum, but better cameras push resolutions up to about 800×600 pixels.
- On-camera storage: PC Card storage is the most flexible, but you should make sure that you have at least two of these cards, so that you can swap out a full card for an empty one.
- Controls: Zooming, adjustable photo quality settings, and the ability to view and delete images from the camera are all useful.

Color Depth

The decision here is very simple: Accept nothing less than 24-bit color. Fortunately, most cameras today provide this level of color capability, making them a good match for printers and graphics display subsystems that are also tuned for 24-bit operation.

Resolution

Expect resolutions to continually improve. Two years ago, 320×240 was the resolution offered on affordable digital cameras. Now, even 640×480 resolution is considered low-end, with 1,024×768 becoming mainstream.

Unless your needs are very specific, you'll want to buy a model that provides a resolution higher than 640×480 pixels. These cameras produce attractive output that looks great when printed on new photo-quality ink jet printers. Of course, the highest resolutions push camera prices up, with top-end models selling for close to $1,000.

Keep in mind that not all resolutions are created equal. Lens quality and image compression both affect the end result. You should try to purchase all the resolution you can afford, but be sure to read the latest comparative reviews to get the skinny on which models do the best job. Keep in mind that this technology moves fast. What was a winning product six months ago will probably be in the middle of the pack today.

Short-Term Memory

Storage is a big deal. A camera with a small integrated memory store will have you running back to your PC every 10 shots or so, so that you can make space for more pictures. And if you take that camera with you on a vacation, your PC probably won't be close at hand.

If possible, consider a camera that uses PC Card Flash memory (see Figure 28.7). These credit-card-sized modules plug into the back of your camera and hold 2 to 10MB of images. To transfer the data to your PC, you simply plug the card into a PC Card reader (often sold separately) and download the files.

FIGURE 28.7.
Flash memory is good stuff. This Konica digital camera uses a 2MB Flash memory card to store images. (Photo courtesy of Intel Corp.)

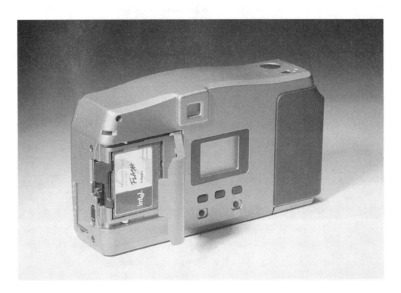

PC Card memory enjoys two major advantages over the built-in stuff found in most low-cost cameras. First, it's swappable. When you run out of storage space, you simply pull out the module and plug in a fresh one. You're then ready to snap another round of photos without having to go back to your PC, fire up the camera's desktop software, and move images to the hard disk. Of course, after you've downloaded your images, the card is free to accept another round of photos.

Second, PC Card memory can get images into your computer much faster than a serial cable can. Downloading a full set of photos over a serial cable can take 10 minutes or more—an agonizing process when you want to just grab a couple of images quickly.

Viewing Options

Another key feature is viewer options. All digital cameras include an inline viewer, which you must hold up to your eye to aim the camera. However, like camcorders, many digital cameras offer tiny color LCD-view panels. Often available as an option (expect to pay $150 to $250 for this perk), the LCD lets you size up images without putting your face to the camera.

The big attraction of the LCD panel is viewing. The LCD lets you immediately view any photo stored in the camera's memory. Although the screens are tiny—about 1½ inches on a side—their active-matrix design provides a crisp, bright display that can be viewed in sunlight.

Another advantage of the display is the fact that you can manage images without the PC. Cryptic but usable controls can often be found on the top or back of the camera. They enable you to delete the active image, making it easy to reclaim valuable storage space when you're on the road. The ability to proof images before downloading them can be helpful as well, prompting you to retake a picture that didn't work out, for example.

The Battery Issue

Digital cameras might seem to be the soul of convenience—no film strips to thread, no rushing to Walgreens to make the 11:30 a.m. deadline for next-day processing. What you will be doing is buying batteries and fretting about existing charge in the cells.

Digital cameras chew up batteries at a ferocious pace, particularly if you use an LCD attachment and take flash pictures. If possible, look for a unit that has a rechargeable battery pack rather than one that uses common but nonrechargeable AA or AAA batteries.

> **Tip:** Save yourself some money by practicing good power management. Try to minimize the use of the LCD display when possible—it's a big consumer of power. Also, make sure that you purchase the optional AC adapter and power cord when you get the camera. Downloading images can take a while for many of these products, and doing this on a battery shortens its life considerably.

Diagnosing/Troubleshooting

Digital cameras are highly integrated sealed-box peripherals. If something goes wrong with them, you won't be able to effect repairs without voiding the warranty and potentially damaging the product. As with so many computer components and peripherals, your best bet is to pursue a warranty repair or replacement of the camera through the manufacturer. Failing that, you can try to have the unit serviced.

The outlook for damaged cameras might be gloomy, but often things aren't as bad as they seem. A camera that fails to download images, for example, might simply be suffering from a loose connector or a dying battery. Here are a few simple things to look for:

- Check those batteries: Digital cameras consume batteries at an alarming pace. A fresh set of batteries can wear down fast if you've been using the LCD viewer or you've monkeyed with the power-down settings so that the camera fails to turn itself off when left unattended.

- Tighten connections: Cables can get bumped and stretched when you're downloading images. Make sure that the connectors are fitted tightly.

- Watch those modules: By the same token, you need to make sure that PC Card memory modules are fitted firmly in their sockets. Also, when you're juggling multiple memory cards, it's easy to accidentally swap an empty card for one that has the photos you want. Make a point to mark your modules with an indelible ink pen so that you can keep track.

- Use fresh batteries: Be careful not to team fresh batteries with older ones. This mismatch can result in wacky behavior, including lost data and unexpected shut-downs. When you replace batteries, replace them all at the same time.

- Check the Twain drivers: If your PC can't see the camera, this might be a software problem. Make sure that the proper Twain drivers are installed (they're included with the camera) and that you're using the correct serial or other bus port.

Connecting to the Desktop

Of course, those digital snapshots aren't much use if you can't get them out of the camera. And the local one-hour photo shop isn't going to know what to do with that Flash memory card, either. In order for your photos to be useful, you need to get them to your desktop.

There are three primary means to transfer photos:

- Serial cable

- USB cable

- Flash memory or other physical media

In all cases, you'll have to install camera-specific software that tells Windows 95 or 98 to look out for the camera and provides a way to handle image transfers. Often, you may be able to select from transfer options (such as serial or USB) depending on your camera model, system configuration, and the connection you choose. You should follow the directions in your documentation to make sure the software installs properly before you start using the camera.

Connecting Via Serial Port

The most popular PC-camera interconnection today is the serial port, though that is changing rapidly. If you've connected a modem or other serial device, you already know the drill. You must tell the camera interface software to look for the camera at a specific COM port. But you must be careful not to cause modem or mouse conflicts, which can occur if you assign both the camera and modem to COM1, for example.

Before you select the port in the camera software, check your modem and, if necessary, mouse COM port settings from the Windows Control Panel.

1. Click Start, Settings, Control Panel and open the Modem icon.

2. Click the Properties button and check the listed COM port.

3. Close up the Modem Properties dialog box.

4. If you have a serial mouse, launch the Mouse item in the Control Panel and click the General tab.

5. Note any COM port designation for the mouse. Close the Mouse Properties dialog box.

With the information you've gathered, you can now try to assign a nonconflicting address for your serial camera. If you already have two devices set up (probably on COM1 and COM2) you will probably have to share a port. Your best bet is to share the modem settings, because the modem can be easily shut down and unplugged for your transfer sessions, whereas the mouse remains critical to operation. If you do this, simply unplug the modem and plug the camera into the serial port that the modem occupied. Provided your camera software is set to the proper COM port, it should find the camera.

Connecting Via USB

For Windows 98 users, USB connectivity is much simpler. Just plug in the camera, power it on, and USB will detect its presence and invoke the proper drivers or software installation routines. (You may need to set the camera to a connect mode in order for the PC to recognize the device).

If this is the first time you've used the camera, you'll need the device driver and application CD-ROM that came with the unit. When prompted, place the disk in the drive and tell the setup program where to find the camera drivers. Follow the onscreen instructions to complete the installation. When complete, the camera is available to Windows 98. Subsequent connections automatically invoke the camera software. Just plug in the camera using the USB wire—your PC will find the camera and fire up the application.

Connecting Via Flash Card or Floppy

If you are using a physical media to transfer images, you'll want to follow the documentation closely. The simplest of the bunch is Sony's innovative Digital Mavica camera. It stores photos to a standard 1.44MB floppy disk—all you do is put the floppy into your floppy drive and copy the JPEG files over using Windows Explorer.

Many digital cameras use solid state Flash memory, which is often readable using standard PC Card readers found on virtually all notebook PCs. Unfortunately, few desktops include these readers, posing a problem if you want to take advantage of fast transfers available from the physical medium. You can purchase a PC Card reader for your PC, but these entail more expense, more drivers, and the hassle of installation.

Olympus came up with a solution in the form of its FlashPath floppy disk adapter. This $99 module lets you read Flash memory using your standard floppy drive. All you do is insert the Flash memory into the adapter, place the adapter into the drive, and then drag the JPEG files over using Windows Explorer. It's not as fast as a direct PC Card connection, but it's a lot more convenient. You will, however, need to install the Windows 9x drivers that come with the FlashPath adapter—otherwise Windows won't recognize the media.

Summary

Digital cameras are where the geek culture meets the mainstream. With Web sites turning into an accepted means of keeping ties among scattered family members, a good digital camera can help bring people closer together. Meanwhile, professionals can greatly enhance their productivity and speed to market by using all-digital photography.

And more is on the way. Intel is pushing for lower-cost cameras by shifting the burden of image compression and other operations to fast, MMX-enabled PCs. The FlashPix file format, developed by Kodak and promoted by Intel, employs variable-resolution output, making it easy to use one shot for high-resolution printing and low-resolution Web pages—without converting formats.

Just be warned: Digital photography is not for the meek. You still won't get the quality provided by 35mm film—that is still years away. You'll also want enough system horsepower and available storage to manage, manipulate, and store your growing library of digital snapshots. All that said, digital photography is one of the coolest—and most useful—things to come out of PCs since the spreadsheet.

Scanners

The past few years have seen an explosion of devices connected to the personal computer. PC speakers, monitor-top cameras, personal photo printers, and connected PDAs have all staked out a piece of turf on your desk. You can add scanners to that list. These useful peripherals can turn your boring old PC into a desktop photo studio, document imaging center, or fax machine—all for as little as $200.

This chapter introduces you to scanner upgrades, ranging from inexpensive monochrome handheld devices to full-blown color flatbed models that are appropriate for professional artwork. In this chapter, you will learn

- How the different types of scanners work, including the interaction of the hardware and software
- What to consider when purchasing a new scanner, including what type of scanner is best for you
- How to install a new scanner and its software and make sure it's operating properly
- Tips and tricks for creating good scans
- How to resolve scanner problems ranging from software tweaks to mechanical problems

Assessing Scanners

When it comes right down to it, a scanner upgrade might be one of the best ways to extend your PC's capabilities. After all, a faster CPU or a large hard disk won't give you the ability to grab objects in the real world and turn them into digital images and documents. But a low-cost desktop scanner can. And it can do so—in full color—for as little as $200.

Scanners are basically desktop analog-to-digital converters. They take analog visual things—documents, magazine pages, photos, business cards, and so on—and turn them into digitized bitmaps that your PC can understand. Bundled software lets you capture data and change settings that affect the visual quality of the captured images. In addition, optical character recognition (OCR) software is usually included to enable you to scan text and have the digitized information converted into usable text.

All scanners take the same basic approach to capturing visual information. A light source is aligned horizontally across the face of the scanner and is used to illuminate the target document. Reflected light passes through a lens, where it is detected by a row of charge-coupled devices (CCDs). The CCDs convert the reflected light into electrical impulses that vary in voltage according to the intensity of the reflected light. There is one CCD per pixel of resolution, so a 600dpi scanner would have 600 CCDs arrayed across the scanner's sensor head. Finally, one or more analog-to-digital converters turn the analog electrical signals into the 1s and 0s that your PC can understand.

Types of Scanners

You'll find a real variety of scanners on the market, ranging from precise, high-resolution scanners intended for professional artwork to small, quick-reading models designed to grab documents at a moment's notice. With the size, shape, and capabilities of scanners varying so widely, it's important to understand how they work and what you want before going in.

There are three types of scanners for the PC:

- Flatbed scanners
- Sheet-fed scanners
- Handheld scanners

Flatbed Scanners

The most popular and versatile type of scanner is the flatbed scanner (see Figure 29.1). As prices come down, the flatbed is the scanner of choice for more and more users. Flatbed scanners look like a rectangular box, usually 10-inches wide by about 12- or 13-inches long, which enables them to conveniently scan an 8½×17-inch piece of paper.

FIGURE 29.1.
The UMAX Astra 1200S flatbed scanner provides top resolution and quiet operation. (Photo courtesy of UMAX)

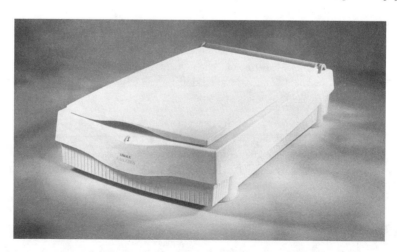

In the same manner as a photocopier, flatbed products scan documents by running a sensor across the length of the document. The sensor itself lies underneath a glass scanning surface, while a top door closes over the scan table to control lighting, allowing for better results.

Flatbed scanners enjoy the highest level of accuracy because the document isn't moved during the scan. In addition, the sensor array travels along a finely controlled path in a sealed environment, allowing for fine control that can enhance effective resolutions. However, you have to manually feed each page to the flatbed scanner unless you want to invest in a document feeder that can move paper in and out of the scan table automatically.

Sheet-Fed Scanners

Sheet-fed scanners (see Figure 29.2) are a popular alternative because of their attractive price—black-and-white models often sell for less than $100. Those working in crowded offices and other tight spaces also appreciate the small footprint of sheet-fed devices, as they take up a small fraction of the space consumed by flatbed scanners. Sheet-fed models use a motor to pull documents past a scanning head that is about 8½ inches wide. The biggest advantage is that sheet-feds can capture an entire standard page in one pass, without consuming a lot of desk space.

FIGURE 29.2.

The Umax PageOffice 11C is compact, yet it provides color-scanning capability. (Photo courtesy of UMAX)

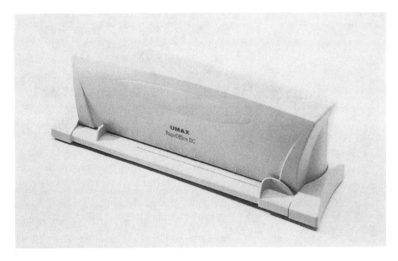

Sheet-fed models have a few telling shortfalls. For one, they can handle only loose-leaf pages. You can't scan material from a book or magazine without first ripping out the page to be scanned. For another, these products can choke on thicker media, such as cardboard, and they can be tricky to use with small or odd-shaped paper, such as business cards. And because pages are pulled through the device past the scanning head, the scan isn't as accurate as that of a flatbed, where the medium is stationary.

Sheet-fed scanners range in price from about $100 to $250, and resolution ranges from 200 to 400dpi. In general, sheet-fed scanners are excellent for OCR work, as well as serving as input scanners for faxing. Some, such as Visioneer's popular PaperPort Vx, provide a software interface to launch fax, OCR, and image-editing software directly from the program.

Handheld Scanners

Handheld scanners (see Figure 29.3) have been a diminishing breed in the scanner market. As its name implies, you use a handheld scanner by moving it over the item being scanned. It's no surprise that this type of scanner can be a bit imprecise—especially after that second cup of coffee—but it has the key advantages of being inexpensive and portable.

FIGURE 29.3.
The HP CapShare could be the future of hand-held scanning: A portable device that can capture, transfer, and fax documents on the road.

Traditional handheld scanners use a scan head that is 4- to 6-inches wide, allowing them to take in about half the width of a standard page at a time. To operate the unit, you must pull the scan head slowly and evenly across the document, maintaining a constant rate of speed to avoid overtaking the scanner's capacity to capture the data. A tracking roller records the distance and rate of travel, allowing the scanner to know exactly where each visual bit of information belongs.

Because the scan head is only half the width of a piece of paper, most units come with software that lets you stitch scan passes together into a single bitmap. The software attempts to anchor the two scans together to provide a close match, but the results are usually disappointing. If you need capture entire 8½×11-inch documents, a handheld scanner probably won't be suitable. Drastic drops in flatbed and sheet-fed scanner prices have also helped push handhelds out of the market.

The exception comes in the form of Hewlett-Packard's CapShare scanner, a handheld scanner and information appliance tailored for traveling executives. This battery-powered device lets you scan documents anywhere. IR and serial connections enable you to transfer scanned documents to a PC for storing or processing. A built-in LCD screen allows you to view scanned documents, while the unit itself can store up to 50 letter-sized scanned pages. The drawback: At more than $600, you won't mistake this advanced 400dpi scanner for a cheap handheld.

Color Scanning: Three Times the Work and Worth It

Not more than three years ago, it was hard to decide whether to go with color or black-and-white. A black-and-white scanner could be had at a reasonable price, but color-capable scanners still commanded a premium. Compact scanners, meanwhile, might lack color capability all together. Today, color pervades the entire range of scanner products, from low-cost handheld and sheet-fed models to powerful flatbed scanners.

The reason it took color a while to hit the mainstream is that capturing all the color data gets complex. For now, you need to understand how scanners see color. Just as a dog, a scanner's CCDs see only in shades of gray—or, more accurately, in levels of voltages that can be assumed to be gray. To process color, scanners must take three separate snapshots, each tailored to a specific area of the color spectrum, and composite them to yield a color scan.

Here's how it works: By limiting the scanned light to one area of the spectrum, a typical flatbed scanner can capture eight bits of color data for that color. By doing this for three building-block colors—usually red, green, and blue—the device can composite the information from the three scans to yield a range of 16.7 million distinct colors per pixel—more than the human eye can fathom.

Scanners can take color-specific snapshots in one of two ways: They employ a light filter to limit the reflected light to the desired wavelength, or they shine a specific color of light onto the document. In either case, by applying three different color looks to each line of the document, the scanner can put together an accurate picture of the colors it is seeing.

Of course, moving to color means that you are, in effect, scanning your document three times. In this case, there are two approaches:

- Take three passes at the document: An option available only to flatbed scanners, this approach has the scan head scan the document three times—once each for red, green, and blue light. After this is done, the three images are merged using software to create the composited full-color image. Of course, even a slight variation in scanner movement yields registration problems, possibly causing the individual red, blue, and green colors to become visible.

- Alternate the light or filters in a single pass: Every color handheld and sheet-fed scanner takes this approach. The scanner switches rapidly among the three color settings as it scans, yielding three color looks in a single pass. Although this is useful for limiting possible registration problems, the quick alternating of filters or lights poses a design challenge. Also, much more data is being grabbed in a single pass, so the scanner must capture and transfer information quickly enough to avoid data overruns.

A Look Inside Colors

Here's where things get weird. The way your scanner deals with color depends on whether it uses color filters or different colors of scanning lights to read color information from documents. It all goes back to the area of *color modeling*—elaborate logical systems for specifying colors in digital equipment. Don't panic. Unless you want to delve into the arcane art of color matching to make sure your screen-based designs look just so when printed professionally, you can still lead a full and rewarding life without mastering this stuff. Still, it's useful to know whether or not you're printing scanned images to a color printer.

Here's how the process works: If your scanner employs a light filter, it is built around the RGB color scheme, which keys on red, green, and blue to build 16.7 million possible colors. To come up with colors such as maroon, yellow, and aqua, the PC mixes varying levels of red, green, and blue inside each visible pixel. By applying a certain number of bits (usually eight of them) to represent each color value in a pixel, you get the relative color depth available to the scanner.

The RGB color model is *additive*. In other words, RGB devices combine elements from building-block color to produce the desired color for each point. Both monitors and scanners that use color filters employ the RGB color model. The common bond is that color is perceived after it is passed through a filtering medium (such as color-specific phosphors or filters).

A different color-modeling scheme is used by printers and by scanners that employ different scanning light colors instead of filters. In this case, color isn't achieved by filtering through a medium. Instead, bouncing back the desired spectrum to the viewer produces color. Called *subtractive mixing,* this approach works based on what light does *not* get passed through or absorbed by the target. What is left is bounced back to the eye—thus the phrase *subtractive mixing*. (Can you tell that this name was thought up by someone who spent *way* too much time in a lab?)

In the subtractive universe, the color model is called *CMYK,* or cyan, magenta, yellow, and black. (K is used for black to avoid confusion with blue.) Cyan, magenta, and yellow are the primary colors in this scheme. Black gets thrown in to ensure that true black can be produced, because mixing cyan, magenta, and yellow really yields a brown or gray rather than true black. (With additive mixing, black is produced by the absence of light—you just turn off the pixel.)

Dots, Spots, and Spurious Specs

Of course, one of the first things any buyer looks for in a scanner is resolution. How many dots per square inch can the device detect? This seems like a straightforward question. Unfortunately, scanner marketers and engineers have teamed up to create really innovative ways to make this a tough question to answer.

Basically, there are three types of resolution in a scanner, all of which can come into play:

- Optical resolution
- Mechanical resolution
- Interpolated resolution

Let's walk through each.

Optical Resolution

This is the one that really matters. Optical resolution is directly associated with the number of CCDs (those small light-gathering sensors) mounted on the scan head. The quality of the scanner lens also comes into play.

If a scanner has 300 CCDs strung across each inch of the array, its optical resolution is 300dpi. If it has 600 or 1,200 CCDs per inch, the optical resolution is 600 or 1,200dpi, respectively (see Figure 29.4). Optical resolution defines the scanner's horizontal resolution—what it can see from side to side as it reads each line.

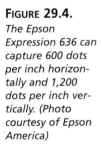

FIGURE 29.4.

The Epson Expression 636 can capture 600 dots per inch horizontally and 1,200 dots per inch vertically. (Photo courtesy of Epson America)

Mechanical Resolution

Our first step down the slippery slope starts here. The number of steps per inch that the scanner's sensor array takes as it passes over the target determines mechanical resolution. A 300dpi mechanical resolution means that the sensor array stops every 1/300th of an inch to take a snapshot of the line, while a 600dpi unit stops every 1/600th of an inch.

Although mechanical resolution is a legitimate measure of fidelity, it works only along the vertical access. The optical resolution always defines the horizontal fidelity of the scan.

The limiting issue is the precision of the scanner's motor. Flatbed scanners, with their sealed sensor array and stable document platform, enjoy the biggest advantage here. These tabletop units can achieve mechanical resolutions of 1,200dpi by providing minute control over the travel of the sensor array.

Although this is all based on good principles, problems arise in how this capability is reported to consumers. Often, vendors put the mechanical resolution ahead of the true optical resolution, calling their device a 1,200×600dpi scanner. (The bigger number looks really impressive up front, no?) Worse, these products might be referred to only by their mechanical resolution when you're shopping at a store or talking to friends. So what you think is a 1,200×1,200dpi scanner is actually a 600×1,200dpi scanner.

Interpolated Resolution

Finally, scanner makers talk about the top resolution that their products can provide. Using software to guess what lies between its CCDs, scanners can produce effective resolutions of up to 2,400dpi. Called *interpolation,* this process simply averages the known values of adjacent points and fills in the result between them.

Interpolation can be useful, particularly if you need to blow up a small image to a large size. If you captured a 300×300dpi image and increased it to 600×600dpi in a graphics program, the result would be a blocky graphic. By processing the picture using your scanner's interpolation software, you can get much better results, because the original dots aren't just replicated, but smoothed out.

In general, interpolation happens on your PC, not inside the scanner. For this reason, a quick system with lots of RAM can help speed up this kind of scanning. However, no amount of processing power can overcome the basic fallacy of interpolation. You simply can't reliably produce something that isn't there.

Think about it. Unexpected changes in color information between CCDs can yield unrealistic results. And when you double the resolution of an image, basically, half the dots *aren't really there.* If someone tries to sell you a scanner based on the interpolated resolution, look elsewhere.

> **Tip:** Be aware that the interpolation algorithms within image-editing packages such as Adobe PhotoShop might be superior to those supplied with your scanner's software. If you have a new scanner and a favorite photo editor, you might run a little contest to see which really does a better job.

Software

Don't underestimate the importance of software. Virtually all scanners include a bundle of photo- and image-editing software, as well as utilities for managing and tweaking images. There are four main areas:

- Twain driver software
- Photo-editing applications
- Optical character recognition
- Utilities

Twain Software

Virtually all scanners come with so-called Twain software, an industry-standard interface designed to take the guesswork out of scanning. Established as a software driver, Twain lets any compliant application provide instant scanning capability. A Twain-compliant word processor, for example, could offer a Scan menu option that activates any installed Twain-compliant scanner.

Over the years, Twain has grown from a software driver layer (plumbing, if you will) into a useful interface for scanning hardware. Depending on which product you buy, you might find that any Twain-compliant application has access to powerful scanning controls. In fact, your word processor or spreadsheet might have all the trappings of a photo-editing applet.

Photo-Editing Software

You might think you're buying hardware, but the software bundles that scanners provide can be attractive—particularly if you don't already own any image-editing software. Adobe PhotoShop or PhotoDeluxe, Ulead's PhotoImpact, and Kai's PowerGoo are just a sample of the powerful programs often included with scanners.

Also included might be image-management utilities that enable you to organize and search for graphics files. For example, you can assign key words to captured images—say, "beach" and "swim" with a scanned image of your family on the beach—so that you can use quick text searches to find images later.

Keep in mind that any serious photo editing work requires serious hardware. A large, 600-dpi image scan can grab tens of megabytes of RAM and monopolize even a fast Pentium II CPU for nearly a minute at a time. If you intend to conduct any sort of high-resolution editing, you'll want to make sure your PC has 64MB of RAM—at least—and a fast CPU.

Optical Character Recognition

One of the key components of many scanners bound for business duty is optical character recognition (OCR) software. This software processes the scanned bitmap image and converts the legible images of text into text that can be imported into a word processing program. The software allows for quick conversion of paper documents into digital format.

Here, even low-cost handheld and sheet-fed scanners provide adequate resolution for OCR work. What is more important is the quality of the OCR software—some *serious* math goes into character recognition. The raw horsepower of your system makes a big difference as well, because a slower 486 grinds to a halt trying to work through the complex recognition algorithms. A fast Pentium-II CPU and plenty of system RAM goes a long way toward enabling efficient OCR processing.

Bus Interface: Connecting to the PC

Today, most scanners hook to your PC in one of two ways: over the parallel port or over a SCSI connection—but that is changing. With the arrival of Windows 98 on PCs equipped with Universal Serial Bus ports, scanner vendors have begun marketing USB-based products in earnest. You'll also find a few serial port scanners available, though the port really lacks the bandwidth for high-resolution work.

Parallel Port Scanners

Most handheld and sheet-fed scanners will join the clamor of peripherals vying for your parallel port. If you don't have too many parallel devices, this won't be a problem. Setup is almost always painless, and virtually all PCs have a parallel port. Most of these scanners include a parallel pass-through device that lets you keep your printer hooked up along with the scanner.

> **Note:** If you end up using a pass-through port with your scanner, keep a couple of things in mind to avoid trouble. First, don't try to print and scan at the same time. The pass-through device is there as a convenience to eliminate the troublesome plugging and unplugging of connectors—it can't juggle multiple jobs on the same port. Second, be aware that enhanced parallel port operation might not work over a pass-through device. If you experience printer trouble after installing a pass-through device, you should check your system CMOS utility and try setting the parallel port to standard Centronics operation.

SCSI Scanners

Until very recently, flatbed scanners and SCSI were a joint proposition—and no wonder. The SCSI bus has more than enough bandwidth for high-resolution scan jobs, provides standard external access, and has the flexibility that enables other devices to daisy chain off the scanner. What's more, SCSI was a fixture on computers usually used by people who needed tabletop scanners—graphics professionals who had Macintosh computers or high-end workstations.

Unfortunately, for many PC users, SCSI has spelled trouble. Until the arrival of user-friendly 32-bit operating systems and useful SCSI tools such as Corel's EZ SCSI software, SCSI peripherals could be very difficult to install and manage. There was also the little problem of added expense: Often purchasing a SCSI scanner meant shelling out for a SCSI card to match. That extra expense typically adds $100 or more to the cost of the scanner.

Today, SCSI headaches are subsiding as drivers and operating systems improve. However, unless you have an existing SCSI interface on the outside of your PC, a SCSI-based scanner means that you will have to add an add-in card to your system.

USB Scanners

If you're in the market for a scanner, it might be a good idea to look for one that has USB capability. Provided that your PC includes USB connectors and is running Windows 98, this Plug and Play external bus can greatly ease hardware setups. Plug the scanner in and Windows 98 automatically detects, identifies, and loads the drivers for the new device—of course, you might have to insert a driver disc along the way. And like SCSI, you can string USB peripherals to each other, making it easy to find enough connector ports and avoid evil cable tangles behind your PC. The bus also supports 12MBps data rates, more than enough for scanning purposes.

If you don't have a USB connector, you might consider an upgrade as part of your scanner purchase. Vendors such as CMD sell ISA and PCI based add-in cards that offer a pair of USB ports, allowing older Pentium and Pentium MMX-class systems to support USB. Just be sure you have Windows 98 running on your PC. Windows 95 provides only partial USB support, and many devices lack the extra software needed to run smoothly with it. Windows NT, meanwhile, won't support USB until version 5.0.

Buying a Scanner

How do you go about buying a new scanner? If you read the preceding section, you probably have a pretty good idea of what's out there. Now you just have to figure out what you want to do.

Table 29.1 provides a breakdown of common scanner usage scenarios and the hardware for the job. Keep in mind that these are minimum requirements—you might want to buy more scanner than you need right now, with the expectation that you'll make use of those features down the road.

Table 29.1. Scanners for every job.

Task	Mechanism	Minimum Requirements
Professional artwork	Flatbed	1,200×1,200dpi resolution, 36-bit color
Business and home artwork	Flatbed	600×600dpi resolution, 24-bit color
Business and home documents	Sheet-fed	300×300dpi resolution, monochrome
Portable	Handheld	300×300dpi resolution, monochrome

Professional Artwork

If you're buying a scanner to create accurate reproductions of photos for publication or distribution, image quality is your overriding concern. Your scanner must provide optical resolutions of 1,200dpi to ensure fine detail under close scrutiny. Color depths should be 30 or 36 bits, which is high enough to smooth subtle color gradients and enhance dark images.

Scanners in this range can get pricey, mainly because of the added expense involved in scanning 30-bit and greater color depths. Expect to pay $3,000 or more for a scanner that has these capabilities. Here are things you should look for in a top-of-the-line scanner:

- Optical resolutions of 1,200dpi
- Color depths ranging from 30 to 36 bits
- Fast SCSI or USB interface
- An optional slide scanner attachment for making scans of 35mm slides and transparencies (see Figure 29.5)
- Professional photo-editing software, such as Adobe PhotoShop

FIGURE 29.5.
The UMAX PowerLook 2000 includes a transparency adapter for scanning photographic slides. (Photo courtesy of UMAX)

General Business and Home Graphics

This fast-growing area of the market offers greater capabilities and lower prices than ever before. Expect scanners to be pulled into mixed duty, capturing high-quality color photographs one minute and scanning a five-page technical report bound for OCR processing the next.

Depending on the relative demands you put on image-capture quality, a flatbed model is probably best for this type of work. This is certainly the most versatile design, because it can scan pages directly from books, magazines, and boxes—scans that a sheet-fed model can't cope with. Prices are very competitive: Many top-notch flatbed scanners sell for $200 to $500 and offer more than enough resolution and color handling for heavy artwork.

If you're looking for lower prices and smaller footprints, a color sheet-fed scanner is a good idea. Generally, you'll give up a couple hundred dots of resolution (400dpi is a frequent sheet-fed spec), as well as the capability to read thick media. But scanners such as Visioneer's PaperPort Strobe offer unmatched automation (stick a piece of paper in the slot, and it starts scanning) and provide neat hooks to your day-to-day applications, turning your scanner into a real part of your PC's tool set. These scanners run $120 to $300.

Here's what you should look for in a scanner bound for home and business use:

- 300×300dpi optical resolution
- 24-bit color support
- SCSI, USB, or parallel port interface
- Good OCR software
- Photo-editing software, such as Adobe Photo Deluxe, that stresses usability more than esoteric feature sets

Business and Home Document Scanning

Suppose you don't care about art or images but you need something to turn your bills and documents into electronic files. If you don't want to spend extra money for the ability to keep your records stored on your PC, a low-cost black-and-white sheet-fed model is your best bet. Resolutions really don't have to go beyond 300dpi, because that is enough to support effective OCR processing.

Note that if you're scanning many documents, you might need to buy a flatbed scanner that has an optional paper feeder attachment. Unfortunately, these can get expensive, so be sure to shop around for availability and cost of attachments for various scanners before deciding on one.

You can expect prices for these scanners to be at $150 and below. Here's what you should look for in a document scanner:

- 300×300dpi optical resolution
- 256 grayscale support
- USB or parallel port interface
- Good OCR software
- Small footprint and automation features

Portable Scanning

Portable scanning is a niche application, to be sure, but this is one of the few markets left for handheld scanners. And it's an intriguing one. Partnered with a notebook, a parallel port-based handheld scanner can capture business cards, legal documents, and other business-related fare—whether in a trade show booth or in a hotel meeting room.

In fact, handheld scanners may be the most intriguing part of the market as we approach the year 2000. HP's innovative CapShare device is a battery-powered handheld that can scan and store up to 50 letter-sized pages, and uses IR or serial connections to move documents to PCs or printers. Unlike typical scanners, the CapShare lets you store, view, and manage documents directly from the scanner itself using a small, monochrome LCD screen.

Meanwhile, traditional handheld scanners are hard to find. They lack the stability or resolution of desktop and even sheet-fed models, and no longer provide a cost benefit. Color sheet-fed scanners can be had for about $100.

Working with Scanners

You've got your new scanner home, so now what? That's a good question. Just as any external peripheral, a scanner needs to be connected to your system and given resources to be able to access what it needs to work. More importantly, actually making scans can be very tricky. This section helps you install and effectively use your scanner.

Installing a Scanner

Installing a scanner can be tricky, usually because you must deal with connectivity issues associated with the parallel port or SCSI bus. The following sections give you a heads-up on obstacles that you might encounter during installation.

Installing a Parallel Port Scanner

The good news is that you won't have to tear the case off your PC and fish around for free bus slots. The bad news is that, depending on your parallel port settings, you might have to fish around in your system CMOS and Windows 95 Device Manager to free up parallel port resources.

The easiest way to install a scanner is to closely follow the manufacturer's installation instructions. Scanners often provide a fully automated installation from a CD-ROM or floppy disk. However, if you choose to use Windows 95's Add New Hardware Wizard, do the following:

1. Shut off the PC. Place the scanner on a flat, stable surface within a few feet of the PC.

2. Plug the 25-pin female end of the supplied parallel cable into your PC, and plug the pincher or end that mates with the scanner's port into the scanner.

3. Plug the scanner's power cord into an outlet. Make sure that all cables and cords are firmly seated. Also watch out for retaining pins, which are used to hold the scanning mechanism in place during shipping. These need to be removed.

4. Turn on the scanner (in some cases, the scanner comes on as soon as it's plugged in). You should hear the motor initiate. Turn on the PC.

5. Windows 95 detects new hardware and launches the Add New Hardware Wizard.

6. In the Hardware Type box, select Other (it has a yellow question mark icon).

7. Click Next. When prompted to detect the hardware, click the No option button and then click Next.

8. From the Manufacturers list, scroll down to Unknown Device and select it.

9. In the Models box, select Unsupported Devices.

10. Place the scanner's driver floppy disk into drive A: of your PC.

11. Click Have Disk and double-click the .INF file for your scanner.

12. Windows 95 updates the drivers and then presents a dialog box prompting you to select which port to connect the device to.

Parallel Problems

Parallel port devices are supposed to be easy to use. And although I complain vigorously about overcrowding on the parallel port, in general, these devices are simpler to use than those using SCSI or proprietary bus cards. Still, the parallel port has its moments. And when it does, it's usually bad news, because your printer and perhaps a few other devices will all get dragged down with it.

Parallel port scanners often require that you turn off enhanced parallel capabilities. If you're having problems, check your system BIOS to see whether the parallel port is set to Enhanced Parallel Port or Enhanced Capabilities Port. If it is, set it back to Bi-Directional Parallel Port.

Many scanners feature a pass-through connector to enable you to hook both a printer and a scanner to the parallel port. Be sure not to try to use both peripherals at the same time, because the conflicting signals could cause both jobs to fail.

Installing SCSI Scanners

Installing a SCSI scanner isn't too tough, provided that you already have a working SCSI daisy chain on your system. If you're familiar with the workings of SCSI, you'll be ready to deal with terminator plugs, SCSI ID settings, and even the vagaries of what-goes-where on a daisy chain to make everything work properly.

If you don't already have a SCSI adapter installed in your system, you can find out what you need to do in Chapter 10, "Control Freaks: IDE and SCSI Controllers." In fact, many scanners come bundled with a basic SCSI card. In this case, of course, you'll need to install that card first, before you get around to the scanner itself (again, Chapter 10 has what you need). After that is done, you can install the new SCSI scanner. Do the following:

1. Shut off the PC. Place the scanner on a flat, stable surface within a few feet of the PC.

2. Locate the peripheral you want the scanner to operate off of. Or, if the scanner is the only external SCSI device, plug the SCSI cable into the SCSI port on the back of the PC.

3. Set the scanner's ID number to a unique value between 1 and 7. The control for this setting can usually be found on the back of the scanner.

4. Most consumer scanners are preterminated—that is, they need to sit at the end of the SCSI daisy chain and do not need manual termination. If your scanner is not configured in this way, you'll need to terminate the device by placing the supplied terminator plug into the outbound port on the back of the scanner.

5. Turn on the scanner (in some cases, the scanner comes on as soon as it is plugged in). You should hear the motor initiate.

> **Tip:** In general, it's a good idea to power up external SCSI devices, such as scanners, before you start the computer. This ensures that the devices are up and ready when the SCSI bus interrogates them.

6. Windows 95 detects new hardware and launches the Add New Hardware Wizard.

7. In the Hardware Type box, select Other (it has a yellow question mark icon).

8. Click Next. When prompted to detect the hardware, click the No option button and then click Next.

9. From the Manufacturers list, scroll down to Unknown Device and select it.

10. In the Models box, select Unsupported Devices.

11. Place the scanner's driver floppy disk into drive A: of your PC.

12. Click Have Disk and double-click the .INF file for your scanner.

13. Windows 95 updates the drivers and then presents a dialog box prompting you to select which port to connect the device to.

Installing a USB Scanner

If you want to avoid the hassle of scanner installations, check out a USB scanner. If your system has a couple USB ports on the back and you are running Windows 98, you should be able to enjoy lower cost, better performance, and easier setup using a USB-based product. If you already have a couple USB devices, however, you may be fresh out of free ports to plug into. You can get a separate USB hub to provide addition ports for more devices, but you'll have to weigh the additional cost of the hub when making the decision.

Beyond plug and play installation, USB scanners are able to do away with power cords. That's because the USB wire is able to supply electricity to lower power devices (a USB laser printer, for example, still needs a power cord). With sheet-fed scanners so small these days, it seems that the single bulkiest component is the power transformer that often blocks two or more plugs on a power strip. A USB scanner can help take care of that hassle.

To install a USB scanner under Windows 98, do the following:

1. Exit your various programs so that only Windows 98 is running. If you've been running a lot of different programs for several hours, you might reboot to free up any constrained resources.

2. Plug the scanner's USB wire into one of the free USB ports at the back of the PC.

3. Wait a moment. Windows 98 should detect the presence of a device on the USB port and launch the Hardware Wizard.

4. When prompted, place the scanner's driver CD-ROM or floppy disk into the appropriate drive.

5. If Windows 98 is unable to automatically find the driver files, click the Have Disk button and navigate to the appropriate drive and subdirectory. Double-click the .INF file for your scanner.

6. Windows 98 updates the drivers and initializes the scanner.

7. Install the application software provided by the vendor, following the instructions provided. You will probably have to reboot after installing applications.

Getting Good Scans

If you think using a scanner is like making copies, think again. Scanning can be very complex, particularly if you're trying to optimize your scans for one or more print output devices. Resolutions, color depths, and gamma correction settings all need to be taken into account before you begin your scan.

You get the best results and save a lot of time if you keep a few things in mind as you work.

Don't Overscan

A common mistake is scanning at the top resolution when in fact the graphic is bound for a 300dpi laser printer or, even worse, an onscreen Web graphic. If you capture a 600dpi image and print it on a 300dpi laser printer, you'll have wasted a lot of bits and time.

A related problem occurs when you try to scan a low-resolution image at high resolution. This is classic garbage in, garbage out—only lots of it. You end up with a highly detailed image that records every flaw and blur in the original scan. You're better off stepping back on the resolution, and enhancing performance in the process.

Table 29.2 lists the output resolutions of devices you might be scanning for.

Table 29.2. Output resolutions.

Device	Resolution
High-end laser	1,200dpi
Midrange laser	600dpi
Low-end laser, ink jets	300-400dpi
PC display	72dpi

As you can see, a 600dpi scan won't do you much good on many printers. The situation is even worse on monitors, which can display only about 72 dots per inch. High-resolution scans for these devices only consume bits and time.

The exception is if you plan to enlarge the image after the scan. In this case, the extra resolution is critical to keep the image quality acceptable. A 600dpi scan enlarged to twice its size looks about right for a 300dpi output device.

Work Outside the Box

Although most scanners come with their own utilities for sprucing up scans, you might be well advised to disregard them. In general, you'll get better results from a full-fledged photo-editing package such as Adobe PhotoShop—albeit at a price—than you will from bundled utilities.

Choose Your Media

Don't expect too much from magazine photographs and other printed matter. Newspapers, magazines, and books use halftone graphics to produce visual detail. The use of these mixed dots often creates a distracting moiré pattern in the scan—a perceptible flaw in the image. Where possible, you should use true photographs, because these won't produce a moiré effect.

Scanner Maintenance

Scanners can be troublesome devices. After all, anything on a PC that uses a SCSI interface needs some care and feeding to ensure cooperation. You'll also need to worry about the health of rollers used to move scanning heads or paper through the chassis. Still, depending on how often you use your scanner, your maintenance might amount to little more than occasionally cleaning the scanning table glass.

Summary

Professional-quality scanning became affordable only recently. Flatbed scanners with 600dpi capability can now be purchased for $250 and up, meaning that almost any desktop can afford to become a photography studio.

Of course, not everyone is interested in art. Sheet-fed models make excellent corporate sidekicks, turning printed matter into editable text, faxable documents, or shareable images. Although options such as automatic sheet feeders or slide adapters can run up the cost a bit, they add important features for people who need them.

Perhaps most important, the arrival of USB should launch a new generation of scanners. Gone will be the pricey and challenging SCSI bus for higher-end models. After scanner makers update their designs, USB promises to greatly enhance the ease of use and affordability of flatbed scanners.

APPENDIX

What to Do with a PC That's Beyond Recovery

There comes a time when even the most aggressive upgrade can't save a system. Whether overcome by the ravages of obsolescence or damaged beyond repair, every PC will eventually need to be retired.

What do you do with a PC that can no longer run the applications you need to use every day? Actually, there are a variety of options:

- Donate it to charity
- Cannibalize what parts you can for use in another system
- Place the system into limited, modified duty
- Recycle the PC components with a reclamation company

Donating a PC

Perhaps one of the best ways to dispose of an aging PC is to donate it to charity. Not only do you get the old hardware out of the house, but you also gain a nifty tax deduction. Many organizations are in need of PCs, ranging from schools and churches to nonprofit organizations.

In order for the PC to qualify as a tax-deductible donation, you need to make sure that you meet the following criteria:

- The PC is in reasonable working order
- The receiving organization is a recognized charity
- You receive a dated and itemized receipt from the organization confirming the donation

If you're not sure where to take your PC, a number of charitable organizations specialize in handling PC donations. A further advantage is that these organizations know how to handle the specifics of PC donations, including assessing the market value of your PC.

The following are just a few of the charities specializing in PC donations. These companies will accept your hardware and distribute it to organizations such as schools, churches, and nonprofit institutions:

- Computer Recycling Center
  (415) 428-3700; www.crc.org

- Computer Recycling Project
  (415) 695-7703; www.wco.com/~dale/crp.html

- Computers & You
  (415) 922-7593; www.glide.org/programs/cny_IV.html

- Detwiler Foundation
  (800) 939-6000; www.detwiler.org

- East-West Education Development Foundation
  (617) 261-6699

- Educational Assistance Limited
  (708) 690-0010

- Gifts in Kind International
  (703) 836-2121; www.giftsinkind.org

- Lazarus Foundation
  (410) 740-0735; www.west.net/~recycle/lazarus/
  (805) 563-1009; www.west.net/~recycle/lazarus/

- National Christina Foundation
  (800) 247-4784

- Non-Profit Computing
  (212) 759-2368

If you decide to donate a PC, be aware of the tax implications. Claiming excessive deductions on your return for computer donations can draw the attention of the IRS. You'll also need to keep receipts from your donations in case you face an audit.

Of course, you'll need to itemize your return in order to apply charitable deductions. If you file a 1040EZ return, or if you have less than $6,500 in possible deductions on your 1040 return, you probably won't be able to take a deduction. You should check your current tax situation or consult a tax professional to determine whether a charitable contribution makes sense.

Fine Young Cannibals

That old PC might be beyond help, but it can still help other systems. Several components inside it might be useful to your primary system:

- RAM
- Hard disk
- Modem
- Display

RAM

You won't always be able to use your old RAM in your new system. If your old PC uses 30-pin or 72-pin DRAM SIMMs, it might be incompatible with the 168-pin DIMMs used in modern Pentium MMX and Pentium II class PCs. You need to check the RAM SIMMs closely to ensure that the relative speed and type of RAM are compatible.

If the RAM is incompatible, you might be able to at least get some money back by selling the old memory. But keep in mind that RAM remains incredibly cheap. Unless you have a large amount of RAM to resell, it may not be worth much. Check with local computer stores and memory retailers to find out how much your memory might be worth.

Hard Disk

The hard disk in your old PC might be tiny in comparison to the multigigabyte jobs you see in new PCs, but the disk itself might be in fine shape. If both systems use enhanced IDE drives, it's very easy to plug the drive from the older system into your newer PC. The drive could then be used to archive and back up important data on the faster primary disk, just in case something goes wrong.

Modem

Your new PC probably shipped with a 56KBps modem, but your older system might be equipped with an adequate 28.8KBps or 33.6KBps modem. If so, you can install the old modem into the new system and possibly use it to nearly double your Web-browsing bandwidth.

How? New software can bundle dual data phone calls, enabling two modems to aggregate their bandwidth into a single wide data pipe. Using this capability, you can add the 28.8KBps bandwidth to the 33.6 or 56KBps data capability already present on your PC. Of course, you'll need a second phone line to make this work, and your ISP must offer a so-called modem duplexing service, which may cost you more than standard service to use. Windows 98 adds modem duplexing as part of its dial-up services. You can also buy third-party packages able to turn your dual-modem phone calls into the equivalent of a single higher-bandwidth connection.

Display

Why would you want to use an old graphics card and 14-inch display on your new system? For one thing, Windows 98 allows multiple displays and graphics cards to work together. The interface of a single application can be stretched across two monitors, or you can dedicate the 14-inch display to viewing one thing while the larger monitor displays another. This is useful if you need to compare the data displayed by two separate programs, for example, or if you want to use one monitor to browse the Web while the other displays a program.

Limiting Duty

Just because you have a new PC doesn't mean you have to retire, sell, or trash the old one. Heck, even a creaky, old 486 can offer useful services for those with a small office or home office. In most cases you'll need to set up a modest network to make the old PC's services available to your main system. You may also need to consider an inexpensive upgrade to that aging machine, in order to make it reasonably useful.

What can your old machine do for you? Well, if you have a small network in your office, that 486 can serve as a networked printer server. The old system sits on the network itself, while the printer is connected to it via a standard printer port. You can also set up an old system to act as a primary email gateway or modem server, though the demands of today's Internet are quickly making online operation a task for more powerful systems.

One terrific option is to use that old PC as your data backup center. Instead of buying tape drives or other large format media drives for every PC, set up a single drive on that old PC. Then you can use backup software (such as Adaptec's Easy Exec) to automatically save data on your PC's hard disks to the backup drive. The primary limitation here—depending on the operating systems being used by your client PCs, is that the old system may need an upgrade to run the backup software.

Recycling Components

For true dinosaurs, there may simply be no prospect of giving away or reusing the system or components. In this case, the best option might be to discard the PC. But just throwing the old dog out might not be a great choice. PCs aren't exactly biodegradable—they're built of metal and plastic, and the monitors include hefty glass CRTs.

You might find a more environmentally friendly option by having the old components recycled. Some companies specialize in reclaiming the PCB boards, metal traces, and gold plating found on many PC components. Check with your local recycling company to see if it can make use of these parts, or contact one of the charitable organizations mentioned earlier.

Summary

Even when a PC has grown too old and tired to be of use to you, it might be able to serve others. Donating your old PC is the most attractive option. It effectively disposes of your old PC, helps those who need a system, and even nets you a tax break. Of course, cannibalizing the parts for use in your existing system is a good option as well, because it can help extend the capabilities of the machine you use every day.

Glossary

10BaseT The 10MBps Ethernet LAN that uses a central hub in a star configuration. Uses Category 3 twisted pair wiring that is similar to phone wires.

100BaseT The 100MBps version of Ethernet LAN that uses higher-quality Category 5 twisted pair wiring. Requires 100MBps-capable network cards and hubs.

80x86 or x86 A generic term referring to the Intel CPU architecture established with the 8086 processor used in the first IBM PC. The term *x86-compatible* refers to compatibility with the instruction set used in all Intel processors, including the new Pentium II CPUs.

accelerated graphics port See AGP.

access time The time it takes for a device to retrieve requested information. A critical specification for storage media, including RAM and disk drives, access time is generally measured in milliseconds or nanoseconds, although tape drives can take several seconds to access data.

active-matrix A type of LCD display that produces high brightness and contrast by directly applying an electrical charge to each pixel on the screen.

ActiveMovie The successor to the Media Player applet, ActiveMovie provides the playback and control interface for video, audio, and animation. Developers can use ActiveMovie to create interactive effects-laden video and audio content.

address bus The electrical connections that enable the CPU to send and address information to the system.

ADSL Asymmetric Digital Subscriber Line. A new digital phone service that promises downstream data rates of up to 6MBps. ADSL requires changes to central telephone switches, as well as ADSL-specific modems. It is available in limited markets.

AGP Accelerated Graphics Port. A new graphics bus enabling 3D programs to use main system memory to store large amounts of texture data. Based on the PCI bus specification, AGP runs at 66MHz and adds pipelining and address queuing to optimize performance. Systems must be built with AGP support in order to accept AGP graphics cards.

American Standard Code for Information Interchange   See ASCII.

API   Application Programming Interface. A method of defining a standard set of function calls and other interface elements. It usually defines the interface between a high-level language and the lower-level elements used by a device driver or operating system. The ultimate goal is to provide some type of service to an application that requires access to the operating system or device feature set.

application programming interface   See API.

areal density   An expression of the number of bits that can be stored on a square inch of media. Typically used for hard disks, CD-ROM drives, and other spinning-disk media. The number of bits on each linear inch of track (bit density) is multiplied by the number of concentric tracks on each inch of the medium (track density).

ASCII   American Standard Code for Information Interchange. A standard method of equating the numeric representations available in a computer to human-readable form. For example, the number 32 represents a space. There are 128 characters (7 bits) in the standard ASCII code. The extended ASCII code uses 8 bits for 256 characters. Display adapters from the same machine type usually use the same upper 128 characters. Printers, however, might reserve these upper 128 characters for nonstandard characters. For example, many Epson printers use them for the italic representations of the lower 128 characters.

asymmetric digital subscriber line   See ADSL.

ATA   AT Attachment interface. The standard 40-pin connection and logical interface used in IDE devices. ATA-2 provides faster transfers and logical block addressing, which allows for large and fast hard disk drives.

ATAPI   AT Attachment Packet Interface. Defines a standard interface and behavior for peripherals connected to the IDE bus, including hard disks, CD-ROM drives, and tape drives.

AVI   Audio Video Interleave. The video file format developed by Microsoft that is often used in multimedia titles and software designed for Windows. AVI files combine audio and video into a single track to enhance synchronization of audio and images during playback.

bandwidth   A generic term that expresses the data or signal carrying capacity of a bus, cable, or other connection.

bank   The block of system memory that can be read by the CPU in a single clock cycle. The data width of a bank of memory must match that of the motherboard bus. For example, on a 64-bit Pentium motherboard, two 32-bit SIMMs compose a single bank.

bidirectional parallel port   Defines a printer's ability to transfer information both ways on a printer cable. Input usually contains data or printer control codes. Output usually contains printer status information or error codes.

BIOS Basic Input/Output System. Code burned into read-only memory (ROM) on the motherboard that handles communication between the computer and peripherals.

bps Bits per second. The number of bits transmitted per second. Often used to express the speed of modems and other peripherals.

bus A set of wires or traces that carries data and other electrical signals to one or more devices. ISA, PCI, and USB are all examples of PC buses.

bus master A peripheral that can take control of the bus to transfer data without requiring the CPU's intervention.

cache A generic term describing a small pool of fast data storage used to augment a device's performance.

CardBus An updated 32-bit PC Card specification that provides backward compatibility with existing PC Card peripherals. CardBus allows for 3.3-volt operation, better power management, and DMA capability for video capture and other multimedia applications.

CCD Charge-Coupled Device. A sensor that responds to exposure to light by emitting an electrical impulse. Digital cameras and scanners interpret images from the relative electrical strength at each point on the CCD.

CD-R Compact Disk-Recordable. Up to 640MB of data can reside on 5¼-inch CD-R media, which can be read by standard CD-ROM drives. Desktop CD-R drives use laser light to mark changes into a chemical media layer on CD-R discs, which then behave like standard CD-ROM discs during playback. Once they're altered, CD-R media can't be changed, so multiple writes aren't possible.

CD-ROM Compact Disk-Read Only Memory. Up to 640MB of data resides on 5¼-inch CD-ROM discs, which consist of reflective media marked with pits and lands (non-pits). CD-ROM drives use a yellow laser to read pits and lands, which a microprocessor translates into digital 1s and 0s.

CD-RW Compact Disk-Rewritable. Up to 640MB of data can reside on 5¼-inch CD-RW media, which can be read by standard CD-ROM drives. Desktop CD-RW drives use laser light to mark changes into a phase-changing media layer on CD-RW discs, which then behave like standard CD-ROM discs during playback. The phase-changing CD-RW medium can be rewritten many times.

CDFS Compact Disc File System. The portion of the file subsystem specifically designed to interact with compact disc drives. It also provides the user interface elements required to tune this part of the subsystem. The CDFS takes the place of an FSD for CD-ROM drives.

charge-coupled device See CCD.

CISC Complex Instruction Set Computing. Describes the type of instructions used by a processor. Intel x86-type CPUs feature a large set of instructions that are complex in nature.

client The recipient of data, services, or resources from a file or other server. This term can refer to a workstation or an application. The server can be another PC or an application.

CMOS Complimentary Metal Oxide Semiconductor. Normally refers to a construction method for low-power battery-backed memory. When used in the context of a PC, this term usually refers to the memory used to store system configuration information and the real-time clock status. The configuration information normally includes the amount of system memory, the type and size of floppy drives, the hard drive parameters, and the video display type. Some vendors also include other configuration information as part of this chip.

coaxial cable A type of wiring identical to that used to connect cable TV boxes, that is sometimes used to connect network computers. Coaxial cable is notable for its high bandwidth and heavy shielding.

codec Coder-decoder or compression-decompression. Refers to software used to compress and decompress audio, video, and other media files.

COM port PC serial port.

compact disc file system See CDFS.

complimentary metal oxide semiconductor See CMOS.

coprocessor An additional processor in the PC that takes the load off the CPU by handling various tasks such as graphics operation, video playback, and communications.

CPU Central Processing Unit. The brains of the PC, the CPU is the most complex and most powerful chip in the system, consisting of millions of transistors.

CRT Cathode Ray Tube. The large glass vacuum tube mounted inside the PC monitor. An electron gun mounted inside the tube shoots a focused stream of electrons at a layer of phosphors on the inside of the glass, causing them to emit light.

daisy chain A string of connected devices in which electrical signals move from the first device to the last. The SCSI bus is a daisy-chained bus.

DAT drive Digital Audio Tape drive. A tape drive that uses a cassette to store data. The cassette and the drive use the same technology as the audio version of the DAT drive. However, the internal circuitry of the drive formats the tape for use with a computer system. The vendor must also design the interface circuitry with computer needs in mind. DAT tapes enable you to store large amounts of information in a relatively small amount of space. Typical drive capacities range from 1.2 to 8GB.

Device Bay A proposed industry-standard modular housing and bus connection for all manner of devices. Utilizes the USB and IEEE 1394 interfaces for Plug and Play operation.

device driver Device-specific code that allows the operating system and hardware to speak with each other.

digital audio tape drive See DAT drive.

DIMM Dual Inline Memory Module. The standard module format used by SDRAM system memory found in Pentium MMX and new Pentium II PCs.

direct memory access See DMA.

DirectX A suite of programming APIs and technologies that allows compelling multimedia content under Windows 95. DirectX includes the following components: DirectDraw (graphics and video), Direct3D (3D graphics), DirectSound (audio), DirectInput (game controllers), and DirectPlay (network game play). Hardware devices must use DirectX-aware drivers in order to take advantage of the DirectX services built into the operating system.

disk defragmenter An application used to reorder the data on a long-term storage device such as a hard or floppy disk drive. Reordering the data so that it appears in sequential order (file by file) reduces the time required to access and read it. Sequential order lets you read an entire file without moving the disk head at all in some cases and only a little in others. This reduction in access time normally improves overall system throughput and therefore enhances system efficiency.

DMA Direct Memory Access. A memory-addressing technique in which the processor doesn't perform the actual data transfer. This method of memory access is faster than any other technique.

docking station A hardware module that connects to a notebook and provides desktop-like capabilities such as networking and expandability.

DOS protected-mode interface See DPMI.

dot pitch Defines the width of pixel dots on a monitor. Measured in millimeters. The smaller the measurement, the greater the potential precision of the display.

DPMI DOS Protected-Mode Interface. A method of accessing extended memory from a DOS application using the Windows extended memory manager.

DRAM Dynamic Random Access Memory. The standard memory found in most PCs. DRAM must be constantly refreshed with electrical signals in order to maintain its data state.

dual-ported video RAM See VRAM.

dual-scan passive-matrix display A variation of passive-matrix display technology. The screen is divided into two horizontal sections, doubling the number of transistors available to send charges to pixels on the screen. See passive-matrix display.

DVD-R   DVD-Recordable. The recordable version of DVD-ROM, DVD-R drives can write up to 3.6GB of data to DVD-R media. DVD-R discs can be written to only once.

DVD-RAM   DVD-Random Access Memory. The rewritable version of DVD-ROM, DVD-RAM drives can write up to 2.4GB of data to DVD-RAM media. DVD-RAM discs can be rewritten.

DVD-ROM   DVD-Read Only Memory. A specification for 5¼-inch optical disks able to store up to 17GB of data. DVD-ROM discs provide higher capacities than CD-ROM discs by more closely spacing the pits and lands. DVD-ROM discs can store data on both sides of the disc and on two layers on each side.

DVD+RW   DVD+ReWritable. A competing rewritable DVD format sponsored by HP, Sony, and others.

Dvorak layout   An alternative method of laying out the keyboard so that stress is reduced and typing speed is increased. It's different from the more familiar "QWERTY" layout used by most keyboards and typewriters.

ECP   See enhanced capabilities port.

EMM   Expanded Memory Manager. A device driver such as EMM386.EXE that provides expanded memory services on an 80386 and above machine. (Special drivers work with 80286 and a few 8088/8086 machines.) An application accesses expanded memory using a page frame or other memory-mapping technique from within the conventional or upper-memory area (0 to 124KB). The EMM usually emulates expanded memory using extended memory managed by an extended memory manager (XMM) such as HIMEM.SYS. An application must change the processor's mode to protected in order to use XMS. Some products, such as 386MAX.SYS and QEMM.SYS, provide both EMM and XMM services in one driver.

EMS   Expanded Memory Specification. Several versions of this specification are currently in use. The most popular version is 3.2, even though a newer 4.0 specification is available. This specification defines one method of extending the amount of memory that a processor can address from the conventional memory area. It uses an area outside of system memory to store information. An EMM provides a window view into this larger data area. The old 3.2 specification requires a 64KB window in the UMB. The newer 4.0 specification can create this window anywhere in conventional or UMB memory.

enhanced capabilities port   An extension of the bidirectional parallel port specification that increases performance.

enhanced IDE   Enhanced Integrated Drive Electronics. A standard low-cost interface for internal hard disk, CD-ROM, and other drives.

enhanced parallel port   An extension of the bidirectional parallel port specification that increases performance.

EPP   See enhanced parallel port.

expanded memory manager   See EMM.

expanded memory specification   See EMS.

FAT   File Allocation Table. The method of formatting a hard disk drive used by DOS and other operating systems. This technique is one of the oldest formatting methods available.

FAT32   File Allocation Table 32. An enhanced version of the FAT disk-formatting scheme, introduced in the OSR2 version of Windows 95 and, soon, Windows 98. FAT32 allows enhanced IDE hard disk capacities of up to 9GB in a single partition and reduces the amount of so-called "slack" associated with files, particularly smaller ones.

file allocation table   See FAT.

FireWire   See IEEE 1394.

FTP   File Transfer Protocol. A networking protocol commonly used for Internet downloads and uploads.

full-duplex   Describes a signal flow in two directions along a connection. Full-duplex sound cards allow speakerphone capability, in which both sides of the call can speak simultaneously, or in which a card can record and play back at the same time.

GB   See gigabyte.

GDI   Graphics Device Interface. One of the main Windows root components. It controls the way graphic elements are presented on-screen. Every application must use the API provided by this component to draw or perform other graphics-related tasks.

general protection fault   See GPF.

gigabyte   An amount of data equal to 1,024 megabytes, or 1,073,741,824 bytes.

GPF   General Protection Fault. A processor or memory error that occurs when an application makes a request that the system can't honor. This type of error results in some type of severe action on the part of the operating system. Normally, the operating system terminates the offending application.

graphical user interface   See GUI.

graphics device interface   See GDI.

GUI   Graphical User Interface. A system of icons and graphic images that replaces the character-mode menu system used by many machines. The GUI can ride on top of another operating system (such as DOS or UNIX) or reside as part of the operating system itself (such as Windows or OS/2). Advantages of a GUI include ease of use and high-resolution graphics. Disadvantages include higher workstation hardware requirements and lower performance over a similar system using a character-mode interface.

half duplex   A connection in which signal flow can occur in only one direction at a time. Half-duplex sound cards are unable to allow efficient audio or videoconferencing because of their inability to allow both sides to speak at once.

hard disk   The PC's primary permanent data store. Hard disks consist of a coated medium that is magnetically charged to indicate 1 or 0 bits. The drive head floats over the spinning disk, reading and writing data.

heat sink   A metal or plastic device attached to a chip that helps dissipate heat away from the chip.

hertz   Indicates a signal frequency that cycles once per second.

IDE   Integrated Drive Electronics. Initially described the class of hard disks that had the controller circuitry built into the drive instead of on a separate card. Today IDE is often used to describe ATA-compliant devices.

IEEE 1394   Also known as FireWire. A high-speed Plug and Play external bus designed for applications such as video capture and consumer electronics connectivity.

Industry Standard Architecture   See ISA.

.INF file   A special form of device or application configuration file. It contains all the parameters that Windows requires to install or configure the device or application. For example, an application .INF file might contain the location of data files and the interdependencies of DLLs. Both application and device .INF files contain the registry and .INI file entries required to make Windows recognize the application or device.

ink jet printer   A printer that produces monochrome or color output by spraying ink onto the page.

interlacing   A way of scanning a CRT screen in which the electron gun paints every other line from top to bottom and then paints the remaining alternating lines. Older interlaced displays cause visible flicker, which can result in eye strain.

interrupt request   See IRQ.

IPX   Internet Packet eXchange. The networking communication protocol for Novell's NetWare network operating system.

IrDA   Infrared Device Association. A specification, named after a standards-making body, that provides a standard way for devices to communicate using infrared light. The initial 152KBps data rate was later improved to 4MBps.

IRQ   Interrupt Request. The set of special address lines that connect a peripheral to the processor. Think of an IRQ as an office telephone that has multiple incoming lines. Every time a device calls, its entry lights up on the front of the phone. The processor selects the desired line and picks up the receiver to find out what the device wants. Everything works fine as long as there is one line for each device that needs to call the processor. If more than one device were to try to call in on the same line, the processor wouldn't know what was at the other end. This is the source of IRQ. Older PC-class machines provided eight interrupt lines. The newer AT-class machines provide 16. However, only 15 of those can be used, because one of them is used for internal purposes.

ISA   Industry Standard Architecture. The standard expansion bus on PCs since their inception. The current ISA bus runs at 8MHz and features a 16-bit connection. Common ISA peripherals include sound cards, internal modems, and LAN adapters.

ISDN   Integrated Services Digital Network. A digital phone service provided by telephone companies that can transport up to 128KBps of data. PC-based ISDN communication requires an ISDN adapter, often called an ISDN modem.

jumper   Used to set hardware resources on motherboards and peripherals, a jumper is a plastic-covered contact that fits over dual pins protruding from a circuit board.

LAN   Local Area Network. A combination of hardware and software used to connect a group of PCs to each other and/or a mini or mainframe computer. Two main networking models are in use: peer-to-peer and client-server. The peer-to-peer model doesn't require a dedicated server. In addition, all the workstations in the group can share resources. The client-server model uses a central server for resource sharing, but some special methods are provided for using local resources in a limited fashion.

laser printer   A printer that works like a copier to cook toner onto the page. An image of the page is etched onto a rotating drum, so that toner adheres to the etched area.

LCD   Liquid Crystal Display. Flat-panel displays used in notebook PCs. Images are displayed by charging individual liquid crystals suspended between glass panels.

liquid crystal display   See LCD.

local area network   See LAN.

magneto-optical (MO) drive   High-capacity disk media and drives, often used to archive and exchange files. MO drives use a laser to heat the underlying magnetic medium to a state where it can be rewritten. The thermal threshold of MO disks makes them less susceptible to data loss than magnetic media such as hard disks.

MCA   Microchannel Architecture. A specialized bus introduced by IBM. It's faster than the old ISA bus and gives the operating system information about the peripheral devices connected to the bus. It also provides the means for devices to become self-configuring.

mean time between failure   Also called MTBF, this is a measure of the statistical probability that a device will fail within the indicated time. Usually expressed in hours.

microchannel architecture   See MCA.

MIDI   Musical Instrument Digital Interface. A standard scheme for expressing musical notes using a series of instructions. MIDI files are very compact, but they allow MIDI-aware sound cards to play back realistic-sounding musical scores.

miniport driver   A specialized Windows component that provides access to a resource, normally a peripheral device of some type. It's also used to access pseudo-devices and network resources.

modem   Short for modulate-demodulate. Modems enable PCs to send and receive data over standard phone lines by translating digital bits into analog sound.

motherboard   The PC's main board, upon which the CPU, chipset, system memory, and expansion slots are all mounted.

Motion Picture Experts Group   See MPEG.

MPEG   Motion Picture Experts Group. A standards group that provides file formats and other specifications in regard to full-motion video and other types of graphic displays. MPEG-2 is a high-quality video format used in DVD-ROM titles, and MPEG-1 provides low-bandwidth playback for use on CD-ROM titles.

multiple-boot configuration   A method of creating a configurable environment that was first introduced with DOS 5.0. The user simply selects the operating environment from a list of environments presented prior to the boot sequence. This technique provides an additional layer of flexibility and enables the user to optimize the operating environment to perform specific tasks.

multitasking   The ability of some processor and environment/system combinations to perform more than one task at a time. The applications appear to run simultaneously. For example, you can download messages from an online service, print from a word processor, and recalculate a spreadsheet all at the same time. Each application receives a slice of time before the processor moves to the next application. Because the time slices are fairly small, it appears to the user that these actions are occurring simultaneously.

near-line storage   A generic term that describes large, fast, removable media that can be used to augment existing hard disk capacity. Magneto-optical drives and Jaz drives are examples of near-line media. Also called near-disk storage.

nested objects   Two or more objects that are coupled in some fashion. The objects normally appear within the confines of a container object. Object nesting allows multiple objects to define the properties of a higher-level object. It also enables the user to associate different types of objects with each other.

network interface card   See NIC.

NIC   Network Interface Card. The device responsible for allowing a workstation to communicate with the file server and other workstations. It provides the physical means of creating the connection. The card plugs into an expansion slot in the computer. A cable that attaches to the back of the card completes the communication path.

NTFS Windows NT File System. The method of formatting a hard disk drive used by Windows NT. Although it provides significant speed advantages over other formatting techniques, only the Windows NT operating system and applications designed to work with that operating system can access a drive formatted using this technique.

NTSC National Television Standards Committee. Used to describe the video format standard employed in television broadcasts.

parity A type of random access memory (RAM) that incorporates additional bits to confirm that data wasn't corrupted.

passive-matrix display Inexpensive LCD display. Individual pixels are lit when charges from the horizontal and vertical edge of the screen intersect. Passive-matrix displays lack brightness and contrast because pixels are not frequently refreshed.

PCI Peripheral Component Interconnect. A high-speed general-purpose peripheral bus, often used for graphics cards, network interface cards, and other high-speed devices.

PCI-X Peripheral Component Interconnect-X. A proposed extension to the PCI bus, which initially will run at 66MHz over a 32-bit bus, effectively doubling performance. Targeted for high-performance servers and workstations.

peripheral component interconnect See PCI.

Plug and Play The combination of BIOS, operating system, and peripheral device components that provides a self-configuring environment. This self-configuring feature enables the operating system to avoid potential hardware conflicts by polling the peripheral devices, assessing their requirements, and determining and implementing optimal settings for each device.

POST Power-On Self Test. The set of diagnostic and configuration routines the BIOS runs during system initialization. For example, the memory counter you see during the boot sequence is part of this process.

power-on self test See POST.

protected mode The processor mode in which the processor can access all of the extended memory. This mode also provides a better level of application error detection as part of the processing cycle.

QIC Quarter-Inch Cartridge. A specification for tape backup cartridges. QIC-40 and QIC-80 cassettes hold 40MB and 80MB of data, respectively.

RAM Random Access Memory. The generic term for the volatile, silicon-based data storage used in PCs.

RDRAM Rambus DRAM. A type of memory that uses fast-and-thin bus interface to provide bandwidth that is double that of SDRAM. Found on some graphics cards and expected to be used in system motherboards by mid-1999.

real mode   A Windows operating mode supporting the capabilities of the 8088/8086 processor. This essentially limits you to loading one application within the confines of conventional memory. Windows versions after 3.0 don't support this mode. You must use these versions with workstations containing an 80286 or higher processor.

remote access   The ability to use a remote resource as you would a local resource. In some cases, this also means downloading the remote resource to use as a local resource.

RISC   Reduced Instruction Set Computing. A type of processor instruction set that runs very quickly using a few simple instructions rather than a larger set of complex instructions.

SCSI   Small Computer System Interface. The fast internal and external bus standard frequently used for scanners, hard disk drives, and other high-bandwidth peripherals. Types of SCSI include Fast SCSI, Wide SCSI, and FastWide SCSI, which tops out at 40MBps.

SCSI manager   Windows NT introduced something called the miniport driver. With Windows 95, you can use the Windows NT miniport binaries. However, before you can actually do this, Windows 95 must translate its commands to a format that the miniport driver understands. The SCSI manager performs this service.

SDRAM   Synchronous Dynamic Random Access Memory. A type of memory that improves performance by working in lockstep with the system clock.

SEC   See Single Edge Connector.

server   An application or workstation that provides services, resources, or data to a client application or workstation. The client usually makes requests in the form of OLE, DDE, or other command formats.

Single Edge Connector   The proprietary edge-on connector—similar to add-in cards— used for Intel's Pentium II, Xeon, and Celeron CPUs.

small computer system interface   See SCSI.

SMP   Symmetric Multiprocessing. PCs equipped with more than one CPU, with all CPUs able to take part in all tasks. SMP systems require an SMP-aware operating system, such as Windows NT Workstation or OS/2 SMP.

symmetric multiprocessing   See SMP.

system resource   Data, peripheral devices, or other system components used to create, delete, or manipulate documents and produce output.

TAPI   Telephony API. An interface used by applications to interface with various types of communication equipment. This currently includes both modems and fax devices.

task switching   The ability of an operating system to support more than one application or thread of execution at a time. The foreground application or task is the only one that executes. All other threads of execution are suspended in the background. Contrast this with multitasking, in which all threads—background and foreground—execute.

Telephony API   See TAPI.

texture maps   Images that are laid over 3D objects to add the illusion of reality to rendered 3D scenes.

UAE   Unrecoverable Application Error. A processor or memory error that occurs when an application makes a request that the system can't honor. The operating system normally doesn't detect this type of error. The result is that the system freezes or becomes unstable to the point of being unusable. Also see GPF.

ultra ATA   An enhancement to the enhanced IDE specification that allows for 33MBps data rates, double that of earlier drives.

universal serial bus   See USB.

unrecoverable application error   See UAE.

USB   Universal Serial Bus. A medium-speed (12MBps) Plug and Play external bus designed for devices such as mice, keyboards, scanners, and digital cameras.

VESA   Video Electronics Standards Association. A standards group responsible for creating display adapter and monitor specifications. This group has also worked on other standards, such as the VL bus used in some PCs.

VESA Local Bus   See VL-bus.

VFAT   Virtual File Allocation Table. An enhanced method of disk formatting based on the FAT system. It allows for additional functionality, such as long filenames.

Video Electronics Standards Association   See VESA.

virtual device driver   See VxD.

virtual file allocation table   See VFAT.

VL-bus   VESA Local Bus. A 32-bit 33MHz bus found in 486 systems. The first industry-standard, high-speed expansion bus, it was replaced by PCI in Pentium-based PCs.

VRAM   Dual-Ported Video RAM. A special form of memory that allows simultaneous reads and writes. It provides a serial read interface and a parallel write interface. The advantage of using VRAM is that it's much faster and doesn't require as much detection code on the part of the application or device driver.

VxD   Virtual Device Driver. A 32-bit driver DLL that allows dynamic loading and unloading and other low-level features under Windows 95.

wave audio   A digital representation of analog sound that is made up of sine waves of varying frequency and amplitude. Wave audio files can produce accurate recordings but take up a great deal of hard disk space.

WDM   A common device driver scheme for the Windows 95 and Windows NT operating systems that allows peripheral makers to write a single 32-bit driver for both OSs.

Win32 Driver Model   See WDM.

Windows NT   A 32-bit operating system tailored for network servers, corporate workstations, and high-end graphics. Windows NT provides greater reliability than Windows 95.

Windows NT file system   See NTFS.

wizard   A specialized application that reduces the complexity of using or configuring your system. For example, the Printer Wizard makes it easier to install a new printer.

Index

C

D

F

H

H

LTO (Linear Tape-Open), 386-387
physical characteristics, 382-383
QIC-format Travan, 383-385
six-cartridge weekly backups, 395
software for, 387-389
three-cartridge weekly backups, 395
types of media, 383-384
turbo switch, disabling, 220
upgrading, buying strategies, 100-102
UPSs, 204-205
   buying, 213
   features of, 208
   line-interactive, 207-208
   online, 207
   standby, 207
   VA ratings, 205-206
video capture, 484
   applications for, 484-485
   buying, 494-496
   cameras, 493-494
   installing, 503-506
   low-end video capture, 486-487
   setup, 496-498
   troubleshooting, 496-499
   upgrading to videoconferencing, 499-503
   video capture boards, 487-493
   videoconferencing, 485-486
Hardware Device Manager (sound board settings), 450-451
HDSL (high bit rate DSL), 539
head-mounted displays, 471
heat (hostile environments), 77-80
Hewlett-Packard's PCL language, 609
HiFD drives, 328-329
high bandwidth modems (future of PCs), 20
high bit rate DSL (HDSL), 539
high-end systems, buying chipsets, 233
high-level hard disk formatting, 303
history of PCs, 9-11
home offices
   buying profile, 96-97
   upgrading I/O buses, 564-566
home theater 3D audio, 440

home-based networks, 582
   phone lines, 582-583
   power lines, 583-584
   radio, 584-585
HomePNA (Home Phone Networking Alliance), 582
hostile environments, 77
   airborne hazards, 80-82
   electrical problems, 82-84
   heat, 77-80
HP CapShare handheld scanner, 676-677
hubs, 586
   USB, 554

I

I/O (input/output) buses, 551
   buying, 563
      consumer electronics/video capture, 566-567
      home offices, 564-566
      notebook computers, 567
      when not to upgrade, 568
      when to upgrade, 563-564
   CardBus, 561-562
   FireWire, 555-556
      advantages of, 556-557
      installing, 570-571
      operational overview, 557-558
   infrared (IR), 558-559
      advantages of, 559
      installing, 572-573
      operational overview, 559-560
   PC Cards, 561
      installing, 571-572
   technology overview, 551-553
   USB, 553
      advantages of, 553-554
      installing, 568-570
      operational overview, 554-555
I/O port conflicts, troubleshooting networks, 592-593
IBM, history of PCs, 9-11
IBM TrackPoint, 646
iCOMP index, 120

Q-R